Texas Principles of Real Estate

ELEVENTH EDITION

Charles J. Jacobus
D.R.E.I., C.R.E.I.

CENGAGE Learning™

Australia • Brazil • Japan • Korea • Mexico • Singapore • Spain • United Kingdom • United States

CENGAGE Learning™

Texas Principles of Real Estate, Eleventh Edition
Charles J. Jacobus

Vice President/Editor-in-Chief: Dave Shaut

Acquisitions Editor: Sara Glassmeyer

Developmental Editor: Arlin Kauffman, LEAP Publishing Services

Senior Marketing and Sales Manager: Mark Linton

Content Project Management: PreMediaGlobal

Production Manager: Jennifer Ziegler

Senior Frontlist Buyer, Manufacturing: Charlene Taylor

Senior Art Director: Pamela Galbreath

Rights Acquisitions Specialist: John Hill

Cover Image: © Getty Images

Library of Congress Control Number: 2011926710

ISBN-13: 978-1-111-42772-6

ISBN-10: 1-111-42772-0

Cengage Learning
5191 Natorp Boulevard
Mason, OH 45040
USA

Cengage Learning products are represented in Canada by Nelson Education, Ltd.

For your course and learning solutions, visit **www.cengage.com.**
Purchase any of our products at your local college store or at our preferred online store **www.cengagebrain.com.**

Printed in the United States of America
1 2 3 4 5 6 7 15 14 13 12 11

A Letter From The Owners

Welcome!

Congratulations on your decision to get into real estate and welcome to The Austin Institute, where you will learn more than you ever imagined!

More than just a licensing school, we provide courses on business building, investing, negotiations and finance, as well as world-class coaching and professional designation courses.

Real estate is the best business in the world, offering opportunities in both the residential and commercial arenas. Whether you decide on apartment locating, leasing, sales, investing or development, you will find endless financial opportunities, long term financial security, and freedom from the ordinary.

Here you will be exposed to the most progressive, cutting edge business building and investing course curriculum in the country. **No other real estate school in America teaches what we teach**: **The Three Step Success System**, which shows how to design your life and build a business that provides the income to live that life exactly the way ***you*** want.

We are committed to your success as a REALTOR® and have used our experience from years in this business to design a full-blown course curriculum that no other licensed course provider offers. We will take you through the licensing process, then into the exciting and profitable world of business and investing, where those with the desire, the heart, and commitment to do so will make all their dreams come true.

We saw this quote years ago and it has inspired us:

"Real estate is the best business in the world. We help make other people's dreams come true…while achieving our own."- Unknown

We truly appreciate your business, and we thank you for spending your time and money with us. We have assembled a first class staff, course curriculum, team of instructors and professional development programs in an ongoing effort to thank you for the honor to serve you and to make sure you get more than you paid for.

Please take the time to read through this guide for a thorough understanding of the benefits of making The Austin Institute of Real Estate your real estate education provider for life.

Constantly striving to exceed your expectations, we are

Sincerely yours,

Wayne and Lynn Morgan, owners
The Austin Institute of Real Estate
The Business School For Real Estate Pros

AIRE Class Agreement

Please check these agreements as they are discussed by you and your instructor:

- ☐ I agree to park only in The Institute parking lot and on Putnam Street. If I park in front of any other business I will be towed immediately.
- ☐ I agree to use tobacco (smoke & smokeless) outside the building and place my cigarette butts in the ashtrays provided.
- ☐ I agree not to use the large decorative vases outside as trash cans.
- ☐ I agree to notify the front office of any make-up or schedule changes because it may effect credit received for class.
- ☐ I agree to raise my hand when I have something to say in class, as it may also be important to someone else.
- ☐ I agree not to use my cellphone in the front office, as it is disruptive to the staff and my fellow students.
- ☐ I agree to be courteous to others and make sure that my cell phone or pager is on vibrate, so as not to disturb the class.
- ☐ I will not use class time to answer phone calls or take care of personal business. To do so constitutes a violation of TREC attendance policies and will result in the need for make-up time.
- ☐ I will refer to my enrollment agreement for make-up time on any missed class hours. I agree to check in at the front desk when I leave early or come in late.
- ☐ I understand that all make-up hours must be completed before any final exam is given (exams are given Monday-Friday, during normal business hours).
- ☐ I agree to allow the instructors their break time and agree to bring up questions I have during class time.
- ☐ I agree to push in my chair, straighten my table(s), and throw away my trash before I leave each day.
- ☐ I agree to not move chairs and tables from class to class.
- ☐ I agree to stay out of classrooms other than the one in which my course is being held.
- ☐ I agree to the following final examination schedule: Four day classes: 4:00pm on the 4th day. Evening classes: 8:40pm on the 8th night. Three day classes: 7:20pm on the 3rd day.
- ☐ I agree not to audio or videotape any portion of any class provided by The Austin Institute of Real Estate.
- ☐ MESSAGES: We will take messages and faxes for your convenience during our office hours (8am-6pm Mon-Fri) and hold them at the front desk. We will not interrupt class to deliver messages unless it is an emergency.
- ☐ TEMPERATURE: The temperature is set for optimum learning conditions. Students are NOT allowed to adjust the temperature. If you would like to request a change in temperature, please ask for assistance from your instructor or the front office. Classrooms can occasionally be cooler than normal; please dress accordingly.
- ☐ I understand these guidelines and agree to abide by them.

Brief Contents

Contents

16 TAXES AND ASSESSMENTS 410

17 TITLE CLOSING AND ESCROW 426

Preface

Is your goal a full-time or part-time career in real estate? Do you own or plan to own your own home or an investment property? Are you a student of real estate desiring to broaden your knowledge of this subject? If you answered "Yes" to one or more of these questions, the content of this book will be of immense help to you. After all, in the United States and in Texas, real estate is part of the great American dream. It touches all of our lives. We share stories about it, invest in it, live in it and on it, sell it, and hire people to advise us about it. The subject of real estate is always fun and interesting, but often complex. With the current state of the economy and given the recent past, this statement has never been more true.

Texas is on the forefront of real estate education, law, and practice. Our state currently has one of the highest educational requirements for real estate licensees. The Texas Real Estate Center in College Station is the premier real estate research facility in the country. The State Bar of Texas is widely acknowledged as the leading bar association in the country for research and education. Texas offers many resources for students and practitioners, and this eleventh edition of *Texas Principles of Real Estate* is a primary beneficiary of (and, we hope, an example of) Texas's efforts to pursue excellence in real estate education.

In this book you will learn about Texas real estate brokerage, appraisal, financing, contracts, closing, and investment. Additionally, you will learn about land descriptions, rights and interests, fair housing, taxes, leases, condominiums, zoning, licensing, and the use of computers in real estate. You will find particularly valuable the attention given to such timely topics as a real estate agent's professional obligation to buyers and sellers, buyer brokerage, new RESPA rules, foreclosure, and new contract forms. Included throughout the book are numerous examples from the actual practice of real estate in Texas.

This book is written in a clear and easily readable style to help you understand and apply the important information contained in these chapters. Figures and tables will help you to visualize real estate rights and interests, financing techniques, appraisal methods, closing statements, and map reading. Simplified, plain English examples of real estate documents are used in some areas of this text so their key elements can be easily identified and not lost in a haze of legal language.

I have attempted to cover most substantive Texas topics in such depth that this book can be used for future reference as well as for an introduction to Texas real estate. For your convenience, the most current version of the Texas Occupations Code has been included. The official regulations are detailed and voluminous. Both are readily available from the Texas Real Estate Commission website: http://www.trec.state.tx.us. As a first assignment, you should download the information and become acquainted with it.

NEW TO THIS EDITION

This edition has been updated to reflect the 2009 legislature changes. More specifically changes include:

Chapter 2: Updated Table 2-1, Real Estate Education and experience requirements. Figure 2-1, Code of Ethics has been updated to the most recent version. Updated Real Estate License Act.

Chapter 6: Update Table 6-1, Concurrent Ownership by States.

Chapter 10: Updated One to Four Family Residential Contract form. Added text to reflect changes in updated contract form.

Chapter 12: Added most recent FHA coverage effective Jan, 2009. Added new material to Mortgage Insurance topic.

Chapter 13: Updated Uniform Residential Loan Applications form.

Chapter 14: New topics added on OFHEO, and GNMA. Updated topic of Private Conduits.

Chapter 17: Updated topic "The Transaction" under section "Real Estate Agent Duties". Updated numbers for Sample Closing, Buyers Side and Settlement Charges topics. Updated HUD Settlement Statement 17-3. New paragraph added on RESPA topic. Updated Figure 17-4, Good Faith Estimate.

Chapter 22: Updated Figure 22-1, Seller's Disclosure Notice.

SPECIAL FEATURES OF THIS BOOK

- Beginning with Chapter 2, each chapter offers a list of key terms and their definitions. Key terms are also boldfaced and italic at first use within the chapter.
- Chapters also begin with a chapter overview that previews the chapter's main topics.
- Within chapters you'll encounter "Putting It to Work," brief capsules of practical information that help you understand how the discussion relates to the everyday practice of real estate in Texas.
- Each chapter ends with multiple-choice questions. These questions will help you review the material and will alert you to areas that may need more study if you are preparing for your Texas real estate licensing examination. The questions are much like the ones you will encounter on your real estate exam

and should provide valuable practice for that exam. The answers to these chapter-end questions are found in the Answer Key in the back of the book so that you can check your responses.

- For those of you preparing for your licensing exam, the book now offers two Practice Examinations. These tests contain 90 questions each, in the multiple-choice format used by Texas's testing service. Although answers for the Practice Exams are also found in the Answer Key, take the exam in its completion, timing yourself as will be the case when you take the real exam. Then use the Answer Key to identify the areas in which you need to review.
- To aid your review and help you locate topics, this book offers a comprehensive Glossary and a detailed Index.
- Finally, this book includes a useful, concise math review. Many of you probably worry that you will be unprepared for the math you'll encounter in this book and in your profession. This appendix will help you identify the basic skills you'll use and help you review and develop those skills.
- All of these features and the book's readable style make it perfect for distance learning courses. If you are taking the course via computer, telecourse, mail, or any other distance learning method, you'll find the book easy to use.

STUDY AIDS

Texas Real Estate Exam Prep CD. This interactive prep guide helps you prepare for the license exam with 220 questions, answers, and rationale to help you effectively and efficiently prepare for the exam.

SUPPLEMENTS

The complete Instructor's Manual available with adoption of this text includes chapter outlines and a test bank of extra review/test questions (40-50 per chapter) for each chapter.

Classroom PowerPoint® presentation slides also support each chapter by outlining learning objectives, emphasizing key concepts, and highlighting real-world applications to help further engage learners and generate classroom discussion. These instructional support materials are available online at www.cengage.com/realestate/jacobus.

ACKNOWLEDGMENTS

Special thanks to the following individuals for their help in preparing this and previous editions of the book: Katy Peeples, Minor Peeples, Dorothy A. Lewis, Ken Sheffield, Kevin Morris, Loretta DeHay, Richard Chumbley, Jim Howze, Rita Santamaria, Ralph Tamper, Ken Combs, Drue Combs, Jerry Rutledge, Bill Proctor, Dorothy Haley, Joe Goeters, Jessica Flair, Joe Irwin, Frankie Jefferson, Alex Binkley, Pat Streeter, John Banman, and John P. Wiedemer. I appreciate their assistance and support.

Texas Principles of Real Estate

Chapter 1

IN THIS CHAPTER

Real estate is a unique subject, and because it is unique, real estate has spawned complex legal theories and very unusual situations. No two situations are ever exactly alike, and the subject never ceases to be intellectually stimulating. Everyone has a favorite story about real estate, and it has remained a fascinating topic for centuries. This fascination is what makes the real estate business such a fun, interesting business.

As a new real estate student, one must be prepared to learn a lot of new concepts and be willing to commit the time and effort to that end. Some say that the only way to learn real estate is by experience. Many years ago this was the traditional concept. Real estate was then considered to be a "marketing" or "salesmanship" business, and experience was the best teacher. Recent years, however, have seen the development of extensive academic applications in real estate education. Real estate has come to the academic forefront; undergraduate degrees in real estate are becoming more common, as are graduate level degree programs. There is also a resulting emphasis on the professionalism and duty of these new real estate professionals. Unlike many other academic subjects, however, real estate continues to emphasize the "people-oriented" aspects of the business. Experience and hard work have a very high correlation with success in the real estate business.

With these combinations in mind, this book has been written to provide an understanding of the basic principles and business fundamentals of real estate. Emphasis is placed on an easily readable presentation that combines explanations of the basic principles of the subject with "why" things are done and "how" these principles apply to everyday activities.

Introduction to Real Estate

HOW TO READ THIS BOOK

Chapters 2 through 25 include a list of the new "Key Terms" that you will learn, along with brief definitions. Read these before starting your work in each chapter. In the body of each chapter these terms are set in ***boldface italic type*** and given an in-depth discussion. At the end of each chapter are questions designed to help you test yourself on your comprehension of the material in the chapter you've just read. The answers are given in Appendix D in the back of the book.

A glossary is also included at the back of this book to help reinforce your familiarity with the language of real estate.

TRANSACTION OVERVIEW

Figure 1.1 provides a visual summary of the real estate transaction cycle. It is included here to give you an overview of the different steps involved in the sale of real property and to show how the steps are related to each other. The chapter in which each step is discussed is also shown. Whether your point of view is that of a real estate agent, owner, buyer, or seller, you will find the chapters that follow to be informative and valuable.

CHAPTER ORGANIZATION

This text is organized so as to carefully build your knowledge of real estate. For example, land description methods and rights and interests in land are necessary to sales contracts, abstracts, deeds, mortgages, and listings and therefore are discussed early in the text.

Chapter 3 includes topics such as metes and bounds and tract maps. It also discusses what is real estate and what is not, and how land is physically and economically different from other commodities. Having described real estate, the next logical step is to look at the various rights and interests that exist in a given

FIGURE 1.1 An overview of a real estate transaction.

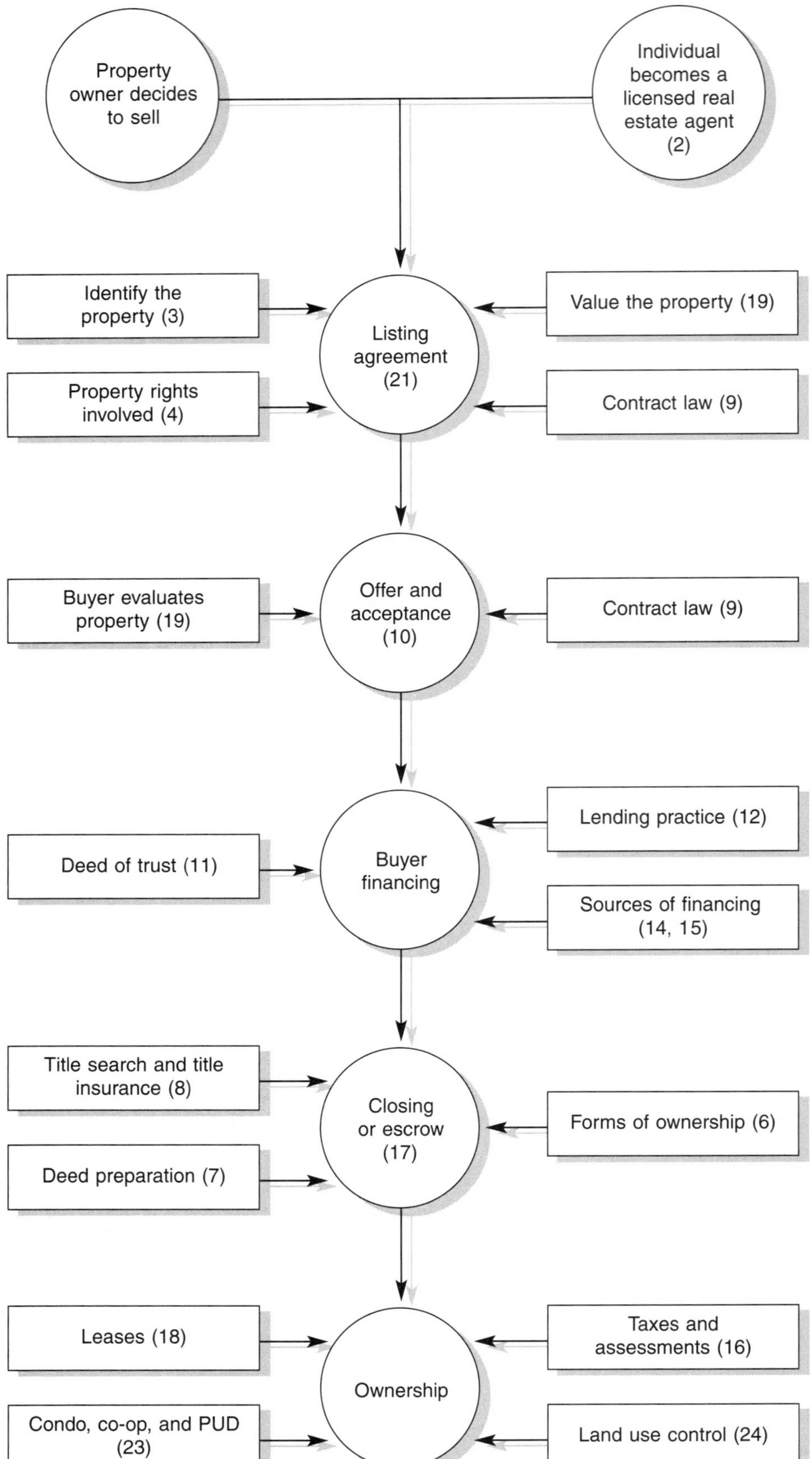

Source: © 2012 Cengage Learning

parcel of land. In Chapter 4 you will see that there is much more to ownership of land than meets the eye! In Chapter 6 we look at how a given right or interest in land can be held by an individual, by two or more persons, or by a business entity. Included in this chapter are discussions of joint tenancy, tenancy in common, and community property.

Chapters 7 and 8 deal with the process by which the ownership of real estate is transferred from one person to another. In particular, Chapter 7 discusses deeds and wills, and Chapter 8 deals with how a person gives evidence to the world that he possesses a given right or interest in land. Abstracts and title insurance are among the topics included.

In Chapters 9 and 10 we turn to contract law and its application to offers and acceptances. Because so much of what takes place in real estate is in the form of contracts, you will want to have a solid understanding of what makes a contract legally binding and what doesn't.

Chapters 11 through 15 are devoted to real estate finance. Chapter 11 explains mortgages and the laws regarding their use. Amortized loans, points, FHA and VA programs, loan application, and mortgage insurance are discussed in Chapter 12. Consumer loan issues are discussed in Chapter 13. Mortgage lenders, the secondary mortgage market, due-on-sale clauses, adjustable rate mortgages, and financing alternatives are covered in Chapters 14 and 15.

Chapter 16 shows how property taxes and assessments are calculated, and Chapter 17 explains title closing and escrow. Chapter 18 deals with leasing real estate and includes and describes a sample lease document. Chapter 19 explores the language, principles, and techniques of real estate appraisal.

In Chapters 2, 21 and 22 we examine the relationship between real estate agents, buyers, and sellers. Chapter 2 deals with real estate license law requirements, how a salesperson goes about choosing a broker to affiliate with, and professional ethics. Chapter 21 discusses an agent's employment, commission issues, and ethics. Chapter 22 explains the concepts of agency and intermediary status. Chapter 5 introduces you to fair housing, equal credit opportunity, and the Americans with Disabilities Act (ADA).

The remaining chapters deal with a number of individual and specialized real estate topics. Chapter 23 explores the condominium, cooperative, and planned unit development and time-share forms of real estate ownership. Included is a look at how they are created and the various rights and interests in land that are created by them.

Zoning, land planning, and deed restrictions are covered in Chapter 24. These are important topics because any limitations on a landowner's right to develop and use land can have a substantial effect on the value of the property. Finally, Chapter 25 is an introduction to the opportunities available to you as a real estate investor. Topics include tax shelter, equity build-up, what to buy, and when to buy.

Following the final chapter are several appendices that you will find useful. Appendices include the Texas Real Estate License Act and the Texas Canons of Professional Conduct. In addition, you will find a short real estate math review section, and the answers to the problems found at the end of Chapters 2 through 25.

CAREER OPPORTUNITIES

The contents and organization of this book are designed for people who are interested in real estate because they now own or plan to own real estate, and for people who are interested in real estate as a career. It is to those who are considering real estate as a profession that the balance of this chapter is devoted.

Most people who are considering a career in real estate think of becoming a real estate agent who specializes in selling homes. This is quite natural because home selling is the most visible segment of the real estate industry. It is the area of business most people enter and the one in which most practicing real estate licensees make their living. Residential sales experience is a good way to find out whether real estate sales appeals to you and whether residential property is the type of property in which you wish to specialize.

RESIDENTIAL BROKERAGE

Residential brokerage requires a broad knowledge of the community and its neighborhoods, finance, real estate law, economics, and the money market. Working hours will often include nights and weekends because these times are usually most convenient to buyers and sellers. A residential agent must also possess an automobile that is suitable for taking clients to see property.

A person who is adept at interpersonal relations, who can identify clients' buying motives, and find the property to fit, will probably be quite successful in this business.

PUTTING IT TO WORK

In only a few real estate offices are new residential salespersons given a minimum guaranteed salary or a draw against future commissions. Therefore, a new comer should have enough capital to survive until the first commissions are earned—and that can take four to six months. Additionally, the salesperson must be capable of developing and handling a personal budget that will withstand the feast and famine cycles that can occur in real estate.

COMMERCIAL BROKERAGE

Commercial brokers specialize in income-producing properties such as apartment and office buildings, retail stores, and warehouses. In this specialty, the salesperson is primarily selling monetary benefits. These benefits are the income, appreciation, mortgage reduction, and tax shelter that a property can reasonably be expected to produce.

To be successful in commercial brokerage, one must be very competent in mathematics, know how to finance transactions, and be aware of current tax laws. One must also have a sense of what makes a good investment, what makes an investment salable, and what the growth possibilities are in the neighborhood where a property is located.

Commission income from commercial brokerage is likely to be less frequent but in larger amounts compared residential brokerage. The time required to break into the business is longer, but once in the business, agent turnover is low. The working hours of a commercial broker are much closer to regular business hours than those in residential selling.

INDUSTRIAL BROKERAGE

Industrial brokers specialize in finding suitable land and buildings for industrial concerns. This includes leasing and developing industrial property as well as listing and selling it. An industrial broker must be familiar with industry requirements such as proximity to raw materials, water and power, labor supplies, and transportation. He must also know about local building, zoning, environmental, and tax laws as they pertain to possible sites, and about the schools, housing, and cultural and recreational facilities that would be used by future employees of the plant.

Commissions are irregular, but are usually substantial. Working hours are regular business hours, and sales efforts are primarily aimed at locating facts and figures and presenting them to clients in an orderly fashion. Industrial clients are usually sophisticated business people. Gaining entry to an industrial brokerage and acquiring a client list can be slow.

FARM BROKERAGE

With the rapid disappearance of the family farm, the farm broker's role is changing. Today a farm broker must be equally capable of handling the 160-acre spread of Farmer Jones and the 10,000-acre operation owned by an agribusiness corporation. College training in agriculture is an advantage and on-the-job training is a must. Knowledge of soil types, seeds, fertilizers, production methods, new machinery, government subsidies, and tax laws is vital to success. Farm brokerage offers as many opportunities to earn commissions and fees from leasing and property management as from listing and selling property.

PROPERTY MANAGEMENT

For an investment property, the property manager's job is to supervise every aspect of a property's operation so as to produce the highest possible financial return over the longest period of time. The manager's tasks include renting, tenant relations, building repair and maintenance, accounting, advertising, and supervision of personnel and tradespeople.

The expanded development of condominiums has resulted in a growing demand for property managers to maintain them. In addition, large businesses that own property for their own use hire property managers.

PUTTING IT TO WORK

Property managers are usually paid a salary and, if the property is a rental, a bonus for keeping the building fully occupied. To be successful, a property manager should be at ease with tenants, a public relations expert, handy with tools, a good bookkeeper, and knowledgeable about laws applicable to rental units.

APARTMENT LOCATORS

In recent years, the service of helping tenants find rental units and helping landlords find tenants has become increasingly popular. This is normally a free service to the public. Locators are paid commissions by management companies and owners of apartment projects for finding qualified tenants. A locating agent must have an in-depth knowledge of the apartment complexes in the community and their requirements for tenants. The locating business has expanded in the last few years to include the leasing of condominiums, townhouses, and single-family homes.

An offshoot of apartment locators are roommate locators. These are especially popular in cities with substantial numbers of single persons. Roommate locators are central places where people who are looking for other people willing to share living space can meet. The locator service maintains files on people with space to share (such as the second bedroom in a two-bedroom apartment) and those looking for space. The files will contain information on location, rent, male or female, smoking or nonsmoking, etc.

PUTTING IT TO WORK

Most roommate and tenant locator services have been started by individual entrepreneurs and are not affiliated with real estate offices. In Texas, a real estate license is required to operate as an apartment locator or a roommate locator.

REAL ESTATE APPRAISING

The job of the real estate appraiser is to gather and evaluate all available facts affecting a property's value. Appraisal is a real estate career opportunity that demands a special set of skills: practical experience, technical education, and good judgment. If you have an analytical mind and like to collect and interpret data, you might consider becoming a real estate appraiser. The job combines office work and field work, and the income of an expert appraiser can match that of a top real estate salesperson. You can be an independent appraiser or work as a salaried appraiser for local tax authorities or lending institutions. The appraisal process is becoming more complex, however. Most lenders and taxing authorities require that their appraisers have some advanced credential designation to ensure an adequate level of competence.

GOVERNMENT SERVICE

Approximately one-third of the land in the United States is government owned. This includes vacant and forested lands, office buildings, museums, parks, zoos, schools, hospitals, public housing, libraries, fire and police stations, roads and highways, subways, airports, and courthouses. All of these are real estate and all require government employees who can negotiate purchases and sales, appraise, finance, manage, plan, and develop. Cities, counties, and state governments, all have extensive real estate holdings. At the federal level, the Forest Service, Park Service, Department of Agriculture, Army Corps of Engineers, Bureau of Land Management, and General Services Administration are all major landholders. In addition to outright real estate ownership, government agencies such as the Federal Housing Administration, Department of Veterans Affairs, and Federal Home Loan Bank employ thousands of real estate specialists to keep their real estate lending programs operating.

LAND DEVELOPMENT

Most new houses in the United States are built by developers who in turn sell them to homeowners and investors. Some houses are built by small-scale developers who produce only a few a year. Others are part of 400-house subdivisions and 40-story condominiums that are developed and constructed by large corporations that have their own planning, appraising, financing, construction, title, and marketing personnel. There is equal opportunity for success in development whether you build four houses a year or work for a firm that builds 400 a year.

URBAN PLANNING

Urban planners work with local governments and civic groups for the purpose of anticipating future growth and land use changes. The urban planner makes recommendations for new streets, highways, sewer and water lines, schools, parks, and libraries. The current emphasis on environmental protection and controlled growth has made urban planning one of real estate's most rapidly expanding specialties. An urban planning job is usually a salaried position and does not emphasize sales ability.

MORTGAGE FINANCING

Specialists in mortgage financing have a dual role: (1) to find economically sound properties for lenders, and (2) to locate money for borrowers. A mortgage specialist can work independently, receiving a fee from the borrower for locating a lender, or as a salaried employee of a lending institution. The commission paid to a mortgage specialist on a multimillion dollar loan can be quite substantial. Texas requires mortgage brokers to be licensed.

SECURITIES AND SYNDICATIONS

Limited partnerships and other forms of real estate syndications that combine the investment capital of a number of investors to buy large properties number in the thousands. The investment opportunities and professional management offered by syndications are eagerly sought after by people with money to invest in real estate. As a result, there are job opportunities in creating, promoting, and managing real estate syndications.

CONSULTING

Real estate consulting involves giving others advice about real estate for a fee. A consultant must have a very broad knowledge of real estate—including financing, appraising, brokerage, management, development, construction, investing, leasing, zoning, taxes, title, economics, and law. To remain in business as a consultant, one must develop a good track record of successful suggestions and advice. Because it is difficult to be a consultant without performing a brokerage function, most consultants have a real estate license.

RESEARCH AND EDUCATION

A person interested in real estate research can concentrate on such matters as improved construction materials and management methods, or on finding answers to economic questions such as "What is the demand for homes going to be next year in this community (state, country)?"

Opportunities abound in real estate education. Nearly all states require the completion of specified real estate courses before a real estate license can be issued. All states require continuing education for license renewal. As a result, people with experience in the industry and an ability to effectively teach the subject are much sought after as instructors.

Real estate teachers organizations, such as the Texas Real Estate Teachers Association (TRETA) with their CREI (Certified Real Estate Instructor) designation and the Real Estate Educators Association (REEA) with their DREI (Distinguished Real Estate Instructor) designation, are now also making a significant impact on improving the quality of real estate education.

FULL-TIME INVESTOR

One of the advantages of the free-enterprise system is that you can choose to become a full-time investor solely for yourself. A substantial number of people have quit their jobs to work full time with their investment properties and have done quite well at it. A popular and successful route for many has been to purchase, inexpensively and with a low down payment, a small apartment building that has not been well maintained but is in a good neighborhood. The property is then thoroughly reconditioned and rents are raised. This process increases the value of the property. The increase is parlayed into a larger building—often through a tax-deferred exchange—and the process is repeated. Alternatively, the investor can increase the mortgage loan on the building and take the cash he receives as a "salary" for himself or use it as a down payment on another not-too-well maintained apartment building in a good neighborhood.

Other individual investors have done well financially by searching newspaper advertisements and regularly visiting real estate brokerage offices looking for underpriced properties that can be sold at a mark-up. A variation of this is to write to out-of-town property owners in a given neighborhood to see if any wish to sell at a bargain price. Another approach is to become a small-scale developer and contractor. (No license is needed if you work with your own property.) Through your own personal efforts you create value in your projects and then hold them as investments. One should be cautioned, however, that there are very few legitimate "get rich quick" schemes in the real estate business.

LICENSE REQUIREMENTS

As stated previously, property owners who deal only with their own property are not required to hold a real estate license. However, any person who *for another*, and for compensation or the promise of compensation, lists or offers to list, sells or offers to sell, buys or offers to buy, negotiates or offers to negotiate, either directly or indirectly, for the purpose of bringing about a sale, purchase, or options to purchase, exchange, auction, lease, or rental of real estate, or any interest in real estate, is required to hold a valid real estate license. Texas also requires people offering their services as property managers to hold real estate licenses.

If your real estate plans are such that you may need a license, you should turn to Chapter 2 and read the material on real estate licensing.

Chapter 2

KEY TERMS

Broker: a person or legal entity licensed to act independently in conducting a real estate brokerage business

Independent contractor: one who contracts to do work according to personal methods and is responsible to the employer only for the results of that work

License revocation: to recall and make void a license

License suspension: to temporarily make a license ineffective

Licensee: one who holds a license

REALTOR®: a registered trademark owned by the National Association of REALTORS® for use by its members

Recovery fund: a state-operated fund that can be tapped to pay for uncollectible judgments against real estate licensees

Sales associate: a salesperson or broker employed by a broker

Salesperson: a person employed by a broker to list, negotiate, sell, or lease real property for others

Texas Real Estate Commission: the state board that advises and sets policies regarding real estate licensees and transaction procedures

Licensing Laws and Professional Affiliation

IN THIS CHAPTER

In this chapter we will cover the various licensing law requirements, emphasizing the provisions of the Texas Real Estate License Act. The License Act defines the **licensees,** explains the licensing procedure, and describes the obligations of the licensees with special emphasis on license suspension and revocation. This chapter also covers the purpose and function of the real estate commission recovery fund, securities licensing, affiliating with a broker, franchise offices, and the independent contractor issue. The chapter concludes with coverage of professional real estate associations.

For most owners of real estate the decision to sell means hiring a broker to find a buyer. Although some owners choose to market their properties themselves, most find it advantageous to turn the job over to a real estate broker and pay a commission for the service of finding a buyer and carrying the deal through closing. The next three chapters are for the owner who plans to use a broker and for the person who plans to be a real estate salesperson or broker. First, Chapter 2 discusses examination and licensing requirements and an overview of how states regulate the real estate profession, including a section on how to choose a broker with whom to affiliate and professional real estate associations, in particular the Texas Association of REALTORS®, and the National Association of REALTORS®. In Chapter 21, we discuss employment, utilizing a simplified real estate listing contract. Next we take a close look at the agency responsibilities a broker has toward a seller together with the seller's obligations toward the broker. Then we discuss seller and broker responsibilities toward persons who are interested in purchasing the listed property, and buyer brokerage.

RATIONALE FOR REAL ESTATE LICENSING

Does the public have a vested interest in seeing that real estate salespersons and brokers have the qualifications of honesty, truthfulness, good reputation, and real estate knowledge before they are allowed to negotiate real estate transactions on behalf of others? It was this concern that brought about real estate licensing laws as we know them today. Until 1917, no state required real estate agents to be licensed. Anyone who wanted to be an agent could simply hang up a sign stating that he or she was an agent. In larger cities there were persons and firms who specialized in bringing buyers and sellers together. In smaller towns, a local banker, attorney, or barber would know who had what for sale and be the person a buyer would ask for property information.

The first attempt to require that persons acting as real estate agents be licensed was made by the California legislature in 1917. That law was declared unconstitutional, with the main opposition being that the state was unreasonably interfering with the right of every citizen to engage in a useful and legitimate occupation. Two years later, in 1919, the California legislature passed a second real estate licensing act. This time it was upheld by the Supreme Court. That same year, Michigan, Oregon, and Tennessee also passed real estate licensing acts. Today, all 50 states and the District of Columbia require that persons who offer their services as real estate agents be licensed.

The Real Estate License Act (the "Act") of Texas (Occupation Code, § 1101) was first passed in 1939. The Act defines the functions and duties of a broker and establishes explicit provisions for ***license revocation*** and suspension. The interpretation of the Act is administered literally, requiring a higher standard of care from the licensee.

The licensing laws prevent complete freedom of entry into the profession. The public has a vested interest in seeing that salespersons and brokers have the qualifications of honesty, truthfulness, and good reputation. This was the intent of the first license laws. Some years later the additional requirements of license examinations and real estate education were added in the belief that a person who wants to be a real estate agent should meet special knowledge qualifications. To further protect consumers, the Texas Real Estate Commission (TREC) requires that each active real estate broker display a Consumer Information Form in a prominent location in each place of business the broker maintains. The form informs the consumer of the broker's recovery fund (discussed later) and how to direct complaints to the Texas Real Estate Commission.

The penalties for a violation of the License Act are severe. Each violation is set in an amount not to exceed $5,000. Each day a violation continues may be considered a separate violation for purposes of penalty assessment, if the Commission finds that the charged person: (1) engaged in an activity for which a real estate broker or real estate salesperson's license is required without a legal license, and (2) was not licensed by the Commission as a real estate broker or a real estate salesperson at any time in the four years preceding the date of the violation. The License Act also provides for imprisonment for up to one year.

Experience to date clearly indicates that the Texas Real Estate License Act has helped to upgrade technical competency and has increased public confidence in brokers and salespersons. Moreover, the Act is an important and powerful tool in reducing fraudulent real estate practices because the state can suspend or revoke a person's license to operate. A complete copy of the Act current as of the date of this publication is shown in Appendix A, and the current Texas Real Estate License Act is available on the Internet at http://www.trec.state.tx.us. It is suggested that it be read several times, in detail. It is a primary basis for test questions at every level, and there is no excuse for not knowing it. TREC regulations and form information are also available at the TREC website.

The Act currently defines two levels of licensure: broker and salesperson.

BROKER DEFINED

A real estate ***broker***, as statutorily defined in Texas, means a person (*person* is defined as an "individual or any other entity including but not limited to a governmental body, limited liability company, limited liability partnership, partnership, or corporation, foreign or domestic") who, *for another person* and for a fee, commission, or other valuable consideration, or with the intention or in the expectation or on the promise of receiving or collecting a fee, commission, or other valuable consideration from another person:

1. Sells, exchanges, purchases, rents, or leases real estate.
2. Offers to sell, exchange, purchase, rent, or lease real estate.
3. Negotiates, or attempts to negotiate, the listing, sale, exchange, purchase, rental, or leasing of real estate.
4. Lists, or offers or attempts or agrees to list, real estate for sale, rental, lease, exchange, or trade.
5. Appraises, or offers or attempts or agrees to appraise, real estate.
6. Auctions, or offers or attempts or agrees to auction, real estate.
7. Buys or sells, or offers to buy or sell, or otherwise deals in options on real estate.
8. Aids, attempts, or offers to aid, in locating or obtaining for purchase, rent, or lease, any real estate.
9. Procures, or assists in the procuring of, prospects for the purpose of effecting the sale, exchange, lease, or rental of real estate.
10. Procures, or assists in the procuring of, properties for the purpose of effecting the sale, exchange, lease, or rental of real estate.

The statutory definition of *real estate broker* in Texas also includes a person employed by, or on behalf of, the owner or owners of lots or other parcels of real estate, at a salary, fee, commission, or any other valuable consideration, employed to sell real estate in lots or parcels, or any other disposition thereof. The term *broker* also includes a person who charges an advance fee, or contracts for collection of a fee in connection with a contract, whereby he undertakes primarily to promote the sale of real estate either through its listing in a publication issued primarily for such purpose, or for referral of information concerning the real estate to brokers, or both.

SALESPERSON DEFINED

The definition of real estate ***salesperson*** is a person associated with a Texas-licensed real estate broker for the purposes of performing acts or transactions comprehended by the term of *real estate broker* as defined in the Act. It is specifically provided that a salesperson shall not accept compensation for real estate transactions from any person other than the broker under whom the salesperson is licensed at the time that the salesperson is paid, or under whom the salesperson was licensed when the salesperson earned the right to compensation. Thus, a salesperson who takes a listing on a property does so in the name of the salesperson's broker. In the event of a legal dispute caused by a salesperson, the dispute would be between the principal and the broker. Thus, some brokers take considerable care to oversee the documents that their salespeople prepare and sign. Other brokers do not, relying instead on the knowledge and sensibility of their salespeople, and accepting a certain amount of risk in the process.

The above definitions are intended to be all-inclusive so that almost any act affecting real property is construed to be one that constitutes brokerage. The objective is to maintain higher standards in the real estate industry through licensing. The only people not required to be licensed are specifically exempted from the Act and are persons operating in unique capacities, as discussed next.

Exemptions From Licensing

Not everybody in the office needs to be licensed. Clarification of the licensing provisions are set out in the TREC rules pertaining to the provisions of The Texas Real Estate Licensing Act. These rules state that an office sales manager who deals only with licensees and office personnel does not have to be licensed, nor does an officer of a corporation acting in behalf of the Board of Directors of the corporation, provided no special compensation is received.

Other exemptions from licensing include the following:

1. An attorney licensed in any state.
2. An attorney-in-fact authorized under a power of attorney to conduct a real estate transaction.
3. A public official in the conduct of official duties.
4. A person conducting an auction under the authority of a license issued by this state, provided the person does not perform any other act of a real estate broker or salesman as defined by this Act.
5. A person acting under a court order or under the authority of a will or a written trust instrument.
6. A person employed by an owner in the sale of structures and land on which said structures are located if the structures are erected by the owner in the course of the owner's business.
7. An on-site manager of an apartment complex.
8. An owner or his employees in renting or leasing his own real estate whether improved or unimproved.

9. A partnership or limited liability partnership performing an act constituting an act of a broker or salesperson, as defined by the Act, through a partner who is duly licensed as a real estate broker.
10. Transactions involving the sale, lease, or transfer of any mineral or mining interest in real property.
11. Transactions involving the sale, lease, or transfer of cemetery lots.
12. Transactions involving the renting, leasing, or management of hotels or motels.
13. The sale of real property under a power of sale conferred by a deed of trust or other contract lien.

Sales Associate

The term ***sales associate*** is not a license category. It merely refers to anyone with a real estate license who is employed by and "associated" with a broker. Most often this associate will be a real estate salesperson. However, a person who holds a broker license can work for another broker. Such a person is a regular member of the employing broker's sales force just like someone with a salesperson license. The salesperson and brokers who work for a broker are known collectively as the broker's sales associates or sales force or sales staff. You will also hear the term *real estate agent* used in a general sense. Correctly speaking, the broker is a special agent of the property owner and the sales associate is a general agent of the broker. In nontechnical language, real estate agent today means anyone, broker or salesperson, who negotiates real estate transactions for others.

License Eligibility

To be eligible for a real estate salesperson's license in Texas, an individual must be a resident of Texas and be at least 18 years of age. An applicant for a brokerage license shall additionally have not less than two years' active experience as a licensed real estate practitioner. He or she must further satisfy the Commission, through its application procedures, as to honesty, trustworthiness, integrity, and competency. Competency is determined by passing the licensing examination.

The Act further requires that any applicant for broker licensure shall furnish the Commission satisfactory evidence: (1) that the applicant has satisfied the educational requirements required by the Act, (2) that the applicant has satisfied the requirements for broker licensure, (3) that the applicant was a licensed real estate broker in another state and that the applicant has had not less than two years active experience in that other state as a licensed real estate broker or salesperson during the 36-month period immediately preceding the filing of the application and that the applicant satisfied the educational requirements for broker licensure provided for by the Act, or (4) the applicant has within one year previous to the filing of the application been licensed in the state as a broker.

The 2007 Legislature added a new requirement. An applicant for a license or renewal of an unexpired license must submit a complete and legible set of fingerprints, on a form prescribed by the commission, to the commission or to the Department of Public Safety for the purposes of obtaining criminal history record information from DPS and the Federal Bureau of Investigation. If he refuses to do so, the commission will refuse to issue the license.

Education Requirements—Brokers

In recent years, the education requirements have also become an increasingly important part of license qualifications. Nearly all states (including Texas) require that applicants take real estate education courses at community colleges, universities, private real estate schools, or through adult education programs at high schools.

An applicant for a Texas real estate brokerage license must furnish evidence of successful completion of 60 semester hours (900 classroom hours) of real estate core courses or related courses accepted by the Real Estate Commission. Eighteen of the 60 hours must be completed in core real estate courses, two semester hours of which is required to be real estate brokerage.

Education Requirements—Salespersons

An applicant for real estate salesperson license must furnish evidence of successful completion of 14 semester hours (210 classroom hours) of post secondary education. Ten hours of these 14 hours must be in real estate core courses as defined by the Act. Four of the 10 hours must be completed in a course described as Principles of Real Estate, which must include at least three classroom hours of instruction on federal, state, and local laws relating to housing discrimination, housing credit discrimination, and community reinvestment. Applicants must also show evidence of completion of two hours (30 classroom hours) of a course in the Law of Agency, a minimum of two hours in the Law of Contracts, and an additional two hours of core real estate courses. There is an additional educational requirement for the salesperson's first renewal: completion of 18 semester hours; 14 of which must be in core real estate courses.

Continuing Education

Once the minimum education requirements have been satisfied, the licensee must provide the Commission proof of attendance of at least 15 classroom hours of continuing education courses approved by the Commission during the term of the current license. At least six hours of the instruction must be devoted to the rules of the Commission, fair housing laws, agency laws, antitrust laws, the Deceptive Trade Practices-Consumer Protection Act, disclosures to buyers and sellers, current contract and addendum forms, the unauthorized practice of law, and case studies involving violations of laws and regulations, current federal housing administration, veterans administration regulations, tax laws, property tax consulting laws, and other legal topics approved by the Commission. The nine remaining hours may be devoted to other real estate related topics approved by the Commission. The Commission has approved the publication of two courses, Law Update (a three-hour course) and Ethics (another three-hour course), that are now mandatory for all licensees taking courses for their MCE credit. Real estate related courses approved by the State Bar of Texas also qualify for credit. The only exception to this rule is that if a licensee is a member of the legislature, that person is only required to complete three hours of continuing education in the legal topics. The Commission may not require examinations except for correspondence courses. Daily course segments must be at least one hour long, but not more than 10 hours long.

If a license is renewed for less than two years, the licensee must provide the commission proof of attendance of at least eight classroom hours of continuing education within the term of the current license, three classroom hours of which must have been devoted to the legal topics. Core courses can qualify for MCE credit.

Table 2.1 shows the education and experience requirements in effect in the United States at the time this book was printed. The table is included to give you an overview of the emphasis currently being placed on education and experience by the various states. For up-to-the-minute information on education and experience requirements in Texas, you should go online to http://www.trec.state.tx.us.

LICENSING PROCEDURE

When a license applicant has completed or is close to completing the education and experience requirements, formal application for licensure is begun by filling out a license application form furnished by the Texas Real Estate Commission. When the application is completed, it is returned to the Commission along with a fee to cover application processing and the examination charge. After the Commission receives the application, an examination authorization letter is issued that gives the applicant one year in which to take and pass the exam.

Examination

License examinations in Texas are now administered by PSI Examination Services (PSI), a nationally recognized testing organization, with testing centers throughout Texas. Applicants can make reservations with PSI via a toll-free number, mail, online at http://psiexams.com, or facsimile, and seats are scheduled on a first-come first-serve basis. A fee is charged each time the exam is taken. An applicant may reschedule an appointment without forfeiting the fee if PSI is timely notified.

The examination consists of two parts: a theory portion (based on general principles) and a Texas law portion. The theory portion contains 80 questions on both exams. The law portion is 30 questions on a salesperson's exam, and 40 questions on the broker's exam. Two and a half hours are allowed to complete both exams, which also includes questions on closing statements that are not on the salesperson's exam. Each applicant must take both parts the first time; if one part is passed it need not be retaken. Test results are provided immediately following the exam. Each test differs and another fee is required each time the

TABLE 2.1 Real estate education and experience requirements

	Salesperson License		Broker License (Total Hours)		
State	Education Requirement	Continuing Education	Education Requirement	Experience Requirement	Continuing Education
Alabama	60 hours	Yes	60 hours	2 years	Yes
Alaska	20 hours	Yes	35 hours		Yes
Arizona	90 hours	Yes	180 hours	3 years	Yes
Arkansas	60 hours	Yes	120 hours	2 years	Yes
California	135 hours	Yes	five additional college-level courses	2 years	Yes
Colorado	N/A	Yes	360 hours	N/A	Yes
Connecticut	60 hours	Yes	168 hours	2 years	Yes
Delaware	99 hours	Yes	198 hours	5 years	Yes
Dist. of Col.	60 hours	Yes	195 hours	2 years	Yes
Florida	63 hours	Yes	180 hours	1 year	Yes
Georgia	75 hours	Yes	135 hours	3 years	Yes
Hawaii	60 hours	Yes	140 hours	3 years	Yes
Idaho	90 hours	Yes	180 hours	2 years	Yes
Illinois	45 hours	Yes	120 hours	N/A	Yes
Indiana	54 hours	Yes	56 hours	N/A	Yes
Iowa	60 hours	Yes	132 hours	2 years	Yes
Kansas	60 hours	Yes	84 hours	2 years	Yes
Kentucky	96 hours	Yes	192 hours	N/A	Yes
Louisiana	90 hours	Yes	240 hours	2 years	Yes
Maine	60 hours	Yes	165 hours	3 years	Yes
Maryland	60 hours	Yes	195 hours	3 years	Yes
Massachusetts	24 hours	No	54 hours	1 year	Yes
Michigan	40 hours	Yes	130 hours	3 years	Yes
Minnesota	90 hours	Yes	120 hours	2 years	Yes
Mississippi	60 hours	Yes	120 hours	1 year	Yes
Missouri	72 hours	Yes	120 hours	1 year	Yes
Montana	60 hours	Yes	120 hours	2 years	Yes

Explanation: Hours are clock-hours in the classroom; experience requirement is experience as a licensed real estate salesperson; continuing education refers to education required for license renewal. Some states credit completed salesperson education toward the broker education requirement.

(continued)

exam is taken. Retaking the exam immediately is not a good idea, because you may not see any of the same questions on the second exam that you experienced on the first exam. A word of caution: The exam tests knowledge of the subject matter, not how to take a test. Study hard and often!

Renewal

Once licensed, as long as a person remains active in real estate the license may be renewed by paying the required annual certification fee, and confirming to the

TABLE 2.1 Real estate education and experience requirements (*continued*)

	Salesperson License		Broker License (Total Hours)		
State	Education Requirement	Continuing Education	Education Requirement	Experience Requirement	Continuing Education
Nebraska	60 hours	Yes	120 hours	N/A	Yes
Nevada	90 hours	Yes	64 college or credit hours	N/A	Yes
New Hampshire	40 hours	Yes	100 hours or 2,000 hours part time	1 year/5 years	Yes
New Jersey	75 hours	No	225 hours	3 years	No
New Mexico	60 hours	Yes	180 hours	2 years	Yes
New York	45 hours	Yes	90 hours	1 year	Yes
North Carolina	N/A	Yes	75 hours	N/A	Yes
North Dakota	45 hours	Yes	105 hours	2 years	Yes
Ohio	120 hours	Yes	360 hours	2 years	Yes
Oklahoma	45 hours	Yes	120 hours	2 years	Yes
Oregon	N/A	Yes	150 hours	N/A	Yes
Pennsylvania	60 hours	Yes	300 hours	3 years	Yes
Rhode Island	18 hours	No	108 hours	1 year	Yes
South Carolina	60 hours	No	120 hours	3 years	Yes
South Dakota	None	Yes	100 hours	2 years	No
Tennessee	90 hours	Yes	120 hours	3 years	Yes
Texas	210 hours	Yes	900 hours	2 years	Yes
Utah	90 hours	Yes	210 hours	3 years	Yes
Vermont	40 hours	Yes	80 hours	2 years	Yes
Virginia	60 hours	Yes	240 hours	4 years	Yes
Washington	60 hours	Yes	180 hours	2 years	Yes
West Virginia	90 hours	Yes	180 hours	2 years	Yes
Wisconsin	72 hours	Yes	108 hours	N/A	Yes
Wyoming	54 hours	Yes	108 hours	2 years	Yes

Source: Association of Real Estate License Law Officials, P.O. Box 230139, Montgomery, AL, 36123-0159, or http://www.ARELLO.org. Check with your state for any subsequent changes.

Texas Real Estate Commission that the licensee has not been convicted of a felony. If the licensee has met all of the educational requirements, license renewal is put on a biennial renewal (every two years). No additional exam is required.

If a license expires, the Real Estate Commission must waive the examination of an applicant for a broker or salesperson license who has, within one year previous to the filing of the application, been licensed in Texas as a broker or salesperson. The Commission may, at its discretion, also provide for a waiver of some or all of the requirements for a license under the Act for an applicant who was licensed under the Act within six years preceding the date of filing the renewal application.

The Act also allows a nonresident who was formerly licensed in Texas as a salesperson or broker to apply for licensure in Texas not later than the first anniversary of the date of the expiration of the previous license. The nonresident is subject to the same requirements as a resident applicant, however.

Inactive Status

All salesperson licenses are initially issued as "inactive" until the salesperson becomes affiliated with a sponsoring broker. When the association of a salesperson with the sponsoring broker is terminated, the broker must immediately return the salesperson's license to the Commission. The Real Estate Commission Regulations provide that if the sponsorship has ended because the broker terminated the sponsorship, the broker *must* immediately notify the salespeople *in writing*. If the sponsorship has ended because the salesperson has left the sponsorship, the salesperson *must* immediately notify the broker *in writing*. The salesperson is then placed on "inactive" status by the Commission. That salesperson's license may be activated if, within the calendar year, a request, accompanied by the required fee, is filed with the Commission by a licensed broker advising that she assumes sponsorship of the salesperson. A salesperson may also elect to remain inactive indefinitely so long as the salesperson continues to pay the annual fee to the Commission.

A real estate broker who is not acting as a broker or sponsoring a salesperson may also apply to the Commission in writing to be placed on the inactive status list maintained by the Commission and must do so before the expiration of the broker's license. The broker must terminate the broker's association with any salesperson sponsored by the broker by getting written notice to the salesperson before the thirtieth day before the date the broker applies for inactive status. A broker on inactive status is still required to pay the annual renewal fees. If the broker has been on inactive status, the Commission must remove the person from the inactive list on application and proof of attendance of at least 15 classroom hours of continuing education as specified under the Act.

NONRESIDENT LICENSING

The general rule regarding license requirements is that a person must be licensed in the state within which he negotiates. Thus, if a broker or one of his salespeople sells an out-of-state property, but conducts the negotiations entirely within the borders of his own state, he does not need to be licensed to sell in the state where the land is actually located. State laws also permit the broker of one state to split a commission with the broker of another state provided each conducts negotiations only within the state where he is licensed. Therefore, if a Texas Broker B takes a listing at its office on a parcel of land located in Texas, and a Broker C in Oklahoma sells it to one of his clients, conducting the sale negotiations within State C, then Brokers B and C can split the commission. If, however, the Oklahoma Broker C comes to Texas to negotiate a contract, then a license in Texas is necessary. The standard practice has been to apply for a *nonresident license* and meet substantially the same exam and experience requirements as demanded of resident brokers.

The Texas Real Estate Licensing Act allows a licensed real estate broker in another state to apply for broker licensure if he has been a licensed real estate broker in another state with not less than two years' active experience during the 36-month period immediately preceding the filing of his application, and the educational requirements for broker licensure in the state of Texas are satisfied.

License Reciprocity

In recent years, there has been considerable effort to design real estate licensing systems that permit a broker and the broker's sales staff to conduct negotiations in other states without having to obtain nonresident licenses. The result is *license reciprocity* and it applies when one state honors another's license. In permitting reciprocity, state officials are primarily concerned with the nonresident's knowledge of real estate law and practice as it applies to the state in which the applicant wishes to operate.

A few states accept real estate licenses issued by other states. This is called *full reciprocity* and means that a licensee can operate in another state without having to take that state's examination and meet its education and experience requirements. More commonly, most states have *partial reciprocity* that gives credit to the licensees of another state for experience, education, and examination. Texas does not reciprocate with any state. Instead, the Texas Real Estate License Act provides that a resident broker in another state may apply for a nonresident Texas broker license by meeting the nonresident broker requirements.

Notice of Consent

When a broker operates outside of his home state, he may be required to file a **notice of consent** in each state in which he intends to operate, usually with the secretary of state. This permits the secretary of state to receive legal summonses on behalf of the nonresident broker and provides a state resident an avenue by which he can sue a broker who is a resident of another state. Texas has this requirement.

LICENSING THE BUSINESS FIRM

When a real estate broker wishes to establish a brokerage business, the simplest method is a sole proprietorship under the broker's own name, such as Kathleen B. Jones, Real Estate Broker. Some states, including Texas, permit a broker to operate out of his or her residence. However, operating a business in a residential neighborhood can be bothersome to neighbors.

Assumed Name

When a person operates under a name other than his own, he must register that name by filing an *assumed name certificate* with his county clerk and the state real estate licensing authority. Thus, if John B. Jones wishes to call his brokerage business Great Texas Realty, his business certificate would show "John B. Jones, doing business as Great Texas Realty." (Sometimes "doing business as" is shortened to dba or d/b/a.)

A sole proprietorship, whether operated under the broker's name or an assumed name, offers a broker advantages in the form of absolute control, flexibility, ease of organization, personal independence, ownership of all the profits and losses, and the freedom to expand by sponsoring all the salespeople and staff he can manage and afford. Against this the sole proprietor must recognize that he is the sole source of capital for the business and the only owner available to manage it.

Recognizing the need to accumulate capital and management expertise within a single brokerage operation, Texas also permits corporations, limited liability companies, and partnerships to be licensed. Because a corporation is an artificial being (not an individual), it cannot take a real estate examination. Therefore, Texas laws require that an officer of the corporation be a Texas-licensed real estate broker and qualified to act as the designated person for a corporation holding Texas broker licensure. A corporation incorporated in a state other than Texas may be accepted as a Texas resident for purposes of licensure if it is qualified to do business in Texas; its corporate officers, its principal place of business, and all of its assets are located in Texas; and all of its officers and directors are Texas residents. Similarly, a limited liability company must have a manager as a designated broker. Texas law does not require that a partnership entity be licensed, provided that each individual partner or non-partner employee who acts as a real estate agent in the partnership's name is licensed as a real estate broker or salesperson. The partnership must also file an assumed name certificate showing the names of the partners and the name of the partnership.

Branch Offices

If a broker expands by establishing branch offices that are geographically separate from the main or home office, each branch must have a branch office license.

LICENSING REAL ESTATE INSPECTORS

A common problem for real estate purchasers, and an area of continuing liability for real estate agents, has been that of defective property. Purchasers frequently feel that the expertise of real estate agents should shield them from the duty to investigate too closely, because the agent sees and inspects property all the time. The agent also has a duty to disclose material defects in the property under the License Act. The difficulty in relying on the agent is that the agent often doesn't have the expertise, and in many cases the defect is too technical or complicated to be discovered by the agent.

In an effort to alleviate this situation, Texas provides for the licensing of **real estate inspectors.** The statute provides that a person may not act as a real estate inspector for a buyer or seller unless the person possesses a real estate inspector license issued by the Texas Real Estate Commission. The statute further provides for minimum standards of education and a recovery fund, similar to that required of real estate salespersons or brokers. The law is also designed to eliminate certain potential for conflicts of interest, specifically prohibiting the inspector from:

1. Accepting an assignment if the employment is contingent on the reporting of a specific, predetermined condition or on reporting findings other than those known to the inspector to be facts at the time of accepting the assignment.
2. Acting in a manner or engaging in a practice that is dishonest or fraudulent or that involves deceit or misrepresentation.
3. Performing the inspection in a negligent or incompetent manner.
4. Acting in the dual capacity of inspector and undisclosed principal.
5. Acting in the dual capacity of real estate inspector and real estate broker or salesperson.
6. Performing any repairs in connection with the real estate inspection.

There are additional prohibitions and specific references to prohibiting the inspector's violations of the Deceptive Trade Practices Act. The statute also provides for recovery of attorney's fees, at the discretion of the court, if they are incurred in obtaining a recovery from a licensed inspector for a violation of the Act.

PUTTING IT TO WORK

Since the statute has been in effect, it has opened a whole new industry in the real estate profession. In addition, it has given the home purchaser a licensed, competent person for protection against defects in the property. The real estate licensee, too, has a person to recommend for the inspections of a more technical nature, which may help to eliminate another potential liability.

REGISTRATION

The Texas Real Estate License Act also provides for *registration* for those who sell, buy, lease, or transfer an easement or a right-of-way for compensation, or with the intention or in the expectation, or on the promise of receiving or collecting compensation, for use and connection with telecommunication, utility, railroad, or pipeline service. These people, as a part of their daily business, engage in the transfer or sale of real estate for others, but there has been a "gray" area as to whether they needed to be licensed. They don't market real estate for consumers in the regular course of business. Most of their activities are specialized in right-of-way acquisitions. To eliminate this confusion, we now have a registration procedure under Section 1101.502 of the Texas

Real Estate License Act. It does not require the same educational requirements of real estate licensing, and has Commission procedures for investigating complaints for revoking or suspending the registration if a registrant had engaged in conduct that violates the Act.

TEXAS REAL ESTATE COMMISSION

The administration of the provisions of the Texas Real Estate License Act is vested in the ***Texas Real Estate Commission.*** The Commission consists of nine members appointed by the Governor with the consent of two-thirds of the Senate present. The commissioners hold office for staggered terms of six years, with the terms of three members expiring January 31 of each odd-numbered year. The governor designates one of the licensed broker members as the chairperson.

A person who is appointed to serve as a Commissioner may not vote, deliberate, or be counted as member in attendance at a meeting of the Commission until that person completes a training program that complies with state law.

Commission Membership

Six members of the Commission must have been engaged in the real estate brokerage business as licensed real estate brokers as their major occupation for at least five years preceding their appointments to the Commission, although a broker appointee cannot hold an office in a real estate industry trade association. The other three members must be representatives of the general public who are not licensed under the Texas Real Estate License Act and who do not have a financial interest in the practice of real estate broker or real estate salesperson, other than as consumers, and who are not acting for anyone holding such an interest.

An existing commissioner can be removed from the commission if as broker member he or she ceases to be a licensed real estate broker, or if as a public member he or she acquires a real estate license or financial interest in the practice of real estate, or if that commissioner becomes an employee or paid consultant of any real estate trade association or an officer in a statewide real estate trade association, or if a commissioner misses more than one-half of the regularly scheduled meetings. All appointments to the Commission must be made without regard to the race, creed, sex, religion, or national origin of the appointee.

The Commission has a regular meeting in October of each year, although it usually meets at least once per month. It has the power to make and enforce all rules and regulations in performance of its duties and institute actions to enjoin any violation of any provision of the Texas Real Estate License Act.

Any rule promulgated by the Commission may be blocked or rescinded by a majority vote of the standing committee of the Texas House or Texas Senate having jurisdiction over the affairs of the Texas Real Estate Commission.

Commissioners' Duties

The duties of the commissioners do not normally include the daily operation of the Real Estate Commission. Their compensation as commissioners is only token compensation for time actually spent on their duties, and they are not employees of the Commission. Therefore, to administer the day-to-day activities of the Commission, the Commission selects an Administrator, who has the complete authority to exercise the powers, rights, and duties of the Commission. The Administrator and his or her staff are salaried employees of the Commission and all business of the Commission, service of process, notices, and applications are considered filed with the Administrator or Assistant Administrator.

LICENSE SUSPENSION AND REVOCATION

The most important control a state has over its real estate salespersons and brokers is that it can **suspend** (temporarily make ineffective) or **revoke** (recall and make void) a real estate license. Without one, it is unlawful for a person to engage in real estate activities for the purpose of earning a commission or fee. Unless an agent has a valid license, a court of law will not uphold the agent's claim for a commission from a client.

The Texas Real Estate Licensing Act gives certain reasons for which a license can be revoked or suspended. The Commission can revoke or suspend a license if:

1. The licensee has entered a plea of guilty or nolo contendere, or been found guilty or been convicted of, a felony, in which fraud is an essential element, and the time for appeal has elapsed or the judgment or conviction has been affirmed on appeal, irrespective of an order granting probation following such conviction, suspending the imposition of sentence.

2. The licensee has procured, or attempted to procure, a real estate license for himself or herself or a salesperson, by fraud, misrepresentation, or deceit, or by making a material misstatement of fact in an application for a real estate license.

3. The licensee, when selling, trading, or renting real property in his or her own name, or in the name of a relative within the first degree of consanguinity, engaged in misrepresentation or dishonest or fraudulent action.

4. The licensee fails within a reasonable time to make good a check issued to the Commission after the Commission has mailed a request for payment by certified mail to the licensee's last known business address as reflected by the Commission's records.

5. The licensee fails or refused to produce on request, for inspection by the Commission or Commission representative, a document, book, or record, that is in the license holder's possession and relates to a real estate transaction conducted by the license holder.

6. The licensee fails to provide, within a reasonable time, information the Commission requested that relates to a formal or informal complaint to the Commission that would indicate a violation of the Texas Real Estate License Act.

7. The licensee fails to surrender to the owner, without just cause, a document or instrument that is requested by the owner and is in the license holder's possession.

8. The licensee fails to use a contract form required by the Commission.

9. The licensee fails to inform the Commission, not later than the 30th day after the date of the final conviction or the entry of a plea of nolo contendre, that the person has been convicted of or entered a plea of nolo contendre with a felony or criminal offense involving fraud; or

10. The licensee has disregarded or violated a provision of this Act.

The licensee, **while performing an act constituting a broker or salesperson:**

1. Acts negligently or incompetently.

2. Engages in conduct that is dishonest or in bad faith or demonstrates untrustworthiness.

3. Makes a material misrepresentation, or fails to disclose to a potential purchaser any latent structural defect or any other defect known to the broker or salesperson. Latent structural defects and other defects do not refer to trivial or insignificant defects, but to those defects that would be significant factors to a reasonable and prudent purchaser in making a decision to purchase.

4. Fails to disclose to a potential buyer a defect described under 3. above, that is known to the license holder.

5. Makes a false promise of a character likely to influence, persuade, or induce any person to enter into a contract or agreement when the licensee could not or did not intend to keep such promise.

6. Pursues a continued and flagrant course of misrepresentation or makes false promises through agents, salespersons, advertising, or otherwise.

7. Fails to make clear, to all parties to a transaction, for which party the licensee is acting.

8. Receives compensation from more than one party except with the full knowledge and consent of all parties.

9. Fails within a reasonable time to properly account for or remit money coming into his or her possession that belongs to others.

10. Commingles money belonging to others with the licensee's own funds.

11. Pays a commission or fees to, or divides a commission or fee with, anyone not licensed as a real estate broker or salesperson in this state or in any other state, for compensation for services as a real estate agent.

Note: This provision (coupled with sec. 14A) now subjects a real estate licensee to license revocation for splitting a fee with an attorney who is not a principal in the transaction.

12. Fails to specify a definite termination date that is not subject to prior notice in a contract, other than a contract to perform property management services, in which the licensee agrees to perform services for which a license is required under this Act.

13. Accepts, receives, or charges an undisclosed commission, rebate, or direct profit on expenditures made for a principal.

14. Solicits, sells, or offers for sale real property by means of a lottery.

15. Solicits, sells, or offers real property by means of a deceptive trade practice.

16. Acts in the dual capacity of broker and undisclosed principal in a transaction.

17. Guarantees, authorizes, or permits a person to guarantee that future profits will result from a resale of real property.

18. Places a sign on real property offering it for sale, lease, or rent without the written consent of the owner or his authorized agent.

19. Offers real property for sale or for lease without the knowledge and consent of the owner or his or her authorized agent, or on terms other than those authorized by the owner or the owner's authorized agent.

20. Offers to sell or lease real estate on terms other than those authorized by the owner of the real property or the owner's authorized agent.

21. Induces or attempts to induce a party to a contract of sale or lease to break the contract for the purpose of substituting in lieu thereof a new contract.

22. Negotiates or attempts to negotiate the sale, exchange, lease, or rental of real property with an owner or lessor, knowing that the owner or lessor had a written out-standing contract, granting exclusive agency in connection with the property to another real estate broker.

23. Publishes, or causes to be published, an advertisement including, but not limited to, advertising by newspaper, radio, television, or display that is misleading, or which is likely to deceive the public, or which in any manner tends to create a misleading impression, or which fails to identify the person causing the advertisement to be published as a licensed real estate broker or agent.

24. Withholds from, or inserts in a statement of account or invoice, a statement that made it inaccurate in a particular material.

25. Publishes or circulates an unjustified or unwarranted threat of legal proceedings, or other action.

26. Establishes an association, by employment or otherwise, with an unlicensed person who is expected or required to act as a real estate licensee, or aiding or abetting or conspiring with a person to circumvent the requirements of this Act.

27. Aids, abets, or conspires with another person to circumvent this statute.

28. Fails or refuses on demand to furnish copies of a document pertaining to a transaction dealing with real estate to a person whose signature is affixed to the document.

29. Fails to advise a purchaser in writing before the closing of a transaction that the purchaser should either have the abstract covering the real estate which is the subject of the contract examined by an attorney of the purchaser's own selection, or be furnished with or obtain a policy of title insurance.

30. Fails within a reasonable time to deposit money received as escrow agent in a real estate transaction, either in trust with a title company authorized to do

business in this state, or in a custodial, trust, or escrow account maintained for that purpose in a banking institution authorized to do business in this state.

31. Disburses money deposited in a custodial, trust, or escrow account, before the transaction concerned has been consummated or finally otherwise terminated.

32. Discriminates against an owner, potential purchaser, lessor, or potential lessee on the basis of race, color, religion, sex, national origin, or ancestry, including directing prospective home buyers or lessees interested in equivalent properties to different areas according to the race, color, religion, sex, national origin, or ancestry of the potential owner or lessee.

33. Disregards or violates a provision of this Statute.

The Commission is required to maintain a system to promptly and efficiently act on complaints filed with the commission and must maintain a file on each complaint. The Commission must also ensure that they give priority to the investigation of complaints filed by a consumer and the enforcement case resulting from the consumer complaint. The Commission is required to assign priorities and investigate complaints using a risk-based approach based on the degree of potential harm to the consumer, potential for immediate harm to a consumer, overall severity of the allegations and the complaint, number of license holders potentially involved in the complaint, previous complaint history of the license holder, and number of potential violations in the complaint.

The Commission may revoke a license if the Commission makes a payment from the real estate recovery trust account. If revoked, a person is not eligible for a license until the person had repaid in full the amount paid from the account.

In addition to suspension and revocation, the Commission may order a licensee to pay a refund to a consumer as provided in an agreement resulting from an informal settlement conference, or an enforcement order, in addition to imposing an administrative penalty or other sanctions.

The Commission is also required to adopt procedures governing informal disposition of the contested case. These new informal dispositions must provide the complainant and the license holder the opportunity to be heard and require the presence of a public member of the Commission for a case involving a consumer complaint, and at least two staff members of the Commission with experience in the regulatory area that is the subject of the proceeding. The presiding officer of the Commission for a case involving a consumer is also required to appoint a disciplinary panel consisting of three Commission members to determine whether a person's license to practice should be temporarily suspended. If the disciplinary panel determines from the information that a person licensed to practice would, by the person's continuing to practice, constitute a continuing threat to the public welfare, the panel shall temporarily suspend the license of that person.

Recovery Fund

The Texas Real Estate Commission has established a ***recovery fund***, with specified limits, to pay damages in the event a judgment is obtained against the licensee and there are no other funds recoverable from the licensee. The recovery fund is funded solely from fees paid by licensees. In order to proceed against the recovery fund the complainant must have received a final judgment in a court of competent jurisdiction. The amounts to be recovered are limited to $50,000 per transaction or $100,000 against any one licensed real estate broker or salesperson. The complainant must also prove that there were no attachable assets belonging to the broker or salesperson.

The Texas Real Estate License Act provides that if a person files a complaint with the Commission relating to a real estate broker or salesperson, the Commission shall furnish to that complainant an explanation of the remedies that are available to that person under the Act. The Commission must also provide information about appropriate state or local agencies or officials with which the person may file a complaint. The Commission shall furnish the same explanatory information to the person against whom the complaint is filed. The Commission is required to keep an information file about each complaint filed with the Commission, and it shall inform the complainant and person against whom the complaint is filed as to the status of the complaint at least as often as every three months. If the Commission revokes a person's license issued under the Act, the Commission may not issue another license to that person for one year after the revocation.

The requirement for bonds and the establishment of the recovery funds are not perfect solutions to the problem of uncollectible judgments because the wronged party must expend considerable effort to recover the loss, and it is quite possible that the maximum amount available per transaction or licensee will not fully compensate for the losses suffered. However, either system is better than none at all, which is still the case in some states.

SECURITIES LICENSE

There may be times when a real estate licensee also needs a securities license. This is so whenever the property being sold is an investment contract in real estate rather than real estate itself. A prime example is a real estate partnership. Timeshare units and rental pools where condominium owners put their units into a pool for a percentage of the pool's income may also fall into this category. Securities licenses are issued by the National Association of Securities Dealers based on successful completion of their examination. Legal counsel is advised if there is the possibility you may be selling securities. Counsel will also advise on state and federal laws requiring the registration of real estate securities before they are sold.

The Real Estate License Act

CHAPTER 1101. REAL ESTATE BROKERS AND SALESPERSONS

SUBCHAPTER A. GENERAL PROVISIONS

Sec. 1101.001. SHORT TITLE. This chapter may be cited as The Real Estate License Act. (V.A.C.S. Art. 6573a, Sec. 1(a).)

Sec. 1101.002. DEFINITIONS. In this chapter:

(1) "Broker":

(A) means a person who, in exchange for a commission or other valuable consideration or with the expectation of receiving a commission or other valuable consideration, performs for another person one of the following acts:

(i) sells, exchanges, purchases, or leases real estate;

(ii) offers to sell, exchange, purchase, or lease real estate;

(iii) negotiates or attempts to negotiate the listing, sale, exchange, purchase, or lease of real estate;

(iv) lists or offers, attempts, or agrees to list real estate for sale, lease, or exchange;

(v) appraises or offers, attempts, or agrees to appraise real estate;

(vi) auctions or offers, attempts, or agrees to auction real estate;

(vii) deals in options on real estate, including buying, selling, or offering to buy or sell options on real estate;

(viii) aids or offers or attempts to aid in locating or obtaining real estate for purchase or lease;

(ix) procures or assists in procuring a prospect to effect the sale, exchange, or lease of real estate; or

(x) procures or assists in procuring property to effect the sale, exchange, or lease of real estate; and

(B) includes a person who:

(i) is employed by or for an owner of real estate to sell any portion of the real estate; or

(ii) engages in the business of charging an advance fee or contracting to collect a fee under a contract that requires the person primarily to promote the sale of real estate by:

(a) listing the real estate in a publication primarily used for listing real estate; or

(b) referring information about the real estate to brokers.

(2) "Certificate holder" means a person registered under Subchapter K.

(3) "Commission" means the Texas Real Estate Commission.

(4) "License holder" means a broker or salesperson licensed under this chapter.

(5) "Real estate" means any interest in real property, including a leasehold, located in or

outside this state. The term does not include an interest given as security for the performance of an obligation.

(6) "Residential rental locator" means a person who offers for consideration to locate a unit in an apartment complex for lease to a prospective tenant. The term does not include an owner who offers to locate a unit in the owner's complex.

(7) "Salesperson" means a person who is associated with a licensed broker for the purpose of performing an act described by Subdivision (1).

(8) "Subagent" means a license holder who:

(A) represents a principal through cooperation with and the consent of a broker representing the principal; and

(B) is not sponsored by or associated with the principal's broker.

(V.A.C.S. Art. 6573a, Secs. 2(1), (2), (3), (4), (6), 15C(m)(3), (5), 24(a); New.)

Sec. 1101.003. CORE REAL ESTATE COURSES. (a) For purposes of this chapter, "core real estate courses" include:

(1) agency law, which includes the following topics:

(A) the relationship between a principal and an agent;

(B) an agent's authority;

(C) the termination of an agent's authority;

(D) an agent's duties, including fiduciary duties;

(E) employment law;

(F) deceptive trade practices;

(G) listing or buying representation procedures; and

(H) the disclosure of agency;

(2) contract law, which includes the following topics:

(A) elements of a contract;

(B) offer and acceptance;

(C) statute of frauds;

(D) remedies for breach, including specific performance;

(E) unauthorized practice of law;

(F) commission rules relating to use of adopted forms; and

(G) owner disclosure requirements;

(3) principles of real estate, which includes:

(A) an overview of:

(i) licensing as a broker or salesperson;

(ii) ethics of practice as a license holder;

(iii) titles to and conveyance of real estate;

(iv) legal descriptions;

(v) deeds, encumbrances, and liens;

(vi) distinctions between personal and real property;

(vii) appraisal;

(viii) finance and regulations;

(ix) closing procedures; and

(x) real estate mathematics; and

(B) at least three hours of classroom instruction on federal, state, and local laws relating to housing discrimination, housing credit discrimination, and community reinvestment;

(4) property management, which includes the following topics:

(A) the role of a property manager;

(B) landlord policies;

(C) operational guidelines;

(D) leases;

(E) lease negotiations;

(F) tenant relations;

(G) maintenance;

(H) reports;

(I) habitability laws; and

(J) the Fair Housing Act (42 U.S.C. Section 3601 et seq.);

(5) real estate appraisal, which includes the following topics:

(A) the central purposes and functions of an appraisal;

(B) social and economic determinants of the value of real estate;

(C) appraisal case studies;

(D) cost, market data, and income approaches to value estimates of real estate;

(E) final correlations; and

(F) reporting;

(6) real estate brokerage, which includes the following topics:

(A) agency law;

(B) planning and organization;

(C) operational policies and procedures;

(D) recruitment, selection, and training of personnel;

(E) records and control; and

(F) real estate firm analysis and expansion criteria;

(7) real estate finance, which includes the following topics:

(A) monetary systems;

(B) primary and secondary money markets;

(C) sources of mortgage loans;

(D) federal government programs;

(E) loan applications, processes, and procedures;

(F) closing costs;

(G) alternative financial instruments;

(H) equal credit opportunity laws;

(I) community reinvestment laws, including the Community Reinvestment Act of 1977 (12 U.S.C. Section 2901 et seq.); and

(J) state housing agencies, including the Texas Department of Housing and Community Affairs;

(8) real estate investment, which includes the following topics:

(A) real estate investment characteristics;

(B) techniques of investment analysis;

(C) the time value of money;

(D) discounted and nondiscounted investment criteria;

(E) leverage;

(F) tax shelters depreciation; and

(G) applications to property tax;

(9) real estate law, which includes the following topics:

(A) legal concepts of real estate;

(B) land description;

(C) real property rights and estates in land;

(D) contracts;

(E) conveyances;

(F) encumbrances;

(G) foreclosures;

(H) recording procedures; and (I) evidence of titles;

(10) real estate marketing, which includes the following topics:

(A) real estate professionalism and ethics;

(B) characteristics of successful salespersons;

(C) time management;

(D) psychology of marketing;

(E) listing procedures;

(F) advertising;

(G) negotiating and closing;

(H) financing; and

(I) Subchapter E, Chapter 17, Business & Commerce Code; and

Page 3

(11) real estate mathematics, which includes the following topics:

(A) basic arithmetic skills and review of mathematical logic;

(B) percentages;

(C) interest;

(D) the time value of money;

(E) depreciation;

(F) amortization;

(G) proration; and

(H) estimation of closing statements.

(b) The commission may designate a course as an equivalent of a course listed in Subsection (a).

(c) The commission by rule may prescribe:

(1) The content of the core real estate courses listed in Subsection (a); and

(2) the title and content of additional core real estate courses.

(V.A.C.S. Art. 6573a, Secs. 7(a) (part), (b).)

Sec. 1101.004. ACTING AS BROKER OR SALESPERSON. A person acts as a broker or salesperson under this chapter if the person, with the expectation of receiving valuable consideration, directly or indirectly performs or offers, attempts, or agrees to perform for another person any act described by Section 1101.002(1), as a part of a transaction or as an entire transaction.

(V.A.C.S. Art. 6573a, Sec. 4 (part).)

Sec. 1101.005. APPLICABILITY OF CHAPTER. This chapter does not apply to:

(1) an attorney licensed in any state;

(2) an attorney-in-fact authorized under a power of attorney to conduct a real estate transaction;

(3) a public official while engaged in official duties;

(4) an auctioneer licensed under Chapter 1802 while conducting the sale of real estate by auction if the auctioneer does not perform another act of a broker or salesperson;

(5) a person conduction a real estate transaction under a court order or the authority of a will or written trust instrument;

(6) a person employed by an owner in the sale of structures and land on which structures are located if the structures are erected by the owner in the course of the owner's business;

(7) an on-site manager of an apartment complex;

(8) an owner or the owner's employee who leases the owner's improved or unimproved real estate;

(9) a partnership or limited liability partnership acting as a broker or salesperson through a partner who is a licensed broker; or

(10) a transaction involving:

(A) the sale, lease, or transfer of a mineral or mining interest in real property;

(B) the sale, lease, or transfer of a cemetery lot;

(C) the lease or management of a hotel or motel; or

(D) the sale of real property under a power of sale conferred by a deed of trust or other contract lien.

(V.A.C.S. Art. 6573a, Sec. 3 (part).)

Sec. 1101.0055. NONAPPLICABILITY OF LAW GOVERNING CANCELLATION OF CERTAIN TRANSACTIONS. A service contract that a license holder enters into for services governed by this chapter is not a good or service governed by Chapter 39, Business & Commerce Code.

Sec. 1101.006. APPLICATION OF SUNSET ACT. The Texas Real Estate Commission is subject to Chapter 325, Government Code (Texas Sunset Act). Unless continued in existence as provided by that chapter, the commission is abolished and this chapter, Chapter 1102 and Chapter 1303 of this code and Chapter 221, Property Code, expire September 1, 2019.

(V.A.C.S. Art. 6573a, Sec. 5(n).)

Sec. 1101.007. COMPLIANCE WITH SUNSET RECOMMENDATIONS. (a) The commission shall:

(1) comply with and implement the management action recommendations regarding the commission adopted by the Sunset Advisory Commission on January 10, 2007, as a result of its review of the commission; and

(2) report to the Sunset Advisory Commission not later than November 1, 2008, the information the Sunset Advisory Commission requires regarding the commission's implementation of the recommendations under Subdivision (1).

(b) This section expires June 1, 2009.

[Sections 1101.008-1101.050 reserved for expansion]

SUBCHAPTER B. TEXAS REAL ESTATE COMMISSION

Sec. 1101.051. COMMISSION MEMBERSHIP. (a) The Texas Real Estate Commission consists of nine members appointed by the governor with the advice and consent of the senate as follows:

(1) six members who have been engaged in the brokerage business as licensed brokers as their major occupation for the five years preceding appointment; and

(2) three members who represent the public.

(b) Each member of the commission must be a qualified voter.

(c) Appointments to the commission shall be made without regard to the race, color, disability, sex, religion, age, or national origin of the appointee.

(V.A.C.S. Art. 6573a, Secs. 5(a) (part), (c) (part).)

Sec. 1101.052. PUBLIC MEMBER ELIGIBILITY. A person is not eligible for appointment as a public member of the commission if the person or the person's spouse:

(1) is registered, certified, or licensed by an occupational regulatory agency in the real estate industry;

(2) is employed by or participates in the management of a business entity or other organization regulated by the commission or receiving funds from the commission;

(3) owns or controls, directly or indirectly, more than a 10 percent interest in a business entity or other organization regulated by the commission or receiving funds from the commission; or

(4) uses or receives a substantial amount of tangible goods, services, or funds from the commission, other than compensation or reimbursement authorized by law for commission membership, attendance, or expenses.

(V.A.C.S. Art. 6573a, Sec. 5(c) (part).)

Sec. 1101.053. MEMBERSHIP AND EMPLOYEE RESTRICTIONS. (a) In this section, "Texas trade association" means a cooperative, and voluntarily joined statewide association of business or professional competitors in this state designed to assist its members and its industry or profession in dealing with mutual business or professional problems and in promoting their common interest.

(b) A person may not be a member of the commission and may not be a commission employee employed in a "bona fide executive, administrative, or professional capacity," as that phrase is used for purposes of establishing an exemption to the overtime provisions of the federal Fair Labor Standards Act of 1938 (29 U.S.C. Section 201 et seq.) if:

(1) the person is an officer, employee, or paid consultant of a Texas trade association in the real estate industry; or

(2) the person's spouse is an officer, manager, or paid consultant of a Texas trade association in the real estate industry.

(c) A person may not serve as a commission member or act as the general counsel to the commission if the person is required to register as a lobbyist under Chapter 305, Government Code, because of the person's activities for compensation on behalf of a profession related to the operation of the commission.

(V.A.C.S. Art. 6573a, Secs. 5(b)(1) (part), (2).)

Sec. 1101.054. OFFICIAL OATH; BOND. Not later than the 15th day after the date of appointment, each appointee must take the constitutional oath of office.

(V.A.C.S. Art. 6573a, Sec. 5(a) (part).)

Sec. 1101.055. TERMS; VACANCY. (a) Commission members serve staggered six-year terms, with the terms of three members expiring January 31 of each odd-numbered year.

(b) If a vacancy occurs during a member's term, the governor shall appoint a person to fill the unexpired term.

(V.A.C.S. Art. 6573a, Sec. 5(a) (part).)

Sec. 1101.056. OFFICERS. (a) The governor shall designate a commission member who is a licensed broker as presiding officer. The presiding officer serves in that capacity at the pleasure of the governor.

(b) At a regular meeting in February of each year, the commission shall elect an assistant presiding officer and secretary from its membership.

(V.A.C.S. Art. 6573a, Sec. 5(a) (part).)

Sec. 1101.057. GROUNDS FOR REMOVAL. (a) It is a ground for removal from the commission that a member:

(1) does not have at the time of appointment the qualifications required by Section 1101.051(a) or (b) or 1101.052;

(2) does not maintain during service on the commission the qualifications required by Section 1101.051(a) or (b) or 1101.052;

(3) is ineligible for membership under Section 1101.053;

(4) cannot discharge the member's duties for a substantial part of the member's term; or

(5) is absent from more than half of the regularly scheduled commission meetings that the member is eligible to attend during each calendar year, unless the absence is excused by majority vote of the commission.

(b) The validity of an action of the commission is not affected by the fact that it is taken when a ground for removal of a commission member exists.

(c) If the administrator has knowledge that a potential ground for removal exists, the administrator shall notify the presiding officer of the commission of the potential ground. The presiding officer shall then notify the governor and the attorney general that a potential ground for removal exists. If the potential ground for removal involves the presiding officer, the administrator shall notify the next highest ranking officer of the commission, who shall then notify the governor and the attorney general that a potential ground for removal exists.

(V.A.C.S. Art. 6573a, Secs. 5(d), (e), (f).)

Sec. 1101.058. PER DIEM; REIMBURSEMENT. A commission member is entitled to receive:

(1) $75 for each day the member performs the member's official duties; and

(2) reimbursement for actual and necessary expenses incurred in performing the member's official duties.

(V.A.C.S. Art. 6573a, Sec. 5(g).)

Sec. 1101.059. TRAINING. (a) A person who is appointed to and qualifies for office as a member of the commission may not vote, deliberate, or be counted as a member in attendance at a meeting of the commission until the person completes a training program that complies with this section.

(b) The training program must provide the person with information regarding:

(1) this chapter and other laws regulated by the commission;

(2) the programs, functions, rules, and budget of the commission;

(3) the results of the most recent formal-audit of the commission;

(4) the requirements of laws relating to open meetings, public information, administrative procedure, and conflicts of interest; and

(5) any applicable ethics policies adopted by the commission or the Texas Ethics Commission.

(c) A person appointed to the commission is entitled to reimbursement, as provided by the General Appropriations Act, for the travel expenses incurred in attending the training program regardless of whether the attendance at the program occurs before or after the person qualifies for office.

[Sections 1101.060-1101.100 reserved for expansion]

SUBCHAPTER C. ADMINISTRATOR AND OTHER COMMISSION PERSONNEL

Sec. 1101.101. ADMINISTRATOR AND OTHER PERSONNEL. (a) The commission shall appoint an administrator.

(b) The commission may designate a subordinate officer as assistant administrator to act for the administrator in the administrator's absence.

(c) The commission may employ other subordinate officers and employees necessary to administer and enforce this chapter and Chapter 1102, including a general counsel, attorneys, investigators, and support staff.

(d) The commission shall determine the salaries of the administrator, officers, and employees of the commission. The amounts of the salaries may not exceed the amounts specified by the General Appropriations Act.

(V.A.C.S. Art. 6573a, Secs. 5(i) (part), (t) (part).)

Sec.1101.102. DIVISION OF RESPONSIBILITIES. The commission shall develop and implement policies that clearly separate the policymaking responsibilities of the commission and the management responsibilities of the administrator and the staff of the commission.

(V.A.C.S. Art. 6573a, Sec. 5(s).)

Sec. 1101.103. CODE OF ETHICS; STANDARDS OF CONDUCT. Each member, officer, employee, and agent of the commission is subject to the code of ethics and standards of conduct imposed by Chapter 572, Government Code.

(V.A.C.S. Art. 6573a, Sec. 5(b)(1) (part).)

Sec. 1101.104. QUALIFICATIONS AND STANDARDS OF CONDUCT INFORMATION. The commission shall

Page 7

provide, as often as necessary, to its members and employees information regarding their:

(1) qualifications for office or employment under this chapter and Chapter 1102; and

(2) responsibilities under applicable laws relating to standards of conduct for state officers or employees.

(V.A.C.S. Art. 6573a, Sec. 5(x).)

Sec. 1101.105. CAREER LADDER PROGRAM; PERFORMANCE EVALUATIONS. (a) The administrator or the administrator's designee shall develop an intra-agency career ladder program. The program must require intra-agency postings of all nonentry level positions concurrently with any public posting.

(b) The administrator or the administrator's designee shall develop a system of annual performance evaluations. All merit pay for commission employees must be based on the system established under this subsection.

(V.A.C.S. Art. 6573a, Sec. 5(i) (part).)

Sec. 1101.106. EQUAL EMPLOYMENT OPPORTUNITY POLICY; REPORT. (a) The administrator or the administrator's designee shall prepare and maintain a written policy statement to ensure implementation of an equal employment opportunity program under which all personnel transactions are made without regard to race, color, disability, sex, religion, age, or national origin. The policy statement must include:

(1) personnel policies, including policies relating to recruitment, evaluation, selection, appointment, training, and promotion of personnel;

(2) a comprehensive analysis of the commission workforce that meets federal and state guidelines;

(3) procedures by which a determination can be made of significant underuse in the commission workforce of all persons for whom federal or state guidelines encourage a more equitable balance; and

(4) reasonable methods to appropriately address those areas of underuse.

(b) A policy statement prepared under Subsection (a) must:

(1) cover an annual period;

(2) be updated at least annually; and

(3) be filed with the governor.

(c) The governor shall deliver a biennial report to the legislature based on the information received under Subsection (b). The report may be made separately or as a part of other biennial reports made to the legislature.

(V.A.C.S. Art. 6573a, Secs. 5(u), (v), (w).)

[Sections 1101.107-1101.150 reserved for expansion]

SUBCHAPTER D. COMMISSION POWERS AND DUTIES

Sec. 1101.151. GENERAL POWERS AND DUTIES OF COMMISSION. (a) The commission shall:

(1) administer this chapter and Chapter 1102;

(2) adopt rules and establish standards relating to permissible forms of advertising by a license holder acting as a residential rental locator;

(3) maintain a registry of certificate holders; and

(4) design and adopt a seal.

(b) The commission may:

(1) adopt and enforce rules necessary to administer this chapter and Chapter 1102; and

(2) establish standards of conduct and ethics for persons licensed under this chapter and Chapter 1102 to:

(A) fulfill the purposes of this chapter and Chapter 1102; and

(B) ensure compliance with this chapter and Chapter 1102.

(V.A.C.S. Art. 6573a, Secs. 5(a) (part), (h) (part), (j) (part), (t) (part), 9A(b), (d), 24(c).)

Sec. 1101.152. FEES. (a) The commission shall adopt rules to charge and collect fees in amounts reasonable and necessary to cover the costs of administering this chapter, including a fee for:

(1) filing an original application for a broker license;

(2) annual renewal of a broker license;

(3) filing an original application for a salesperson license;

(4) annual renewal of a salesperson license;

(5) annual registration;

(6) filing an application for a license examination;

(7) filing a request for a branch office license;

(8) filing a request for a change of place of business, change of name, return to active status, or change of sponsoring broker;

(9) filing a request to replace a lost or destroyed license or certificate of registration;

(10) filing an application for approval of an education program under Subchapter G;

(11) annual operation of an education program under Subchapter G;

(12) filing an application for approval of an instructor of core real estate courses;

(13) transcript evaluation;

(14) preparing a license or registration history;

(15) filing an application for a moral character determination; and

(16) conducting a criminal history check for issuing or renewing a license.

(16) conducting a criminal background check in connection with the annual renewal of a license under this chapter.

(b) The commission shall adopt rules to set and collect fees in amounts reasonable and necessary to cover the costs of implementing the continuing education requirements for license holders, including a fee for:

(1) an application for approval of a continuing education provider;

(2) an application for approval of a continuing education course of study;

(3) an application for approval of an instructor of continuing education courses; and

(4) attendance at a program to train instructors of a continuing education course prescribed under Section 1101.455.

(c) Notwithstanding Subsection (a), if the commission issues an original inactive salesperson license under Section 1101.363(b) to a salesperson who is not sponsored by a licensed broker and the salesperson is subsequently sponsored by a licensed broker, the commission may not charge:

(1) the salesperson a fee for filing a request to place the salesperson license on active status; or

(2) the broker a fee for filing a request to sponsor the salesperson.

(V.A.C.S. Art. 6573a, Secs. 7A(d) (part), 11 (part).)

Amended by SB 862, 81st Legislative Session, 2009, Sections 1 and II

Sec. 1101.153. FEE INCREASE. (a) The fee for filing an original application for an individual broker license and the fee for annual renewal of an individual broker license is the amount of the fee set by the commission under Section 1101.152 and a fee increase of $200.

(b) Of each fee increase collected under Subsection (a):

(1) $50 shall be transmitted to Texas A&M University for deposit in a separate banking account that may be appropriated only to support, maintain, and carry out the purposes, objectives, and duties of the Texas Real Estate Research Center;

(2) $50 shall be deposited to the credit of the foundation school fund; and

(3) $100 shall be deposited to the credit of the general revenue fund.

(V.A.C.S. Art. 6573a, Secs. 11A(a), (b) (part).)

Amended by SB 862, 81st Legislative Session, 2009, Section III

Sec. 1101.154. ADDITIONAL FEE: TEXAS REAL ESTATE RESEARCH CENTER. (a) The fee for the issuance or renewal of a:

(1) broker license is the amount of the fee set under Sections 1101.152 and 1101.153 and an additional $20 fee;

(2) salesperson license is the amount of the fee set under Section 1101.152 and an additional $20 fee; and

(3) certificate of registration is the amount of the fee set under Section 1101.152 and an additional $20 fee.

(b) The commission shall transmit quarterly the additional fees collected under Subsection (a) to Texas A&M University for deposit in a separate banking account that may be appropriated only to support, maintain, and carry out the purposes, objectives, and duties of the Texas Real Estate Research Center.

(V.A.C.S. Art. 6573a, Secs. 5(m) (part), 11 (part).)

Amended by SB 862, 81st Legislative Session, 2009, Section IV

Sec. 1101.155. RULES RELATING TO CONTRACT FORMS. (a) The commission may adopt rules in the public's best interest that require license holders to use contract forms prepared by the Texas Real Estate Broker-Lawyer Committee and adopted by the commission.

(b) The commission may not prohibit a license holder from using for the sale, exchange, option, or lease of an interest in real property a contract form that is:

(1) prepared by the property owner; or

(2) prepared by an attorney and required by the property owner.

(c) A listing contract form adopted by the commission that relates to the contractual obligations between a seller of real estate and a license holder acting as an agent for the seller must include:

(1) a provision informing the parties to the contract that real estate commissions are negotiable; and

(2) a provision explaining the availability of Texas coastal natural hazards information important to coastal residents, if that information is appropriate.

(V.A.C.S. Art. 6573a, Secs. 16(e) (part), 18A.)

Sec. 1101.156. RULES RESTRICTING ADVERTISING OR COMPETITIVE BIDDING. (a) The commission may not adopt a rule restricting advertising or competitive bidding by a person regulated by the commission except to prohibit a false, misleading, or deceptive practice by the person.

(b) The commission may not include in rules to prohibit false, misleading, or deceptive practices by a person regulated by the commission a rule that:

(1) restricts the use of any advertising medium;

(2) restricts the person's personal appearance or use of the person's voice in an advertisement;

(3) relates to the size or duration of an advertisement used by the person; or

(4) restricts the person's advertisement under a trade name.

(V.A.C.S. Art. 6573a, Sec. 5(z).)

Sec. 1101.157. SUBPOENA AUTHORITY. (a) The commission may request and, if necessary, compel by subpoena:

(1) the attendance of witnesses for examination under oath; and

(2) the production for inspection and copying of records, documents, and other evidence relevant to the investigation of an alleged violation of this chapter.

(b) A subpoena may be issued throughout the state and may be served by any person designated by the commission.

(c) If a person fails to comply with a subpoena issued under this section, the commission, acting through the attorney general, may file suit to enforce the subpoena in a district court in Travis County or in the county in which a hearing conducted by the commission may be held.

(d) The court shall order compliance with the subpoena if the court finds that good cause exists to issue the subpoena.

Sec. 1101.158. ADVISORY COMMITTEES.

(a) The commission may appoint advisory committees to perform the advisory functions assigned to the committees by the commission. An advisory committee under this section is subject to Section 2110, Government Code.

(b) A member of an advisory committee who is not a member of the commission may not receive compensation for service on the committee. The member may receive reimbursement for actual and necessary expenses incurred in performing committee functions as provided by Section 2110.004, Government Code.

(c) A member of an advisory committee serves at the will of the commission.

(d) An advisory committee may hold a meeting by telephone conference call or other video or broadcast technology.

(e) Advisory committee meetings are subject to Chapter 551, Government Code.

Sec. 1101.159. USE OF TECHNOLOGY. The commission shall implement a policy requiring the commission to use appropriate technological solutions to improve the commission's ability to perform its functions. The policy must ensure that the public is able to interact with the commission on the Internet.

Sec. 1101.160. NEGOTIATED RULEMAKING AND ALTERNATIVE DISPUTE RESOLUTION PROCEDURES. (a) The commission shall develop and implement a policy to encourage the use of:

(1) negotiated rulemaking procedures under Chapter 2008, Government Code, for the adoption of commission rules; and

(2) appropriate alternative dispute resolution procedures under Chapter 2009, Government Code, to assist in the resolution of internal and external disputes under the commission's jurisdiction.

(b) The commission's procedures relating to alternative dispute resolution must conform, to the extent possible, to any model guidelines issued by the State Office of Administrative

Hearings for the use of alternative dispute resolution by state agencies.

(c) The commission shall designate a trained person to:

(1) coordinate the implementation of the policy adopted under Subsection (a);

(2) serve as a resource for any training needed to implement the procedures for negotiated rulemaking or alternative dispute resolution; and

(3) collect data concerning the effectiveness of those procedures, as implemented by the commission.

(V.A.C.S. Art. 6573a, Secs. 15(e), 17(b).)

[Sections 1101.161-1101.200 reserved for expansion]

SUBCHAPTER E. PUBLIC INTEREST INFORMATION AND COMPLAINT PROCEDURES

Sec.1101.201. PUBLIC INTEREST INFORMATION. (a) The commission shall prepare information of public interest describing the functions of the commission.

(b) The commission shall make the information available to the public and appropriate state agencies.

(V.A.C.S. Art. 6573a, Sec. 5(r).)

Sec.1101.202. COMPLAINTS. (a) The commission by rule shall establish methods by which consumers and service recipients are notified of the name, mailing address, and telephone number of the commission for the purpose of directing a complaint to the commission. The commission may provide for that notice:

(1) on each application for a license or certificate of registration or written contract for services of a person regulated under this chapter or Chapter 1102;

(2) on a sign prominently displayed in the place of business of each person regulated under this chapter or Chapter 1102;

(b) The commission shall provide to a person who files a complaint with the commission relating to a license holder and to the license holder against whom the complaint is filed:

(1) an explanation of the remedies that are available to the person under this chapter; and

(2) information about appropriate state or local agencies or officials with whom the person may file a complaint.

(3) in a bill for services provided by a person regulated under this chapter or Chapter 1102; or

(4) in conjunction with the notice required by Section 1101.615; or

(5) to be prominently displayed on the Internet website of a person regulated under this chapter or Chapter 1102.

(V.A.C.S. Art. 6573a, Secs. 5(q), 18B(a).)

Sec.1101.203. COMPLAINT INFORMATION. (a) The commission shall maintain a system to promptly and efficiently act on complaints filed with the commission. The commission shall maintain a file on each complaint. The file must include:

(1) information relating to the parties to the complaint;

(2) the subject matter of the complaint;

(3) a summary of the results of the review or investigation of the complaint; and

(4) the disposition of the complaint.

(b) The commission shall make information available describing its procedures for complaint investigation and resolution.

(c) The commission, shall periodically notify the parties to the complaint of the status of the complaint until final disposition, unless the notice would jeopardize an undercover investigation authorized under Section 1101.204.

(V.A.C.S. Art. 6573a, Secs. 18B(b), (c).)

Sec.1101.204. COMPLAINT INVESTIGATION AND DISPOSITION. (a) The commission or commission staff may file a complaint and conduct an investigation as necessary to enforce this chapter, Chapter 1102, or a rule adopted under those chapters.

(b) The commission shall investigate the actions and records of a license holder if:

(1) a person submits a signed, written complaint; and

(2) the complaint and any evidence presented with the complaint provide reasonable cause for an investigation.

(c) The commission may not conduct an investigation of a person licensed under this chapter or Chapter 1102 in connection with a complaint submitted later than the fourth anniversary of the date of the incident that is the subject of the complaint.

(d) The commission shall promptly provide a written notice to a person licensed under this chapter or Chapter 1102 who is the subject of an investigation unless after deliberation the commission decides against notification.

(e) Notwithstanding any other provision of this chapter, an undercover or covert investigation may not be conducted unless the commission expressly authorizes the investigation after considering the circumstances and determining that the investigation is necessary to implement this chapter.

(f) An investigation or other action against a person licensed under this chapter or Chapter 1102 may not be initiated on the basis of an anonymous complaint.

(g) Repealed by Acts 2007, 80th Leg., R.S., Ch. 1411, Sec. 59(1), eff. September 1, 2007.

(h) The commission shall ensure that the commission gives priority to the investigation of a complaint filed by a consumer and an enforcement case resulting from the consumer complaint. The commission shall assign priorities and investigate complaints using a risk-based approach based on the:

(1) degree of potential harm to a consumer;

(2) potential for immediate harm to a consumer;

(3) overall severity of the allegations in the complaint;

(4) number of license holders potentially involved in the complaint;

(5) previous complaint history of the license holder; and

(6) number of potential violations in the complaint.

(V.A.C.S. Art. 6573a, Secs. 15(a) (part), (d), 15B(a), (e).)

Sec. 1101.205. COMPLAINT INVESTIGATION OF CERTIFICATE HOLDER. The commission shall investigate a signed complaint received by the commission that relates to an act of a certificate holder or a person required to hold a certificate under Subchapter K.

(V.A.C.S. Art. 6573a, Sec. 9A(c) (part).)

Sec. 1101.206. PUBLIC PARTICIPATION. (a) The commission shall develop and implement policies that provide the public with a reasonable opportunity to appear before the commission and to speak on any issue under the commission's jurisdiction.

(b) The commission shall prepare and maintain a written plan that describes how a person who does not speak English or who has a physical, mental, or developmental disability may be provided reasonable access to the commission's programs.

Page 13

(V.A.C.S. Art. 6573a, Secs. 5(p), (y).)

[Sections 1101.207-1101.250 reserved for expansion]

SUBCHAPTER F. TEXAS REAL ESTATE BROKER-LAWYER COMMITTEE

Sec. 1101.251. DEFINITION OF COMMITTEE. In this subchapter, "committee" means the Texas Real Estate Broker-Lawyer Committee.

Sec. 1101.252. COMMITTEE MEMBERSHIP. (a) The Texas Real Estate Broker-Lawyer Committee consists of 13 members appointed as follows:

(1) six members appointed by the commission; and

(2) six members of the State Bar of Texas appointed by the president of the state bar; and

(3) one public member appointed by the governor.

(b) Appointments to the committee shall be made without regard to the race, creed, sex, religion, or national origin of the appointee.

V.A.C.S. Art. 6573a, Sec. 16(d) (part).)

Sec. 1101.253. TERMS; VACANCIES. (a) Committee members serve staggered six-year terms, with the terms of two commission appointees and two State Bar of Texas appointees expiring every two years and the term of the public member expiring every six years.

(b) A committee member shall hold office until the member's successor is appointed.

(c) If a vacancy occurs during a member's term, the entity making the original appointment shall appoint a person to fill the unexpired term.

(V.A.C.S. Art. 6573a, Sec. 16(d) (part).)

Sec. 1101.254. POWERS AND DUTIES. (a) In addition to other delegated powers and duties, the committee shall draft and revise contract forms that are capable of being standardized to expedite real estate transactions and minimize controversy.

(b) The contract forms must contain safeguards adequate to protect the principals in the transaction.

(V.A.C.S. Art. 6573a, Sec. 16(c).)

[Sections 1101.255-1101.300 reserved for expansion]

SUBCHAPTER G. ACCREDITATION AND APPROVAL OF REAL ESTATE EDUCATIONAL PROGRAMS AND COURSES OF STUDY

Sec. 1101.301. ACCREDITATION OF PROGRAMS AND COURSES OF STUDY. (a) The commission, as necessary for the administration of this chapter and Chapter 1102, may:

(1) establish standards for the accreditation of educational programs or courses of study in real estate and real estate inspection conducted in this state, excluding programs and courses offered by accredited colleges and universities;

(2) establish by rule reasonable criteria for the approval of real estate and real estate inspection courses; and

(3) inspect and accredit real estate and real estate inspection educational programs or courses of study.

(b) The commission shall determine whether a real estate or real estate inspection course satisfies the requirements of this chapter and Chapter 1102.

(c) In establishing accreditation standards for an educational program under Subsection (a), the commission shall adopt rules that require a program to establish that at least 55 percent of the program's graduates have passed a licensing exam the first time the exam has been taken by the graduates before the commission may renew the program's accreditation.

(V.A.C.S. Art. 6573a, Sec. 7(f) (part).)

Sec. 1101.302. BOND REQUIRED. (a) In this section, "educational institution" means a school, excluding an accredited college or university, authorized by the commission under this chapter to offer a real estate or real estate inspection educational program or course of study.

(b) An educational institution shall maintain a corporate surety bond or other security acceptable to the commission that is:

(1) in the amount of $20,000;

(2) payable to the commission; and

(3) for the benefit of a party who suffers damages caused by the failure of the institution to fulfill obligations related to the commission's approval.

(V.A.C.S. Art. 6573a, Sec. 7(f) (part).)

Sec. 1101.303. APPROVAL OF CONTINUING EDUCATION PROVIDER OR COURSE OF STUDY. (a) If the commission determines that an applicant for approval as a continuing education provider satisfies the requirements of this subchapter or Section 1102.205 and any rule adopted under this subchapter or Section 1102.205, the commission may authorize the applicant to offer continuing education for a two-year period.

(b) If the commission determines that an applicant for approval of a continuing education course of study satisfies the requirements of this subchapter or Section 1102.205 and any rule adopted under this subchapter or Section 1102.205, the commission may authorize the applicant to offer the course of study for a two-year period.

(V.A.C.S. Art. 6573a, Sec. 7A(d) (part).)

Sec. 1101.304. EXAMINATION PASSAGE RATE DATA. (a) The commission shall adopt rules regarding the collection and publication of data relating to examination passage rates for graduates of accredited educational programs.

(b) Rules adopted under this section must provide for a method to:

(1) calculate the examination passage rate;

(2) collect the relevant data from the examination administrator or the accredited program; and

(3) post the examination passage rate data on the commission's Internet website, in a manner aggregated by educational program and by license group.

(c) In determining the educational program a graduate is affiliated with for purposes of this section, the educational program is the program the graduate last attended.

Sec. 1101.305. REVIEW COMMITTEE. (a) The commission may appoint a committee to review the performance of an educational program performing below the standards set by the commission under Section 1101.301. The committee shall consist of:

(1) at least one commission member;

(2) at least one member of the commission staff;

(3) individuals licensed under this chapter or Chapter 1102; and

(4) a representative from the Texas Real Estate Research Center.

(b) A committee formed under this section shall review and evaluate any factor causing an educational program's poor performance and report findings and recommendations to improve performance to the program and to the commission.

Page 15

(c) A committee formed under this section may not revoke the accreditation of an educational program. The commission may temporarily suspend a program in the same manner as a license under Subchapter N.

[Sections 1101.306-1101.350 reserved for expansion]

SUBCHAPTER H. LICENSE REQUIREMENTS

Sec. 1101.351. LICENSE REQUIRED. (a) Unless a person holds a license issued under this chapter, the person may not:

(1) act as or represent that the person is a broker or salesperson; or

(2) act as a residential rental locator.

(b) An applicant for a broker or salesperson license may not act as a broker or salesperson until the person receives the license evidencing that authority.

(c) A licensed salesperson may not act or attempt to act as a broker or salesperson unless the salesperson is associated with a licensed broker and is acting for that broker.

(V.A.C.S. Art. 6573a, Secs. 1(b), 4 (part), 9(b) (part), 24(b) (part).)

Sec. 1101.352. LICENSE APPLICATION. (a) Each applicant for a broker or salesperson license must submit an application on a form prescribed by the commission.

(b) Each applicant for a broker or salesperson license must disclose in the license application whether the applicant has:

(1) entered a plea of guilty or nolo contendere to a felony; or

(2) been convicted of a felony and the time for appeal has elapsed or the judgment or conviction has been affirmed on appeal.

(c) The disclosure under Subsection (b) must be provided even if an order has granted community supervision suspending the imposition of the sentence.

(V.A.C.S. Art. 6573a, Secs. 6(a), (part), 9 (e) (part).)

Sec. 1101.3521. CRIMINAL HISTORY RECORD INFORMATION REQUIREMENT FOR LICENSE. (a) The commission shall require that an applicant for a license or renewal of an unexpired license submit a complete and legible set of fingerprints, on a form prescribed by the commission, to the commission or to the Department of Public Safety for the purpose of obtaining criminal history record information from the Department of Public Safety and the Federal Bureau of Investigation.

(b) The commission shall refuse to issue a license to or renew the license of a person who does not comply with the requirement of Subsection (a).

(c) The commission shall conduct a criminal history check of each applicant for a license or renewal of a license using information:

(1) provided by the individual under this section; and

(2) made available to the commission by the Department of Public Safety, the Federal Bureau of Investigation, and any other criminal justice agency under Chapter 411, Government Code.

(d) The commission may:

(1) enter into an agreement with the Department of Public Safety to administer a criminal history check required under this section; and

(2) authorize the Department of Public Safety to collect from each applicant the costs incurred by the department in conducting the criminal history check.

Sec. 1101.353. MORAL CHARACTER DETERMINATION. (a) If before applying for a license under this chapter a person requests that the commission determine whether the person's moral character complies with the commission's moral character requirements for licensing under this chapter and pays the fee prescribed by Section 1101.152, the commission shall make its determination of the person's moral character.

(b) Not later than the 30th day after the date the commission makes its determination, the commission shall notify the person of the determination.

(c) If a person applies for a license after receiving notice of a determination, the commission may conduct a supplemental moral character determination of the person. The supplemental determination may cover only the period after the date the person requests a moral character determination under this section.

(d) The commission may issue a provisional moral character determination. The commission by rule shall adopt reasonable terms for issuing a provisional moral character determination.

(V.A.C.S. Art. 6573a, Sec. 6A.)

Sec. 1101.354. GENERAL ELIGIBILITY REQUIREMENTS. To be eligible to receive a license under this chapter, a person must:

(1) at the time of application:

(A) be at least 18 years of age;

(B) be a citizen of the United States or a lawfully admitted alien; and

(C) be a resident of this state;

(2) satisfy the commission as to the applicant's honesty, trustworthiness, and integrity;

(3) demonstrate competence based on an examination under Subchapter I;

(4) complete the required courses of study, including any required core real estate courses prescribed under this chapter; and

(5) complete at least:

(A) three classroom hours of course work on federal, state, and local laws governing housing discrimination, housing credit discrimination, and community reinvestment; or

(B) three semester hours of course work on constitutional law.

(V.A.C.S. Art. 6573a, Secs. 6(b), 7(a) (part), (j).)

Sec. 1101.355. ADDITIONAL GENERAL ELIGIBILITY REQUIREMENTS FOR CERTAIN BUSINESS ENTITIES. (a) To be eligible for a license under this chapter:

(1) a corporation must designate one of its officers as its agent for purposes of this chapter; and

(2) a limited liability company must designate one of its managers as its agent for purposes of this chapter.

(b) A corporation or limited liability company may not act as a broker unless the entity's designated agent is a licensed broker according to the commission's records.

(V.A.C.S. Art. 6573a, Sec. 6(c) (part).)

Sec. 1101.356. BROKER LICENSE: EXPERIENCE AND EDUCATION REQUIREMENTS. (a) An applicant for a broker license must provide to the commission satisfactory evidence that the applicant:

(1) has had at least two years of active experience in this state as a license holder during the 36 months preceding the date the application is filed; and

(2) has successfully completed at least 60 semester hours, or equivalent classroom hours, of postsecondary education, including:

(A) at least 18 semester hours or equivalent classroom hours of core real estate courses, two semester hours of which must be real estate brokerage; and

(B) at least 42 hours of core real estate courses or related courses accepted by the commission.

(b) Subsection (a) does not apply to an applicant who, at the time of application, is licensed as a real estate broker by another state that has license requirements comparable to the requirements of this state.

(c) An applicant for a broker license who is licensed as a salesperson and is subject to the annual education requirements prescribed by Section 1101.454 must provide to the commission satisfactory evidence that the applicant has satisfied the requirements of that section. The hours completed under Section 1101.454 shall be applied to the number of hours required of the applicant under Subsection (a) (2) of this section.

(V.A.C.S. Art. 6573a, Secs. 7(d), (g) (part).)

Sec. 1101.357. BROKER LICENSE: ALTERNATE EXPERIE NCE REQUIREMENTS FOR CERTAIN APPLICANTS. An applicant for a broker license who does not satisfy the experience requirements of Section 1101.356 must provide to the commission satisfactory evidence that:

(1) the applicant:

(A) is a licensed real estate broker in another state;

(B) has had at least two years of active experience in that state as a licensed real estate broker or salesperson during the 36 months preceding the date the application is filed; and

(C) has satisfied the educational requirements prescribed by Section 1101.356; or

(2) the applicant was licensed in this state as a broker in the year preceding the date the application is filed.

(V.A.C.S. Art. 6573a, Secs. 7(g) (part), 14 (b) (part).)

Sec. 1101.358. SALESPERSON LICENSE: EDUCATION REQUIREMENTS. (a) An applicant for a salesperson license must provide to the commission satisfactory evidence that the applicant has completed at least 14 semester hours, or equivalent classroom hours, of postsecondary education, including:

(1) at least four semester hours of core real estate courses on principles of real estate;

(2) at least two semester hours of each of the following core real estate courses:

(A) agency law;

(B) contract law; and

(C) one additional core real estate course; and

(3) at least four semester hours of core real estate courses or related courses.

(b) The commission shall waive the education requirements of Subsection (a) if the applicant has been licensed in this state as a broker or salesperson within the year preceding the date the application is filed.

(c) If an applicant for a salesperson license was licensed as a salesperson within the year preceding the date the application is filed and the license was issued under the conditions prescribed by Section 1101.454, the commission shall require the applicant to provide the evidence of successful completion of education requirements that would have been required if the license had been maintained without interruption during the preceding year.

(V.A.C.S. Art. 6573a, Secs. 7(e) (part), (h).)

Sec. 1101.359. ALTERNATE EDUCATION REQUIREMENTS FOR CERTAIN LICENSE HOLDERS. An applicant for a broker license who is not subject to the education requirements of Section 1101.356(a)(2) and an applicant for a salesperson license who is not subject to the education requirements of Section 1101.358 or 1101.454 must provide to the commission satisfactory evidence that the applicant has completed the number of classroom hours of continuing education that would have been required for a timely renewal under Section 1101.455 during the two years preceding the date the application is filed.

Added by S.B. 810, effective January 1, 2006

(V.A.C.S. Art. 6573a, Sec. 7A(b).)

Sec. 1101.360. ELIGIBILITY REQUIREMENTS FOR CERTAIN NONRESIDENT APPLICANTS. (a) A resident of another state who is not a licensed real estate broker and who was formerly licensed in this state as a broker or salesperson may apply for a license under this chapter not later than the first anniversary of the date of the expiration of the former license.

(b) A nonresident applicant is subject to the same license requirements as a resident. The commission may refuse to issue a license to a nonresident applicant for the same reasons that it may refuse to issue a license to a resident applicant.

(c) A nonresident applicant must submit with the application an irrevocable consent to a legal action against the applicant in the court of any county in this state in which a cause of action may arise or in which the plaintiff may reside. The action may be commenced by service of process or pleading authorized by the laws of this state or by delivery of process on the administrator or assistant administrator of the commission. The consent must:

(1) stipulate that the service of process or pleading is valid and binding in all courts as if personal service had been made on the nonresident in this state;

(2) be acknowledged; and

(3) if made by a corporation, be authenticated by its seal.

(d) A service of process or pleading served on the commission under this section shall be by duplicate copies. One copy shall be filed in the commission's office, and the other copy shall be forwarded by registered mail to the last known principal address recorded in the commission's records for the nonresident against whom the process or pleading is directed.

(e) A default judgment in an action commenced as provided by this section may not be granted:

(1) unless the commission certifies that a copy of the process or pleading was mailed to the defendant as provided by Subsection (d); and

(2) until the 21st day after the date the process or pleading is mailed to the defendant.

(V.A.C.S. Art. 6573a, Secs. 14(b) (part), (c) (part).)

Sec. 1101.361. ADDITIONAL ELIGIBILITY REQUIREMENTS FOR CERTAIN NONRESIDENT APPLICANTS. (a) Notwithstanding Section 1101.360, a nonresident applicant for a license who resides in a municipality whose boundary is contiguous at any point with the boundary of a municipality in this state is eligible to be licensed under this chapter in the same manner as a resident of this state if the nonresident has been a resident of that municipality for at least the 60 days preceding the date the application is filed.

(b) A person licensed under this section shall maintain at all times a place of business in the municipality in which the person resides or in the municipality in this state that is contiguous to the municipality in which the person resides. The place of business must meet all the requirements of Section 1101.552. A place of business located in the municipality in which the person resides is considered to be in this state.

(c) A person licensed under this section may not maintain a place of business at another location in this state unless the person complies with Section 1101.356 or 1101.357.

(V.A.C.S. Art. 6573a, Sec. 14(c) (part).)

Sec. 1101.362. WAIVER OF LICENSE REQUIREMENTS: PREVIOUS LICENSE HOLDERS. The commission by rule may waive some or all of the requirements for a license under this chapter for an applicant who was licensed under this chapter within the six years preceding the date the application is filed.

(V.A.C.S. Art. 6573a, Sec. 7(c) (part).)

Sec. 1101.363. ISSUANCE OF LICENSE. (a) The commission shall issue an appropriate license to an applicant who meets the requirements for a license.

(b) The commission may issue an inactive salesperson license to a person who applies for a salesperson license and satisfies all requirements for the license. The person may not act as a salesperson unless the person is sponsored by a licensed broker who has notified the commission as required by Section 1101.367(b). Notwithstanding Section 1101.367(b), the licensed broker is not required to pay the fee required by that subsection.

(c) A license remains in effect for the period prescribed by the commission if the license holder complies with this chapter and pays the appropriate renewal fees.

(V.A.C.S. Art. 6573a, Sec. 9(a) (part).)

Sec. 1101.364. DENIAL OF LICENSE. (a) The commission shall immediately give written notice to the applicant of the commission's denial of a license.

(b) A person whose license application is denied under this section is entitled to a hearing under Section 1101.657.

(V.A.C.S. Art. 6573a, Secs. 10(a) (part), (b).)

Sec. 1101.365. PROBATIONARY LICENSE. (a) The commission may issue a probationary license.

(b) The commission by rule shall adopt reasonable terms for issuing a probationary license.

(V.A.C.S. Art. 6573a, Sec. 10(c).)

Sec. 1101.366. INACTIVE LICENSE: BROKER. (a) The commission may place on inactive status the license of a broker if the broker:

(1) is not acting as a broker;

(2) is not sponsoring a salesperson; and

(3) submits a written application to the commission before the expiration date of the broker's license.

(b) The commission may place on inactive status the license of a broker whose license has expired if the broker applies for inactive status on a form prescribed by the commission not later than the first anniversary of the expiration date of the broker's license.

(c) A broker applying for inactive status shall terminate the broker's association with each salesperson sponsored by the broker by giving written notice to each salesperson before the 30th day preceding the date the broker applies for inactive status.

(d) A broker on inactive status:

(1) may not perform any activity regulated under this chapter; and

(2) must pay annual renewal fees.

(e) The commission shall maintain a list of each broker whose license is on inactive status.

(f) The commission shall remove a broker's license from inactive status if the broker:

(1) submits an application to the commission;

(2) pays the required fee; and

(3) submits proof of attending at least 15 classroom hours of continuing education as specified by Section 1101.455 during the two years preceding the date the application under Subdivision (1) is filed.

(V.A.C.S. Art. 6573a, Secs. 6(a) (part), 13A.)

Sec. 1101.367. INACTIVE LICENSE: SALESPERSON. (a) When the association of a salesperson with the salesperson's sponsoring broker terminates, the broker shall immediately return the salesperson license to the commission. A salesperson license returned under this subsection is inactive.

(b) The commission may remove a salesperson license from inactive status under Subsection (a) if, before the expiration date of the salesperson license, a licensed broker files a request with the commission advising the commission that the broker assumes sponsorship of the salesperson, accompanied by the appropriate fee.

(c) As a condition of returning to active status, an inactive salesperson whose license is not subject to the annual education requirements of Section 1101.454 must provide to the commission proof of attending at least 15 hours of continuing education as specified by Section 1101.455 during the two years preceding the date the application to return to active status is filed.

(V.A.C.S. Art. 6573a, Secs. 6(a) (part), 7A(c), 13.)

[Sections 1101.368-1101.400 reserved for expansion]

SUBCHAPTER I. EXAMINATIONS

Sec. 1101.401. EXAMINATION REQUIRED. (a) The competency requirement prescribed under Section 1101.354(3) shall be established by an examination prepared or contracted for by the commission.

(b) The commission shall determine the time and place in the state for offering the examination.

(c) The examination must be of sufficient scope in the judgment of the commission to determine whether a person is competent to act as a broker or salesperson in a manner that will protect the public.

(d) The examination for a salesperson license must be less exacting and less stringent than the broker examination.

(e) The commission shall provide each applicant with study material and references on which the examination is based.

(f) An applicant must satisfy the examination requirement not later than six months after the date the license application is filed.

(V.A.C.S. Art. 6573a, Sec. 7(a) (part).)

Sec. 1101.402. WAIVER OF EXAMINATION. The commission shall waive the examination requirement for an applicant for:

(1) a broker license if:

(A) the applicant was previously licensed in this state as a broker; and

(B) the application is filed before the first anniversary of the expiration date of that license; and

(2) a salesperson license if:

(A) the applicant was previously licensed in this state as a broker or salesperson; and

(B) the application is filed before the first anniversary of the expiration date of that license.

(V.A.C.S. Art. 6573a, Sec. 7(c) (part).)

Page 21

Sec. 1101.403. ADMINISTRATION OF EXAMINATION; TESTING SERVICE. (a) The commission shall administer any examination required by this chapter or Chapter 1102 unless the commission enters into an agreement with a testing service to administer the examination.

(b) The commission may accept an examination administered by a testing service if the commission retains the authority to establish the scope and type of the examination.

(c) The commission may negotiate an agreement with a testing service relating to examination development, scheduling, site arrangements, administration, grading, reporting, and analysis.

(d) The commission may require a testing service to:

(1) correspond directly with license applicants regarding the administration of the examination;

(2) collect fees directly from applicants for administering the examination; or

(3) administer the examination at specific locations and specified frequencies.

(e) The commission shall adopt rules and standards as necessary to implement this section.

(V.A.C.S. Art. 6573a, Sec. 7(k).)

Sec. 1101.404. EXAMINATION RESULTS. (a) Not later than the 30th day after the date an examination is administered, the commission shall notify each examinee of the results of the examination. If an examination is graded or reviewed by a national testing service, the commission shall notify each examinee of the results of the examination not later than the 14th day after the date the commission receives the results from the testing service.

(b) If the notice of the results of an examination graded or reviewed by a national testing service will be delayed for more than 90 days after the examination date, the commission shall notify each examinee of the reason for the delay before the 90th day.

(c) If requested in writing by a person who fails an examination, the commission shall provide to the person an analysis of the person's performance on the examination.

(V.A.C.S. Art. 6573a, Sec. 7(i).)

Sec. 1101.405. REEXAMINATION. An applicant who fails an examination may apply for reexamination by filing a request accompanied by the proper fee.

(V.A.C.S. Art. 6573a, Sec. 7(a) (part).)

[Sections 1101.406-1101.450 reserved for expansion]

SUBCHAPTER J. LICENSE RENEWAL

Sec. 1101.451. LICENSE EXPIRATION AND RENEWAL. (a) The commission may issue or renew a license for a period not to exceed 24 months.

(b) The commission by rule may adopt a system under which licenses expire on various dates during the year. The commission shall adjust the date for payment of the renewal fees accordingly.

(c) For a year in which the license expiration date is changed, renewal fees payable shall be prorated on a monthly basis so that each license holder pays only that portion of the fee that is allocable to the number of months during which the license is valid. On renewal of the license on the new expiration date, the total renewal fee is payable.

(d) Except as provided by Subsection (e), a renewal fee for a license under this chapter may not exceed, calculated on an annual basis, the amount of the sum of the fees established under Sections 1101.152, 1101.154, and 1101.603.

(e) A person whose license has been expired for 90 days or less may renew the license by paying to the commission a fee equal to 1-1/2 times the required renewal fee. If a license has been expired for more than 90 days but less than one year, the person may renew the license by paying to the commission a fee equal to two times the required renewal fee.

(f) If a person's license has been expired for one year or longer, the person may not renew the license. The person may obtain a new license by submitting to reexamination and complying with the requirements and procedures for obtaining an original license.

(V.A.C.S. Art. 6573a, Secs. 9(c) (part), (d) (part).)

Sec. 1101.452. INFORMATION REQUIRED FOR LICENSE RENEWAL. (a) To renew an active license that is not subject to the annual education requirements of Section 1101.454, the license holder must provide to the commission proof of compliance with the continuing education requirements of Section 1101.455.

(b) Each applicant for the renewal of a license must disclose in the license application whether the applicant has:

(1) entered a plea of guilty or nolo contendere to a felony; or

(2) been convicted of a felony and the time for appeal has elapsed or the judgment or conviction has been affirmed on appeal.

(c) The disclosure under Subsection (b) must be provided even if an order has granted community supervision suspending the imposition of the sentence.

(V.A.C.S. Art. 6573a, Secs. 7A(a) (part), 9(e) (part).)

Sec. 1101.4521. CRIMINAL HISTORY RECORD INFORMATION FOR RENEWAL. An applicant for the renewal of an unexpired license must comply with the criminal history record check requirements of Section 1101.3521.

Sec. 1101.453. ADDITIONAL RENEWAL REQUIREMENTS FOR CERTAIN BUSINESS ENTITIES. (a) To renew a license under this chapter:

(1) a corporation must designate one of its officers as its agent for purposes of this chapter; and

(2) a limited liability company must designate one of its managers as its agent for purposes of this chapter.

(b) A corporation or limited liability company may not act as a broker unless the entity's designated agent is a licensed broker according to the commission's records.

(V.A.C.S. Art. 6573a, Sec. 6(c) (part).)

Sec. 1101.454. SALESPERSON LICENSE RENEWAL. (a) An applicant applying for the first renewal of a salesperson license must provide to the commission satisfactory evidence of completion of at least 18 semester hours, or equivalent classroom hours, of postsecondary education, including 14 hours of core real estate courses.

(b) The commission may not waive the requirements for renewal under this section.

Added by S.B. 810, effective January 1, 2006

(V.A.C.S. Art. 6573a, Secs. 7(e) (part), 9 (d) (part).)

Sec. 1101.455. CONTINUING EDUCATION REQUIREMENTS. (a) In this section, "property tax consulting laws and legal issues" includes the Tax Code, preparation of property tax reports, the unauthorized practice of law, agency law, tax law, law relating to property tax or property assessment, deceptive trade practices, contract forms and addendums, and other legal topics approved by the commission.

(b) A license holder who is not subject to the annual education requirements of Section 1101.454 must attend during the term of the current license at least 15 classroom hours of continuing education courses approved by the commission.

(c) The commission by rule may:

(1) prescribe the title, content, and duration of continuing education courses that a license holder must attend to renew a license; and

(2) approve as a substitute for the classroom attendance required by Subsection (b):

(A) relevant educational experience; and

(B) correspondence courses.

(d) In addition, the commission may approve supervised video instruction as a course that may be applied toward satisfaction of the classroom hours of continuing education courses required by Subsection (b).

(e) At least six of the continuing education hours required by Subsection (b) must cover the following legal topics:

(1) commission rules;

(2) fair housing laws;

(3) Property Code issues, including landlord-tenant law;

(4) agency law;

(5) antitrust laws;

(6) Subchapter E, Chapter 17, Business & Commerce Code;

(7) disclosures to buyers, landlords, tenants, and sellers;

(8) current contract and addendum forms;

(9) unauthorized practice of law;

(10) case studies involving violations of laws and regulations;

(11) current Federal Housing Administration and Department of Veterans Affairs regulations;

(12) tax laws;

(13) property tax consulting laws and legal issues; or

(14) other legal topics approved by the commission.

(f) The remaining nine hours may be devoted to other real estate-related topics approved by the commission.

(g) The commission may consider courses equivalent to those described by Subsections (e) and (f) for continuing education credit.

(h) The commission shall automatically approve the following courses as courses that satisfy the mandatory continuing education requirements of Subsection (f):

(1) core real estate courses; and

(2) real estate-related courses approved by the State Bar of Texas for minimum continuing legal education participatory credit.

(i) The commission may not require an examination for a course under this section unless the course is a correspondence course or a course offered by an alternative delivery system, including delivery by computer.

(j) Daily classroom course segments must be at least one hour and not more than 10 hours.

(k) An online course offered under this section may not be completed in less than 24 hours.

(l) Notwithstanding the number of hours required by Subsection (e), a member of the legislature licensed under this chapter is only required to complete three hours of continuing education on the legal topics under Subsection (e).

(V.A.C.S. Art. 6573a, Sec. 7A(a).)

Sec. 1101.456. EXEMPTION FROM CONTINUING EDUCATION REQUIREMENTS FOR CERTAIN BROKERS. Notwithstanding any other provision of this chapter, a broker who, before October 31, 1991, qualified under former Section 7A(f), The Real Estate License Act (Article 6573a, Vernon's Texas Civil Statutes), as added by Section 1.041, Chapter 553, Acts of the 72nd Legislature, Regular Session, 1991, for an exemption from continuing education requirements is not required to comply with the mandatory continuing education requirements of this subchapter to renew the broker's license.

(V.A.C.S. Art. 6573a, Sec. 7A(f) (part).)

Sec. 1101.457. DEFERRAL OF CONTINUING EDUCATION REQUIREMENTS. (a) The commission by rule may establish procedures under which an applicant may have the applicant's license issued, renewed, or returned to active status before the applicant completes continuing education requirements.

(b) The commission may require an applicant under this section to:

(1) pay a fee, not to exceed $200, in addition to any fee for late renewal of a license under this chapter; and

(2) complete the required continuing education not later than the 60th day after the date the license is issued, renewed, or returned to active status.

(V.A.C.S. Art. 6573a, Sec. 7A(g).)

[Sections 1101.458-1101.500 reserved for expansion]

SUBCHAPTER K. CERTIFICATE REQUIREMENTS

Sec. 1101.501. CERTIFICATE REQUIRED. A person may not sell, buy, lease, or transfer an easement Or right-of-way for another, for compensation or with the expectation of receiving compensation, for use in connection with telecommunication, utility, railroad, or pipeline service unless the person:

(1) holds a license issued under this chapter; or

(2) holds a certificate of registration issued under this subchapter.

(V.A.C.S. Art. 6573a, Secs. 4 (part), 9(b) (part), 9A(a).)

Sec. 1101.502. ELIGIBILITY REQUIREMENTS FOR CERTIFICATE. (a) To be eligible to receive a certificate of registration or a renewal certificate under this subchapter, a person must be:

(1) at least 18 years of age; and

(2) a citizen of the United States or a lawfully admitted alien.

(b) To be eligible to receive a certificate of registration or a renewal certificate under this subchapter, a corporation, limited liability company, partnership, limited liability partnership, or other entity must designate as its agent one of its officers, partners, or managers who is registered under this subchapter.

(V.A.C.S. Art. 6573a, Sec. 6(d).)

Sec. 1101.503. ISSUANCE OF CERTIFICATE. (a) The commission shall issue a certificate of registration to an applicant who meets the requirements for a certificate of registration.

(b) The certificate remains in effect for the period prescribed by the commission if the certificate holder complies with this chapter and pays the appropriate renewal fees.

(V.A.C.S. Art. 6573a, Sec. 9(a) (part).)

Sec. 1101.504. CERTIFICATE EXPIRATION. The duration, expiration, and renewal of a certificate of registration are subject to the same provisions as are applicable under Section 1101.451 to the duration, expiration, and renewal of a license.

(V.A.C.S. Art. 6573a, Secs. 9(c) (part), (d) (part).)

Sec. 1101.505. DENIAL OF CERTIFICATE. The denial of a certificate of registration is subject to the same provisions as are applicable under Section 1101.364 to the denial of a license.

(V.A.C.S. Art. 6573a, Secs. 10(a) (part), (b).)

Sec. 1101.506. CHANGE OF ADDRESS. Not later than the 10th day after the date a certificate holder moves its place of business from a previously designated address, the holder shall:

(1) notify the commission of the move; and

(2) obtain a new certificate of registration that reflects the address of the new place of business.

(V.A.C.S. Art. 6573a, Sec. 12(e) (part).)

Sec. 1101.507. DISPLAY OF CERTIFICATE. A certificate holder shall prominently display at all times the holder's certificate of registration in the holder's place of business.

(V.A.C.S. Art. 6573a, Sec. 12(e) (part).)

[Sections 1101.508-1101.550 reserved for expansion]

SUBCHAPTER L. PRACTICE BY LICENSE HOLDER

Sec. 1101.551. DEFINITIONS. In this subchapter:

(1) "Intermediary" means a broker who is employed to negotiate a transaction between the parties to a transaction and for that purpose may act as an agent of the parties.

(2) "Party" means a prospective buyer, seller, landlord, or tenant or an authorized representative of a buyer, seller, landlord, or tenant, including a trustee, guardian, executor, administrator, receiver, or attorney-in-fact. The term does not include a license holder who represents a party.

(V.A.C.S. Art. 6573a, Secs. 15C(m)(2) (part), (4).)

Sec. 1101.552. FIXED OFFICE REQUIRED; CHANGE OF ADDRESS; BRANCH OFFICES. (a) A resident broker shall maintain a fixed office in this state. The address of the office shall be designated on the broker's license.

(b) Not later than the 10th day after the date a broker moves from the address designated on the broker's license, the broker shall submit an application, accompanied by the appropriate fee, for a license that designates the new location of the broker's office. The commission shall issue a license that designates the new location if the new location complies with the requirements of this section.

(c) A broker who maintains more than one place of business in this state shall obtain a branch office license for each additional office maintained by the broker by submitting an application, accompanied by the appropriate fee.

(d) A nonresident licensed broker is not required to maintain a place of business in this state.

(V.A.C.S. Art. 6573a, Secs. 12(a), (b), 14 (b) (part).)

Sec. 1101.553. DISPLAY OF LICENSE. A residential rental locator shall prominently display in a place accessible to clients and prospective clients:

(1) the locator's license;

(2) a statement that the locator is licensed by the commission; and

(3) the name, mailing address, and telephone number of the commission as provided by Section 1101.202(a).

(V.A.C.S. Art. 6573a, Secs. 12(c), (d), 24(d).)

Sec. 1101.554. CUSTODY OF SALESPERSON LICENSE. (a) The commission shall deliver or mail each salesperson license to the broker with whom the salesperson is associated.

(b) The broker shall keep the license under the broker's custody and control.

(V.A.C.S. Art. 6573a, Sec. 9(a) (part).)

Sec. 1101.555. NOTICE TO BUYER REGARDING ABSTRACT OR TITLE POLICY. When an offer to purchase real estate in this state is signed, a license holder shall advise each buyer, in writing, that the buyer should:

(1) have the abstract covering the real estate that is the subject of the contract examined by an attorney chosen by the buyer; or

(2) be provided with or obtain a title insurance policy.

(V.A.C.S. Art. 6573a, Sec. 20(c) (part).)

Sec. 1101.556. DISCLOSURE OF CERTAIN INFORMATION RELATING TO OCCUPANTS. Notwithstanding other law, a license holder is not required to inquire about, disclose, or release information relating to whether:

(1) a previous or current occupant of real property had, may have had, has, or may have AIDS, an HIV-related illness, or an HIV infection as defined by the Centers for Disease Control and Prevention of the United States Public Health Service; or

(2) a death occurred on a property by natural causes, suicide, or accident unrelated to the condition of the property.

(V.A.C.S. Art. 6573a, Sec. 15E.)

Sec. 1101.557. ACTING AS AGENT; REGULATION OF CERTAIN TRANSACTIONS.

(a) A broker who represents a party in a real estate transaction or who lists real estate for sale under an exclusive agreement for a party is that party's agent.

(b) A broker described by Subsection (a):

(1) may not instruct another broker to directly or indirectly violate Section 1101.652 (b)(22);

(2) must inform the party if the broker receives material information related to a transaction to list, buy, sell, or lease the party's real estate, including the receipt of an offer by the broker; and

(3) shall, at a minimum, answer the party's questions and present any offer to or from the party.

(c) For the purposes of this section:

(1) a license holder who has the authority to bind a party to a lease or sale under a power of attorney or a property management agreement is also a party to the lease or sale;

(2) an inquiry to a person described by Section 1101.005(6) about contract terms or forms required by the person's employer does not violate Section 1101.652(b)(22) if the person does not have the authority to bind the employer to the contract; and

(3) the sole delivery of an offer to a party does not violate Section 1101.652(b)(22) if:

(A) the party's broker consents to the delivery;

(B) a copy of the offer is sent to the party's broker, unless a governmental agency using a sealed bid process does not allow a copy to be sent; and

(C) the person delivering the offer does not engage in another activity that directly or indirectly violates Section 1101. 652(b)(22).

(V.A.C.S. Art. 6573a, Sec. 15C(c).)

Sec. 1101.558. REPRESENTATION DISCLOSURE. (a) In this section, "substantive dialogue" means a meeting or written communication that involves a substantive discussion relating to specific real property. The term does not include:

(1) a meeting that occurs at a property that is held open for any prospective buyer or tenant; or

(2) a meeting or written communication that occurs after the parties to a real estate transaction have signed a contract to sell, buy, or lease the real property concerned.

(b) A license holder who represents a party in a proposed real estate transaction shall disclose, orally or in writing, that representation at the time of the license holder's first contact with:

(1) another party to the transaction; or

(2) another license holder who represents another party to the transaction.

(c) A license holder shall provide to a party to a real estate transaction at the time of the first substantive dialogue with the party the written statement prescribed by Subsection (d) unless:

(1) the proposed transaction is for a residential lease for not more than one year and a sale is not being considered; or

(2) the license holder meets with a party who is represented by another license holder.

(d) The written statement required by Subsection (c) must be printed in a format that uses at least 10-point type and read as follows:

"Before working with a real estate broker, you should know that the duties of a broker depend on whom the broker represents. If you are a prospective seller or landlord (owner) or a prospective buyer or tenant (buyer), you should know that the broker who lists the property for sale or lease is the owner's agent. A broker who acts as a subagent represents the owner in cooperation with the listing broker. A broker who acts as a buyer's agent represents the buyer. A broker may act as an intermediary between the parties if the parties consent in writing. A broker can assist you in locating a property, preparing a contract or lease, or obtaining financing without representing you. A broker is obligated by law to treat you honestly.

"IF THE BROKER REPRESENTS THE OWNER: The broker becomes the owner's agent by entering into an agreement with the owner, usually through a written listing agreement, or by agreeing to act as a subagent by accepting an offer of subagency from the listing broker. A subagent may work in a different real estate office. A listing broker or subagent can assist the buyer but does not represent the buyer and must place the interests of the owner first. The buyer should not tell the owner's agent anything the buyer would not want the owner to know because an owner's agent must disclose to the owner any material information known to the agent.

"IF THE BROKER REPRESENTS THE BUYER: The broker becomes the buyer's agent by entering into an agreement to represent the buyer, usually through a written buyer representation agreement. A buyer's agent can assist the owner but does not represent the owner and must place the interests of the buyer first. The owner should not tell a buyer's agent anything the owner would not want the buyer to know because a buyer's agent must disclose to the buyer any material information known to the agent.

"IF THE BROKER ACTS AS AN INTERMEDIARY: A broker may act as an intermediary between the parties if the broker complies with The Texas Real Estate License Act. The broker must obtain the written consent of each party to the transaction to act as an intermediary. The written consent must state who will pay the broker and, in conspicuous bold or underlined print, set forth the broker's obligations as an intermediary. The broker is required to treat each party honestly and fairly and to comply with The Texas Real Estate License Act. A broker who acts as an intermediary in a transaction: (1) shall treat all parties honestly; (2) may not disclose that the owner will accept a price less than the asking price unless authorized in writing to do so by the owner; (3) may not disclose that the buyer will pay a price greater than the price submitted in a written offer unless authorized in writing to do so by the buyer; and (4) may not disclose any confidential information or any information that a party specifically instructs the broker in writing not to disclose unless authorized in writing to disclose the information or required to do so by The Texas Real Estate License Act or a court order or if the information materially relates to the condition of the property. With the parties' consent, a broker acting as an intermediary between the parties may appoint a person who is licensed under The Texas Real Estate License Act and associated with the broker to communicate with and carry out instructions of one party and another person who is licensed under that Act and associated with the broker to communicate with and carry out instructions of the other party.

"If you choose to have a broker represent you, you should enter into a written agreement with the broker that clearly establishes the broker's obligations and your obligations. The agreement should state how and by whom the broker will be paid. You have the right to choose the type of representation, if any, you wish to receive. Your payment of a fee to a broker does not necessarily establish that the broker represents you. If you have any questions regarding the duties and responsibilities of the broker, you should resolve those questions before proceeding."

(e) The license holder may substitute "buyer" for "tenant" and "seller" for "landlord" as appropriate in the written statement prescribed by Subsection (d).

(V.A.C.S. Art. 6573a, Secs. 15C(a), (b), (d), (e), (f), (g), (m)(1).)

Sec. 1101.559. BROKER ACTING AS INTERMEDIARY. (a) A broker may act as an intermediary between parties to a real estate transaction if:

(1) the broker obtains written consent from each party for the broker to act as an intermediary in the transaction; and

(2) the written consent of the parties states the source of any expected compensation to the broker.

(b) A written listing agreement to represent a seller or landlord or a written agreement to represent a buyer or tenant that authorizes a broker to act as an intermediary in a real estate transaction is sufficient to establish written consent of the party to the transaction if the written agreement specifies in conspicuous bold or underlined print the conduct that is prohibited under Section 1101.651(d).

(c) An intermediary shall act fairly and impartially. Appointment by a broker acting as an intermediary of an associated license holder under Section 1101.560 to communicate with, carry out the instructions of, and provide opinions and advice to the parties to whom that associated license holder is appointed is a fair and impartial act.

(V.A.C.S. Art. 6573a, Secs. 15C(h), (i), (m)(2) (part).)

Page 29

Sec. 1101.560. ASSOCIATED LICENSE HOLDER ACTING AS INTERMEDIARY. (a) A broker who complies with the written consent requirements of Section 1101.559 may appoint:

(1) a license holder associated with the broker to communicate with and carry out instructions of one party to a real estate transaction; and

(2) another license holder associated with the broker to communicate with and carry out instructions of any other party to the transaction.

(b) A license holder may be appointed under this section only if:

(1) the written consent of the parties under Section 1101.559 authorizes the broker to make the appointment; and

(2) the broker provides written notice of the appointment to all parties involved in the real estate transaction.

(c) A license holder appointed under this section may provide opinions and advice during negotiations to the party to whom the license holder is appointed.

(V.A.C.S. Art. 6573a, Sec. 15C(k) (part).)

Sec. 1101. 561. DUTIES OF INTERMEDIARY PREVAIL. (a) The duties of a license holder acting as an intermediary under this subchapter supersede the duties of a license holder established under any other law, including common law.

(b) A broker must agree to act as an intermediary under this subchapter if the broker agrees to represent in a transaction:

(1) a buyer or tenant; and

(2) a seller or landlord.

(V.A.C.S. Art. 6573a, Sec. 15C(l).)

[Sections 1101.562-1101.600 reserved for expansion]

SUBCHAPTER M. REAL ESTATE RECOVERY TRUST ACCOUNT

Sec. 1101.601. REAL ESTATE RECOVERY TRUST ACCOUNT. (a) The commission shall maintain a real estate recovery trust account to reimburse aggrieved persons who suffer actual damages caused by an act described by Section 1101.602 committed by:

(1) a license holder;

(2) a certificate holder; or

(3) a person who does not hold a license or certificate and who is an employee or agent of a license or certificate holder.

(b) The license or certificate holder must have held the license or certificate at the time the act was committed.

(V.A.C.S. Art. 6573a, Sec. 8(a) (part).)

Sec. 1101.602. ENTITLEMENT TO REIMBURSEMENT. An aggrieved person is entitled to reimbursement from the trust account if a person described by Section 1101.601 engages in conduct described by Section 1101.652(a)(3) or (b) or 1101.653(1), (2), (3), or (4).

(V.A.C.S. Art. 6573a, Sec. 8(a) (part).)

Sec. 1101.603. PAYMENTS INTO TRUST ACCOUNT. (a) In addition to other fees required by this chapter, an applicant for an original license must pay a fee of $10.

(b) In addition to other fees required by this chapter, an applicant for an original certificate of registration or renewal certificate must pay a fee of $50.

(c) The commission shall deposit to the credit of the trust account:

(1) fees collected under Subsections (a) and (b); and

(2) an administrative penalty collected under Subchapter O for a violation by a person licensed as a broker or salesperson.

(d) A administrative penalty collected under Subchapter O for a violation by a person who is not licensed under this chapter or Chapter 1102 shall be deposited to the credit of the trust account or the real estate inspection recovery fund, as determined by the commission.

(e) On a determination by the commission at any time that the balance in the trust account is less than $1 million, each license holder at the next license renewal must pay, in addition to the renewal fee, a fee that is equal to the lesser of $10 or a pro rata share of the amount necessary to obtain a balance in the trust account of $1.7 million. The commission shall deposit the additional fee to the credit of the trust account.

(f) To ensure the availability of a sufficient amount to pay anticipated claims on the trust account, the commission by rule may provide for the collection of assessments at different times and under conditions other than those specified by this chapter.

(V.A.C.S. Art. 6573a, Secs. 8(b), (c) (part), 11 (part), 19A(o) (part).)

Sec. 1101.604. MANAGEMENT OF TRUST ACCOUNT. (a) The commission shall hold money credited to the trust account in trust to carry out the purpose of the trust account.

(b) Money credited to the trust account may be invested in the same manner as money of the Employees Retirement System of Texas, except that an investment may not be made that would impair the liquidity necessary to make payments from the trust account as required by this subchapter.

(c) Interest from the investments shall be deposited to the credit of the trust account.

(d) If the balance in the trust account on December 31 of a year is more than the greater of $3.5 million or the total amount of claims paid from the trust account during the preceding four fiscal years, the commission shall transfer the excess amount of money in the trust account to the credit of the general revenue fund.

(V.A.C.S. Art. 6573a, Secs. 8(c) (part), (j).)

Sec. 1101.605. DEADLINE FOR ACTION; NOTICE TO COMMISSION. (a) An action for a judgment that may result in an order for payment from the trust account may not be brought after the second anniversary of the date the cause of action accrues.

(b) When an aggrieved person brings an action for a judgment that may result in an order for payment from the trust account, the license or certificate holder against whom the action is brought shall notify the commission in writing of the action.

(V.A.C.S. Art. 6573a, Sec. 8(d).)

Sec. 1101.606. CLAIM FOR PAYMENT FROM TRUST ACCOUNT. (a) Except as provided by Subsection (c), an aggrieved person who obtains a court judgment against a license or certificate holder for an act described by Section 1101.602 may, after final judgment is entered, execution returned nulla bona, and a judgment lien perfected, file a verified claim in the court that entered the judgment.

(b) After the 20th day after the date the aggrieved person gives written notice of the claim to the commission and judgment debtor, the person may apply to the court that entered the judgment for an order for payment from the trust account of the amount unpaid on the judgment. The court shall proceed promptly on the application.

(c) If an aggrieved person is precluded by action of a bankruptcy court from executing a judgment or perfecting a judgment lien as required by Subsection (a), the person shall verify to the commission that the person has made a good faith effort to protect the judgment from being discharged in bankruptcy.

(d) The commission by rule may prescribe the actions necessary for an aggrieved person to demonstrate that the person has made a good faith effort under Subsection (c) to protect a judgment from being discharged in bankruptcy.

(V.A.C.S. Art. 6573a, Secs. 8(e), (f) (part).)

Amended by SB 862, 81st Legislative Session, 2009, Section V

Sec. 1101.607. ISSUES AT HEARING. At the hearing on the application for payment from the trust account, the aggrieved person must show:

(1) that the judgment is based on facts allowing recovery under this subchapter;

(2) that the person is not:

(A) the spouse of the judgment debtor or the personal representative of the spouse; or

(B) a license or certificate holder who is seeking to recover compensation, including a commission, in the real estate transaction that is the subject of the application for payment;

(3) that, according to the best information available, the judgment debtor does not have sufficient attachable assets in this or another state to satisfy the judgment;

(4) the amount that may be realized from the sale of assets liable to be sold or applied to satisfy the judgment; and

(5) the balance remaining due on the judgment after application of the amount under Subdivision (4).

(V.A.C.S. Art. 6573a, Sec. 8(f) (part).)

Sec. 1101.608. COMMISSION RESPONSE. (a) On receipt of notice under Section 1101.606 and the scheduling of a hearing, the commission may notify the attorney general of the commission's desire to enter an appearance, file a response, appear at the hearing, defend the action, or take any other action the commission considers appropriate.

(b) The commission and the attorney general may act under Subsection (a) only to:

(1) protect the trust account from spurious or unjust claims; or

(2) ensure compliance with the requirements for recovery under this subchapter.

(c) The commission may relitigate in the hearing any material and relevant issue that was determined in the action that resulted in the judgment in favor of the aggrieved person.

(V.A.C.S. Art. 6573a, Secs. 8(h) (part), (k).)

Sec. 1101.609. COURT ORDER FOR PAYMENT. The court shall order the commission to pay from the trust account the amount the court finds payable on the claim under this subchapter if at a hearing the court is satisfied:

(1) of the truth of each matter the aggrieved person is required by Section 1101.607 to show; and

(2) that the aggrieved person has satisfied each requirement of Sections 1101.606 and 1101.607.

(V.A.C.S. Art. 6573a, Secs. 8(a) (part), (h) (part).)

Sec. 1101.610. PAYMENT LIMITS; ATTORNEY'S FEES. (a) Payments from the trust account for claims, including attorney's fees, interest, and court costs, arising out of a single transaction may not exceed a total of $50,000, regardless of the number of claimants.

(b) Payments from the trust account for claims based on judgments against a single license or certificate holder may not exceed a total of $100,000 until the license or certificate holder has reimbursed the trust account for all amounts paid.

(c) If the court finds that the total amount of claims against a license or certificate holder exceeds the limitations in this section, the court shall proportionately reduce the amount payable on each claim.

(d) A person receiving payment from the trust account is entitled to receive reasonable attorney's fees in the amount determined by the court, subject to the limitations prescribed by this section.

(V.A.C.S. Art. 6573a, Secs. 8(h) (part), (n), (p).)

Sec. 1101.611. APPLICATION OF JUDGMENT RECOVERY. An aggrieved person who receives a recovery on a judgment against a single defendant before receiving a payment from the trust account must apply the recovery first to actual damages.

(V.A.C.S. Art. 6573a, Sec. 8(g).)

Sec. 1101.612. SUBROGATION. (a) The commission is subrogated to all rights of a judgment creditor to the extent of an amount paid from the trust account, and the judgment creditor shall assign to the commission all right, title, and interest in the judgment up to that amount.

(b) The commission has priority for repayment from any subsequent recovery on the judgment.

(c) The commission shall deposit any amount recovered on the judgment to the credit of the trust account.

(V.A.C.S. Art. 6573a, Sec. 8(l).)

Sec. 1101.613. EFFECT ON DISCIPLINARY PROCEEDINGS. (a) This subchapter does not limit the commission's authority to take disciplinary action against a license or certificate holder for a violation of this chapter or a commission rule.

(b) A license or certificate holder's repayment of all amounts owed to the trust account does not affect another disciplinary proceeding brought under this chapter.

(V.A.C.S. Art. 6573a, Sec. 8(o).)

Sec. 1101.614. WAIVER OF RIGHTS. An aggrieved person who does not comply with this subchapter waives the person's rights under this subchapter.

(V.A.C.S. Art. 6573a, Sec. 8(m).)

Sec. 1101.615. NOTICE TO CONSUMERS AND SERVICE RECIPIENTS. (a) Each license and certificate holder shall provide notice to consumers and service recipients of the availability of payment from the trust account for aggrieved persons:

(1) in conjunction with the notice required by Section 1101.202;

(2) on a written contract for the license or certificate holder's services;

(3) on a brochure that the license or certificate holder distributes;

(4) on a sign prominently displayed in the license or certificate holder's place of business; or

(5) in a bill or receipt for the license or certificate holder's services; or

(6) in a prominent display on the Internet website of a person regulated under this chapter.

(b) The notice must include:

(1) the commission's name, mailing address, and telephone number; and

(2) any other information required by commission rule.

(V.A.C.S. Art. 6573a, Sec. 8(q).)

[Sections 1101.616-1101.650 reserved for expansion]

Page 33

SUBCHAPTER N. PROHIBITED PRACTICES AND DISCIPLINARY PROCEEDINGS

Sec. 1101.651. CERTAIN PRACTICES PROHIBITED. (a) A licensed broker may not pay a commission to or otherwise compensate a person directly or indirectly for performing an act of a broker unless the person is:

(1) a license holder; or

(2) a real estate broker licensed in another state who does not conduct in this state any of the negotiations for which the commission or other compensation is paid.

(b) A salesperson may not accept compensation for a real estate transaction from a person other than the broker with whom the salesperson is associated or was associated when the salesperson earned the compensation.

(c) A salesperson may not pay a commission to a person except through the broker with whom the salesperson is associated at that time.

(d) A broker and any broker or salesperson appointed under Section 1101.560 who acts as an intermediary under Subchapter L may not:

(1) disclose to the buyer or tenant that the seller or landlord will accept a price less than the asking price, unless otherwise instructed in a separate writing by the seller or landlord;

(2) disclose to the seller or landlord that the buyer or tenant will pay a price greater than the price submitted in a written offer to the seller or landlord, unless otherwise instructed in a separate writing by the buyer or tenant;

(3) disclose any confidential information or any information a party specifically instructs the broker or salesperson in writing not to disclose, unless:

(A) the broker or salesperson is otherwise instructed in a separate writing by the respective party;

(B) the broker or salesperson is required to disclose the information by this chapter or a court order; or

(C) the information materially relates to the condition of the property;

(4) treat a party to a transaction dishonestly; or

(5) violate this chapter.

(V.A.C.S. Art. 6573a, Secs. 1(d), (e), 14 (a), 15C(j), (k) (part).)

Sec. 1101.652. GROUNDS FOR SUSPENSION OR REVOCATION OF LICENSE. (a) The commission may suspend or revoke a license issued under this chapter or take other disciplinary action authorized by this chapter if the license holder:

(1) enters a plea of guilty or nolo contendere to or is convicted of a felony or a criminal offense involving fraud, and the time for appeal has elapsed or the judgment or conviction has been affirmed on appeal, without regard to an order granting community supervision that suspends the imposition of the sentence;

(2) procures or attempts to procure a license under this chapter for the license holder or a salesperson by fraud, misrepresentation, or deceit or by making a material misstatement of fact in an application for a license;

(3) engages in misrepresentation, dishonesty, or fraud when selling, buying, trading, or leasing real property in the name of:

(A) the license holder;

(B) the license holder's spouse; or

(C) a person related to the license holder within the first degree by consanguinity;

(4) fails to honor, within a reasonable time, a check issued to the commission after the commission has sent by certified mail a

request for payment to the license holder's last known business address according to commission records;

(5) fails or refuses to produce on request, for inspection by the commission or a commission representative, a document, book, or record that is in the license holder's possession and relates to a real estate transaction conducted by the license holder;

(6) fails to provide, within a reasonable time, information requested by the commission that relates to a formal or informal complaint to the commission that would indicate a violation of this chapter;

(7) fails to surrender to the owner, without just cause, a document or instrument that is requested by the owner and that is in the license holder's possession;

(8) fails to use a contract form required by the commission under Section 1101.155;

(9) fails to notify the commission, not later than the 30th day after the date of a final conviction or the entry of a plea of guilty or nolo contendere, that the person has been convicted of or entered a plea of guilty or nolo contendere to a felony or a criminal offense involving fraud; or

(10) disregards or violates this chapter.

(b) The commission may suspend or revoke a license issued under this chapter or take other disciplinary action authorized by this chapter if the license holder, while acting as a broker or salesperson:

(1) acts negligently or incompetently;

(2) engages in conduct that is dishonest or in bad faith or that demonstrates untrustworthiness;

(3) Makes a material misrepresentation to a potential buyer concerning a significant defect, including a latent structural defect, known to the license holder that would be a significant factor to a reasonable and prudent buyer in making a decision to purchase real property;

(4) fails to disclose to a potential buyer a defect described by Subdivision (3) that is known to the license holder;

(5) makes a false promise that is likely to influence a person to enter into an agreement when the license holder is unable or does not intend to keep the promise;

(6) pursues a continued and flagrant course of misrepresentation or makes false promises through an agent or salesperson, through advertising, or otherwise;

(7) fails to make clear to all parties to a real estate transaction the party for whom the license holder is acting;

(8) receives compensation from more than one party to a real estate transaction without the full knowledge and consent of all parties to the transaction;

(9) fails within a reasonable time to properly account for or remit money that is received by the license holder and that belongs to another person;

(10) commingles money that belongs to another person with the license holder's own money;

(11) pays a commission or a fee to or divides a commission or a fee with a person other than a license holder or a real estate broker or salesperson licensed in another state for compensation for services as a real estate agent;

(12) fails to specify a definite termination date that is not subject to prior notice in a contract, other than a contract to perform property management services, in which the license holder agrees to perform services for which a license is required under this chapter;

(13) accepts, receives, or charges an undisclosed commission, rebate, or direct profit on an expenditure made for a principal;

(14) solicits, sells, or offers for sale real property by means of a lottery;

(15) solicits, sells, or offers for sale real property by means of a deceptive practice;

(16) acts in a dual capacity as broker and undisclosed principal in a real estate transaction;

(17) guarantees or authorizes or permits a person to guarantee that future profits will result from a resale of real property;

(18) places a sign on real property offering the real property for sale or lease without obtaining the written consent of the owner of the real property or the owner's authorized agent;

(19) offers to sell or lease real property without the knowledge and consent of the owner of the real property or the owner's authorized agent;

(20) offers to sell or lease real property on terms other than those authorized by the owner of the real property or the owner's authorized agent;

(21) induces or attempts to induce a party to a contract of sale or lease to break the contract for the purpose of substituting a new contract;

(22) negotiates or attempts to negotiate the sale, exchange, or lease of real property with an owner, landlord, buyer, or tenant with knowledge that that person is a party to an outstanding written contract that grants exclusive agency to another broker in connection with the transaction;

(23) publishes or causes to be published an advertisement, including an advertisement by newspaper, radio, television, the Internet or display, that misleads or is likely to deceive the public, tends to create a misleading impression, or fails to identify the person causing the advertisement to be published as a licensed broker or agent;

(24) withholds from or inserts into a statement of account or invoice a statement that the license holder knows makes the statement of account or invoice inaccurate in a material way;

(25) publishes or circulates an unjustified or unwarranted threat of a legal proceeding or other action;

(26) establishes an association by employment or otherwise with a person other than a license holder if the person is expected or required to act as a license holder;

(27) aids, abets, or conspires with another person to circumvent this chapter;

(28) fails or refuses to provide, on request, a copy of a document relating to a real estate transaction to a person who signed the document;

(29) fails to advise a buyer in writing before the closing of a real estate transaction that the buyer should:

(A) have the abstract covering the real estate that is the subject of the contract examined by an attorney chosen by the buyer; or

(B) be provided with or obtain a title insurance policy;

(30) fails to deposit, within a reasonable time, money the license holder receives as escrow agent in a real estate transaction:

(A) in trust with a title company authorized to do business in this state; or

(B) in a custodial, trust, or escrow account maintained for that purpose in a banking institution authorized to do business in this state;

(31) disburses money deposited in a custodial, trust, or escrow account, as provided in Subdivision (30), before the completion or termination of the real estate transaction;

(32) discriminates against an owner, potential buyer, landlord, or potential tenant on the basis of race, color, religion, sex,

disability, familial status, national origin, or ancestry, including directing a prospective buyer or tenant interested in equivalent properties to a different area based on the race, color, religion, sex, disability familial status, national origin, or ancestry of the potential owner or tenant; or

(33) disregards or violates this chapter.

(V.A.C.S. Art. 6573a, Secs. 15(a) (part), 16(e) (part).) Amended by SB 862, 81st Legislative Session, 2009, Section VI

Sec. 1101.653. GROUNDS FOR SUSPENSION OR REVOCATION OF CERTIFICATE. The commission may suspend or revoke a certificate of registration issued under this chapter if the certificate holder:

(1) engages in dishonest dealing, fraud, unlawful discrimination, or a deceptive act;

(2) makes a misrepresentation;

(3) acts in bad faith;

(4) demonstrates untrustworthiness;

(5) fails to honor, within a reasonable time, a check issued to the commission after the commission has mailed a request for payment to the certificate holder's last known address according to the commission's records;

(6) fails to provide to a party to a transaction a written notice prescribed by the commission that:

(A) must be given before the party is obligated to sell, buy, lease, or transfer a right-of-way or easement; and

(B) contains:

(i) the name of the certificate holder;

(ii) the certificate number;

(iii) the name of the person the certificate holder represents;

(iv) a statement advising the party that the party may seek representation from a lawyer or broker in the transaction; and

(v) a statement generally advising the party that the right-of-way or easement may affect the value of the property; or

(7) disregards or violates this chapter or a commission rule relating to certificate holders.

(V.A.C.S. Art. 6573a, Sec. 9A(c) (part).)

Sec. 1101.654. SUSPENSION OR REVOCATION OF LICENSE OR CERTIFICATE FOR UNAUTHORIZED PRACTICE OF LAW. (a) The commission shall suspend or revoke the license or certificate of registration of a license or certificate holder who is not a licensed attorney in this state and who, for consideration, a reward, or a pecuniary benefit, present or anticipated, direct or indirect, or in connection with the person's employment, agency, or fiduciary relationship as a license or certificate holder:

(1) drafts an instrument, other than a form described by Section 1101.155, that transfers or otherwise affects an interest in real property; or

(2) advises a person regarding the validity or legal sufficiency of an instrument or the validity of title to real property.

(b) Notwithstanding any other law, a license or certificate holder who completes a contract form for the sale, exchange, option, or lease of an interest in real property incidental to acting as a broker is not engaged in the unauthorized or illegal practice of law in this state if the form was:

(1) adopted by the commission for the type of transaction for which the form is used;

(2) prepared by an attorney licensed in this state and approved by the attorney for the type of transaction for which the form is used; or

(3) prepared by the property owner or by an attorney and required by the property owner.

(V.A.C.S. Art. 6573a, Secs. 16(a), (b).)

Sec. 1101.655. REVOCATION OF LICENSE OR CERTIFICATE FOR CLAIM ON ACCOUNT. (a) The commission may revoke a license, approval, or registration issued under this chapter or Chapter 1102 if the commission makes a payment from the real estate recovery trust account to satisfy all or part of a judgment against the license or certificate registration holder.

(b) The commission may probate an order revoking a license under this section.

(c) A person is not eligible for a license or certificate until the person has repaid in full the amount paid from the account for the person, plus interest at the legal rate.

(V.A.C.S. Art. 6573a, Sec. 8(i).)

Sec. 1101.656. ADDITIONAL DISCIPLINARY AUTHORITY OF COMMISSION. (a) In addition to any other authority under this chapter, the commission may suspend or revoke a license, place on probation a person whose license has been suspended, or reprimand a license holder if the license holder violates this chapter or a commission rule.

(b) The commission may probate a suspension, revocation, or cancellation of a license under reasonable terms determined by the commission.

(c) The commission may require a license holder whose license suspension or revocation is probated to:

(1) report regularly to the commission on matters that are the basis of the probation;

(2) limit practice to an area prescribed by the commission; or

(3) continue to renew professional education until the license holder attains a degree of skill satisfactory to the commission in the area that is the basis of the probation.

(V.A.C.S. Art. 6573a, Secs. 15B(b), (c), (d).)

Sec. 1101.657. HEARING. (a) If the commission proposes to deny, suspend, or revoke a person's license or certificate of registration, the person is entitled to a hearing conducted by the State Office of Administrative Hearings.

(b) The commission shall adopt procedures by which all decisions to suspend or revoke a license or certificate are made by or are appealable to the commission.

(c) A hearing under this section is governed by the contested case procedures under Chapter 2001, Government Code.

(V.A.C.S. Art. 6573a, Sec. 17(a).)

Sec. 1101.658. APPEAL. (a) A person aggrieved by a ruling, order, or under this subchapter is entitled to appeal to a district court in the county in which the administrative hearing was held.

(b) An appeal is governed by the procedures under Chapter 2001, Government Code.

(V.A.C.S. Art. 6573a, Sec. 18.)

Sec. 1101.659. REFUND. (a) Subject to Subsection (b), the commission may order a person regulated by the commission to pay a refund to a consumer as provided in an agreement resulting from an informal settlement conference or an enforcement order instead of or in addition to imposing an administrative penalty or other sanctions.

(b) The amount of a refund ordered as provided in an agreement resulting from an informal settlement conference or an enforcement order may not exceed the amount the consumer paid to the person for a service or accommodation regulated by this commission. The commission may not require payment of other damages or estimate harm in a refund order.

Sec. 1101.660. INFORMAL PROCEEDINGS. (a) The commission by rule shall adopt procedures governing informal disposition of a contested case.

(b) Rules adopted under this section must:

(1) provide the complainant and the license holder, certificate holder, or regulated entity an opportunity to be heard; and

(2) require the presence of:

(A) a public member of the commission for a case involving a consumer complaint; and

(B) at least two staff members of the commission with experience in the regulatory area that is the subject of the proceeding.

Sec. 1101.661. FINAL ORDER. The commission may issue a final order in a proceeding under this subchapter or Subchapter O regarding a person whose license has expired during the course of an investigation or administrative proceeding.

Sec. 1101.662. TEMPORARY SUSPENSION. (a) The presiding officer of the commission shall appoint a disciplinary panel consisting of three commission members to determine whether a person's license to practice under this chapter should be temporarily suspended.

(b) If the disciplinary panel determines from the information presented to the panel that a person licensed to practice under this chapter would, by the person's continued practice, constitute a continuing threat to the public welfare, the panel shall temporarily suspend the license of that person.

(c) A license may be suspended under this section without notice or hearing on the complaint if:

(1) institution of proceedings for a hearing before the commission is initiated simultaneously with the temporary suspension; and

(2) a hearing is held under Chapter 2001, Government Code, and this chapter as soon as possible.

(d) Notwithstanding Chapter 551, Government Code, the disciplinary panel may hold a meeting by telephone conference call if immediate action is required and convening the panel at one location is inconvenient for any member of the panel.

[Sections 1101.663-1101.700 reserved for expansion]

SUBCHAPTER O. ADMINISTRATIVE PENALTY

Sec. 1101.701. IMPOSITION OF ADMINISTRATIVE PENALTY. (a) The commission may impose an administrative penalty on a person who violates this chapter or a rule adopted or order issued by the commission under this chapter.

(b) The commission shall periodically review the commission's enforcement procedures and ensure that administrative penalty and disciplinary proceedings are combined into a single enforcement procedure.

(c) The commission may combine a proceeding to impose an administrative penalty with another disciplinary proceeding, including a proceeding to suspend or revoke a license.

(V.A.C.S. Art. 6573a, Sec. 19A(a).)

Sec. 1101.7015. DELEGATION OF ADMINISTRATOR'S AUTHORITY. The commission may authorize the administrator to delegate to another commission employee the administrator's authority to act under this subchapter.

Sec. 1101.702. AMOUNT OF PENALTY. (a) The amount of an administrative penalty may not exceed $5,000 for each violation. Each day a violation continues or occurs may be considered a separate violation for purposes of imposing a penalty.

(b) In determining the amount of the penalty, the administrator shall consider:

(1) the seriousness of the violation, including the nature, circumstances, extent, and gravity of the prohibited acts;

(2) the history of previous violations;

(3) the amount necessary to deter a future violation;

(4) efforts to correct the violation; and

(5) any other matter that justice may require.

(c) The commission by rule shall adopt a schedule of administrative penalties based on the criteria listed in Subsection (b) for violations subject to an administrative penalty under this section to ensure that the amount of a penalty imposed is appropriate to the violation. The rules adopted under this subsection must provide authority for the commission to suspend or revoke a license in addition to or instead of imposing an administrative penalty.

(V.A.C.S. Art. 6573a, Secs. 19A(b), (c).)

Sec. 1101.703. NOTICE OF VIOLATION AND PENALTY. (a) If, after investigation of a possible violation and the facts relating to that violation, the administrator determines that a violation has occurred, the administrator may issue a notice of violation stating:

(1) a brief summary of the alleged violation;

(2) the administrator's recommendation on the imposition of the administrative penalty or another disciplinary sanction, including a recommendation on the amount of the penalty; and

(3) that the respondent has the right to a hearing to contest the alleged violation, the recommended penalty, or both.

(b) Not later than the 14th day after the date the report is issued, the administrator shall give written notice of the report to the person charged with the violation. The notice must:

(1) include a brief summary of the charges;

(2) state the amount of the recommended penalty; and

(3) inform the person of the person's right to a hearing on the occurrence of the violation, the amount of the penalty, or both.

(V.A.C.S. Art. 6573a, Secs. 19A(d) (part), (e).)

Sec. 1101.704. PENALTY TO BE PAID OR HEARING REQUESTED. (a) Not later than the 20th day after the date the person receives the notice under Section 1101.703, the person may:

(1) accept the administrator's determination, including the recommended administrative penalty; or

(2) request in writing a hearing on the occurrence of the violation, the amount of the penalty, or both.

(b) If the person accepts the administrator's determination, or fails to respond in a timely manner to the notice, the commission by order shall approve the determination and order payment of the recommended penalty or impose the recommended action.

(V.A.C.S. Art. 6573a, Secs. 19A(f), (g).)

Sec. 1101.705. HEARING; DECISION. (a) If the person requests a hearing, the administrator shall set a hearing and give notice of the hearing to the person.

(b) An administrative law judge of the State Office of Administrative shall conduct the hearing. The administrative law judge shall:

(1) make findings of fact and conclusions of law; and

(2) promptly issue to the commission a proposal for decision regarding the occurrence of the violation and the amount of any proposed administrative penalty.

(c) Based on the findings of fact, conclusions of law, and proposal for decision of the administrative law judge, the commission by order may determine that:

(1) a violation occurred and impose an administrative penalty; or

(2) a violation did not occur.

(d) A proceeding under this section is subject to Chapter 2001, Government Code.

(e) The notice of the commission's order given to the person under Chapter 2001, Government Code, must include a statement of the person's right to judicial review of the order.

(V.A.C.S. Art. 6573a, Sec. 19A(h).)

Sec. 1101.706. NOTICE OF ORDER. The administrator shall give notice of the commission's order to the person. The notice must:

(1) include the findings of fact and conclusions of law, separately stated;

(2) state the amount of any penalty imposed;

(3) inform the person of the person's right to judicial review of the order; and

(4) include other information required by law.

(V.A.C.S. Art. 6573a, Sec. 19A(i).)

Sec. 1101.707. OPTIONS FOLLOWING DECISION: PAY OR APPEAL. (a) Not later than the 30th day after the date the commission's order becomes final, the person shall:

(1) pay the administrative penalty; or

(2) file a petition for judicial review contesting the occurrence of the violation, the amount of the penalty, or both.

(b) Within the 30-day period prescribed by Subsection (a), a person who files a petition for judicial review may;

(1) stay enforcement of the penalty by:

(A) paying the penalty to the court for placement in an escrow account; or

(B) giving the court a supersedeas bond in a form approved by the court that:

(i) is for the amount of the penalty; and

(ii) is effective until judicial review of the order is final; or

(2) request the court to stay enforcement by:

(A) filing with the court an affidavit of the person stating that the person is financially unable to pay the penalty and is financially unable to give the supersedeas bond; and

(B) giving a copy of the affidavit to the administrator by certified mail.

(c) If the administrator receives a copy of an affidavit under Subsection (b)(2), the administrator may file with the court, within five days after the date the copy is received, a contest to the affidavit.

(d) The court shall hold a hearing on the facts alleged in the affidavit as soon as practicable and shall stay the enforcement of the penalty on finding that the alleged facts are true. The person who files an affidavit has the burden of proving that the person is financially unable to pay the penalty and to give a supersedeas bond.

(V.A.C.S. Art. 6573a, Secs. 19A(j), (k), (l) (part), (m) (part).)

Sec. 1101.708. COLLECTION OF PENALTY. If the person does not pay the administrative penalty and the enforcement of the penalty is not stayed, the administrator may refer the matter to the attorney general for collection of the penalty.

Sec. 1101.7085. DETERMINATION BY COURT. (a) If the court sustains the determination that a violation occurred, the court may uphold or reduce the amount of the administrative penalty and order the person to pay the full or reduced amount of the penalty.

(b) If the court does not sustain the finding that a violation occurred, the court shall order that a penalty is not owed.

(V.A.C.S. Art. 6573a, Sec. 19A(l) (part).)

Sec. 1101.709. REMITTANCE OF PENALTY AND INTEREST. (a) If after judicial review the administrative penalty is reduced or is not upheld by the court, the court shall remit the appropriate amount, plus accrued interest, to the person if the person paid the penalty.

(b) The interest accrues at the rate charged on loans to depository institutions by the New York Federal Reserve Bank.

(c) The interest shall be paid for the period beginning on the date the penalty is paid and ending on the date the penalty is remitted.

(d) If the person gave a supersedeas bond and the penalty is not upheld by the court, the court shall order, when the court's judgment becomes final, the release of the bond.

(e) If the person gave a supersedeas bond and the amount of the penalty is reduced, the court shall order the release of the bond after the person pays the reduced amount.

Sec. 1101.710. ADMINISTRATIVE PROCEDURE. A proceeding under this subchapter is subject to Chapter 2001, Government Code.

(V.A.C.S. Art. 6573a, Sec. 19A(n).)

[Sections 1101.711-1101.750 reserved for expansion]

SUBCHAPTER P. OTHER PENALTIES AND ENFORCEMENT PROVISIONS

Sec. 1101.751. INJUNCTIVE ACTION BROUGHT BY COMMISSION. (a) In addition to any other action authorized by law, the commission may bring an action in its name to enjoin a violation of this chapter or a commission rule.

(b) To obtain an injunction under this section, the commission is not required to allege or prove that:

(1) an adequate remedy at law does not exist; or

(2) substantial or irreparable damage would result from the continued violation.

(V.A.C.S. Art. 6573a, Sec. 5(h) (part).)

Sec. 1101.752. ADDITIONAL INJUNCTIVE AUTHORITY. (a) In addition to any other action authorized by law, the commission, acting through the attorney general, may bring an action to abate a violation or enjoin a violation or potential violation of this chapter or a commission rule if the commission determines that a person has violated or is about to violate this chapter.

(b) The action shall be brought in the name of the state in the district court in the county in which:

(1) the violation occurred or is about to occur; or

(2) the defendant resides.

(c) An injunctive action may be brought to abate or temporarily or permanently enjoin an act or to enforce this chapter.

(d) The commission is not required to give a bond in an action under Subsection (a), and court costs may not be recovered from the commission.

(e) If the commission determines that a person has violated or is about to violate this chapter, the attorney general or the county attorney or district attorney in the county in which the violation has occurred or is about to occur or in the county of the defendant's residence may bring an action in the name of the state in the district court of the county to abate or temporarily or permanently enjoin the violation or to enforce this chapter. The plaintiff in an action under this subsection is not required to give a bond, and court costs may not be recovered from the plaintiff.

(V.A.C.S. Art. 6573a, Secs. 19(c), (d) (part).)

Sec. 1101.753. CIVIL PENALTY FOR CERTAIN VIOLATIONS BY BROKER, SALESPERSON, OR CERTIFICATE HOLDER. (a) In addition to injunctive relief under Sections 1101.751 and 1101.752, a person who receives a commission or other consideration as a result of acting as a broker or salesperson without holding a license or certificate of registration under this chapter is liable to the state for a civil penalty of not less than the amount of money received or more than three times the amount of money received.

(b) The commission may recover the civil penalty, court costs, and reasonable attorney's fees on behalf of the state.

(c) The commission is not required to give a bond in an action under this section, and court costs may not be recovered from the commission.

(V.A.C.S. Art. 6573a, Sec. 19(d) (part).)

Sec. 1101.754. PRIVATE CAUSE OF ACTION FOR CERTAIN VIOLATIONS BY BROKER, SALESPERSON, OR CERTIFICATE HOLDER. (a) A person who receives a commission or other consideration as a result of acting as a broker or salesperson without holding a license or certificate of registration under this chapter is liable to an aggrieved person for a penalty of not less than the amount of money received or more than three times the amount of money received.

(b) The aggrieved person may file suit to recover a penalty under this section.

(V.A.C.S. Art. 6573a, Sec. 19(b).)

Sec. 1101.755. APPEAL BOND EXEMPTION. The commission is not required to give an appeal bond in an action to enforce this chapter.

(V.A.C.S. Art. 6573a, Sec. 5(h) (part).)

Sec. 1101.756. GENERAL CRIMINAL PENALTY. (a) A person commits an offense if the person willfully violates or fails to comply with this chapter or a commission order.

(b) An offense under this section is a Class A misdemeanor.

(V.A.C.S. Art. 6573a.1.)

Sec. 1101.757. CRIMINAL PENALTY FOR CERTAIN VIOLATIONS BY RESIDENTIAL RENTAL LOCATOR. (a) A person commits an offense if the person engages in business as a residential rental locator in this state without a license issued under this chapter.

(b) An offense under this section is a Class A misdemeanor.

(V.A.C.S. Art. 6573a, Sec. 24(f).)

Sec. 1101.758. CRIMINAL PENALTY FOR CERTAIN VIOLATIONS BY BROKER, SALESPERSON, OR CERTIFICATE HOLDER. (a) A person commits an offense if the person acts as a broker or salesperson without holding a license under this chapter or engages in an activity for which a certificate of registration is required under this chapter without holding a certificate.

Page 43

(b) An offense under this section is a Class A misdemeanor.

(V.A.C.S. Art. 6573a, Sec. 19(a).)

Sec. 1101.759. CEASE AND DESIST ORDER. (a) If it appears to the commission that a person is violating this chapter or Chapter 1102 or a rule adopted under this chapter or Chapter 1102, the commission, after notice and opportunity for a hearing, may issue a cease and desist order prohibiting the person from engaging in the activity.

(b) A violation of an order under this section constitutes grounds for imposing an administrative penalty under Subchapter O.

[Sections 1101.759-1101.800 reserved for expansion]

SUBCHAPTER Q. GENERAL PROVISIONS RELATING TO LIABILITY ISSUES

Sec. 1101.801. EFFECT OF DISCIPLINARY ACTION ON LIABILITY. Disciplinary action taken against a person under Section 1101.652 does not relieve the person from civil or criminal liability.

(V.A.C.S. Art. 6573a, Sec. 15(b).)

Sec. 1101.802. LIABILITY RELATING TO HIV INFECTION OR AIDS. Notwithstanding Section 1101.801, a person is not civilly or criminally liable because the person failed to inquire about, make a disclosure relating to, or release information relating to whether a previous or current occupant of real property had, may have had, has, or may have AIDS, an HIV-related illness, or HIV infection as defined by the Centers for Disease Control and Prevention of the United States Public Health Service.

(V.A.C.S. Art. 6573a, Sec. 15(c).)

Sec. 1101.803. GENERAL LIABILITY OF BROKER. A licensed broker is liable to the commission, the public, and the broker's clients for any conduct engaged in under this chapter by the broker or by a salesperson associated with or acting for the broker.

(V.A.C.S. Art. 6573a, Sec. 1(c).)

Sec. 1101.804. LIABILITY FOR PROVIDING CERTAIN INFORMATION. A license holder or nonprofit real estate board or association that provides information about real property sales prices or the terms of a sale for the purpose of facilitating the listing, selling, leasing, financing, or appraisal of real property is not liable to another person for providing that information unless the disclosure of that information is specifically prohibited by statute.

(V.A.C.S. Art. 6573a, Sec. 15D.)

Sec. 1101.805. LIABILITY FOR MIS REPRESENTATION OR CONCEALMENT. (a) In this section, "party" has the meaning assigned by Section 1101.551.

(b) This section prevails over any other law, including common law.

(c) This section does not diminish a broker's responsibility for the acts or omissions of a salesperson associated with or acting for the broker.

(d) A party is not liable for a misrepresentation or a concealment of a material fact made by a license holder in a real estate transaction unless the party:

(1) knew of the falsity of the misrepresentation or concealment; and

(2) failed to disclose the party's knowledge of the falsity of the misrepresentation or concealment.

(e) A license holder is not liable for a misrepresentation or a concealment of a material fact made by a party to a real estate transaction unless the license holder:

(1) knew of the falsity of the misrepresentation or concealment; and

(2) failed to disclose the license holder's knowledge of the falsity of the misrepresentation or concealment.

(f) A party or a license holder is not liable for a misrepresentation or a concealment of a material fact made by a subagent in a real estate transaction unless the party or license holder:

(1) knew of the falsity of the misrepresentation or concealment; and

(2) failed to disclose the party's or license holder's knowledge of the falsity of the misrepresentation or concealment.

(V.A.C.S. Art. 6573a, Sec. 15F.)

Sec. 1101.806. LIABILITY FOR PAYMENT OF COMPENSATION OR COMMISSION. (a) This section does not:

(1) apply to an agreement to share compensation among license holders; or

(2) limit a cause of action among brokers for interference with business relationships.

(b) A person may not maintain an action to collect compensation for an act as a broker or salesperson that is performed in this state unless the person alleges and proves that the person was:

(1) a license holder at the time the act was commenced; or

(2) an attorney licensed in any state.

(c) A person may not maintain an action in this state to recover a commission for the sale or purchase of real estate unless the promise or agreement on which the action is based, or a memorandum, is in writing and signed by the party against whom the action is brought or by a person authorized by that party to sign the document.

(d) A license holder who fails to advise a buyer as provided by Section 1101.555 may not receive payment of or recover any commission agreed to be paid on the sale.

AFFILIATING WITH A BROKER

If you plan to enter real estate sales, selecting a broker to work for is one of the most important decisions you must make. The best way to approach it is to stop and carefully consider what you have to offer the real estate business and what you expect in return. And look at it in that order! It is easy to become captivated by the big commission income you visualize coming your way. But if that is your only perspective, you will meet with disappointment. People are willing to pay you money because they expect to receive some product or service in return. That is their viewpoint and it would probably be yours if you were in their position. Your clients are not concerned with your income goal; it is only incidental to their goals. If you help them attain their goals, you will reach yours.

Before applying for a real estate license ask yourself if the working hours and conditions of a real estate agent are suitable to you. Specifically, are you prepared to work on a commission-only basis? Evenings and weekends? On your own? With people you've never met before? If you can comfortably answer yes to these questions, then start looking for a broker to sponsor you. As discussed earlier, salesperson license educational requirements can be completed without broker sponsorship, but a salesperson must have a sponsoring broker in order to make application for a salesperson license.

Training

Your next step is to look for those features and qualities in a broker that will complement, enhance, and encourage your personal development in real estate. If you are new to the industry, training and education will most likely be at the top of your list. Therefore, in looking for a broker you will want to find one who will in one fashion or another teach you the trade. (What you have learned to date from books, classes, and license examination preparation will be helpful, but you will need additional specific training.)

PUTTING IT TO WORK

Real estate franchise operations and large brokerage offices usually offer extensive training. In smaller offices, the broker in charge is usually responsible for seeing that newcomers receive training. An office that offers no training to a newcomer should be avoided.

Compensation

Another question high on your list will be compensation. Compensation for salespersons is usually a percentage of the commissions they earn for the broker. How much each receives is open to negotiation between the broker and each salesperson working for him. A broker who offers the sales staff office space, extensive secretarial help, a large advertising budget, a mailing program, and generous long-distance telephone privileges might take 40% to 50% of each incoming commission dollar for office overhead. A broker who provides fewer services might take 25% or 30%.

Salespersons with proven sales records can sometimes reduce the portion of each earned commission dollar that must go to the broker. This is because the broker may feel that with an outstanding sales performer, a high volume of sales will offset a smaller percentage for overhead. Conversely, a new and untried salesperson, or one with a mediocre past sales record, may have to give up a larger portion of each dollar for the broker's overhead.

PUTTING IT TO WORK

Many brokers feel that one must produce to be paid and the hungrier the salesperson, the quicker that salesperson will produce. A broker who pays salespersons regardless of sales produced simply must siphon the money from those who are producing. The old saying, "There's no such thing as a free lunch" applies to sales commissions.

When one brokerage agency lists a property and another locates the buyer, the commission is split according to any agreement the two brokers wish to make. After splitting, each broker pays a portion of the money received to the salesperson involved in accordance with the commission agreements.

While investigating commission arrangements, one should also inquire about incentive and bonus plans, automobile expense reimbursement, health insurance, life insurance, and retirement plans.

An alternative commission arrangement is the **100% commission** wherein the salesperson does not share the commission with the broker. Instead the salesperson is charged a fee for office space, advertising, telephone, multiple listings, and any other expenses the broker incurs on behalf of the salesperson. Generally speaking, 100% arrangements are more popular with proven performers than with newcomers.

Broker Support

Broker support will have an impact on any salesperson's success. Specifically: Will you have your own desk to work from? Are office facilities efficient and modern? Does the broker provide secretarial services? What is the broker's advertising policy and who pays for ads? Does the broker have sources of financing for clients? Does the broker allow his salespersons to invest in real estate? Does the broker have a good reputation in the community? Who pays for signs, business cards, franchise fees, and realty board dues?

Finding a Broker

Many salespersons associate with a particular broker as a result of a friendship or word-of-mouth information. However, there are other ways to find a suitable position. An excellent way to start your search is to decide what geographical area you want to work in. If you choose the same community or neighborhood in which you live, you will already possess a valuable sense and feel for that area.

Having selected a geographical area to specialize in, look in the Sunday newspaper real estate advertisements section and the telephone book Yellow Pages for names of brokers. Hold interviews with several brokers and as you do, remember that you are interviewing them just as intensively as they are interviewing you. At your visits with brokers be particularly alert to your feelings. Intuition can be as valuable a guide to a sound working relationship as a list of questions and answers regarding the job.

As you narrow your choices, revisit the offices of brokers who particularly impressed you. Talk with some of the salespersons who have worked or are working there. They can be very candid and valuable sources of information. Be wary of individuals who are extreme in their opinions: Rely instead on the consensus of opinion. Locate clients who have used the firm's services and ask them their opinions of the firm. You might also talk to local appraisers, lenders, and escrow agents for candid opinions. If you do all this advance work, the benefits to you will be greater enjoyment of your work, more money in your pocket, and less likelihood of wanting to quit or move to another office.

Employment Contract

Having selected a broker with whom to associate, your next step is to make an employment contract. An **employment contract** formalizes the working arrangement between the broker and the salespersons. An oral contract may be legally binding, but a written one is preferred because it sets forth the relationship with a higher degree of specificity. This greatly reduces the potential for future controversy and litigation.

The employment contract will cover such matters as compensation (how much and under what circumstances), training (how often and if required), hours of work (including assigned office hours and open houses), company identification (distinctive articles of clothing and name tags), fees and dues (license and realty board), expenses (automobile, advertising, telephone), fringe benefits (health and life insurance, pension and profit-sharing plans), withholding (income taxes and social security), territory (assigned area of the community), termination of employment (quitting and firing), federal tax obligations, and general office policies and procedures (office manual).

INDEPENDENT CONTRACTOR STATUS

Is the real estate sales associate an employee of the broker or an independent contractor? The answer is both. On one hand, the sales associate acts like an **employee** because the associate works for the broker, usually at the broker's place of business. There the associate prepares listings and sales documents on forms specified by the broker and upon closing receives payment from the broker. On the other hand, the sales associate acts like an ***independent contractor*** because the associate is paid only if the associate brings about a sale that produces a commission. An important distinction between the two is whether or not the broker must withhold income taxes and social security from the associate's commission checks. If the sales associate is considered by the Internal Revenue Service (IRS) to be an employee for tax purposes, the broker must withhold. If classed as an independent contractor for tax purposes, the sales associate is responsible for personal income taxes and social security. The IRS prefers employee status because it is easier to collect taxes from an employer than from an employee.

As a result of federal legislation that took effect January 1, 1983, the IRS will treat real estate sales associates as independent contractors if they meet all of the following three requirements. First, the associate must be a licensed real estate agent. Second, virtually all of the associate's payment for services as a real estate agent must be directly related to sales and not to hours worked. Third, a written agreement must exist between the associate and the broker stating that the associate will be treated as an independent contractor for tax purposes. If an agent and that agent's sponsoring broker do not comply with this statute, they run the risk of losing their independent contractor status, and the sponsoring broker would be subject to the same filing requirements as any other employer in the normal course of business.

These are highlights of the issue. If you plan to work for a broker, you may find it valuable to have this matter as well as your entire employment contract reviewed by an attorney before you sign it.

FRANCHISED OFFICES

Prior to the early 1970s, a real estate brokerage was typically a small business. In fact, most brokerages were one-office firms. A brokerage was considered large if it had four or five branch offices, handling perhaps 200 properties a year. Then real estate franchise organizations entered the real estate business in a big way. By offering *franchises,* large organizations such as Century-21, Prudential, Better Homes and Garden, ERA, and ReMax offered national identification, large-scale advertising, sales staff training programs, management advice, customer referrals, financing help for buyers, and guaranteed sales plans to small brokerage offices. In return, the brokerage firm (the *franchisee*) paid a fee to the national organization of from 3% to 8% of its gross commission income. The new marketing system flourished, and by the mid-1990s approximately half of the real estate licensees affiliated with the National Association of REALTORS® were working as franchised offices. Meanwhile, the number of franchisers grew to more than 60 large organizations including those mentioned above and many more, offering attractive franchises to the small firms.

Statistics show that franchising appeals mostly to middle-sized firms with 10 to 50 sales associates. Larger firms are able to provide the advantages of a franchise for themselves, while the smallest firms tend to occupy special market niches and often consist of one or two licensees who do not bring in additional sales associates. For a newly licensed salesperson wishing to affiliate with a firm, a franchised firm can offer immediate public recognition, extensive training opportunities, established office routines, regular sales meetings, and access to a nationwide referral system. Franchise affiliation is not magic however. Success still depends on the individual who makes sales calls, values property, gets listings, advertises, shows property, qualifies, negotiates, and closes transactions.

National Real Estate Firms

During the late 1970s a large real estate firm in California—Coldwell Banker—began an expansion program by purchasing multi-branch real estate firms in other states. Today, a number of national franchises have several hundred offices across the United States. Cendant Corp. has acquired three major franchises to create a huge network of firms that may offer a number of other services to complement their brokerage services—some refer to it as “full service.” The additional services can include access to auto dealers, interior decorators, contractors, and other commonly used services by home buyers. Between the national firms and the local firms in size are several well-established regional firms such as Ebby Halliday in Dallas and Heritage Texas Properties in Houston.

For a newcomer, affiliation with a national or regional real estate firm offers benefits like those of a franchised firm (recognition, training, routines, etc.). The main difference is who owns the firm. A franchised firm will be locally owned and locally managed; that is, it is an independent firm. Regional and national firms are locally managed but not locally owned. The sales associates will only occasionally, if ever, meet the owner(s).

PROFESSIONAL REAL ESTATE ASSOCIATIONS

Even before laws required real estate agents to have licenses, there were professional real estate organizations. Called real estate boards, they joined together agents within a city or county on a voluntary basis. The push to organize came from real estate people who saw the need for some sort of controlling organization that could supervise the activities of individual agents and elevate real estate licensees to professional status in the public’s mind. Next came the gradual grouping of local boards into state associations, and finally, in 1908, the National Association of Real Estate Boards (NAREB) was formed. In 1914, the NAREB developed a model license law that became the basis for real estate license laws in many states.

National Association of REALTORS® (NAR)

Today the local boards are still the fundamental units of the **National Association of REALTORS® (NAR).** Local membership is open to anyone holding a real estate license. Called boards of REALTORS®, real estate boards, Associations of REALTORS®, and realty boards, they promote fair dealing among their members and with the public and protect members from dishonest and irresponsible licensees. They also promote legislation that protects property rights, offer short seminars to keep members up-to-date with current laws and practices, and, in general, do whatever is necessary to build the dignity, stability, and professionalization of the industry. Local boards often operate the local multiple listing service, although in some communities it is a privately owned and operated business.

State associations are composed of the members of local boards plus salespeople and brokers who live in areas where no local board exists. The purposes of the state associations are to unite members statewide, to encourage legislation that benefits and protects the real estate industry and safeguards the public in their real estate transactions, and to promote economic growth and development in the state. Also, state associations hold conventions to educate members and encourage networking among them. A plethora of information about NAR is available at their website, http://www.realtor.org.

Texas Association of REALTORS® (TAR)

The **Texas Association of REALTORS® (TAR),** with approximately 80,000 members, is the Texas organization of REALTORS® authorized to use the REALTOR® emblem. They maintain an active program of continuing education throughout the NAR Institute and its Real Estate Institute. They publish and distribute information on state legislation (material legislation), licensing laws, and professional standards. They also publish a book of forms for members' use called *The REALTOR® Reference.*

A great deal of information is available through the TAR library of tapes and books. Standardized legal forms are available through the Texas Association of REALTORS®. The mailing address is

Texas Association of REALTORS®
1115 San Jacinto Blvd., Suite 200
Austin, Texas 78701-1906
Website: http://texasrealtors.com

REALTOR® and NAR

The NAR is made up of local boards and state associations in the United States. The term ***REALTOR®*** is a registered trade name that belongs to the NAR. *REALTOR®* is not synonymous with real estate agent. It is reserved for the exclusive use of members of the National Association of REALTORS®, who as part of their membership pledge themselves to abide by the Association's Code of Ethics. The term *REALTOR®* cannot be used by nonmembers, and in some states the unauthorized use of the term is a violation of the real estate law. Prior to 1974, the use of the term *REALTOR®* was primarily reserved for principal brokers. Then in November of that year, by a national membership vote, the decision was made to create an additional membership class, the **REALTOR®-Associate**, for salespersons working for member REALTORS®.

Code of Ethics

The *Code of Ethics* has been revised several times since it was developed in 1913, and it now contains 17 articles that pertain to the REALTOR'S® relationship to clients, to other real estate agents, and to the public as a whole. The full Code is reproduced in Figure 2.1. The NATIONAL ASSOCIATION OF REALTORS® reserves exclusively unto itself the right to officially comment on and interpret the Code and particular provisions thereof. For the NATIONAL ASSOCIATION'S official interpretation of the Code, see Interpretations of the Code of Ethics; NATIONAL ASSOCIATION OF REALTORS®.

Although a complete review of each article is beyond the scope of this chapter, the Code shows that some articles parallel existing laws. For example, Article 10 speaks against racial discrimination and Article 2 speaks for full disclosure. However, as a whole the Code of Ethics addresses itself to the aspirations and obligations of a REALTOR® that may be beyond the written law. In other words, to be recognized as a REALTOR®, one must not only comply with the letter of the law, but also observe the ethical standards by which the industry operates.

In some states, ethical standards such as those in the NAR Code of Ethics have been legislated into law. Called **canons,** their intent is to promote ethical practices by all brokers and salespersons, not just by those who join the National Association of REALTORS®. The Texas Real Estate Commission promulgates its own Canons of Professional Ethics, set out in Appendix B. Read it. It is almost as important as the License Act, and all licensees should familiarize themselves with it.

In addition to its emphasis on real estate brokerage, the National Association of REALTORS® also contains a number of specialized professional groups within itself. These include the American Institute of Real Estate Appraisers, the Farm and Land Institute, the Institute of Real Estate Management, the REALTORS® National Marketing Institute, the Society of Industrial REALTORS®, the Real Estate Securities and Syndication Institute, the American Society of Real Estate Counselors, the American Chapter of the International Real Estate Federation, and the Women's Council of REALTORS®. In each case, membership is open to REALTORS® interested in these specialties.

Realtist and NAREB

The National Association of Real Estate Brokers (NAREB) is a national trade association representing minority real estate professionals actively engaged in the industry. Founded in 1947, its members use the trade name **Realtist.** The organization extends through 14 regions across the country with more than 60 active local boards. NAREB education and certification programs include the Real Estate Management Brokers Institute, National Society of Real Estate Appraisers, Real Estate Brokerage Institute, and United Developers Council. The organization's purposes are to promote high standards of service and conduct and to protect the public against unethical, improper, or fraudulent real estate practices. Their website is http://www.nareb.com.

FIGURE 2.1 Code of ethics

Code of Ethics and Standards of Practice of the NATIONAL ASSOCIATION OF REALTORS®

Effective January 1, 2011

Where the word REALTORS® is used in this Code and Preamble, it shall be deemed to include REALTOR-ASSOCIATE®s.

While the Code of Ethics establishes obligations that may be higher than those mandated by law, in any instance where the Code of Ethics and the law conflict, the obligations of the law must take precedence.

Preamble

Under all is the land. Upon its wise utilization and widely allocated ownership depend the survival and growth of free institutions and of our civilization. REALTORS® should recognize that the interests of the nation and its citizens require the highest and best use of the land and the widest distribution of land ownership. They require the creation of adequate housing, the building of functioning cities, the development of productive industries and farms, and the preservation of a healthful environment.

Such interests impose obligations beyond those of ordinary commerce. They impose grave social responsibility and a patriotic duty to which REALTORS® should dedicate themselves, and for which they should be diligent in preparing themselves. REALTORS®, therefore, are zealous to maintain and improve the standards of their calling and share with their fellow REALTORS® a common responsibility for its integrity and honor.

In recognition and appreciation of their obligations to clients, customers, the public, and each other, REALTORS® continuously strive to become and remain informed on issues affecting real estate and, as knowledgeable professionals, they willingly share the fruit of their experience and study with others. They identify and take steps, through enforcement of this Code of Ethics and by assisting appropriate regulatory bodies, to eliminate practices which may damage the public or which might discredit or bring dishonor to the real estate profession. REALTORS® having direct personal knowledge of conduct that may violate the Code of Ethics involving misappropriation of client or customer funds or property, willful discrimination, or fraud resulting in substantial economic harm, bring such matters to the attention of the appropriate Board or Association of REALTORS®. *(Amended 1/00)*

Realizing that cooperation with other real estate professionals promotes the best interests of those who utilize their services, REALTORS® urge exclusive representation of clients; do not attempt to gain any unfair advantage over their competitors; and they refrain from making unsolicited comments about other practitioners. In instances where their opinion is sought, or where REALTORS® believe that comment is necessary, their opinion is offered in an objective, professional manner, uninfluenced by any personal motivation or potential advantage or gain.

The term REALTOR® has come to connote competency, fairness, and high integrity resulting from adherence to a lofty ideal of moral conduct in business relations. No inducement of profit and no instruction from clients ever can justify departure from this ideal.

In the interpretation of this obligation, REALTORS® can take no safer guide than that which has been handed down through the centuries, embodied in the Golden Rule, "Whatsoever ye would that others should do to you, do ye even so to them."

Accepting this standard as their own, REALTORS® pledge to observe its spirit in all of their activities whether conducted personally, through associates or others, or via technological means, and to conduct their business in accordance with the tenets set forth below. *(Amended 1/07)*

Duties to Clients and Customers

Article 1

When representing a buyer, seller, landlord, tenant, or other client as an agent, REALTORS® pledge themselves to protect and promote the interests of their client. This obligation to the client is primary, but it does not relieve REALTORS® of their obligation to treat all parties honestly. When serving a buyer, seller, landlord, tenant or other party in a non-agency capacity, REALTORS® remain obligated to treat all parties honestly. *(Amended 1/01)*

- **Standard of Practice 1-1**
  REALTORS®, when acting as principals in a real estate transaction, remain obligated by the duties imposed by the Code of Ethics. *(Amended 1/93)*

- **Standard of Practice 1-2**
  The duties imposed by the Code of Ethics encompass all real estate-related activities and transactions whether conducted in person, electronically, or through any other means.

  The duties the Code of Ethics imposes are applicable whether REALTORS® are acting as agents or in legally recognized non-agency capacities except that any duty imposed exclusively on agents by law or regulation shall not be imposed by this Code of Ethics on REALTORS® acting in non-agency capacities.

  As used in this Code of Ethics, "client" means the person(s) or entity(ies) with whom a REALTOR® or a REALTOR®'s firm has an agency or legally recognized non-agency relationship; "customer" means a party to a real estate transaction who receives information, services, or benefits but has no contractual relationship with the REALTOR® or the REALTOR®'s firm; "prospect" means a purchaser, seller, tenant, or landlord who is not subject to a representation relationship with the REALTOR® or REALTOR®'s firm; "agent" means a real estate licensee (including brokers and sales associates) acting in an agency relationship as defined by state law or regulation; and "broker" means a real estate licensee (including brokers and sales associates) acting as an agent or in a legally recognized non-agency capacity. *(Adopted 1/95, Amended 1/07)*

- **Standard of Practice 1-3**
  REALTORS®, in attempting to secure a listing, shall not deliberately mislead the owner as to market value.

- **Standard of Practice 1-4**
  REALTORS®, when seeking to become a buyer/tenant representative, shall not mislead buyers or tenants as to savings or other benefits that might be realized through use of the REALTOR®'s services. *(Amended 1/93)*

NATIONAL ASSOCIATION *of* REALTORS®

FIGURE 2.1 Code of ethics (*continued*)

- **Standard of Practice 1-5**
REALTORS® may represent the seller/landlord and buyer/tenant in the same transaction only after full disclosure to and with informed consent of both parties. *(Adopted 1/93)*

- **Standard of Practice 1-6**
REALTORS® shall submit offers and counter-offers objectively and as quickly as possible. *(Adopted 1/93, Amended 1/95)*

- **Standard of Practice 1-7**
When acting as listing brokers, REALTORS® shall continue to submit to the seller/landlord all offers and counter-offers until closing or execution of a lease unless the seller/landlord has waived this obligation in writing. REALTORS® shall not be obligated to continue to market the property after an offer has been accepted by the seller/landlord. REALTORS® shall recommend that sellers/landlords obtain the advice of legal counsel prior to acceptance of a subsequent offer except where the acceptance is contingent on the termination of the pre-existing purchase contract or lease. *(Amended 1/93)*

- **Standard of Practice 1-8**
REALTORS®, acting as agents or brokers of buyers/tenants, shall submit to buyers/tenants all offers and counter-offers until acceptance but have no obligation to continue to show properties to their clients after an offer has been accepted unless otherwise agreed in writing. REALTORS®, acting as agents or brokers of buyers/tenants, shall recommend that buyers/tenants obtain the advice of legal counsel if there is a question as to whether a pre-existing contract has been terminated. *(Adopted 1/93, Amended 1/99)*

- **Standard of Practice 1-9**
The obligation of REALTORS® to preserve confidential information (as defined by state law) provided by their clients in the course of any agency relationship or non-agency relationship recognized by law continues after termination of agency relationships or any non-agency relationships recognized by law. REALTORS® shall not knowingly, during or following the termination of professional relationships with their clients:
1) reveal confidential information of clients; or
2) use confidential information of clients to the disadvantage of clients; or
3) use confidential information of clients for the REALTOR®'s advantage or the advantage of third parties unless:
   a) clients consent after full disclosure; or
   b) REALTORS® are required by court order; or
   c) it is the intention of a client to commit a crime and the information is necessary to prevent the crime; or
   d) it is necessary to defend a REALTOR® or the REALTOR®'s employees or associates against an accusation of wrongful conduct.

Information concerning latent material defects is not considered confidential information under this Code of Ethics. *(Adopted 1/93, Amended 1/01)*

- **Standard of Practice 1-10**
REALTORS® shall, consistent with the terms and conditions of their real estate licensure and their property management agreement, competently manage the property of clients with due regard for the rights, safety and health of tenants and others lawfully on the premises. *(Adopted 1/95, Amended 1/00)*

- **Standard of Practice 1-11**
REALTORS® who are employed to maintain or manage a client's property shall exercise due diligence and make reasonable efforts to protect it against reasonably foreseeable contingencies and losses. *(Adopted 1/95)*

- **Standard of Practice 1-12**
When entering into listing contracts, REALTORS® must advise sellers/landlords of:
1) the REALTOR®'s company policies regarding cooperation and the amount(s) of any compensation that will be offered to subagents, buyer/tenant agents, and/or brokers acting in legally recognized non-agency capacities;
2) the fact that buyer/tenant agents or brokers, even if compensated by listing brokers, or by sellers/landlords may represent the interests of buyers/tenants; and
3) any potential for listing brokers to act as disclosed dual agents, e.g., buyer/tenant agents. *(Adopted 1/93, Renumbered 1/98, Amended 1/03)*

- **Standard of Practice 1-13**
When entering into buyer/tenant agreements, REALTORS® must advise potential clients of:
1) the REALTOR®'s company policies regarding cooperation;
2) the amount of compensation to be paid by the client;
3) the potential for additional or offsetting compensation from other brokers, from the seller or landlord, or from other parties;
4) any potential for the buyer/tenant representative to act as a disclosed dual agent, e.g., listing broker, subagent, landlord's agent, etc., and
5) the possibility that sellers or sellers' representatives may not treat the existence, terms, or conditions of offers as confidential unless confidentiality is required by law, regulation, or by any confidentiality agreement between the parties. *(Adopted 1/93, Renumbered 1/98, Amended 1/06)*

- **Standard of Practice 1-14**
Fees for preparing appraisals or other valuations shall not be contingent upon the amount of the appraisal or valuation. *(Adopted 1/02)*

- **Standard of Practice 1-15**
REALTORS®, in response to inquiries from buyers or cooperating brokers shall, with the sellers' approval, disclose the existence of offers on the property. Where disclosure is authorized, REALTORS® shall also disclose, if asked, whether offers were obtained by the listing licensee, another licensee in the listing firm, or by a cooperating broker. *(Adopted 1/03, Amended 1/09)*

Article 2

REALTORS® shall avoid exaggeration, misrepresentation, or concealment of pertinent facts relating to the property or the transaction. REALTORS® shall not, however, be obligated to discover latent defects in the property, to advise on matters outside the scope of their real estate license, or to disclose facts which are confidential under the scope of agency or non-agency relationships as defined by state law. *(Amended 1/00)*

- **Standard of Practice 2-1**
REALTORS® shall only be obligated to discover and disclose adverse factors reasonably apparent to someone with expertise in those areas required by their real estate licensing authority. Article 2 does not impose upon the REALTOR® the obligation of expertise in other professional or technical disciplines. *(Amended 1/96)*

- **Standard of Practice 2-2**
(Renumbered as Standard of Practice 1-12 1/98)

- **Standard of Practice 2-3**
(Renumbered as Standard of Practice 1-13 1/98)

- **Standard of Practice 2-4**
REALTORS® shall not be parties to the naming of a false consideration in any document, unless it be the naming of an obviously nominal consideration.

FIGURE 2.1 Code of ethics (*continued*)

- **Standard of Practice 2-5**
  Factors defined as "non-material" by law or regulation or which are expressly referenced in law or regulation as not being subject to disclosure are considered not "pertinent" for purposes of Article 2. *(Adopted 1/93)*

Article 3

REALTORS® shall cooperate with other brokers except when cooperation is not in the client's best interest. The obligation to cooperate does not include the obligation to share commissions, fees, or to otherwise compensate another broker. *(Amended 1/95)*

- **Standard of Practice 3-1**
  REALTORS®, acting as exclusive agents or brokers of sellers/landlords, establish the terms and conditions of offers to cooperate. Unless expressly indicated in offers to cooperate, cooperating brokers may not assume that the offer of cooperation includes an offer of compensation. Terms of compensation, if any, shall be ascertained by cooperating brokers before beginning efforts to accept the offer of cooperation. *(Amended 1/99)*

- **Standard of Practice 3-2**
  To be effective, any change in compensation offered for cooperative services must be communicated to the other REALTOR® prior to the time that REALTOR® submits an offer to purchase/lease the property. *(Amended 1/10)*

- **Standard of Practice 3-3**
  Standard of Practice 3-2 does not preclude the listing broker and cooperating broker from entering into an agreement to change cooperative compensation. *(Adopted 1/94)*

- **Standard of Practice 3-4**
  REALTORS®, acting as listing brokers, have an affirmative obligation to disclose the existence of dual or variable rate commission arrangements (i.e., listings where one amount of commission is payable if the listing broker's firm is the procuring cause of sale/lease and a different amount of commission is payable if the sale/lease results through the efforts of the seller/landlord or a cooperating broker). The listing broker shall, as soon as practical, disclose the existence of such arrangements to potential cooperating brokers and shall, in response to inquiries from cooperating brokers, disclose the differential that would result in a cooperative transaction or in a sale/lease that results through the efforts of the seller/landlord. If the cooperating broker is a buyer/tenant representative, the buyer/tenant representative must disclose such information to their client before the client makes an offer to purchase or lease. *(Amended 1/02)*

- **Standard of Practice 3-5**
  It is the obligation of subagents to promptly disclose all pertinent facts to the principal's agent prior to as well as after a purchase or lease agreement is executed. *(Amended 1/93)*

- **Standard of Practice 3-6**
  REALTORS® shall disclose the existence of accepted offers, including offers with unresolved contingencies, to any broker seeking cooperation. *(Adopted 5/86, Amended 1/04)*

- **Standard of Practice 3-7**
  When seeking information from another REALTOR® concerning property under a management or listing agreement, REALTORS® shall disclose their REALTOR® status and whether their interest is personal or on behalf of a client and, if on behalf of a client, their relationship with the client. *(Amended 1/11)*

- **Standard of Practice 3-8**
  REALTORS® shall not misrepresent the availability of access to show or inspect a listed property. *(Amended 11/87)*

- **Standard of Practice 3-9**
  REALTORS® shall not provide access to listed property on terms other than those established by the owner or the listing broker. *(Adopted 1/10)*

- **Standard of Practice 3-10**
  The duty to cooperate established in Article 3 relates to the obligation to share information on listed property, and to make property available to other brokers for showing to prospective purchasers/tenants when it is in the best interests of sellers/landlords. *(Adopted 1/11)*

Article 4

REALTORS® shall not acquire an interest in or buy or present offers from themselves, any member of their immediate families, their firms or any member thereof, or any entities in which they have any ownership interest, any real property without making their true position known to the owner or the owner's agent or broker. In selling property they own, or in which they have any interest, REALTORS® shall reveal their ownership or interest in writing to the purchaser or the purchaser's representative. *(Amended 1/00)*

- **Standard of Practice 4-1**
  For the protection of all parties, the disclosures required by Article 4 shall be in writing and provided by REALTORS® prior to the signing of any contract. *(Adopted 2/86)*

Article 5

REALTORS® shall not undertake to provide professional services concerning a property or its value where they have a present or contemplated interest unless such interest is specifically disclosed to all affected parties.

Article 6

REALTORS® shall not accept any commission, rebate, or profit on expenditures made for their client, without the client's knowledge and consent.

When recommending real estate products or services (e.g., homeowner's insurance, warranty programs, mortgage financing, title insurance, etc.), REALTORS® shall disclose to the client or customer to whom the recommendation is made any financial benefits or fees, other than real estate referral fees, the REALTOR® or REALTOR®'s firm may receive as a direct result of such recommendation. *(Amended 1/99)*

- **Standard of Practice 6-1**
  REALTORS® shall not recommend or suggest to a client or a customer the use of services of another organization or business entity in which they have a direct interest without disclosing such interest at the time of the recommendation or suggestion. *(Amended 5/88)*

Article 7

In a transaction, REALTORS® shall not accept compensation from more than one party, even if permitted by law, without disclosure to all parties and the informed consent of the REALTOR®'s client or clients. *(Amended 1/93)*

Article 8

REALTORS® shall keep in a special account in an appropriate financial institution, separated from their own funds, monies coming into their possession in trust for other persons, such as escrows, trust funds, clients' monies, and other like items.

FIGURE 2.1 Code of ethics (*continued*)

Article 9

REALTORS®, for the protection of all parties, shall assure whenever possible that all agreements related to real estate transactions including, but not limited to, listing and representation agreements, purchase contracts, and leases are in writing in clear and understandable language expressing the specific terms, conditions, obligations and commitments of the parties. A copy of each agreement shall be furnished to each party to such agreements upon their signing or initialing. *(Amended 1/04)*

- **Standard of Practice 9-1**
  For the protection of all parties, REALTORS® shall use reasonable care to ensure that documents pertaining to the purchase, sale, or lease of real estate are kept current through the use of written extensions or amendments. *(Amended 1/93)*

- **Standard of Practice 9-2**
  When assisting or enabling a client or customer in establishing a contractual relationship (e.g., listing and representation agreements, purchase agreements, leases, etc.) electronically, REALTORS® shall make reasonable efforts to explain the nature and disclose the specific terms of the contractual relationship being established prior to it being agreed to by a contracting party. *(Adopted 1/07)*

Duties to the Public

Article 10

REALTORS® shall not deny equal professional services to any person for reasons of race, color, religion, sex, handicap, familial status, national origin, or sexual orientation. REALTORS® shall not be parties to any plan or agreement to discriminate against a person or persons on the basis of race, color, religion, sex, handicap, familial status, national origin, or sexual orientation. *(Amended 1/11)*

REALTORS®, in their real estate employment practices, shall not discriminate against any person or persons on the basis of race, color, religion, sex, handicap, familial status, national origin, or sexual orientation. *(Amended 1/11)*

- **Standard of Practice 10-1**
  When involved in the sale or lease of a residence, REALTORS® shall not volunteer information regarding the racial, religious or ethnic composition of any neighborhood nor shall they engage in any activity which may result in panic selling, however, REALTORS® may provide other demographic information. *(Adopted 1/94, Amended 1/06)*

- **Standard of Practice 10-2**
  When not involved in the sale or lease of a residence, REALTORS® may provide demographic information related to a property, transaction or professional assignment to a party if such demographic information is (a) deemed by the REALTOR® to be needed to assist with or complete, in a manner consistent with Article 10, a real estate transaction or professional assignment and (b) is obtained or derived from a recognized, reliable, independent, and impartial source. The source of such information and any additions, deletions, modifications, interpretations, or other changes shall be disclosed in reasonable detail. *(Adopted 1/05, Renumbered 1/06)*

- **Standard of Practice 10-3**
  REALTORS® shall not print, display or circulate any statement or advertisement with respect to selling or renting of a property that indicates any preference, limitations or discrimination based on race, color, religion, sex, handicap, familial status, national origin, or sexual orientation. *(Adopted 1/94, Renumbered 1/05 and 1/06, Amended 1/11)*

- **Standard of Practice 10-4**
  As used in Article 10 "real estate employment practices" relates to employees and independent contractors providing real estate-related services and the administrative and clerical staff directly supporting those individuals. *(Adopted 1/00, Renumbered 1/05 and 1/06)*

Article 11

The services which REALTORS® provide to their clients and customers shall conform to the standards of practice and competence which are reasonably expected in the specific real estate disciplines in which they engage; specifically, residential real estate brokerage, real property management, commercial and industrial real estate brokerage, land brokerage, real estate appraisal, real estate counseling, real estate syndication, real estate auction, and international real estate.

REALTORS® shall not undertake to provide specialized professional services concerning a type of property or service that is outside their field of competence unless they engage the assistance of one who is competent on such types of property or service, or unless the facts are fully disclosed to the client. Any persons engaged to provide such assistance shall be so identified to the client and their contribution to the assignment should be set forth. *(Amended 1/10)*

- **Standard of Practice 11-1**
  When REALTORS® prepare opinions of real property value or price, other than in pursuit of a listing or to assist a potential purchaser in formulating a purchase offer, such opinions shall include the following unless the party requesting the opinion requires a specific type of report or different data set:
  1) identification of the subject property
  2) date prepared
  3) defined value or price
  4) limiting conditions, including statements of purpose(s) and intended user(s)
  5) any present or contemplated interest, including the possibility of representing the seller/landlord or buyers/tenants
  6) basis for the opinion, including applicable market data
  7) if the opinion is not an appraisal, a statement to that effect *(Amended 1/10)*

- **Standard of Practice 11-2**
  The obligations of the Code of Ethics in respect of real estate disciplines other than appraisal shall be interpreted and applied in accordance with the standards of competence and practice which clients and the public reasonably require to protect their rights and interests considering the complexity of the transaction, the availability of expert assistance, and, where the REALTOR® is an agent or subagent, the obligations of a fiduciary. *(Adopted 1/95)*

- **Standard of Practice 11-3**
  When REALTORS® provide consultive services to clients which involve advice or counsel for a fee (not a commission), such advice shall be rendered in an objective manner and the fee shall not be contingent on the substance of the advice or counsel given. If brokerage or transaction services are to be provided in addition to consultive services, a separate compensation may be paid with prior agreement between the client and REALTOR®. *(Adopted 1/96)*

- **Standard of Practice 11-4**
  The competency required by Article 11 relates to services contracted for between REALTORS® and their clients or customers; the duties expressly imposed by the Code of Ethics; and the duties imposed by law or regulation. *(Adopted 1/02)*

FIGURE 2.1 Code of ethics (*continued*)

Article 12

REALTORS® shall be honest and truthful in their real estate communications and shall present a true picture in their advertising, marketing, and other representations. REALTORS® shall ensure that their status as real estate professionals is readily apparent in their advertising, marketing, and other representations, and that the recipients of all real estate communications are, or have been, notified that those communications are from a real estate professional. *(Amended 1/08)*

- **Standard of Practice 12-1**
  REALTORS® may use the term "free" and similar terms in their advertising and in other representations provided that all terms governing availability of the offered product or service are clearly disclosed at the same time. *(Amended 1/97)*

- **Standard of Practice 12-2**
  REALTORS® may represent their services as "free" or without cost even if they expect to receive compensation from a source other than their client provided that the potential for the REALTOR® to obtain a benefit from a third party is clearly disclosed at the same time. *(Amended 1/97)*

- **Standard of Practice 12-3**
  The offering of premiums, prizes, merchandise discounts or other inducements to list, sell, purchase, or lease is not, in itself, unethical even if receipt of the benefit is contingent on listing, selling, purchasing, or leasing through the REALTOR® making the offer. However, REALTORS® must exercise care and candor in any such advertising or other public or private representations so that any party interested in receiving or otherwise benefiting from the REALTOR®'s offer will have clear, thorough, advance understanding of all the terms and conditions of the offer. The offering of any inducements to do business is subject to the limitations and restrictions of state law and the ethical obligations established by any applicable Standard of Practice. *(Amended 1/95)*

- **Standard of Practice 12-4**
  REALTORS® shall not offer for sale/lease or advertise property without authority. When acting as listing brokers or as subagents, REALTORS® shall not quote a price different from that agreed upon with the seller/landlord. *(Amended 1/93)*

- **Standard of Practice 12-5**
  REALTORS® shall not advertise nor permit any person employed by or affiliated with them to advertise real estate services or listed property in any medium (e.g., electronically, print, radio, television, etc.) without disclosing the name of that REALTOR®'s firm in a reasonable and readily apparent manner. This Standard of Practice acknowledges that disclosing the name of the firm may not be practical in electronic displays of limited information (e.g., "thumbnails", text messages, "tweets", etc.). Such displays are exempt from the disclosure requirement established in this Standard of Practice, but only when linked to a display that includes all required disclosures. *(Adopted 11/86, Amended 1/11)*

- **Standard of Practice 12-6**
  REALTORS®, when advertising unlisted real property for sale/lease in which they have an ownership interest, shall disclose their status as both owners/landlords and as REALTORS® or real estate licensees. *(Amended 1/93)*

- **Standard of Practice 12-7**
  Only REALTORS® who participated in the transaction as the listing broker or cooperating broker (selling broker) may claim to have "sold" the property. Prior to closing, a cooperating broker may post a "sold" sign only with the consent of the listing broker. *(Amended 1/96)*

- **Standard of Practice 12-8**
  The obligation to present a true picture in representations to the public includes information presented, provided, or displayed on REALTORS®' websites. REALTORS® shall use reasonable efforts to ensure that information on their websites is current. When it becomes apparent that information on a REALTOR®'s website is no longer current or accurate, REALTORS® shall promptly take corrective action. *(Adopted 1/07)*

- **Standard of Practice 12-9**
  REALTOR® firm websites shall disclose the firm's name and state(s) of licensure in a reasonable and readily apparent manner.

  Websites of REALTORS® and non-member licensees affiliated with a REALTOR® firm shall disclose the firm's name and that REALTOR®'s or non-member licensee's state(s) of licensure in a reasonable and readily apparent manner. *(Adopted 1/07)*

- **Standard of Practice 12-10**
  REALTORS®' obligation to present a true picture in their advertising and representations to the public includes the URLs and domain names they use, and prohibits REALTORS® from:
  1) engaging in deceptive or unauthorized framing of real estate brokerage websites;
  2) manipulating (e.g., presenting content developed by others) listing content in any way that produces a deceptive or misleading result; or
  3) deceptively using metatags, keywords or other devices/methods to direct, drive, or divert Internet traffic, or to otherwise mislead consumers. *(Adopted 1/07)*

- **Standard of Practice 12-11**
  REALTORS® intending to share or sell consumer information gathered via the Internet shall disclose that possibility in a reasonable and readily apparent manner. *(Adopted 1/07)*

- **Standard of Practice 12-12**
  REALTORS® shall not:
  1) use URLs or domain names that present less than a true picture, or
  2) register URLs or domain names which, if used, would present less than a true picture. *(Adopted 1/08)*

- **Standard of Practice 12-13**
  The obligation to present a true picture in advertising, marketing, and representations allows REALTORS® to use and display only professional designations, certifications, and other credentials to which they are legitimately entitled. *(Adopted 1/08)*

Article 13

REALTORS® shall not engage in activities that constitute the unauthorized practice of law and shall recommend that legal counsel be obtained when the interest of any party to the transaction requires it.

Article 14

If charged with unethical practice or asked to present evidence or to cooperate in any other way, in any professional standards proceeding or investigation, REALTORS® shall place all pertinent facts before the proper tribunals of the Member Board or affiliated institute, society, or council in which membership is held and shall take no action to disrupt or obstruct such processes. *(Amended 1/99)*

- **Standard of Practice 14-1**
  REALTORS® shall not be subject to disciplinary proceedings in more than one Board of REALTORS® or affiliated institute, society, or council in which they hold membership with respect to alleged violations of the Code of Ethics relating to the same transaction or event. *(Amended 1/95)*

FIGURE 2.1 Code of ethics (*continued*)

- **Standard of Practice 14-2**
REALTORS® shall not make any unauthorized disclosure or dissemination of the allegations, findings, or decision developed in connection with an ethics hearing or appeal or in connection with an arbitration hearing or procedural review. *(Amended 1/92)*

- **Standard of Practice 14-3**
REALTORS® shall not obstruct the Board's investigative or professional standards proceedings by instituting or threatening to institute actions for libel, slander, or defamation against any party to a professional standards proceeding or their witnesses based on the filing of an arbitration request, an ethics complaint, or testimony given before any tribunal. *(Adopted 11/87, Amended 1/99)*

- **Standard of Practice 14-4**
REALTORS® shall not intentionally impede the Board's investigative or disciplinary proceedings by filing multiple ethics complaints based on the same event or transaction. *(Adopted 11/88)*

Duties to REALTORS®

Article 15

REALTORS® shall not knowingly or recklessly make false or misleading statements about competitors, their businesses, or their business practices. *(Amended 1/92)*

- **Standard of Practice 15-1**
REALTORS® shall not knowingly or recklessly file false or unfounded ethics complaints. *(Adopted 1/00)*

- **Standard of Practice 15-2**
The obligation to refrain from making false or misleading statements about competitors, competitors' businesses, and competitors' business practices includes the duty to not knowingly or recklessly publish, repeat, retransmit, or republish false or misleading statements made by others. This duty applies whether false or misleading statements are repeated in person, in writing, by technological means (e.g., the Internet), or by any other means. *(Adopted 1/07, Amended 1/10)*

- **Standard of Practice 15-3**
The obligation to refrain from making false or misleading statements about competitors, competitors' businesses, and competitors' business practices includes the duty to publish a clarification about or to remove statements made by others on electronic media the REALTOR® controls once the REALTOR® knows the statement is false or misleading. *(Adopted 1/10)*

Article 16

REALTORS® shall not engage in any practice or take any action inconsistent with exclusive representation or exclusive brokerage relationship agreements that other REALTORS® have with clients. *(Amended 1/04)*

- **Standard of Practice 16-1**
Article 16 is not intended to prohibit aggressive or innovative business practices which are otherwise ethical and does not prohibit disagreements with other REALTORS® involving commission, fees, compensation or other forms of payment or expenses. *(Adopted 1/93, Amended 1/95)*

- **Standard of Practice 16-2**
Article 16 does not preclude REALTORS® from making general announcements to prospects describing their services and the terms of their availability even though some recipients may have entered into agency agreements or other exclusive relationships with another REALTOR®. A general telephone canvass, general mailing or distribution addressed to all prospects in a given geographical area or in a given profession, business, club, or organization, or other classification or group is deemed "general" for purposes of this standard. *(Amended 1/04)*

  Article 16 is intended to recognize as unethical two basic types of solicitations:

  First, telephone or personal solicitations of property owners who have been identified by a real estate sign, multiple listing compilation, or other information service as having exclusively listed their property with another REALTOR® and

  Second, mail or other forms of written solicitations of prospects whose properties are exclusively listed with another REALTOR® when such solicitations are not part of a general mailing but are directed specifically to property owners identified through compilations of current listings, "for sale" or "for rent" signs, or other sources of information required by Article 3 and Multiple Listing Service rules to be made available to other REALTORS® under offers of subagency or cooperation. *(Amended 1/04)*

- **Standard of Practice 16-3**
Article 16 does not preclude REALTORS® from contacting the client of another broker for the purpose of offering to provide, or entering into a contract to provide, a different type of real estate service unrelated to the type of service currently being provided (e.g., property management as opposed to brokerage) or from offering the same type of service for property not subject to other brokers' exclusive agreements. However, information received through a Multiple Listing Service or any other offer of cooperation may not be used to target clients of other REALTORS® to whom such offers to provide services may be made. *(Amended 1/04)*

- **Standard of Practice 16-4**
REALTORS® shall not solicit a listing which is currently listed exclusively with another broker. However, if the listing broker, when asked by the REALTOR®, refuses to disclose the expiration date and nature of such listing, i.e., an exclusive right to sell, an exclusive agency, open listing, or other form of contractual agreement between the listing broker and the client, the REALTOR® may contact the owner to secure such information and may discuss the terms upon which the REALTOR® might take a future listing or, alternatively, may take a listing to become effective upon expiration of any existing exclusive listing. *(Amended 1/94)*

- **Standard of Practice 16-5**
REALTORS® shall not solicit buyer/tenant agreements from buyers/tenants who are subject to exclusive buyer/tenant agreements. However, if asked by a REALTOR®, the broker refuses to disclose the expiration date of the exclusive buyer/tenant agreement, the REALTOR® may contact the buyer/tenant to secure such information and may discuss the terms upon which the REALTOR® might enter into a future buyer/tenant agreement or, alternatively, may enter into a buyer/tenant agreement to become effective upon the expiration of any existing exclusive buyer/tenant agreement. *(Adopted 1/94, Amended 1/98)*

- **Standard of Practice 16-6**
When REALTORS® are contacted by the client of another REALTOR® regarding the creation of an exclusive relationship to provide the same type of service, and REALTORS® have not directly or indirectly initiated such discussions, they may discuss the terms upon which they might enter into a future agreement or, alternatively, may

FIGURE 2.1 Code of ethics (*continued*)

enter into an agreement which becomes effective upon expiration of any existing exclusive agreement. *(Amended 1/98)*

- **Standard of Practice 16-7**
The fact that a prospect has retained a REALTOR® as an exclusive representative or exclusive broker in one or more past transactions does not preclude other REALTORS® from seeking such prospect's future business. *(Amended 1/04)*

- **Standard of Practice 16-8**
The fact that an exclusive agreement has been entered into with a REALTOR® shall not preclude or inhibit any other REALTOR® from entering into a similar agreement after the expiration of the prior agreement. *(Amended 1/98)*

- **Standard of Practice 16-9**
REALTORS®, prior to entering into a representation agreement, have an affirmative obligation to make reasonable efforts to determine whether the prospect is subject to a current, valid exclusive agreement to provide the same type of real estate service. *(Amended 1/04)*

- **Standard of Practice 16-10**
REALTORS®, acting as buyer or tenant representatives or brokers, shall disclose that relationship to the seller/landlord's representative or broker at first contact and shall provide written confirmation of that disclosure to the seller/landlord's representative or broker not later than execution of a purchase agreement or lease. *(Amended 1/04)*

- **Standard of Practice 16-11**
On unlisted property, REALTORS® acting as buyer/tenant representatives or brokers shall disclose that relationship to the seller/landlord at first contact for that buyer/tenant and shall provide written confirmation of such disclosure to the seller/landlord not later than execution of any purchase or lease agreement. *(Amended 1/04)*

  REALTORS® shall make any request for anticipated compensation from the seller/landlord at first contact. *(Amended 1/98)*

- **Standard of Practice 16-12**
REALTORS®, acting as representatives or brokers of sellers/landlords or as subagents of listing brokers, shall disclose that relationship to buyers/tenants as soon as practicable and shall provide written confirmation of such disclosure to buyers/tenants not later than execution of any purchase or lease agreement. *(Amended 1/04)*

- **Standard of Practice 16-13**
All dealings concerning property exclusively listed, or with buyer/tenants who are subject to an exclusive agreement shall be carried on with the client's representative or broker, and not with the client, except with the consent of the client's representative or broker or except where such dealings are initiated by the client.

  Before providing substantive services (such as writing a purchase offer or presenting a CMA) to prospects, REALTORS® shall ask prospects whether they are a party to any exclusive representation agreement. REALTORS® shall not knowingly provide substantive services concerning a prospective transaction to prospects who are parties to exclusive representation agreements, except with the consent of the prospects' exclusive representatives or at the direction of prospects. *(Adopted 1/93, Amended 1/04)*

- **Standard of Practice 16-14**
REALTORS® are free to enter into contractual relationships or to negotiate with sellers/landlords, buyers/tenants or others who are not subject to an exclusive agreement but shall not knowingly obligate them to pay more than one commission except with their informed consent. *(Amended 1/98)*

- **Standard of Practice 16-15**
In cooperative transactions REALTORS® shall compensate cooperating REALTORS® (principal brokers) and shall not compensate nor offer to compensate, directly or indirectly, any of the sales licensees employed by or affiliated with other REALTORS® without the prior express knowledge and consent of the cooperating broker.

- **Standard of Practice 16-16**
REALTORS®, acting as subagents or buyer/tenant representatives or brokers, shall not use the terms of an offer to purchase/lease to attempt to modify the listing broker's offer of compensation to subagents or buyer/tenant representatives or brokers nor make the submission of an executed offer to purchase/lease contingent on the listing broker's agreement to modify the offer of compensation. *(Amended 1/04)*

- **Standard of Practice 16-17**
REALTORS®, acting as subagents or as buyer/tenant representatives or brokers, shall not attempt to extend a listing broker's offer of cooperation and/or compensation to other brokers without the consent of the listing broker. *(Amended 1/04)*

- **Standard of Practice 16-18**
REALTORS® shall not use information obtained from listing brokers through offers to cooperate made through multiple listing services or through other offers of cooperation to refer listing brokers' clients to other brokers or to create buyer/tenant relationships with listing brokers' clients, unless such use is authorized by listing brokers. *(Amended 1/02)*

- **Standard of Practice 16-19**
Signs giving notice of property for sale, rent, lease, or exchange shall not be placed on property without consent of the seller/landlord. *(Amended 1/93)*

- **Standard of Practice 16-20**
REALTORS®, prior to or after their relationship with their current firm is terminated, shall not induce clients of their current firm to cancel exclusive contractual agreements between the client and that firm. This does not preclude REALTORS® (principals) from establishing agreements with their associated licensees governing assignability of exclusive agreements. *(Adopted 1/98, Amended 1/10)*

Article 17

In the event of contractual disputes or specific non-contractual disputes as defined in Standard of Practice 17-4 between REALTORS® (principals) associated with different firms, arising out of their relationship as REALTORS®, the REALTORS® shall submit the dispute to arbitration in accordance with the regulations of their Board or Boards rather than litigate the matter.

In the event clients of REALTORS® wish to arbitrate contractual disputes arising out of real estate transactions, REALTORS® shall arbitrate those disputes in accordance with the regulations of their Board, provided the clients agree to be bound by the decision.

The obligation to participate in arbitration contemplated by this Article includes the obligation of REALTORS® (principals) to cause their firms to arbitrate and be bound by any award. *(Amended 1/01)*

- **Standard of Practice 17-1**
The filing of litigation and refusal to withdraw from it by REALTORS® in an arbitrable matter constitutes a refusal to arbitrate. *(Adopted 2/86)*

- **Standard of Practice 17-2**
Article 17 does not require REALTORS® to arbitrate in those circumstances when all parties to the dispute advise the Board in writing that they choose not to arbitrate before the Board. *(Amended 1/93)*

FIGURE 2.1 Code of ethics (*continued*)

- **Standard of Practice 17-3**
REALTORS®, when acting solely as principals in a real estate transaction, are not obligated to arbitrate disputes with other REALTORS® absent a specific written agreement to the contrary. *(Adopted 1/96)*

- **Standard of Practice 17-4**
Specific non-contractual disputes that are subject to arbitration pursuant to Article 17 are:

1) Where a listing broker has compensated a cooperating broker and another cooperating broker subsequently claims to be the procuring cause of the sale or lease. In such cases the complainant may name the first cooperating broker as respondent and arbitration may proceed without the listing broker being named as a respondent. When arbitration occurs between two (or more) cooperating brokers and where the listing broker is not a party, the amount in dispute and the amount of any potential resulting award is limited to the amount paid to the respondent by the listing broker and any amount credited or paid to a party to the transaction at the direction of the respondent. Alternatively, if the complaint is brought against the listing broker, the listing broker may name the first cooperating broker as a third-party respondent. In either instance the decision of the hearing panel as to procuring cause shall be conclusive with respect to all current or subsequent claims of the parties for compensation arising out of the underlying cooperative transaction. *(Adopted 1/97, Amended 1/07)*

2) Where a buyer or tenant representative is compensated by the seller or landlord, and not by the listing broker, and the listing broker, as a result, reduces the commission owed by the seller or landlord and, subsequent to such actions, another cooperating broker claims to be the procuring cause of sale or lease. In such cases the complainant may name the first cooperating broker as respondent and arbitration may proceed without the listing broker being named as a respondent. When arbitration occurs between two (or more) cooperating brokers and where the listing broker is not a party, the amount in dispute and the amount of any potential resulting award is limited to the amount paid to the respondent by the seller or landlord and any amount credited or paid to a party to the transaction at the direction of the respondent. Alternatively, if the complaint is brought against the listing broker, the listing broker may name the first cooperating broker as a third-party respondent. In either instance the decision of the hearing panel as to procuring cause shall be conclusive with respect to all current or subsequent claims of the parties for compensation arising out of the underlying cooperative transaction. *(Adopted 1/97, Amended 1/07)*

3) Where a buyer or tenant representative is compensated by the buyer or tenant and, as a result, the listing broker reduces the commission owed by the seller or landlord and, subsequent to such actions, another cooperating broker claims to be the procuring cause of sale or lease. In such cases the complainant may name the first cooperating broker as respondent and arbitration may proceed without the listing broker being named as a respondent. Alternatively, if the complaint is brought against the listing broker, the listing broker may name the first cooperating broker as a third-party respondent. In either instance the decision of the hearing panel as to procuring cause shall be conclusive with respect to all current or subsequent claims of the parties for compensation arising out of the underlying cooperative transaction. *(Adopted 1/97)*

4) Where two or more listing brokers claim entitlement to compensation pursuant to open listings with a seller or landlord who agrees to participate in arbitration (or who requests arbitration) and who agrees to be bound by the decision. In cases where one of the listing brokers has been compensated by the seller or landlord, the other listing broker, as complainant, may name the first listing broker as respondent and arbitration may proceed between the brokers. *(Adopted 1/97)*

5) Where a buyer or tenant representative is compensated by the seller or landlord, and not by the listing broker, and the listing broker, as a result, reduces the commission owed by the seller or landlord and, subsequent to such actions, claims to be the procuring cause of sale or lease. In such cases arbitration shall be between the listing broker and the buyer or tenant representative and the amount in dispute is limited to the amount of the reduction of commission to which the listing broker agreed. *(Adopted 1/05)*

- **Standard of Practice 17-5**
The obligation to arbitrate established in Article 17 includes disputes between REALTORS® (principals) in different states in instances where, absent an established inter-association arbitration agreement, the REALTOR® (principal) requesting arbitration agrees to submit to the jurisdiction of, travel to, participate in, and be bound by any resulting award rendered in arbitration conducted by the respondent(s) REALTOR®'s association, in instances where the respondent(s) REALTOR®'s association determines that an arbitrable issue exists. *(Adopted 1/07)*

The* Code of Ethics *was adopted in 1913. Amended at the Annual Convention in 1924, 1928, 1950, 1951, 1952, 1955, 1956, 1961, 1962, 1974, 1982, 1986, 1987, 1989, 1990, 1991, 1992, 1993, 1994, 1995, 1996, 1997, 1998, 1999, 2000, 2001, 2002, 2003, 2004, 2005, 2006, 2007, 2008, 2009, and 2010.

Explanatory Notes

The reader should be aware of the following policies which have been approved by the Board of Directors of the National Association:

In filing a charge of an alleged violation of the Code of Ethics by a REALTOR®, the charge must read as an alleged violation of one or more Articles of the Code. Standards of Practice may be cited in support of the charge.

The Standards of Practice serve to clarify the ethical obligations imposed by the various Articles and supplement, and do not substitute for, the Case Interpretations in *Interpretations of the Code of Ethics*.

Modifications to existing Standards of Practice and additional new Standards of Practice are approved from time to time. Readers are cautioned to ensure that the most recent publications are utilized.

166-288 (12/10 JBK)

NATIONAL ASSOCIATION *of* REALTORS®

430 North Michigan Avenue • Chicago, IL 60611-4087
800.874.6500 • www.REALTOR.org

TEXAS ASSOCIATION OF REALTORS®

INDEPENDENT CONTRACTOR AGREEMENT FOR SALES ASSOCIATE

1. **PARTIES.** The parties to this agreement are:
   Broker: ______________________________; and
   Associate: ______________________________.

2. **TERM:** This agreement commences on ____________________ (Commencement Date) and ends at such time as either party terminates this agreement in accordance with Paragraph 21.

3. **DEFINITIONS:**

   A. *"Brokerage services"* means assistance and services to prospects that are reasonably necessary to negotiate and bring about the successful closing of transactions for the sale, purchase, or lease of real estate.

   B. *"Files"* means any documents, instruments, contracts, written agreements, disclosures, memoranda, books, publications, records, correspondence, reports, data, lists, compilations, studies, surveys, images, and all other data, whether in written or electronic format, which are related to Broker's real estate business. The term "files" ❑ includes ❑ excludes Associate's prospect lists.

   C. *"Prospect"* means: (1) a buyer, prospective buyer, seller, prospective seller, landlord, prospective landlord, tenant, or prospective tenant of real estate; or (2) a client or customer of Broker or Associate.

   D. *"Real estate business"* means all business related to the acts of a real estate broker as defined by Section 1101.002, Occupations Code (the Real Estate License Act).

4. **BEST EFFORTS:** Associate will use Associate's best professional efforts to:
   A. solicit listings and prospects for Broker's real estate business; and
   B. provide brokerage services to prospects procured by or assigned to Associate.

5. **EXCLUSIVE ASSOCIATION:** Associate will perform the services contemplated by this agreement exclusively for Broker. Associate may not engage in the brokerage of businesses or in the management of property without Broker's knowledge and written consent.

6. **LEGAL AND ETHICAL COMPLIANCE:** When delivering brokerage services to prospects and when otherwise performing under this agreement, the parties agree to comply with all applicable laws and standards of practice, including but not limited to the Real Estate License Act, the Rules of the Texas Real Estate Commission, the Code of Ethics of the National Association of REALTORS®, the bylaws of the national, state, and applicable local associations of REALTORS®, any rules and regulations of any listing services to which the parties may subscribe, and any standards or policies Broker adopts.

7. **LICENSES AND TRADE ASSOCIATIONS:**

   A. Broker's License and Membership Status: Broker is a licensed real estate broker in the State of Texas and is a member of the National Association of REALTORS®, the Texas Association of REALTORS®, and the following local associations of REALTORS®: ______________________________ ______________________________. Broker will maintain Broker's license and REALTOR® membership status active and in good standing at all times while this agreement is in effect.

Independent Contractor Agreement between________________________________

B. Associate's License and Membership Status: Associate is a licensed real estate ❑ salesperson ❑ broker in the State of Texas and ❑ is ❑ will become a member of the National Association of REALTORS®, the Texas Association of REALTORS®, and the following local associations of REALTORS®:________________________________

________________________________.

Associate will maintain Associate's license and REALTOR® membership status active and in good standing at all times while this agreement is in effect.

8. INDEPENDENT CONTRACTOR:

A. Contractor: Associate is an independent contractor and is not Broker's employee. Broker will not withhold any amounts for taxes from the fees paid to Associate under this agreement, unless ordered to do so by a court of law or the Internal Revenue Service. Broker will not pay any amounts for FICA, unemployment compensation, or worker's compensation for Associate.

B. Statement of Understanding: On or about the first day of ________________________ of each calendar year this agreement is in effect, Associate will execute and deliver to Broker a Statement of Understanding, a copy of which is attached to this agreement.

C. Not a Partnership: This agreement does not create a partnership between the parties. Except as provided by this agreement, neither party is liable to the other party for any expense or obligation incurred by the other party.

9. ASSOCIATE'S AUTHORITY:

A. Signing Brokerage Service Agreements: Associate may sign listing agreements, buyer or tenant representation agreements, and commission agreements on Broker's behalf provided that Associate complies with Paragraph 6 and any standards and policies Broker adopts with respect to signing such agreements.

B. Submission of Agreements: All listings, representation agreements, commission agreements, and other agreements for brokerage services that Associate procures or signs must be taken in Broker's name and must be submitted to Broker within ____________ days after the listing, representation agreement, commission agreement, or other agreement is taken by Associate.

C. Cancellations or Termination of Brokerage Service Agreements: Associate may not cancel, terminate, or compromise any agreement to which Broker is a party without Broker's written approval.

D. Other Agreements: Unless specifically authorized by this agreement or by Broker in writing, Associate may not bind or obligate Broker to any agreement or relationship.

10. FILES AND CONFIDENTIALITY OF OPERATIONS:

A. Obligation to Maintain a File: In any transaction related to Broker's real estate business in which Associate is involved, Associate must maintain a file at Broker's office that contains all applicable items described under the definition of "files" under Paragraph 3B. Associate will maintain the file in a format that Broker regularly maintains such files in Broker's office.

B. Confidentiality of Files: The parties agree that all files related to Broker's real estate business are Broker's confidential business property. Associate agrees to hold all files and information in the files confidential and not disclose such information to any person without Broker's knowledge and consent unless:
(1) required by law or a court order to disclose such information; or
(2) such information is otherwise public information.

C. Prospects and Operations: Unless required by law or expressly permitted by Broker, Associate may not furnish any person with information about:
(1) Broker's prospects or Broker's relationship with any prospects; or
(2) Broker's policies and business operations.

D. Survival: This Paragraph 10 survives termination of this agreement.

E. NOTICE: *All Internet data that is composed, transmitted, or received on the Broker's computers or network is considered to be part of the Broker's records and, as such, is subject to: (1) Broker's review; and (2) disclosure to law enforcement agencies or as the law may otherwise require. The unauthorized use, installation, copying, or distribution of trademark or patented material on the Internet or by other means is prohibited.*

11. **OWNERSHIP OF LISTINGS AND REPRESENTATION AGREEMENTS:** All listings, representation agreements, commission agreements, and other agreements for brokerage services in which Broker is named as a party are owned exclusively by Broker.

12. **RECEIPT OF MONEY BY ASSOCIATE:**

A. Compliance with Contracts: Associate must promptly deposit all checks or funds Associate receives in trust for others in accordance with the contracts under which the checks or funds are received. Associate may not maintain a separate trust, escrow, or management account for real estate business purposes.

B. Receipt of Brokerage Fees: Unless otherwise authorized by Broker, Associate must deliver any compensation for brokerage services received from any client, customer, escrow agent, title company, prospect, or any other person to Broker for disbursement in accordance with this agreement, including but not limited to any check, credit card, debit card, draft, or any negotiable instrument made payable or issued to Associate.

13. **FACILITIES:** Broker will furnish to Associate the following office facilities at Broker's office for uses related to Broker's real estate business: ____
____
____
____
____.

Performance under this agreement does not require Associate to be present in Broker's office.

14. **ADVERTISING:**

A. All advertising related to Broker's real estate business, including brokerage services performed by Associate, may be placed only by Broker or only with Broker's knowledge and consent. Broker will, at Broker's discretion, include Associate's name in such advertising when appropriate. Associate will not cause any advertisement that is related to Broker's real estate business to be published without Broker's prior knowledge and consent.

B. "Advertising" includes any written or oral statement which is intended to induce the public to use Associate's or Broker's services, and includes without limitation all publications, newsletters, radio or television broadcasts, all electronic media including e-mail and the Internet, business stationary, business cards, signs, and billboards.

15. **ASSIGNMENT OF PROSPECTS:**

A. Definition: Under this Paragraph 15, "*assign*" means to appoint an associate to deal with a prospect on Broker's behalf.

B. Assignments: Broker gives to Associate the right, together with Broker, to deal with prospects that Associate procures and with prospects that Broker assigns to Associate. Broker retains the right and sole discretion to assign leads and prospects that are procured by Broker through Broker's real estate business to any of Broker's associates as Broker determines appropriate.

C. Reassignments: Broker may reassign a prospect with whom Associate deals to another associate if: (1) Broker determines that a reassignment of the prospect is necessary for the orderly, ethical, or lawful operation of Broker's real estate business; (2) Associate is not capable of continuing to service the prospect; or (3) this agreement terminates. This provision applies to all prospects, regardless of who procured the prospect.

D. No Interference: Associate may not interfere with any assignments or reassignments of prospects or leads that Broker may make.

16. ASSOCIATE'S FEES:

A. Brokerage Fees are Paid to Broker: All fees and compensation that Broker or Associate earn for providing brokerage services to prospects (for example, fees earned under listing agreements, buyer or tenant representation agreements, agreements between brokers) are payable to and belong to Broker.

B. Amount of Associate's Fees: Broker will pay Associate fees for the brokerage services that Associate provides under this agreement at the rates or in the amounts specified in:

❑ (1) the attached fee schedule.

❑ (2) ____,
which is incorporated into this agreement.

C. When Associate's Fees are Earned and Payable: Associate's fees under this agreement are earned at the time Broker's fees are earned under the applicable agreements for brokerage services that Associate performs for Broker. Associate's fees under this agreement are payable when Broker receives Broker's fees under the applicable agreements for brokerage services, unless the fees are subject to arbitration, litigation, or a court order.

D. Disputes between Associates: If another associate of Broker claims a fee from a transaction for which Associate also claims a fee, the amount of the fee payable to Associate will be divided between Associate and the other associate claiming the fee in accordance with an agreement between them. If no such agreement is reached, the dispute will be resolved by Broker's internal dispute resolution policy; and, if no such policy exists, by arbitration. Before disbursing any fee, Broker may require written authorization from any associate claiming the fee. Associate agrees not to hold Broker liable for holding, in trust, any disputed funds between associates.

E. Delinquent Brokerage Fees: Broker is not liable to Associate for any fees not collected from a prospect. Broker retains complete discretion to enforce or not enforce any agreement for brokerage services with a prospect.

F. Bonuses: Associate may not accept any fee, bonus, or other compensation directly; whether such is in money, gift cards, credit cards, trips, or other benefits or personal property. All fees, bonuses, and other compensation must be paid to Broker for distribution in accordance with this agreement. Unless otherwise agreed in writing between the parties to this agreement, bonuses will be considered as part of the gross compensation Broker receives under the applicable agreements for brokerage services and will be disbursed in accordance with:

❑ (1) the attached fee schedule.

❑ (2) ____,
which is incorporated into this agreement.

G. Fees upon Reassignment of Prospects: If Broker reassigns a prospect with whom Associate deals to another associate or if Broker reassigns a prospect with whom another associate deals to Associate, Broker will pay Associate a fee in accordance with:

❑ (1) the attached fee schedule.

❑ (2) ____,
which is incorporated into this agreement.

H. Other: If an attached fee schedule or other document incorporated into this agreement does not specifically address the amount of the fee or compensation due to Associate under any given circumstances, the amount of the fee or compensation will be an amount that Broker determines is reasonable and equitable.

I. Assignment of Fees: Associate may not assign any interest in fees or compensation due under this agreement to any other person.

17. EXPENSES:

A. No Liability for Another's Expense: Unless the parties agree otherwise, Broker is not liable for any expense incurred by Associate. Unless the parties agree otherwise, Associate is not liable to Broker for the expenses for the office facilities that Broker will provide under this agreement.

B. Special Expenses: "*Special expenses*" means expenses that Broker incurs for ____________________
____
____.

(Note: Special expenses may include items such as desk fees, transaction fees, E&O premiums, franchise fees, etc.). Special expenses will be:

❑ (1) deducted from the gross fees that Broker receives under this agreement for brokerage services and paid to the providers of the special services before calculating Associate's fees payable under this agreement.

❑ (2) invoiced to Associate by Broker and will become payable upon receipt of the invoice.

❑ (3) charged to Associate in accordance with:

❑ (a) the attached fee schedule.

❑ (b) ____,
which is incorporated into this agreement.

C. License and Membership Fees: Each party is responsible to pay all their respective license and membership fees. Associate must immediately reimburse Broker any fee, expense, or penalty that Broker incurs as a result of:

(1) the parties' association; or

(2) Associate's failure to maintain Associate's license or REALTOR® membership status as required by this agreement.

D. Automobile Expenses: Associate will furnish his or her own automobile and pay all such expenses. Broker is not liable or responsible for Associate's automobile or its expenses. Associate must maintain liability and property damage insurance satisfactory to Broker and must name Broker as an additional insured in any such policy. Upon execution of this agreement, Associate must deliver to Broker satisfactory evidence of the insurance required by this agreement and must deliver evidence of the renewal of such insurance at the time the insurance policy is renewed. If Associate fails to maintain the required insurance in full force and effect at times this agreement is in effect, Broker may:

(1) purchase insurance that will provide Broker with the same coverage as required by this paragraph and Associate must immediately reimburse Broker for such expense; or

(2) terminate this agreement.

E. Other Expenses: Associate is responsible for all of Associate's expenses necessary to perform the services required of Associate under this agreement, including but not limited to, license fees, association dues, entertainment costs, club dues, mobile phone expenses, education expenses, computer service access charges, periodical expenses, and other related expenses. Although not obligated to do so, if Broker pays any such expense for or on behalf of Associate, Associate will reimburse Broker such amount upon demand.

18. OFFSET: Broker retains the right of offset for all purposes. Broker may deduct amounts Associate owes Broker from any amounts Broker owes to Associate under this agreement.

19. DEFENSE OF DISPUTES AND LITIGATION:

A. Cooperation: If a dispute, litigation, or complaint against Broker or Associate occurs in a transaction in which Associate is involved and which is related to Broker's real estate business, the parties will cooperate fully with each other in defending the action.

B. Insurance Deductible: If Broker and Associate are named as defendants in a dispute, litigation, or complaint, any deductible for errors and omissions insurance that may cover the defense or payment of any liability under the dispute, litigation, or complaint will be paid as follows: ____________________

____.

C. Mutual Defense: If any defense expenses are not paid by an errors and omissions insurer, Broker and Associate will share all such expenses and costs related to defend the dispute, litigation, or complaint in the same proportion as they would share the fee resulting from the transaction as if there were no dispute, litigation, or complaint; provided that both Broker and Associate are named as defendants or respondents to the dispute, litigation, or complaint. If either party determines that it cannot mutually defend a dispute, litigation, or complaint with the other party, each party will be responsible for its own costs to defend the dispute, litigation, or complaint from the time one party notifies the other of such a determination.

D. Defense Management in a Mutual Defense: If the parties mutually defend a dispute, litigation, or complaint, Broker maintains sole discretion to:
(1) determine whether to defend or compromise the dispute, litigation, or complaint;
(2) employ attorneys or other experts;
(3) direct the course of any defense strategy; and
(4) determine the terms and conditions of any compromise or settlement, provided that Broker may not obligate Associate to pay anything of value without Associate's written consent.

E. Liability for Damages: Except as provided in Paragraph 19F, each party is responsible for the payment of any amounts for which it is found liable. The sharing of defense costs provided in this Paragraph 19 does not apply to the payment of damages for which a party is found liable by a court of law, arbitrator, or state agency.

F. Reimbursement and Indemnity: If Broker is found to be liable by a court, arbitrator, or government agency as a result of Associate's negligence, misrepresentations, fraud, false statements, violation of the Real Estate License Act, or violation of any other state or federal statute, Associate will indemnify and reimburse Broker all such amounts and all attorney's fees, costs, and other expenses necessary to defend the action including those defense costs that were previously shared under this Paragraph 19.

G. Survival: This Paragraph 19 survives the termination of this agreement.

20. PROSECUTION OF CLAIMS: For all matters related to Broker's real estate business, Broker retains sole discretion to prosecute, complain, compromise, or settle any claim that Broker may have against any other person, including but not limited to other brokers, and Broker's or Associate's clients, customers, and prospects.

21. TERMINATION:

A. Either Party may Terminate: Either party may terminate this agreement, with or without cause, by providing written notice to the other party.

B. Entitlement to Fees: Any fee to Associate that remains unpaid on the date of termination will be paid in accordance with:

❑ (1) the attached fee schedule.
❑ (2) ______________________________, which is incorporated into this agreement.

C. Services to Prospects: Upon termination of this agreement, all negotiations and other brokerage services with prospects commenced by Associate before termination will be assumed by Broker. Associate will cooperate with Broker to provide for an orderly transition and assumption of such service by Broker.

D. Associate's Obligations upon Termination: At the time this agreement ends, Associate must:
(1) cease all negotiations and other dealings that concern Broker's real estate business commenced by Associate before this agreement ends;
(2) provide Broker a written list of all current listings and pending sales and leases;
(3) turn over to Broker all files related to Broker's real estate business and that Associate may have or control; and
(4) turn over to Broker all Broker's personal property including but not limited to keysafes, signs, equipment, supplies, manuals, forms, and keys.

E. Files: Associate may not remove any files related to Broker's real estate business from Broker's office without Broker's prior knowledge and consent. Associate is entitled to copies of relevant documents concerning pending transaction in which Associate has a bona fide interest. Broker will not unreasonably withhold copies of such documents.

22. NOTICES: All notices under this agreement must be in writing and are effective when hand-delivered, mailed, sent by facsimile transmission, or sent by electronic mail from one party to the other.

23. SPECIAL PROVISIONS:

24. AGREEMENT OF THE PARTIES:

A. Addenda: Attached to and incorporated into this agreement are:
❑ (1) the Fee Schedule dated ______________;
❑ (2) the Statement of Understanding (which should be reviewed and signed each year);
❑ (3) IRS Form I-9; and
❑ (4) ______________________________
______________________________.

B. Entire Agreement: This document contains the entire agreement between the parties and may not be changed except by written agreement.

C. No Assignment: Neither party may assign this agreement or any interest in this agreement without the written consent of the other party.

D. Heirs and Successors: The parties' obligations under this agreement and the parties' entitlement to any compensation, reimbursement, or indemnity under this agreement inures to the benefit of the respective party's successors, permitted assigns, heirs, executors, and administrators.

E. Controlling Law: The laws of the State of Texas govern the interpretation, validity, performance, and enforcement of this agreement.

F. Severable Clauses: If any clause in this agreement is found to be invalid or unenforceable by a court of law, the remainder of this agreement will not be affected and all other provisions of this agreement will remain valid and enforceable.

G. Waiver: Waiver of any provision in this agreement by any party is effective only if the waiver is in writing. A waiver, whether in writing or otherwise, may not be construed as a waiver of any subsequent breach or failure of the same provision or any other provision of this agreement.

This is intended to be a legally binding agreement. READ IT CAREFULLY. If you do not understand the effect of this agreement, consult your attorney BEFORE signing.

____________________ Associate's Name Printed (as it appears on license)	____________________ Broker's Name Printed License No.
____________________ Associate's Signature Date	By:____________________ Signature Date
____________________ License No. License Expiration Date	____________________ Title
____________________ Home Address	____________________ Office Address
____________________ City, State, Zip Code	____________________ City, State, Zip Code
____________________ Home Phone Mobile Phone	____________________ Office Phone Fax Number
____________________ E-mail	____________________ E-mail

TEXAS ASSOCIATION OF REALTORS®

STATEMENT OF UNDERSTANDING

It is suggested that this statement be executed annually.

CONCERNING THE INDEPENDENT CONTRACTOR AGREEMENT BETWEEN

______________________________ **(Broker)**

and

______________________________ **(Associate)**

I, the above-named Associate, state as follows:

(1) I am a ☐ broker ☐ salesperson duly licensed in the State of Texas and am affiliated as an independent contractor with the above-named Broker.

(2) I have paid all my own license fees and membership dues required under the Independent Contractor Agreement with Broker and have not received reimbursement from Broker.

(3) I have paid all of my own automobile and transportation expenses and have not received reimbursement from Broker.

(4) I have paid all entertainment and other incidental expenses in connection with soliciting listings and procuring prospects and have not received reimbursement from Broker.

(5) Broker has not required me to maintain any specific schedule.

(6) I have not had to consult with Broker regarding scheduling of my vacations or working hours.

(7) I have received no salary or sick pay and I am compensated on a commission basis.

(8) I have paid my own income and FICA taxes.

(9) My association with Broker may be terminated by either party at any time upon notice given to the other party; but the rights of the parties to any fees which accrued before termination are not divested by the termination.

____

Associate Date

(TAR-2302) 8-16-07 Page 1 of 1

REVIEW QUESTIONS

Answers to these questions are found in the Answer Key section at the back of the book.

1. Real estate licensing laws represent a government's effort to ascertain that real estate brokers and salespersons
   A. are persons of good reputation as to honesty and truthfulness.
   B. are competent.
   C. both A and B.
   D. neither A nor B.

2. The two levels of license under the Texas Real Estate License Act are:
   A. broker and appraiser.
   B. salesman and appraiser.
   C. salesman and agent.
   D. broker and salesperson.

3. Which of the following may conduct a real estate brokerage business without a proper license?
   A. Members of the state bar
   B. Attorneys-in-fact
   C. Both A and B
   D. Neither A nor B

4. A real estate broker differs from a real estate salesperson under the law in that
   A. the broker may act independently in conducting a brokerage business.
   B. a salesperson may operate in the brokerage business only under the supervision of a real estate broker.
   C. both A and B.
   D. neither A nor B.

5. Which of the following could be licensed as a real estate broker?
   A. A corporation
   B. A limited liability company
   C. An actual person
   D. A sole proprietorship
   E. All of the above

6. A person who holds a real estate license is a
   A. licensor.
   B. licensee.
   C. vestee.
   D. vestor.

7. Which of the following is NOT a real estate license category?
   A. Salesperson
   B. Broker
   C. Attorney-in-fact
   D. Both A and C

8. A real estate salesperson, under the Texas Real Estate License Act, may
   A. take a listing in the name of the broker.
   B. accept compensation from real estate owners.
   C. both A and B.
   D. neither A nor B.

9. The ultimate responsibility for a mistake in a document prepared by a real estate salesperson rests
   A. equally upon the salesperson and the employing broker.
   B. upon the employing broker.
   C. both A and B.
   D. neither A nor B.

10. The term "sales associate" may refer to
    A. a licensed salesperson employed by a real estate broker.
    B. a licensed real estate broker employed by another licensed broker.
    C. both A and B.
    D. neither A nor B.

11. An applicant for a Texas real estate brokerage license must complete
    A. 60 clock-hours of real estate core courses.
    B. 900 clock-hours of real estate related courses.
    C. 20 clock-hours of real estate core courses.
    D. 900 clock-hours of real estate core and related courses.

12. An applicant for a salesperson's license in Texas must complete how may clock-hours in real estate core courses?
    A. 120
    B. 180
    C. 12
    D. 30

13. Before being granted an original salesperson's license, an applicant must
    A. pass the examination for salesperson licensure.
    B. name the broker with whom the applicant will be associated.
    C. complete any state-mandated continuing education requirements.
    D. All of the above.

14. After licensure as a real estate broker or salesperson, a licensee must, in order to maintain the license, do all the following EXCEPT:
    A. meet any continuing education requirements.
    B. retake the original license examination and pass it.
    C. pay license renewal fees.
    D. renew the license prior to the expiration of any allowable grace period.

15. A real estate broker may share a commission on a real estate sale with any of the following EXCEPT:
    A. a salesperson licensed in his employ.
    B. a broker licensed in another state.
    C. another broker licensed in his state of licensure.
    D. a salesperson licensed with another broker in the state of licensure.

16. Real estate brokers may operate their businesses as sole proprietorships under
    A. their own name.
    B. a fictitious name.
    C. both A and B.
    D. neither A nor B.

17. For a corporation to be granted a license as a real estate broker,
    A. all officers must be licensed as real estate brokers.
    B. all stockholders must be licensees.
    C. the chief executive officer must be a licensed broker.
    D. salespersons may NOT hold office in the corporation.

18. In Texas, the requirement that a real estate agent hold a real estate license is set by the
    A. real estate commission.
    B. legislature.
    C. real estate director or commissioner.
    D. governor.

19. The composition of the Texas Real Estate Commission includes
    A. six representatives of the general public.
    B. six real estate brokers.
    C. three real estate brokers and three public representatives.
    D. four representatives of the public.

20. A license can be suspended or revoked for:
    A. placing a sign on a property offering it for sale without the written consent of the owner.
    B. offering property for sale without the consent of the owner.
    C. publishing an unjustified threat of legal proceedings.
    D. all of the above.

Chapter 3

KEY TERMS

Base line: an east-west or geographer's line selected as a basic reference in the rectangular survey system

Fixture: an object that has been attached to land so as to become real estate

Improvements: any form of land development, such as buildings, roads, fences, pipelines, etc.

Meridian: imaginary lines running north and south, used as references in mapping land

Metes and bounds: a detailed method of land description that identifies a parcel by specifying its shape and boundaries

Monument: an iron pipe, stone, tree, or other fixed point used in making a survey

Personal property: a right or interest in things of a temporary or movable nature; anything not classed as real property

Real estate: land and improvements in a physical sense as well as the rights to own or use them

Recorded plat: a subdivision map filed in the county recorder's office that shows the location and boundaries of individual parcels of land

Riparian right: the right of a landowner whose land borders a river or stream to use and enjoy that water

Nature and Description of Real Estate

IN THIS CHAPTER

In this chapter you will be introduced to the terminology used to define and describe real estate. Real estate is defined, and rights in land are also described. Other topics include fixtures, appurtenances, water rights, and land descriptions. The metes and bounds description of land and the rectangular survey system of describing land are also covered as are other land descriptive survey systems. The chapter concludes with coverage of the physical and economic characteristics of land. Key terms, such as scarcity, homogeneity, immobility, fixity, and situs, are also defined. These and the other terms defined within this second chapter should be studied thoroughly and be remembered to enhance your understanding of material in subsequent chapters.

What is real estate? **Real estate** or real property is land and the improvements made to land and the rights to use them. Let's begin in this chapter by looking more closely at what is meant by land and improvements. Then in the next chapter we shall focus our attention on the various rights one may possess in land and improvements.

LAND

Often we think of land as only the surface of the earth. But it is substantially more than that. As Figure 3.1 illustrates, land starts at the center of the earth, passes through the earth's surface, and continues on into space. An understanding of this concept is important because, given a particular parcel of land, it is possible for one person to own the rights to use its surface **(surface rights)**, another to own the rights to drill or dig below its surface **(subsurface rights)**, and still another to own the rights to use the air space above it **(air rights)**.

Realty refers to land and buildings and other improvements from a physical standpoint; **real property** refers to the right to own land and improvements;

FIGURE 3.1 Land includes the surface of the earth and the sky above and everything to the center of the earth.

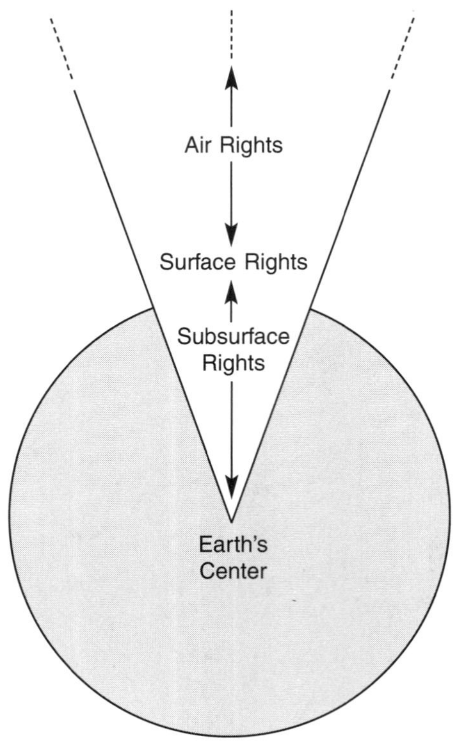

Source: © 2012 Cengage Learning

and ***real estate*** refers to land and improvements and the rights to own or use them. As a practical matter, however, these three terms are used interchangeably in everyday usage.

IMPROVEMENTS

Anything affixed to land with the intent of being permanent is considered to be part of the land and therefore real estate. Thus, houses, schools, factories, barns, fences, roads, pipelines, and landscaping are real estate. As a group, these are referred to as ***improvements*** because they improve or develop land.

Being able to identify what is real estate and what is not is important. For example, in conveying ownership to a house, only the lot is described in the deed. It is not necessary to describe the dwelling unit itself, or the landscaping, driveways, sidewalks, wiring, or plumbing. Items that are not a part of the land, such as tables, chairs, beds, desks, automobiles, farm machinery, and the like, are classified as ***personal property***, or **personalty**.

If the right to use them is to be transferred to the buyer, the seller should sign a separate **bill of sale** (a document that transfers title to personal property), in addition to the deed.

FIXTURES

When an object that was once personal property is attached to land (or a building thereon) so as to become real estate, it is called a ***fixture***. As a rule, a fixture is the property of the landowner and when the land is conveyed to a new owner, it is automatically included with the land.

Tests of a Fixture

Whether or not an object becomes real estate depends on whether the object was affixed or installed with the apparent intent of permanently improving the land. In Texas, the determination of what constitutes a fixture has primarily revolved around three criteria:

1. Method of annexation to the real estate
2. Fitness or adaptation to a particular use of the premises
3. The intention of the parties

Annexation

The first test, **method of annexation**, refers to how the object is attached to the land. Ordinarily, when an object that was once personal property is attached to land by virtue of its being imbedded in the land or affixed to the land by means of cement, nails, bolts, etc., it becomes a fixture. To illustrate, when asphalt and concrete for driveways and sidewalks are still on the delivery truck, they are movable and therefore personal property. But once they are poured into place, the asphalt and concrete become part of the land. Similarly, lumber, wiring, pipes, doors, toilets, sinks, water heaters, furnaces, and other construction materials change from personal property to real estate when they become part of a building. Items brought into the house that do not become permanently affixed to the land remain personal property; for example, furniture, clothing, cooking utensils, radios, and television sets.

Adaptation

Historically, the **manner of attachment** was the only method of classifying an object as personal property or real estate, but as time progressed, this test alone was no longer adequate. For example, how would you classify custom-made drapes made for an unusual window? For the answer, we must apply a second test: *How is the article adapted* to the building? If the drapes were custom cut for the windows in the building, they are automatically included in the purchase or rental of the building. Drapes of a standard size that may be suitable for use in other buildings are personal property and are not automatically included with the building. Note the difference: In the first case, the drapes are specifically adapted to the building; in the second case, they are not.

Intention

Of the three tests, pre-eminence is given to the question of intention of the parties. **Intention** is inferred from the nature of the article, the relationship and situation of the parties involved, the policy of the law, the mode of annexation, and the purpose or use for which the annexation is made. So intention, in its broadest sense, includes the other two criteria. It is always a good idea to confirm the party's intent, in writing, in the contract for sale.

Prior Liens Against Fixtures

In addition to the misunderstandings that often arise between buyer and seller in determining the intention of the parties regarding fixtures, there are also priorities given in the law that create a priority interest in fixtures if that interest is timely and properly recorded. If the interest is of record, the buyer may find that an important fixture may have prior claims by a supplier or vendor that gives the purchaser an inferior priority in the event of nonpayment or subsequent default by the seller. For instance, if a homeowner purchased a central air conditioning unit, the air conditioning contractor or vendor would probably record and properly file a chattel mortgage (which is recorded *before* the item becomes a fixture) in the real property records to reflect their interest in the air conditioning system until it is fully paid for.

PUTTING IT TO WORK

The air conditioning system once affixed to the real estate is a part of that real estate. However, Texas statute gives that air conditioning contractor, as a materialman and supplier, the right to put a lien on the property and remove that air conditioner in the event that the contractor is not paid. Therefore, even a subsequent purchaser may discover that the air conditioning unit can be removed after they take possession of the premises.

Trade Fixtures

Normally, when a tenant makes permanent additions to the property they are renting, the additions belong to the landlord when the lease or rental agreement expires. However, this can work a particular hardship on tenants operating a trade or business. For example, a supermarket moves into a rented building, then buys and bolts to the floor various **trade fixtures** such as display shelves, meat and dairy coolers, frozen food counters, and checkout stands. When the supermarket later moves out, do these items, by virtue of their attachment, become the property of the building owner? Modern courts hold that tenant-owned trade fixtures do not become the property of the landlord. However, for the tenant to keep the trade fixtures, they must be removed in a timely manner before the expiration of the lease and without seriously damaging the building.

Plants, Trees, and Crops

Trees, cultivated perennial plants, and uncultivated vegetation of any sort are classed as **fructus naturales** and are considered part of the land. Annual cultivated crops are called **fructus industriales** or **emblements** and most courts of law regard them as personal property even though they are attached to the soil.

APPURTENANCES

The conveyance of land carries with it any appurtenances to the land. An **appurtenance** is a right or privilege or improvement that belongs to and passes with land but is not necessarily a part of the land. Examples of appurtenances are easements and rights-of-way (discussed in Chapter 4), condominium parking stalls, and shares of stock in a mutual water company that services the land.

WATER RIGHTS

Water rights vary across the country. Some have noted the "30-inch" rule. This concept divides the country from north to south between the eastern areas that receive more than 30 inches of annual rainfall and the western areas that receive less than 30 inches of annual rainfall (roughly paralleling Interstate Highway 35, from Texas to Minnesota). Eastern areas generally have an ample supply of water, so their water laws are largely the law of surface waters and are modeled after the English riparian system. Western areas regularly experience varying degrees of water shortages and drought conditions, resulting in water law rules being based on the concept that the State is the owner of the water (in fee or in trust for the public) and allowing a person to establish a state-permitted right to use the water by putting it to beneficial use.

The ownership of land that borders on a river or stream carries with it the right to use that water in common with the other landowners whose land borders on the same watercourse. This is known as a ***riparian right***. The landowners do not have absolute ownership of the water that flows through or past their land, but they may use it in a reasonable manner. Where land borders on a lake or sea, it is said to carry **littoral rights** rather than riparian rights. Littoral rights allow landowners to use and enjoy the water touching their land provided they do not alter the water's position by artificial means.

Ownership of land normally includes the right to drill for and remove water found below the surface. Where water is not confined to a defined underground waterway, it is known as **percolating water**. When speaking of underground water, the term **water table** refers to the upper limit of percolating water below the earth's surface. It is also called the **groundwater level**. This may be only a few feet below the surface or hundreds of feet down.

Texas Commission on Environmental Quality

The laws of the State of Texas with respect to water rights are contained in the State's Water Code. The agency of the state given primary responsibility for implementing the provisions of the Constitution and laws of the State of Texas is the Texas Commission on Environmental Quality (TCEQ). This agency is responsible for carrying out legislative, executive, and judicial functions provided under the Texas Water Code, delegated to it by the Constitution and other laws of the State of Texas.

The commission is composed of three members who are appointed by the Governor with the advice and consent of the Senate. Each must be from a different section of the state. They hold staggered terms for six years, and no person may serve more than two six-year terms. This agency has the function of holding hearings to authorize the issuing of permits and judicial review. Any person affected by a ruling, order, decision, or other act of the department may file a petition to review, set aside, modify, or suspend the act of the department.

Water Development Board

The Texas Water Development Board (TWDB) is composed of six members who are appointed by the Governor with the advice and consent of the state Senate. The board establishes and approves all general policies of the state regarding agricultural water funding and water-related research, administrating the Texas Water Bank (which facilitates the transfer, sale, or lease of water rights throughout the state), and administers the Texas Water Trust (water rights that are held for environmental flow maintenance purposes). The TWDB also maintains a centralized databank on information on the state's natural resources called the Texas Natural Information System. In addition, the TWDB manages the strategic mapping program, a Texas-based program to develop consistent, large-scale, computerized-based maps describing basic geographic features of Texas. In an ever-growing world, it also administers the drinking water state revolving fund, and provides loans to local governments for local water supply projects and water quality projects. It also supports regions in developing a regional water plan that would be incorporated into a statewide water plan for orderly development.

Ownership of Waterways

The Texas Water Code specifies that the water of the ordinary flow, underflow, and tides of every flowing river, natural stream, and lake, and of every bay or arm of the Gulf of Mexico, and the storm water, flood water, and rain water of every river, natural stream, canyon, ravine, depression, and watershed in the State is the property of the State.

Water imported from any source outside the boundaries of the State for use in the State that is transported through the beds and banks of any applicable stream within the State or by using any facilities owned or operated by the State, is the property of the State. The State may authorize the use of state water that may be acquired by appropriation in the manner provided for by statute. Once the permit has been obtained from the Texas Water Development Board, the right to use the state water under that permit is limited not only to the amount specifically appropriated, but also to the amount that can be beneficially used for the purposes specified in the appropriation. All water not used within the specified limits is not considered as having been appropriated. If one doesn't use their appropriation, it may be limited or prohibited in future years.

Texas also reserves, under the Open Beaches Act, the free and unrestricted right of ingress or egress to and from the state-owned beaches on the shore of the Gulf of Mexico. This area extends from the line of mean low tide to the line of vegetation bordering on the Gulf of Mexico.

Underground Water

Texas has not adopted the appropriative system with respect to groundwater rights. The Texas Supreme Court has adopted the English common law **rule of capture**, which allows the owner of the surface pump unlimited quantities of water from under the land. Therefore, groundwater is considered the property of the owner of the surface estate and is treated like mineral ownership. Water usage has become a significant issue in Texas. A lot of Texas groundwater is now regulated in many areas by ground-water districts, which have authority over the drilling, completion, and pumping of groundwater wells. So checking with the Texas Water Development Board should be a part of every buyer's due diligence if there is a plan for using groundwater in any significant quantities.

Conflicting Claims

If water appropriation has two conflicting claimants, the first in time is first in right. The only exception to the doctrine of appropriation by the Department of Water Resources is that any city or town can make further appropriations of the water for domestic or municipal use without paying for the water. When persons use water under the terms of a certified filing or permit for a period of three years, they acquire title to the appropriation against any other claimant of the water. Conversely, if any lawful appropriation or use of state water is willfully abandoned during the three years, the right to use the water is forfeited and the water is again subject to appropriation. All persons having an appropriation by the State must file by March 1 of each and every year a written report to the Department on forms prescribed by the Department or be subject to a statutory penalty.

State Rights

The Water Code basically vests water rights in the State. It does not recognize any riparian rights in the owner of any land to which the title passed out of the State of Texas after July 1, 1895. Current owners who can trace their riparian rights to a date prior to that date may still claim them.

State Water Agencies

Other state agencies are also concerned with specific requirements for water use and water development. They include Water Control and Improvement Districts, Underground Water Conservation Districts, Fresh Water Supply Districts, Municipal Utility Districts, Water Improvement Districts, Drainage Districts, Levee Improvement Districts, Public Improvement Districts, and Navigation Districts. There have recently been established Subsidence Districts that affect control and permit procedures for development along the Texas coastal areas. There is a very good chance that if any development is to take place, one or several of the preceding districts or agencies will significantly affect the proposed project.

LAND DESCRIPTIONS

There are six commonly used methods of describing the location of land: (1) metes and bounds, (2) rectangular survey system, (3) recorded plat, (4) reference to documents other than maps, (5) assessor parcel number, and (6) informal references. We shall look at each in detail. Methods (1) through (4) are generally considered to be **legal descriptions**. That is, they sufficiently identify the land so that it cannot be confused with another tract. Methods (5) and (6) are informal references. Although commonly used, they are not sufficient for legally identifying the land. For instance, if a home is located on Pine, it could be Pine Street, Pine Avenue, Pine Lane, or Pine Court. They are often confused with each other when a person lives "on Pine." Finally, some houses have one address but are located on two lots, some single-family lots have two houses with different addresses, or tax assessors misidentify tracts (their employees identify tracts for tax purposes only and can make mistakes). This is why a proper legal description is so important.

Metes and Bounds

A ***metes and bounds*** land description is one that identifies a parcel by specifying its shape and boundaries. Early land descriptions in the United States depended on convenient natural or man-made objects. A stream might serve to mark one side of a parcel, an old oak tree to mark a corner, a road another side, a pile of rocks a second corner, a fence another side, and so forth. This method was handy, but it had two major drawbacks: there might not be a convenient corner or boundary marker where one was needed, and over time, oak trees died, stone heaps were moved, streams and rivers changed course, stumps rotted, fences were removed, and unused roads became overgrown with vegetation.

Possible drawbacks of the metes and bounds method of land description are resolved by setting a permanent man-made ***monument*** at one corner of the parcel, and then describing the parcel in terms of distance and direction from that point. From the monument, the surveyor runs the parcel's outside lines by compass and distance so as to take in the land area being described. Distances are measured in feet, usually to the nearest tenth or one-hundredth of a foot. Direction is shown in degrees, minutes, and seconds. There are 360 degrees (°) in a circle, 60 minutes (') in each degree, and 60 seconds (") in each minute. The abbreviation 29°14'52" would be read as 29 degrees, 14 minutes, and 52 seconds. Figure 3.2 illustrates a modern metes and bounds land description.

At the corner where the survey begins, a monument in the form of an iron pipe or bar one to two inches in diameter is driven into the ground. Alternatively, concrete or stone monuments are sometimes used. To guard against the possibility that the monument might later be destroyed or removed, it is referenced by means of a **connection line** to a nearby **permanent reference mark** established by a government survey agency. The corner where the parcel survey begins is called the **point of beginning** or **point of commencement**. From this point in Figure 3.2, we travel clockwise along the parcel's perimeter, reaching the next corner by going in the direction 80 degrees east of south for a distance of

FIGURE 3.2 Describing land by metes and bounds.

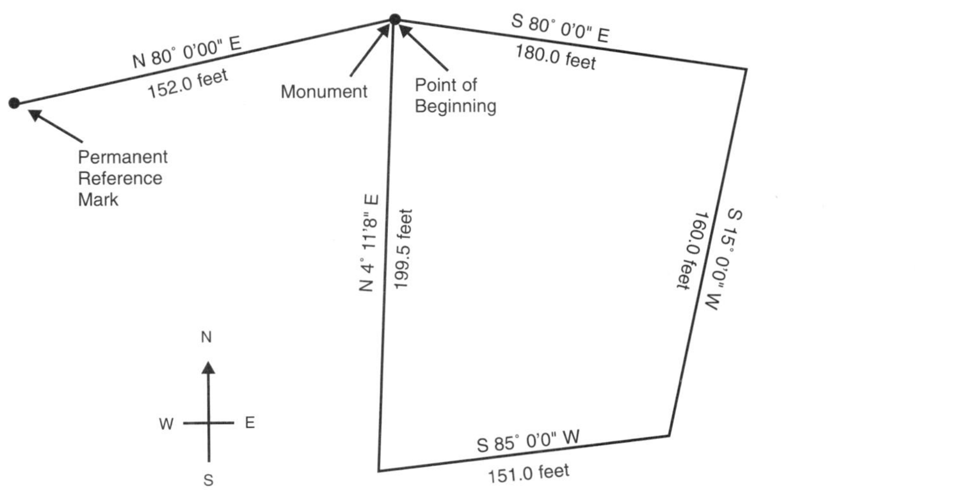

Source: © 2012 Cengage Learning

180 feet. We then travel in a direction 15 degrees west of south for 160 feet, thence 85 degrees west of south for 151 feet, and thence 4 degrees, 11 minutes, and 8 seconds east of north for 199.5 feet back to the point of beginning.

In mapping shorthand, this parcel would be described by first identifying the monument, then the county and state within which it lies, and "thence S80°0'0", 180.0'; thence S15°0'0"W, 160.0'; thence S85°0'0"W, 151.0'; thence N4° 11'18"E, 199.5' back to the p.o.b." It is customary, but not required, to describe a parcel as if traveling clockwise around it.

Compass Directions

The compass illustrated in Figure 3.3A shows how the direction of travel along each side of the parcel in Figure 3.2 is determined. Note that the same line can be labeled two ways depending on which direction you are traveling. To illustrate, look at the line from *P* to *Q*. If you are traveling toward *P* on the line, you are going N45°W. But, if you are traveling toward point *Q* on the line, you are going S45°E.

Curved boundary lines are produced by using arcs of a circle. The length of the arc is labeled *L* or *A*; the radius of the circle producing the arc is labeled *R*. The symbol (delta) indicates the angle used to produce the arc (see Figure 3.3B). **Bench marks** are commonly used as permanent reference markers. A bench mark is a fixed marker of known location and elevation. It may be as simple as an iron post or as elaborate as an engraved 3¾" brass disc set into concrete. The mark is usually set in place by a government survey team from the U.S. Geological Survey (USGS) or the U.S. Coast and Geodetic Survey (USCGS). Bench marks are referenced to each other by distance and direction. The advantages of this type of reference point, compared to trees, rocks, and the like, are permanence and accuracy to within a fraction of an inch. Additionally, even though it is possible to destroy a reference point or monument, it can be replaced in its

FIGURE 3.3 Metes and bounds mapping.

(A) Naming Directions for a Metes and Bounds Survey

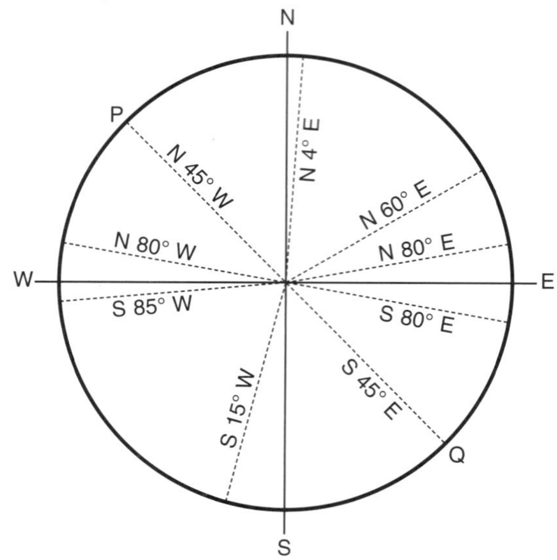

Moving in a clockwise direction from the point of beginning, set the center of a circle compass (like the one shown above) on each corner of the parcel to find the direction of travel to the next corner.

(B) Mapping a Curve

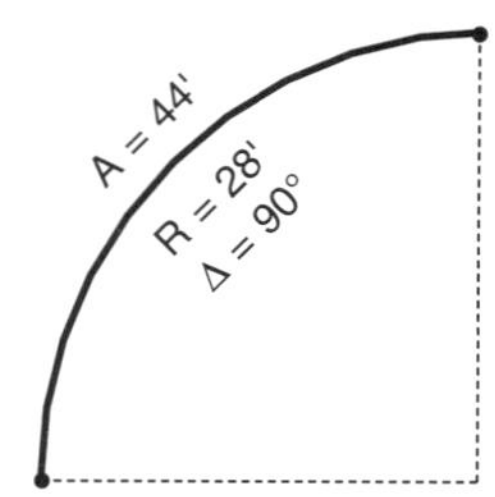

A = Length of the arc. (Some maps use the letter 'L')

R = Radius of the circle necessary to make the required arc (shown here by the broken lines)

Δ = Angle necessary to make the arc, i.e., the angle between the broken lines

exact former position because the location of each is related to other reference points.

It is also possible to describe a parcel using metes and bounds when there is no physical monument set in the ground. This is done by identifying a corner of a parcel of land by using the rectangular survey system or a recorded plat map, and then using that corner as a reference point to begin a metes and bounds description. As long as the starting place for a metes and bounds description can be accurately located by future surveyors, it will serve the purpose.

Rectangular Survey System

The **rectangular survey system** was authorized by Congress in May 1785 in order to systematically divide the land north and west of the Ohio River into six-mile squares, now called congressional townships. It was also designed to provide a faster and simpler method than metes and bounds for describing land in newly annexed territories and states. Rather than using physical monuments, the rectangular survey system, also known as the **government survey** or **U.S. public lands survey**, is based on the system of mapping lines first imagined by ancient geographers and navigators. These are the east-west **latitude lines** and the north-south **longitude lines** that encircle the earth.

Certain longitude lines were selected to act as principal ***meridians***. For each of these an intercepting latitude line was selected as a ***base line***. Every 24 miles north and south of a base line, **correction lines** or **standard parallels** were

FIGURE 3.4 Selected latitude and longitude lines serve as base lines and meridians.

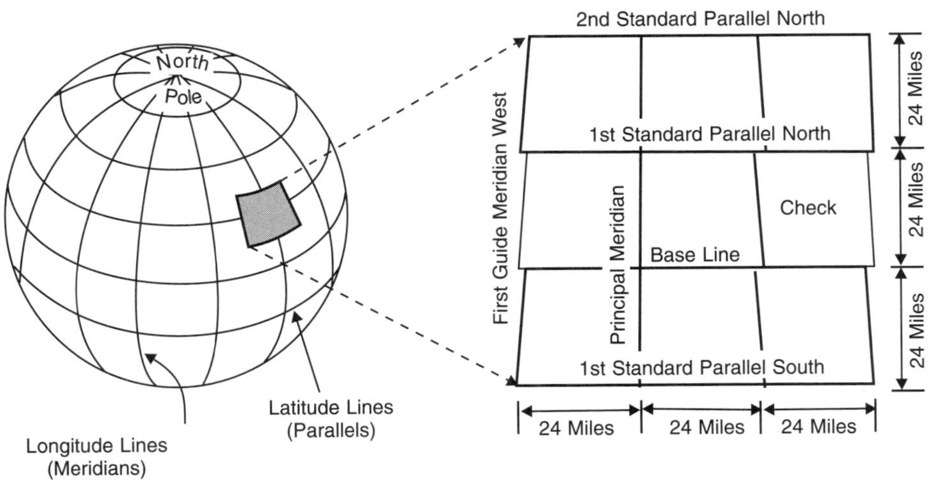

Source: © 2012 Cengage Learning

established. Every 24 miles east and west of a principal meridian, **guide meridians** were established to run from one standard parallel to the next. These are needed because the earth is a sphere, not a flat surface. As one travels north in the United States, longitude (meridian) lines come closer together; that is, they converge toward the pole. Figure 3.4 shows how guide meridians and correction lines adjust for this problem. Each 24-by-24 mile area created by the guide meridians and correction lines is called a **check**.

There are 36 principal meridians and their intersecting base lines in the U.S. public land survey system. Figure 3.5 shows the states in which this system is used and the land area for which each principal meridian and base line act as a reference. For example, the Sixth Principal Meridian is the reference point for land surveys in Kansas, Nebraska, and portions of Colorado, Wyoming, and South Dakota. In addition to the U.S. public land survey system, a portion of western Kentucky was surveyed into townships by a special state survey. Also, the state of Ohio contains eight public land surveys that are rectangular in design, but which use state boundaries and major rivers rather than latitude and longitude as reference lines.

Range

Figure 3.6 shows how land is referenced to a principal meridian and base line. Every six miles east and west of each principal meridian, parallel survey lines are drawn. The resulting six-mile-wide columns are called **ranges** and are numbered consecutively east and west of the principal meridian. For example, the first range west is called Range 1 West and abbreviated R1W. The next range west is R2W, and so forth. The fourth range east is R4E.

Township

Every six miles north and south of a base line, township lines are drawn. They intersect with the range lines and produce six-by-six-mile mapped squares called **townships** (not to be confused with the word *township* as applied to political

FIGURE 3.5 The public lands survey of the United States.

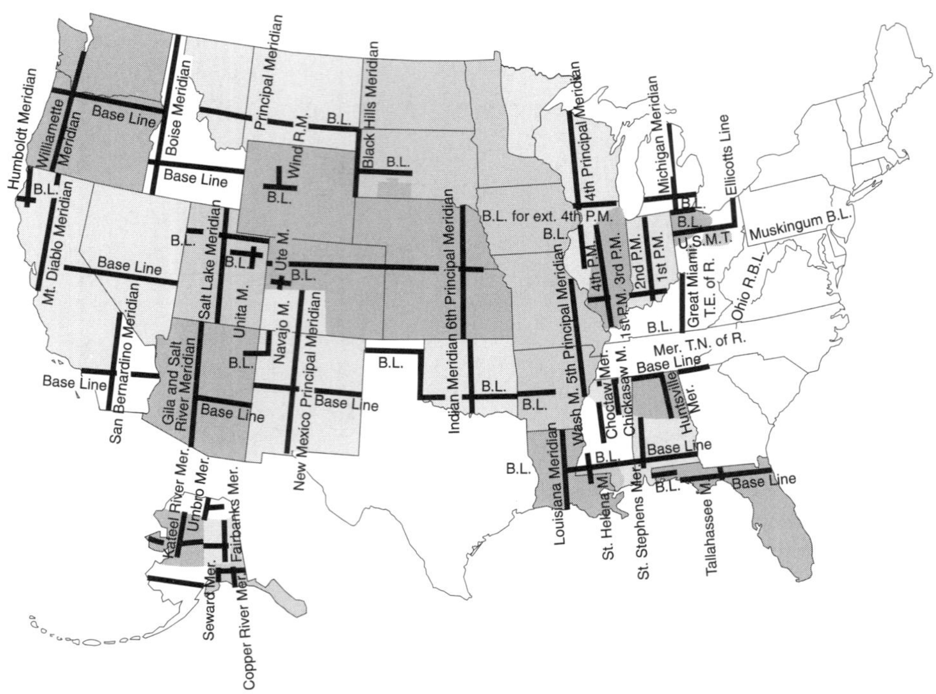

Source: © 2012 Cengage Learning

FIGURE 3.6 Identifying townships and sections.

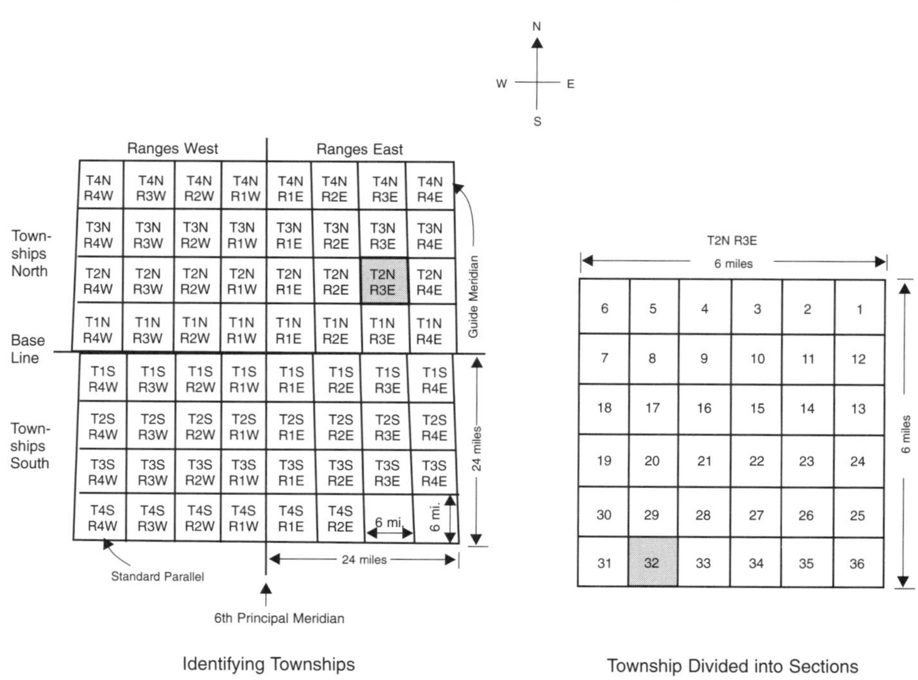

Source: © 2012 Cengage Learning

subdivisions). Each tier or row of townships thus created is numbered with respect to the base line. Townships lying in the first tier north of a base line all carry the designation Township 1 North, abbreviated T1N. Townships lying in the first tier south of the base line are all designated T1S, and in the second tier south, T2S. By adding a range reference, an individual township can be identified. Thus, T2S, R2W would identify the township lying in the second tier south of the base line and the second range west of the principal meridian. T14N, R52W would be a township 14 tiers north of the base line and 52 ranges west of the principal meridian.

Section

Each 36-square-mile township is divided into 36 one-square-mile units called **sections**. When one flies over farming areas, particularly in the Midwest, the checkerboard pattern of farms and roads that follow section boundaries can be seen. Sections are numbered 1 through 36, starting in the upper-right corner of the township. With this numbering system, any two sections with consecutive numbers share a common boundary. The section numbering system is illustrated in the right half of Figure 3.6 where the shaded section is described as Section 32, T2N, R3E, 6th Principal Meridian.

Acre

Each square-mile section contains 640 acres, and each **acre** contains 43,560 square feet. Any parcel of land smaller than a full 640-acre section is identified by its position in the section. This is done by dividing the section into quarters and halves as shown in Figure 3.7. For example, the shaded parcel shown at A is described by

FIGURE 3.7 Subdividing a section.

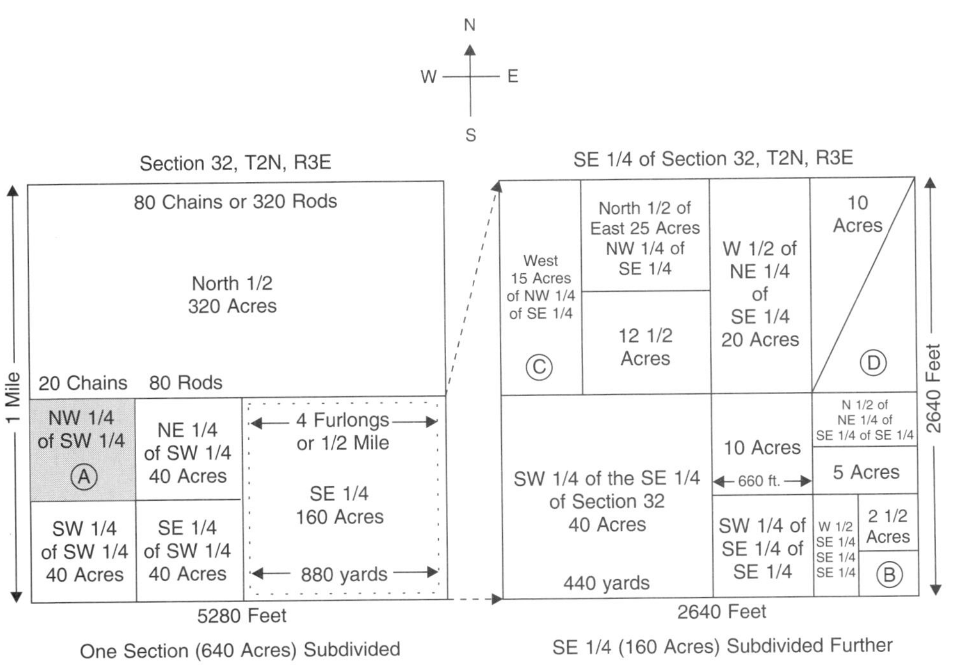

Source: © 2012 Cengage Learning

dividing the section into quarters and then dividing the southwest quarter into quarters. Parcel A is described as the NW ¼ of the SW ¼ of Section 32, T2N, R3E, 6th P.M. Additionally, it is customary to name the county and state in which the land lies. How much land does the NW ¼ of the SW ¼ of a section contain? A section contains 640 acres; therefore, a quarter-section contains 160 acres. Dividing a quarter-section again into quarters results in four 40-acre parcels. Thus, the northwest quarter of the southwest quarter contains 40 acres.

The rectangular survey system is not limited to parcels of 40 or more acres. To demonstrate this point, the SE ¼ of section 32 is exploded in the right half of Figure 3.7. Parcel B is described as the SE ¼ of the SE ¼ of the SE ¼ of the SE ¼ of section 32 and contains 2½ acres. Parcel C is described as the west 15 acres of the NW ¼ of the SE ¼ of section 32. Parcel D would be described in metes and bounds using the northeast corner of the SE ¼ of section 32 as the starting point.

Not all sections contain exactly 640 acres. Some are smaller because the earth's longitude lines converge toward the North Pole. Also, a section may be larger or smaller than 640 acres due to historical accommodations or survey errors dating back 100 years or more. For the same reasons, not all townships contain exactly 36 square miles.

In terms of surface area, more land in the United States is described by the rectangular survey system than by any other survey method. But in terms of number of properties, the recorded plat is the most important survey method.

As shown on the map in Figure 3.5, Texas has not seen fit to adopt it. Note, however, that it has had limited use in parts of west Texas, and can be included on the Texas real estate license exam.

Recorded Plat

When a tract of land is ready for subdividing into lots for homes and businesses, reference by ***recorded plat*** provides the simplest and most convenient method of land description. A **plat** is a map that shows the location and boundaries of individual properties. Also known as the lot-block-tract system, recorded map, or recorded survey, this method of land description is based on the filing of a surveyor's plat in the county clerk's office where the land is located. Figure 3.8 illustrates a plat. Notice that a metes and bounds survey has been made and a map prepared to show in detail the boundaries of each parcel of land. Each parcel is then assigned a lot number. Each block in the tract is given a block number, and the tract itself is given a name or number. A plat showing all the blocks in the tract is delivered to the county recorder's office, where it is placed in **map books** or **survey books**, along with plats of other subdivisions in the county.

Each plat is given a book and page reference number, and all map books are available for public inspection. From that point on, it is no longer necessary to give a lengthy metes and bounds description to describe a parcel. Instead, one need only provide the lot and block number, tract name, map book reference, county, and state. To find the location and dimensions of a recorded lot in Texas, one simply looks at the map book at the county clerk's office.

FIGURE 3.8 Land description by recorded plat.

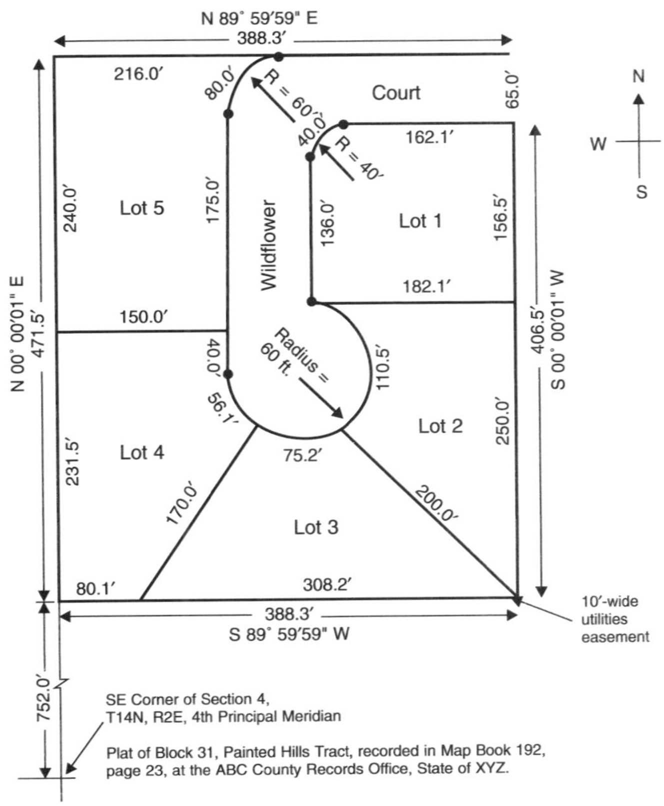

Source: © 2012 Cengage Learning

Note that the plat in Figure 3.8 combines both of the land descriptions just discussed. The boundaries of the numbered lots are in metes and bounds. These, in turn, are referenced to a section corner in the rectangular survey system.

Assessor Parcel Number

In many Texas counties, the appraisal district assigns an **assessor parcel number** to each parcel of land in the county. The primary purpose is to aid in the assessment of property for tax collection purposes. However, these parcel numbers are public information and real estate brokers, appraisers, and investors can and do use them extensively to assist in identifying real properties.

The method used in Texas is to divide the county into map books. Each book is given a number and covers a given portion of the county. Depending on the size of the county and the number of separate parcels of land in the county, the number of map books necessary to cover a county can range from less than a dozen to several hundred. On each page of the map book are parcel maps, each with its own number. For subdivided lots, these maps are based on the plats submitted by the subdivider to the county clerk's office when the subdivision was made. For unsubdivided land, the appraisal district prepares its own maps.

FIGURE 3.9 Assessor's map.

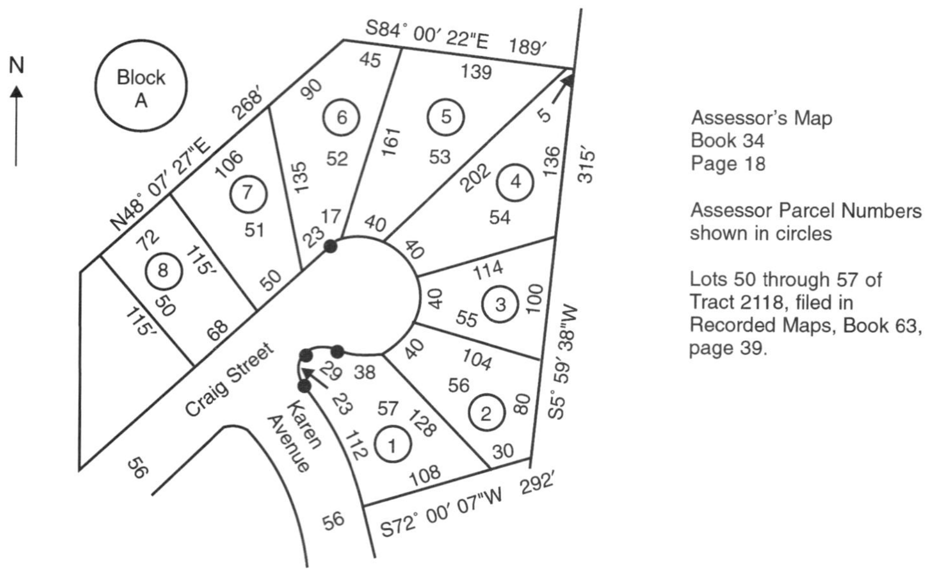

The tax assessor assigns every parcel of land in the county its own parcel number. For example, the western-most parcel (Lot 50) in the map would carry the number 34-18-8, meaning Book 34, Page 18, Parcel 8.

Source: © 2012 Cengage Learning

Each parcel of land on the map is assigned a parcel number by the appraisal district. The assessor parcel number may or may not be the same as the lot number assigned by the subdivider. To reduce confusion, the parcel number is either circled or underlined. Figure 3.9 illustrates a page out of an appraisal district's map book.

The appraisal district's maps are open to viewing by the public at the appraisal district's office. In many counties, private firms reproduce the maps and rolls and make them available to real estate brokers, appraisers, lenders, etc., for a fee.

PUTTING IT TO WORK

Before leaving the topic of the appraisal district's maps, a word of caution is in order. These maps should not be relied upon as the final authority for the legal description of a parcel. That can come only from a title search that will include looking at the current deed to the property and the recorded copy of the subdivider's plat. Note also that the assessor parcel number is never used as a legal description in a deed.

Reference to Documents other than Maps

Land can also be described by referring to another publicly recorded document, such as a deed or a mortgage, that contains a full legal description of the parcel in question. For example, suppose that several years ago Baker received a deed from

Adams that contained a long and complicated metes and bounds description. Baker recorded the deed in the public records office, where a photocopy was placed in Book 1089, Page 456. If Baker later wants to deed the same land to Cooper, Baker can describe the parcel in his deed to Cooper by saying, "all the land described in the deed from Adams to Baker recorded in Book 1089, Page 456, county of ABC, state of XYZ, at the public recorder's office for said county and state." Because these books are open to the public, Cooper (or anyone else) could go to Book 1089, Page 456, and find a detailed description of the parcel's boundaries.

Informal References

Street numbers and place names are **informal references**: the house located at 7216 Maple Street; the apartment identified as Apartment 101, 875 First Street; the office identified as Suite 222, 3570 Oakview Boulevard; or the ranch known as the Rocking K Ranch—in each case followed by the city (or county) and state where it is located. The advantage of an informal reference is that it is easily understood. The disadvantage from a real estate standpoint is that it is not a precise method of land description: A street number or place name does not provide the boundaries of the land at that location (i.e., it could include more than one lot), and these numbers and names change over the years. Consequently, in real estate the use of informal references is limited to situations in which convenience is more important than precision. Thus, in a rental contract, Apartment 101, 875 First Street, City and State, is sufficient for a tenant to find the apartment unit. The apartment need not be described by one of the following more formal land descriptions.

PUTTING IT TO WORK

The key test of a land description is: "Can another person, reading what I have written or drawn, understand my description and go out and locate the boundaries of the parcel?"

VERTICAL LAND DESCRIPTION

In addition to surface land descriptions, land may also be described in terms of vertical measurements. This type of measurement is necessary when air rights or subsurface rights need to be described.

A point, line, or surface from which a distance, vertical height, or depth is measured is called a **datum**. The most commonly used datum plane in the United States is mean sea level, although a number of cities have established other data surfaces for use in local surveys. Starting from a datum, bench marks are set at calculated intervals by government survey teams; thus, a surveyor need not travel to the original datum to determine an elevation. These same bench marks are used as reference points for metes and bounds surveys.

In selling or leasing subsurface drilling or mineral rights, the chosen datum is often the surface of the parcel. For example, an oil lease may permit the extraction

FIGURE 3.10 Air lot and contour lines.

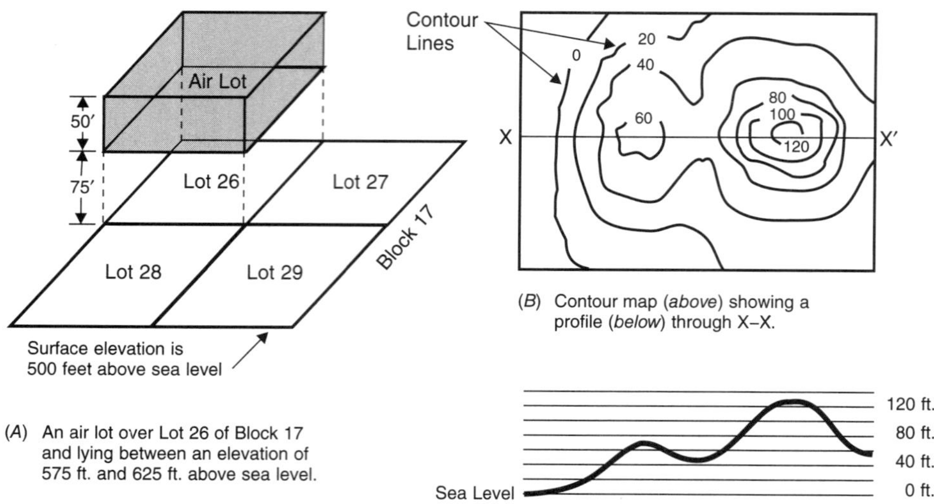

(*A*) An air lot over Lot 26 of Block 17 and lying between an elevation of 575 ft. and 625 ft. above sea level.

(*B*) Contour map (*above*) showing a profile (*below*) through X–X.

Source: © 2012 Cengage Learning

of oil and gas from a depth greater than 500 feet beneath the surface of a parcel of land. (Subsurface rights are discussed more in the next chapter.)

An **air lot** (a space over a given parcel of land) is described by identifying both the parcel of land beneath the air lot and the elevation of the air lot above the parcel (see Figure 3.10A). Multi-story condominiums use this system of land description.

Contour maps (topographic maps) indicate elevations. On these maps, **contour lines** connect all points having the same elevation. The purpose is to show hills and valleys, slopes, and water runoff. If the land is to be developed, the map shows where soil will have to be moved to provide level building lots. Figure 3.10B illustrates how vertical distances are shown using contour lines.

PHYSICAL CHARACTERISTICS OF LAND

The physical characteristics of land are immobility, indestructibility, and nonhomogeneity. This combination of characteristics makes land different from other commodities and directly and indirectly influences our use of it.

Immobility

A parcel of land cannot be moved. It is true that soil, sand, gravel, and minerals can be moved by the action of nature (erosion) or humans (digging); however, the parcel itself still retains its same geographical position on the globe. Because land is **immobile**, a person must go to the land; it cannot be brought to him. When land is sold, the seller cannot physically deliver his land to the buyer. Instead, the seller gives the buyer a document called a deed that transfers to the buyer the right to go onto that land and use it. Because land is immobile, real estate offices nearly always limit their sales activities to nearby properties. Even so, a great deal of a salesperson's effort consists of traveling to show properties to clients. Immobility also creates a need for property-management firms, because unless an owner of rental property lives on the property or nearby, neither land nor buildings can be efficiently managed.

Indestructibility

Land is **indestructible,** that is, durable. For example, today one can travel to the Middle East and walk on the same land that was walked on in Biblical days, and most of the land that we use in the United States today is the same land used by the American Indians a thousand years ago.

The characteristic of physical durability encourages many people to buy land as an investment because they feel that paper money, stocks and bonds, and other commodities may come and go, but land will always be here. Although this is true in a physical sense, whether a given parcel has and will have economic value depends on one's ability to protect his ownership and on subsequent demand for that land by other people. In other words, physical durability must not be confused with economic durability.

Nonhomogeneity

The fact that no two parcels of land are exactly alike because no two parcels can occupy the same position on the globe is known as **nonhomogeneity** (heterogeneity). Courts of law recognize this characteristic of land and consequently treat land as a **nonfungible** commodity; that is, nonsubstitutable. Thus, in a contract involving the sale or rental of land (and any improvements to that land), the courts can be called upon to enforce specific performance of the contract. For example, in a contract to sell a home, if the buyer carries out his obligations and the seller fails to convey ownership to the buyer, a court of law will force the seller to convey ownership of *that* specific home to the buyer. The court will not require the buyer to accept a substitute home. This is different from a homogeneous or **fungible** commodity that is freely substitutable in carrying out a contract. For example, one bushel of No. 1 grade winter wheat can be freely replaced by another bushel of the same grade, and one share of common stock can be substituted for another because all are identical.

Although land is nonhomogeneous, there can still be a high degree of physical and economic similarity. For example, in a city block containing 20 house lots of identical size and shape, there will be a high degree of similarity even though the lots are still nonhomogeneous. Finding similar properties is, in fact, the basis for the market-comparison approach to appraising real estate.

ECONOMIC CHARACTERISTICS OF LAND

The dividing line between the physical and economic characteristics of land is sometimes difficult to define because the physical aspects of land greatly influence our economic behavior toward land. However, four economic characteristics are generally recognized: scarcity, modification, permanence of investment (fixity), and area preference (situs).

Scarcity

The shortage of land in a given geographical area where there is great demand for land is referred to as **scarcity**. It is a man-made characteristic. For example, land is scarce in Dallas and Houston, because a relatively large number of people want to use a relatively small area of land. Yet outside of Texas cities there is plenty of uncrowded land available for purchase at very reasonable prices.

Land scarcity is also influenced by our ability to use land more efficiently. To illustrate, in agricultural areas production per acre of land has more than doubled for many crops since 1940. This is not due to any change in the land, but is the result of improved fertilizers and irrigation systems, better seeds, and modern crop management. Likewise, in urban areas, an acre of land that once provided space for five houses can be converted to high-rise apartments to provide homes for 100 or more families.

Thus, although there is a limited physical amount of land on the earth's surface, scarcity is chiefly a function of demand for land in a given geographical area and the ability of man to make land more productive. The persistent notion that all land is scarce has led to periodic land sale booms in undeveloped areas, which can be followed by a collapse in land prices when it becomes apparent that that particular land is not economically scarce.

Modification

Land use and value are greatly influenced by **modification**, that is, improvements made by individuals to surrounding parcels of land. For example, the construction of an airport will increase the usefulness and value of land parallel to runways, but will have a negative effect on the use and value of land at the ends of runways because of noise from landings and takeoffs. Similarly, land subject to flooding will become more useful and valuable if government-sponsored flood control dams are built upriver.

PUTTING IT TO WORK

One of the most widely publicized cases of land modification occurred near Orlando, Florida when Disney World was constructed. Nearby land previously used for agricultural purposes suddenly became useful as motel, gas station, restaurant, house, and apartment sites, and increased rapidly in value.

Fixity

The fact that land and buildings and other improvements to land require long periods of time to pay for themselves is referred to as **fixity** or **investment permanence**. For example, it may take 20 or 30 years for the income generated by an apartment or office building to repay the cost of the land and building plus interest on the money borrowed to make the purchase. Consequently, real estate investment and land use decisions must consider not only how the land will be used next month or next year, but also the usefulness of the improvements 20 years from now. There is no economic logic in spending money to purchase land and improvements that will require 20 to 30 years to pay for themselves, if their usefulness is expected to last only 5 years. Fixity also reflects the fact that land cannot be moved from its present location to another location where it will be more valuable. With very few exceptions, improvements to land are also fixed. Even with a house, the cost of moving it plus building a foundation at the new site can easily exceed the value of the house after the move. Thus, when an investment is made in real estate, it is regarded as a **fixed** or **sunk cost**.

Situs

Situs, or **location preference**, refers to location from an economic rather than a geographic standpoint. It has often been said that the single most important word in real estate is "location." What this means is the preference of people for a given area. For a residential area, these preferences are the result of **natural factors,** such as weather, air quality, scenic views, and closeness to natural recreation areas, and man-made factors, such as job opportunities, transportation facilities, shopping, and schools. For an industrial area, situs depends on such things as an available labor market, adequate supplies of water and electricity, nearby rail lines, and highway access. In farming areas, situs includes soil and weather conditions, water and labor availability, and transportation facilities.

Situs is the reason that house lots on street corners sell for more than identical-sized lots not on corners. This reflects a preference for open space. The same is true in apartments; corner units usually rent for more than similar-sized noncorner units. In a high-rise apartment building, units on the top floors, if they offer a view, command higher prices than identical units on lower floors. On a street lined with stores, the side of the street that is shaded in the afternoon will attract more shoppers than the unshaded side. Consequently, buildings on the shaded side will generate more sales and, as a result, will be worth more.

It is important to realize that because situs is a function of people's preferences and preferences can change with time, situs can also change. For example, the freeway and expressway construction boom that started up in the 1950s and accelerated during the 1960s increased the preference for suburban areas. This resulted in declining property values in inner city areas and increasing land values in the suburbs. Today, people are starting to show a preference for living closer to the centers of cities, due to transportation convenience and proximity to work.

REVIEW QUESTIONS

Answers to these questions are found in the Answer Key section at the back of the book.

1. In determining whether an article of personal property has become a fixture, which of the following tests would NOT be applied?
   A. The manner of attachment
   B. The cost of the article
   C. The adaptation of the article to the land
   D. The existence of an agreement between the parties

2. The term "real estate" includes
   A. the right to use land.
   B. anything affixed to land with the intent of being permanent.
   C. rights to the air above the land.
   D. rights to subsurface minerals.
   E. All of the above.

3. Determining what is a fixture and what is not is important when
   A. property taxes are calculated.
   B. real estate is mortgaged.
   C. a tenant attaches an object to a rented building.
   D. hazard insurance is purchased.
   E. All of the above.

4. In remodeling their home, the Wades put the items described below in the home. Once in place all would be fixtures EXCEPT:
   A. an oriental throw rug in the front entry hall.
   B. the built-in kitchen range.
   C. the built-in dishwasher.
   D. custom fitted wall-to-wall carpet installed over plywood subflooring.

5. Which of the following are NOT classified as real property?
   A. Fixtures
   B. Emblements
   C. A shrub planted in the ground
   D. Air rights

6. The right of an owner to use water from a stream for his own use is called
   A. an emblement right.
   B. a riparian right.
   C. a littoral right.
   D. a percolated right.

7. Which of the following land description methods identifies a parcel of land by specifying its shape and boundaries?
   A. Metes and bounds
   B. Government survey
   C. Recorded plat
   D. Assessor's parcel number
   E. All of the above

8. Which of the following have been used as monuments to designate the corner of a parcel of land in the metes and bounds description of the land?
   A. An iron pipe driven in the ground
   B. A tree
   C. A fence corner
   D. All of the above
   E. None of the above

9. The term "point of beginning" refers to
   A. a permanent reference marker.
   B. the first corner of the parcel to be surveyed.
   C. a benchmark.
   D. the intersection of a principal meridian with its base line.

10. 1/60th of 1/60th of 1/360th of a circle is known as a
   A. degree.
   B. minute.
   C. second.
   D. None of the above.

11. The major drawbacks of the early land descriptions were
   A. the possible lack of convenient monuments or boundaries.
   B. the possibility that monuments or boundaries could be moved or might disappear.
   C. both A and B.
   D. neither A nor B.

12. As measured from the north, an angular bearing of 135 degrees would be equivalent to which of the following in a surveyor's description of the same angle?
   A. S 45 degrees W
   B. N 45 degrees W
   C. N 45 degrees E
   D. S 45 degrees E

13. Goodwin, a surveyor, was called upon to make a metes and bounds survey of an irregularly shaped parcel of land. Which of the following statements would be correct?
   A. Goodwin could travel in either a clockwise or counterclockwise direction in making the survey.
   B. Goodwin must always travel in a clockwise direction in making the survey.
   C. The angular bearings of all boundary lines would be measured from the north.
   D. The corner where the survey was begun would be identified as the point of beginning.
   E. Both A and D.

14. A township is
   A. six miles square.
   B. one mile square.
   C. six square miles.
   D. one square mile.

15. Forty-three thousand, five hundred and sixty is the number of square feet in
   A. an acre.
   B. a section.
   C. a township.
   D. a tier.

16. The NW ¼ of the NW ¼ of the NW ¼ of a section contains
   A. 80 acres.
   B. 10 acres.
   C. 20 acres.
   D. 40 acres.

17. An assessor's parcel number
   A. is the final authority for the legal description of a parcel of land.
   B. is often used as a legal description in a deed.
   C. both A and B.
   D. neither A nor B.

Chapter 4

KEY TERMS

Chattel: an article of personal property

Easement: the right or privilege one party has to use land belonging to another for a special purpose not inconsistent with the owner's use of the land

Eminent domain: the right of government to take privately held land for public use provided fair compensation is paid

Encroachment: the unauthorized intrusion of a building or other improvement onto another person's land

Encumbrance: any impediment to a clear title, such as a lien, lease, or easement

Fee simple: the largest, most complete bundle of rights one can hold in land; land ownership

Homestead protection: state laws that protect against the forced sale of a person's home

Lien: a hold or claim that one person has on the property of another to secure payment of a debt or other obligation

Title: the right to or ownership of something; also the evidence of ownership, such as a deed or bill of sale

Rights and Interests in Land

IN THIS CHAPTER

This chapter provides general and legal information concerning rights and interests in land. It begins with a brief discussion of government rights in land, individual rights, easements, encroachments, deed restrictions, and types of liens. Other topics covered in this chapter include various types of estates, homestead rights, chattels, and subsurface rights.

FEUDAL AND ALLODIAL SYSTEMS

Early humans were nomadic and had no concept of real estate. Roaming bands followed game and the seasons and did not claim the exclusive right to use a given area. When humans began to cultivate crops and domesticate animals, the concept of an exclusive right to the use of land became important. This right was claimed for the tribe as a whole, and each family in the tribe was given the right to the exclusive use of a portion of the tribe's land. In turn, each family was obligated to aid in defending the tribe's claim against other tribes.

Feudal System

As time passed, individual tribes allied with each other for mutual protection; eventually these alliances resulted in political states. In the process, land ownership went to the head of the state, usually a king. The king, in turn, gave the right (called a feud) to use large tracts of land to select individuals, called lords. The lords did not receive ownership. They were tenants of the king, and were required to serve and pay duties to the king and to help fight the king's wars. It was customary for the lords to remain tenants for life, subject, of course, to the defeat of their king by another king. This system, wherein all land ownership rested in the name of the king, became known as the **feudal system.**

The lords gave their subjects the right to use small tracts of land. For this, the subjects owed their lord a share of their crops and their allegiance in a time of war.

The subjects (vassals) were, in effect, tenants of the lord and subtenants of the king. Like the lord, the vassal could not sell his rights nor pass them to his heirs.

Allodial System

The first major change in the feudal system occurred in 1285 when King Edward I of England gave his lords the right to pass their tenancy rights to their heirs. Subsequently, tenant vassals were permitted to convey their tenancy rights to others. By the year 1650, the feudal system had come to an end in England; in France it ended with the French Revolution in 1789. In its place arose the **allodial system** of land ownership under which individuals were given the right to own land. Initially, lords became owners and the peasants remained tenants of the lord. As time passed, the peasants became landowners either by purchase or by a gift from the lord.

When the first European explorers reached North American shores, they claimed the land in the name of the king or queen whom they represented. When the first settlers later came to America from England, they claimed the land in the name of their mother country. However, because the feudal system had been abolished in the meantime, the king of England granted the settlers private ownership of the land upon which they settled while retaining the claim of ownership to the unsettled lands.

Claims by the king of England to land in the 13 colonies ended with the American Revolution. Subsequently, the U.S. government acquired the ownership right to additional lands by treaty, wars, and purchase, resulting in the borders of the United States as we know them today. The United States adopted the allodial system of ownership and not only permits, but also encourages, its citizens to own land within its borders.

GOVERNMENT RIGHTS IN LAND

Under the feudal system, the king was responsible for organizing defense against invaders, making decisions on land use, providing services such as roads and bridges, and the general administration of the land and his subjects. An important aspect of the transition from feudal to allodial ownership was that the need for these services did not end. Consequently, even though ownership could now be held by private citizens, it became necessary for the government to retain the rights of taxation, eminent domain, police power, and escheat. Let's look at each of these more closely.

Property Taxes

Under the feudal system, governments financed themselves by requiring lords and vassals to share a portion of the benefits they received from the use of the king's lands. With the change to private ownership, the need to finance governments did not end. Thus, the government retained the right to collect **property taxes** from landowners. Before the advent of income taxes, taxes levied against land were the main source of government revenues. Taxing land was a logical method of raising revenue for two reasons: (1) until the Industrial Revolution, which started in the mid-eighteenth century, land and agriculture were the primary sources of income; the more land one owned, the wealthier one was considered to be and therefore the better able to pay taxes to support the government; and (2) land is impossible to hide, making it easily identifiable for taxation. This is not true of other valuables such as gold or money.

The real property tax has endured over the centuries, and today it is still a major source of government revenue. The major change in real estate taxation is that initially it was used to support all levels of government, including defense. Today, defense is supported by the income tax, and real estate taxes are sources of city, county, and, in some places, state revenues. At state and local government levels, the real property tax provides money for such things as schools, fire and police protection, parks, and libraries.

PUTTING IT TO WORK

To encourage property owners to pay their taxes in full and on time, the right of taxation also enables the government to seize ownership of real estate upon which taxes are delinquent and to sell the property to recover the unpaid taxes.

Eminent Domain

The right of government to take ownership of privately held real estate regardless of the owner's wishes is called ***eminent domain.*** Land for schools, freeways, streets, parks, urban renewal, public housing, public parking, and other social and public purposes is obtained this way. Quasi-public organizations, such as utility companies and railroads, are also permitted by state law to obtain land needed for utility lines, pipes, and tracks. The legal proceeding involved in eminent domain is **condemnation** and the property owner must be paid the fair market value of the property taken from him. The actual condemnation is usually preceded by negotiations between the property owner and an agent of the public body wanting to acquire ownership. If the agent and the property owner can arrive at a mutually acceptable price, the property is purchased outright. If an agreement cannot be reached, a formal proceeding in eminent domain is filed against the property owner in a court of law. The court hears expert opinions from appraisers brought by both parties, and then sets the price the property owner must accept in return for the loss of ownership.

When only a portion of a parcel of land is being taken, **severance damages** may be awarded in addition to payment for land actually being taken. For example, if a new highway requires a 40-acre strip of land through the middle of a 160-acre farm, the farm owner will not only be paid for the 40 acres; she will also receive severance damages to compensate for the fact that her farm will be more difficult to work because it is no longer in one piece.

An **inverse condemnation** is a proceeding brought about by a property owner demanding that his land be purchased from him. In a number of cities, homeowners at the end of airport runways have forced airport authorities to buy their homes because of the deafening noise of jet aircraft during takeoffs. Damage awards may also be made when land itself is not taken but its usefulness is reduced because of a nearby condemnation. These are **consequential damages** and might be awarded, for instance, when land is taken for a sewage treatment plant, and privately owned land downwind from the plant suffers a loss in value owing to the prevalence of foul odors.

Police Power

The right of government to enact laws and enforce them for the order, safety, health, morals, and general welfare of the public is called **police power.** Examples of police power applied to real estate are zoning laws; planning laws; building, health, and fire codes; and rent control. A key difference between police power and eminent domain is that although police power restricts how real estate may be used, there is no legally recognized "taking" of property. Consequently, there is no payment to an owner who suffers a loss of value through the exercise of police power, unless the regulation results in the property having no value (i.e., required open space). If the property is valueless as a result of the regulation, it becomes a taking, and the owner must be compensated. A government may not use police power in an offhand or capricious manner; any law that restricts how an owner may use his real estate must be deemed in the public interest and applied evenhandedly to be valid. The breaking of a law based upon police power results in either a civil or criminal penalty rather than in the seizure of real estate, as in the case of unpaid property taxes. Of the various rights the government holds in land, police power has the most impact on land value.

Escheat

When a person dies and leaves no heirs and no instructions as to how to dispose of her real and personal property, or when property is abandoned, the ownership of that property reverts to the state. This reversion to the state is called **escheat** from the Anglo-French word meaning *to fall back*. Escheat solves the problem of property becoming ownerless.

PROTECTING OWNERSHIP

It cannot be overemphasized that in order to have real estate there must be a system or means of protecting rightful claims to the use of land and the improvements thereon. In the United States, the federal government is given the task of organizing a defense system to prevent confiscation of those rights by a foreign power. The federal government, in combination with state and local governments, also establishes laws and courts within the country to protect the ownership rights of one citizen in relation to another citizen. Whereas the armed forces protect against a foreign takeover from outside, written deeds, public records, contracts, and other documents have replaced the need for brute force to prove and protect ownership of real estate within the country.

FEE SIMPLE

The concept of real estate ownership can be more easily understood when viewed as a collection or bundle of rights. Under the allodial system, the rights of taxation, eminent domain, police power, and escheat are retained by the government. The remaining bundle of rights, called ***fee simple***, is available for private ownership. The fee simple bundle of rights can be held by a person and his heirs forever or until his government can no longer protect those rights. Figure 4.1 illustrates the fee simple bundle of rights concept.

The term **estate** refers to one's legal interest or rights in land. A fee simple is the largest estate one can hold in land. Most real estate sales are for the fee simple estate. When a person says she "owns" or has "title" to real estate, it is usually the fee simple estate that is being discussed. The word ***title*** refers to the ownership of something. All other lesser estates in land, such as life estates and leaseholds, are created from the fee estate.

Real estate is concerned with the "sticks" in the bundle—how many there are, how useful they are, and who possesses the sticks not in the bundle. With that in mind, let us describe what happens when sticks are removed from the bundle.

ENCUMBRANCES

Whenever a stick is removed from the fee simple bundle, it creates an impediment to the free and clear ownership and use of that property. These impediments to title are called encumbrances. An ***encumbrance*** is defined as any claim, right, lien, estate, or liability that limits the fee simple title to property. An encumbrance is, in effect, a stick that has been removed from the bundle. Commonly found encumbrances are easements, encroachments, deed restrictions, liens, leases, and air and subsurface rights. In addition, qualified fee estates are encumbered estates, as are life estates.

The party holding a stick from someone else's fee simple bundle is said to hold a claim to or a right or interest in that land. In other words, what is one

FIGURE 4.1 The fee simple bundle of rights

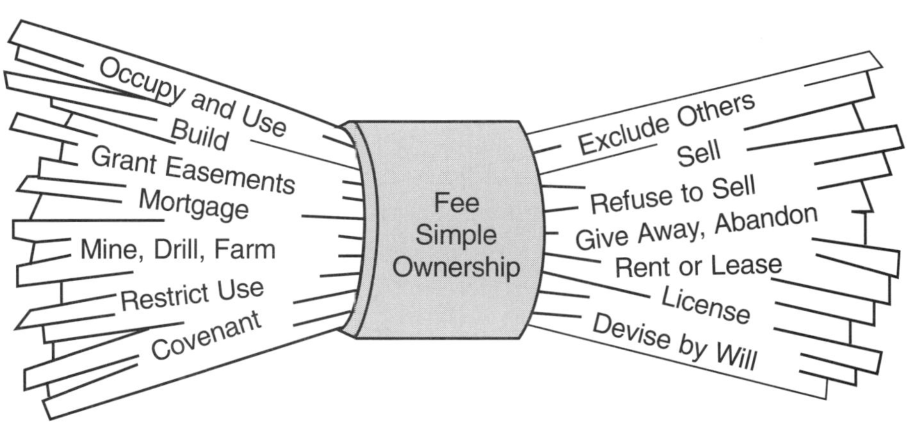

Real estate ownership is, in actuality, the ownership of rights to land. The largest bundle available for private ownership is called "fee simple."

Source: © 2012 Cengage Learning

person's encumbrance is another person's right or interest or claim. For example, a lease is an encumbrance from the standpoint of the fee simple owner. But from the tenant's standpoint, it is an interest in land that gives the tenant the right to the exclusive use of land and buildings. A mortgage is an encumbrance from the fee owner's viewpoint, but a right to foreclose from the lender's viewpoint. A property that is encumbered with a lease and a mortgage is called "a fee simple subject to a lease and a mortgage." Figure 4.2 illustrates how a fee simple bundle shrinks as rights are removed from it. Meanwhile, let us turn our attention to a discussion of individual sticks found in the fee simple bundle.

Easements

An ***easement*** is a right or privilege one party has to the use of the land of another for a special purpose consistent with the general use of the land. The landowner is

FIGURE 4.2 Removing sticks from the fee simple bundle

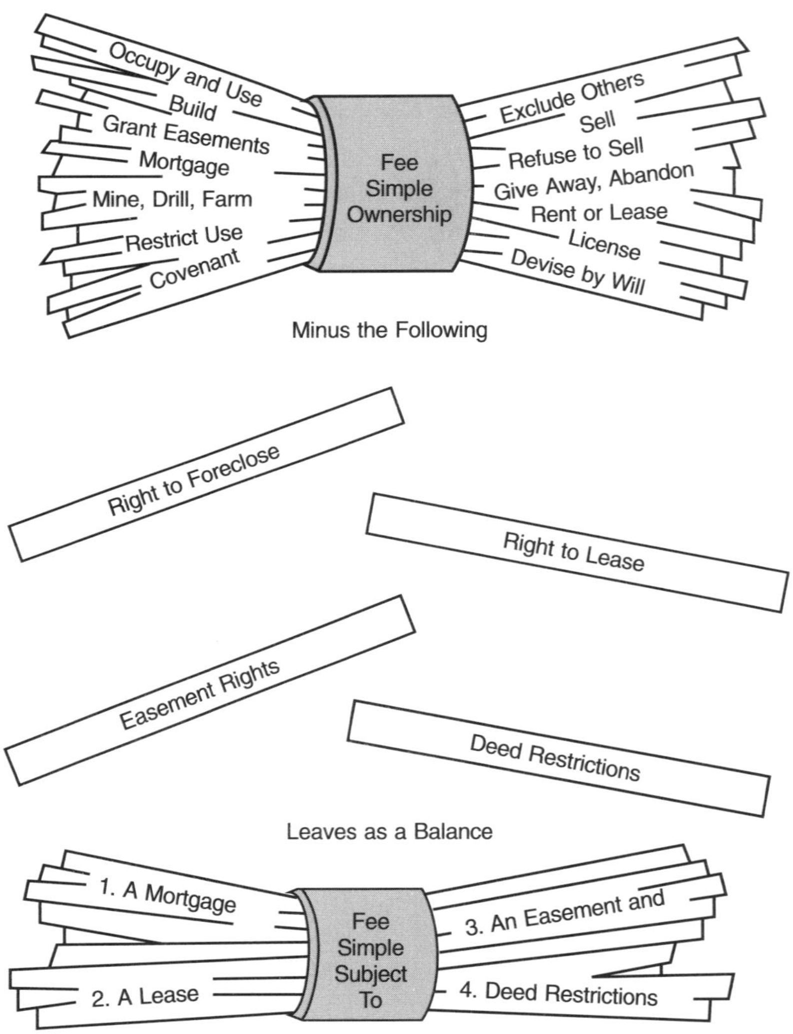

Note that the fee simple bundle shrinks as an owner voluntarily removes rights from it.

Source: © 2012 Cengage Learning

not dispossessed from his land, but rather coexists side by side with the holder of the easement. Examples of easements are those given to telephone and electric companies to erect poles and to run lines over private property, easements given to people to drive or walk across someone else's land, and easements given to gas and water companies to run pipelines to serve their customers. Figure 4.3 illustrates several examples of easements.

The usual procedure in creating an easement is for the landowner to use a written document to specifically grant an easement to someone else or to reserve an easement to himself in the deed when he sells the property. A land developer may reserve easements for utility lines and then grant them to the utility companies that will service the lots.

It is also possible for an easement to arise without a written document. For example, a parcel of land fronts on a road and the owner sells the back half of the parcel. If the only access to the back half is by crossing over the front half, even if the seller did not expressly grant an easement, the law may protect the buyer's right to travel over the front half to get to his land. This may create an **easement by implication,** or an **easement by necessity,** depending on the circumstances. Another method of acquiring an easement without a written document is by constant use, or **easement by prescription:** If a person acts as though she owns an easement long enough, she will have a legally recognized easement. Persons using a private road without permission for a long enough period of time can acquire a legally recognized easement by this method.

FIGURE 4.3 Commonly found easements

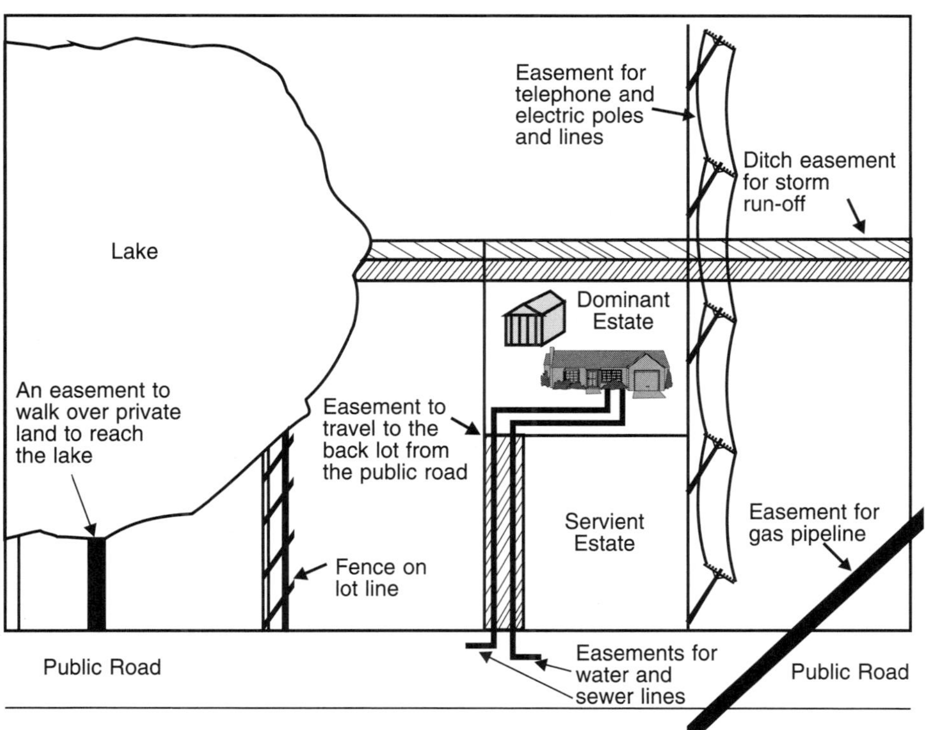

Source: © 2012 Cengage Learning

Easement Appurtenant

In Figure 4.3, the driveway from the road to the back lot is called an **easement appurtenant.** This driveway is automatically included with the back lot whenever the back lot is sold or otherwise conveyed. This is so because this easement is physically and legally connected (appurtenant) to the back lot, which is the dominant estate. Please note that just as the back lot benefits from this easement, the front lot is burdened by it. Whenever the front lot is sold or otherwise conveyed, the new owners must continue to respect the easement to the back lot. The owner of the front lot owns all the front lot, but cannot put a fence across the easement, or plant trees on it or grow a garden on it or otherwise hamper access to the back lot. The front lot, being burdened by the easement, is called the **servient estate,** and the back lot, which benefits from the easement, is called the **dominant estate.**

Easement in Gross

An **easement in gross** is given to a person or business, and a subsequent sale of the land does not usually affect ownership of the easement. It benefits the user only and is an encumbrance to the fee estate (no benefit to the contiguous land owner). Therefore, there is neither a dominant or a servient estate. Telephone, electricity, and gas line easements are examples of easements in gross. The holder of a commercial easement usually has the right to sell, assign, or devise it. However, easements in gross are limited to the specified user, are not transferable, and terminate with the death of the person holding the easement.

Party Wall Easement

Party wall easements exist when a single wall straddles the lot line that separates two parcels of land. The wall may be either a fence or the wall of a building. In either case, each lot owner owns that portion of the wall on his land, plus an easement in the other half of the wall for physical support. Party walls are common where stores and office buildings are built right up to the lot line. Such a wall can present an interesting problem when the owner of one lot wants to demolish his building. Because the wall provides support for the building next door, it is usually her responsibility to either leave the wall or provide special supports for the adjacent building during demolition and until another building is constructed on the lot.

Easement Termination

Easements may be terminated when the purpose for the easement no longer exists (e.g., a public road is built adjacent to the back half of the lot mentioned earlier), or when the dominant and servient estates are combined with the intent of extinguishing the easement, or by release from the owner of the dominant estate to the servient estate, or by lack of use.

Encroachments

The unauthorized intrusion of a building or other improvement onto another person's land is called an ***encroachment.*** A tree that overhangs into a neighbor's yard or a building or eave of a roof that crosses a property line are examples of

FIGURE 4.4 Commonly found encroachments

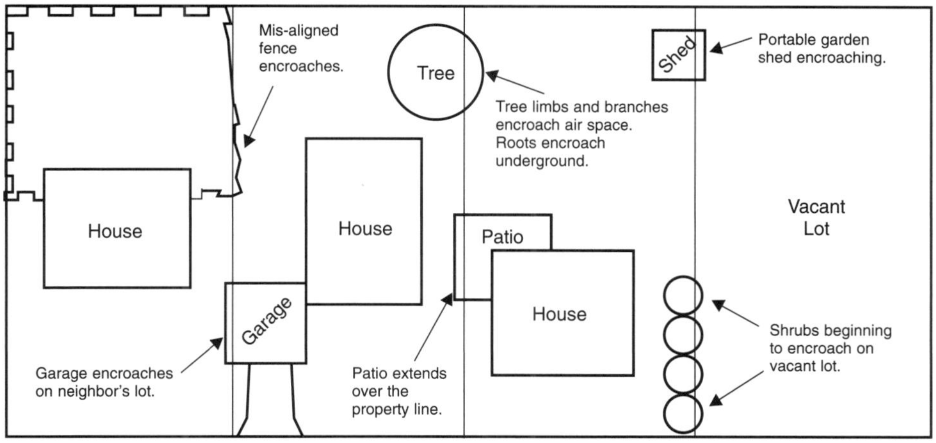

Most commonly found encroachments are not intentional but are due to poor or nonexistent planning. For example, a weekend garden shed, fence, or patio project is built without surveying to find the lot line, or a tree or bush grows so large it encroaches upon a neighbor's land.

Source: © 2012 Cengage Learning

encroachments. The owner of the property being encroached upon has the right to force the removal of the encroachment. Failure to do so may eventually injure his title and make his land more difficult to sell. Ultimately, inaction may result in the encroaching neighbor claiming a legal right to continue his use. Figure 4.4 illustrates several commonly found encroachments.

Deed Restrictions

Private agreements that govern the use of land are known as **deed restrictions** or **deed covenants.** For example, a land subdivider can require that persons who purchase lots from her build only single-family homes containing 1,200 square feet or more. The purpose would be to protect those who have already built houses from an erosion in property value due to the construction of nearby buildings not compatible with the neighborhood. Where scenic views are important, deed restrictions may limit the height of buildings and trees to 15 feet. A buyer would still obtain fee simple ownership, but at the same time would voluntarily give up some of his rights to do as he pleases. As a buyer, he is said to receive a fee simple title subject to deed restrictions.

PUTTING IT TO WORK

The right to enforce the deed restrictions is usually given by the developer to the subdivision's homeowner association. Violation of a deed restriction can result in a civil court action brought by other property owners who are bound by the same deed restriction.

Liens

A hold or claim that one person has on the property of another to secure payment of a debt or other obligation is called a ***lien.*** Common examples are property tax liens, mechanic's liens, judgment liens, and mortgage liens. From the standpoint of the property owner, a lien is an encumbrance on his title. Note that a lien does not transfer title to property. The debtor retains title until the lien is foreclosed. When there is more than one lien against a property, the lien that was recorded first usually has the highest priority in the event of foreclosure.

Property Tax Lien

Property tax liens are superior to other liens. A **property tax lien** results from the right of government to collect taxes from property owners. At the beginning of each tax year, a tax lien is placed on taxable property and remains until the property taxes are paid. If they are not paid, the lien gives the government the right to force the sale of the property in order to collect the unpaid taxes.

Mechanic's Lien

Mechanic's lien laws give anyone who has furnished labor or materials for the demolition or improvement of land the right to place a lien against that land if payment has not been received. A sale of the property can then be forced to recover the money owed. To be entitled to a mechanic's lien, the work or materials must have been provided pursuant to an agreement with the property owner or his representative.

The legal theory behind mechanic's lien rights is that the labor and materials supplied enhance the value of the property. Therefore, the property should be security for payment. If the property owner does not pay voluntarily, the lien can be enforced with a court-supervised foreclosure sale. To be valid, a mechanic's lien must be recorded in the county clerk's office within the time limits set by state law.

Judgment Lien

Judgment liens arise from lawsuits for which money damages are awarded. The law permits a hold to be placed against the real and personal property of the debtor until the judgment is paid. Usually the lien created by the judgment covers property only in the county where the judgment was awarded. However, the creditor can extend the lien to property in other counties by filing an **abstract of judgment** in each of those counties. If the debtor does not repay the lien voluntarily, and the property is not the debtor's homestead (or is in excess of allowable homestead limits), the creditor can ask the court to issue a **writ of execution** that directs the county sheriff to seize and sell a sufficient amount of the debtor's property to pay the debt and expenses of the sale. If a writ of execution is not issued, the creditor must renew the abstract of judgment every 10 years or it will expire and be of no further effect.

PUTTING IT TO WORK

If a landowner hires a contractor to build a house or add a room to his existing house, and then fails to pay the contractor, the contractor may file a mechanic's lien against the land and its improvements. Furthermore, if the landowner pays the contractor, but the contractor does not pay his subcontractors, the subcontractors are entitled to file a mechanic's lien against the property. In this situation, the owner may have to pay twice. The Texas legislature has also extended the lien rights to architects, engineers, and surveyors, provided that certain requirements are met.

Mortgage Lien

A **mortgage lien** is a pledge of property by its owner to secure the repayment of a debt. In contrast to a property tax lien that is imposed by law, a mortgage lien is a voluntary lien created by the property owner. In contrast to a judgment lien, which applies to all the debtor's property, a mortgage lien covers only the specific property that its owner elects to pledge. If the debt secured by the mortgage lien is not repaid, the creditor can foreclose and sell the pledged property. If this is insufficient to repay the debt, some states allow the creditor to petition the court for a judgment lien for the balance due. (Mortgage law is covered in more detail in Chapter 11.)

Voluntary and Involuntary Liens

A **voluntary lien** is a lien created by the property owner. A mortgage lien is an example of a voluntary lien; the owner voluntarily creates a lien against his or her own property in order to borrow money. An **involuntary lien** is one that is created by operation of law, against the wishes of the owner. Examples are property tax liens and judgment liens.

Specific and General Liens

A **specific lien** is a lien on a specific property. A property tax lien is a specific lien because it is a lien against a specific property and no other. Thus, if a person owns five parcels of land scattered throughout a given county and fails to pay the taxes on one of those parcels, the county can force the sale of just that one parcel; the others cannot be touched. Mortgages and mechanic's liens are also specific liens in that they apply to only the property receiving the materials or labor. In contrast, a **general lien** is a lien on all the property of a person in a given jurisdiction. For example, a judgment lien is a lien on all the debtor's property in the county or counties in which the judgment has been filed. Federal tax liens are also general liens.

QUALIFIED FEE ESTATES

A **qualified fee estate** is a fee estate that is subject to certain limitations imposed by the person creating the estate. Qualified fee estates fall into three categories: determinable, condition subsequent, and condition precedent. They will be discussed only briefly because they are uncommon.

A **fee on conditional limitation,** also called a **fee simple determinable estate,** results when the estate created is limited by the happening of a certain event. For example, Mr. Smith donates a parcel of land to a church so long as the land is used for religious purposes. The key words are "so long as." So long as the land is used for religious purposes the church has all the rights of fee simple ownership. But, if some other use is made of the land, it reverts to the grantor (Mr. Smith) or someone else named by Mr. Smith (called a **remainderman**). Note that the termination of the estate is automatic if the land is used contrary to the limitation stated in the deed.

A **fee simple subject to condition subsequent** is similar to a determinable fee except that it gives the grantor the right to terminate the estate rather than wait for it to terminate automatically. Continuing the above example, Mr. Smith would have the right to reenter the property and take it back if it was no longer being used for religious purposes.

With a **fee simple upon condition precedent,** the title will not take effect until a condition is performed. For example, Mr. Smith could deed his land to a church with the condition that the deed will not take effect until a religious sanctuary is built.

Occasionally, qualified fees have been used by land developers in lieu of deed restrictions or zoning. For example, the buyer has the fee title so long as she uses the land for a single-family residence. In another example, a land developer might use a condition precedent to encourage lot purchasers to build promptly. This would enhance the value of her unsold lots. From the standpoint of the property owner, a qualification is an encumbrance to her title.

LIFE ESTATES

A **life estate** conveys an estate for the duration of someone's life. The duration of the estate can be tied to the land of the **life tenant** (the person holding the life estate) or to a third party. In addition, someone must be named to acquire the estate upon its termination. The following example will illustrate the life estate concept. Suppose you have an aunt who needs financial assistance and you have decided to grant her, for the rest of her life, a house to live in. When you create the life estate, she becomes the life tenant. Additionally, you must decide who gets the house upon her death. If you want it back, you would want a **reversionary interest** for yourself. This way the house reverts to you, or if you predecease her, to your heirs. If you want the house to go to someone else, your son or daughter for example, you could name him or her as the **remainderman.** Alternatively, you could name a friend, relative, or charity as the remainderman. While your aunt is alive, the remainderman is said to hold a **remainder interest** in the house. When she dies, that interest changes to a fee simple estate.

A life estate does not have to be based on the life span of the life tenant. It can be based on the life span of a third party in which case it is called a life estate **pur autre vie** (i.e., for the life of another). Continuing the above example, suppose that you know your rich uncle is naming your aunt to receive a substantial portion of his wealth upon his death. If this would adequately take care of her future financial needs, you could grant your aunt a life estate until your uncle dies. Sometimes a life estate is used to avoid the time and expense of probating a will and to reduce estate taxes. For example, an aging father could deed his real estate to his children but retain a life estate for himself.

Prohibition of Waste

Because a life estate arrangement is temporary, the life tenant must not commit **waste** by destroying or harming the property. Furthermore, the life tenant is required to keep the property in reasonable repair and to pay any property taxes, assessments, and interest on debt secured by the property. During the tenancy, the life tenant is entitled to the use and/or income generated by the property, and may sell, lease, rent, or mortgage his or her interest. Note, however, that it is impossible for the life tenant to sell, lease, or mortgage any greater interest than the life tenant holds.

STATUTORY ESTATES

Statutory estates are created by state law. They include **dower,** which gives a wife rights in her husband's real property; **curtesy,** which gives a husband rights in his wife's real property; and **community property,** which gives each spouse a one-half interest in marital property. Additionally there are **homesteads,** which are designed to protect the family's home from certain debts and, upon the death of one spouse, provide the other with a home for life. In Texas there is ***homestead protection*** and community property, but no dower or curtesy.

Dower

Historically, **dower** came from old English common law, in which the marriage ceremony was viewed as merging the wife's legal existence into that of her husband's. From this viewpoint, property bought during marriage belongs to the husband, with both husband and wife sharing the use of it. As a counterbalance, the dower right recognizes the wife's efforts in marriage and grants her legal ownership to one-third (in some states one-half) of the family's real property for the rest of her life. This prevents the husband from conveying ownership of the family's real estate without the wife's permission and protects her even if she is left out of her husband's will.

Because the wife's dower right does not ripen into actual ownership until her husband's death, her right is described as being **inchoate** until then. Once she obtains her life estate, she can sell, give, rent, or mortgage it, as described previously. Recognizing the impractical nature of an undivided life estate and the need for equal rights between husband and wife, some states award the wife an undivided fee simple estate rather than a life estate.

In real estate sales, the effect of dower laws is that when a husband and wife sell their property, the wife must relinquish her dower rights. This is usually accomplished by the wife signing the deed with her husband or by signing a separate quit claim deed. If she does not relinquish her dower rights, the buyer (or even a future buyer) may find that, upon the husband's death, the wife may return to legally claim an undivided ownership in the property. This is an important reason why, if you are buying real estate, you should have the property's ownership researched by a competent abstractor and have the title you receive insured by a title insurance company. Because the wife's dower right is inchoate while her husband is alive, she cannot sell it or otherwise part with it except when they mutually sell family real estate.

Curtesy

Roughly the opposite of dower, **curtesy** gives the husband benefits in his deceased wife's property as long as he lives. However, unlike dower, the wife can defeat those rights in her will. Furthermore, state law may require the couple to have had a child in order for the husband to qualify for curtesy. In some states, husbands are given dower rights rather than curtesy.

Community Property

Ten states (Alaska, Arizona, California, Idaho, Louisiana, Nevada, New Mexico, Texas, Washington, and Wisconsin) subscribe to the legal theory that during marriage each spouse has an equal interest in all property acquired by their joint efforts during the marriage. This jointly produced property is called **community property.** Upon the death of one spouse, one-half of the community property passes to his or her heirs. The other one-half is retained by the surviving spouse. When community property is sold or mortgaged, both spouses should sign the document. Community property rights arise upon marriage (either formal or common law) and terminate upon divorce or death. Community property is discussed at greater length in Chapter 6.

Homestead Protection

Forty-two of the fifty states have passed **homestead** laws, usually with two purposes in mind: (1) to provide some legal protection for the homestead claimants from debts and judgments against them that might result in the forced sale and loss of the home, and (2) to provide a home for a widow, and sometimes a widower, for life. Homestead laws also restrict one spouse from acting without the other when conveying the homestead or using it as collateral for a loan. Dower, curtesy, and community property rights are automatic in those states that have them. In some states the homestead right may require that a written declaration be recorded in the public records. This is not required in Texas, however. Additionally, the "homestead" exemption from forced sale should not be confused with the "homestead exemption," which Texas grants to homeowners in order to reduce their property taxes.

TEXAS HOMESTEAD RIGHTS

In Texas, the homestead right is constitutional and, as a constitutional right, cannot be waived through any contractual agreement or change in state law. Basically, homestead rights are expressed as exemptions from forced sale. All rights vested under the homestead laws are rights secure in the homestead claimant. The independence and security of a home may be enjoyed without the danger of its loss or harassment by reason of the improvidence or misfortune of a head, *or any member,* of the family. That is, the homestead claimant cannot be deprived of the homestead by creditors in the normal course of business. Therefore, a homeowner could own a very expensive house, which falls within the homestead exemption limits, and *no creditor,* regardless of the amount of the debt, could force the homeowner to sell her home to satisfy the debt, except under certain constitutionally specified circumstances.

Article 16, Section 50, of the Texas Constitution specifically states that the homestead of a family, or a single adult person, is protected from forced sale for payment of all debts, with the following exceptions: (1) purchase money mortgages, which secure the payment of the purchase price of the house; (2) taxes; (3) mechanics' and materialmen's liens levied because of construction improvements to the homestead, *if* the improvements were contracted for in writing and signed by the husband and wife before any work was performed in constructing said improvements; (4) federal tax liens of both spouses; (5) refinancing of liens against the homestead; (6) an owelty of partition imposed against the whole for the acquisition of a partial interest; (7) a home equity lien; (8) a reverse mortgage; and (9) real estate liens on mobile homes. There is also court authority that a homestead can be foreclosed on for nonpayment of subdivision maintenance fund liens.

The homestead may not be conveyed without the consent of the spouse.

Protection Is Automatic

There is no official document one must sign to create homestead rights. The fact that the realty is in the possession of the owner and that the owner resides upon it as his principal residence makes it the homestead of the family in law and in fact. Additionally, even if the homestead is not occupied by the owner, the intent of making it the owner's homestead, accompanied by circumstances manifesting said intention, is enough to vest the homestead character of the property and make the exemption rights applicable to it. There must be a declaration of homestead, however, in order to get the benefit of certain tax exemptions provided for under state and county taxing authorities. However, this declaration is not required to create homestead rights. Note that in both situations only one property (the principal residence) can be claimed as a homestead.

Once the homestead rights have vested in a certain parcel of real property, it maintains its homestead character during the entire life of the occupant and loses its homestead character only by (1) death, (2) abandonment, or (3) alienation (subsequent sale).

Whereas death and alienation are self-explanatory, abandonment is a fact question. Abandonment of a homestead property cannot be accomplished by mere intention. There must be a discontinuance of use of the property coupled with an intention not to use it again as a home before it constitutes abandonment.

Homestead Limitations

There are limits established as to the homestead, however, depending on the type of homestead exemption one wishes to claim. The Constitution of Texas states that a **rural homestead** for married claimants consists of not more than 200 acres of land, which may be in one or more parcels, with the improvements thereon. If more than 200 acres is owned, the owner may designate which 200 acres constitutes the homestead, so long as the designated 200 acres do contain the owner's home. A state statute limits the homestead of a single person to only 100 acres.

An **urban homestead** is a homestead in a city, town, or village and can consist of a lot or lots amounting to not more than 10 acres of land, together with any improvement on the land. The 10 acres must be contiguous. The urban homestead can consist of both a business and a residential homestead, provided that the amount of both homestead claims does not exceed 10 acres. The value of the improvements has no bearing whatsoever in the homestead designation. The temporary renting of a homestead does not change the character of the homestead when no other homestead has been acquired; and, even if another house had been acquired, there must have been sufficient abandonment of the previous homestead before the homestead rights vest in the newly acquired home.

Homestead rights are constitutional and can be changed only by constitutional amendment, ratified by the voters of the State of Texas.

Home Equity Liens

In 1997 Texas passed a constitutional amendment to allow home equity loans in Texas. This proposal is very restrictive, allowing for only *one* such loan at a time, with no personal liability, without prepayment penalty, that cannot be called (accelerated) because of the home's decrease in market value. The amendment allows the homeowner a *3-day* right to rescind, and allows many other protections for consumers. They will be discussed in greater detail in a later chapter.

FREEHOLD ESTATES

In a carryover from the old English court system, estates in land are classified as either **freehold estates** or **leasehold estates.** The main difference is that freehold estate cases are tried under real property laws, whereas leasehold (also called non freehold or less-than-freehold) estates are tried under personal property laws.

The two distinguishing features of a freehold estate are the following: (1) there must be actual ownership of the land, and (2) the estate must be of unpredictable duration. Fee estates, life estates, and estates created by statute are freehold estates.

LEASEHOLD ESTATES

The distinguishing features of a leasehold estate are (1) although there is possession of the land, there is no ownership; and (2) the estate is of definite duration.

As previously noted, the user of a property need not be its owner. Under a lease-hold estate, the user is called the **lessee** or **tenant,** and the person from whom he leases is the **lessor** or **landlord.** As long as the tenant has a valid lease, abides by it, and pays the rent on time, the owner, even though he owns the property, cannot occupy it until the lease has expired. During the lease period, the freehold estate owner is said to hold a **reversionary interest.** This is his right to recover possession at the end of the lease period. Meanwhile, the lease is an encumbrance against the property.

There are four categories of leasehold estates: (1) estate for years; (2) periodic estate; (3) estate at will; and (4) tenancy at sufferance. Note that in this chapter, we will be examining leases primarily from the standpoint of estates in land. Leases as financing tools are discussed in Chapter 15, and lease contracts are covered in Chapter 18.

Estate for Years

Also called a tenancy for years, the **estate for years** is somewhat misleadingly named because it implies that a lease for a number of years has been created. Actually, the key criterion is that the lease has a specific starting time and a specific ending time. It can be for any length of time, ranging from less than a day to many years. An estate for years does not automatically renew itself. Neither the landlord nor the tenant must act to terminate it, because the lease agreement itself specifies a termination date.

Usually the lessor is the freehold estate owner. However, the lessor could be a lessee. To illustrate, a fee owner leases property to a lessee, who, in turn, leases the right to another person. By doing this, the first lessee has become a **sublessor** and is said to hold a **sublease.** The person who then leases is a **sublessee.** It is important to realize that in no case can a sublessee acquire from the lessee any more rights than the lessee has under the lease. Thus, if a lessee has a five-year lease with three years remaining, only the remaining three years or a portion of that can be subleased to the sublessee.

Periodic Estate

Also called an estate from year-to-year or a periodic tenancy, a **periodic estate** has an original lease period with a fixed length; when it runs out, unless the tenant or his landlord acts to terminate it, renewal is automatic for another like period of time. A month-to-month apartment rental is an example of this arrangement. To avoid last-minute confusion, rental agreements usually require that advance notice be given if either the landlord or the tenant wishes to terminate the tenancy.

Estate at Will

Also called a tenancy at will, an **estate at will** is a landlord-tenant relationship with all the normal rights and duties of a lessor-lessee relationship, except that the estate may be terminated by either the lessor or the lessee at anytime. However, most states recognize the inconvenience a literal interpretation of "anytime" can cause and require that reasonable advance notice be given.

Tenancy at Sufferance

A **tenancy at sufferance** occurs when a tenant stays beyond legal tenancy without the consent of the landlord. In other words, the tenant wrongfully holds the property against the owner's wishes. In a tenancy at sufferance, the tenant is commonly called a **holdover tenant,** although once he stays beyond his legal tenancy he is not actually a tenant in the normal landlord-tenant sense. The landlord is entitled to evict him and recover possession of the property, provided the landlord does so in a timely manner. A tenant at sufferance differs from a trespasser only in that his original entry was rightful. If, during the holdover period, the tenant pays and the landlord accepts rent, the tenancy at sufferance changes to a periodic estate.

SUBSURFACE RIGHTS

In Texas, oil and mineral rights are subsurface estates in real estate and occupy a unique position. Once the subsurface rights have been leased or conveyed, there is an immediate conflict of rights as to surface control. The subsurface mineral owner has the dominant estate in Texas; that is, an owner of mineral rights has the right, unless otherwise specified, to reasonably enter upon any property to extract the minerals to which he holds a fee or leasehold estate. A mineral owner or lessee may waive these rights by relinquishing surface control of the property so that the surface estate owner can develop his property without worry of interference from the subsurface interest below.

This has become a key issue in residential real estate in some areas of the state. Oil and gas reserves have been discovered in paying quantities (the price of oil and gas has increased dramatically) in areas that may be under existing subdivisions. In those cases, the oil company must contact every owner in the subdivision regarding their respective interest in the oil rights. Oil and gas rights are complicated. The Texas Real Estate Commission has recently promulgated a new addendum to the contract forms to provide for this contingency.

Any rights to the subsurface oil, gas, or minerals are always subject to prior notices of record, local land use legislation and regulation, and any other prior existing interests that may affect the surface estate as well as the subsurface estate. Therefore, one could assume that any oil, gas, or mineral rights acquired after the property has been deed restricted would be subject to those deed restrictions, and owners of any oil, gas, and mineral rights within a municipality that has an ordinance against drilling would probably not be allowed to drill without a special permit from the city's governing body.

Although the oil or minerals in the ground are considered real property, once they are extracted from the ground they become personalty. Texas courts have held that once oil and minerals are extracted from the ground and then later injected into the ground for storage purposes, the oil and minerals still maintain their character as personal property and do not revert to real estate.

PUTTING IT TO WORK

It is important for a developer in Texas to recognize that even though he has built on a parcel of land, the mineral estate owner has the right to extract his mineral interests, regardless of the nuisance or inconvenience to the subsequent property owner. This may create a serious problem in subdivision property or fully developed property where the mineral rights have not been waived, or surface control has not been relinquished by the mineral estate owner.

LICENSE

A **license** is not a right or an estate in land, but a personal privilege given to someone to use land. It is nonassignable and can be canceled by the person who issues it. A license to park is typically what an automobile parking lot operator provides for persons parking in her lot. The contract creating the license is usually written on the stub that the lot attendant gives the driver, or it is posted on a sign on the lot. Tickets to theaters and sporting events also fall into this category. Because it is merely a personal privilege, a license is not an encumbrance against land.

CHATTELS

A ***chattel*** is an article of personal property. Chattels are divided into two categories: chattels personal and chattels real. Examples of **chattels personal** are automobiles, clothes, food, and furniture. **Chattels real** are interests in real estate that remain personal property; for example, a contract for the purchase of real estate or a lease. In the United States, chattels are governed by personal property laws. Freehold estates are governed by real property laws.

PICTORIAL SUMMARY

Let's conclude this chapter by combining what has been discussed in Chapter 3 regarding the physical nature of land with what has been covered in this chapter regarding estates and rights in land. The results, diagrammed in Figure 4.5, show why real estate is both complicated and exciting. A single parcel of land can be divided into subsurface, surface, and air-space components, and each of these carries its own fee simple bundle of rights, which can be divided into the various estates and rights discussed in this chapter.

To more clearly convey this idea, let us turn our attention to Figure 4.5. In Parcel A, the fee landowner has leased the bulk of her surface and air rights, plus the right to draw water from her wells, to a farmer for the production of crops and livestock. This leaves the fee owner with the right to lease or sell subterranean rights for mineral, oil, and gas extraction. With a single parcel of land, the fee owner has created two estates, one for farming and another for oil and gas production. With the minor exception of the placement of the well platforms, pumps, and

FIGURE 4.5 Cross section of estates and rights in land

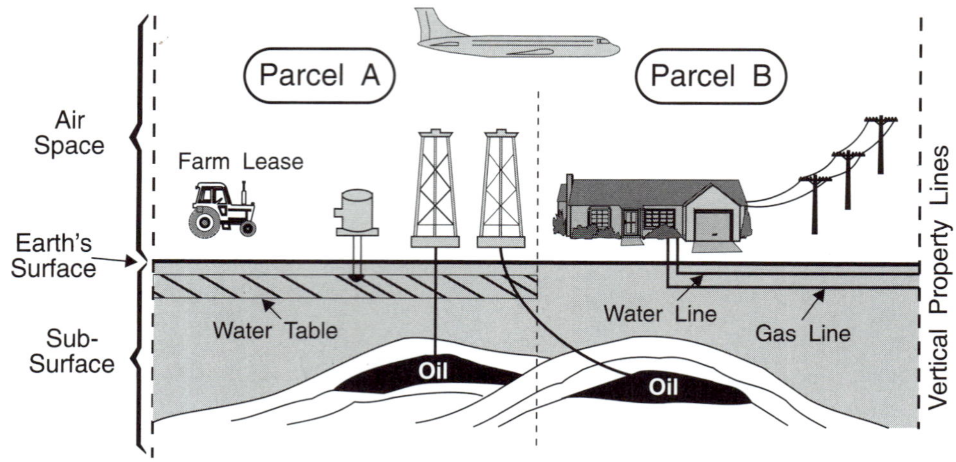

Source: © 2012 Cengage Learning

pipes, neither use interferes with the other and both bring income to the landowner. The farmer, in turn, can personally use the leasehold estate he possesses or sublease it to another farmer. The oil company, if it has leased its rights, can sublease them; if it has purchased them, it can sell or lease them. A variation would be for an oil company to buy the land in fee, conduct its drilling operations, and lease the remainder to a farmer. In the public interest, the government has claimed the right to allow aircraft to fly over the land. Although technically a landowner owns from the center of the earth out to the heavens, the right given to an aircraft to fly overhead creates a practical limit on that ownership.

OVERVIEW OF RIGHTS AND INTERESTS IN THE LAND

Figure 4.6 provides an overview of the various rights and interests in land that are discussed in this chapter and the previous chapter. This chart is designed to give you an overall perspective of what the term **real estate** includes.

FIGURE 4.6 Rights and interests in land

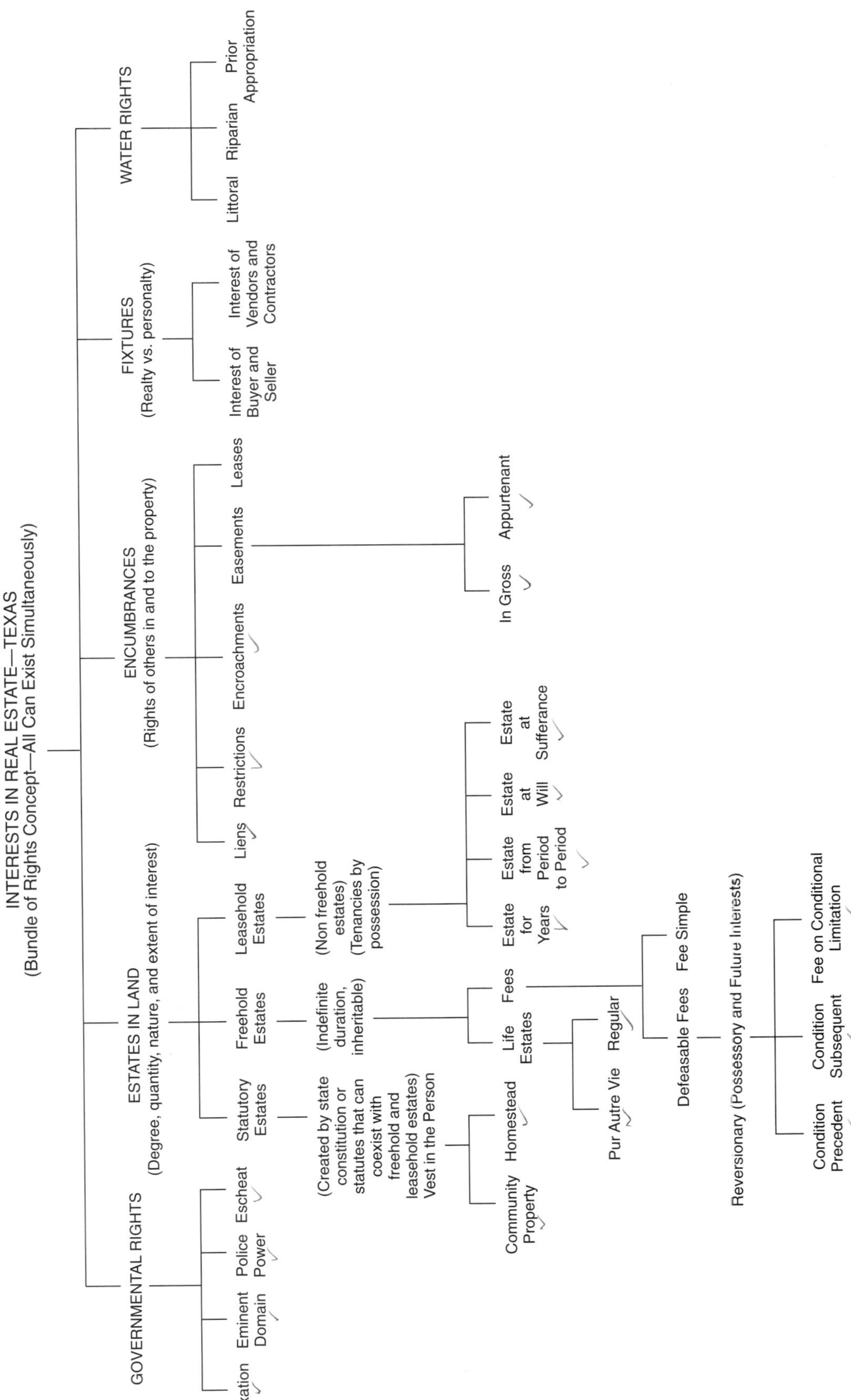

Source: © 2012 Cengage Learning

REVIEW QUESTIONS

Answers to these questions are found in the Answer Key section at the back of the book.

1. The system under which individuals are given the right to own land is known as the
   A. feudal system.
   B. allodial system.
   C. chattel system.
   D. fee system.

2. By which of the following processes may a government acquire ownership of privately held land?
   A. Condemnation
   B. Taxation
   C. Police power
   D. Escheat
   E. Both A and D

3. The right of the government to place reasonable restrictions on the use of privately held land is known as
   A. a restrictive covenant.
   B. police power.
   C. escheat.
   D. estate.

4. Which of the following is NOT an example of a government's exercise of its police power?
   A. Rent controls
   B. Building codes
   C. Zoning laws
   D. Restrictive covenants

5. Property owned by a person who dies intestate and without heirs will escheat to the
   A. city.
   B. county.
   C. state.
   D. federal government.

6. A property owner who holds fee simple title to land will have all of the following "sticks" in his bundle of rights EXCEPT the right to:
   A. occupy and use it.
   B. restrict the use of the land.
   C. devise it by will.
   D. violate building, health, and safety codes.

7. The term "estate" refers to
   A. the quantity of land as shown on a plat of the property.
   B. one's legal rights in the land.
   C. both A and B.
   D. neither A nor B.

8. All of the following constitute an encumbrance on the fee simple title to real property EXCEPT
   A. a will conveying the property to the owner's heirs upon death of the owner.
   B. a restrictive covenant in the deed to the property.
   C. a mortgage.
   D. a lease.

9. Which of the following easements could be created without a written document?
   A. An easement by necessity
   B. An easement by prescription
   C. Both A and B
   D. Neither A nor B

10. An easement is
  A. an appurtenance to the holder of the dominant tenement.
  B. an encumbrance to the holder of the servient tenement.
  C. both A and B.
  D. neither A nor B.

11. Morris sold the back half of her lot to Katz and gave Katz a permanent easement across her land in order for Katz to have access to the road. Which of the following statements is true?
  A. The easement is an easement in gross.
  B. The easement is an easement appurtenant.
  C. The servient estate is held by Katz.
  D. The dominant estate is held by Morris.

12. An easement appurtenant may NOT be terminated
  A. by combination of the dominant and servient tenements.
  B. when the purpose for the easement no longer exists.
  C. by lack of use.
  D. unilaterally by the holder of the servient tenement.

13. All of the following may constitute a lien on real property EXCEPT:
  A. a mortgage.
  B. unpaid real property taxes.
  C. a restrictive covenant in a deed.
  D. a judgment against the owner.

14. Which of the following are examples of specific liens?
  A. Mechanic's liens
  B. Judgment liens
  C. Property tax liens
  D. Federal income tax liens
  E. Both A and C

15. Which of the following is NOT classified as a freehold estate?
  A. An estate created by statute
  B. A life estate
  C. A fee simple estate
  D. A leasehold estate

16. Real estate held as a leasehold
  A. is used by the owner rather than by the tenant.
  B. reverts to the tenant upon termination of the lease.
  C. both A and B.
  D. neither A nor B.

17. Unless the landlord or tenant acts to terminate it, an estate from period-to-period
  A. automatically renews itself.
  B. continues for an indefinite time.
  C. both A and B.
  D. neither A nor B.

18. The lessor holds a reversion in which of the following situations?
  A. Estate for years
  B. Periodic estate
  C. Estate at will
  D. Tenancy at sufferance
  E. All of the above

19. A tenant at sufferance is
  A. a legal tenant.
  B. a trespasser.
  C. a licensee.
  D. a guest.

20. A chattel is
  A. an item of personal property.
  B. an item of real property such as a building.
  C. a freehold estate in land.
  D. a term that refers to land used for cattle ranching.

Chapter 5

KEY TERMS

Americans with Disabilities Act (ADA): a federal law giving disabled individuals the right to access commercial facilities open to the public

Block busting: the illegal practice of inducing panic selling in a neighborhood for financial gain

Community Reinvestment Act: a federal statute encouraging federally regulated lenders to participation in low-income areas

Familial status: one or more individuals under the age of 18 who are domiciled with a parent or other person having custody

Handicapped: having a physical or mental impairment that substantially limits one or more life activities, or having a record of such impairment

Protected class: a class of people that by law are protected from discrimination

Steering: the practice of directing home seekers to particular neighborhoods based on race, color, religion, sex, national origin, handicapped, or adults-only status

Tester: an individual or organization that responds to or tests for compliance with fair housing laws

Texas Fair Housing Act: a Texas statute enforcing federal and state guidelines against discrimination

Fair Housing, ADA, Equal Credit, and Community Reinvestment

IN THIS CHAPTER

This chapter concentrates on federal and state legislation that has had a strong impact on expanding the ability of individuals to own real estate. The concept of fair housing prohibits discrimination in the purchase of real property. Equal credit has made lending sources available for thousands who could not previously qualify for loans. The Community Reinvestment Act encourages lenders to make loans in disadvantaged areas.

It is almost impossible to fully explain the effects of federal legislation on real estate over the last 30 years. The scope and effect of the changes resulting from federal legislation is felt daily and has touched virtually every aspect of the real estate business. The federal government's emphasis on protection of individual rights was imposed because many states found this goal politically difficult to pursue, and in many cases a long history of prejudice was an overwhelming obstacle.

Federal legislation has been liberally applied to virtually all areas of discrimination—race, color, creed, national origin, alienage, sex, marital status, age, familial status, and handicapped status. The theories supporting these federal laws are applied differently though, depending on the source of the law and enforcement of the applicable statute. Let's review these theories in greater detail.

CONSTITUTIONAL IMPACT ON OWNERSHIP OF REAL PROPERTY

The most fundamental rights in real property are obtained in the U.S. Constitution. These rights are so firmly established and so broadly affect real estate that they deserve discussion at the outset. The Declaration of Independence declared that all [people] are created equal and set the stage for an attitude of the government that we enjoy in the United States. It was with this forethought that our founders wrote the United States Constitution that instilled in all citizens certain inalienable rights of which they can never be deprived. As far as real property ownership is concerned, the most significant of these rights are stated in the Fifth, Fourteenth, and Thirteenth Amendments to the Constitution.

The Fifth Amendment clearly states that no person shall "... be deprived of life, liberty, or property without due process of law...." It was from this fundamental statement that we have developed the inherent right that nobody can have their property taken from them without court proceedings. This concept has been expanded over the last 40 years or so to include the prohibition of certain types of discrimination, creating certain ***protected classes*** of people who may not be discriminated against (denied housing because of one's race, for instance).

To date, the types of discrimination that have been deemed "suspect" and unconstitutional by the United States Supreme Court have included discrimination on the basis of race, color, religion, national origin, and alienage. *Everyone* is entitled to own property. This is logical. A citizen of the United States cannot alter his race, color, national origin, or alienage, and is entitled to practice the religion of his choice. Very strict constitutional prohibitions have been established by the courts to eliminate this type of discrimination for any citizen in the United States. It should be emphasized that there is no *constitutional* prohibition of discrimination on the basis of sex, age, or marital status.

One of the most significant areas of litigation has been based on racial discrimination. This has been applied to all federal enforcement through the Fifth Amendment and to state and individual actions through the Thirteenth and Fourteenth Amendments to the Constitution.

The Fourteenth Amendment prohibits any state (as distinguished from the federal government) from depriving a person of life, liberty, or property without due process of law, and prohibits any state from denying any person within its jurisdiction the equal protection of the laws. The significant case in interpreting the Fourteenth Amendment as it applies to the states was *Shelley* v. *Kraemer*. In this Supreme Court case, some white property owners were attempting to enforce a deed restriction that required that all property owners must be Caucasian. The state courts granted the relief sought. The Supreme Court, however, reversed the case, stating that the action of state courts in enforcing the restrictions deprives parties of their substantive right, without due process of law, to have access to housing. The Court stated that equality and the enjoyment of property rights were regarded by the framers of the Fourteenth Amendment as an essential precondition to realization of other basic civil rights and liberties that the Fourteenth Amendment was intended to guarantee. Therefore, it was concluded that the "equal protection" clause of the Fourteenth Amendment should prohibit the judicial enforcement by state courts of restrictive covenants based on race or color.

The Thirteenth Amendment to the United States Constitution prohibits slavery and involuntary servitude. This amendment formed the basis for the most significant landmark case on discrimination, *Jones* v. *Alfred H. Mayer Company*. That case basically held that any form of discrimination, even by individuals, creates a "badge of slavery" that in turn results in the violation of the Thirteenth Amendment. The Supreme Court stated that in enforcing the Civil Rights Act of 1866, Congress is empowered under the Thirteenth Amendment to secure to all citizens the right to buy whatever a white man can buy and the right to live wherever a white man can live. The Court further stated, "If Congress cannot say that being a free man means at least this much, then the Thirteenth Amendment has a promise the Nation cannot keep." This case effectively prohibits discrimination of all types and is applicable to real estate transactions.

FAIR HOUSING LAWS

In addition to the constitutional issues, two major federal laws prohibit discrimination in housing. The first is the *Civil Rights Act of 1866*. It states that, "All citizens of the United States shall have the same right in every State and Territory, as is enjoyed by the white citizens thereof to inherit, purchase, lease, sell, hold, and convey real and personal property." In 1968, the Supreme Court affirmed that the 1866 Act prohibits "all racial discrimination, private as well as public, in the sale of real property." The second is the *Fair Housing Law,* officially known as Title VIII of the Civil Rights Act of 1968, as amended. This law makes it illegal to discriminate on the basis of race, color, religion, sex, national origin, physical handicap, or familial status in connection with the sale or rental of housing and any vacant land offered for residential construction or use.

There are three ways that a Fair Housing Act violation can be proven. The first is obvious, an intentional discrimination against someone in a protected class, such as: "I refuse to sell to the Irish." The second requires that a regulation, while appearing neutral, creates a discriminatory impact. For instance, a "one bedroom/single occupant" restriction that effectively eliminates occupancy by families or children has a discriminatory impact, even though it isn't specifically set out in the restriction. The third way a fair housing violation can be proven is if the owner fails to "reasonably accommodate" members of a protected class. For instance, if an occupant develops a disability, the owner or landlord must attempt to reasonably accommodate that occupant's needs. Once a fair housing violation has been demonstrated, the burden shifts to the defendant to produce evidence that shows the defendant's conduct was for a legitimate, nondiscriminatory purpose. If the owner can prove that, there is no fair housing violation.

Understanding that one cannot discriminate on the basis of race, color, religion, national origin, and sex (gender) seems fundamental today. In 1988, the president signed an amendment to the Civil Rights Act of 1968. It expands the Act to provide for housing for the handicapped as well as people with children under the age of 18. The Act now provides protection for any form of discrimination based on race, color, religion, national origin, sex, familial status, or handicapped status. The law's application is very broad, and needs to be discussed in more detail.

Handicapped

The amendment defines ***handicapped*** as:

1. Having a physical or mental impairment that substantially limits one or more major life activities.
2. Having a record of having such an impairment.
3. Being regarded as having such an impairment.

This includes recovered mental patients as well as those who are presently suffering from a mental handicap.

This legislation has changed our attitude about certain restrictions. It is assumed, for instance, that a blind person can live with a guide dog in a housing project that prohibits pets. The handicapped are also allowed to make reasonable modifications to existing units, as long as it is at the handicapped's expense. The handicapped renter must also restore the unit to its original use upon termination of occupancy. The law also makes it unlawful for a landlord or owner to refuse to make reasonable accommodations, rules, policies, practices, or services when it is necessary to afford a handicapped person an equal opportunity to use and enjoy the dwelling. In addition, all new multifamily dwellings with four or more units must be constructed to allow access and use by handicapped persons. If the building has no elevators, only first floor units are covered by this provision. Doors and hallways in the buildings must be wide enough to accommodate wheelchairs. Light switches and other controls must be in convenient locations. Most rooms and spaces must be on an accessible route, and special accommodations such as grab bars in the bathrooms must be provided.

There are some exceptions under the handicapped person provision. The term *handicapped* for instance, does not include current illegal use of or addiction to a controlled substance, but it *does* include recovering addicts. Handicapped status also does not include any person whose tenancy imposes a direct threat to the health, safety, and property of others.

Since the statute was enacted, some cases have held that recovering drug addicts and alcoholics are handicapped, as are people infected with the HIV virus. Therefore, they cannot be discriminated against, and denial of housing as a result of this "handicap" is a violation of the Fair Housing Act. This may result in unusual situations in which recovering drug addicts (perhaps criminals) could be moving into a neighborhood and the neighbors are prohibited from discriminating against them or denying them housing (by enforcing deed restrictions or zoning ordinances) because it would have a discriminatory effect on the handicapped.

Familial Status

Familial status is defined as one or more individuals (who have not obtained the age of 18 years) being domiciled with a parent or another person having legal custody of such individual or individuals or the designee of such parent or other person having such custody, with the written permission of such parent or other person. These protections also apply to any person who is pregnant or in the process of securing legal custody of any individual who has not obtained the age of 18 years.

The most significant effect of this amendment is that all homeowner association property, apartment projects, and condominiums now have to have facilities adapted for children and cannot discriminate against anyone on the basis of familial status when leasing, selling, or renting property.

There are also specific exemptions to this portion of the Act. A building can qualify for an exemption if it: (1) provides housing under the state or federal program that the Secretary of Housing and Urban Development determines is specifically designed and operated to assist elderly persons; (2) provides housing intended for, and is generally occupied only by, persons 62 years of age or older; or (3) provides housing generally intended and operated for at least one person 55 years of age or older per unit and at least 80% of the occupied units are occupied by at least one person who is 55 years of age or older; and (4) meets certain policies, rules, and regulations that are adopted by the Secretary of Housing and Urban Development. There is often confusion over whether or not housing for the elderly is truly that. A large number of housing projects that primarily house the elderly do not qualify under the two exemptions under the Fair Housing Act. If a person is genuinely concerned about not having children around, they need to determine whether or not the housing project qualifies under the familial status exemption.

The penalties for violation of the Act are severe. The first violation of the Act results in a fine of not more than $50,000, and for subsequent violations a fine of not more than $100,000. The fines are in addition to other civil damages, potential injunctions, reasonable attorney's fees, and costs.

These amendments to the Fair Housing Law have a significant impact for all licensees attempting to sell, list, lease, or rent real estate. It is unlawful to refuse to sell or rent or to refuse to negotiate the sale or rental of any property based on familial status or handicapped status. Any printing and advertising cannot make any reference to preference based on handicapped or familial status. As stated previously, the landlord cannot deny the right of a handicapped tenant to make any changes in the physical structure of the building provided that the tenant agrees to reinstate the building back to its original form when leaving.

It is safe to say that many circumstances that may occur have not been specifically addressed by the statute. It is critically important that licensees recognize these two new prohibitions against discrimination and deem them just as serious violations of an individual's civil rights as are more traditional theories of race, color, religion, national origin, and sex. The difficulty, though, is that a real estate agent cannot tell if a person is handicapped (a recovering drug addict, for instance) or has children, unless the agent inquires. So it is prudent to inquire, *then* handle their requests. Otherwise one could violate the Act without knowing it.

Specifically, what do these two federal statutes prohibit, and what do they allow? The 1968 Fair Housing Law provides protection against the following acts if they discriminate against one or more of the protected classes:

1. Refusing to sell or rent to, deal or negotiate with any person.
2. Discriminating in the terms or conditions for buying or renting housing.
3. Discriminating by advertising that housing is available only to persons of a certain race, color, religion, sex, national origin, those who are not handicapped, or adults only.
4. Denying that housing is available for inspection, sale, or rent when it really is available.
5. Denying or making different terms or conditions for home loans by commercial lenders.
6. Denying to anyone the use of or participation in any real estate services, such as brokers' organizations, multiple listing services, or other facilities related to the selling or renting of housing.
7. Steering or block busting.

Steering

Steering is the practice of directing home seekers to particular neighborhoods based on race, color, religion, sex, national origin, nonhandicapped, or adult-only housing. Steering includes efforts to exclude minority members from one area of a city as well as to direct them to minority or changing areas. Examples include showing only certain neighborhoods, slanting property descriptions, and downgrading neighborhoods. Steering is often subtle, sometimes no more than a word, phrase, or facial expression. Nonetheless, steering accounts for the bulk of the complaints filed against real estate licensees under the Fair Housing Act.

A new issue has arisen, sometimes referred to as benign steering. In these situations, a buyer may request a particular neighborhood based on race, culture, or diversity (i.e., a purchaser may request a neighborhood that is "ethnically diverse") and request that he be taken there. How can a licensee or an agent take them to a chosen neighborhood without running the risk of steering? At least one case has indicated that when a buyer requests a particular neighborhood based on diversity, race, culture, or other discriminatory reasons, the agent should simply not respond to these questions. No matter what the response is, it could be misconstrued by the other party and deemed by a court to be a discriminatory practice. Therefore, a better procedure seems to be to never answer the questions relating to potential discriminatory practice.

Block Busting

Block busting is the illegal practice of inducing panic selling in a neighborhood for financial gain. Block busting typically starts when one person induces another to sell property cheaply by stating that an impending change in the racial or religious composition of the neighborhood will cause property values to fall, school quality to decline, and crime to increase. The first home thus acquired is sold (at a mark-up) to a minority member. This event is used to reinforce fears that the neighborhood is indeed changing. The process quickly snowballs as residents panic and sell at progressively lower prices. The homes are then resold at higher prices to incoming residents.

Note that block busting is not limited to fears over people moving into a neighborhood. In a Virginia case, a real estate firm attempted to gain listings in a certain neighborhood by playing upon residents' fears regarding an upcoming expressway project.

Housing Covered by the Fair Housing Law

The Fair Housing Law applies to the following types of housing:

1. Single-family houses owned by private individuals when (1) a real estate broker or other person in the business of selling or renting dwellings is used, and/or (2) discriminatory advertising is used.
2. Single-family houses not owned by private individuals.
3. Single-family houses owned by a private individual who owns more than three such houses or who, in any two-year period, sells more than one in which the individual was not the most recent resident.
4. Multifamily dwellings of five or more units.
5. Multifamily dwellings containing four or fewer units, if the owner does not reside in one of the units.

Acts Not Prohibited by the Fair Housing Law

Not covered by the Fair Housing Law are the sale or rental of single-family houses owned by a private individual who owns three or fewer such single-family houses if (1) a broker is not used, (2) discriminatory advertising is not used, and (3) no more than one house in which the owner was not the most recent resident is sold during any two-year period. Not covered by the 1968 Act are rentals of rooms or units in owner-occupied multidwellings for two to four families, if discriminatory advertising is not used. The Act also does not cover the sale, rental, or occupancy of dwellings that a religious organization owns or operates for other than a commercial purpose to persons of the same religion, if membership in that religion is not restricted on account of race, color, or national origin. It also does not cover the rental or occupancy of lodgings that a private club owns or operates for its members for other than a commercial purpose. Housing for the elderly may also allow discrimination in not permitting children or young adult occupants in the development or building, provided that the housing is primarily intended for the elderly, has minimum age requirements (55 or 62), and meets certain HUD guidelines.

Note, however, that the above listed acts *not* prohibited by the Fair Housing Law *are* prohibited by the 1866 Civil Rights Act when discrimination based on race occurs in connection with such acts.

Fair Housing Enforcement

Adherence to the 1968 Act can be enforced in any of three ways by someone who feels discriminated against. The first is to file a written complaint with the Department of Housing and Urban Development (HUD) in Washington, D.C. The second is to file court action directly in a U.S. District Court or state or local court. The third is to file a complaint with the U.S. Attorney General. If a complaint is filed, HUD may: investigate to see if the law has been broken; attempt to resolve the problem by conference, conciliation, or persuasion; refer the matter to a state or local fair housing authority; or recommend that the complaint be filed in court. If HUD finds that a Fair Housing violation has occurred, it will schedule a hearing before a HUD administrative law judge, where the defendant is given the opportunity to explain the justification for the discrimination charge. Either party, the complainant or the defendant, can cause the HUD scheduled administrative proceeding to be terminated, if they elect to have the matter litigated in federal court instead. HUD has a "complaints" section on its website, at http://www.hud.gov/complaints/housediscrim.cfm. A person seeking enforcement of the 1866 Act must file a suit in a federal court.

No matter which route is taken, the burden of proving illegal discrimination under the 1968 Act is the responsibility of the person filing the complaint. If successful, the following remedies are available: (1) an injunction to stop the sale or rental of the property to someone else making it available to the complainant, (2) money for actual damages caused by the discrimination, (3) punitive damages, and (4) court costs. There are also criminal penalties for those who coerce, intimidate, threaten, or interfere with a person's buying, renting, or selling of housing.

Agent's Duties

A real estate agent's duties are to uphold the Fair Housing Law and the 1866 Civil Rights Act. If a property owner asks an agent to discriminate, the agent must refuse to accept the listing. An agent is in violation of fair housing laws by giving a minority buyer or seller less than favorable treatment or by ignoring or referring this individual to an agent of the same minority. Violation also occurs when an agent fails to use best efforts or does not submit an offer because of race, color, religion, sex, national origin, physical handicap, or occupancy by children.

Testers

From time to time a licensee may be approached by fair housing ***testers***. These are individuals or organizations that respond to advertising and visit real estate offices to test for compliance with fair housing laws. The tester does not announce himself or herself as such or ask if the office follows fair housing practices. Rather, the tester plays the role of a person looking for housing to buy or rent and observes whether or not fair housing laws are being followed. If not followed, the tester lodges a complaint with the appropriate fair housing agency. Additional information on fair housing is available through the Internet on http://www.hud.gov.

TEXAS FAIR HOUSING LAW

In 1989, Texas passed the ***Texas Fair Housing Act***, which in most respects parallels the Federal Fair Housing Law. The statute creates a Commission on Human Rights that is authorized to receive, investigate, and seek to conciliate any active complaints violating the Texas Fair Housing Act. The Commission must investigate discriminatory housing practices if the complaints filed are: (1) in writing, (2) under oath, and (3) in the form prescribed by the Commission, not later than one year after the discriminatory housing practice has occurred or terminated, whichever is later. On the filing of a complaint, the Commission shall give the aggrieved person notice that the complaint has been received, and notify the respondent of the alleged discriminatory housing practice. The respondent may then file an answer that must also be: (1) in writing, (2) under oath, and (3) in the form prescribed by the Commission. The Commission is then required to investigate the complaint and to encourage conciliation if possible. If the Commission concludes that prompt judicial action is necessary, it shall file an investigative report to the Attorney General, who shall then file an action on behalf of the aggrieved person in district court and seek relief from the alleged discriminatory housing practice that has occurred.

It should also be kept in mind that other states, as well as local jurisdictions (cities or counties), may have more restrictive statutes or ordinances regarding discrimination. For example, it some states it is illegal to discriminate on the basis of obesity, presence of children, sexual orientation, and welfare status. The important thing to remember is that the more restrictive statute or ordinance will control.

Enforcement by Private Persons

A person may also file a civil action in district court not later than the second year after the occurrence or the termination of an alleged discriminatory housing practice; or the breach of a conciliation agreement entered into under the Texas Fair Housing Act, whichever occurs last; or to obtain relief of the breach or discriminatory housing practice. If the court finds that discriminatory practice has occurred or is about to occur, the court may award to the plaintiff actual and punitive damages, reasonable attorney's fees and court costs, and a permanent or temporary injunction.

Criminal Penalties

The Texas Fair Housing Act also provides criminal penalties for a person who commits an offense under the Act by force or threat of force, or who intentionally intimidates or interferes with a person because of race, color, religion, sex, handicap, familial status, or national origin. The offense is a Class A misdemeanor.

THE AMERICANS WITH DISABILITIES ACT

The ***Americans with Disabilities Act (ADA)*** was enacted in 1992 and deals primarily with commercial property. Generally stated, it provides access requirements and prohibits discrimination against people with disabilities in public accommodations, state and local government, transportation, telecommunications, and employment. Anyone who has, or is "perceived" as having, a physical or mental handicap such that it interferes with a "major life activity" is covered by the Act.

The Act specifically affects the real estate brokerage industry in that real estate licensees need to determine whether or not the product the licensee is selling, managing, or leasing is in compliance with the Act. A licensee should always be cautioned, however, that the statute is very detailed and that a number of gray areas still lack clear interpretation.

Scope

The antidiscrimination and removal of barrier requirements of the ADA apply to "places of public accommodations," and the accessibility requirements of the ADA with respect to new construction and alterations apply to public accommodations and "commercial facilities."

"Places of public accommodations" encompasses 12 categories of retail and service businesses, including places of lodging; food and drink establishments; places of exhibitionary entertainment; places of public gathering; sales and rental establishments; services establishments such as law firms, accounting firms, and banks; public transportation stations; places of public display or collection; places of recreation; educational facilities; social service center establishments; and exercise clubs. It is presumed that this definition includes brokerage offices, even if they are located in private homes.

"Commercial facility" is defined as a facility (1) whose operations affect commerce, (2) that is intended for nonresidential use, and (3) that is not a facility expressly exempted from coverage under the Fair Housing Act of 1968.

The ADA contains a broad prohibition affecting public accommodations; it prohibits discriminating against those with disabilities by denying them the full and equal enjoyment of goods, services, facilities, privileges, advantages, and the accommodations of any place of public accommodation. Facilities need to be usable by those with disabilities.

All commercial facilities must also be accessible to the maximum extent feasible whenever alterations are being performed on the facility. Alteration is defined as any change that affects the usability of a facility. If the alterations are made to a lobby or work area of the public accommodation, a path of travel to the altered area and to the bathrooms, telephones, and drinking fountains serving that area must be made accessible to the extent that the added accessibility costs are not disproportionate to the overall cost of the original alteration. Disproportionate cost is defined for the purposes of the Act as costs that exceed 20% of the original alteration. The cost of alteration means all costs, and renovating in particular, in proportion to the facility in a three-year period.

The Act requires modifications to procedures so that disabled individuals are not excluded from regular programs. Places of public accommodations must make reasonable modifications to the policies and procedures in order to accommodate individuals with disabilities and not create restrictions that tend to screen out individuals with disabilities, such as requiring a person to produce a driver's license or not allowing more than one person in a clothes changing area when a disabled person needs the assistance of another. The Act also requires auxiliary aids and services to ensure effective communication with individuals with hearing, vision, or speech impairments. These requirements would include interpreters, listening headsets, television closed caption decoders, telecommunication devices for the deaf, video tech displays, braille materials, and large print materials.

Several defenses and exclusions are available under the Act, but most are extremely narrow in scope. In addition, there are few court precedents to help us interpret the ADA. Problems in compliance will occur. For example, if a water fountain is placed low enough for someone in a wheelchair to use, what happens to the tall person who has difficulty in bending? Lowering a fire extinguisher for easier access to the person in the wheelchair also gives easier access to small children. Something that is "child proof" will also be inaccessible to someone with limited use of their hands.

Both the Department of Justice and private individuals may maintain a cause of action to enforce Title III against commercial building owners. The Department may seek monetary damages or injunctive relief, but private individuals are entitled only to seek injunctive relief under the statute. Apparently a tort claim may create a cause of action for monetary damages.

EQUAL CREDIT OPPORTUNITY ACT

The Equal Credit Opportunity Act (ECOA) was originally passed to provide for equal credit for borrowers by making it unlawful to discriminate against an applicant for credit based on sex or marital status. In 1976, the Act was amended to prohibit discrimination in any credit transaction based on race, color, religion, national origin, sex, marital status, age (not including minors), receipt of income from a public assistance program, and the good faith exercise of rights under the ECOA or other consumer protection laws.

Prohibited Requests

To effect this prohibition on discrimination, a creditor is prohibited from requiring certain information from the borrower:

1. Information concerning a spouse or former spouse, except when that spouse will be contractually obligated for repayment or if the spouse resides in a community property state.
2. Information regarding the applicant's marital status unless the credit requested is for an individual's unsecured account, or unless the applicant resides in a community property state and the community property is to be relied upon to repay the credit. Inquiries as to the applicant's marital status are limited, however, to categories of "married," "unmarried," and "separated." "Unmarried" includes single, divorced, and widowed persons and may be specified in the application.

3. Information concerning the source of an applicant's income without disclosing that information regarding alimony, child support, or separate maintenance is to be furnished only at the option of the applicant. The big exception to the rule is when the applicant expects to use any of those sources of income for repayment. If so, the lender may request this information.
4. Information regarding an applicant's birth control practices or any intentions concerning the bearing or rearing of children, although a lender still has the right to ask an applicant about the number and ages of any dependents or about dependent-related financial obligations.
5. Questions regarding race, color, religion, or national origin of the applicant.

There are minor exceptions when a real estate loan is involved. These exceptions are allowed in order to provide certain information that may be used by the federal government for the purposes of monitoring conformance with the Equal Credit Opportunity Act. When the information is requested, the lender is required to advise the applicants that the furnishing of the specific information is for purposes of monitoring the lender's compliance and is requested on a voluntary basis only. If the applicant does not wish to answer the questions, the lender simply notes the refusal on the application form. The refusal to give the information requested cannot be used in any way in considering whether or not credit is granted to the applicant. If the applicant agrees to provide the information on a voluntary basis, the following information can be furnished:

1. Race or national origin.
2. Sex, relating to gender only (not sexual preference).
3. Marital status (using the categories of married, unmarried, or separated).

When considering race and national origin only the following categories can be used: American Indian or Alaskan Native, Asian or Pacific Islander, Black, White, Hispanic or "other."

Evaluating Credit Applications

As previously stated, the lender cannot use information obtained from an applicant that might be considered to be discriminatory. Each applicant has to be evaluated on the same basic information as any other individual person. Lenders can't refuse credit based on individual category, such as newlyweds, recent divorcees, etc. The lender's rules must be applied uniformly to all applicants. The areas in which there can be no discrimination have already been discussed (sex, marital status, race, color, religion, national origin, age, public assistance) but some of these areas need to be discussed in greater detail.

Age

A lender is prohibited from taking an applicant's age into account in determining his ability to repay, as well as income from any public assistance program. The only exception to this prohibition is minors, who lack contractual capacity and cannot enter into real estate transactions.

Children

As discussed in the previous sections on fair housing, the Equal Credit Opportunity Act has always provided that there can be no assumptions or statistics relating to the likelihood that a group of persons may bear children. In prior years, lenders required nonpregnancy affidavits and other indications that a young newly married couple would not endanger the income-producing capacity of the wife.

Part-Time Income

Income from part-time employment or retirement income cannot be discounted because of the basis of its source. However, the creditor may still consider the amount and probability of continuance of such income.

Alimony and Child Support

Alimony and child support and separate maintenance cannot be considered in evaluating a loan application unless the creditor determines that such payments are not likely to be made consistently. In such cases, the lender has the right to determine whether or not the applicant has the ability to compel payment and the creditworthiness of the party who is obligated to make such payments.

Credit History

The Equal Credit Opportunity Act requires a creditor to consider the separate record of the applicant. This prohibits the lender from tying the applicant's credit history to the past record of the spouse or former spouse.

Immigration Residency

A creditor may consider an applicant's immigration status and whether or not he or she is a permanent resident of the United States.

Sex

A lender may not ask about the sex of an applicant but may ask an applicant to designate a title on the application form (Ms., Miss, Mrs., or Mr.) if the form indicates the designation of the title is optional.

Marital Status

If an applicant applies for individual credit, the lender may not ask the applicant for marital status unless the applicant resides in a community property state (Texas!) or is relying on property located in a community property state to repay the loan. Similarly, a lender may not seek information about a spouse or former spouse unless a spouse will be permitted to use the account, the spouse is contractually liable on the account, or the borrower is relying on the spouse's income as a basis for repayment of the loan.

Credit Denial

If an applicant is denied credit, the lender must give a written notice of decline, also referred to as "Notice of Adverse Action," to the applicant and advise the rejected applicant of the federal agency that administers compliance with the

Equal Credit Opportunity Act for that particular loan transaction. The statement of specific reasons must give the precise reason or reasons for the denial of credit. There are suggested guidelines for giving reasons for credit denial including:

1. Unable to verify credit references.
2. Temporary or irregular employment.
3. Insufficient length of employment.
4. Insufficient income.
5. Excessive obligations.
6. Inadequate collateral.
7. Too short a period of residency.
8. Delinquent credit obligation.

An application can also be denied if it is incomplete.

Penalties

Failure to comply with the Equal Credit Opportunity Act or the accompanying federal regulations makes a creditor subject to a civil liability for damages limited to $10,000 in individual actions and the lesser of $500,000 or 1% of the creditor's net worth in class actions. The court may also award court costs and reasonable attorney's fees to an aggrieved applicant.

Copies of Appraisal Reports

A lender or loan broker must provide a copy of an appraisal report to an applicant for a loan to be secured by a lien on the dwelling. The report may be provided either routinely as a part of the lender's standard process or when the loan applicant requests a copy. If the lender decides to provide the appraisal only upon request, it must notify the applicant in writing of the right to receive a copy of the appraisal report. The lender must promptly (generally within 30 calendar days) mail or deliver the copy of the appraisal report after he receives the borrower's request.

COMMUNITY REINVESTMENT ACT

The ***Community Reinvestment Act*** expands the concept that regulated financial institutions must serve the needs of their communities. Whenever a financing institution regulated by the federal government applies for a charter, branch facility, office relocation, or acquisition of another financing institution, the record of the institution's help in meeting local credit needs must be one of the factors considered by the federal supervising agencies.*

Federal regulators are required to evaluate each financial institution's actual performance in meeting the credit needs of its community, using lending, investment, and service tests to review an institution's performance. Some financial

* The supervising agencies include the Office of the Controller of the Currency, the Board of Governors of the Federal Reserve System, the Federal Deposit Insurance Corporation, and the Office of Thrift Supervision.

institutions may choose to adopt a strategic plan that sets forth specific goals that must be obtained.

For larger institutions, and some smaller institutions, the lending, investment, and service tests are measured by home mortgage loan originations, small business and small firm loans, community development loans, and consumer loans. The investment test evaluates the extent to which an institution has been meeting community needs through qualified investment. A service test reviews the availability and responsiveness of an institution's system for delivering retail banking and community development of services.

In addition, the retail institution must delineate an assessment area consisting of one or more metropolitan's statistical areas or contiguous subdivisions, such as counties, cities, and towns, focusing on the location of where the lender has its main office, branches, and automatic teller machines.

CRA Statement

The institution must post in the public lobby of its main office and each branch office a "Community Reinvestment Act" (CRA) notice. This notice informs consumers that they are entitled to certain information about the operations of the lender and their performance under the CRA, the schedules for the CRA examination, and the availability of any federal regulatory report covered by the CRA.

REVIEW QUESTIONS

Answers to these questions are found in the Answer Key section at the back of the book.

1. Discrimination in the availability of housing on the basis of race is prohibited by the
   A. Civil Rights Act of 1866.
   B. Fair Housing Act of 1968.
   C. Both A and B.
   D. Neither A nor B.

2. Vera, a real estate broker, was offered a rental listing by a homeowner who stated that he would not rent the property to a person of certain religious beliefs. Vera should
   A. refuse to accept the listing on these terms.
   B. accept the listing and leave it up to the owner to refuse any offers received from persons of that religion.
   C. accept the listing and steer persons of that religion to other properties.
   D. file a complaint of discrimination against the owner.

3. Under federal law, the owner of one single-family dwelling, in which he has resided for ten years, who does not employ an agent and does not use discriminatory advertising, may discriminate in the sale or rental of the property on any of the following bases EXCEPT:
   A. religion.
   B. race.
   C. color.
   D. national origin.

4. State and local laws that restrict or prohibit discrimination in the availability of rental housing may
   A. be more restrictive than federal statutes.
   B. prohibit additional forms of discrimination.
   C. both A and B.
   D. neither A nor B.

5. The Civil Rights Act of 1866 prohibits
   A. racial discrimination.
   B. steering.
   C. block busting.
   D. discrimination for any reason.

6. All of the following are prohibited by the Fair Housing Act of 1968, as amended, EXCEPT:
   A. discrimination in advertising.
   B. denial of availability of housing on the basis of religion.
   C. discrimination in terms or conditions for sale or rent.
   D. discrimination on the basis of age.

7. An amendment to the Fair Housing Act of 1968, signed by the president in 1988 prohibits:
   A. discrimination on the basis of physical handicap.
   B. the offering of different loan terms by commercial lenders based on race or religion of the loan applicant.
   C. the refusal to sell, rent, or negotiate with any person.
   D. steering and block busting.

8. The practice of directing homeseekers to particular neighborhoods based on race, color, religion, sex, or national origin
   A. is known as steering.
   B. is prohibited by the Civil Rights Act of 1866.
   C. constitutes block busting.
   D. none of the above.
   E. all of the above.

9. All of the following are true for the inducement of panic selling in a neighborhood for financial gain EXCEPT:
   A. it is prohibited by the Fair Housing Act of 1968.
   B. it is limited to the fear of loss of value because of the changing of the racial composition of a neighborhood.
   C. it is known as block busting.
   D. the prohibition applies to licensed real estate agents.

10. The Fair Housing Act of 1968 applies to
    A. single-family housing.
    B. multiple dwellings.
    C. both A and B.
    D. neither A nor B.

11. A church that operates housing for the elderly may restrict occupancy to members of the church if
    A. membership in the church is open to all persons.
    B. the units are to be rented, but not if they are being offered for sale.
    C. both A and B.
    D. neither A nor B.

12. A victim of discrimination in housing may seek enforcement of the 1968 Fair Housing Act by any of the following means EXCEPT:
    A. filing a complaint with HUD.
    B. filing an action in federal court.
    C. filing a complaint with the U.S. Attorney General.
    D. filing a complaint with the state real estate department.

13. A person seeking enforcement of the Civil Rights Act of 1866 may do so by filing
    A. an action in federal court.
    B. a complaint with the U.S. Attorney General.
    C. an action in county court.
    D. a complaint with HUD.

14. A licensed real estate agent is offered a listing by an owner who stipulates that she will not sell to any person of a certain national origin. The agent should
    A. accept the listing and leave it up to the owner to reject offers from these persons.
    B. refuse to accept the listing.
    C. report the owner to the real estate department.
    D. file a complaint against the owner with HUD.

15. The Sunset Hills Country Club has several guest bedrooms that are made available to members and guests for a nominal charge, but are not available to the general public. Does this constitute a violation of the federal fair housing laws?
    A. Yes, because rental housing of this nature must be open to the public.
    B. Yes, because the charging of a fee constitutes a commercial purpose.
    C. No, because the club is exempt under the provisions of the Fair Housing Act of 1968.
    D. No, because this does not constitute steering or block busting.

Chapter 6

KEY TERMS

Association: a not-for-profit organization that can own property and transact business in its own name

Community property: a property in which spouses are treated as equal partners, with each owning a one-half interest

Estate in severalty: an estate owned by one person; sole ownership

Financial liability: the amount of money one can lose; one's risk exposure

Joint tenancy: a form of property co-ownership that features the right of survivorship

Joint venture: an association of two or more persons or firms in order to carry out a single business project

Limited liability company: a company consisting of members or managers that is governed by its bylaws

Partnership: two or more persons engaged in business for a profit

Right of survivorship: a feature of joint tenancy whereby the surviving joint tenants automatically acquire all the rights, title, and interest of the deceased joint tenant

Tenants in common: shared ownership of a single property among two or more persons; interests need not be equal and no right of survivorship exists

Undivided interest: ownership by two or more persons that gives each the right to use the entire property

Forms of Ownership

IN THIS CHAPTER

This chapter looks at how a given right or interest in land is held by one or more individuals. It covers such topics as sole ownership, tenants in common, joint tenancy, tenancy by the entirety, and community property. In Chapter 3 we looked at land from a physical standpoint: the size and shape of a parcel, where it is located, and what was affixed to it. In Chapter 4 we explored various legal rights and interests that can be held in land. In this chapter, we look at how a given right or interest in land can be held by one or more individuals.

SOLE OWNERSHIP

When title to property is held by one person, it is called an ***estate in severalty*** or **sole ownership**. Although the word "severalty" seems to imply that several persons own a single property, the correct meaning can be easily remembered by thinking of "severed" (separated) ownership. Sole ownership is available to single and married persons. However, in the case of married persons, most states require one spouse to waive community property, dower, or curtesy rights in writing. Businesses usually hold title to property in severalty. It is from the estate in severalty that all other tenancies are carved.

The major advantage of sole ownership for an individual is flexibility. As a sole owner you can make all the decisions regarding a property without having to get the agreement of co-owners. You can decide what property or properties to buy, when to buy, and how much to offer. You can decide whether to pay all cash or to seek a loan using the property as collateral. Once bought, you control (within the bounds of the law) how the property will be used, how much will be charged if it is rented, and how it will be managed. If you decide to sell, you alone decide when to offer the property for sale and at what price and terms.

But freedom and responsibility go together. For example, if you purchase a rental property you must determine the prevailing rents, find tenants, prepare contracts, collect the rent, and keep the property in repair; or you must hire and pay someone else to manage the property. Another deterrent to sole ownership is the high entry cost. This form of real estate ownership is not possible for someone with only a few hundred dollars to invest.

TENANTS IN COMMON

When two or more persons wish to share the ownership of a single property, they may do so as ***tenants in common.*** As tenants in common, each owns an ***undivided interest*** in the whole property. This means that each owner has a right to possession of the entire property. None can exclude the others nor claim any specific portion. In a tenancy in common, these interests need not be the same size, and each owner can independently sell, mortgage, give away, or devise his individual interest. This independence is possible because each tenant in common has a separate legal title to his undivided interest.

Suppose that you invest $20,000 along with two of your friends, who invest $30,000 and $50,000, respectively; together you buy 100 acres of land as tenants in common. Presuming that everyone's ownership interest is proportional to his or her cash investment, you will hold a 20% interest in the entire 100 acres and your two friends will hold 30% and 50%. You cannot pick out 20 acres and exclude the other co-owners from them, nor can you pick out 20 acres and say, "These are mine and I'm going to sell them"; nor can they do that to you. You do, however, have the legal right to sell or otherwise dispose of your 20% interest (or a portion of it) without the permission of your two friends. Your friends have the same right. If one of you sells, the purchaser becomes a new tenant in common with the remaining co-owners.

Wording of the Conveyance

As a rule, a tenancy in common is indicated by naming the co-owners in the conveyance and adding the words "as tenants in common." For example, a deed might read, "Samuel Smith, John Jones, and Robert Miller, as tenants in common." If nothing is said regarding the size of each co-owner's interest in the property, the law presumes that all interests are equal. Therefore, if the co-owners intend their interests to be unequal, the size of each co-owner's undivided interest must be stated as a percent or a fraction, such as 60 and 40 or one-third and two-thirds.

PUTTING IT TO WORK

In Texas, if two or more persons are named as owners, and there is no specific indication as to how they are taking title, they are presumed to be tenants in common. Thus, if a deed is made out to "Donna Adams and Barbara Kelly," the law would consider them to be tenants in common, each holding an undivided one-half interest in the property. An important exception to this presumption is when the co-owners are married to each other. In this case, they may be automatically considered to be taking ownership as community property.

No Right of Survivorship

When a tenancy in common exists, if a co-owner dies the undivided interest passes to the heirs or devisees, who then become tenants in common with the remaining co-owners. There is no ***right of survivorship***; that is, the remaining co-owners do not acquire the deceased's interest unless they are named in the deceased's last will and testament to do so. When a creditor has a claim on a co-owner's interest and forces its sale to satisfy the debt, the new buyer becomes a tenant in common with the remaining co-owners. If one co-owner wants to sell (or give away) only a portion of his undivided interest, he may; the new owner becomes a tenant in common with the other co-owners.

Any income generated by the property belongs to the tenants in common in proportion to the size of their interests. Similarly, each co-owner is responsible for paying his proportionate share of property taxes, repairs, upkeep, and so on, plus interest and debt repayment, if any. If any co-owner fails to contribute his proportionate share, the other co-owners can pay on his behalf and then sue him for that amount. If co-owners find that they cannot agree on how the property is to be run and cannot agree on a plan for dividing or selling it, it is possible to request a court-ordered partition. A **partition** divides the property into distinct portions so that each person can hold his or her proportionate interest in severalty. If this is physically impossible, such as when three co-owners each have a one-third interest in a house, the court will order the property sold and the proceeds divided among the co-owners.

The major advantage of tenancy in common is that it allows two or more persons to achieve goals that one person could not accomplish alone. However, prospective co-owners should give advance thought to what they will do (short of going to court) if (1) a co-owner fails to pay his share of ownership expenses; (2) differences arise regarding how the property is to be operated; (3) an agreement cannot be reached as to when to sell, for how much, and on what terms; and (4) what happens if a co-owner dies and those who inherit his interest have little in common with the surviving co-owners. The counsel of an attorney experienced in property ownership can be very helpful when considering the co-ownership of property.

JOINT TENANCY

Another form of multiple-person ownership is ***joint tenancy.*** The most distinguishing characteristic of joint tenancy is the right of survivorship. Upon the death of a joint tenant, his interest does not descend to his heirs or pass by his will. Rather, the entire ownership remains in the surviving joint tenant(s). In other words, there is just one less owner.

Four Unities

To create a joint tenancy, **four unities** must be present. They are the unities of time, title, interest, and possession.

Unity of time means that each joint tenant must acquire his or her ownership interest at the same moment. Once a joint tenancy is formed, it is not possible to add new joint tenants later unless an entirely new joint tenancy is formed among the existing co-owners and the new co-owner. To illustrate, suppose that *A*, *B*, and *C* own a parcel of land as joint tenants. If *A* sells his interest to *D*, then *B*, *C*, and *D* must sign documents to create a new joint tenancy among them. If this is not done, *D* automatically becomes a tenant in common with *B* and *C* who, between themselves, remain joint tenants. *D* will then own an undivided one-third interest in common with *B* and *C* who will own an undivided two-thirds interest as joint tenants.

Unity of title means that the joint tenants acquire their interests from the same source; that is, the same deed or will. (Some states allow a property owner to create a valid joint tenancy by conveying to himself, or herself, and another without going through a third party.)

PUTTING IT TO WORK

Texas requires that the joint tenancy be expressly agreed to in writing by the parties involved. Any automatic presumption of joint tenancy has been abolished by statute.

Unity of interest means that the joint tenants own one interest together and each joint tenant has exactly the same right in that interest. (This, by the way, is the foundation upon which the survivorship feature rests.) If the joint tenants list differing individual interests, they lack unity of interest and will be treated as tenants in common. Unity of interest also means that if one joint tenant holds a fee simple interest in the property, the others cannot hold anything but a fee simple interest.

Unity of possession means that the joint tenants must enjoy the same undivided possession of the whole property. All joint tenants have the use of the entire property, and no individual owns a particular portion of it. By way of contrast, unity of possession is the only unity essential to a tenancy in common.

Right of Survivorship

The feature of joint tenancy ownership that is most widely recognized is its **right of survivorship**. Upon the death of a joint tenant, that interest in the property is extinguished. In a two-person joint tenancy, when one person dies, the other immediately becomes the sole owner. With more than two persons as joint tenants, when one dies the remaining joint tenants are automatically left as owners. Ultimately, the last survivor becomes the sole owner. The legal philosophy is that the joint tenants constitute a single owning unit. The death of one joint tenant does not destroy that unit—it only reduces the number of persons owning the unit. For the public record, a copy of the death certificate and an affidavit of death of the joint tenant is recorded in the county where the property is located. The property must also be released from any estate tax liens.

The right of survivorship has made joint tenancy a popular form of ownership among married couples in other states. Married couples often want the surviving spouse to have sole ownership of the marital property. Any property held in joint tenancy goes to the surviving spouse without the delay of probate and usually with less legal expense. Community property (discussed later in this chapter) may not be held in joint tenancy.

"Poor Man's Will"

Because of the survivorship feature, joint tenancy has loosely been labeled a "poor man's will." However, it should not replace a properly drawn will because it affects only that property held in joint tenancy. Moreover, a will can be changed if the persons named therein are no longer in one's favor. But once a joint tenancy is formed, the title is permanently conveyed and no further opportunity for change exists, unless the joint tenancy is terminated. A joint tenant cannot name someone in his will to receive the joint tenant interest because his interest ends upon his death. One should also be aware of the possibility that ownership in joint tenancy may result in additional estate taxes.

Another important aspect of joint tenancy ownership is that it can be used to defeat dower or curtesy rights. If a married man forms a joint tenancy with someone other than his wife (such as a business partner) and then dies, his wife has no dower rights in that joint tenancy. As a result, courts have begun to look with disfavor upon the right of survivorship. Louisiana, Ohio, and Oregon either do not recognize joint tenancy or have abolished it. The remaining 47 states and the District of Columbia recognize joint tenancy ownership, but 14 (including Texas) have abolished the automatic presumption of survivorship (see Table 6.1). In those 14 states, if the right of survivorship is desired in a joint tenancy, it must be clearly stated in the conveyance. For example, a deed might read, "Karen Carson and Judith Johnson, as joint tenants with the right of survivorship and not as tenants in common." Even in those states not requiring it, this wording is often used to ensure that the right of survivorship is intended. In community property states, one spouse cannot take community funds and establish a valid joint tenancy with a third party.

There is a popular misconception that a debtor can protect himself from creditors' claims by taking title to property as a joint tenant. It is true that in a joint tenancy, the surviving joint tenant(s) acquire(s) the property free and clear of any liens against the deceased. However, this can happen only if the debtor dies before the creditor seizes the debtor's interest.

Only a human being can be a joint tenant. A corporation cannot be a joint tenant. This is because a corporation is an artificial legal being and can exist in perpetuity; that is, never die. Joint tenancy ownership is not limited to the ownership of land; any estate in land and any chattel interest may be held in joint tenancy.

TENANCY BY THE ENTIRETY

Tenancy by the entirety (also called tenancy by the entireties) is a form of joint tenancy specifically for married persons. To the four unities of a joint tenancy is added a fifth: **unity of person**. The basis for this is the legal premise that a husband and wife are an indivisible legal unit. Two key characteristics of a

TABLE 6.1 Concurrent ownership by states

	L.L.P.*	L.L.C.**	Tenancy in common	Joint tenancy	Tenancy by the entirety	Community property
Alabama	X	X	X	X		
Alaska		X	X	X	X	X
Arizona	X	X	X	X		X
Arkansas		X	X	X	X	
California		X	X	X		X
Colorado		X	X	X		
Connecticut		X	X	X		
Delaware	X	X	X	X	X	
District of Columbia	X	X	X	X	X	
Florida		X	X	X	X	
Georgia	X	X	X	X		
Hawaii		X	X	X	X	
Idaho	X	X	X	X		X
Illinois		X	X	X		
Indiana		X	X	X	X	
Iowa	X	X	X	X		
Kansas	X	X	X	X		
Kentucky		X	X	X	X	
Louisiana	X	X				X
Maine		X	X	X		
Maryland	X	X	X	X	X	
Massachusetts		X	X	X	X	
Michigan	X	X	X	X	X	
Minnesota	X	X	X	X		
Mississippi	X	X	X	X	X	
Missouri		X	X	X	X	
Montana		X	X	X		
Nebraska		X	X	X		
Nevada		X	X	X		X
New Hampshire		X	X	X		
New Jersey	X	X	X	X	X	
New Mexico		X	X	X		X
New York		X	X	X	X	
North Carolina	X	X	X	X	X	
North Dakota		X	X	X		
Ohio	X	X	X		X	
Oklahoma		X	X	X	X	
Oregon		X	X		X	
Pennsylvania		X	X	X	X	
Rhode Island		X	X	X	X	
South Carolina		X	X	X		
South Dakota		X	X	X		
Tennessee		X	X	X	X	
Texas	X	X	X	X		X
Utah	X	X	X	X	X	
Vermont		X	X	X	X	
Virginia	X	X	X	X	X	
Washington		X	X	X		X
West Virginia		X	X	X	X	
Wisconsin		X	X	X		X
Wyoming		X	X	X	X	

*Limited Liability Partnership
**Limited Liability Company
In Ohio and Oregon other means are available to achieve rights of survivorship between nonmarried persons. When two or more persons own property together in Louisiana, it is termed an "ownership in indivision" or a "joint ownership." Louisiana law is based on an old French civil law.
Source: © 2012 Cengage Learning

tenancy by the entirety are the following: (1) the surviving spouse becomes the sole owner of the property upon the death of the other, and (2) neither spouse has a disposable interest in the property during the lifetime of the other. Thus, while both are alive and married to each other, both signatures are necessary to convey title to the property. With respect to the first characteristic, tenancy by the entirety is similar to joint tenancy because both feature the right of survivorship. They are quite different, however, with respect to the second characteristic. A joint tenancy can be terminated by one tenant's conveyance of his or her interest, but a tenancy by the entirety can be terminated only by joint action of husband and wife. Because Texas has community property laws, tenancy by the entireties is not recognized here.

States that recognize tenancy by the entirety are listed in Table 6.1. Some of these states automatically assume that a tenancy by the entirety is created when married persons buy real estate. However, it is best to use a phrase such as "John and Mary Smith, husband and wife as tenants by the entirety with the right of survivorship" on deeds and other conveyances. This avoids later questions as to whether their intention might have been to create a joint tenancy or a tenancy in common.

COMMUNITY PROPERTY

Due largely to its Spanish heritage, Texas has adopted community property laws that vest particular rights in property as a result of the marital community. Table 6.1 identifies the 10 community property states. The laws of each community property state vary slightly, but the underlying concept is that the husband and wife contribute jointly and equally to their marriage and thus should share equally in any property purchased during marriage. Whereas English law is based on the merging of husband's and wife's interest upon marriage, community property law treats husband and wife as equal partners, with each owning an undivided one-half interest.

Community Property, Separate Property

Community property rights do not come into effect until there is a marriage and, similarly, end with the dissolution of that marriage. The law in Texas presumes that all property acquired after marriage is ***community property.***

Property that is not community property is referred to as **separate property**. The Texas Constitution defines separate property as property acquired prior to marriage (even if the owner subsequently marries, the real estate remains separate property) and property acquired by gift, devise, or descent after marriage. In addition, spouses can agree in writing, before or during marriage, that property can be separate rather than community. Courts have held that property purchased after marriage with separate funds can also be construed as separate property, and an increase in the value of separate property stays separate property. However, rents and revenues from separate property are construed to be community property, unless the spouses agree otherwise.

Spouses can also agree, in writing, to convert one spouse's separate property into community property. This creates a significant change in property rights, because one's separate property would then be subject to joint management control and disposition by both spouses and subject to the liabilities of the other spouse. When a separate property agreement is executed, the law requires special language in the document warning the parties of the potential risks of executing the agreement.

Community property cannot be generally conveyed without both spouses' signatures. There are statutes that will allow property under the sole management and control of one spouse to be sold without the signature of the other spouse. As a good business practice, however, the wise real estate agent should obtain the other spouse's signature on any pertinent documents for real estate believed to be community property.

The major advantage of the community property system is found in its philosophy: It treats the spouses as equal partners in property acquired through their mutual efforts during marriage. Even if the wife elects to be a full-time homemaker and all the money brought into the household is the result of her husband's job (or vice versa), the law treats them as equal co-owners in any property bought with that money. This is true even if only one spouse is named as the owner.

In the event of divorce, if the parting couple cannot amicably decide how to divide their community property, the courts will usually do so. If the courts do not, the ex-spouses will become tenants in common with each other. If it later becomes necessary, either can file suit for partition.

Community Property Right of Survivorship

The Texas Constitution also provides that husbands and wives can own community property with rights of survivorship. Don't confuse this with joint tenancy. In joint tenancy, you will recall, each spouse is liable for their proportionate share of ownership. In community property, both spouses are jointly and severally liable for all community debts. To create the right of survivorship, a written agreement signed by both spouses must be recorded in the county courthouse. This type of ownership can have unexpected results. Legal counsel should be consulted before using this form of ownership.

PARTNERSHIP

A ***partnership*** exists when two or more persons, as partners, unite their property, labor, and skill as a business to share the profits created by it. The agreement between the partners can be oral or written. The partners can hold the partnership property either in their own names (as tenants in common or as joint tenants) or in the name of the partnership (which would hold title in severalty). For convenience, especially in a large partnership, the partners can designate two or three of their group to make contracts and sign documents on behalf of the entire partnership. There are four types of partnerships: general partnerships made up entirely of general partners, limited partnerships composed of general and limited partners, limited liability partnerships that limit the liability of a general partner from the misconduct of other general partners, and joint ventures.

General Partnership

The **general partnership** is an outgrowth of common law. In 2003, Texas enacted the Business Organizations Code, which provides that (1) title to partnership property can be held in the partnership's name, (2) each partner has an equal right of possession of partnership property—but only for partnership purposes, (3) upon the death of one partner their rights in the partnership property vest in the surviving partners— but the decedent's estate must be reimbursed for the value of their interest in the partnership, (4) a partner's right to specific partnership property is not subject to dower or curtesy, and (5) partnership property can be attached by creditors only for debts of the partnership, not for debts of a partner.

As a form of property ownership, the partnership is a method of combining the capital and expertise of two or more persons. It is equally important to note that the profits and losses of the partnership are taxable directly to each individual partner in proportion to his or her interest in the partnership. Although the partnership files a tax return, it is only for information purposes. The partnership itself does not pay taxes. Negative aspects of this form of ownership center around financial liability, illiquidity, and in some cases, management.

Financial liability means each partner is personally responsible for all the debts of the partnership. Thus, each general partner can lose not only what they have invested in the partnership, but more, up to the full extent of their personal financial worth. If one partner makes a commitment on behalf of the partnership, all partners are responsible for making good on that commitment. If the partnership is sued, each partner is fully responsible, although a recent legislative change requires the creditor to proceed against partnership assets before pursuing the individual partners. **Illiquidity** refers to the possibility that it may be very difficult to sell one's partnership interest on short notice in order to raise cash. **Management** means that each general partner is expected to take an active part in the operation of the partnership.

Texas Partnership Statutes

The nature of the Texas community property laws has generally dictated that a partnership has three distinct interests, which are set out by the Texas partnership statutes. They are as follows:

1. A partner's right to specific partnership property (such as desks, typewriters, machinery, etc.), which is *not* community property.
2. A partner's interest in the partnership (usually determined by a dollar amount), which *may be* community property.
3. A partner's right to management in the partnership, which is *not* community property.

Limited Partnership

Because of unlimited financial liability and management responsibility, an alternative partnership form, the **limited partnership**, has developed. Also included in the new Business Organizations Code, the Code requires that a limited partnership be formed by a written document.

A limited partnership is composed of general and limited partners. The general partners organize and operate the partnership, contribute some capital, and agree to accept the full financial liability of the partnership. The **limited partners** provide the bulk of the investment capital, have little say in the day-to-day management of the partnership, share in the profits and losses, and contract with their general partners to limit the financial liability of each limited partner to the amount he or she invests. Additionally, a well-written partnership agreement will allow for the continuity of the partnership in the event of the death of either a general or limited partner.

The advantages of limited liability, minimum management responsibility, and direct pass-through of profits and losses for taxation purposes have made this form of ownership popular. However, being free of management responsibility is advantageous to the investors only if the general partners are capable and honest. If they are not, the only control open to the limited partners is to vote to replace the general partners.

PUTTING IT TO WORK

Before investing in a limited partnership, one should investigate the past record of the general partners, because this is usually a good indication of how the new partnership will be managed. The investigation should include checking their previous investments, talking to past investors, and checking court records for any legal complaints brought against them. Additionally, the prospective partner should be prepared to stay in for the duration of the partnership as the resale market for limited partnership interests is small.

Limited Liability Partnerships

The Texas legislature also enacted another form of ownership called a **limited liability partnership**. This form of ownership attempts to limit the liability of the general partner from the misconduct of other general partners. For instance, in a law firm or a brokerage firm organized as a general partnership, all the general partners have the right to bind the partnership and all general partners have 100% liability for partnership obligations. The limited liability partnership, however, limits the liability of the partners such that if one partner commits malfeasance or malpractice (for example, a partner in the tax section of a law firm), it would not create a 100% liability for a partner in the real estate section of the law firm. Only the partners who have direct supervisory control over the misconduct will have liability for it. Note that most large law firms now have "L.L.P." behind their names.

To create the limited liability partnership, the firm must register with the Secretary of State and carry a specified amount of malpractice insurance.

Joint Venture

A ***joint venture*** is a partnership of two or more persons or firms to carry out a single business project. A joint venture is treated as a partnership for tax purposes. However, whereas a general partner can bind her partnership to a contract, a joint venturer cannot bind the other joint venturers to a contract for anything outside the scope of that single business project. Examples of joint ventures in real estate are the purchase of land by two or more persons with the intent of grading it and selling it as lots, the association of a landowner and builder to build and sell, and the association of a lender and builder to purchase land and develop buildings on it to sell to investors. Each member of the joint venture makes a contribution in the form of capital or talent, and all have a strong incentive to make the joint venture succeed. If more than one project is undertaken, the relationship may become a general partnership rather than a joint venture.

LIMITED LIABILITY COMPANIES

There has been legitimate, and probably justified, concern over liabilities of defendants in a business environment. One understands that if a person is harmed, there should be an ability to recover from the wrongdoer, yet many juries award significant sums of money, and attempt to pursue personal liability for officers and directors of corporations because of their duties of care in the business entity (including real estate brokers!).

All states (see Table 6.1) have passed laws creating a new form of entity called a ***limited liability company***, often referred to as an *"L.C."* or *"L.L.C."* The statutes tend to be lengthy and complicated, and only the most general descriptions can be explained here. A lot of case law and perhaps amendments to the statutes will be forthcoming in the future.

Formation

Generally, most states allow two or more (Texas allows only one) persons 18 years of age or older to act as organizers of a limited liability company by signing the Articles of Organization of such limited liability company and giving the original copy of the Articles to the Secretary of State. The Articles of Organization should include:

1. The name of the limited liability company.
2. The period of duration that may have limitations in some states.
3. The purpose for which the limited liability company is organized (which may include any or all lawful business).
4. The address of the principal place of business and the name of the initial registered agent in the State.
5. The names of the managers or members who are to manage the company.

The Secretary of State then issues a Certificate of Organization, and the existence of the limited liability company begins at that time.

A member or manager of a limited liability company is not liable for debts, obligations, or liabilities of a limited liability company. A membership interest is considered to be personal property and the member has no interest in specific limited liability company property.

Operations of a Limited Liability Company

The limited liability company name must include the word "Limited" or the abbreviation "Ltd." or "L.C." It must maintain the registered office and registered agent (similar to a corporation), and all real or personal property owned or purchased by the limited liability company shall be held and owned, and the conveyance shall be made, in the name of the limited liability company. All instruments and documents providing for the acquisition, mortgage, or disposition of the limited liability company shall be valid and binding upon the company if they are executed by one or more persons acting as a manager or member (if the management of the limited liability company is retained by the members).

Please note that limited liability companies are not corporations, nor partnerships, nor limited partnerships. They borrow attributes from both the general partnership and the corporation but mix them differently than they are mixed in the limited partnership. They are a totally new theory of ownership enacted by the state legislatures and, as stated previously, there is a lot of law yet to be made in this area. A major advantage in using a limited liability company is its classification as a partnership for federal income tax purposes. It is important that the organizers and owners of the limited liability company operate the company other than as a corporation so it will not be taxed as a corporation. Most limited liability companies do not have a continuity of life as a corporation, and the transferability of interest is limited.

The Treasury regulations basically identify six "corporate" characteristics. If the limited liability company is operated too much like a corporation, it could have serious adverse tax consequences, so professional help is critical in establishing and operating the limited liability company, both from a legal and tax perspective.

CORPORATIONS

Each state has passed laws to permit groups of people to create **corporations** that can buy, sell, own, and operate in the name of the corporation. The corporation, in turn, is owned by stockholders, who possess shares of stock as evidence of their ownership.

Texas, by statute, gives corporations the right to acquire, purchase, and sell real property. To effect a conveyance, the conveying instrument must be signed by the corporation's president, vice president, or attorney-in-fact and be accompanied by a resolution by the Board of Directors of the corporation. A sale, mortgage, or pledge of substantially all the assets of the corporation must have approval of a majority of the shareholders.

Because the corporation is an entity (or legal being) in the eyes of the law, the corporation must pay income taxes on its profits. What remains after taxes can be used to pay dividends to the stockholders, who, in turn, pay personal income taxes on their dividend income. This double taxation of profits is the most important negative factor in the corporate form of ownership. On the positive side, the entity aspect shields the investor from liability. Even if the corporation falls on the hardest of financial times and owes more than it owns, the worst that can happen to the stockholder is that the value of her stock will drop to zero. Another advantage is that shares of stock are much more liquid than any previously discussed form of real estate ownership, even sole ownership. Stockbrokers and stock exchanges who specialize in the purchase and sale of corporate stock usually complete a sale in a week or less. Furthermore, shares of stock in most corporations sell for less than $100, thus enabling an investor to operate with small amounts of capital. In a corporation, the stockholders elect a board of directors, who, in turn, hire the management needed to run the day-to-day operations of the company. As a practical matter, however, unless a person is a major shareholder in a corporation, he or she will have little control over management. The alternative is to buy stock in firms where shareholder likes the management and sell where she does not.

Subchapter S Corporations

Several large real estate corporations are traded on the New York Stock Exchange, and the corporation is a popular method of organization for real estate brokers and developers. Nevertheless, most real estate investors shun corporations because of the double taxation feature and because the tax benefits of owning real estate are trapped inside the corporation.

In 1958, the Internal Revenue Code first allowed stockholders to organize **Subchapter S corporations** that provided the liability protection of a corporation with the profit-and-loss pass-through of a partnership. Although the initial 10 stockholder maximum was a drawback, the real problem for real estate investors was that no more than 20% of a Subchapter S's gross receipts could come from passive income. And rent is passive income. Effective in 1997, Congress revised the rules and increased the maximum number of shareholders to 75. (Regular corporations are now called C Corporations.) The advantages of S corporations were further enhanced by the Internal Revenue Code, which reduced the top personal tax rate below the top rate on corporations.

ASSOCIATIONS

An ***association*** is an organization that can own property and transact business in its own name. Several examples of associations are the homeowner associations found in condominiums and planned unit developments. There are also professional associations organized for business purposes, such as doctors' associations and architects' associations. If properly incorporated, an association will shield its members from personal liability in the event of lawsuits against the association. In Texas, if it is not properly incorporated, creates proportional liability for all its members.

UNINCORPORATED NONPROFIT ASSOCIATIONS

An **unincorporated nonprofit association** is defined under Texas law as "an unincorporated organization, other than one created by a trust, consisting of three or more persons joined by mutual consent for a common, nonprofit purpose." A nonprofit association may hold title to real estate in its own name and can transfer unencumbered real estate. In effect, the statute gives nonprofit associations, regardless of their lack of organization, separate status as an entity under Texas law. The individual members of a nonprofit organization are not liable for a breach of the association's contracts, nor tortious conduct, merely because a person is a member. This prevents personal liability for a member "by accident" if they are merely a member of a church congregation, volunteer organization, or other unincorporated nonprofit venture.

REAL ESTATE INVESTMENT TRUSTS

The idea of creating a trust that in turn carries out the investment objectives of its investors is not new. In 1961 Congress passed a law allowing trusts that specialize in real estate investments to avoid double taxation by following strict rules. Texas has also passed a REIT act that sets forth state guidelines and requirements. These **real estate investment trusts (REITs)** pool the money of many investors for the purchase of real estate, much as mutual funds do with stocks and bonds. Investors in a REIT are called **beneficiaries** and they purchase **beneficial interests** somewhat similar to shares of corporate stock. The trust officers, with the aid of paid advisors, buy, sell, mortgage, and operate real estate investments on behalf of the beneficiaries. If a REIT confines its activities to real estate investments, and if the REIT has at least 100 beneficiaries and distributes at least 95% of its net income every year, the Internal Revenue Service will collect tax on the distributed income only once—at the beneficiaries' level. Failure to follow the rules results in double taxation.

The REIT is an attempt to combine the advantages of the corporate form of ownership with single taxation status. Like stock, the beneficial interests are freely transferable and usually sell for $100 each or less, a distinct advantage for the investor with a small amount of money to invest in real estate. Beneficial interests in the larger REITs are sold on a national basis, thus enabling a REIT to have thousands of beneficiaries and millions of dollars of capital for real estate purchases.

INTER VIVOS AND TESTAMENTARY TRUSTS

In all states, the trust form of ownership can be used to provide for the well-being of another person. Basically, this is an arrangement whereby title to real and/or personal property is transferred by its owner (the **trustor**) to a trustee. The **trustee** holds title and manages the property for the benefit of another (the **beneficiary**) in accordance with instructions given by the trustor. Two popular forms are the inter vivos trust, also called a living trust, and the testamentary trust.

An **inter vivos trust** takes effect during the life of its creator. For example, you can transfer property to a trustee with instructions that it be managed and that income from the trust assets be paid to your children, spouse, relatives, or a charity.

A **testamentary trust** takes effect after death. For example, you could place instructions in your will that upon your death your property is to be placed into a trust. You can name whomever you want as trustee (a bank or trust company or friend, for example) and whom you want as beneficiaries. You can also give instructions as to how the assets are to be managed and how much (and how

FIGURE 6.1 Methods of holding title (Texas)

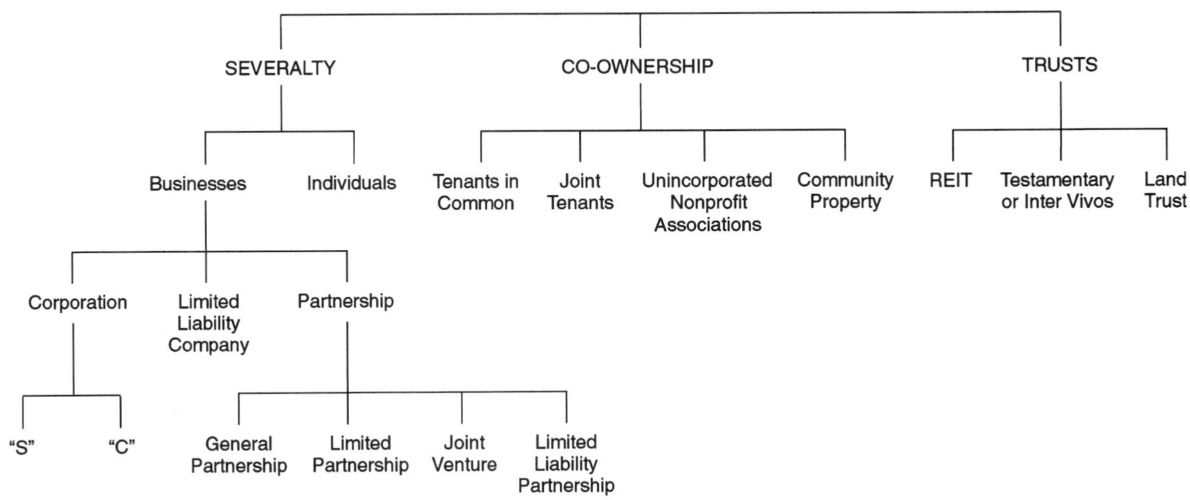

Source: © 2012 Cengage Learning

often) to pay the beneficiaries. Because trusts provide property management and financial control as well as a number of tax and estate planning advantages, this form of property ownership is growing in popularity.

LAND TRUSTS

In several states, an owner of real estate may create a trust wherein he is both the trustor and the beneficiary. Called a **land trust**, the landowner conveys his real property to a trustee, who in turn manages the property according to the beneficiary's (owner's) instructions. Because the beneficial interest created by the trust is considered personal property, the land trust effectively converts real property to personal property. Originally, the land trust gained popularity because true ownership could be cloaked in secrecy behind the name of a bank's trust department. Today, however, its popularity is mainly because it is a useful vehicle for group ownership and may not be subject to legal attachment like real property, which is held in the name of the beneficiary. Land trusts are commonly used in Texas although there is no specific statutory authority for their existence.

CAVEAT

The purpose of this chapter has been to acquaint you with the fundamental aspects of the most commonly used forms of real estate ownership in the United States. You undoubtedly saw instances where you could apply these. Unfortunately, it is not possible in a real estate principles book to discuss each detail of Texas law (many of which change frequently), nor to take into consideration the specific characteristics of a particular transaction. In applying the principles in this book to a particular transaction, you should add competent legal advice regarding legal interpretation of these principles.

REVIEW QUESTIONS

Answers to these questions are found in the Answer Key section at the back of the book.

1. Able, Baker, and Charles are going to purchase an investment property as co-owners and will take title as joint tenants. Which of the following statements are incorrect?
   A. All will acquire their interests at the same moment in time.
   B. Each will receive a separate deed for his share.
   C. All may have equal interest in the property.
   D. All will enjoy equal rights of possession.

2. A married person can hold as separate property
   A. property bought by that person before marriage.
   B. property inherited by that person after marriage.
   C. both A and B.
   D. neither A nor B.

3. A tenant in common may NOT
   A. claim a portion of the property for his own use.
   B. convey his interest by will.
   C. use his share of the property as collateral for a mortgage loan.
   D. sell his share without the agreement of the other tenants.

4. All of the following are true of joint tenancy EXCEPT:
   A. Unities of time, title, interest, and possession must be present.
   B. New joint tenants may be added without forming a new joint tenancy.
   C. Survivorship exists among joint tenants.
   D. A husband and wife may hold title as joint tenants.

5. Joint tenants must acquire their interests in jointly held property
   A. at the same time.
   B. from the same source.
   C. in the same instrument.
   D. all of the above.

6. If any unity of joint tenancy is broken, the law will regard the estate as
   A. a tenancy by the entireties.
   B. community property.
   C. a tenancy in common.
   D. an estate in severalty.

7. In Texas, if two or more persons are named as owners and there is no specific indication as to how they are taking title, they are presumed to be
   A. joint tenants.
   B. tenants in common.
   C. separate owners.
   D. joint owners.

8. Community property laws are derived from legal concepts that have their origin in
   A. Spanish law.
   B. English common law.
   C. American statutory law.
   D. English parliamentary law.

9. Mr. and Mrs. Marvin live in a community property state. Which of the following would most likely be considered their community property?
   A. Property that is inherited by either spouse.
   B. Property conveyed as a gift to either spouse.
   C. Property purchased after they were married.
   D. Property owned by either spouse prior to their marriage.

10. In community property states, which of the following exists?
    A. Dower
    B. Curtesy
    C. Both A and B
    D. Neither A nor B

11. A business entity owned by stockholders who possess shares of stock as evidence of their ownership is
    A. a general partnership.
    B. an S corporation.
    C. a C corporation.
    D. all of the above.
    E. both B and C.

12. The possibility of double taxation on income is a negative factor in
    A. the corporation form of ownership.
    B. the limited partnership form of ownership.
    C. major corporations only.
    D. all of the above.

13. The day-to-day operations of a corporation are the responsibility of its
    A. stockholders.
    B. board of directors.
    C. both A and B.
    D. neither A nor B.

14. Before investing in a limited partnership, one should:
    A. determine if the partnership is suitable for his personal objectives.
    B. investigate the past performance of the general partners.
    C. both A and B.
    D. neither A nor B.

15. The Texas Constitution provides that husbands and wives
    A. can own community property with rights of survivorship
    B. can no longer own any property with rights of survivorship.
    C. are liable only for their proportional share of ownership as in joint tenancy.
    D. both A and C.
    E. none of the above.

Chapter 7

KEY TERMS

Adverse possession: acquisition of land through prolonged and unauthorized occupation

Bargain and sale deed: a deed that contains no covenants, but does imply that the grantor owns the property being conveyed

Cloud on the title: any claim, lien, or encumbrance that impairs title to property

Color of title: some plausible, but not completely clear-cut indication of ownership rights

Consideration: anything of value given to induce another to enter into a contract

Covenant: a written agreement or promise

Deed: a written document that when properly executed and delivered conveys title to land

Grantee: the person named in a deed who acquires ownership

Grantor: the person named in a deed who conveys ownership

Quitclaim deed: a legal instrument used to convey whatever title the grantor has; it contains no covenants, warranties, nor implication of the grantor's ownership

Warranty: an assurance or guarantee that something is true as stated

Transferring Title

IN THIS CHAPTER

In this chapter you will learn how the ownership of real estate is conveyed from one owner to another. Voluntary conveyance of real estate by deed, conveyance after death, and conveyance by occupancy, accession, public grant, dedication, and forfeiture are covered. An important part of this chapter, and a part that you should review very carefully, is the coverage of the essential elements of a deed. Likewise, the various covenants and warranties should be reviewed.

The previous three chapters emphasized how real estate is described, the rights and interests available for ownership, and how title can be held. In this chapter we shall discuss how ownership of real estate is conveyed from one owner to another. We begin with the voluntary conveyance of real estate by deed, and then continue with conveyance after death, and conveyance by occupancy, accession, public grant, dedication, and forfeiture.

DEEDS

A ***deed*** is a written legal document by which ownership of real property is conveyed from one party to another. Deeds were not always used to transfer real estate. In early England, when land was sold its title was conveyed by inviting the purchaser onto the land. In the presence of witnesses, the seller picked up a clod of earth and handed it to the purchaser. Simultaneously, the seller stated that he was delivering ownership of the land to the purchaser. In times when land sales were rare, because ownership usually passed from generation to generation, and when witnesses seldom moved from the towns or farms where they were born, this method worked well. However, as transactions became more common and people more mobile, this method of title transfer became less reliable. Furthermore, it was susceptible to fraud if enough people could be bribed or forced to make false statements. In 1677, England passed a law known as the **Statute of Frauds.** This law, subsequently adopted by each of the American states, requires that contracts for the sale of real estate be in writing and signed in order to be enforceable in a court of law. Texas also has a statute that specifically requires deeds to be in writing.

Essential Elements of a Deed

What makes a written document a deed? What special phrases, statements, and actions are necessary to convey the ownership rights one has in land and buildings? First, a deed must identify the ***grantor***, who is the person giving up ownership, and the ***grantee***, the person who is acquiring that ownership. The actual act of conveying ownership is known as a **grant.** To be legally enforceable, the grantor must be of legal age (18 years in Texas) and of sound mind.

Second, the deed must state that ***consideration*** was given by the grantee to the grantor. In Texas it is common to use the phrase, "For ten dollars ($10.00) and other good and valuable consideration," or the phrase, "For valuable consideration." These meet the legal requirement that consideration be shown, but retain privacy regarding the exact amount paid.

If the conveyance is a gift, the phrase, "For love and affection," may be used, provided the gift is not for the purpose of defrauding the grantor's creditors. In these situations, consideration is not required, and the conveyance is still valid.

Third, the deed must contain **words of conveyance.** With these words the grantor clearly states that the grantor is making a grant of real property to the grantee and identifies the quantity of the estate being granted. Usually, this is the fee simple estate, but it may also be a lesser estate (such as a life estate) or an easement.

A land *description* is the fourth requirement. Acceptable legal descriptions are made by the metes and bounds method, by the government survey system, by recorded plat, or by reference to another recorded document that, in turn, uses one of these methods. Street names and numbers are not used because they do not identify the exact boundaries of the land and because street names and numbers can and do change over time. Appraisal district parcel numbers are subject to change, and are not used either. If the deed conveys only an easement or air right, the deed states that fact along with the legal description of the land. The key point is that a deed must clearly specify what the grantor is granting to the grantee.

Fifth, the grantor must execute the deed by signing it. If the grantor is unable to write his name, he may make a mark, usually an X, in the presence of witnesses. They in turn print his name next to the X and sign as witnesses. If the grantor is a business entity (corporation, partnership, LLC), the authorized party signs the deed.

Figure 7.1 illustrates the essential elements that combine to form a deed. Notice that the example includes an identification of the grantor and grantee, fulfills the requirement for consideration, has words of conveyance, a legal description of the land involved, and the grantor's signature. The words of conveyance are "grant" and the phrase, "to have and to hold forever," says that the grantor is conveying all future benefits, not just a life estate or a tenancy for years. Ordinarily, the grantee does not sign the deed.

FIGURE 7.1 Essential elements of a deed

John Stanley, *grantor, for valuable consideration given by* Robert Brenner, *grantee, does hereby grant unto the grantee, his heirs and assigns to have and to hold forever, the following described land: [insert legal description here].*

John Stanley
Grantor's signature

As a sixth and final requirement, there must also be *delivery and acceptance.* Although a deed may be completed and signed, it does not transfer title to the grantee until the grantor voluntarily delivers it to the grantee and the grantee willingly accepts it. At that moment title passes.

Under Texas law, if a deed has been recorded it is presumed that a proper delivery has been effected. Delivery of the deed into escrow may also constitute delivery. When a deed has been irrevocably delivered into escrow, and the condition of the escrow is thereafter performed, title is said to have passed from the seller when the deed is deposited into escrow. This is sometimes referred to as the *relation back doctrine,* which effects a full and valid delivery for the grantor. For instance, when a grantor delivers title into escrow, but dies before closing of escrow, the conveyance would still be accomplished.

Covenants and Warranties

Although legally adequate, a deed meeting the preceding requirements can still leave a very important question unanswered in the grantee's mind: "Does the grantor possess all the right, title, and interest she is purporting to convey by this deed?" As a protective measure, the grantee can ask the grantor to include certain ***covenants*** and ***warranties*** in the deed. These are written promises by the grantor that the condition of title is as stated in the deed together with the grantor's guarantee that if title is not as stated she will compensate the grantee for any loss suffered. They are implied by law in Texas if the grantor uses the term "grant" or "convey."

Texas law generally recognizes two basic warranties. One is a warranty that the grantor has not previously conveyed the same estate or any right, title, or interest therein to a person other than the grantee named in the deed. The second is a warranty that the estate passed is free from encumbrances other than those therein specified at the time of the execution of the deed. These warranties basically provide that in the event there is a third-party claimant at some later date claiming title to the property, the grantee has the right to recover against the grantor any damages that he may suffer as a result of the failure of the warranties of the grantor in his general warranty deed.

Date and Acknowledgment

Although it is customary to show on the deed the *date* it was executed by the grantor, it is not essential to the deed's validity. Remember that title passes upon *delivery* of the deed to the grantee and that this may not necessarily be the date it was signed.

It is standard practice to have the grantor appear before a notary public or other public officer and formally declare that he signed the deed as a voluntary act. This is known as an **acknowledgment.** An acknowledgment is not necessary in Texas to make the deed a valid conveyance. However, without the acknowledgment the deed is binding only between the parties to the instrument. To protect against third-party claimants, the deed must be recorded in the county clerk's office in the county courthouse in the county in which the land is located. Acknowledgments and the importance of recording deeds will be covered in more detail in Chapter 8. Meanwhile, let's turn our attention to examples of the most commonly used deeds in Texas.

GENERAL WARRANTY DEED

Figure 7.2 illustrates a typical Texas general warranty deed. The name of the deed is shown in **[1]**, although this usually has no effect if the deed is in fact something other than a general warranty deed. An introduction to the deed is usually combined with the location of the property as shown in **[2]**. This is usually the recording jurisdiction, that is, the county where the property is located. The designation of the grantors, as shown in **[3]** and **[4]**, generally shows the marital status of the grantor(s). This helps keep the chain of title intact in the event there are any conflicts or discrepancies regarding the grantor and grantee in future conveyances. Consideration, a requirement for deeds generally, although it need not be valuable consideration, is shown at **[5]**. Consideration is usually stated as "$10.00 and other good and valuable consideration" to show that consideration was in fact paid, but to keep the actual amount of the transaction out of the public record. The granting clause is shown in **[6]**. The use of the word "grant" or "convey" in Texas implies general warranty covenants, and unless otherwise stated, Texas law presumes fee simple title. The names of the grantees are shown in [7]. If a deed does not have a grantee, it is void because no effective conveyance took place. A legal description, a requirement for all deeds, is shown at **[8]**. The habendum and warranty clauses, which define the obligations of the grantor with respect to the warranties, are shown at **[9]**. Although not legally required, the deed is generally dated, as shown in **[10]**. The important date is not the date of the deed but the date the deed was recorded. The Texas Recording Act provides that priority interests are determined by the first to record, therefore the date of conveyance is not technically as important as the recording date. The final requirement for a deed is that it has the signature of the grantor(s), shown at **[11]**. Although not required to convey property, an acknowledgment of the grantors' signatures before a notary public is usually attached so that the deed can be recorded. Texas does not require a seal in order to make the deed valid. However, the acknowledgment must have a seal to be effective.

The exact style or form of a deed is not critical as long as it contains all the essentials clearly stated and in conformity with state law. For example, one

FIGURE 7.2 Typical texas general warranty deed

[1] **GENERAL WARRANTY DEED**
(Cash)

THE STATE OF TEXAS §
§ KNOW ALL MEN BY THESE PRESENTS:
COUNTY OF HARRIS [2] §

[3] [4]

THAT THE UNDERSIGNED, I.M. Seller and wife, Happy Seller, hereinafter referred to as "Grantor", whether one or more, for and in consideration of the sum of TEN DOLLARS ($10.00) [5] cash, and other good and valuable consideration in hand paid by the Grantee, herein named, the receipt and sufficiency of which is hereby fully acknowledged and confessed, has GRANTED, SOLD and [6] CONVEYED, and by these presents does hereby GRANT, SELL and CONVEY unto N. Debted and wife, May B. Debted, herein referred to as "Grantee", whether one or more, the real property described [7] to-wit:

[8] Lot 1, Block 1, Shakey Acres Subdivision, Harris County, Texas, as shown of record at Volume 7, Page 3, of the Map Records of Harris County, Texas.

This conveyance, however, is made and accepted subject to any and all validly existing encumbrances, conditions and restrictions, relating to the hereinabove described property as now reflected by the records of the County Clerk of Harris County, Texas.

TO HAVE AND TO HOLD the above described premises, together with all and singular the rights and appurtenances thereto in anywise belonging unto the said Grantee, Grantee's heirs, executors, administrators, successors and/or assigns forever; and Grantor does hereby bind Grantor, Grantor's heirs, executors, administrators, successors and/or assigns to WARRANT AND FOREVER [9] DEFEND all and singular the said premises unto the said Grantee, Grantee's heirs, executors, administrators, successors and/or assigns, against every person whomsoever claiming or to claim the same or any part thereof.

Current ad valorem taxes on said property having been prorated, the payment thereof is assumed by Grantee.

[10]

EXECUTED this 28th day of February, 200x.

____
I.M. SELLER

Grantee's Address: [11]

____
____________________________ HAPPY SELLER

THE STATE OF TEXAS §
§
COUNTY OF HARRIS §

The foregoing instrument was acknowledged before me on the 28th day of February, 200x, by I.M. Seller and Happy Seller.

____
NOTARY PUBLIC, STATE OF TEXAS

commonly used warranty deed format begins with the words "Know all men by these presents," is written in the first person, and has the date at the end. Although a person may prepare his own deed, the writing of deeds should be left to experts in the field. In fact, Texas permits only attorneys to write deeds for other persons. Even the preparation of preprinted deeds from stationery stores and title companies should be left to knowledgeable persons. Preprinted deeds contain several pitfalls for the unwary. First, the form may have been prepared and printed in another state and, as a result, may not meet the requirements of Texas law. Second, if the blanks are incorrectly filled in, the deed may not be legally recognized. This is a particularly difficult problem when neither the grantor nor grantee realizes it until several years after the deed's delivery. Third, the use of a form deed presumes that the grantor's situation can be fitted to the form and that the grantor will be knowledgeable enough to select the correct form.

SPECIAL WARRANTY DEED

In a **special warranty deed,** the grantor covenants and warrants the property's title only against defects occurring during the grantor's ownership and not against defects existing before that time. The special warranty deed is often used by executors and trustees who convey on behalf of an estate or principal because the executor or trustee has no authority to warrant and defend the acts of previous holders of title. The grantee can protect against the gap in warranty by purchasing title insurance.

BARGAIN AND SALE DEED

The basic ***bargain and sale deed*** contains no covenants, and only the minimum essentials of a deed (note the habendum and warranty clause in Figure 7.3). It has a date, identifies the grantor and grantee, recites consideration, describes the property, contains words of conveyance, and has the grantor's signature. But lacking covenants, what assurance does the grantee have that she is acquiring title to anything? Actually, none. In this deed the grantor purports to own the property described in the deed and that he is granting it to the grantee. Logically, then, a grantee will prefer a warranty deed over a bargain and sale deed, or will require title insurance.

QUITCLAIM DEED

A ***quitclaim deed*** has no covenants or warranties (see Figure 7.4). Moreover, the grantor makes no statement, nor does he even imply that he owns the property he is quitclaiming to the grantee. Whatever rights the grantor possesses at the time the deed is delivered are conveyed to the grantee. If the grantor has no interest, right, or title to the property described in the deed, none is conveyed to the grantee. However, if the grantor possesses fee simple title, fee simple title will be conveyed to the grantee.

The critical wording in a quitclaim deed is the grantor's statement that he does hereby "quitclaim." The word *quitclaim* means to renounce all possession, right, or interest. Sometimes the words "remise" or "release" may also be used. If the grantor subsequently acquires any right or interest in the property, he is not obligated to convey it to the grantee.

At first glance it may seem strange that such a deed should even exist, but it does serve a very useful purpose. Situations often arise in real estate transactions when a person claims to have a partial or incomplete right or

FIGURE 7.3 Bargain and sale deed

DEED
(Without Warranties)

THE STATE OF TEXAS §
§ KNOW ALL MEN BY THESE PRESENTS:
COUNTY OF HARRIS §

THAT the undersigned, I.M. Seller and wife, Happy Seller, hereinafter referred to as "Grantor", whether one or more, of the County of Harris and State of Texas, for and in consideration of the sum of TEN AND NO/100 DOLLARS ($10.00) and other good and valuable consideration in hand paid by N. Debted and wife, May B. Debted, hereinafter referenced "Grantee", whether one or more, the receipt and sufficiency of which is hereby acknowledged, have granted, sold and quitclaimed, and by these presents do grant, sell and convey unto Grantee, of the County of Harris and State of Texas, the real property described to-wit:

Lot 1, Block 1, Shakey Acres Subdivision, Harris County, Texas, as shown of record at Volume 7, Page 3, of the Map Records of Harris County, Texas.

TO HAVE AND HOLD the above described property and premises unto the said Grantee, Grantee's heirs, administrators, executors, successors and/or assigns forever. This conveyance is made without warranty, express or implied.

EXECUTED this 28th day of February, 200x.

____
I.M. SELLER

Grantee's Address:

____
____

____
HAPPY SELLER

THE STATE OF TEXAS §
§
COUNTY OF HARRIS §

The foregoing instrument was acknowledged before me on the 28th day of February, 200x, by I.M. Seller and Happy Seller.

____
NOTARY PUBLIC, STATE OF TEXAS

interest in a parcel of land. Such a right or interest, known as a ***cloud on the title***, may have been due to an inheritance, community property right, or an old, unreleased mortgage. By releasing that claim to the fee simple owner through the use of a quitclaim deed, the cloud on the fee owner's title is removed.

After-Acquired Title

The basic bargain and sale deed contains no covenants of warranty. It does purport to pass an interest in real estate, but with no warranties. It is superior to the quitclaim deed in that it passes *after-acquired title*. While generally

FIGURE 7.4 Quitclaim deed

QUITCLAIM DEED

THE STATE OF TEXAS	§	
	§	KNOW ALL MEN BY THESE PRESENTS:
COUNTY OF HARRIS	§	

That the undersigned, I.M. Seller and wife, Happy Seller, hereinafter referred to as "Grantor", whether one or more, for and in consideration of the sum of TEN AND NO/100 DOLLARS ($10.00) in hand paid by Grantee herein named, and other good and valuable consideration, the receipt and sufficiency of which is hereby acknowledged, has QUITCLAIMED, and by these presents does QUITCLAIM unto N. Debted and wife, May B. Debted, of the County of Harris, State of Texas, herein referred to as "Grantee", whether one or more, the real property described to-wit:

Lot 1, Block 1, Shakey Acres Subdivision, Harris County, Texas, as shown of record at Volume 7, Page 3, of the Map Records of Harris County, Texas.

TO HAVE AND TO HOLD all of Grantor's right, title and interest in and to the above described property and premises unto the Grantee, and Grantee's heirs, administrators, executors, successors and/or assigns forever; so that neither Grantor nor Grantor's heirs, administrators, executors, successors and/or assigns shall have, claim or demand any right or title to the aforesaid property, premises or appurtenances or any part thereof.

EXECUTED this 28th day of February, 200x.

____
I.M. SELLER

Grantee's Address:

____
____

____
HAPPY SELLER

THE STATE OF TEXAS	§
	§
COUNTY OF HARRIS	§

The foregoing instrument was acknowledged before me on the 28th day of February, 200x, by I.M. Seller and Happy Seller.

____
NOTARY PUBLIC, STATE OF TEXAS

Source: © 2012 Cengage Learning

considered a legal technicality, the after-acquired title doctrine generally states that if a grantor conveys an interest in property that the grantor does not own at the time of the conveyance, and if the grantor ever acquires that property subsequent to her initial conveyance, title automatically passes to the initial grantee. A quitclaim deed contains no warranties; the grantor does not claim to own an interest in property. A quitclaim deed is merely a relinquishment of all right, title, and interest that the grantor *may* have. Because of the loose wording of the quitclaim deed, it does not pass after-acquired title. Therefore, for most real estate situations a bargain and sale deed is preferred to a quitclaim deed.

OTHER TYPES OF DEEDS

All deeds used in Texas are of one of the types discussed above. People often refer to other deeds used for special purposes by name, but actually all of these deeds must have the characteristics of one of the foregoing deeds. Since these alternate deed terms are commonly used, we will describe them briefly.

A **gift deed** is created by simply replacing the recitation or money and other valuable consideration with the statement, "in consideration of his [her, their] love and affection." This phrase may be used in a warranty, special warranty, or grant deed. However, it is most often used in quitclaim or bargain and sale deeds as these permit the grantor to avoid committing himself to any warranties regarding the property.

A **guardian's deed** is used to convey a minor's interest in real property. It contains only one covenant, that the guardian and minor have not encumbered the property. The deed must state the legal authority (usually a court order) that permits the guardian to convey the minor's property.

A **sheriff's deed** or **trustee's deed** in the event of a foreclosure is issued to the new buyer when a person's real estate is sold as the result of a mortgage or other court-ordered foreclosure sale. The deed should state the source of the sheriff's or referee's authority and the amount of consideration paid. Such a deed conveys only the foreclosed party's title, and, at the most, carries only one covenant: that the sheriff or referee has not damaged the property's title.

A **correction deed,** also called a *deed of confirmation,* is used to correct an error in a previously executed and delivered deed. For example, a name may have been misspelled or an error found in the property description.

A *tax deed* is used to convey title to property that has been sold by the state or local government because of the nonpayment of real property taxes.

CONVEYANCE AFTER DEATH

If a person dies without leaving a last will and testament (or leaves one that is subsequently ruled void by the courts because it was improperly prepared), he is said to have died **intestate,** which means without a testament. When this happens, state law directs how the deceased's assets shall be distributed. This is known as **title by descent** or **intestate succession.**

Under Texas law, when a person dies, whether testate or intestate, his real or personal property passes immediately upon his death to his heirs or to his beneficiaries, subject to the payments of any debts, except those which are exempted by law.

Upon the death of a spouse, all of the community property of the deceased spouse passes to the surviving spouse if: (1) there are no children, or (2) if all the surviving children of the deceased spouse are also children of the surviving spouse.

If there are children of the decedent that are not the children of the surviving spouse, one-half of the community estate is retained by the surviving spouse and one-half passes to the children of the decedents of the deceased spouse. One-third of the separate property of a spouse passes to the surviving spouse as a life estate. The children of the decedent inherit two-thirds and the remainder interest of the life estate of the surviving spouse.

If there is no spouse or children, the deceased's grandchildren receive the next share. If there are no lineal descendants, the deceased's parents, brothers and sisters, and their children receive the next largest share. These are known as the deceased's **heirs.** The amount each heir receives, if anything, depends on state law and on how many persons with superior positions in the succession are alive. If no heirs can be found, the deceased's property escheats (reverts) to the state. These rules apply to real property. Personal property rules are slightly different: If there is separate personal property, the surviving spouse inherits one-third of these items.

Testate, Intestate

A person who dies and leaves a valid will is said to have died **testate,** which means that he or she died leaving a testament telling how the property shall be distributed. The person who made the will, now deceased, is known as the **testator** (male) or **testatrix** (female). In the will, the testator names the persons or organizations who are to receive their real and personal property after they die. Real property that is willed is known as a **devise** and the recipient, a **devisee.** Personal property that is willed is known as a **bequest** or **legacy,** and the recipient, a **legatee.** The will usually names an **executor** (male) or **executrix** (female) to carry out its instructions. If one is not named, the court will appoint an **administrator** (male) or **administratrix** (female).

Notice an important difference between the transfer of real estate ownership by deed and by will: once a deed is made and delivered, the ownership transfer is permanent; the grantor cannot change their mind and take back the property. With respect to a will, the devisees, although named, have no rights to the testator's property until the testator dies. Until that time the testator/testatrix can change their mind and their will.

Probate Court

Upon death, the deceased's will must be filed with a court having power to admit and certify wills, called a **probate court** in Texas. In lesser populated Texas counties, the county court performs this function. This court determines if the will meets all the requirements of law: in particular, that it is genuine, properly signed and witnessed, and that the testator was of sound mind when he made it. At this time anyone may step forward and contest the validity of the will. If the court finds the will to be valid, the executor/executrix is permitted to carry out its terms. If the testator owned real property, its ownership is conveyed using an executor's deed prepared and signed by the executor. The executor's deed is used both to transfer title to a devisee and to sell real property to raise cash. The executor's deed is usually a special warranty deed.

Protecting the Deceased's Intentions

Because the deceased are not present to protect their assets, state laws attempt to ensure that fair market value is received for the deceased's real estate by requiring court approval of proposed sales, and in some cases by sponsoring open bidding in the courtroom. To protect one's interests, a purchaser should ascertain that the executor/executrix has the authority to convey title.

For a will to be valid, and subsequently bind the executor to carry out the instructions, it must meet specific legal requirements. All states, including Texas, recognize the **formal** or **witnessed will,** a written document prepared, in most cases, by an attorney. The testator must declare it to be his or her will and sign it in the presence of two witnesses, who, at the testator's request and in his or her presence, sign the will as witnesses. A formal will prepared by an attorney is the preferred method because the will then conforms explicitly to the law. This greatly reduces the likelihood of its being contested after the testator's death. Additionally, an attorney may offer valuable advice on how to word the will to reduce inheritance taxes.

Holographic Wills

Holographic wills are wills that are entirely handwritten, dated, and signed by the testator; but there are no witnesses. Nineteen states, including Texas, recognize holographic wills as legally binding. People selecting this form of will generally do so because it saves the time and expense of seeking professional legal aid, and because it is entirely private. Besides the fact that holographic wills are considered to have no effect in 31 states, they often result in much legal argument in states that do accept them. This can occur when the testator is not fully aware of the law as it pertains to the making of wills. Many otherwise happy families have been torn apart by dissension when a relative dies and they read the will only to find that there is a question as to whether or not it was properly prepared and hence valid. Unfortunately, what follows is not what the deceased intended; those who would receive more from intestate succession will contest that the will be declared void and of no effect. Those with more to gain if the will stands as written will muster legal forces to argue for its acceptance by the probate court.

Codicil

A **codicil** is a written supplement or amendment made to a previously existing will. It is used to change some aspect of the will or to add a new instruction, without the work of rewriting the entire will. The codicil must be dated, signed, and witnessed in the same manner as the original will. The only valid way to change a will is with a codicil or by writing a completely new will. The law does not recognize cross-outs, notations, or other alterations made on the will itself.

ADVERSE POSSESSION

Through the unauthorized occupation of another person's land for a long enough period of time, it is possible under certain conditions to acquire ownership by ***adverse possession.*** The historical roots of adverse possession go back many centuries to a time before written deeds were used as evidence of ownership. At that time, in the absence of any claims to the contrary, a person who occupied a parcel of land was presumed to be its owner. Today, adverse possession is, in effect, a statute of limitations that bars a legal owner from claiming title to land when they have done nothing to oust an adverse occupant during the statutory period. From the adverse occupant's standpoint, adverse possession is a method of acquiring title by possessing land for a specified period of time under certain conditions.

Courts of law are quite demanding of proof before they will issue a decree in favor of a person claiming title by virtue of adverse possession. The claimant must have maintained actual, visible, continuous, hostile, exclusive, and notorious possession, and be publicly claiming ownership to the property. These requirements mean that the claimant's use must have been visible and obvious to the legal owner, continuous and not just occasional, and exclusive enough to give notice of the claimant's individual claim. Furthermore, the use must have been without permission and the claimant must have acted as though the claimant was the owner, even in the presence of the actual owner. Finally, the adverse claimant must be able to prove that they have met these requirements for a period ranging from 3 to 30 years.

Adverse possession is statutorily defined in Texas and consists of four types: 3-year, 5-year, 10-year, and 25-year adverse possession.

Under the *3-year possession* statute, the possessor must claim title to the property under "some title" or "color of title," which might even be "irregular." (One or more of the documents of title in the chain of title may be missing.)

Title means a regular chain of transfers from or under the sovereignty of the soil. ***Color of title*** means a consecutive chain of transfers down to such person in possession, which may be irregular, as long as said defect does not extend to or include the want to intrinsic fairness or honesty.

The *5-year adverse possession* statute requires that the adverse claimant have peaceable and adverse possession of the property; cultivating, using, enjoying, and paying taxes on it; and claiming under a deed or deeds duly registered.

The *10-year adverse possession* statute requires that the adverse claimant have peaceable and adverse possession of the property; cultivating, using, and enjoying the same; and has a restriction of 160 acres unless the property has been fenced off, and unless the claimant has some memorandum of title that fixes the boundaries of the property. The memorandum of title as used in the 10-year statute does not require a deed, but merely a memorandum of title.

The *25-year adverse possession* statute requires peaceable and adverse possession of the real estate for a period of 25 years under a claim of right in good faith under any instrument purporting to convey the same, which has been recorded in the records of the county in which the real estate is located. This type of adverse possession is valid against minors and incompetents.

It is important to realize that any adverse possession in Texas under a fraudulent claim or under a forged document does not comply with the adverse possession requirements as set out by statute. Also, it is easy to understand why the owner of a large ranch would "ride the range" to maintain his fence and boundaries against poachers or other adverse claimants to either maintain his own title or perfect his own adverse possession interest.

Tacking On

In accumulating the required number of years, an adverse claimant may **tack on** the period of possession to that of a prior adverse occupant. This could be done through the purchase of that right. The current adverse occupant could in turn sell the property to a still later adverse occupant until enough years were accumulated to present a claim in court.

Although the concept of adverse possession often creates the mental picture of a trespasser moving onto someone else's land and living there long enough to acquire title in fee, this is not the usual application. More often, adverse possession is used to extinguish weak or questionable claims to title. For example, if a person buys property at a tax sale, takes possession, and pays the property taxes each year afterward, adverse possession laws act to cut off claims to title by the previous owner.

EASEMENT BY PRESCRIPTION

An easement can also be acquired by prolonged adverse use. This is known as acquiring an *easement by prescription*. As with adverse possession, the laws are strict: the usage must be openly visible, continuous, and exclusive, as well as hostile and adverse to the owner. The use must have occurred over a period of 10 years. All these facts must be proved in a court of law before the court will issue the claimant a document legally recognizing ownership of the easement. As an easement is a right to use land for a specific purpose, not ownership of the land itself. Texas courts do not require the payment of property taxes to acquire a prescriptive easement.

As may be seen from the foregoing discussion, a landowner must be given obvious notification *at the location* of his land that someone is attempting to claim ownership or an easement. Because an adverse claim must be continuous and hostile, an owner can break it by ejecting the trespassers or by preventing them from trespassing or by simply giving them permission to be there. Any of these actions would demonstrate the landowner's superior title. Owners of stores and office buildings with private sidewalks or streets used by the public can take action to break any possible claims to a public easement by either periodically barricading the sidewalk or street or by posting signs giving permission to pass. These signs are often seen in the form of brass plaques embedded in the sidewalk or street. In certain states, a landowner may record with the public records office a **notice of consent.** This is evidence that subsequent uses of his land for the purposes stated in the notice are permissive and not adverse. The notice may be revoked later by recording a **notice of revocation.** There is no authority in Texas creating easements by prescription to the public, except for public roads through dedication. Federal, state, and local governments protect themselves against adverse claims to their lands by passing laws making themselves immune from adverse possession claims.

OWNERSHIP BY ACCESSION

The extent of one's ownership of land can be altered by the process of **accession.** This can result from natural or man-made causes. With regard to natural causes, the owner of land fronting on a lake, river, or ocean may acquire additional land because of the gradual accumulation of rock, sand, and soil. This process is called **accretion,** and the results are referred to as alluvion and reliction. **Alluvion** is the increase of land that results when waterborne soil is gradually deposited to produce firm dry ground. **Reliction** (or dereliction) results when a lake, sea, or river permanently recedes, exposing dry land. When land is rapidly washed away by the action of water, it is known as **avulsion.** Man-made accession occurs by *annexation* when personal property is permanently attached to the real estate. For example, when lumber, nails, and cement are used to build a house, they alter the extent of one's land ownership.

PUBLIC GRANT OF LAND

A transfer of land by a government body to a private individual is called a **public grant** or *patent.* The Homestead Act passed by the U.S. Congress in 1862 permits persons wishing to settle on otherwise unappropriated federal land to acquire fee simple ownership by paying a small filing charge and occupying and cultivating the land for five years. Similarly, for only a few dollars, a person may file a mining claim to federal land for the purpose of extracting whatever valuable minerals they can find. To retain the claim, a certain amount of work must be performed on the land each year. Otherwise, the government will consider the claim abandoned and another person may claim it. If the claim is worked long enough, a public grant can be sought and fee simple title obtained. In 1976, the U.S. government ended the homesteading program in all states except Alaska.

DEDICATION OF LAND

When an owner makes a voluntary gift of land to the public, it is known as **dedication.** To illustrate, a land developer buys a large parcel of vacant land and develops it into streets and lots. The lots are sold to private buyers, but what about the streets? In all probability they will be dedicated to the town, city, or county. By doing this, the developer, and later the lot buyers, will not have to pay taxes on the streets, and the public will be responsible for maintaining them. The fastest way to accomplish the transfer is by either statutory dedication or dedication by deed. In *statutory dedication,* the developer prepares a map showing the streets, has the map approved by local government officials, and then records it as a public document. In *dedication by deed,* the developer prepares a deed that identifies the streets and grants them to the city.

Common law dedication takes place when landowners, by their acts or words, show that they intend part of their land to be dedicated even though they have never officially made a written dedication. For example, a landowner may encourage the public to travel on his roads in an attempt to convince a local road department to take over maintenance.

REVERSION

Reversion can occur when a deed contains a condition or limitation. For example, a grantor states in his deed that the land conveyed may be used for residential purposes only. If the grantee constructs commercial buildings, the grantor can reacquire title on the grounds that the grantee forfeited his interest by not using the land for the required purpose. Note the discussion on qualified fee estates and life estates in Chapter 4. Similarly, a deed may prohibit certain uses of land. If the land is used for a prohibited purpose, the grantor can claim forfeiture has occurred.

ALIENATION

A change in ownership of any kind is known as an *alienation.* In addition to the forms of alienation discussed in this chapter, alienation can result from court action in connection with escheat, eminent domain, partition, foreclosure, execution sales, quiet title suits, and marriage. These topics are discussed in other chapters.

REVIEW QUESTIONS

Answers to these questions are found in the Answer Key section at the back of the book.

1. A written legal document by which ownership of real property is transferred from one party to another is
   A. a bill of sale.
   B. a lease.
   C. a contract of sale.
   D. a deed.

2. Which of the following is essential to the validity of a deed?
   A. The grantor must be of legal age.
   B. The grantor must be of sound mind.
   C. Both A and B.
   D. Neither A nor B.

3. Which of the following may not be conveyed by deed?
   A. Fee simple estate
   B. Life estate
   C. Easements
   D. Leasehold estate

4. With the words conveyance in a deed, the grantor
   A. states that he is making a grant of the property to the grantee.
   B. warrants that he has the right to convey title to the property.
   C. Both A and B.
   D. Neither A nor B.

5. In order to convey title to real property, a deed must be signed by the
   A. grantee.
   B. grantor.
   C. agent.
   D. buyer.

6. In order to convey title, a deed must be
   A. delivered by the grantor to the grantee.
   B. accepted by the grantee.
   C. Both A and B.
   D. Neither A nor B.

7. The "relation back doctrine" in Texas applies when
   A. a grantor delivers title directly to the grantee.
   B. a grantor does not deliver title to the grantee.
   C. the grantor delivers title into escrow.
   D. the grantee refuses to accept title.

8. Texas law recognizes which two basic deed warranties:
   A. No previous conveyance and covenant of further assurance.
   B. No previous conveyance and covenant against encumbrances.
   C. Covenant against encumbrances and covenant of quiet possession.
   D. No previous conveyance and covenant of warranty forever.

9. The deed considered to be the best deed a grantee can receive is a
   A. general warranty deed.
   B. special warranty deed.
   C. bargain and sale deed.
   D. quitclaim deed.

10. Which of the following are the same?
    A. Grantor—Party conveying title
    B. Grantee—Party acquiring title
    C. Both A and B
    D. Neither A nor B

11. The phrase "the grantee's heirs and assigns forever" indicates the conveyance of a
    A. fee simple estate.
    B. life estate.
    C. leasehold estate.
    D. less than freehold estate.

12. The most important date on a deed in Texas is the date that the deed is
    A. signed.
    B. conveyed.
    C. recorded.
    D. written.

13. Quitclaim deeds are often used
    A. to remove a cloud from the title.
    B. to convey the grantor's interest without imposing any future obligations to defend the title upon the grantor.
    C. both A and B.
    D. neither A nor B.

14. You would expect to find the words "remise" and "release" in a
    A. warranty deed.
    B. special warranty deed.
    C. grant deed.
    D. quitclaim deed.

15. A court of law with the power to admit and certify wills is called a
    A. probate court.
    B. surrogate court.
    C. both A and B.
    D. neither A nor B.

16. Title acquired as the result of inheritance from a person who dies intestate is known as
    A. title by descent.
    B. a devise.
    C. title by intestate succession.
    D. both A and C.
    E. both B and C.

17. A handwritten will signed by the testator but not witnessed is known as a
    A. nuncupative will.
    B. holographic will.
    C. oral will.
    D. formal will.

18. An easement acquired by prolonged adverse use is acquired by
    A. implied grant.
    B. necessity.
    C. prescription.
    D. condemnation.

19. An owner can break a claim of adverse possession by
    A. ejecting the trespasser.
    B. giving the trespasser permission to trespass.
    C. both A and B.
    D. neither A nor B.

20. The process of increasing land due to the gradual deposition of waterborne soil is known as
    A. reliction.
    B. avulsion.
    C. accretion.
    D. alluvion.

Chapter 8

KEY TERMS

Abstract: a summary of all recorded documents affecting title to a given parcel of land

Acknowledgment: a formal declaration by a person signing a document that he or she, in fact, did sign the document

Actual notice: knowledge gained from what one has actually seen, heard, read, or observed

Chain of title: the linkage of property ownership that connects the present owner to the original source of title

Constructive notice: notice given by the public records and by visible possession, coupled with the legal presumption that all persons are thereby notified

Marketable title: title that is free from reasonable doubt as to who is the owner

Mechanic's lien: a lien placed against real property by any unpaid workman or supplier who has done work or furnished building materials

Quiet title suit: court-ordered hearings held to determine land ownership

Title insurance: an insurance policy against defects in title not listed in the title report or abstract

Recordation, Abstracts, and Title Insurance

IN THIS CHAPTER

This chapter focuses on (1) the need for a method of determining real property ownership, (2) the process by which current and past ownership is determined from public records, and (3) the availability of insurance against errors made in determining ownership. The chapter also covers the need for public records, requirements for recording, public records organization, chain of title, abstract, title insurance, and quiet title suits.

NEED FOR PUBLIC RECORDS

Until the enactment of the Statute of Frauds in England in 1677, determining who owned a parcel of land was primarily a matter of observing who was in physical possession. A landowner gave notice to the world of his claim to ownership by visibly occupying his land. After 1677 written deeds were required to show transfers of ownership. The problem then became one of finding the person holding the most current deed to the land. This was easy if the deedholder also occupied the land, but was more difficult if he did not. The solution was to create a government-sponsored public recording service where a person could record his deed. These records would then be open free of charge to anyone. In this fashion, an owner could post notice to all that he claimed ownership of a parcel of land. A purchaser seeks ***marketable title***—one that is reasonably free from doubt as to who the owner is. Although Texas recognizes the term *marketable title* generally, it has not adopted a Marketable Title Act (as some states have), and marketable title is not insured under Texas title insurance policies.

Constructive Notice

There are two ways for a person to give notice of a claim or right to land. One is by recording documents in the public records that give written notice to that effect. The other is by visibly occupying or otherwise visibly making use of the land. The law holds the world at large responsible for looking at the public records and looking at the land for this notice of right or claim. This is called ***constructive notice.*** Constructive notice charges the public with the responsibility of looking in the public records *and* at the property itself to obtain knowledge of all who are claiming a right or interest.

Actual Notice

Actual notice is knowledge that one has actually gained based on what one has seen, heard, read, or observed. For example, if you read an unrecorded deed from Jones to Smith, you have actual notice of the deed and Smith's claim to the property. If you go to the property and you see someone in possession, you have actual notice of their claim to be there.

Actual notice also includes notice the law presumes you to have when circumstances, appearances, or rumors warrant further inquiry. For example, suppose you are considering the purchase of vacant acreage and upon inspecting it see a dirt road cutting across the land that is not mentioned in the public records. The law expects you to make further inquiry. The road may be a legal easement across the property. Another example is that anytime you buy rental property, you are expected to make inquiry as to the rights of the occupants. They may hold substantial rights you would not know about without asking them.

Remember that anyone claiming an interest or right is expected to make it known either by recorded claim or visible use of the property. Anyone acquiring a right or interest is expected to look in the public records and go to the property to make a visual inspection for claims and inquire as to the extent of those claims.

Recording Acts

All states have passed **recording acts** to provide for the recording of every instrument (i.e., document) by which an estate, interest, or right in land is created, transferred, or encumbered. In Texas, each county has a county clerk's office. Located at the seat of county government, each county clerk's office will record documents submitted to it that pertain to real property in that county. Thus, a deed to property in Tarrant County is recorded with the county clerk in Tarrant County. Similarly, anyone seeking information regarding ownership of land in Tarrant County would go to the county clerk's office in Tarrant County. The recording process itself involves photocopying the documents and filing them for future reference.

To encourage people to use public recording facilities Texas law holds that (1) a deed, mortgage, or other instrument affecting real estate is not effective as far as subsequent purchasers and lenders are concerned if it is not recorded, and (2) prospective purchasers, mortgage lenders, and the public at large are presumed notified when a document is recorded. Figure 8.1 illustrates the concept of public recording.

Example of Notice Laws

To illustrate the effect of constructive and actual notice laws, suppose that Brown offers to sell his land to Carver. Carver then inspects both the land and the public

FIGURE 8.1 The concept of public recording

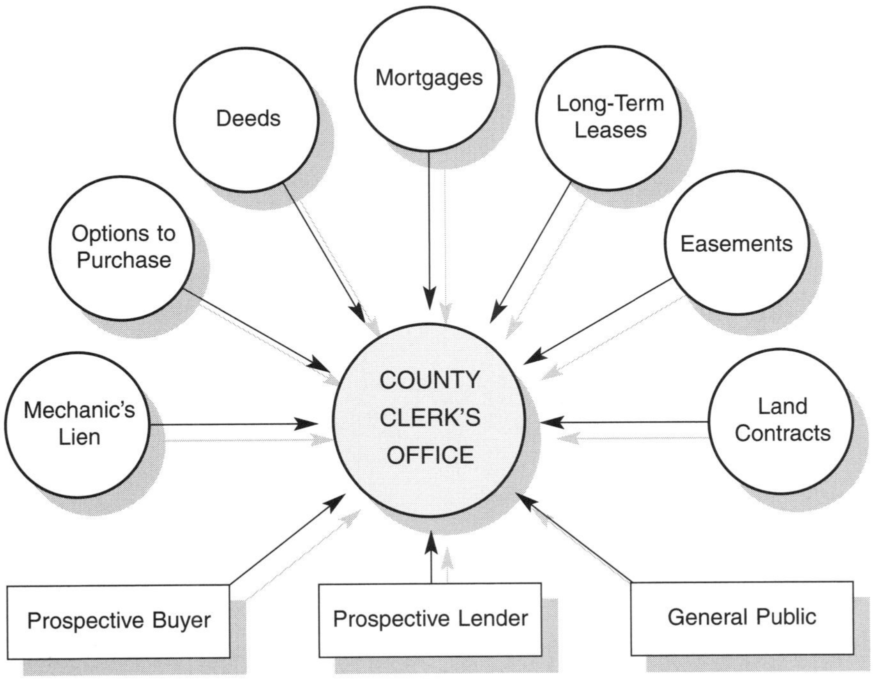

The county clerk's office serves as a central information station for changes in rights, estates, and interests in land.

Source: © 2012 Cengage Learning

records and finds Brown to be the owner. Satisfied as to Brown's ownership, Carver pays Brown and receives a deed in return. Suppose that Carver does not occupy the land, but he does record his deed with the county clerk's office in the county where the land is located. If Brown now approaches Dawson and attempts to sell the same land, Dawson will find, upon visiting the public records office, that Brown has already conveyed title to Carver.

But what if Dawson assumes that Brown is telling the truth and does not trouble himself to inspect the land or the records? Even though Dawson pays for the land and receives a deed from Brown, the law will not regard Dawson as the rightful owner, even if Dawson records his deed. When Dawson discovers that Carver is the true owner, the only recourse open to Dawson is to sue Brown for the return of his money, presuming he can still locate Brown.

What would the result be if Carver did not record the deed he received and did not occupy the land? If Dawson became interested in buying the land and inspected the public records, he would find Brown to be the owner of the record. Upon inspecting the land, Dawson would find no notice of Carver's ownership either. Having satisfied the law and himself regarding the land's ownership, Dawson would pay Brown and receive a deed to the land. If Dawson records his deed before Carver does, the law will consider Dawson to be the new owner. At this point, the only recourse open to Carver is to try to get his money back from Brown. Even if Carver later records his deed and claims that the date on his deed is earlier than the date on Dawson's deed, it is of no avail. Priority is established by the date of recording, not by the date written on the deed. Failure to record does not invalidate the deed itself. It is still binding between the parties who made it, but it is not valid with respect to the rest of the world.

If Carver does not record the deed he receives, but does occupy the land, the law holds Dawson responsible for visiting the land and asking Carver what his rights are. At that point Dawson would learn of Brown's deed to Carver. Anytime a person buys property knowing that it has been sold before to another and the deed has not been recorded, he will not receive good title.

Although recording acts permit the recording of any estate, right, or interest in land, many lesser rights are rarely recorded because of the cost and effort involved. Month-to-month rentals and leases for a year or less fall into this category. Consequently, only an on-site inspection would reveal their existence, or the existence of any developing adverse possession or prescriptive easement claim.

PUTTING IT TO WORK

With respect to actual and constructive notice, we can draw two important conclusions. First, a prospective purchaser (or lessee or lender) is presumed by law to have inspected both the land itself and the public records to determine the present rights and interests of others. Second, upon receiving a deed, mortgage, or other document relating to an estate, right, or interest in land, one should have it immediately recorded in the county in which the land is located so that others will have notice of the recording party's interest in the land.

REQUIREMENTS FOR RECORDING

Texas requires that a document be *acknowledged* before it is eligible to be recorded or it will permit *proper witnessing* or a *jurat* as a substitute.

To effect a proper witnessing, the witness must personally appear before some officer authorized to take acknowledgments (notary public) and state under oath that (1) the witness saw the person execute the instrument and that said person executed the instrument for the purposes and consideration therein stated; and (2) that the witness signed the instrument as a witness at the request of the person who executed such instrument.

A **jurat** is a sworn statement by the person who signed the document that the information contained in the document is true. It is usually sworn to before a notary public or other authorized officer. A form of jurat is shown in Figure 8.2.

FIGURE 8.2 A form of jurat

Subscribed and sworn to before me on this ______ day of __________, 20______.

____

Notary Public in and for

______________ County, Texas

Source: © 2012 Cengage Learning

The objective of these requirements is to make certain that the person who signs the document is the same person named in the document and that the signing was a free and voluntary act. This is done to ensure the accuracy of the public records and to eliminate the possibility of forgery and fraud. To illustrate, suppose that you own 50 acres of vacant land and someone is intent on stealing it from you. Because the physical removal of your land is an impossibility, an attempt could be made to change the public records. A deed would be typed and the forger would sign your name to it. If he were successful in recording the deed, and then attempted to sell the land, the buyer would, upon searching the records, find a deed conveying the land from you to the forger. A visual inspection of the vacant 50 acres would not show you in actual possession. Although innocent of any wrongdoing and buying in good faith, the buyer would be left with only a worthless piece of paper, as there was no intent on your part to convey title to him.

Acknowledgment

An ***acknowledgment*** is a formal declaration by a person signing a document that he or she, in fact, did sign the document. Persons authorized to take acknowledgments include notaries public, recording office clerks, commissioners of deeds, judges of courts of record, justices of the peace, and certain others as authorized by Texas law. Commissioned military officers are authorized to take the acknowledgments of persons in the military; foreign ministers and consular agents can take acknowledgments abroad. In Texas, a notary public can take an acknowledgment anywhere in the state. If an acknowledgment is taken outside the state where the document will be recorded, either the recording county must already recognize the out-of-state official's authority or the out-of-state official must provide certification that he or she is qualified to take acknowledgments. The official seal of the notary on the acknowledgment normally fulfills this requirement.

The acknowledgment illustrated in Figure 8.3 is typical of those used by an individual in Texas. Note that a description of the identity card is required. A short form acknowledgment, shown in Figure 8.4, is also used in Texas. No

FIGURE 8.3 An acknowledgment

THE STATE OF TEXAS §
§
COUNTY OF §

BEFORE ME, ____________, on this day personally appeared ____________, known to me (or proved to me on the oath of ____________, or through ____________, (description of identity card or other document)) to be the person whose name is subscribed to the forgoing instrument and acknowledged to me that he executed the same for purposes and consideration therein expressed.

Given under my hand and seal of office this ____________ day of ____________, A.D., ____________.

____
NOTARY PUBLIC

Source: © 2012 Cengage Learning

FIGURE 8.4 A short form acknowledgment

The State of Texas
County of ________________ *ss*

This instrument was acknowledged before me on (date) by (name or names of person acknowledging).

(Signature of officer) ____________________
(Title of officer) ____________________
My commission expires: ____________________

identity card is referenced in the short form. The person signing the document must personally appear before the notary, and that the notary states that he or she knows that person to be the person described in the document. If they are strangers, the notary will require proof of identity. The person executing the document states that he or she acknowledges executing the document. Note that it is the signer who does the acknowledging, not the notary. At the completion of the signing, a notation of the event is supposed to be made in a permanent record book kept by the notary.

State law also allows a notary public to sign the name of an individual who is physically unable to do so, if authorized to do so by the disabled person in the presence of a disinterested witness.

PUBLIC RECORDS ORGANIZATION

Each document brought to the county clerk's office for recordation is photocopied and then returned to its owner. The photocopy is arranged in chronological order with photocopies of other documents and bound into a book. These books are placed in chronological order on shelves that are open to the public for inspection. References are simply *book* and *page* of the recorded documents.

Filing incoming documents in chronological order makes sense for the recorder's office, but it does not provide an easy means for a person to locate all the documents relevant to a given parcel of land. To illustrate, suppose that you are planning to purchase a parcel of land and want to make certain that the person selling it is the legally recognized owner. Without an index to guide you, you would have to inspect every document in every volume, starting with the most recent book, until you located the current owner's deed. In a heavily populated county, your search might require you to look through hundreds of books, each containing up to 1,000 pages of documents. Consequently, recording offices have developed systems of indexing called grantor and grantee indexes.

In addition to the book and page records that are used in most counties in Texas, the legislature has specifically enacted legislation that provides for the microfilming of records by counties. Rather than record them under mortgage records, deed records, or other similar records, all records relating to or affecting real property are recorded under the heading of "Real Property Records" or "Official Public Records of Real Property." Then, instead of getting a volume and page number, the document is given a Clerk's File Number and a Film Code Number. Texas has also provided for a *fixture* recording system for property, which is personalty but is to become attached to realty. These are commonly termed **UCC liens** or *chattel mortgage liens* (UCC liens are liens that attach pursuant to the provisions of the Uniform Commercial Code, which Texas has adopted as the Texas Business and Commerce Code). As discussed in the fixture portion of this text, there are certain criteria under which the lien created by a supplier of certain fixtures may even be superior to that of a first lien deed of trust. Therefore it is important that the fixture records be searched as well as the lis pendens records, judgment rolls, and mechanics' liens filings in those counties that have those extra records.

Tract Indexes

Of the two indexing systems, the **tract index** is the simplest to use. In it, one page is allocated to either a single parcel of land or to a group of parcels, called a tract. On that page you will find a reference to all the recorded deeds, mortgages, and other documents at the recorder's office that relate to that parcel. Each reference gives the book and page where the original document is recorded. Title companies organize their records this way. The county clerks in Texas do not.

Grantor and Grantee Indexes

Grantor and grantee indexes are alphabetical indexes and are usually bound in book form. There are several variations in use in the United States, but the basic principle is the same. For each calendar year, the **grantor index** lists in alphabetical order all grantors named in the documents recorded that year. Next to each grantor's name is the name of the grantee named in the document, the book and page where a photocopy of the document can be found, and a few words describing the document. The **grantee index** is arranged by grantee names and gives the name of the grantor and the location and description of the document. This type of indexing system is required for county clerk's offices in Texas.

Electronic Recording

Texas adopted a new Electronic Recording Act which provides that an electronic document (a document that is received by the county clerk in electronic form) can be recorded in the county clerk's office in the county in which the land is located, in addition to the traditional paper documents that are recorded. Not surprisingly, this will prove to be a highly technical issue. The Texas State Library and Archives Commission was charged with the responsibility of creating rules and adopting standards to implement the new electronic recording procedure. This process will be relatively simple; the document will be prepared at the closing in electronic format, and you can execute this document with your "electronic signature." An electronic signature is an electronic sound, symbol, or process attached to or logically associated with the document, and executed or adopted by a person with the intent to sign the document. It can be as simple as typing your name at the bottom of the document or signing the document onscreen rather than on paper. The title company, bank, or other recording entity will then e-mail the document to the courthouse where it will be recorded with the traditional grantor-grantee index format. In the future, you will be able to search for a title in your own computer and copy documents from the courthouse by simply downloading them at home.

CHAIN OF TITLE

A ***chain of title*** shows the linkage of property ownership that connects the present owner to the original source of title. In most cases it starts with the original sale or grant of the land from the government to a private citizen. It is used to prove how title came to be **vested** in (i.e., possessed by) the current owner. Figure 8.5 illustrates the chain-of-title concept.

FIGURE 8.5 Chain of title

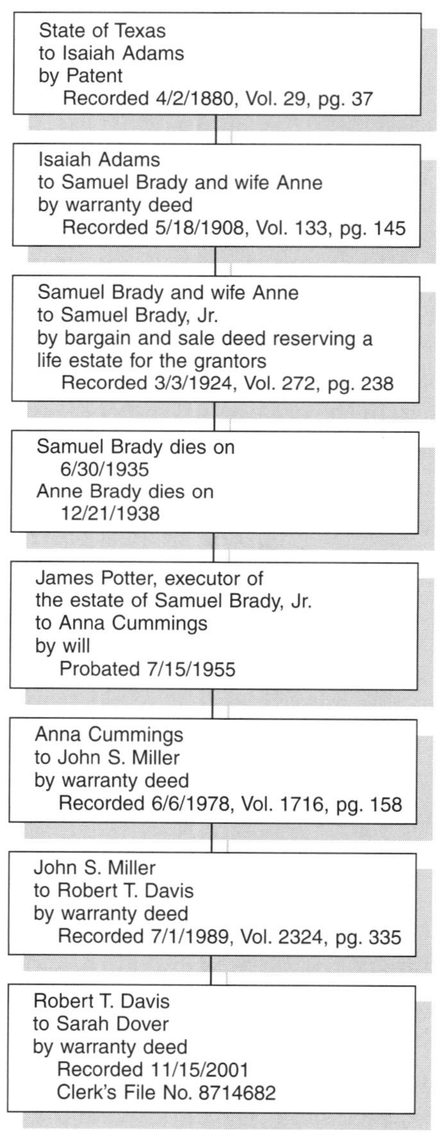

Source: © 2012 Cengage Learning

Sometimes, while tracing (running) a chain of title back through time, an apparent break or dead end will occur. This can happen because the grantor is an administrator, executor, sheriff, or judge, or because the owner died or because a mortgage against the land was foreclosed. To regain the title sequence, one must search outside the recorder's office by checking probate court records in the case of a death or by checking civil court actions in the case of a foreclosure.

In addition to looking for grantors and grantees, a search must be made for any outstanding mortgages, judgments, actions pending, liens, and unpaid taxes that may affect the title. In Texas, mortgages are placed in the general grantor and grantee indexes, listing the borrower (mortgagor) as the grantor and the lender (mortgagee) as the grantee. The process involves looking for the name of the property owner in each annual **mortgagor index** published while he owned the land. If a mortgage is found, a further check will reveal whether or not it has been satisfied and released. If it has been released, the recorder's office will have noted on the margin of the recorded mortgage the book and page where the release is located. When one knows the lender's name, the mortgage location and its subsequent release can also be found by searching the **mortgagee index.**

Public records must also be checked to learn if any lawsuits have resulted in judgments against recent owners, or if any lawsuits are pending that might later affect title. This information is found, respectively, on the **judgment rolls** and in the *lis pendens index* at the office of the county clerk. The term *lis pendens* is Latin for pending lawsuits that may affect title to the real property. A separate search must also be made for ***mechanics' liens*** against the property that may have been filed by unpaid workmen and material suppliers. This step should also include an on-site inspection of the land for any recent construction activity or material deliveries. A visit must also be made to the local tax assessor's office to check the tax rolls for unpaid property taxes. This does not exhaust all possible places that must be visited to do a thorough title search. A title searcher may also research birth, marriage, divorce, and adoption records, probate records, military files, and federal tax liens in an effort to identify all the parties with an interest or potential interest in a given parcel of land and its improvements.

ABSTRACT OF TITLE

Although it is useful for the real estate practitioner to be able to find a name or document in the public records, full-scale title searching should be left to professionals. In a sparsely populated county, title searching is usually done on a part-time basis by an attorney. In more heavily populated counties, a full-time **abstractor** (also spelled **abstracter**) will search the records. These persons are experts in the field of title search, and for a fee they will prepare an abstract of title for a parcel of land.

An **abstract of title** is a complete historical summary of all recorded documents affecting the title of a property. It recites all recorded grants and conveyances and identifies and summarizes recorded easements, mortgages, wills, tax liens, judgments, pending lawsuits, marriages, divorces, etc., that might affect the title. The abstract also includes a list of the public records searched, and not searched, in preparing the abstract.

The ***abstract*** is next sent to an attorney. On the basis of the knowledge of law and the abstract, the attorney renders an **opinion** as to who the fee owner is and names anyone else who has a legitimate right or interest in the property. Generally speaking, the seller usually pays the cost of updating the abstract, and the buyer pays the attorney to give the opinion.

TITLE INSURANCE

Despite the diligent efforts of conveyancers, abstracters, and attorneys to give as accurate a picture of land ownership as possible, there is no guarantee that the finished abstract, or its certification, is completely accurate. Persons preparing abstracts and opinions are liable for mistakes due to their own negligence, and they can be sued if that negligence results in a loss to a client. But what if a recorded deed in the title chain is a forgery? Or what if a married person represented himself on a deed as a single person, thus resulting in unextinguished dower rights? Or what if a deed was executed by a minor or an otherwise legally incompetent person? Or what if a document was misfiled, or there were undisclosed heirs, or a missing will later came to light, or there was confusion because of similar names on documents? These situations can result in substantial losses to a property owner, yet the fault may not lie with the conveyancer, abstracter, or attorney. The solution has been the organization of private companies to sell insurance against losses arising from title defects such as these as well as from errors in title examination.

Efforts to insure titles date back to the last century and were primarily organized by and for the benefit of attorneys who wanted protection from errors that they might make in the interpretation of abstracts. As time passed, ***title insurance*** became available to anyone wishing to purchase it. The basic principle of title insurance is similar to any form of insurance: Many persons pay a small amount into an insurance pool that is then available if any one of them should suffer a loss.

Title Commitment

When a title company receives a request for a title insurance policy, the first step is an examination of the public records. This is done either by an independent abstracter or attorney or by an employee of the title company. The company then reviews the findings and renders an opinion as to who the fee owner is and lists anyone else he feels has a legitimate right or interest in the property such as a mortgage lender or easement holder. This information is typed up and becomes the **title commitment,** which obligates the title insurance company to issue a policy of title when curative requirements, if any, have been satisfied. An example of a title commitment is illustrated in plain language in Figure 8.6. The Texas Department of Insurance publishes standard forms for commitments, the use of which is required by all title companies in Texas. They are much longer and in much greater detail than the sample shown.

Notice how a title commitment differs from an abstract of title. Whereas an abstract is a summary of all recorded events that have affected the title to a given

FIGURE 8.6 Title commitment

The title company will issue an insurance policy to you upon payment of the premium and upon compliance with the requirements contracted herein.
Land Description: Lot 17, Block M, Atwater's Addition, Jefferson County, State of Texas.
Date and Time of Search: March 3, 200x at 9:00 am
Title Appears to be in: Stan Dupp, a single man
Proposed Insured: Barbara Baker, a single woman
Fee or Interest: Fee simple
Exceptions:

1. *A lien in favor of Jefferson County for property taxes, in the amount of $645.00, due on or before April 30, 200x.*
2. *A mortgage in favor of the First National Bank in the amount of $30,000, recorded June 2, 1974, in Vol. 2975, Page 245 of the Official County Records.*
3. *An easement in favor of the Southern Telephone Company along the eastern five feet of said land for telephone poles and conduits. Recorded on June 15, 1946, in Vol. 1210, Page 133 of the Official County Records.*
4. *An easement in favor of Coastal States Gas and Electric Company along the north ten feet of said land for underground pipes. Recorded on June 16, 1946, in Vol. 1210, Page 137 of the Official County Records.*

Source: © 2012 Cengage Learning

parcel of land, a title commitment is more like a snapshot that shows the condition of title at a specific moment in time. A title commitment does not tell who the previous owners were; it only tells who the current owner appears to be as of the date of the commitment. A title commitment does not list all mortgage loans ever made against the land, but only those that have not been removed.

Texas Title Policy

The standard Texas title insurance policy form provides insurance coverage for loss of title. It must be issued on a form promulgated by the Texas Department of Insurance. Ordinarily, it contains ten exceptions from coverage, including the following:

1. Restrictive covenants of record itemized below. (This normally refers to any deed restrictions or covenants that may have been reserved by a prior deed holder, such as those used for land-use control. If there are none, the provision is deleted.)
2. Any discrepancies, conflicts, or shortages in area or boundary lines, or any encroachments, or any overlapping of improvements. (This exception to the title policy may be amended to read "shortages in area" upon request and, in the case of an owner's policy, payment of an additional premium.)
3. Homestead or community property or survivorship rights, if any, of any spouse of any insured.
4. Any titles or rights asserted by anyone, including, but not limited to, persons, the public, corporations, governments, or other entities (a) to tidelands, or

lands comprising the shores or beds of navigable or parental rivers and streams, lakes, bays, gulf, or oceans, or (b) to land beyond the line of the harbor or boat headlines as established or changed by any government, or (c) to filled-in lands, or artificial islands, or (d) to statutory water rights, including riparian rights, or (e) to the area extending from the line of mean low tide to the line of vegetation, or the right of access to that area or easement along across that area.

5. Standby fees and taxes for the current year and subsequent years, and for subsequent years due to changes in usage or ownership. (The title policy only warrants that taxes due prior to the closing have been paid and are up-to-date.)

Texas Residential Owner Policies (Form T-1R) are now required for use on all 1–4 family residential transactions. In all other cases, a Texas Owner Policy Form T-1 is used.

Policy Premium

In Texas, it is generally customary for the seller to pay the cost of the insurance (the title commitment is issued at no cost). However, this is always negotiable between the buyer and the seller. When a property is sold, it is insured for an amount equal to the purchase price. This insurance remains effective as long as the buyer or owner or his heirs (or qualified family trust) have an interest in the property.

The insurance premium consists of a single payment. Title policy rates are set by the Texas Department of Insurance and are the same for all title companies (each company does a complete title search). Each time the property is sold, a new policy must be purchased. The old policy cannot be assigned to the new owner.

Loan Policy

Thus far our discussion of title insurance has centered on what is called an **owner's policy.** Title insurance companies also offer what is called a **loan policy.** This protects a lender who has taken real estate as collateral for a loan. There are three significant differences between an owner's and a loan policy. First, the owner's policy is good for the full amount of coverage stated on the policy for as long as the insured or the insured's heirs have an interest in the property. In contrast, the loan policy protects only for the amount owed on the mortgage loan. Thus, the coverage on a loan policy declines and finally terminates when the loan is fully repaid. The second difference is that the loan policy does not make exceptions for claims to ownership that could have been determined by physically inspecting the property. The third difference is that the mortgagee's title policy provides coverage to subsequent holders of the same mortgage loan.

The cost of a loan policy (also known as a lender's policy) is similar to an owner's policy. Although the insurance company takes added risks by eliminating some exceptions found in the owner's policy, this is balanced by the fact that the liability decreases as the loan is repaid. When an owner's policy and a loan policy are purchased at the same time, as in the case of a sale with new financing, the combined cost is only a little more than the cost of the owner's policy alone. The loan policy covers only title problems. It does not insure that the loan will be repaid by the borrower.

Claims for Losses

When an insured defect arises, the title insurance company reserves the right to either pay the loss or fight the claim in court. If it elects to fight, any legal costs the company incurs are in addition to the amount of coverage stated in the policy. If a loss is paid, the amount of coverage is reduced by that amount and any unused coverage is still in effect. If the company pays a loss, it acquires the right to collect from the party who caused the loss. In Texas, the title policy now provides for payment of actual damages, but if 100% of the title fails, coverage is limited to the face value of the policy.

In comparing title insurance to other forms of insurance (e.g., life, fire, automobile), note that title insurance protects against something that has already happened but has not been discovered. A forged deed may result in a disagreement over ownership: the forgery is a fact of history, the insurance is in the event of its discovery. But in some cases the problem will never be discovered. For example, heirs may be totally unaware of their property rights and fail to timely claim them. If they never claim them, the rights extinguish themselves by limitations, and the intervening property owners will have been unaffected.

Only a small part of the premiums collected by title insurance companies are used to pay claims, largely because they take great pains to maintain on their own premises complete copies of the public records for each county in which they do business. These are called **title plants;** in most cases they are actually more complete and better organized than those available at the county clerk's office. This is because the State Board of Insurance requires that the records be maintained on an *abstract indexing system,* rather than the grantor-grantee indexing system. The philosophy is that the better the quality of the title search, the fewer the claims that must be paid.

The Growth of Title Insurance

The title insurance business has mushroomed due to three important reasons. First, in a warranty deed, the grantor makes several strongly worded covenants. As you will recall, the grantor covenants that he is the owner, that there are no encumbrances except as stated in the deed, and that the grantor will warrant and forever defend the premises. Thus, signing a warranty deed places a great obligation on the grantor. By purchasing title insurance and using only a special warranty, the grantor can transfer a significant portion of that obligation to an insurance company.

Second, a grantee is also motivated to have title insurance. Even with a warranty deed, there is always the lingering question of whether or not the seller would be financially capable of making good on her covenants and warranties. They are useless if one cannot enforce them.

Third, the broad use of title insurance has made mortgage lending more attractive and borrowing a little easier and cheaper for real property owners. This is because title insurance has removed the risk of loss due to defective titles while insuring the lender's lien priority. Secondary market purchasers of loans such as FNMA and FHLMC (Chapter 14) require title insurance on any loan they purchase.

QUIET TITLE SUIT

When a title defect (or **title cloud**) must be removed, it is logical to remove it by using the path of least resistance. For example, if an abstract or title report shows unpaid property taxes, the buyer may require the seller to pay them in full before the deal is completed. Similarly, a distant relative with ownership rights might be willing, upon negotiation, to quitclaim them for a price.

Sometimes a stronger means is necessary to remove title defects. For example, the distant relative may refuse to negotiate, or the lender may refuse to remove a mortgage lien despite pleas from the borrower that it has been paid. The solution is a ***quiet title suit*** (also called a quiet title action). In Texas, a property owner can ask the courts to hold hearings on the ownership of his land. At these hearings anyone claiming to have an interest or right to the land in question may present verbal or written evidence of that claim. A judge, acting on the evidence presented and the laws of his state, rules on the validity of each claim. The result is to legally recognize those with a genuine right or interest and to "quiet" those without a genuine interest.

REVIEW QUESTIONS

Answers to these questions are found in the Answer Key section at the back of the book.

1. Once a person is aware of another's rights or interest in property, that person is said to have
   A. constructive notice.
   B. legal notice.
   C. inquiry notice.
   D. actual notice.

2. Constructive notice requires that
   A. a landowner give public notice of his or her claim of ownership.
   B. anyone interested in the property inspect the property and the public records.
   C. both A and B.
   D. neither A nor B.

3. The county clerk's office
   A. serves as a central information station for documents pertaining to interests in land.
   B. is an agency of the federal government.
   C. both A and B.
   D. neither A nor B.

4. Farmer Sorensen leases 320 acres adjacent to his ranch. Sorensen can give notice to the world at large by
   A. plowing the land.
   B. storing his equipment on it.
   C. putting a fence around it.
   D. all of the above.
   E. none of the above.

5. Priority of a recorded instrument is determined by the date of
   A. acknowledgment.
   B. delivery to the grantee.
   C. the instrument.
   D. recordation.

6. Deeds and other instruments that affect land titles should be recorded
   A. immediately after delivery or execution.
   B. in order to provide constructive notice.
   C. both A and B.
   D. neither A nor B.

7. The purpose of having a person's signature acknowledged is to
   A. make certain the person signing the document is the same person named in the document and that the signing was voluntary.
   B. make the document admissible to the public records.
   C. both A and B.
   D. neither A nor B.

8. In a jurisdiction that indexes recorded instruments by grantee and grantor, if one knew the name of the current owner of a property and wished to search the records to verify that ownership, one would look in the
   A. grantee index.
   B. grantor index.
   C. both A and B.
   D. neither A nor B.

9. Instruments are recorded in the public records in what order?
   A. Alphabetical order, based on the grantee's last name.
   B. Chronological order, as received for recordation.
   C. According to the date of the instrument.
   D. Alphabetical order, based on the grantor's last name.

10. The name of the borrower would be filed alphabetically in the
    A. mortgagee index.
    B. grantor index.
    C. lis pendens.
    D. lender's index.

11. Which of the following would not ordinarily be checked in searching a title to a parcel of land?
    A. Judgment records
    B. Lien records
    C. Chattel mortgage records
    D. Lis pendens index

12. A lis pendens index is
    A. an index of existing leases on property.
    B. an index of pending lawsuits.
    C. a tract index.
    D. a chain of title.

13. Which of the following are among the provisions of a typical owner's title insurance policy?
    A. The insurer is responsible for having searched the records pertaining to the property and insures its findings.
    B. The insurer is not responsible for pertinent information that is not found in the public records.
    C. The insurer has not make a visual inspection of the land for signs of notice.
    D. All of the above.

14. Summary of all recorded documents affecting title to a given parcel of land is called
    A. a chain of title.
    B. an abstract of title.
    C. a title report.
    D. all of the above.

15. Protection against a loss occasioned by which of the following would not be covered by title insurance?
    A. Forged deeds, or deeds by incompetents
    B. Unextinguished dower or curtesy rights
    C. Claims by undisclosed or missing heirs
    D. Destruction of improvements by a tornado

16. Should a title insurance company elect to fight a claim in court, the legal expenses incurred will be
    A. deducted from the coverage under the policy.
    B. assumed by the title insurance company without affecting the policy coverage.
    C. shared by the insured and the insurance company.
    D. paid by the insured.

17. The purchase of title insurance eliminates the need for
    A. casualty insurance.
    B. a survey of the property.
    C. constructive notice.
    D. none of the above.
    E. all of the above.

18. All of the following are true of a quiet title suit EXCEPT that it
    A. is a judicial proceeding.
    B. removes all claims to title other than the owner's.
    C. quiets those without a genuine interest in the property.
    D. can be used to clear up a disputed title.

19. The premium for a title insurance policy is
    A. paid annually.
    B. paid semiannually.
    C. a single premium, paid upon issuance.
    D. included in the mortgage payment.

Chapter 9

KEY TERMS

Breach of contract: failure, without legal excuse, to perform as required by a contract

Competent parties: persons considered legally capable of entering into a binding contract

Contract: a legally enforceable agreement to do (or not to do) a particular thing

Duress: the application of force to obtain an agreement

Fraud: an act intended to deceive for the purpose of inducing another to give up something of value

Liquidated damages: an amount of money specified in a contract as compensation to be paid if the contract is not satisfactorily completed

Minor, Infant: a person under the age of legal competence; in most states, under 18 years

Specific performance: contract performance according to the precise terms agreed upon

Void contract: a contract that has no binding effect on the parties who made it

Voidable contract: a contract that is able to be voided by one of its parties

Contract Law

IN THIS CHAPTER

This chapter will introduce you to contract law and how a contract is created. The essentials of a valid contract are also covered in detail. Other topics covered include offer and acceptance, fraud, mistake, lawful objective, consideration, performance, and breach of contract. Although this is a short chapter, it is very important.

HOW A CONTRACT IS CREATED

A *contract* is a legally enforceable agreement to do or not to do a specific thing. In this chapter we shall see how a contract is created and what makes it legally binding. Topics covered include offer and acceptance, fraud, mistake, lawful objective, consideration, performance, and breach of contract. In Chapter 10 we will turn our attention to the earnest money contract, tax-deferred exchange, and installment contract as they relate to the buying and selling of real estate.

Express Contract

A contract can be either expressed or implied. An **express contract** occurs when the parties to the contract declare their intentions either orally or in writing. The word **party** [plural, **parties**] is a legal term that refers to a person or group involved in a legal proceeding. A lease or rental agreement, for example, is an expressed contract. The lessor landlord expresses the intent to permit the lessee tenant to use the premises, and the lessee agrees to pay the rent. A contract to purchase real estate is also an expressed contract.

Implied Contract

An **implied contract** is created by neither words nor writing but rather by actions of the parties indicating that they intend to create a contract. For example, when you step into a taxicab, you imply that you will pay the fare. The cab driver, by allowing you in the cab, implies that you will be taken where you want to go. The same thing occurs at a restaurant. The presence of tables, silverware, menus, waiters, and waitresses implies that you will be served food. When you order, you imply that you are going to pay when the bill is presented.

Bilateral Contract

A contract can be either bilateral or unilateral. A **bilateral contract** results when a promise is exchanged for a promise. In the typical real estate sale, the buyer promises to pay the agreed price, and the seller promises to deliver title to the buyer. In a lease contract the lessor promises the use of the premises to the lessee, and the lessee promises to pay rent in return. A bilateral contract is basically an "I will do this *and* you will do that" arrangement.

PUTTING IT TO WORK

In real estate, certain terms are not included in the listing agreement (exactly how the property will be marketed, advertised, etc.), but it is implied through custom in the industry that certain marketing efforts will be made.

Unilateral Contract

A **unilateral contract** results when a promise is exchanged for performance. For instance, during a campaign to get more listings, a real estate office manager announces to the firm's sales staff that an extra $1,000 bonus will be paid for each salable new listing. No promises or agreements are necessary from the salespersons. The offer is accepted by the salesperson's performance. Each time the salesperson performs by bringing in a salable listing, he or she is in entitled to the promised $1,000 bonus. An option to purchase is also a unilateral contract. It is an offer by the optionor to sell his property in the future in return for an option fee. At the time the option is exercised (and the optionee has the obligation to close), it becomes a bilateral contract for sale (i.e., the optionor has agreed to the conveyance and the optionee has agreed to purchase at some time in the near future). Similarly, a listing can be structured as a unilateral contract. The seller agrees to pay a commission if the broker finds a buyer. When the broker starts to perform, the contract becomes more bilateral, because the agent has expended time and money and would be entitled to reimbursement. When the broker produces the buyer, the broker has completed the performance. At this point, the commission is due and the seller's promise to pay the commission is enforceable. The broker has accepted the offer (discussed later), and the agreement to pay the commission becomes a valid, binding contract because of the broker's performance. A unilateral contract is basically an "I will do this *if* you will do that" arrangement. The offer is made, and it is accepted by performance.

Executory

An **executory** contract is one in which both parties have work to be done after the contract is signed. A contract for the sale of real estate is the classic executory contract. After the parties have signed, both parties have duties to perform in order to complete the final closing.

Executed

An **executed** contract is one that is complete upon signing. The rights have transferred immediately from one party to another. A deed, for instance, when signed and delivered to the grantee, is complete. The parties need to perform no further duties after the delivery of the contract.

All contracts are either (1) express or implied, (2) unilateral or bilateral, or (3) executed or executory. Every contract falls into these three classifications.

Legal Effect

A contract can be construed by the courts to be valid, void, or unenforceable.

A **valid contract** is one that meets all the requirements of law. It is binding upon its parties and legally enforceable in a court of law. A ***void contract*** has no legal effect and, in fact, is not a contract at all. Even though the parties may have gone through the motions of attempting to make a contract, no legal rights are created and any party thereto may ignore it at her pleasure. A ***voidable contract*** binds one party but not the other. An **unenforceable contract** is one that may have been valid, but its enforcement is now barred by the statute of limitations or the doctrine of laches. For instance, in Texas if you try to sue on a contract six years after default, the suit would be barred by the four-year statute of limitations. Let's now turn our attention to the requirements of a valid contract.

ESSENTIALS OF A VALID CONTRACT

For a contract to be *legally valid,* and hence binding and enforceable, the following five requirements must be met:

1. Competent parties
2. Mutual agreement
3. Lawful objective
4. Consideration or cause
5. Contract in writing when required by law

If these conditions are met, any party to the contract may, if the need arises, call upon a court of law to either enforce the contract as written or award money damages for nonperformance. In reality, a properly written contract seldom ends up in court because each party knows it will be enforced as written. It is the poorly written and unenforceable contract that ends up in court. A judge must then decide if a contract actually exists and determine the obligations of each party. It is much better if the contract is correctly prepared in the first place. Let's look more closely at the five requirements of an enforceable contract.

COMPETENT PARTIES

For a contract to be legally enforceable, all parties entering into it must be legally competent. In deciding competency, the law provides a mixture of objective and subjective standards. The most objective standard is that of age. A person must reach the age of *majority* to be legally capable of entering into a contract. ***Minors*** do not have contractual capability. Until the voting age in national elections was reduced from 21 to 18 years by Congress, persons were considered to be minors by most states until the age of 21. Since then state legislatures (including Texas) have lowered the age for entering into legally binding contracts to 18 years. The purpose of majority laws is to protect minors (also known as ***infants*** in legal terminology) from entering into contracts that they may not be old enough to understand. In Texas, a contract entered into by a minor is voidable; some other states hold that they are void.

PUTTING IT TO WORK

In Texas, contracts with minors are voidable. For example, the adult might be bound, but the minor could withdraw. If a contract with a minor is required, it is possible to obtain a binding contract by working through the minor's legal guardian.

Persons of unsound mind who have been declared incompetent by a judge may not make a valid contract, and any attempt to do so results in a void contract. The solution is to contract through the person appointed to act on behalf of the incompetent. If a person has not been judged legally incompetent but nonetheless appears incapable of understanding the transaction in question, that person has no legal power to contract. In some states, persons convicted of felonies may not enter into valid contracts without the prior approval of the parole board.

Regarding intoxicated persons, if there was a deliberate attempt to intoxicate a person for the purpose of approving a contract, the intoxicated person, upon sobering up, can call upon the courts to void the contract. If the contracting party was voluntarily drunk to the point of incompetence, when he is sober he may ratify or deny the contract if he does so promptly. However, some courts look at the matter strictly from the standpoint of whether or not the intoxicated person had the capability of formulating the intent to enter into a contract. Obviously, there are some fine and subjective distinctions among these three categories, and a judge may interpret them differently than the parties to the contract. Most other mind-altering drugs are dealt with in the same manner as alcohol.

Power of Attorney

An individual can give another person the power to act on his behalf: for example to buy or sell land, or to sign lease documents. This is called **power of attorney.** The person holding the power of attorney is called an **attorney-in-fact.** With regard to real estate, a power of attorney must be stated in writing because the real estate documents to be signed must be in writing. Any document signed with a power of attorney should be executed as follows: "Paul Jones, principal, by

Deborah Smith, agent, his attorney-in-fact." If the agent has power to convey title to land, then the document granting him power of attorney should be acknowledged by the principal and recorded. The agent is legally competent to the extent of the powers granted to him by the principal as long as the principal remains alive. The power of attorney can, of course, be terminated by the principal at any time. A recorded notice of revocation is needed to revoke a recorded power of attorney.

Texas also recognizes a statutory **durable power of attorney.** It does not lapse because of the passage of time unless a time limitation is specifically stated in the instrument creating it. The durable power of attorney has additional requirements, however. To be enforceable, it must:

1. Be in writing, designating another person as attorney-in-fact or agent.
2. Be signed by the principal who is an adult.
3. Contain the words "this power of attorney is not affected by subsequent disability or incapacity of the principal," or similar words.
4. Be acknowledged by a principal before an officer authorized to take acknowledgments to deeds or conveyances and to administer oaths under the laws of this state or any other state.

A durable power of attorney can be terminated by express revocation, divorce, annulment, termination by its own terms, the death of the principal, or the appointment of a guardian for the principal. Even those terminations are limited.

However, the statute provides that the revocation, divorce, annulment, death, or qualification of a guardian of the estate of the principal doesn't revoke or terminate the agency as to the attorney-in-fact who doesn't have actual knowledge of the termination.

How does the attorney-in-fact prove he didn't have knowledge? The statute merely requires that he sign an affidavit saying that he did not have, at the time, the exercise of his power; actual knowledge of the termination of the power of attorney by revocation, death, or qualification of the guardian; and that the affidavit is "conclusive proof as between the attorney-in-fact or agent and a person other than the principal." The same is true of people's reliance on the durable power of attorney when the principal becomes disabled or incapacitated. The affidavit is, again, "conclusive proof" of a disability or incapacity of the principal at the time.

A revocation of the durable power of attorney is not effective as to a third party relying on the power of attorney until the third party receives *actual notice* of the revocation.

If the durable power of attorney is for a real property transaction, the durable power of attorney is required to be recorded in the office of the county clerk of the county in which the land is located. The statute even provides a form power of attorney to be used. The form is not exclusive, and other forms of power attorney can be used. Third parties who rely in good faith on the acts of the agent within the scope of the power of attorney may do so *without fear of liability to the principal.*

Corporations and Other Entities

Corporations are considered legally ***competent parties.*** However, the individual contracting on behalf of the corporation must have authority from the board of directors. Some states also require that the corporate seal be affixed to contracts, although Texas does not. A partnership can contract either in the name of the partnership or in the name of any of its general partners. Trustees, executors, and administrators can legally contract on behalf of trusts and estates, provided that they have proper authorization.

MUTUAL AGREEMENT

The requirement of **mutual agreement** (also called *mutual consent,* or *mutual assent,* or **meeting of the minds**) means that there must be agreement to the provisions of the contract by the parties involved. In other words, there must be a mutual willingness to enter into a contract. This means that their intention is to be bound by the agreement, thus precluding jokes or jests from becoming valid contracts. The existence of mutual agreement is evidenced by the words and acts of the parties indicating that there is a valid offer and an unqualified acceptance. In addition, there must be no fraud, misrepresentation, or mistake, and the agreement must be genuine and freely given. Let us consider each of these points in more detail.

Offer

Offer and acceptance requires that one party (the **offeror**) make an offer to another party (the **offeree**). If the offer is acceptable, the offeree must then communicate that acceptance to the offeror. The means of communication may be spoken or written or an action that implies acceptance. To illustrate, suppose that you own a house and want to sell it. You tell your listing broker that you will accept $300,000 and that you would deliver a general warranty deed and pay the normal closing costs for the area. Within a few days, the broker submits a signed document from a prospective buyer. This constitutes an offer, and the buyer (the offeror) has just communicated it to you (the offeree). One requirement of a valid offer is that the offer be specific in its terms. Mutual agreement cannot exist if the terms of the offer are vague or undisclosed and/or the offer does not clearly state the obligations of each party involved. If the seller were to say to a prospective purchaser, "Do you want to buy this house?" without stating the price, and the prospective purchaser said "Yes," the law would not consider this to be a valid offer.

It should also be pointed out that an offer can be revoked by the offeror at any time prior to the offeror hearing of its acceptance. For example, if you submit an offer to purchase a house for $290,000 and while waiting for a response you find another house that you prefer, you can revoke your first offer at any time prior to hearing of its acceptance, then make your contract with the second homeowner. An offeror should be strongly advised, however, not to initiate more than one offer at a time because considerable confusion can be caused by multiple offers, revocations, and acceptances in one transaction.

Acceptance

For an offer to become binding, the seller must accept everything in it. The rejection of even the smallest portion of the offer is a rejection of the entire offer. If the seller wishes to reject the offer but keep negotiations alive, he can make a **counteroffer.** This is a written offer to sell to the buyer at a new price and with terms that are closer to the buyer's offer than the seller's original asking price and terms. The agent prepares the counteroffer by filling out a fresh purchase contract identical in all ways to the buyer's offer except for these changes, or by writing on the back of the offer (or on another sheet of paper) that the seller offers to sell at the terms the buyer had offered except for the stated changes. The counteroffer is then dated and signed by the seller. A time limit may be given to the buyer to accept. The seller keeps a copy, and the counteroffer is delivered to the buyer for a decision. If the counteroffer is acceptable to the buyer, she signs and dates it, and the contract is complete. Another commonly used, but less desirable, practice is to take the buyer's offer, cross out each item unacceptable to the seller, and write above or below it what the seller will accept. Each change is then initialed by the seller and buyer. If the offer is rejected, it is good practice to have the seller write the word *rejected* on the offer followed by his signature.

Counteroffer

Upon receiving the offer, the offeree has three options: agree to it, reject it, or make a counteroffer. If the offeree agrees, he must agree to every item of the offer. An offer is considered by law to be rejected not only if the offeree rejects it outright but also if any change in the terms is made. Any change in the terms is considered a counteroffer. Although it may appear that the offeree is only amending the offer before she accepts it, the offeree has actually rejected it, and is making a new offer. This now makes the seller the offeror. To illustrate, suppose the prospective purchaser submits an offer to the listing broker to purchase the property for $295,000, but instead of accepting the $295,000 offer, the seller amends the contract to reflect a selling price of $300,000. This is a rejection of the original offer, which creates a counteroffer to the purchaser. The purchaser now has the right to accept or reject this counteroffer. If, however, the original $295,000 offer is agreeable to the offeree (seller), she must communicate the acceptance to the purchaser. A spoken "Yes, I'll take it," would not be legally adequate; a real estate licensee should obtain the signature of the seller on a contract, without any further changes.

Fraud

Mutual agreement requires that there be no fraud, misrepresentation, or mistake in the contract if it is to be valid. A ***fraud*** is an act intended to deceive for the purpose of inducing another to part with something of value. It can be as blatant as knowingly telling a lie or making a promise with no intention of performance. For example, you are showing your home, and a prospective buyer asks if there is frequent bus service nearby. There isn't, but you say, "Yes," as you sense this is important and you want to sell the home. The prospective tenant, relying on this information from you, buys the home and moves in. The next day he calls and says that there is no public transportation and he wants to break the agreement immediately. Because mutual agreement was lacking, the buyer can *rescind* (cancel) the contract and get his money back.

Fraud can also result from failing to disclose important information, thereby inducing someone to accept an offer. For example, the day you show your apartment to a prospective tenant the weather is dry. But you know that during every rainstorm the tenant's automobile parking space becomes a lake of water six inches deep. This would qualify as fraud if the prospective tenant was not made aware of it before agreeing to the rental contract. Once again, the law will permit the aggrieved party to rescind the contract. However, the tenant does not have to rescind the contract. If he likes the other features of the apartment enough, he can elect to live with the flooded parking space.

PUTTING IT TO WORK

If a real estate agent commits fraud to make a sale and the deceived party later rescinds the sales contract, not only is the commission lost, but explanations will be necessary to the other parties of the contract. Moreover, state license laws provide for a suspension or revocation of a real estate license for fraudulent acts.

Innocent Misrepresentation

Innocent misrepresentation differs from fraud (intentional misrepresentation) in that the party providing the wrong information is not doing so to deceive another for the purpose of reaching an agreement. To illustrate, suppose that over the past year you have observed that city buses stop near your apartment building. If you tell a prospective tenant that there is bus service, only to learn the day after the tenant moves in that service stopped last week, this is innocent misrepresentation. Although there was no dishonesty involved, the tenant still has the right to rescind the contract. If performance has not begun on the contract (in this case the tenant has not moved in), the injured party may give notice that he *disaffirms* (revokes) the contract. However, if the tenant wants to break the contract, he must do so in a timely manner; otherwise the law will presume that the situation is satisfactory to the tenant.

Mistake

Mistake as applied in contract law has a very narrow meaning. It does not include innocent misrepresentation nor does it include ignorance, inability, or poor judgment. If a person enters into a contract that he later regrets because he did not investigate it thoroughly enough, or because it did not turn out to be beneficial, the law will not grant relief to him on the grounds of mistake, even though he may now consider it a "mistake" to have made the contract in the first place. Mistake as used in contract law arises from ambiguity in negotiations and mistake of material fact. For example, you offer to sell your mountain cabin to an acquaintance. He has never seen your cabin, and you give him instructions on how to get there to look at it. He returns and accepts your offer; however, he made a wrong turn and the cabin he looked at was not your cabin. A week later he discovers his error. The law considers this ambiguity in negotiations. In this case the buyer, in his mind, was purchasing a different cabin than the seller was selling; therefore, there is no mutual agreement and any contract signed is void.

To illustrate a mistake of fact, suppose that you show your apartment to a prospective tenant and tell her that she must let you know by tomorrow whether or not she wants to rent it. The next day she visits you and together you enter into a rental contract. Although neither of you is aware of it, there has just been a serious fire in the apartment. Because a fire-gutted apartment is not what the two of you had in mind when the rental contract was signed, there is no mutual agreement.

Occasionally, "mistake of law" will be claimed as grounds for relief from a contract. However, mistake as to one's legal rights in a contract is not generally accepted by courts of law unless it is coupled with a mistake of fact. Ignorance of the law is not considered a mistake.

Duress

The last requirement of mutual agreement is that the offer and acceptance be genuine and freely given. ***Duress*** (use of force), **menace** (threat of violence), or **undue influence** (unfair advantage) cannot be used to obtain agreement. The law permits a contract made under any of these conditions to be revoked by the aggrieved party.

LAWFUL OBJECTIVE

To be enforceable, a contract cannot call for performing an illegal act. This is because a court of law cannot be called upon to enforce a contract that requires that a law be broken. Such a contract is void, or if already in operation, it is unenforceable in a court of law. For example, a debt contract requiring interest rates in excess of those allowed by state law would be void. If the borrower had started repaying the debt and then later stopped, the lender would not be able to look to the courts to enforce collection of the balance. Contracts contrary to good morals and general public policy are also unenforceable.

CONSIDERATION

For an agreement to be enforceable, it must be supported by **consideration.** Money is usually thought of as meeting this requirement. Yet in the vast majority of contracts, the consideration requirement is met by a promise for a promise. For example, in selling real estate the promise of a purchaser to buy and the promise of an owner to sell constitute sufficient consideration to support their agreement. No deposit money is necessary.

The purpose of requiring consideration is to demonstrate that a bargain has been struck between the parties to the contract. The size, quantity, nature, or amount of what is being exchanged is irrelevant as long as it is present. Consideration can be money, property, personal services, or a promise to do something. For example, there can be an exchange of a promise for a promise, money for a promise, money for property, goods for services, etc. Forbearance also qualifies as consideration.

In a deed, discussed in Chapter 7, the consideration requirement is usually met with a statement such as "For ten dollars and other good and valuable consideration." In a lease, the periodic payment of rent is the consideration for the use of the premises.

A contract fails to be legally binding if consideration is lacking from any party to the contract. The legal philosophy is that a person cannot promise to do something of value for someone else without receiving in turn some form of consideration. Stated another way, each party must give up something, for example, each must suffer a detriment. For example, if I promise to give you my car, the consideration requirement is not met because you promise nothing in return. But if I promise to give you my car when you quit smoking, that meets the consideration requirement.

As a group, money plus promises, property, legal rights, services, and forbearance are classified as **valuable consideration,** if they are worth money. There is one exception to the requirement that each party must provide valuable consideration. That is the case of a gift. If a person wishes to give something of value to a friend or loved one, courts have ruled that "love and affection" will meet the consideration requirement.

PUTTING IT TO WORK

In a typical offer to purchase a home, the consideration is the mutual exchange of promises by the buyer and seller to obligate themselves to do something they were not previously required to do. In other words, the seller agrees to sell on the terms agreed and the buyer agrees to buy the property on those same terms. The earnest money the buyer may put down is not the consideration necessary to make the contract valid. Rather, earnest money is a tangible indication of the buyer's intent and may become a source of compensation (damages) to the seller in the event the buyer does not carry out his promises.

Although this is not valuable consideration, it is nonetheless **good consideration** and as such fulfills the legal requirement that consideration be present. The law generally will not inquire as to the adequacy of the consideration unless there is evidence of fraud, mistake, duress, threat, or undue influence. For instance, if a man gave away his property or sold it very cheaply to keep it from his creditors, the creditors could ask the courts to set aside those transfers.

CONTRACT IN WRITING

In each state (including Texas) there is a law that is commonly known as a **statute of frauds.** The purpose of such laws is to prevent frauds by requiring that all contracts for the sale of land, or an interest in land, be in writing and signed in order to be enforceable in a court of law. This includes such things as offers, acceptances, binders, land contracts, deeds, escrows, and options to purchase. Mortgages and trust deeds (and their accompanying bonds and notes) and leases whose obligations cannot be completed within one year must be in writing to be enforceable. In addition, most states (including Texas) have also adopted the *Uniform Commercial Code* that requires, among other things, that the sale of property with a value in excess of $500 be in writing. Texas also requires that real estate employment contracts be expressed in writing in order for the agent to sue the principal for a commission.

The purpose of requiring that a contract be written and signed is to prevent perjury and fraudulent attempts to seek legal enforcement of a contract that never existed. It is not necessary that a contract be a single formal document. It can consist of a series of signed letters or memorandums as long as the essentials of a valid contract are present. Note that the requirement for a written contract relates only to the enforceability of the contract. Thus, if Mr. Cheddar orally agrees to sell his land to Mr. Cheese and they carry out the deal, neither can come back after the contract was performed and ask a court to rescind the deal because the agreement to sell was oral.

The most common real estate contract that does not need to be in writing to be enforceable is a month-to-month rental agreement that can be terminated by either landlord or tenant on one-month notice. Nonetheless, most are in writing, because people tend to forget oral promises. While the unhappy party can go to court, the judge may have a difficult time determining what oral promises were made, particularly if there were no witnesses other than the parties to the agreement. Hence, it is advisable to put all important contracts in writing and for each party to recognize the agreement by signing it. It is also customary to date written contracts, although most can be enforced without showing the date the agreement was reached.

PUTTING IT TO WORK

A written contract will supersede an oral one. Thus, if two parties orally promise one thing and then write and sign something else, the written contract will prevail. This has been the basis for many complaints against overzealous real estate practitioners who make oral promises that do not appear anywhere in the written contract.

Parol Evidence Rule

Under certain circumstances, the **parol evidence rule** permits oral evidence to complete an otherwise incomplete or ambiguous written contract. However, the application of this rule is quite narrow. If a contract is complete and clear in its intent, the courts presume that what the parties put into writing is what they agreed upon.

Statue of Frauds; Electronic Transactions

The Electronic Records in Global and National Commerce Act was signed on October 1, 2000 and became effective on March 1, 2001. This act, popularly referred to as "esign," in fact has, as one of its primary purposes, the repeal of state law requirements for written instruments as they apply to electronic agreements. The statute is quite clear that a signature, contract, or other record relating to such transaction may not be denied legal effect, validity, or enforceability solely because it is in electronic form; and a contract relating to such transaction may not be denied legal effect, validity, or enforceability solely because an electronic signature or electronic record was used in its formation.

Almost anything can be an electronic signature rendering a party bound to agreement. For instance, if you were sent an email that said "I'll buy your property at 450 W. Meyer in Chicago for $50,000, and you typed at the top of this message "OK" and hit "return", we might have a binding real estate contract. All you'd have to show is that the typing of the words "OK" indicated my intent to express agreement. The fact that I didn't even type out my name would not matter, because I "attached" an "electronic symbol" to a contract. The contract would still have to meet standards of clarity and certainty. And perhaps an exchange this informal would not meet those standards in some jurisdictions. Relatively simple and perhaps thoughtless acts could result in the formation of a relatively serious contract.

Note that the Act applies only to transactions in "interstate commerce." An email message, when it left my computer, could conceivably bounce to Houston, then to Geneva, then to Mexico City all on its way to your computer, even if your computer was located in the building next door. Further, it was carried on a variety of communications media commonly associated with interstate transactions. The likelihood is quite strong that the Supreme Court will have difficulty interpreting around the conclusion that email transactions are in interstate commerce.

Texas enacted its own Uniform Electronic Transaction Act. As briefly stated, the federal law preempted state law concerning paper and ink writing and signature requirements to allow both electronic authentication and electronic records. The Federal esign law provides that the federal law preemption of state law may in turn be superseded by state law, if the state passes the Uniform Electronic Transactions Act with no substantial modifications. Texas passed the UETA largely intact, so the controlling law for electronic transactions in Texas should no longer be the federal esign law but the Texas Uniform Electronic Transaction Act. It will preempt the state of frauds requirement concerning real estate documents that must be in writing and signed but only to the extent of allowing the writing and signing to be done electronically.

Texas' modification to the federal esign law provides that (1) notices of default, acceleration, repossession, foreclosure, eviction, or the right to cure, under a credit agreement secured by, or a rental agreement for, a primary residence of the individual and (2) notices of utility cutoff must continue and be in writing under the old statute of frauds. It does not apply to transactions governed by other laws concerning the creation of execution of wills, codicils, or testamentary trusts.

One certainly needs to look to the future in this matter. Electronic closings, recordings, and commercial contracts and leases will probably become common in the next few years.

PERFORMANCE AND DISCHARGE OF CONTRACTS

Most contracts are discharged by being fully performed by the contracting parties in accordance with the contract terms. However, alternatives are open to the parties of the contract. One is to sell or otherwise **assign** the contract to another party. Unless prohibited by the contract, rights, benefits, and obligations under a contract can be assigned to someone else. The original party to the contract, however, still remains ultimately liable for its performance. Note, too, that an assignment is a contract in itself and must meet all the essential contract requirements to be enforceable. A common example of an assignment occurs when a lessee wants to move out and sells his lease to another party. When a contract creates a personal obligation, such as a listing agreement with a broker, an assignment may not be made.

Novation

A contract can also be performed by **novation.** Novation is the substitution of a new contract between the same or new parties. For example, novation occurs when a buyer assumes a seller's loan, *and* the lender releases the seller from the loan contract. With novation the departing party is released from the obligation to complete the contract.

If the objective of a contract becomes legally impossible to accomplish, the law will consider the contract discharged. For example, a new statute may forbid what the contract originally intended. If the parties mutually agree to cancel their contract before it is executed, this too is a form of discharge. For instance, you sign a five-year lease to pay $500 per month for an office. Three years later you find a better location and want to move. Meanwhile, rents for similar offices in your building have increased to $575 per month. Under these conditions the landlord might want to cancel your lease.

If one of the contracting parties dies, a contract is considered discharged if it calls for some specific act that only the dead person could have performed. For example, if you hired a freelance gardener to tend your landscaping and he died, the contract would be discharged. However, if your contract is with a firm that employs other gardeners who can do the job, the contract would still be valid. Damage to the premises may also discharge the agreement. As a case in point, it is common in real estate sales contracts to provide that the contract is deemed canceled if the property is destroyed or substantially damaged before title passes. However, if the damage is minor and promptly repaired by the seller, the contract would still be valid.

Risk of Loss

If nothing is said in the contract about damage to the premises, then the general rule in Texas is that if neither possession nor title has passed and there is material destruction to the property, the seller cannot enforce the contract and the purchaser is entitled to his money back. If damage is minor and promptly repaired by the seller, the contract would still be enforceable. If either title or possession has passed and destruction occurs, the purchaser is not relieved of his duty to pay the price, nor is he entitled to a refund of money already paid.

BREACH OF CONTRACT

When one party fails to perform as required by a contract and the law does not recognize the reason for failure to be a valid excuse, there is a ***breach of contract.*** The wronged or innocent party has six alternatives: (1) accept partial performance, (2) rescind the contract unilaterally, (3) sue for specific Performance, (4) sue for money damages, (5) accept liquidated money damages, or (6) mutually rescind the contract. Let's consider each of these.

Partial Performance

Partial performance may be acceptable to the innocent party because there may not be a great deal at stake or because the innocent party feels that the time and effort to sue would not be worth the rewards. Suppose that you contracted with a roofing repairman to fix your roof for $400. When he was finished you paid him. A week later you discover a spot that he had agreed to fix, but missed. After many futile phone calls, you accept the breach and consider the contract discharged, because it is easier to fix the spot yourself than to keep pursuing the repairman.

Unilateral Rescission

Under certain circumstances, the innocent party can **unilaterally rescind** a contract. That is, the innocent party can take the position that if the other party is not going to perform his obligations, then the innocent party will not either. An example would be a rent strike in retaliation to a landlord who fails to keep the premises habitable. Unilateral rescission should be resorted to only after consulting an attorney.

Specific Performance

The innocent party may sue in a court of equity to force the breaching party to carry out the remainder of the contract according to the precise terms, price, and conditions agreed upon. For example, you make an offer to purchase a parcel of land and the seller accepts. A written contract is prepared and signed by both of you. If you carry out all your obligations under the contract, but the seller changes his mind and refuses to deliver title to you, you may bring a lawsuit against the seller for ***specific performance.*** In reviewing your suit, the court will determine if the contract is valid and legal, if you have carried out your duties under the contract, and if the contract is just and reasonable. If you win your lawsuit, the court will force the seller to deliver title to you as specified in the contract.

Money Damages

If the damages to the innocent party can be reasonably expressed in terms of money, the innocent party can sue for **money damages.** For example, you rent an apartment to a tenant. As part of the rental contract you furnish the refrigerator and freezer unit. While the tenant is on vacation, the unit breaks down and $200 worth of frozen meat and other perishables spoil. Because your obligation under the contract is to provide the tenant with a working refrigerator-freezer, the tenant can sue you for $200 in money damages. He can also recover interest on the money awarded to him from the day of the loss to the day you reimburse him.

Comparison of Remedies

Note the difference between suing for money damages and suing for specific performance. When money can be used to restore one's position (such as the tenant who can buy $200 worth of fresh food), a suit for money damages is appropriate. In situations where money cannot provide an adequate remedy, and this is often the case in real estate because no two properties are exactly alike, specific performance is appropriate. Notice, too, that the mere existence of the legal rights of the wronged party is often enough to gain cooperation. In the case of the spoiled food, you would give the tenant the value of the lost food before spending time and money in court to hear a judge tell you to do the same thing. A threat of a lawsuit will often bring the desired results if the defendant knows that the law will side with the wronged party. The cases that do go to court are usually those in which the identity of the wronged party and/or the extent of the damages is not clear.

Liquidated Damages

The parties to a contract may decide in advance the amount of damages to be paid in the event either party breaches the contract. An example is an offer to purchase real estate that includes a statement to the effect that, once the seller accepts the offer, if the buyer fails to complete the purchase, the seller may keep the buyer's deposit (earnest money) as ***liquidated damages.*** If a broker is involved, the seller and broker usually agree to divide the damages, thus compensating the seller for damages and the broker for time and effort. Another case of liquidated damages occurs when a builder promises to finish a building by a certain date or pay the party that hired him a certain number of dollars per day until it is completed. This impresses upon the builder the need for prompt completion and compensates the property owner for losses due to the delay.

Mutual Rescission

Specific performance, money damages, and liquidated damages are all designed to aid the innocent party in the event of a breach of contract. However, as a practical matter, the time and cost of pursuing a remedy in a court of law may sometimes exceed the benefits to be derived. Moreover, there is the possibility that the judge for your case may not agree with your point of view. Therefore, even though you are the innocent party and you feel you have a legitimate case that can be pursued in the courts, you may find it more practical to agree with the other party (or parties) to simply cancel (i.e., rescind or annul) the contract. To properly protect everyone involved, the agreement to cancel must be in writing and signed by the parties to the original contract. Properly executed, mutual rescission relieves the parties to the contract from their obligations to each other.

An alternative to mutual rescission is novation. As noted earlier, this is the substitution of a new contract for an existing one. Novation provides a middle ground between suing and rescinding. Thus, the breaching party may be willing to complete the contract provided the innocent party will voluntarily make certain changes in it. If this is acceptable, the changes should be put into writing (or the contract redrafted) and then signed by the parties involved.

STATUTE OF LIMITATIONS

The **statute of limitations** limits by law the amount of time a wronged party has to seek the aid of a court in obtaining justice. The aggrieved party must start legal proceedings within a certain period of time or the courts will not help him. The amount of time varies from state to state and by the type of legal action involved. Texas recognizes a four year limit on written contracts and a two year limit on oral contracts.

IMPLIED OBLIGATIONS

As was pointed out at the beginning of this chapter, one can incur contractual obligations by implication as well as by oral or written contracts. Home builders and real estate agents provide two timely examples. For many years, if a homeowner discovered poor design or workmanship after he had bought a new home, it was his problem. The philosophy was **caveat emptor,** let the buyer beware *before* he buys. Today, courts of law find that in building a home and offering it for sale, the builder simultaneously implies that it is fit for living. Thus, if a builder installs a toilet in a bathroom, the implication is that it will work. In fact, Texas law now requires builders to guarantee their work for one year.

PUTTING IT TO WORK

Real estate practitioner trade organizations, such as the National Association of REALTORS® and state and local REALTOR® associations, are constantly working to elevate the status of real estate brokers and salespeople to that of competent professionals in the public's mind. And as professional status is gained, there is an implied obligation to dispense professional-quality service. Thus, an individual practitioner will not only be responsible for acting in accordance with written laws, but will also be held responsible for being competent and knowledgeable in the field. Once recognized as a professional by the public, the real estate practitioner will not be able to plead ignorance. In view of the present trend toward consumer protection, it appears that the concept of "Let the buyer beware" is being replaced with "Let the agent beware."

REVIEW QUESTIONS

Answers to these questions are found in the Answer Key section at the back of the book.

1. Which of the following would be defined as a party to a contract?
   A. Buyer
   B. Seller
   C. Landlord
   D. Tenant
   E. All of the above

2. A contract based upon a promise exchanged for a promise is a
   A. semilateral contract.
   B. dilateral contract.
   C. binary contract.
   D. bilateral contract.

3. A contract based upon one party's promise in exchange for an act from the other party is classified as
   A. a bilateral contract.
   B. an unenforceable contract.
   C. an executed contract.
   D. a unilateral contract.

4. A unilateral contract is enforceable against
   A. either party.
   B. the offeror.
   C. the offeree.
   D. neither party.

5. A contract binding on one party but not the other is
   A. unenforceable.
   B. void.
   C. voidable.
   D. illegal.

6. A person who has not reached the age of majority is also known as
   A. a minor.
   B. an infant.
   C. both A and B.
   D. neither A nor B.

7. As a rule, a contract between an adult and a minor is NOT
   A. voidable by the minor.
   B. enforceable against the adult.
   C. enforceable against either party.
   D. enforceable against the minor.

8. Attorneys-in-fact derive their powers from
   A. the state bar association.
   B. a power of attorney.
   C. judicial appointment.
   D. popular election.

9. A partnership may contract in the name of
   A. its general partners.
   B. the partnership.
   C. both A and B.
   D. neither A nor B.

10. When an offeror makes a valid offer and communicates it to the offeree, the offeree may
    A. reject the offer.
    B. accept the offer.
    C. make a counteroffer.
    D. all of the above.

11. An offer may be terminated by
    A. withdrawal of the offer.
    B. refusal from the offeree.
    C. the lapse of time.
    D. all of the above.

12. Mutual agreement is missing when a contract is made under
    A. menace.
    B. undue influence.
    C. duress.
    D. all of the above.

13. An act intended to deceive the other party in a contract is
    A. duress.
    B. menace.
    C. mistake.
    D. fraud.

14. A contract made as a joke or in jest is precluded from becoming a valid contract because it lacks
    A. contractual intent.
    B. mutual agreement.
    C. both A and B.
    D. neither A nor B.

15. In Dallas, Texas, Green sold his home to Blue, who took possession prior to settlement. After moving in but before settlement took place, the house was destroyed by a tornado. Which of the following statements is true?
    A. The loss will be borne by Green.
    B. The loss will be borne by Blue.
    C. Blue is entitled to a refund of money already paid.
    D. Blue is relieved of his duty to pay the purchase price.

16. When a lessee in a rented property assigns his lease to another party, he assumes the role of
    A. assignor.
    B. assignee.
    C. sublessee.
    D. none of the above.

17. Substitution of a new contract and a new party for a previous one is known as
    A. innovation.
    B. assignment.
    C. subrogation.
    D. novation.

18. Legal action to force the breaching party to carry out the remainder of a contract is called a suit for
    A. liquidated damages.
    B. specific performance.
    C. partial performance.
    D. breach of contract.

19. The law that limits the time in which a wronged party may file legal action for obtaining justice is the statute of
    A. frauds.
    B. limitations.
    C. novation.
    D. performance.

20. In view of current trends toward consumer protection, the watchwords for real estate salespersons and brokers might well be
    A. caveat emptor.
    B. caveat agent.
    C. both A and B.
    D. neither A nor B.

Chapter 10

KEY TERMS

"As is": said of property offered for sale in its present condition with no guaranty or warranty of quality provided by the seller

Counteroffer: an offer made in response to an offer

Default: failure to perform a legal duty, such as failure to carry out the terms of a contract

Earnest money deposit: money that accompanies an offer to purchase as evidence of good faith

Equitable title: the right to demand that title be conveyed upon payment of the purchase price

Installment contract: a method of selling and financing property whereby the seller retains title but the buyer takes possession while making the payments

Lease-option: allows the tenant to buy the property at a preset price and terms for a given period of time

Right of first refusal: the right to match or better an offer before the property is sold to someone else

Tax-deferred exchange: a sale of real property in exchange for another parcel of real estate to affect a nontaxable gain

"Time is of the essence": a phrase that means that the time limits of a contract must be faithfully observed or the contract is voidable

Texas Real Estate Sales Contracts

IN THIS CHAPTER

Chapter 10 focuses on real estate contracts, especially Texas promulgated forms. Other contracts covered include the option contract, installment contract, and a lease with the option to buy. The right of first refusal and tax deferred exchange are also discussed.

PURPOSE OF SALES CONTRACTS

What is the purpose of a real estate sales contract? If a buyer and a seller agree on a price, why can't the buyer hand the seller the necessary money and the seller simultaneously hand the buyer a deed? The main reason is that the buyer needs time to ascertain that the seller is, in fact, legally capable of conveying title. For protection, the buyer enters into a written and signed contract with the seller, promising that the purchase price will be paid only after title has been searched and found to be in satisfactory condition. The seller, in turn, promises to deliver a deed to the buyer when the buyer has paid his money. This exchange of promises forms the legal consideration of the contract. A contract also gives the buyer time to arrange financing and to specify how such matters as taxes, mortgage debts, leases, and property inspections will be handled.

A properly prepared contract commits each party to its terms. Once a sales contract is in writing and signed, the seller cannot suddenly change his mind and sell his property to another person. The seller is obligated to convey title to the buyer when the buyer has performed the requirements of the contract. Likewise, the buyer must carry out his promises, including paying for the property, providing the seller has done everything required by the contract.

EARNEST MONEY CONTRACTS

The *One to Four Family Residential Contract,* or express it is still commonly called in Texas, the *earnest money contract,* are express, bilateral contracts, and must basically satisfy five requirements in Texas in order for it to be upheld as an enforceable agreement:

1. It must be in writing.
2. The instrument must be signed by the parties sought to be charged therewith.
3. There must be evidence of an intent to convey an interest at some time in the future.
4. There must be an identifiable vendor and vendee.
5. The subject matter to be conveyed must be identifiable.

For general information purposes, it is also recognized in this state that there is such a thing as an *oral earnest money contract.* However, this is very rare.

All real estate licensees are required to use, when appropriate, the standard contract forms and applicable addendums in all real estate transactions. The forms are promulgated by the Texas Real Estate Commission. Copies of two of these TREC contracts are shown in this chapter. If one of the promulgated forms is not used, the licensee is required to use either a form prepared by an attorney at law licensed in this state, or forms prepared by the owner, or forms prepared by an attorney and required by the property owner.

The Real Estate Commission revises all of the earnest money contract forms regularly replacing the previously promulgated forms. Check the TREC web site for the latest forms. The One to Four Family Residential Contract (Resale) etc. (TREC 20-9) is reprinted here as Figure 10.1 and begins at **[1]** and **[2]** by identifying the buyer and seller by name. This is followed by proper legal description to be filled in at **[3]**, and at **[4]**, a place for the address of the property. Paragraph 2.B identifies those items that are permanently installed and built-in items and are labeled "improvements." Those items that are less likely to be attached to the real estate but are peculiarly adapted to the real estate in most circumstances are set out in Paragraph 2.C and labeled "accessories." Paragraph D provides an exception for items that will not be included in the sale at **[5]**. The cash down payment, payable at closing, is to be filled in at **[6]** with the amount of the note (excluding PMI premium) to be filled in at **[7]**. In Paragraph 3, line C, of the contract there is a provision for the total sales price to be filled in at **[8]**.

Paragraph 4 describes the various types of financing that can be used with this form. There are three alternatives (A through C), which can be selected by checking the appropriate box and filling in the corresponding blanks.

Rather than including all of the financing provisions in the body of the contract, it refers to the applicable addenda that can be attached to the contract.

Note that there are two different contingencies; Paragraph 4.A(1) is whether or not the property (the condition of the house, insurability, or appraised value) satisfies the lender's underwriting requirements, notwithstanding the

FIGURE 10.1 Sample of an earnest money contract

02-14-2011

EQUAL HOUSING OPPORTUNITY

PROMULGATED BY THE TEXAS REAL ESTATE COMMISSION (TREC)

ONE TO FOUR FAMILY RESIDENTIAL CONTRACT (RESALE)

NOTICE: Not For Use For Condominium Transactions

1. **PARTIES:** The parties to this contract are ______1______(Seller) and ______2______(Buyer). Seller agrees to sell and convey to Buyer and Buyer agrees to buy from Seller the Property defined below.

2. **PROPERTY:**
   A. LAND: Lot ______ Block______, ______ Addition, City of ___3___, County of ______, Texas, known as ______4______ (address/zip code), or as described on attached exhibit.
   B. IMPROVEMENTS: The house, garage and all other fixtures and improvements attached to the above-described real property, including without limitation, the following **permanently installed and built-in items,** if any: all equipment and appliances, valances, screens, shutters, awnings, wall-to-wall carpeting, mirrors, ceiling fans, attic fans, mail boxes, television antennas and satellite dish system and equipment, mounts and brackets for televisions and speakers, heating and air-conditioning units, security and fire detection equipment, wiring, plumbing and lighting fixtures, chandeliers, water softener system, kitchen equipment, garage door openers, cleaning equipment, shrubbery, landscaping, outdoor cooking equipment, and all other property owned by Seller and attached to the above described real property.
   C. ACCESSORIES: The following described related accessories, if any: window air conditioning units, stove, fireplace screens, curtains and rods, blinds, window shades, draperies and rods, door keys, mailbox keys, above ground pool, swimming pool equipment and maintenance accessories, artificial fireplace logs, and controls for: (i) satellite dish systems, (ii) garage doors, (iii) entry gates, and (iv) other improvements and accessories.
   D. EXCLUSIONS: The following improvements and accessories will be retained by Seller and must be removed prior to delivery of possession:______5______.

   The land, improvements and accessories are collectively referred to as the "Property".

3. **SALES PRICE:**
   A. Cash portion of Sales Price payable by Buyer at closing ....$___6___
   B. Sum of all financing described below (excluding any loan funding fee or mortgage insurance premium) ....$___7___
   C. Sales Price (Sum of A and B) ....$___8___

4. **FINANCING:** The portion of Sales Price not payable in cash will be paid as follows: (Check applicable boxes below)
   ☐ A. THIRD PARTY FINANCING: One or more third party mortgage loans in the total amount of $___9___ (excluding any loan funding fee or mortgage insurance premium).
   (1) Property Approval: If the Property does not satisfy the lenders' underwriting requirements for the loan(s) (including, but not limited to appraisal, insurability and lender required repairs), Buyer may terminate this contract by giving notice to Seller prior to closing and the earnest money will be refunded to Buyer.
   (2) Credit Approval: (Check one box only)
   ☐ (a) This contract is subject to Buyer being approved for the financing described in the attached Third Party Financing Addendum for Credit Approval.
   ☐ (b) This contract is not subject to Buyer being approved for financing and does not involve FHA or VA financing.
   ☐ B. ASSUMPTION: The assumption of the unpaid principal balance of one or more promissory notes described in the attached TREC Loan Assumption Addendum.
   ☐ C. SELLER FINANCING: A promissory note from Buyer to Seller of $___11___, secured by vendor's and deed of trust liens, and containing the terms and conditions described in the attached TREC Seller Financing Addendum. If an owner policy of title insurance is furnished, Buyer shall furnish Seller with a mortgagee policy of title insurance.

Initialed for identification by Buyer______ ______ and Seller ______ ______ TREC NO. 20-10

buyer's ability to qualify for the loan. There is no time limit on this contingency; so if a lender determines on the day of closing that the property doesn't satisfy the lender's underwriting requirements, this contingency has not been satisfied. The buyer has an "out" up until the day of closing, depending on the lender's underwriting requirements. Paragraph 4.A(2) addresses the buyer's contingency for credit approval. Presumably, if the box 4.A(2)(b) is checked, the buyer either has the cash to close or has guaranteed financing already in place. It may be

FIGURE 10.1 Sample of an earnest money contract (*continued*)

Contract Concerning ______________________________ Page 2 of 9 02-14-2011
(Address of Property)

5. EARNEST MONEY: Upon execution of this contract by all parties, Buyer shall deposit $ 12 as earnest money with 13, as escrow agent, at ______________ (address). Buyer shall deposit additional earnest money of $ 14 with escrow agent within _____ days after the effective date of this contract. If Buyer fails to deposit the earnest money as required by this contract, Buyer will be in default.

6. TITLE POLICY AND SURVEY:

A. TITLE POLICY: Seller shall furnish to Buyer at ❑ Seller's ❑ Buyer's expense an owner policy of title insurance (Title Policy) issued by 15 (Title Company) in the amount of the Sales Price, dated at or after closing, insuring Buyer against loss under the provisions of the Title Policy, subject to the promulgated exclusions (including existing building and zoning ordinances) and the following exceptions:
(1) Restrictive covenants common to the platted subdivision in which the Property is located.
(2) The standard printed exception for standby fees, taxes and assessments.
(3) Liens created as part of the financing described in Paragraph 4.
(4) Utility easements created by the dedication deed or plat of the subdivision in which the Property is located.
(5) Reservations or exceptions otherwise permitted by this contract or as may be approved by Buyer in writing.
(6) The standard printed exception as to marital rights.
(7) The standard printed exception as to waters, tidelands, beaches, streams, and related matters.
(8) The standard printed exception as to discrepancies, conflicts, shortages in area or boundary lines, encroachments or protrusions, or overlapping improvements. Buyer, at Buyer's expense, may have the exception amended to read, "shortages in area".

B. COMMITMENT: Within 20 days after the Title Company receives a copy of this contract, Seller shall furnish to Buyer a commitment for title insurance (Commitment) and, at Buyer's expense, legible copies of restrictive covenants and documents evidencing exceptions in the Commitment (Exception Documents) other than the standard printed exceptions. Seller authorizes the Title Company to deliver the Commitment and Exception Documents to Buyer at Buyer's address shown in Paragraph 21. If the Commitment and Exception Documents are not delivered to Buyer within the specified time, the time for delivery will be automatically extended up to 15 days or the Closing Date, whichever is earlier.

C. SURVEY: The survey must be made by a registered professional land surveyor acceptable to the Title Company and Buyer's lender(s). (Check one box only)

❑(1) Within ______ days after the effective date of this contract, Seller shall furnish to Buyer and Title Company Seller's existing survey of the Property and a Residential Real Property Affidavit promulgated by the Texas Department of Insurance (T-47 Affidavit). **If Seller fails to furnish the existing survey or affidavit within the time prescribed, Buyer shall obtain a new survey at Seller's expense no later than 3 days prior to Closing Date.** If the existing survey or affidavit is not acceptable to Title Company or Buyer's lender(s), Buyer shall obtain a new survey at ❑Seller's ❑Buyer's expense no later than 3 days prior to Closing Date.

❑(2) Within _______ days after the effective date of this contract, Buyer shall obtain a new survey at Buyer's expense. Buyer is deemed to receive the survey on the date of actual receipt or the date specified in this paragraph, whichever is earlier.

❑(3) Within _______ days after the effective date of this contract, Seller, at Seller's expense shall furnish a new survey to Buyer.

D. OBJECTIONS: Buyer may object in writing to defects, exceptions, or encumbrances to title: disclosed on the survey other than items 6A(1) through (7) above; disclosed in the Commitment other than items 6A(1) through (8) above; or which prohibit the following use or activity: ____
____.
Buyer must object the earlier of (i) the Closing Date or (ii) _____ days after Buyer receives the Commitment, Exception Documents, and the survey. Buyer's failure to object within the time

Initialed for identification by Buyer_____ _____ and Seller _____ _____ TREC NO. 20-10

construed as a representation to the seller of the buyer's financial ability to close. If you cannot qualify for a loan after making this representation, does it become a deceptive trade practice? This may create an unexpected liability for a buyer. If there is a financing contingency for the buyer in Paragraphs 4.A.(1), or 4.A(2)(a) the contract requires the use of the Third Party Financing Addendum for Credit Approval.

If THIRD PARTY FINANCING (A) is involved, a provision for the amount of the first lien note is provided at [9].

FIGURE 10.1 Sample of an earnest money contract (*continued*)

Contract Concerning ______________________________ Page 3 of 9 02-14-2011
(Address of Property)

allowed will constitute a waiver of Buyer's right to object; except that the requirements in Schedule C of the Commitment are not waived. Provided Seller is not obligated to incur any expense, Seller shall cure the timely objections of Buyer or any third party lender within 15 days after Seller receives the objections and the Closing Date will be extended as necessary. If objections are not cured within such 15 day period, this contract will terminate and the earnest money will be refunded to Buyer unless Buyer waives the objections.

E. TITLE NOTICES:

(1) ABSTRACT OR TITLE POLICY: Broker advises Buyer to have an abstract of title covering the Property examined by an attorney of Buyer's selection, or Buyer should be furnished with or obtain a Title Policy. If a Title Policy is furnished, the Commitment should be promptly reviewed by an attorney of Buyer's choice due to the time limitations on Buyer's right to object.

(2) PROPERTY OWNERS ASSOCIATION(S) MANDATORY MEMBERSHIP: The Property ❑is ❑is not subject to mandatory membership in a property owners association(s). If the Property is subject to mandatory membership in a property owners association(s), Seller notifies Buyer under §5.012, Texas Property Code, that, as a purchaser of property in the residential community identified in Paragraph 2A in which the Property is located, you are obligated to be a member of the property owners association(s). Restrictive covenants governing the use and occupancy of the Property and a dedicatory instrument governing the establishment, maintenance, and operation of this residential community have been or will be recorded in the Real Property Records of the county in which the Property is located. Copies of the restrictive covenants and dedicatory instrument may be obtained from the county clerk. You are obligated to pay assessments to the property owners association(s). The amount of the assessments is subject to change. Your failure to pay the assessments could result in a lien on and the foreclosure of the Property. **If Buyer is concerned about these matters, the TREC promulgated Addendum for Property Subject to Mandatory Membership in a Property Owners Association should be used for each association.**

(3) STATUTORY TAX DISTRICTS: If the Property is situated in a utility or other statutorily created district providing water, sewer, drainage, or flood control facilities and services, Chapter 49, Texas Water Code, requires Seller to deliver and Buyer to sign the statutory notice relating to the tax rate, bonded indebtedness, or standby fee of the district prior to final execution of this contract.

(4) TIDE WATERS: If the Property abuts the tidally influenced waters of the state, §33.135, Texas Natural Resources Code, requires a notice regarding coastal area property to be included in the contract. An addendum containing the notice promulgated by TREC or required by the parties must be used.

(5) ANNEXATION: If the Property is located outside the limits of a municipality, Seller notifies Buyer under §5.011, Texas Property Code, that the Property may now or later be included in the extraterritorial jurisdiction of a municipality and may now or later be subject to annexation by the municipality. Each municipality maintains a map that depicts its boundaries and extraterritorial jurisdiction. To determine if the Property is located within a municipality's extraterritorial jurisdiction or is likely to be located within a municipality's extraterritorial jurisdiction, contact all municipalities located in the general proximity of the Property for further information.

(6) PROPERTY LOCATED IN A CERTIFICATED SERVICE AREA OF A UTILITY SERVICE PROVIDER: Notice required by §13.257, Water Code: The real property, described in Paragraph 2, that you are about to purchase may be located in a certificated water or sewer service area, which is authorized by law to provide water or sewer service to the properties in the certificated area. If your property is located in a certificated area there may be special costs or charges that you will be required to pay before you can receive water or sewer service. There may be a period required to construct lines or other facilities necessary to provide water or sewer service to your property. You are advised to determine if the property is in a certificated area and contact the utility service provider to determine the cost that you will be required to pay and the period, if any, that is required to provide water or sewer service to your property. The undersigned Buyer

Initialed for identification by Buyer_____ _____ and Seller _____ _____ TREC NO. 20-10

The ASSUMPTION provision, (B), provides for assuming the first lien note to the proper payee, shown at [10]. If the buyer is going to assume the loan, the contract now requires the use of the Loan Assumption Addendum.

The Seller Financing provision **(C)**, shown at [11] provides for the amount to be loaned and the interest rate to be charged to the seller. The TREC Seller Financing Addendum provides for more specific information.

In Paragraph 5 the EARNEST MONEY amount is set out at [12], with the depository, usually a title company, shown at [13]. A provision for

FIGURE 10.1 Sample of an earnest money contract (*continued*)

Contract Concerning ______________________________ Page 4 of 9 02-14-2011
(Address of Property)

hereby acknowledges receipt of the foregoing notice at or before the execution of a binding contract for the purchase of the real property described in Paragraph 2 or at closing of purchase of the real property.

(7) PUBLIC IMPROVEMENT DISTRICTS: If the Property is in a public improvement district, §5.014, Property Code, requires Seller to notify Buyer as follows: As a purchaser of this parcel of real property you are obligated to pay an assessment to a municipality or county for an improvement project undertaken by a public improvement district under Chapter 372, Local Government Code. The assessment may be due annually or in periodic installments. More information concerning the amount of the assessment and the due dates of that assessment may be obtained from the municipality or county levying the assessment. The amount of the assessments is subject to change. Your failure to pay the assessments could result in a lien on and the foreclosure of your property.

7. PROPERTY CONDITION:

A. ACCESS, INSPECTIONS AND UTILITIES: Seller shall permit Buyer and Buyer's agents access to the Property at reasonable times. Buyer may have the Property inspected by inspectors selected by Buyer and licensed by TREC or otherwise permitted by law to make inspections. Seller at Seller's expense shall turn on existing utilities for inspections.

B. SELLER'S DISCLOSURE NOTICE PURSUANT TO §5.008, TEXAS PROPERTY CODE (Notice):
(Check one box only)
❑ (1) Buyer has received the Notice.
❑ (2) Buyer has not received the Notice. Within ______ days after the effective date of this contract, Seller shall deliver the Notice to Buyer. If Buyer does not receive the Notice, Buyer may terminate this contract at any time prior to the closing and the earnest money will be refunded to Buyer. If Seller delivers the Notice, Buyer may terminate this contract for any reason within 7 days after Buyer receives the Notice or prior to the closing, whichever first occurs, and the earnest money will be refunded to Buyer.
❑ (3)The Seller is not required to furnish the notice under the Texas Property Code.

C. SELLER'S DISCLOSURE OF LEAD-BASED PAINT AND LEAD-BASED PAINT HAZARDS is required by Federal law for a residential dwelling constructed prior to 1978.

D. ACCEPTANCE OF PROPERTY CONDITION: (Check one box only)
❑ (1) Buyer accepts the Property in its present condition.
❑ (2) Buyer accepts the Property in its present condition provided Seller, at Seller's expense, shall complete the following specific repairs and treatments: ____________ ______________________________.(Do not insert general phrases, such as "subject to inspections" that do not identify specific repairs.)

NOTICE TO BUYER AND SELLER: Buyer's agreement to accept the Property in its present condition under Paragraph 7D(1) or (2) does not preclude Buyer from inspecting the Property under Paragraph 7A, from negotiating repairs or treatments in a subsequent amendment, or from terminating this contract during the Option Period, if any.

E. LENDER REQUIRED REPAIRS AND TREATMENTS: Unless otherwise agreed in writing, neither party is obligated to pay for lender required repairs, which includes treatment for wood destroying insects. If the parties do not agree to pay for the lender required repairs or treatments, this contract will terminate and the earnest money will be refunded to Buyer. If the cost of lender required repairs and treatments exceeds 5% of the Sales Price, Buyer may terminate this contract and the earnest money will be refunded to Buyer.

F. COMPLETION OF REPAIRS AND TREATMENTS: Unless otherwise agreed in writing, Seller shall complete all agreed repairs and treatments prior to the Closing Date. All required permits must be obtained, and repairs and treatments must be performed by persons who are licensed or otherwise authorized by law to provide such repairs or treatments. At Buyer's election, any transferable warranties received by Seller with respect to the repairs and treatments will be transferred to Buyer at Buyer's expense. If Seller fails to complete any agreed repairs and treatments prior to the Closing Date, Buyer may do so and receive reimbursement from Seller at closing. The Closing Date will be extended up to 15 days, if necessary, to complete repairs and treatments.

G. ENVIRONMENTAL MATTERS: Buyer is advised that the presence of wetlands, toxic substances, including asbestos and wastes or other environmental hazards, or the presence of a threatened or endangered species or its habitat may affect Buyer's intended use of the Property. If Buyer is concerned about these matters, an addendum promulgated by TREC or required by the parties should be used.

Initialed for identification by Buyer_____ _____ and Seller ______ _____ TREC NO. 20-10

additional earnest money, if any, is shown at **[14]**. If the earnest money is not deposited, it is a ***default*** by the buyer. Note that the contract does not terminate if the earnest money is not deposited, the buyer is in default. How much earnest money should the buyer put up? It is *always* negotiable. Earnest money, by itself, is not consideration. The consideration in a bilateral contract for sale is the mutual promises the parties make to each other. The earnest money can be agreed to as **liquidated damages** (see the discussion in Chapter 9) in the event of a buyer's default.

FIGURE 10.1 Sample of an earnest money contract (*continued*)

Contract Concerning ____ Page 5 of 9 02-14-2011
(Address of Property)

H. RESIDENTIAL SERVICE CONTRACTS: Buyer may purchase a residential service contract from a residential service company licensed by TREC. If Buyer purchases a residential service contract, Seller shall reimburse Buyer at closing for the cost of the residential service contract in an amount not exceeding $__________________. Buyer should review any residential service contract for the scope of coverage, exclusions and limitations. **The purchase of a residential service contract is optional. Similar coverage may be purchased from various companies authorized to do business in Texas.**

8. **BROKERS' FEES:** All obligations of the parties for payment of brokers' fees are contained in separate written agreements.

9. **CLOSING:**
A. The closing of the sale will be on or before ____________________, 20____, or within 7 days after objections made under Paragraph 6D have been cured or waived, whichever date is later (Closing Date). If either party fails to close the sale by the Closing Date, the non-defaulting party may exercise the remedies contained in Paragraph 15.
B. At closing:
(1) Seller shall execute and deliver a general warranty deed conveying title to the Property to Buyer and showing no additional exceptions to those permitted in Paragraph 6 and furnish tax statements or certificates showing no delinquent taxes on the Property.
(2) Buyer shall pay the Sales Price in good funds acceptable to the escrow agent.
(3) Seller and Buyer shall execute and deliver any notices, statements, certificates, affidavits, releases, loan documents and other documents reasonably required for the closing of the sale and the issuance of the Title Policy.
(4) There will be no liens, assessments, or security interests against the Property which will not be satisfied out of the sales proceeds unless securing the payment of any loans assumed by Buyer and assumed loans will not be in default.
(5) If the Property is subject to a lease, Seller shall (i) deliver to Buyer the lease(s) and the move-in condition form signed by the tenant, if any, and (ii) transfer security deposits (as defined under §92.102, Property Code), if any, to Buyer. In such an event, Buyer shall deliver to the tenant a signed statement acknowledging that the Buyer has received the security deposit and is responsible for the return of the security deposit, and specifying the exact dollar amount of the security deposit.

10. **POSSESSION:** Seller shall deliver to Buyer possession of the Property in its present or required condition, ordinary wear and tear excepted: ☐upon closing and funding ☐according to a temporary residential lease form promulgated by TREC or other written lease required by the parties. Any possession by Buyer prior to closing or by Seller after closing which is not authorized by a written lease will establish a tenancy at sufferance relationship between the parties. **Consult your insurance agent prior to change of ownership and possession because insurance coverage may be limited or terminated. The absence of a written lease or appropriate insurance coverage may expose the parties to economic loss.**

11. **SPECIAL PROVISIONS:** (Insert only factual statements and business details applicable to the sale. TREC rules prohibit licensees from adding factual statements or business details for which a contract addendum, lease or other form has been promulgated by TREC for mandatory use.)

Initialed for identification by Buyer_____ _____ and Seller _____ _____ TREC NO. 20-10

There are provisions in the contracts for title policies and surveys. Note at [15], the owner's title policy of title insurance is to be furnished in the amount of the sales price, and there is a choice as to who will pay. In most Texas counties, it is customary for the seller to pay. In other counties it is customary for the buyer to pay. At other times, a buyer's employer may pay a part of the closing costs.

Paragraph 6.A(8) allows the buyer at buyer's expense to have the exception as to "discrepancies, conflicts, shortages in area for boundary lines, encroachments or protrusions, or overlapping of improvements" amended to read only

FIGURE 10.1 Sample of an earnest money contract (*continued*)

Contract Concerning ______________________________ Page 6 of 9 02-14-2011
(Address of Property)

12. SETTLEMENT AND OTHER EXPENSES:

A. The following expenses must be paid at or prior to closing:

(1) Expenses payable by Seller (Seller's Expenses):

(a) Releases of existing liens, including prepayment penalties and recording fees; release of Seller's loan liability; tax statements or certificates; preparation of deed; one-half of escrow fee; and other expenses payable by Seller under this contract.

(b) Seller shall also pay an amount not to exceed $ ____________ to be applied in the following order: Buyer's Expenses which Buyer is prohibited from paying by FHA, VA, Texas Veterans Land Board or other governmental loan programs, and then to other Buyer's Expenses as allowed by the lender.

(2) Expenses payable by Buyer (Buyer's Expenses): Appraisal fees; loan application fees; adjusted origination charges; credit reports; preparation of loan documents; interest on the notes from date of disbursement to one month prior to dates of first monthly payments; recording fees; copies of easements and restrictions; loan title policy with endorsements required by lender; loan-related inspection fees; photos; amortization schedules; one-half of escrow fee; all prepaid items, including required premiums for flood and hazard insurance, reserve deposits for insurance, ad valorem taxes and special governmental assessments; final compliance inspection; courier fee; repair inspection; underwriting fee; wire transfer fee; expenses incident to any loan; Private Mortgage Insurance Premium (PMI), VA Loan Funding Fee, or FHA Mortgage Insurance Premium (MIP) as required by the lender; and other expenses payable by Buyer under this contract.

B. If any expense exceeds an amount expressly stated in this contract for such expense to be paid by a party, that party may terminate this contract unless the other party agrees to pay such excess. Buyer may not pay charges and fees expressly prohibited by FHA, VA, Texas Veterans Land Board or other governmental loan program regulations.

13. PRORATIONS: Taxes for the current year, interest, maintenance fees, assessments, dues and rents will be prorated through the Closing Date. The tax proration may be calculated taking into consideration any change in exemptions that will affect the current year's taxes. If taxes for the current year vary from the amount prorated at closing, the parties shall adjust the prorations when tax statements for the current year are available. If taxes are not paid at or prior to closing, Buyer shall pay taxes for the current year.

14. CASUALTY LOSS: If any part of the Property is damaged or destroyed by fire or other casualty after the effective date of this contract, Seller shall restore the Property to its previous condition as soon as reasonably possible, but in any event by the Closing Date. If Seller fails to do so due to factors beyond Seller's control, Buyer may (a) terminate this contract and the earnest money will be refunded to Buyer (b) extend the time for performance up to 15 days and the Closing Date will be extended as necessary or (c) accept the Property in its damaged condition with an assignment of insurance proceeds and receive credit from Seller at closing in the amount of the deductible under the insurance policy. Seller's obligations under this paragraph are independent of any other obligations of Seller under this contract.

15. DEFAULT: If Buyer fails to comply with this contract, Buyer will be in default, and Seller may (a) enforce specific performance, seek such other relief as may be provided by law, or both, or (b) terminate this contract and receive the earnest money as liquidated damages, thereby releasing both parties from this contract. If, due to factors beyond Seller's control, Seller fails within the time allowed to make any non-casualty repairs or deliver the Commitment, or survey, if required of Seller, Buyer may (a) extend the time for performance up to 15 days and the Closing Date will be extended as necessary or (b) terminate this contract as the sole remedy and receive the earnest money. If Seller fails to comply with this contract for any other reason, Seller will be in default and Buyer may (a) enforce specific performance, seek such other relief as may be provided by law, or both, or (b) terminate this contract and receive the earnest money, thereby releasing both parties from this contract.

16. MEDIATION: It is the policy of the State of Texas to encourage resolution of disputes through alternative dispute resolution procedures such as mediation. Any dispute between Seller and Buyer related to this contract which is not resolved through informal discussion ☐will ☐will not be submitted to a mutually acceptable mediation service or provider. The parties to the mediation shall bear the mediation costs equally. This paragraph does not preclude a party from seeking equitable relief from a court of competent jurisdiction.

17. ATTORNEY'S FEES: A Buyer, Seller, Listing Broker, Other Broker, or escrow agent who prevails in any legal proceeding related to this contract is entitled to recover reasonable attorney's fees and all costs of such proceeding.

Initialed for identification by Buyer_____ _____ and Seller _____ _____ TREC NO. 20-10

"shortages in area." This provision has been commonly used in commercial contract forms and is now being used in the residential forms. The issue presented is a rather complex one, and now real estate licensees are going to have to become familiar with this issue because many buyers, particularly out-of-state buyers, will want to know about this provision.

If a licensee represents a buyer, they may want to pay particular attention to this provision. Many buyers tend to be extremely picky and they are firmly

FIGURE 10.1 Sample of an earnest money contract (*continued*)

Contract Concerning ______________________________ Page 7 of 9 02-14-2011
(Address of Property)

18. ESCROW:

A. ESCROW: The escrow agent is not (i) a party to this contract and does not have liability for the performance or nonperformance of any party to this contract, (ii) liable for interest on the earnest money and (iii) liable for the loss of any earnest money caused by the failure of any financial institution in which the earnest money has been deposited unless the financial institution is acting as escrow agent.

B. EXPENSES: At closing, the earnest money must be applied first to any cash down payment, then to Buyer's Expenses and any excess refunded to Buyer. If no closing occurs, escrow agent may: (i) require a written release of liability of the escrow agent from all parties, (ii) require payment of unpaid expenses incurred on behalf of a party, and (iii) only deduct from the earnest money the amount of unpaid expenses incurred on behalf of the party receiving the earnest money.

C. DEMAND: Upon termination of this contract, either party or the escrow agent may send a release of earnest money to each party and the parties shall execute counterparts of the release and deliver same to the escrow agent. If either party fails to execute the release, either party may make a written demand to the escrow agent for the earnest money. If only one party makes written demand for the earnest money, escrow agent shall promptly provide a copy of the demand to the other party. If escrow agent does not receive written objection to the demand from the other party within 15 days, escrow agent may disburse the earnest money to the party making demand reduced by the amount of unpaid expenses incurred on behalf of the party receiving the earnest money and escrow agent may pay the same to the creditors. If escrow agent complies with the provisions of this paragraph, each party hereby releases escrow agent from all adverse claims related to the disbursal of the earnest money.

D. DAMAGES: Any party who wrongfully fails or refuses to sign a release acceptable to the escrow agent within 7 days of receipt of the request will be liable to the other party for liquidated damages in an amount equal to the sum of: (i) three times the amount of the earnest money; (ii) the earnest money; (iii) reasonable attorney's fees; and (iv) all costs of suit.

E. NOTICES: Escrow agent's notices will be effective when sent in compliance with Paragraph 21. Notice of objection to the demand will be deemed effective upon receipt by escrow agent.

19. REPRESENTATIONS: All covenants, representations and warranties in this contract survive closing. If any representation of Seller in this contract is untrue on the Closing Date, Seller will be in default. Unless expressly prohibited by written agreement, Seller may continue to show the Property and receive, negotiate and accept back up offers.

20. FEDERAL TAX REQUIREMENTS: If Seller is a "foreign person," as defined by applicable law, or if Seller fails to deliver an affidavit to Buyer that Seller is not a "foreign person," then Buyer shall withhold from the sales proceeds an amount sufficient to comply with applicable tax law and deliver the same to the Internal Revenue Service together with appropriate tax forms. Internal Revenue Service regulations require filing written reports if currency in excess of specified amounts is received in the transaction.

21. NOTICES: All notices from one party to the other must be in writing and are effective when mailed to, hand-delivered at, or transmitted by facsimile or electronic transmission as follows:

To Buyer at: ______________________	**To Seller at:** ______________________
______________________	______________________
______________________	______________________
______________________	______________________
Telephone: ( ) ______________	Telephone: ( ) ______________
Facsimile: ( ) ______________	Facsimile: ( ) ______________
E-mail: ______________	E-mail: ______________

Initialed for identification by Buyer______ ______ and Seller ______ ______ TREC NO. 20-10

convinced that they do not have good title if there is a three inch encroachment of a pool deck into a power line right-of-way. The fact is that they don't have good title if this exists, but, as we just previously discussed, the title insurance company can insure against any damages as a result of the encroachment. Some buyers, however, will worry about their ability to sell the property in the future with this encumbrance and will choose not to purchase. This provision in the contract helps an agent and his buyer focus on alternatives available if this condition exists.

FIGURE 10.1 Sample of an earnest money contract (*continued*)

Contract Concerning ______________________________ Page 8 of 9 02-14-2011
(Address of Property)

22. AGREEMENT OF PARTIES: This contract contains the entire agreement of the parties and cannot be changed except by their written agreement. Addenda which are a part of this contract are (Check all applicable boxes):

- ☐ Third Party Financing Addendum for Credit Approval
- ☐ Addendum for "Back-Up" Contract
- ☐ Seller Financing Addendum
- ☐ Addendum for Coastal Area Property
- ☐ Addendum for Property Subject to Mandatory Membership in a Property Owners Association
- ☐ Environmental Assessment, Threatened or Endangered Species and Wetlands Addendum
- ☐ Buyer's Temporary Residential Lease
- ☐ Seller's Temporary Residential Lease
- ☐ Loan Assumption Addendum
- ☐ Short Sale Addendum
- ☐ Addendum for Sale of Other Property by Buyer
- ☐ Addendum for Property Located Seaward of the Gulf Intracoastal Waterway
- ☐ Addendum for Reservation of Oil, Gas and Other Minerals
- ☐ Addendum for Seller's Disclosure of Information on Lead-based Paint and Lead-based Paint Hazards as Required by Federal Law
- ☐ Other (list): ______________________________

23. TERMINATION OPTION: For nominal consideration, the receipt of which is hereby acknowledged by Seller, and Buyer's agreement to pay Seller $______________ (Option Fee) within 2 days after the effective date of this contract, Seller grants Buyer the unrestricted right to terminate this contract by giving notice of termination to Seller within ________ days after the effective date of this contract (Option Period). If no dollar amount is stated as the Option Fee or if Buyer fails to pay the Option Fee to Seller within the time prescribed, this paragraph will not be a part of this contract and Buyer shall not have the unrestricted right to terminate this contract. If Buyer gives notice of termination within the time prescribed, the Option Fee will not be refunded; however, any earnest money will be refunded to Buyer. The Option Fee ☐will ☐will not be credited to the Sales Price at closing. **Time is of the essence for this paragraph and strict compliance with the time for performance is required.**

24. CONSULT AN ATTORNEY: TREC rules prohibit real estate licensees from giving legal advice. READ THIS CONTRACT CAREFULLY. If you do not understand the effect of this contract, consult an attorney BEFORE signing.

Buyer's	Seller's
Attorney is: ______________________	Attorney is: ______________________
Telephone: ( )	Telephone: ( )
Facsimile: ( )	Facsimile: ( )
E-mail:	E-mail:

EXECUTED the ______day of ____________________, 20____ (EFFECTIVE DATE).
(BROKER: FILL IN THE DATE OF FINAL ACCEPTANCE.)

______________________	______________________
Buyer	Seller
Buyer	Seller

The form of this contract has been approved by the Texas Real Estate Commission. TREC forms are intended for use only by trained real estate licensees. No representation is made as to the legal validity or adequacy of any provision in any specific transactions. It is not intended for complex transactions. Texas Real Estate Commission, P.O. Box 12188, Austin, TX 78711-2188, (512) 459-6544 (http://www.trec.state.tx.us) TREC NO. 20-10. This form replaces TREC NO. 20-8.

TREC NO. 20-10

Note that the title company is required to deliver to the buyer a commitment for title insurance within 20 days after the title company receives a copy of the contract along with legible copies of restrictive covenants and documents evidencing exceptions (at the buyer's expense). This paragraph also authorizes the title company to deliver the commitment and documents to the buyer's address shown in Paragraph 21. If the title commitment and related documents are not delivered in a timely manner, there is an automatic extension for 15 days.

FIGURE 10.1 Sample of an earnest money contract (*continued*)

Contract Concerning ______________________________ Page 9 of 9 02-14-2011
(Address of Property)

BROKER INFORMATION

Other Broker Firm — License No.	Listing Broker Firm — License No.
represents ❑ Buyer only as Buyer's agent ❑ Seller as Listing Broker's subagent	represents ❑ Seller and Buyer as an intermediary ❑ Seller only as Seller's agent
Licensed Supervisor of Associate — Telephone	Licensed Supervisor of Associate — Telephone
Associate — Telephone	Listing Associate — Telephone
Other Broker's Address — Facsimile	Listing Broker's Office Address — Facsimile
City — State — Zip	City — State — Zip
Associate Email Address	Listing Associate's Email Address
	Selling Associate — Telephone
	Selling Associate's Office Address — Facsimile
	City — State — Zip
	Selling Associate's Email Address

Listing Broker has agreed to pay Other Broker____________of the total sales price when the Listing Broker's fee is received. Escrow agent is authorized and directed to pay other Broker from Listing Broker's fee at closing.

OPTION FEE RECEIPT

Receipt of $________________ (Option Fee) in the form of _____________________ is acknowledged.

Seller or Listing Broker ______________ Date ______________

CONTRACT AND EARNEST MONEY RECEIPT

Receipt of ❑Contract and ❑$__________________ Earnest Money in the form of ___________________
is acknowledged.
Escrow Agent: ______________________________________ Date: __________________________

By: ____ Email Address ____________________

Address ______________________________________ Telephone (_____) ________________

City State Zip ______________________________ Facsimile: (_____) ________________

TREC NO. 20-10

Source: Texas Real Estate Commission

Surveys have always been a concern at closings. The contract at [16] provides three alternatives:

(1) The seller can furnish the seller's existing survey of the property and the Residential Real Property Affidavit promulgated by the Texas Department of Insurance. If the Title company, buyer, or buyer's lender do not deem the survey to be acceptable, the buyer or seller shall then have to produce his

own survey. If the seller fails to furnish the existing survey or affidavit within the time prescribed, the buyer has the right to obtain a new survey at the seller's expense.

(2) The buyer provides the survey at the buyer's expense within a prescribed time period. Note that the buyer is deemed to have received the survey within that time period or the date of actual receipt of the survey, whichever is earlier, so one should be careful to put plenty of time to obtain the survey.

(3) The seller can provide a new survey at the seller's expense.

The contract reserves the right of the buyer to object to the survey, title commitment, and exception documents within the time period prescribed in Paragraph 6.D., but the buyer can object no later than the closing date. So if the survey or exception document is not produced until the closing, the buyer has to make a tough decision *at the closing* or he waives his right to object to those items.

If the buyer has a specific concern about his ability to use the property for a specific purpose, he has the right to make that a contingency by inserting that contingency at **[18]**. For instance, the buyer may want to insert "launch pad site," so that if the property could not be used for that purpose, the buyer has no obligation to perform.

The final provisions of Paragraph 6.E give the buyer required notices. The first notice advises the buyer to have an abstract of title covering the property examined by an attorney of the buyer's selection or should be furnished with or obtain a title policy. This automatically provides for a licensee's compliance with the Texas Real Estate License Act. The second disclosure concerns mandatory owners association membership and whether or not the buyer is required to be a member of a homeowner's association in his subdivision. The third notice provides for a required notice if the property is located in a municipal utility district. This is a specific notice required by the Texas Water Code regarding the additional ad valorem taxation that is imposed on the property as a result of being located in a municipal utility district. The fourth notice gives the buyer a specific notice as required by the Texas Natural Resources Code if the property abuts highly influenced waters of this state. The fifth notice is a notification that the property may be subject to annexation as provided under the Texas Property Code.

The 6th Notice deals with property located in a certificated service area of the Utility Service Provider. The 7th Notice advises that the property is in a public improvement district (commonly referred to as a PID). Both the 5th and 6th Notices may require additional funds to be expended through assessments or other fees, and therefore must be disclosed to the buyer as a matter of statute in Texas.

Paragraph 7 gives the buyer the right to inspect the property. Note that Paragraph 7A. gives the buyer the right to access the property at all reasonable times and that there is no limit on how many inspections the buyer can perform. Note the language at **[19]**. Paragraph 7A. does not make inspections or re-inspections a contingency. However, if the property does have significant defects, the buyer may have a cause of action against the seller for misrepresentation or failure to disclose those defects.

A clarification was made in Paragraph 7.D. In the old Paragraph 7.D, licensees, buyers, and sellers were often inserting things into the blank that were not anticipated, such as "subject to inspection" and other vague comments that could render the contract unenforceable. Note that the contract cautions against this and notes the right for the parties to make further amendments. Paragraph 7.D was revised to require that one of two boxes be checked. The first box deals with the property "in its present condition." Several appellate cases have indicated that Paragraph 7.D.(1) will be construed as an "as is" provision.

If box 7.D.(2) is checked, the buyer has noticed a specific item that needs to be repaired on the property (water damage in the master bedroom) and specifies that repair and/or treatment that must be completed prior to closing. In theory, this creates a shift of the burden where the buyer is agreeing to take the property either "as is" or only after the seller has made the specific repairs. So it is up to the buyer to perform inspections during the option period.

What if a defect is discovered during the option period? At this point, the buyer has to make a choice: (1) exercise his right to terminate as set out in Paragraph 23, using TREC Form No. 38-2; or (2) propose an amendment to the contract, using TREC Form 39-6. At that point in time, the seller now has the choice of either agreeing to the repairs or running the risk that the buyer will terminate if the seller does not agree to the amendment.

Note under Paragraph 7.F, that if the seller fails to complete any agreed repairs prior to the closing date, the buyer has the right to do so and receive reimbursement from the seller at closing. This apparently is without regard to the expense, and it seems to give the buyer the unilateral right to do any repairs he thinks are "agreed to," so a prudent licensee should put a price on the "agreed to" repair to clarify this issue. This can be addressed by another TREC form, the Amendment form. It also allows the closing date to be extended up to 15 days to complete those repairs and treatments. There is a practical problem to this. What if the seller won't let the buyer in to make the repairs?

Paragraph 8, although titled Brokers' Fees, provides only that the listing broker is to be identified. The amount of his compensation is specified in the listing agreement and is not a part of this contract between the buyer and seller. A new provision in the contract provides for the brokers to designate who they represent. Under the Texas Real Estate Commission Rules and Regulations, this should have been done prior to signing the contract, and the disclosure in the contract should be nothing more than a confirmation of previously disclosed agency relationships.

Provisions and deadlines for closing are set forth at **[21]**. Possession date for the buyer is stated at **[22]**. The form allows buyer possession of the property either (i) upon closing and funding or (ii) according to the temporary residential lease. There is still no definition for what "funding" means, whether or not the buyer funds, whether or not the lender funds, or if both elements of funding will be required. Often a buyer will fund his proceeds at closing but the lender's funding may be delayed. Does the buyer still get possession in this circumstance? No, if the buyer's lender has not funded, the closing hasn't funded.

A Special Provisions section is provided at Paragraph 11 of the earnest money contract. This particular earnest money contract has very little need for special provisions, except for specifying certain exceptions to the fixtures that the purchaser may expect to be conveyed with the house, because of the all-encompassing type of language set out in Paragraph 2 of the contract. Additional items that are not included in Paragraph 2 may be inserted in Paragraph 11, but the cautious real estate licensee should pay close attention to the fact that only business details can be inserted and not anything that otherwise affects the legal obligations of either party. Note that if there is an applicable TREC Addendum, it *must* be used by the licensee.

Paragraph 12 deals with various expenses the buyer and seller will be expected to pay at or prior to closing. Responsibility for loan appraisal fees is shown at **[23].** (These are generally paid by the party obtaining the loan.) Seller's expenses, which may include the dollar amount for points or commitment fees or discount fees to enable the purchaser to secure his loan, are set out at **[24]**, along with certain other expenses that are incidental to selling.

Paragraphs 13 through 23 are very specific and explanatory provisions that are generally standard to all earnest money contracts. Items generally prorated are taxes, insurance, and rents. Paragraph 14 contains provisions for loss (damage or destruction) of the real estate. If the property is damaged or destroyed by fire or other casualty after the contract date, the seller is required to restore the property to its previous condition as soon as reasonably possible. If seller fails to do so (due to factors beyond seller's control) the buyer has three options: (1) he can terminate the contract and receive a refund of his earnest money; (2) he can extend the time for performance up to 15 days; or (3) accept the property in its damaged condition with an assignment of the insurance proceeds. The seller agrees to pay the deductible on the insurance policy. There is also no agreement as to what "previous condition" might mean. Should the seller reinspect? What if mold has accumulated or other matters not readily discoverable as a result of the damage? No contract can provide for all alternatives (without being sixty pages long). If these new conditions occur, the TREC Amendment form (39-6) is required for licensee's use. Paragraph 15 provides the remedies for default. If the buyer defaults, the seller has two remedies: (1) sue for specific performance, or (2) retain the earnest money. If the seller defaults because of repairs or delivery of the title commitment or survey, the buyer can extend the time for seller's performance up to 15 days or terminate the contract and receive the earnest money. If the seller fails to comply for any other reasons, the buyer may: (1) sue for specific performance and seek other legal remedies, or (2) receive the earnest money.

Paragraph 16 allows for mediation as an alternative method of dispute resolution. Paragraph 18.D was clarified to confirm the award against someone who wrongfully fails to or refuses to sign a release of the earnest money. We have all met these people: They are angry, they may be unreasonable, and they do not want to release or forfeit the earnest money out of spite or hate for the other party. They tend to be emotional and do not want to agree to anything. If a party wrongfully fails or refuses to sign a release for the earnest money, he or she may end up being liable to the other party in an amount equal to the sum of: (1) the forfeiture of the earnest money; (2) three times the earnest money as agreed liquidated damages; (3) reasonable attorneys fees; and (4) all costs of suit. When someone has a $5,000 earnest money dispute, it may be rather shocking to realize they may be responsible for over $20,000 in damages if they wrongfully withhold the release of that earnest money. Hopefully, this will help resolve an awful lot of disputes early on, and, similar to Paragraph 17, result in a resolution of a dispute before it gets to the lawsuit stage.

Paragraph 18 provides for the escrow procedures. In those circumstances, the title company operates as a neutral third party. In the event of a default, the title company deals with the disbursement of the earnest money. Although they can forfeit to the non-defaulting party, the title company will normally require both parties to sign a release of the earnest money. Note that this paragraph, however, imposes a severe penalty in the event that one of the parties refuses to sign the release. Paragraph 18.D. provides that if the parties wrongfully refuse to sign the release, that party will be liable to the other party for liquidated damages equal to three times the amount of the earnest money plus attorney's fees and court costs.

This is in addition to forfeiture of the earnest money, so a party with a "bad attitude" may suffer severe penalties if they unreasonably fail to release the earnest money. Paragraph 21 provides for notices to the seller and the buyer at **[25].** This is more effective than putting it at the end of the contract (past the signatures) and it now makes it part of the body of the contract and is required to be filled in. This was a detail often overlooked by licensees. Putting it in the body of the contract will make that omission much less likely. Paragraph 22 sets out addenda to be attached, if any. Simply check the box and attach the appropriate form. Paragraph 22 is the provision that suggests to the buyer and seller that if they need some legal advice, they should consult an attorney. Paragraph 24, Consult an Attorney, provides for the address, telephone and facsimile numbers for the respective parties' attorney. Those names are inserted at **[26]** and **[27].** The "Notices" paragraph provides for the use of facsimile machines for notices from one party to the other party.

Paragraph 23 is somewhat unique. It gives the buyer (in consideration for the payment of the Option Fee) the right to terminate the contract within the specified number of days. Note that if the blanks of this contract are not filled in, the buyer does not have the termination option; or if, for whatever reason, the buyer has not paid the Option Fee in a timely manner (within 2 days), there is no right to terminate and the buyer and seller have a binding contract for the sale of their real estate. Therefore, if the seller does not receive the Option Fee (or the check bounces) or the contract blanks are not filled in, THIS IS A BINDING EARNEST MONEY CONTRACT ON BOTH PARTIES, SUBJECT TO THE CONDITIONS OF THE AGREEMENT. Note that the right of termination is within the stated number of days after the *effective date* of the contract.

As in the prior contract, the burden is on the buyer to give notice of the termination within the time specified and there is a choice as to whether or not the

Option Fee will be credited to the sales price at closing. The appropriate form has been promulgated by TREC as Form No. 38-2. If the buyer fails to give the notice, the right to terminate is waived. Buyer's agents, mark your calendars!!!

The size of the Option Fee is always negotiable and it is always prudent to negotiate an Option Period long enough to allow for inspections and to obtain costs for repairs. BUT . . . if the buyer finds that the need for extensive repairs exists, the buyer should timely give notice of termination, or amend the Earnest Money Contract, using the TREC amendment form (No. 39-6). This new amendment form is discussed later in this chapter.

Note also that there is a new provision at the end of the contract for seller's receipt of the option money (if Paragraph 23 is used).

The brokers' commission agreement is *after* the contractual agreement between the seller and buyer. It is a separate agreement, *negotiated* between the brokers.

"Time is of the Essence"

Time is of the essence means that the time limit set by the contract must be faithfully observed or the contract is voidable by the nondefaulting party. Moreover, lateness may give a cause for an action for damages. Neither buyer nor seller should expect extensions of time to complete their obligations, because the clause is usually tied into a critical measure of time (e.g., tax deadlines, proration dates, tax deferred exchange compliance, etc.) for one of the parties.

The TREC promulgated form does not provide that "time is of the essence," although it is provided in Paragraph 23 (applicable only to that paragraph) and a few addenda. In an average real estate transaction, many deadlines are outside the control of the parties (providing the title commitment, survey, financing), as a result of which a critical deadline may not be met because of the actions of a third party. Therefore, "time is of the essence" may create a default that neither party anticipates, nor is responsible for.

Federal Clauses

In two instances, the government requires that specific clauses be included in real estate sales contracts. First, an **amendatory language** clause must be included whenever a sales contract is signed by a purchaser prior to the receipt of an FHA Appraised Value or a VA Certificate of Reasonable Value on the property. The purpose is to ensure that the purchaser may terminate the contract without loss when it appears that the agreed purchase price may be significantly above appraised value. The specific clauses, which must be used verbatim, are contained in the TREC promulgated form for FHA-insured or VA-guaranteed financing (TREC No. 40-4). Second, the Federal Trade Commission (FTC) requires that builders and sellers of new houses must include *insulation disclosures* in all earnest money contracts. Disclosures, which may be based upon manufacturer claims, must cite the type, thickness, and R-value of the insulation installed in the home. These disclosures are contained in the TREC promulgated New Home Contracts (TREC Nos. 23-10 and 24-10).

Negotiation

One of the most important principles of real estate contracts in general is that everything is negotiable and nearly everything has a price. In preparing or analyzing any contract, consider what the advantages and disadvantages of each condition are to each party to the contract. A solid contract results when the buyer and seller each feel that they have gained more than they have given up. The prime example is the sales price of the property itself. The seller prefers the money over the property, while the buyer prefers the property over the money. Each small negotiable item in the purchase contract has its price too. For example, the seller may agree to include the refrigerator for $200 more. Equally important in negotiating is the relative bargaining power of the buyer and seller. If the seller is confident he will have plenty of buyers at his asking price, he can elect to refuse offers for less money and reject those with numerous conditions or insufficient earnest money. However, if the owner is anxious to sell and has received only one offer in several months, he may be quite willing to accept a lower price and numerous conditions.

Required Disclosures

Rollback Taxes

Texas laws require other disclosures. Contracts for the sale of vacant land must include a statutory notice about the potential liability for *rollback taxes* if the property has special tax classification, such as religious use, agricultural, or open space use, discussed in Chapter 16. If the seller fails to include the required notice, the seller is liable to the purchaser for any rollback tax liability.

Pipelines

A seller of unimproved land to be used for residential property must also disclose in writing to the purchaser, on or before the effective date of the contract, the *location of any transportation pipeline* on the property, including a pipeline for the transport of natural gas, natural gas liquids, synthetic gas, liquefied petroleum gas, petroleum, or petroleum product, or hazardous substances. If the seller does not know whether pipelines exist under the property, that fact must be stated. If a contract is entered into without the notice, the purchaser may terminate it for any reason not later than the seventh day after the effective date of the contract. This notice doesn't need to be given if the seller is obligated, under the terms of the earnest money contract, to delivery of title commitment to the purchaser, and if the purchaser has a right to terminate the contract if objections to title are not cured. TREC forms already provide for this approval, but the exception does not apply if the seller is going to supply an abstract of title.

Lead-Based Paint

Federal law now requires that before a buyer or tenant becomes obligated under a contract for sale or lease, the sellers and landlords must disclose known lead-based paint and lead-based paint hazards and provide available reports to buyers or tenants. The sellers and landlords must give a buyer a pamphlet "Protect Your Family From Lead In Your Home." Unless otherwise agreed to, homebuyers are entitled to a ten-day period to conduct a lead-based paint inspection or risk assessment at their own expense. Sales contracts and leasing arrangements must include certain language to ensure that disclosure notification actually takes place. The TREC approved lead-based paint disclosure form is shown as Figure 10.2. There is a special burden on real estate agents, who must ensure that sellers and landlords are aware of their obligations and that they disclose the proper information to buyers and tenants. The agent must comply with the law if the seller or landlord fail to do so.

FIGURE 10.2 Lead-based paint disclosure form

APPROVED BY THE TEXAS REAL ESTATE COMMISSION 02-09-2004

EQUAL HOUSING OPPORTUNITY

ADDENDUM FOR SELLER'S DISCLOSURE OF INFORMATION ON LEAD-BASED PAINT AND LEAD-BASED PAINT HAZARDS AS REQUIRED BY FEDERAL LAW

CONCERNING THE PROPERTY AT ______________________________
(Street Address and City)

A. **LEAD WARNING STATEMENT:** "Every purchaser of any interest in residential real property on which a residential dwelling was built prior to 1978 is notified that such property may present exposure to lead from lead-based paint that may place young children at risk of developing lead poisoning. Lead poisoning in young children may produce permanent neurological damage, including learning disabilities, reduced intelligence quotient, behavioral problems, and impaired memory. Lead poisoning also poses a particular risk to pregnant women. The seller of any interest in residential real property is required to provide the buyer with any information on lead-based paint hazards from risk assessments or inspections in the seller's possession and notify the buyer of any known lead-based paint hazards. A risk assessment or inspection for possible lead-paint hazards is recommended prior to purchase."
NOTICE: Inspector must be properly certified as required by federal law.

B. **SELLER'S DISCLOSURE:**
1. PRESENCE OF LEAD-BASED PAINT AND/OR LEAD-BASED PAINT HAZARDS (check on box only):
   - ☐(a) Known lead-based paint and/or lead-based paint hazards are present in the Property (explain): ______________.
   - ☐(b) Seller has no actual knowledge of lead-based paint and/or lead-based paint hazards in the Property.
2. RECORDS AND REPORTS AVAILABLE TO SELLER (check one box only):
   - ☐(a) Seller has provided the purchaser with all available records and reports pertaining to lead-based paint and/or lead-based paint hazards in the Property (list documents): ______________.
   - ☐(b) Seller has no reports or records pertaining to lead-based paint and/or lead-based paint hazards in the Property.

C. **BUYER'S RIGHTS** (check one box only):
- ☐1. Buyer waives the opportunity to conduct a risk assessment or inspection of the Property for the presence of lead-based paint or lead-based paint hazards.
- ☐2. Within ten days after the effective date of this contract, Buyer may have the Property inspected by inspectors selected by Buyer. If lead-based paint or lead-based paint hazards are present, Buyer may terminate this contract by giving Seller written notice within 14 days after the effective date of this contract, and the earnest money will be refunded to Buyer.

D. **BUYER'S ACKNOWLEDGMENT** (check applicable boxes):
- ☐1. Buyer has received copies of all information listed above.
- ☐2. Buyer has received the pamphlet *Protect Your Family from Lead in Your Home*.

E. **BROKERS' ACKNOWLEDGMENT:** Brokers have informed Seller of Seller's obligations under 42 U.S.C. 4852d to: (a) provide Buyer with the federally approved pamphlet on lead poisoning prevention; (b) complete this addendum; (c) disclose any known lead-based paint and/or lead-based paint hazards in the Property; (d) deliver all records and reports to Buyer pertaining to lead-based paint and/or lead-based paint hazards in the Property; (e) provide Buyer a period of up to 10 days to have the Property inspected; and (f) retain a completed copy of this addendum for at least 3 years following the sale. Brokers are aware of their responsibility to ensure compliance.

F. **CERTIFICATION OF ACCURACY:** The following persons have reviewed the information above and certify, to the best of their knowledge, that the information they have provided is true and accurate.

Buyer	Date	Seller	Date
Buyer	Date	Seller	Date
Other Broker	Date	Listing Broker	Date

The form of this addendum has been approved by the Texas Real Estate Commission for use only with similarly approved or promulgated forms of contracts. Such approval relates to this contract form only. TREC forms are intended for use only by trained real estate licensees. No representation is made as to the legal validity or adequacy of any provision in any specific transactions. It is not suitable for complex transactions. Texas Real Estate Commission, P.O. Box 12188, Austin, TX 78711-2188, 1-800-250-8732 or (512) 459-6544 (http://www.trec.state.tx.us)

Form OP-L 01A

Source: Texas Real Estate Commission

Water Districts

Texas law also has special requirements for anyone who proposes to sell or convey real property located in the municipal utility district or other drainage or flood control district that use bonds to finance its improvements. The statute requires that any person who proposes to sell or convey real property located in such a district must first give a notice to the purchaser in a separate written document executed and acknowledged by the seller that the property is located in a water, sewer, drainage, and flood control or protection facilities district, and whether the property is subject to annexation. The notice must be given to the prospective purchaser prior to the execution of a binding contract of sale and purchase, either separately or as a separate portion or paragraph of a purchase contract. If the contract for purchase and sale is entered into without the seller providing the notice required, the purchaser shall be entitled to terminate the contract. The statute specifies the notice to be given and it must be executed, acknowledged, and recorded in the deed records of the county in which the property is located at the closing of the purchase and sale. This statutory provision must also be provided for any executory contract of purchase and sale (i.e., installment land contract) having a performance period of more than six months.

Annexation

A person who sells an interest in real property located in the extraterritorial jurisdiction of a city is required to give the purchaser of the property a written notice that their property is located outside the limits of the municipality, but may now, or later, be included in the extraterritorial jurisdiction of that municipality, and subject to annexation. The seller must deliver the notice to the purchaser before the date of the execution of the contract for sale. The notice is included in the TREC Form under Paragraph 6.B.5.

Property Owners' Association Disclosure

Not later than the tenth day after the date of the written request for subdivision information is received from the seller, seller's agent, or title insurance company, the property owners' association must deliver to the seller, seller's agent, or title insurance company, current copies of the restrictions, a copy of the bylaws and rules of the property owners' association, and a resale certificate. The property owners' association may charge a reasonable fee and is subject to liability if it fails to deliver the resale certificate after two requests.

Property Located in a Certificated Service Area of Utility Service Provider

The Texas Water Code requires that the real property about to be purchased is located in a certificated water or sewer service area, which is authorized by law to provide water and sewer services for the property in a certificated area. If the property is located in this certificated area, the buyer may be required to pay special costs or charges before he can receive the water or sewage. There may also be periods required to construct other facilities necessary to provide water or sewage service to the property. The buyer is then required to inquire as to whether or not those services are available.

Public Improvement District

If the property is located in a public improvement district (PID), the seller is required to notify the buyer that, as a purchaser of the parcel of real property, the buyer might be obligated to pay an assessment to the municipality or county for any improvement projects undertaken by a public improvement district under the local government. It warns the buyer that annual or periodic assessments may be due on those improvements, and that the buyer should inquire the municipality or county levying the assessment as to what the status of the assessment might be.

Licensee Benefits

The use of the foregoing contracts will benefit the licensee in his normal residential real estate transactions. Most of the technical legal questions concerning title, default, escrow, inspections, and closing guarantees, as well as representations and warranties of buyer and seller, are contained as a matter of form in these forms. All the licensee has to do is fill in the blanks. Most clients who are parties to a residential earnest money contract find it easy to understand a fill-in-the-blank type form.

Practicing Law

It should be well understood by all real estate brokers and salespersons that they are not permitted to practice law. This is specifically prohibited under Section 16 of the Texas Real Estate Licensing Act, but the nature of the real estate business has led to some confusion and dissension between lawyers and real estate licensees. For instance, it is common practice for real estate practitioners to fill in the blanks of an earnest money contract, yet not fill in the blanks of a deed. To clarify this matter, an Attorney General's opinion issued in 1972 explained that real estate agents, under law, do not have the right to fill in the blanks of an earnest money contract. However, the opinion went on to say that if the Texas Real Estate Commission wished to require the use of a standard form for certain types of transactions, that such forms could be sanctioned by the Texas Real Estate Commission for use by real estate brokers and salespersons. This enables brokers and salespersons to fill in the blanks of earnest money contracts without violating Section 16 of the Texas Real Estate Licensing Act.

OPTION CONTRACTS

Recall that an earnest money contract is an executory, bilateral contract. In contrast to this, the option contract is a unilateral, executed contract. Once the contract is executed, the buyer then has a right to purchase the property but no obligation to do so. Therefore, the remedy of specific performance against the buyer doesn't exist. The buyer has the right (not the obligation) to buy, but the seller does have the obligation to sell. In return for being granted the option to purchase, and in order for the contract to be enforceable, the buyer must pay consideration to the seller. In most cases, this is a cash payment directly to the seller in lieu of earnest money. In return for the cash payment, the seller takes the property off the market for the term of the option agreement. The buyer does not have to give the seller any reason for the termination, or give the seller copies of any reports, studies, or other investigated matters.

In commercial real estate, it is quite common for large companies wanting to select sites in a given area to option five or ten sites, knowing that they are not obligated to purchase any of the sites. This gives them the opportunity to investigate the sites in more detail, do whatever studies are required, and then purchase one or more sites should they choose to do so.

Exercising the option converts the option contract to an earnest money contract. At that point, the buyer has the duty to perform. Frequently, the contract calls for a very short closing period (e.g. five days), or it may simply convert to a bilateral executory contract under which there are still obligations for both parties to perform prior to closing.

INSTALLMENT CONTRACTS

An ***installment contract,*** also known as a *land contract,* **conditional sales contract, contract for deed,** or **agreement of sale** combines features from a sales contract, deed, and a mortgage. It is used to sell property in situations where the seller does not wish to convey title until all, or at least a substantial portion, of the purchase price is paid by the buyer. This is different from the purchase contract shown in Figure 10.1 wherein the buyer receives possession and a deed at the closing. With an installment contract, the buyer is given possession and the right to use the property upon signing the contract, but he does not acquire title. Instead, he receives a contract promising that a deed will be delivered at a later date. During the period between signing the contract and the seller delivering the deed, the buyer is said to hold ***equitable title*** to the property. That is, he has the exclusive right to acquire the title, along with possession of the property. This equitable title can even be sold, usually by the first buyer who can assign his interest on the contract to the second buyer.

A common use of the installment contract occurs when the buyer does not have the full purchase price in cash or he cannot borrow it from a lender. Under these conditions, the seller must be willing to accept a down payment plus monthly payments until the property is paid for. The seller can either deliver a deed to the buyer at closing and simultaneously have the buyer pledge the property as collateral for the balance due (a mortgage) or the seller can agree to deliver title only after the buyer has completed his payments (an installment contract).

Delivering title after payment is advantageous to the seller because if the buyer fails to make her payments, the title to the property is still in the name of the seller. This avoids the time and costs consumed by foreclosure, a requirement if title has already been conveyed to the buyer.

Sample Contract

Figure 10.3 is a simplified illustration of an installment contract. In paragraph **[1]** the buyer and seller are identified, the purchase price is given and dated, and the amount and terms of the balance due are stated. The buyer is sometimes referred to as the **vendee** and the seller as the **vendor.** In paragraph **[2],** the seller promises

FIGURE 10.3 Sample installment contract

Installment Contract

[1] *RECEIVED this 15th day of October, 200x, from Cliff Fisher and wife Sandy (hereafter called the "buyer") of 7778 Spinner Street, Bridgetown, Anystate the sum of $ 200.00 as down payment toward the sales price of $ 10,000.00. The balance of $9,800.00 is to be paid in equal monthly installments of $ 98.00 until paid in full. The monthly payment includes principal and interest of 10% per annum on the unpaid balance. Payments are to be made on the first of each month to the Sunrise Lake Land Company (hereafter called the "seller").*

[2] *BE IT AGREED: if the buyer makes the payments and performs the agreements stated in this contract, the seller agrees to convey to the buyer in fee simple, clear of all encumbrances whatsoever, by special warranty deed, Lot # 17, Block B-1, Sunrise Lakes Tract, situated and recorded in the County of Sunrise, State of Anywhere.*

[3] *IF THE BUYER fails to make any of the payments herein designated or fails to perform any of the other agreements made herein, this contract shall be terminated and the buyer shall forfeit all payments made on this contract. Such payments will be retained by the seller as accumulated rent on the property described above, and the seller shall have the right to reenter and take possession of the premises.*

[4] *THE BUYER AGREES to pay all property taxes subsequent to the year 19xx.*

[5] *CONSTRUCTION shall be limited to residences built with new materials. Structures must be located at least twenty feet from the front lot line and five feet from the other lot lines. Shacks or unsightly structures are not permitted.*

[6] *THE BUYER AND SELLER agree that this contract, or any assignment thereof, is not to be recorded without the permission of the seller. To do so shall result in any existing balance on this contract becoming due and payable immediately.*

[7] *THE BUYER AND SELLER agree that prompt payment is an essential part of this contract and that this contract is binding upon their assigns, heirs, executors, and administrators.*

[8] *THE BUYER HAS the right to examine the master abstract.*

BUYER[s]	*[9] SELLER*
Cliff Fisher	Salem Bigland
Sandy Fisher	*Salem Bigland President,* *Sunrise Lakes Land Company*

to deliver a deed to the buyer when the buyer has made all the payments stated in paragraph **[1]**. Paragraph **[2]** also describes the property. Paragraph **[3]** deals with the possibility that the buyer may fail to make the required payments or fail to abide by the other contract terms. The strong wording in this paragraph is typical of the installment contract, particularly when it is utilized to sell vacant land. If you read paragraph [3] carefully, you will see that, in the event of the buyer's default, the seller can retain all payments made *and* retake possession of the property. This is the feature that makes the installment contract popular with sellers.

Paragraph [4] deals with property taxes. In this example, the buyer agrees to pay them. Sometimes the seller will agree to pay the property taxes until a deed is delivered to the buyer. This is not an act of kindness but protection for the seller. The seller does not want to risk the possibility of the buyer's failure to pay the taxes, thus giving the county tax collector the right to take the property.

In paragraph [5], the seller sets construction restrictions. The object is to prevent unsightly structures from being built that would have a negative impact on surrounding property values. This enhances the buyer's resale value; for the seller, it means that the property is more valuable if the buyer defaults.

Repossession

In agreement with the provisions in paragraph [3], paragraph [6] provides the seller with a means of smooth recovery of possession and ownership in the event of default by the buyer. If the buyer records his contract with the public recorder, he serves notice that he has an interest in the property. This creates a cloud on the seller's title. If the buyer were to default, the effort necessary to remove this cloud would be inconsistent with the seller's objective of easy recovery. Also, such a cloud makes it more difficult for the seller to borrow against the property. However, a nonrecording provision is definitely not to the advantage of the buyer, as anyone inspecting the public records would not find a record of the buyer's interest. The seller would still be shown as the owner. In view of this, some states outlaw these clauses, but Texas does not.

While repossession and forfeiture in the default of the installment land contract is the same in Texas as it is in most other states, it is important to recognize that the Recording Act in Texas provides that virtually any acknowledged instrument may be recorded. Although there may be a prohibition against recording the land contract itself or of any assignment thereof (provisions that may be legally questionable), it is possible to lease the property, sublet the property, or create some other kind of material interest in the property that can be recorded. The constructive notice will then be effective to show that there is other interest in the property besides that of the owner.

Paragraph [7] reemphasizes that payments must be made promptly and adds that the terms of the contract are binding on anyone to whom the buyer may sell or assign the contract. In the illustrated contract, the buyer does not receive a title report or title insurance for his individual lot when he signs the contract. However, at [8], he is invited to see the abstract; presumably it shows the seller as the owner of the land. The balance of the contract, [9], is for the signatures of the buyer and seller and, when required, witnesses or a notary.

Consumer Criticism

The installment contract has received much consumer criticism because its wording so strongly favors the seller. In numerous instances, buyers, although they have paid a substantial portion of the purchase price, have lost the property and their money due to one or two late payments. Strictly interpreted, that is what the contract says; if the buyer signs it, presumably she agrees. However, the courts and legislatures in several states have found this too harsh.

Texas has provided some statutory relief under the Property Code to this harsh remedy of automatic forfeiture in the installment land contract. The statutes are as follows:

§ 5.064

A seller may enforce a forfeiture of interest and the acceleration of the indebtedness of a purchaser in default under an executory contract for conveyance of real property only if:

(1) the seller notifies the purchaser of:
 (A) the seller's intent to enforce a remedy under this section.
 (B) the purchaser's right to cure the default within the 60-day period described by Section 5.065.
(2) the purchaser fails to cure the default within the 60-day period described by Section 5.065.
(3) Section 5.066 does not apply.

§ 5.063. Notice

(a) Notice under Section 5.064 of this code must be in writing. If the notice is mailed, it must be by registered or certified mail. The notice must be conspicuous and printed in 14 point boldface type or uppercase typewritten letters, and must include the statement:

"NOTICE:

YOU ARE NOT COMPLYING WITH THE TERMS OF THE CONTRACT TO BUY YOUR PROPERTY. UNLESS YOU TAKE THE ACTION SPECIFIED IN THIS NOTICE BY (date) THE SELLER HAS A RIGHT TO TAKE POSSESSION OF YOUR PROPERTY."

The notice must also:

(1) identify and explain the remedy the seller intends to enforce.
(2) if the purchaser has failed to make a timely payment, specify:
 (A) the delinquent amount, itemized into principal and interest.
 (B) any additional charges claimed, such as late charges or attorney's fees.
 (C) the period to which the delinquency and additional charges relate.
(3) if the purchaser has failed to comply with a term of the contract, identify the term violated and the action required to cure the violation.

These statutes strongly restrict the legal title holder's right of forfeiture and acceleration, and the buyer cannot be summarily evicted without the specified notices.

In a never-ending effort to help consumers, the Texas Legislature has recently added new requirements for the use of contracts for deed.

This statute applies only to transactions involving the executory contract of conveyance to be used as the purchaser's residence, or as the residence of a person related to the purchaser within the second degree of consanguinity as determined under the Texas Government code. Any lot measuring one acre or less is presumed to be residential property. If a deed is to be delivered within 180 days after the final execution of the executory contract, the statue does *not* apply.

Before an executory contract is signed by the purchaser, the seller must provide the purchaser with: (1) a tax certificate from the collector for each taxing unit that collects taxes on the property, and (2) a legible copy of the insurance policy, binder, or other evidence relating to the property that indicates: (a) the name of the insurer and the insured, (b) a description of the property insured, and (c) the amount for which the property is insured. If the seller fails to provide this information, it constitutes a deceptive trade practice and entitles the purchaser to cancel and rescind the executory contract and receive a full refund of all payments made to the seller.

In addition, the seller must also provide perspective purchasers with a bold-faced notice in 14 point type, in the contract, or in a separate document, that oral agreements for the conveyance of real estate are invalid and that the contract may not be buried by any oral agreement or discussions that occur before or contemporaneously with the execution of the contract. Again, if seller fails to provide this notification, it constitutes a deceptive trade practice.

Section 5.077 of the statute provides for an annual accounting statement by the owner of the property to the purchaser. The statement must be postmarked not later than January 31st of each year. The new inclusions in the accounting statement are: (1) the amounts paid to insure the property on the purchaser's behalf if collected by the seller, (2) the accounting of any insurance proceeds that the properties had been damaged and the sellers received any insurance proceeds, and (3) if the seller has changed insurance coverage.

If the seller fails to transfer recorded legal title to the property within the 30th day after the seller receives final payment, the seller is liable for liquidated damages in the amount of $250.00 for each day beginning with the 31st day after the seller fails to provide the purchaser with the statement and reasonable attorney's fees. After 90 days the penalty goes to $500 per day. There are some exceptions to these penalties if the seller has died and the heirs have to go to court to probate the estate.

One of the more significant provisions is the seller's remedies on default. The statute gives the purchaser a right to cure the default within a 60-day period (the old statute had a range of cure periods, the lowest being 10 days). If a purchaser defaults after the purchaser has paid 40% or more of the amount due or the equivalent of 48 monthly payments, the seller has to sell the property pursuant to the general foreclosure provisions applicable to a deed of trust (see Chapter 11). The seller may *not* enforce the traditional remedy of forfeiture and acceleration. Another part of the statute provides that the purchaser, at that time, and without paying penalties or charges of any kind, is entitled to convert the purchaser's interest in the property under an executory contract to a recorded, legal title, so long as the buyer executes a deed of trust and note back to the seller for the amounts owed.

Other Pitfalls

Another key weak point in the installment sale contract is that the seller does not deed ownership to the buyer until some later date. Thus, a buyer might make payments for several years only to find that the seller cannot deliver title as promised. At that point, unless the seller is willing to give the buyer a refund, the buyer's only recourse is to sue the seller for specific performance or money damages. However, a lawsuit works only if the buyer has the time and money to pursue the matter, if the suit is successful, and if the seller has the money to pay the judgment. Recent legislation probably tells us that the use of a contract for deed and leases with options to purchase (discussed later) are far too risky to use without extensive legal support. Liabilities are significant and the benefits just aren't that good.

In Chapter 15, the installment contract is discussed as a tool to finance the sale of improved property when other sources of financing are not available.

PUTTING IT TO WORK

If an installment contract is used for the purchase of real estate, it should be done with the help of legal counsel to make certain that it provides adequate safeguards for the buyer as well as the seller.

LEASE WITH OPTION TO BUY

We just discussed the potential horrors and tough requirements placed on sellers under an executory contract. The 2005 Legislature discovered that a number of land owners were attempting to get around the executory contract provisions by using leases with options to purchase rather than traditional contracts for deed. The legislature responded by making an option to purchase real property that includes, or is combined or executed concurrently with, a resident lease agreement, subject to the same rules as a contract for deed. Short-term options and leases (that provide for a deed to be delivered within 180 days) are not affected by these provisions of the Property Code.

An option is an agreement to keep an offer open for a fixed period of time. One of the most popular option contracts in real estate is the *lease with option to buy*. Often simply referred to as a ***lease-option***, it allows the tenant to buy the property at a preset price and terms during the option period. For a residential property, the lease is typically for one year, and the option to buy must be exercised during that time. Let's look more closely.

In this lease-option contract all the normal provisions of a lease are present, such as those shown later in Figure 18.1. All the normal provisions of a purchase contract are present, such as those shown in Figure 10.1. In addition, there will be wording stating that the tenant has the option of exercising the purchase contract, provided the tenant notifies the landlord in writing of that intent during the option period. All terms of the purchase contract must be negotiated and in writing when the lease is signed. Both the tenant and the landlord must sign the lease. Only the landlord must sign the purchase contract and option agreement, although both parties often do so. If the tenant wants to buy during the option period, the tenant notifies the landlord in writing that the tenant wishes to exercise the purchase contract. Together they proceed to carry out the purchase contract as in a normal sale.

If the tenant does not exercise the option within the option period, the option expires and the purchase contract is null and void. If the lease also expires at the end of the option period, the tenant must either arrange with the landlord to continue renting or move out. Alternatively, they can negotiate a new purchase contract or a new lease-option contract.

Popularity

Lease-options are particularly popular in soft real estate markets in which a home seller is having difficulty finding a buyer. One solution is to lower the asking price and/or make the financing terms more attractive. However, the seller may wish to hold out in hopes that prices will rise within a year. In the meantime, the seller needs someone to occupy the property and provide some income.

The lease-option is attractive to a tenant because the tenant has a place to rent plus the option of buying any time during the option period for the price in the purchase contract. In other words, the tenant can wait a year and see if she likes the property and if values rise to or above the price in the purchase contract. If the tenant does not like the property and/or the property does not rise in value, the tenant is under no obligation to buy. Once the lease expires, the tenant is also under no obligation to continue renting either.

Examples

To encourage a tenant to exercise the option to buy, the contract may allow the tenant to apply part or all of the rent paid to the purchase price. In fact, quite a bit of flexibility and negotiation can take place in creating a lease-option. For example, take a house that would rent for $2,000 per month and sell for $300,000 on the open market. Suppose the owner wants $320,000 and won't come down to the market price. Meanwhile the home is vacant and there are mortgage payments to be made. The owner could offer a one-year lease-option with a rental charge of $2,000 each month and an exercise price of $320,000. Within a year, $320,000 may look good to the tenant, especially if the market value of the property has risen significantly above $320,000. The tenant can exercise the option or, if not prohibited by the contract, sell it to someone who intends to exercise it. The owner receives $20,000 more for the property than he could have gotten last year, and the tenant has the benefit of any value increase above that.

Continuing the above example, what if the property rises to $310,000 in value? There is no economic incentive for the tenant to exercise the option at $320,000. The tenant can simply disregard the option and make an offer of $310,000 to the owner. The owner's choice is to sell at that price or continue renting the home, perhaps with another one-year lease-option.

Option Fee

The owner can also charge the tenant extra for the privilege of having the option, but it must make economic sense to a tenant. Suppose in the above example the purchase price is set equal to the current market value—that is, $300,000. This would be a valuable benefit to the tenant, and the owner could charge an up-front cash fee for the option and/or charge above market rent. The amounts would depend on the market's expectations regarding the value of this home a year from now. There is nothing special about a one-year option period, although it is a very popular length of time. The landlord and tenant can agree to a three-month, six-month, or nine-month option if it fits their needs, and the lease can run longer than the option period. Options for longer than one year are generally reserved for commercial properties. For example, a business person just starting out, or perhaps expanding, wants to buy a building but needs one or two years to see how successful the business will be and how much space it will need.

Caveats

Be aware that lease-options may create income tax consequences that require professional tax counseling. Legal advice is also helpful in preparing and reviewing the lease-option papers. This is because the entire deal (lease, option, and purchase contract) must be water-tight from the beginning. One cannot wait until the option is exercised to write the purchase contract or even a material part of it. If a real estate agent puts a lease-option together, the agent is entitled to a leasing commission at the time the lease is signed. If the option is exercised, the agent is due a sales commission on the purchase contract.

Evidence that the option to buy exists should be recorded to establish not only the tenant's rights to purchase the property, but also establish those rights back to the date the option was recorded. An option is an example of a unilateral contract. When it is exercised, it becomes bilateral. The lease portion of a lease-option is a bilateral contract.

The party giving the option is called the **optionor** (the owner in a lease-option). The party receiving the option is the **optionee** (tenant in a lease-option). Sometimes an option to buy is referred to as a *call.* You will see how an option can be used by a home builder to buy land in Chapter 15 and how options can be used to renew leases in Chapter 18.

RIGHT OF FIRST REFUSAL

Sometimes a tenant will agree to rent a property only if given an opportunity to purchase it before someone else does. In other words, the tenant is saying, "Ms. Owner, if you get a valid offer from someone else to purchase this property, show it to me and give me an opportunity to match the offer." This is called a ***right of first refusal.*** If someone presents the owner with a valid offer, the owner must show it to the tenant before accepting it. If the tenant decides not to match it, the owner is free to accept it. The same theory can also apply to a nontenant, perhaps an adjacent property owner who has negotiated this right with the correct owner. A right of first refusal protects a potential purchaser from having the property sold out from under him when, in fact, they knew about the offer, he would have been willing to match it. The owner usually does not care who buys.

It is important to note, however, that under these conditions an owner can never seriously negotiate with the potential purchaser because every facet of the negotiation has to be transmitted to the potential purchaser, effectively giving them veto power. It is only in the unlikely event that the potential purchaser will either (1) pay the seller more money or (2) offer better terms than the tenant that the transaction turns out to be beneficial to the seller. In most circumstances, the right of first refusal is not beneficial to the owner except during a very strong sellers' market.

EXCHANGE AGREEMENTS

Most real estate transactions involve the exchange of real estate for monetary consideration. However, among sophisticated real estate investors, exchanging real property for real property has become popular for two important reasons. First, real estate trades can be accomplished without large amounts of cash by trading a property you presently own for one you want. This sidesteps the intermediate step of converting real estate to cash and then converting cash back to real estate. Second, by using an exchange, you can dispose of one property and acquire another without paying income taxes on the profit in the first property at the time of the transaction. As a result, the phrase *tax-deferred exchange* is often used when talking about trading.

To illustrate, suppose that you own an apartment building (the *"exchange property")* as an investment. The value on your accounting books is $500,000 but its market value today is $750,000. If you sell for cash, you will have to pay income taxes on the difference between the value of the property on your accounting books and the amount you receive for it. If instead of selling for cash, you find another building (the *"replacement property")* that you want and can arrange a trade, then for income tax purposes the new building acquires the accounting book value of the old and no income taxes are due at the time of the trade. Taxes will be due, however, if and when you finally sell rather than trade. The ***tax-deferred exchange*** rules apply to investment properties only. Owner-occupied dwellings are treated differently. The Internal Revenue Service permits a homeowner to sell his home and exclude all gains with the specified limits (see Chapter 16).

Trading Up

Real estate exchanges need not involve properties of equal value. For example, if you own debt-free a small office building worth $100,000, you could trade it for a building worth $500,000 with $400,000 of mortgage debt against it. Alternatively, if the building you wanted was priced at $600,000 with $400,000 in debt against it, you could offer your building plus $100,000 in cash.

The vast majority of tax-deferred exchanges today consist of three transactions: the two conveyances and an escrow agreement with a *qualified intermediary (QI)*. The qualified intermediary can be a title company, an attorney, or in some cases, an independent company providing this service as tax advisors. The QI maintains control over the funds and the closing documents pursuant to the instructions contained in the escrow agreement. This allows the various

FIGURE 10.4 Possible trading combinations.

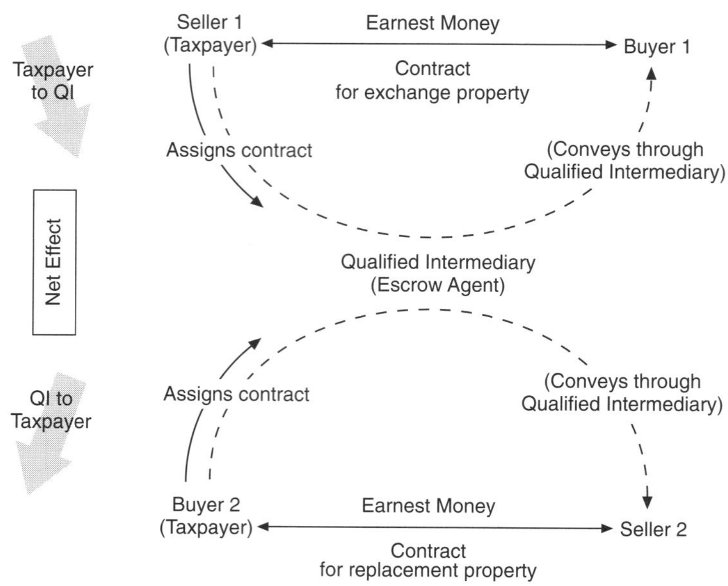

Source: © 2012 Cengage Learning

parties to deposit documents and funds with the QI (often by mail), which makes it much more convenient. As a practical matter, the QI signs all documents relevant to the closing other than the conveyancing documents. The Internal Revenue Service rules allow the conveyancing documents to be executed by the parties to the transaction without involving the formality of the QI's execution. This prevents the QI from becoming "in the chain of title," which could further complicate the transaction.

Assume the party who wants to do the tax-deferred exchange is Seller 1, who signs a contract to convey the exchange property to Buyer 1. After executing a contract of sale, Seller 1 assigns his interest in the contract to the QI, then executes an *escrow agreement* with the QI that defines the QI's role. Seller 1 then locates the replacement property he is interested in purchasing and enters into a purchase contract to acquire that property; he then sends notice of designation of property to the QI, then assigns his interest in the contract as purchaser to the QI. In both transactions, the deed is drafted from Seller to Buyer (so the qualified intermediary owner never takes title to either tract). The QI, who has escrowed the funds from transaction #1, then uses these proceeds to pay Seller 2 to acquire the replacement property.

The key factor is that Seller 1 (taxpayer) has no control over the funds held by the qualified intermediary and cannot be deemed to be in receipt of those funds. In effect, the transaction results in Seller 1 conveying his property to the QI and the qualified intermediary conveying the exchange property to the seller. Note Figure 10.4.

Although trading is a complicated business, it can be very lucrative for real estate agents. Whereas an ordinary sale results in one brokerage commission, a two-party exchange results in two commissions.

Delayed Exchanges

The Internal Revenue Code allows nonsimultaneous exchanges to be tax-deferred under certain circumstances. Such an exchange, commonly called a **delayed exchange,** occurs when property is exchanged for a right to receive property at a future date. It is a helpful technique when one party is willing to exchange out of a property but has not yet chosen a replacement property. Meanwhile the other parties to the exchange are ready and want to close. The delayed exchange allows the closing to take place by giving the seller of the exchange property the right to designate a replacement property and take title after the closing. The 1984 Act specifically allows this, provided (1) the replacement property is identified within 45 days of the original closing, (2) the title to the replacement property is acquired within 180 days of the original closing, and (3) the replacement property is received before the designating party's tax return is due. These rules are strictly construed against the taxpayer. If these rules are not met the transaction will be treated as a sale for the designating party, not an exchange.

Reverse Exchanges

What if a party signs the exchange contracts, but the sale of the exchange property is delayed and the seller has to acquire the replacement property before selling the existing property? Because of the nature of real estate contracts, this is not uncommon, and in 2000 the Internal Revenue Code established a procedure to deal with this issue. The procedure requires that the qualified intermediary, pursuant to a specified arrangement between the taxpayers and the QI, become an Exchange Accommodation Title Holder. The taxpayer transfers the ownership of the replacement property to the Accommodation Title Holder (either paying cash or by getting a loan sufficient to pay the sales price to the seller of the replacement property) and then the Accommodation Title Holder will hold title until the exchange property can be sold. The seller, in effect, "parks" the replacement property with the Accommodation Title Holder until a buyer can be found for the exchange property. Then the standard rules apply in that the conveyance of the relinquished property must occur within 180 days after the property is parked with the Accommodation Title Holder. This has been deemed by the IRS as an "Exchange Last" reverse like-kind exchange.

TYPICAL TRADE CONTRACT

Space does not permit a detailed review of a trade contract. However, very briefly, a typical trade contract identifies the traders involved and their respective properties; names the type of deed and quality of title that will be conveyed; names the real estate brokers involved and how much they are to be paid; discusses prorations, personal property, rights of tenants, and damage to the property; provides a receipt for the deposit that each trader makes; requires each trader to provide a title insurance policy; and sets forth the consequences of defaulting on the contract. If the same broker represents more than one trader, he must disclose this to each trader whom he represents.

11-29-2010

EQUAL HOUSING OPPORTUNITY

PROMULGATED BY THE TEXAS REAL ESTATE COMMISSION (TREC)

THIRD PARTY FINANCING ADDENDUM FOR CREDIT APPROVAL

TO CONTRACT CONCERNING THE PROPERTY AT

____

(Street Address and City)

Buyer shall apply promptly for all financing described below and make every reasonable effort to obtain credit approval for the financing (Credit Approval). Buyer shall furnish all information and documents required by lender for Credit Approval. Credit Approval will be deemed to have been obtained when (1) the terms of the loan(s) described below are available and (2) lender determines that Buyer has satisfied all of lender's requirements related to Buyer's assets, income and credit history. If Buyer cannot obtain Credit Approval, Buyer may give written notice to Seller within ____ days after the effective date of this contract and this contract will terminate and the earnest money will be refunded to Buyer. **If Buyer does not give such notice within the time required, this contract will no longer be subject to Credit Approval. Time is of the essence for this paragraph and strict compliance with the time for performance is required.**

NOTE: Credit Approval does not include approval of lender's underwriting requirements for the Property, as specified in Paragraph 4.A.(1) of the contract.

Each note must be secured by vendor's and deed of trust liens.

CHECK APPLICABLE BOXES:

❑ A. CONVENTIONAL FINANCING:

❑ (1) A first mortgage loan in the principal amount of $ __________________ (excluding any financed PMI premium), due in full in _________ year(s), with interest not to exceed ______% per annum for the first ________year(s) of the loan with Adjusted Origination Charges as shown on Buyer's Good Faith Estimate for the loan not to exceed ________% of the loan.

❑ (2) A second mortgage loan in the principal amount of $_________________(excluding any financed PMI premium), due in full in __________year(s), with interest not to exceed _______% per annum for the first _____________year(s) of the loan with Adjusted Origination Charges as shown on Buyer's Good Faith Estimate for the loan not to exceed ________ % of the loan.

❑ B. TEXAS VETERANS LOAN: A loan(s) from the Texas Veterans Land Board of $____________ for a period in the total amount of _____years at the interest rate established by the Texas Veterans Land Board.

❑ C. FHA INSURED FINANCING: A Section _______________ FHA insured loan of not less than $_________________ (excluding any financed MIP), amortizable monthly for not less than _______years, with interest not to exceed _______% per annum for the first ______year(s) of the loan with Adjusted Origination Charges as shown on Buyer's Good Faith Estimate for the loan not to exceed _______ % of the loan. As required by HUD-FHA, if FHA valuation is unknown, "*It is expressly agreed that, notwithstanding any other provision of this contract, the purchaser (Buyer) shall not be obligated to complete the purchase of the Property described herein or to incur any penalty by forfeiture of earnest money deposits or otherwise unless the purchaser (Buyer) has been given in accordance with HUD/FHA or VA requirements a written statement issued by the Federal Housing Commissioner, Department of Veterans Affairs, or a Direct Endorsement Lender setting forth the appraised value of the Property of not less than $__________________. The purchaser (Buyer) shall have the privilege and option of proceeding with consummation of the contract without regard to the*

____
(Address of Property)

amount of the appraised valuation. The appraised valuation is arrived at to determine the maximum mortgage the Department of Housing and Urban Development will insure. HUD does not warrant the value or the condition of the Property. The purchaser (Buyer) should satisfy himself/herself that the price and the condition of the Property are acceptable."

❑ D. VA GUARANTEED FINANCING: A VA guaranteed loan of not less than $_________________ (excluding any financed Funding Fee), amortizable monthly for not less than________years, with interest not to exceed_________% per annum for the first ________year(s) of the loan with Adjusted Origination Charges as shown on Buyer's Good Faith Estimate for the loan not to exceed _________% of the loan.

VA NOTICE TO BUYER: "*It is expressly agreed that, notwithstanding any other provisions of this contract, the Buyer shall not incur any penalty by forfeiture of earnest money or otherwise or be obligated to complete the purchase of the Property described herein, if the contract purchase price or cost exceeds the reasonable value of the Property established by the Department of Veterans Affairs. The Buyer shall, however, have the privilege and option of proceeding with the consummation of this contract without regard to the amount of the reasonable value established by the Department of Veterans Affairs."*

If Buyer elects to complete the purchase at an amount in excess of the reasonable value established by VA, Buyer shall pay such excess amount in cash from a source which Buyer agrees to disclose to the VA and which Buyer represents will not be from borrowed funds except as approved by VA. If VA reasonable value of the Property is less than the Sales Price, Seller may reduce the Sales Price to an amount equal to the VA reasonable value and the sale will be closed at the lower Sales Price with proportionate adjustments to the down payment and the loan amount.

Buyer hereby authorizes any lender to furnish to the Seller or Buyer or their representatives information relating only to the status of Credit Approval of Buyer.

______________________	______________________
Buyer	Seller
______________________	______________________
Buyer	Seller

REVIEW QUESTIONS

Answers to these questions are found in the Answer Key section at the back of the book.

1. A formal real estate sales contract, prepared at the outset by an agent using prepared forms, may be identified as any of the following EXCEPT
   A. a purchase contract.
   B. an option contract.
   C. an offer and acceptance.
   D. a purchase offer.

2. Martin purchased real estate from Stevens under an agreement that called for him to pay for the property in installments and to receive a deed upon payment of the entire purchase price. This agreement could properly be identified as a
   A. land contract.
   B. contract for deed.
   C. conditional sales contract.
   D. installment contract.
   E. all of the above.

3. In normal real estate brokerage practice, the amount of earnest money deposit paid by the purchaser is
   A. determined by negotiation.
   B. set by state law.
   C. equal to the agent's commission.
   D. the minimum required to make the contract valid.

4. Property taxes, insurance, loan interest, and so forth may be divided between the buyer and seller by the process of
   A. allocation.
   B. appropriation.
   C. proration.
   D. proportioning.

5. In Texas, if a promulgated form is not used, the real estate licensee is required to use a form
   A. prepared by the broker.
   B. prepared by the licensee.
   C. prepared by an attorney at law licensed in Texas.
   D. prepared by the buyer or his agent.

6. Martin is going to purchase a newly built home from the builder. He will finance the purchase by means of a VA-guaranteed loan. The builder must include in the purchase contract
   A. an amendatory clause.
   B. insulation disclosures.
   C. both A and B.
   D. neither A nor B.

7. Mr. and Mrs. Silver entered into a real estate contract with Mr. and Mrs. Gold. If Mr. Gold dies before settlement takes place,
   A. Mr. and Mrs. Silver are obligated to carry out the contract.
   B. Mrs. Gold is obligated to carry out the contract.
   C. Mr. Gold's estate is obligated to carry out the contract.
   D. all of the above.

8. According to the 1989 Legislative Statute on selling or conveying property in a municipal utility district or a flood or drainage control district, the seller
   A. does not have to reveal the type of district to the purchaser.
   B. must give separate written notice to the purchaser acknowledging the type of district in which the property is located.
   C. may give oral or written notice of the type of district.
   D. must provide information on the earnest money contract and deed.

9. Currently, Texas brokers are permitted to fill in the blanks on
   A. a real estate deed.
   B. an earnest money contract.
   C. both A and B.
   D. neither A nor B.

10. When property is sold by means of an installment contract, the
    A. seller delivers a deed at closing.
    B. buyer is NOT given the right to occupy the property until the contract terms have been fulfilled.
    C. both A and B.
    D. neither A nor B.

11. Installment contracts may be used when
    A. the buyer does not have the full purchase price in cash.
    B. the buyer is unable to borrow part of the purchase price from a lender.
    C. both A and B.
    D. neither A nor B.

12. The purchaser under an installment contract may protect his interests by requiring that the
    A. seller place a deed in escrow at settlement.
    B. contract be recorded in the land records.
    C. both A and B.
    D. neither A nor B.

13. Equitable title can be
    A. transferred by sale.
    B. inherited.
    C. mortgaged.
    D. transferred by deed.
    E. all of the above.

14. The option portion of a lease-option contract can be attached to the lease as
    A. a rider.
    B. an accord.
    C. a binder.
    D. a purchase agreement.

15. Lease-option contracts tend to increase in popularity during a
    A. seller's market.
    B. buyer's market.

16. An option to buy is an example of
    A. an executory contract.
    B. a bilateral contract.
    C. a unilateral contract.
    D. both A and B.
    E. both A and C.

17. Under the terms of a right of first refusal, the tenant is given the right to
    A. match an offer to purchase the property
    B. purchase the property at a previously agreed price.
    C. both A and B.
    D. neither A nor B.

18. The party with the least amount of flexibility in a lease-option agreement is the
    A. optionor.
    B. optionee.

19. The phrase "time is of the essence" in a sales contract means that
    A. the time limits set by the contract must be faithfully observed or the contract is voidable.
    B. the parties are prohibited from giving each other an extension.
    C. both A and B.
    D. neither A nor B.

Chapter 11

KEY TERMS

Acceleration clause: allows the lender to demand immediate payment of entire loan if the borrower defaults

Beneficiary: one for whose benefit a trust is created; the lender in a deed of trust arrangement

Deed of Trust: a document that conveys title to a neutral third party trustee as security for a debt

Deficiency judgment: a judgment against a borrower if the foreclosure sale does not bring enough to pay the balance owed

Foreclosure: the procedure by which a person's property can be taken and sold to satisfy an unpaid debt

Junior mortgage: any mortgage on a property that is subordinate to the first mortgage in priority

Mortgage: a document that makes property security for the repayment of a debt

Mortgagee: the party receiving the mortgage; the lender

Mortgagor: the party who gives a mortgage; the borrower

Power of sale: allows a mortgagee to conduct a foreclosure sale without first going to court

Subordination: voluntary acceptance of a lower mortgage priority than one would otherwise be entitled to

Trustee: one who holds property in trust for another

Trustor: one who creates a trust; the borrower in a deed of trusts arrangement

Mortgage Theory and Law

IN THIS CHAPTER

In this chapter we will take a brief look at mortgage theory and law. A mortgage is a pledge of property to secure the repayment of a debt. The chapter includes coverage of lien theory and title theory, pledge methods, promissory notes, the mortgage instrument, the "subject to" clause, loan assumption, and debt priorities. The last part of the chapter deals with the foreclosure process, dividing the discussion between judicial and nonjudicial foreclosure.

EARLY MORTGAGES

A mortgage is a pledge of property to secure the repayment of a debt. If the debt is not repaid as agreed between the lender and borrower, the lender can force the sale of the pledged property and apply the proceeds to repayment of the debt. To better understand current mortgage laws, we should first look at their history.

The concept of pledging property as collateral for a loan is not new. According to historians, the mortgage was in use when the pharaohs ruled Egypt and during the time of the Roman Empire. According to Roman laws, loans could be secured by mortgages on either personal or real property. In the early years of the Empire, nonpayment of a mortgage loan entitled the lender to make the borrower his slave. In the year 326 B.C. Roman law was modified to allow the debtor his freedom while working off his debt. Later, Roman law was again changed, this time to permit an unpaid debt to be satisfied by the sale of the mortgaged property.

Hypothecation

Mortgages were also an important part of English law and, as a result of the English colonization of America, ultimately were incorporated into laws of each state. In England, the concept of pledging real estate by temporarily conveying its title to a lender as security for a debt was in regular use by the eleventh century. However, the Christian church at that time did not allow its members to charge interest. Because of this, the Christian lender took possession of the mortgaged property and collected the rents it produced instead of charging interest.

In contrast, Jewish lenders in England charged interest and left the borrower in possession. It was not until the fourteenth century that charging interest, rather than taking possession, became universal. Leaving the borrower in possession of the pledged property is known as **hypothecation.** The borrower conveys title to the lender, but still has the use of the property. This conveyance of title in the mortgage agreement is conditional. The mortgage states that if the debt it secures is paid on time, the mortgage is defeated and title returns to the borrower. This was and still is known as a **defeasance clause.**

LIEN THEORY VERSUS TITLE THEORY

Although the United States inherited the whole of England's mortgage law, it began to be modified following independence. In 1791 in South Carolina, lawmakers asked the question: "Should a mortgage actually convey title to the lender subject only to the borrower's default? Or does the mortgage, despite its wording, simply create a lien with a right to acquire title only after proper foreclosure?" Their decision was that a mortgage is a lien rather than a conveyance, and South Carolina became the first lien theory state in regard to mortgages. Today, 33 states, including Texas, have adopted this viewpoint.

Fifteen jurisdictions adhere to the older idea that a mortgage is a conveyance of title subject to defeat when the debt it secures is paid. They are classified as **title theory** states. Three states are classified as **intermediate theory** states because they take a position midway between the lien and title theories. In the intermediate states, title does not pass to the lender with the mortgage, but only upon default. In real estate practice, as long as default does not occur, the differences among the three theories are more technical than real.

PLEDGE METHODS

A person can pledge his real estate as collateral for a loan by using any of four methods: the regular mortgage, the equitable mortgage, the deed as security, and the deed of trust.

Regular Mortgage

The *standard* or *regular mortgage* is the mortgage handed down from England and the one commonly found and used in the United States today. In it, the borrower conveys the title to the lender as security for the debt. The mortgage also contains a statement that it will become void if the debt it secures is paid in full and on time. In title theory states, the conveyance feature of the mortgage stands. In lien theory states, such a mortgage is considered to be only a lien against the borrower's property, despite its wording.

Equitable Mortgage

An **equitable mortgage** is a written agreement that, although it does not follow the form of a regular mortgage, is considered by the courts to be one. For example, Black sells his land to Green, with Green paying part of the price now in cash and promising to pay the balance later. Normally, Black would ask Green to execute a regular mortgage as security for the balance due. However, instead of doing this, Black makes a note of the balance due on the deed before handing it to Green. The laws of most states would regard this notation as an equitable mortgage. For all intents and purposes, it is a mortgage, although it is not specifically called one. Another example of an equitable mortgage can arise from the money deposit accompanying an offer to purchase property. If the seller refuses the offer and refuses to return the deposit, the courts will hold that the purchaser has an equitable mortgage in the amount of the deposit against the seller's property. It is important to note that there is no mortgage executed, only the note. Equity imposes the mortgage obligation (and right to foreclose). This is different from using the deed as a security document, discussed below.

Deed as Security

Occasionally, a borrower will give a **deed as security** for a loan. In this situation, the owner owns the home and wants to borrow against it, executing a deed to the lender. On the face of it, he would appear to be able to do whatever he pleases because he has the title. However, if the borrower can prove that the deed was, in fact, security for a loan, the lender must foreclose as with a regular mortgage if the borrower fails to repay. If the loan is repaid in full and on time, the borrower can force the lender to convey the land back to him. Like the equitable mortgage, a deed used as security is treated according to its intent, not its label.

Deed of Trust

Whereas a mortgage is a two-party arrangement with a borrower and a lender, the **trust deed,** also known as a ***deed of trust,*** is a three-party arrangement consisting of the borrower (the trustor), the lender (the beneficiary), and a neutral third party (a trustee). The key aspect of this system is that the borrower executes a deed to the trustee rather than to the lender. If the borrower pays the debt in full and on time, the trustee reconveys title back to the borrower. If the borrower defaults on the loan, the lender asks the trustee to sell the property to pay off the debt. In Texas, debts are most often secured by a deed of trust, and will be covered in more detail later in this chapter.

Chattel Mortgage

A mortgage can also be used to pledge personal property as security for a debt. This is a **chattel mortgage.** The word *chattel* is a legal term for personal property and derives from the Old English word for cattle. As with real property mortgages, a chattel mortgage permits the borrower to use mortgaged personal property as long as the loan payments are made. If the borrower defaults, the lender is permitted to take possession and sell the mortgaged goods. In Texas, the use of chattel mortgages is usually in the form of financing statements and security agreements as provided for in the Texas Business and Commerce Code.

PROMISSORY NOTE

Two documents are involved in a standard mortgage loan—the promissory note and the mortgage. Both are contracts. The **promissory note** establishes who the borrower and lender are, the amount of the debt, the terms of repayment, and the interest rate. A sample of the commonly used FNMA/FHLMC promissory note, usually referred to simply as a **note,** or a **real estate lien note,** is shown in Figure 11.1.

FIGURE 11.1 Real estate lien note

[1] **NOTE**

February 21, , 2006 — [Date] Houston, Texas — [City] [State] [2]

123 Lots Lane, Houston, Texas 77002
[Property Address]

1. BORROWER'S PROMISE TO PAY

[3] In return for a loan that I have received, I promise to pay U.S. $ 183,000.00 [5] (this amount is called "Principal"), plus interest, to the order of the Lender. The Lender is Mort Gage's Mortgage Company [4] . I will make all payments under this Note in the form of cash, check or money order.

I understand that the Lender may transfer this Note. The Lender or anyone who takes this Note by transfer and who is entitled to receive payments under this Note is called the "Note Holder."

2. INTEREST

Interest will be charged on unpaid principal until the full amount of Principal has been paid. I will pay interest at a yearly
[6] rate of 8.5 %.

The interest rate required by this Section 2 is the rate I will pay both before and after any default described in Section 6(B) of this Note.

3. PAYMENTS

(A) Time and Place of Payments

I will pay principal and interest by making a payment every month.

I will make my monthly payment on the 1st day of each month beginning on April 1 , 2006. I will make these payments every month until I have paid all of the principal and interest and any other charges described below that I may owe under this Note. Each monthly payment will be applied as of its scheduled due date and will be applied to interest
[8] before Principal. If, on April 1 , 2032 , I still owe amounts under this Note, I will pay those amounts in full on that date, which is called the "Maturity Date."

I will make my monthly payments at P.O.Box 90210, Beverly Hills, California 90210 or at a different place if required by the Note Holder.

(B) Amount of Monthly Payments

My monthly payment will be in the amount of U.S. $ 1,407.11 . [7]

4. BORROWER'S RIGHT TO PREPAY

[9] I have the right to make payments of Principal at any time before they are due. A payment of Principal only is known as a "Prepayment." When I make a Prepayment, I will tell the Note Holder in writing that I am doing so. I may not designate a payment as a Prepayment if I have not made all the monthly payments due under the Note.

I may make a full Prepayment or partial Prepayments without paying a Prepayment charge. The Note Holder will use my Prepayments to reduce the amount of Principal that I owe under this Note. However, the Note Holder may apply my Prepayment to the accrued and unpaid interest on the Prepayment amount, before applying my Prepayment to reduce the Principal amount of the Note. If I make a partial Prepayment, there will be no changes in the due date or in the amount of my monthly payment unless the Note Holder agrees in writing to those changes.

5. LOAN CHARGES

If a law, which applies to this loan and which sets maximum loan charges, is finally interpreted so that the interest or other loan charges collected or to be collected in connection with this loan exceed the permitted limits, then: (a) any such loan charge shall be reduced by the amount necessary to reduce the charge to the permitted limit; and (b) any sums already collected from me which exceeded permitted limits will be refunded to me. The Note Holder may choose to make this refund by reducing the Principal I owe under this Note or by making a direct payment to me. If a refund reduces Principal, the reduction will be treated as a partial Prepayment.

6. BORROWER'S FAILURE TO PAY AS REQUIRED

[10] **(A) Late Charge for Overdue Payments**

If the Note Holder has not received the full amount of any monthly payment by the end of 10 calendar days after the date it is due, I will pay a late charge to the Note Holder. The amount of the charge will be 18 % of my overdue payment of principal and interest. I will pay this late charge promptly but only once on each late payment.

(B) Default

If I do not pay the full amount of each monthly payment on the date it is due, I will be in default.

MULTISTATE FIXED RATE NOTE—Single Family—Fannie Mae/Freddie Mac UNIFORM INSTRUMENT Form 3200 1/01 *(page 1 of 2 pages)*

Source: © 2012 Cengage Learning

FIGURE 11.1 Real estate lien note (*continued*)

(C) Notice of Default

If I am in default, the Note Holder may send me a written notice telling me that if I do not pay the overdue amount by a certain date, the Note Holder may require me to pay immediately the full amount of Principal which has not been paid and all the interest
[11] that I owe on that amount. That date must be at least 30 days after the date on which the notice is mailed to me or delivered by other means.

(D) No Waiver By Note Holder

Even if, at a time when I am in default, the Note Holder does not require me to pay immediately in full as described above, the Note Holder will still have the right to do so if I am in default at a later time.

(E) Payment of Note Holder's Costs and Expenses

If the Note Holder has required me to pay immediately in full as described above, the Note Holder will have the right to be
[12] paid back by me for all of its costs and expenses in enforcing this Note to the extent not prohibited by applicable law. Those expenses include, for example, reasonable attorneys' fees.

7. GIVING OF NOTICES

Unless applicable law requires a different method, any notice that must be given to me under this Note will be given by delivering it or by mailing it by first class mail to me at the Property Address above or at a different address if I give the Note Holder a notice of my different address.

Any notice that must be given to the Note Holder under this Note will be given by delivering it or by mailing it by first class mail to the Note Holder at the address stated in Section 3(A) above or at a different address if I am given a notice of that different address.

8. OBLIGATIONS OF PERSONS UNDER THIS NOTE

If more than one person signs this Note, each person is fully and personally obligated to keep all of the promises made in this Note, including the promise to pay the full amount owed. Any person who is a guarantor, surety or endorser of this Note is also obligated to do these things. Any person who takes over these obligations, including the obligations of a guarantor, surety or endorser of this Note, is also obligated to keep all of the promises made in this Note. The Note Holder may enforce its rights under this Note against each person individually or against all of us together. This means that any one of us may be required to pay all of the amounts owed under this Note.

9. WAIVERS

I and any other person who has obligations under this Note waive the rights of Presentment and Notice of Dishonor. "Presentment" means the right to require the Note Holder to demand payment of amounts due. "Notice of Dishonor" means the right to require the Note Holder to give notice to other persons that amounts due have not been paid.

10. UNIFORM SECURED NOTE

This Note is a uniform instrument with limited variations in some jurisdictions. In addition to the protections given to the
[13] Note Holder under this Note, a Mortgage, Deed of Trust, or Security Deed (the "Security Instrument"), dated the same date as this Note, protects the Note Holder from possible losses which might result if I do not keep the promises which I make in this Note. That Security Instrument describes how and under what conditions I may be required to make immediate payment in full of all amounts I owe under this Note. Some of those conditions are described as follows:

> If all or any part of the Property or any Interest in the Property is sold or transferred (or if Borrower is not a natural person and a beneficial interest in Borrower is sold or transferred) without Lender's prior written consent, Lender may require immediate payment in full of all sums secured by this Security Instrument. However, this option shall not be exercised by Lender if such exercise is prohibited by Applicable Law.
>
> If Lender exercises this option, Lender shall give Borrower notice of acceleration. The notice shall provide a period of not less than 30 days from the date the notice is given in accordance with Section 15 within which Borrower must pay all sums secured by this Security Instrument. If Borrower fails to pay these sums prior to the expiration of this period, Lender may invoke any remedies permitted by this Security Instrument without further notice or demand on Borrower.

WITNESS THE HAND(S) AND SEAL(S) OF THE UNDERSIGNED

_______________________________ (Seal)
- Borrower

[14] _______________________________ (Seal)
- Borrower

_______________________________ (Seal)
- Borrower

[Sign Original Only]

MULTISTATE FIXED RATE NOTE—Single Family—Fannie Mae/Freddie Mac UNIFORM INSTRUMENT Form 3200 1/01 *(page 2 of 2 pages)*

To be valid as evidence of debt, a note must (1) be in writing, (2) be between a borrower and a lender who both have contractual capacity, (3) state the borrower's promise to pay a certain sum of money, (4) show the terms of payment, (5) be signed by the borrower, and (6) be voluntarily delivered by the borrower and accepted by the lender. If the note is secured by a mortgage or deed of trust or a vendor's lien, it must say so. Otherwise, it is solely a personal obligation of the borrower. Although interest is not required to make the note valid, most loans do carry an interest charge; when they do, the rate of interest must be stated in the note. Finally, in some states it is necessary for the borrower's signature on the note to be acknowledged and/or witnessed.

Borrower-Lender

Referring to Figure 11.1, number [1] identifies the document as a note and [2] gives the location and date of the note's execution (signing). At [3], the borrower states the receipt of something of value and in turn promises to pay the debt described in the note. Typically, the "value received" is a loan of money in the amount described in the note; it could, however, be services or goods or anything else of value.

The section of the note at [4] identifies to whom the obligation is owed and where the payments are to be sent.

Principal and Payments

The **principal** or amount of the obligation, $183,000, is shown at [5]. Number [6] gives the rate of interest on the debt and the date from which it will be charged. The amount of the periodic payment at [7] is calculated from the loan tables like those discussed in Chapter 12. In this case, $1,407.11 each month for 30 years will return the lender's $183,000 plus interest at the rate of 8.5% per year on the unpaid portion of the principal. Number [8] outlines when payments will begin and when subsequent payments will be due. In this example, they are due on the first day of each month until the full $183,000 and interest have been paid. The clause at [9] is a **prepayment privilege** for the borrower. It allows the borrower to pay more than the required $1,407.11 per month and to pay the loan off early without penalty. Without this very important privilege, the note requires the borrower to pay $1,407.11 per month, no more and no less, until the $183,000 plus interest has been paid.

Acceleration Clause

The clause at [10] provides for a late payment fee if payments are not timely made. The provision at [11] allows the lender to demand immediate payment of the entire balance remaining on the note if the borrower misses any of the individual payments. This is called an ***acceleration clause***, because it "speeds up" the remaining payments due on the note and makes them due immediately. Without this clause, the lender can foreclose only on the payments that have come due and have not been paid. In this example, that could take as long as 30 years. This clause also has a certain psychological value: knowing that the lender has the option of calling the entire loan balance due upon default makes the borrower think twice about being late with payments.

Signature

At **[12]**, the borrower agrees to pay any collection costs incurred by the lender if the borrower falls behind in his payments. At **[13]**, the promissory note is tied to the mortgage or deed of trust that secures it, making it a secured loan. Without this reference, it would be like a personal loan. At **[14]**, the borrower signs the note. A person who signs a note is sometimes referred to as a **maker** of the note. If two or more persons sign the note, it is common to include a statement in the note that the borrowers are "jointly and severally liable" for all provisions in the note. Thus, the terms of the note and the obligations it creates are enforceable upon the makers as a group and upon each maker individually. If the borrower is married, lenders generally require both husband and wife to sign. An acknowledgment is not required, because it is the mortgage rather than the note that is recorded in the public records.

THE DEED OF TRUST

The mortgage is a separate agreement from the promissory note. Whereas the note is evidence of a debt and a promise to pay, the mortgage pledges collateral that the lender can sell if the note is not paid.

In Texas, the deed of trust is the same as a mortgage and is almost always used as the mortgage document. Real property is used as security for a debt; if the debt is not repaid, the property is sold and the proceeds are applied to the balance owed. The main legal difference between a deed of trust and a mortgage is diagrammed in Figure 11.2.

FIGURE 11.2 Comparing a mortgage with a deed of trust

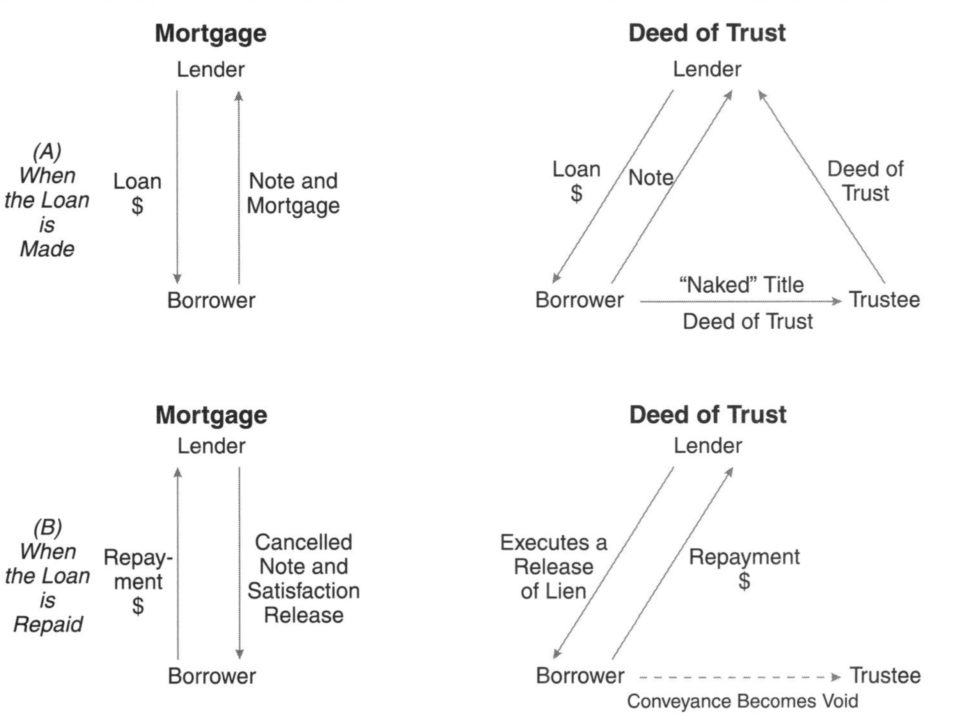

Source: © 2012 Cengage Learning

Parties to a Deed of Trust

Figure 11.2 shows that when a debt is secured by a mortgage the borrower delivers the promissory note and mortgage to the lender, who keeps them until the debt is paid. But when a note is secured by a deed of trust, three parties are involved: the borrower (the ***mortgagor***, ***trustor***, or **grantor**), the lender (the ***mortgagee*** or ***beneficiary***), and a neutral third party (the ***trustee***). The lender makes a loan to the borrower, and the borrower gives the lender a promissory note (like the one shown in Figure 11.1) and a deed of trust. In the deed of trust document, it states that the borrower conveys title to the trustee, to be held in trust until the note is paid in full (you may recall that Texas is a lien theory state, so only a lien interest is actually transferred). The deed of trust is recorded in the county in which the property is located and then is usually given to the lender for safekeeping. A variation used in other areas of the country is to deliver the recorded deed of trust to the trustee to be held in a long-term escrow until the note is paid in full. Anyone searching the title records on the borrower's property would find the deed of trust conveying title to the trustee. This would alert the title searcher to the existence of a debt against the property.

In Texas, the title granted to the trustee is only a conditional conveyance. The title held by the trustee is limited only to what is necessary to carry out the duty as trustee when requested to do so by the beneficiary *(lender)* under the beneficiary's rights as set out in the deed of trust.

When the note is paid in full, the lender cancels the note and issues the grantor **(borrower)** a **release of lien,** which is recorded in the county records to indicate a full discharge of the previously recorded deed of trust lien. Depending on the terms of the deed of trust instrument, the conveyance to the trustee may become void and of no further force and effect.

If a borrower defaults under a deed of trust, the beneficiary (lender) generally instructs the trustee to post the notice of foreclosure at the courthouse and to hold a public sale of the property according to the requirements of the deed of trust and in accordance with Texas statutes. The deed of trust generally specifies this procedure in its ***power of sale*** provision, and the borrower agrees to this provision upon signing the deed of trust.

In Texas, an individual is ordinarily named as a trustee in the deed of trust instrument. This person may be the attorney who draws the papers for the lender, or some other person appointed by the lender. There is normally a provision that allows the lender to appoint a substitute trustee in the event of death or refusal to act by the named trustee. The trustee is supposed to be an impartial third party, although the beneficiary may act as trustee. But because the power of sale remedy is so strict, the instrument and authority of the trustee thereunder is strictly construed to avoid irregularities in the sale. If a person acts as both the trustee and beneficiary, the court may find a conflict of interest or lack of impartiality.

SAMPLE DEED OF TRUST

Figure 11.3 is an example of a deed of trust form that is the standard FNMA/FHLMC uniform instrument commonly used by lenders for residential

FIGURE 11.3 Deed of trust

After Recording Return To:

____

____

____

____

________________ **[Space Above This Line For Recording Data]** ________________

DEED OF TRUST[1]

DEFINITIONS

Words used in multiple sections of this document are defined below and other words are defined in Sections 3, 11, 13, 18, 20 and 21. Certain rules regarding the usage of words used in this document are also provided in Section 16.

(A) "Security Instrument" means this document, which is dated February 21, 2006, together with all Riders to this document.
(B) "Borrower" is N. Debted and wife, May B. Debted. Borrower is the grantor under this Security Instrument. [2]
(C) "Lender" is Mort Gage's Mortgage Company. Lender is a __________ organized and existing under the laws of California __________. Lender's address is P. O. Box 90210, Beverly Hills, California 90210. Lender is the beneficiary under this Security Instrument.
(D) "Trustee" is Charles J. Jacobus. Trustee's address is 6750 West Loop South, Bellaire, Texas 77401.
(E) "Note" means the promissory note signed by Borrower and dated February 21,
[8] 2006. The Note states that Borrower owes Lender ONE HUNDRED EIGHTY-THREE THOUSAND AND 00/100 Dollars (U.S. $183,000.00) plus interest. Borrower has promised to pay this debt in regular Periodic Payments and to pay the debt in full not later than April 1, 2036.
(F) "Property" means the property that is described below under the heading "Transfer of Rights in the Property."
(G) "Loan" means the debt evidenced by the Note, plus interest, any prepayment charges and late charges due under the Note, and all sums due under this Security Instrument, plus interest.

TEXAS--Single Family--Fannie Mae/Freddie Mac UNIFORM INSTRUMENT Form 3044 1/01 *(page 1 of 17 pages)*

mortgage documentation. Other deed of trust forms have provisions that may vary. This example shows the agreement between borrower and lender and states the responsibilities of the trustee. Beginning at [1], the document is identified as a deed of trust. This is followed by the identification of the grantor (borrower) at [2]. Conveyance to the trustee is shown at [3], and the property is legally described at [4]. At [5] and [6] are the habendum and warranty clauses where the borrower states that he will defend the title against claims of others.

Note that the conveyance is made in TRUST at [7] to secure the payment of the promissory note, described at [8].

FIGURE 11.3 Deed of trust (*continued*)

(H) "Riders" means all Riders to this Security Instrument that are executed by Borrower. The following Riders are to be executed by Borrower [check box as applicable]:

☐ Adjustable Rate Rider	☐ Condominium Rider	☐ Second Home Rider
☐ Balloon Rider	☐ Planned Unit Development Rider	☐ Other(s) [specify]________
☐ 1-4 Family Rider	☐ Biweekly Payment Rider	

(I) "Applicable Law" means all controlling applicable federal, state and local statutes, regulations, ordinances and administrative rules and orders (that have the effect of law) as well as all applicable final, non-appealable judicial opinions.
(J) "Community Association Dues, Fees, and Assessments" means all dues, fees, assessments and other charges that are imposed on Borrower or the Property by a condominium association, homeowners association or similar organization.
(K) "Electronic Funds Transfer" means any transfer of funds, other than a transaction originated by check, draft, or similar paper instrument, which is initiated through an electronic terminal, telephonic instrument, computer, or magnetic tape so as to order, instruct, or authorize a financial institution to debit or credit an account. Such term includes, but is not limited to, point-of-sale transfers, automated teller machine transactions, transfers initiated by telephone, wire transfers, and automated clearinghouse transfers.
(L) "Escrow Items" means those items that are described in Section 3.
(M) "Miscellaneous Proceeds" means any compensation, settlement, award of damages, or proceeds paid by any third party (other than insurance proceeds paid under the coverages described in Section 5) for: (i) damage to, or destruction of, the Property; (ii) condemnation or other taking of all or any part of the Property; (iii) conveyance in lieu of condemnation; or (iv) misrepresentations of, or omissions as to, the value and/or condition of the Property.
(N) "Mortgage Insurance" means insurance protecting Lender against the nonpayment of, or default on, the Loan.
(O) "Periodic Payment" means the regularly scheduled amount due for (i) principal and interest under the Note, plus (ii) any amounts under Section 3 of this Security Instrument.
(P) "RESPA" means the Real Estate Settlement Procedures Act (12 U.S.C. §2601 et seq.) and its implementing regulation, Regulation X (24 C.F.R. Part 3500), as they might be amended from time to time, or any additional or successor legislation or regulation that governs the same subject matter. As used in this Security Instrument, "RESPA" refers to all requirements and restrictions that are imposed in regard to a "federally related mortgage loan" even if the Loan does not qualify as a "federally related mortgage loan" under RESPA.
(Q) "Successor in Interest of Borrower" means any party that has taken title to the Property, whether or not that party has assumed Borrower's obligations under the Note and/or this Security Instrument.

TRANSFER OF RIGHTS IN THE PROPERTY

This Security Instrument secures to Lender: (i) the repayment of the Loan, and all renewals, extensions and modifications of the Note; and (ii) the performance of Borrower's covenants and agreements under this Security Instrument and the Note. For this purpose, Borrower irrevocably

TEXAS--Single Family--**Fannie Mae/Freddie Mac UNIFORM INSTRUMENT** **Form 3044 1/01** *(page 2 of 17 pages)*

Covenants of Borrower

At [9] the borrower agrees to provide a fund for *taxes and insurance* by depositing funds equal to one-twelfth of the yearly taxes and assessments that may attain priority over the deed of trust.

The *covenant of insurance* at [10] requires the borrower to carry adequate insurance against damage or destruction of the mortgaged property. This protects the value of the collateral for the loan because without insurance, if the

FIGURE 11.3 Deed of trust *(continued)*

[7]

[3] grants and conveys to Trustee, in trust, with power of sale, the following described property located in the County of Harris:

[Type of Recording Jurisdiction] [Name of Recording Jurisdiction]

[4] Lot One (1), Block Two (2), Shady Acres Subdivision, as recorded in Volume 7, Page 3 of the Map records of Harris County, Texas

which currently has the address of 123 Lois Lane
[Street]
Houston, Texas 77002 ("Property Address"):
[City] [Zip Code]

TOGETHER WITH all the improvements now or hereafter erected on the property, and all
[5] easements, appurtenances, and fixtures now or hereafter a part of the property. All replacements and additions shall also be covered by this Security Instrument. All of the foregoing is referred to in this
[6] Security Instrument as the "Property."

BORROWER COVENANTS that Borrower is lawfully seised of the estate hereby conveyed and has the right to grant and convey the Property and that the Property is unencumbered, except for encumbrances of record. Borrower warrants and will defend generally the title to the Property against all claims and demands, subject to any encumbrances of record.

THIS SECURITY INSTRUMENT combines uniform covenants for national use and non-uniform covenants with limited variations by jurisdiction to constitute a uniform security instrument covering real property.

UNIFORM COVENANTS. Borrower and Lender covenant and agree as follows:

1. Payment of Principal, Interest, Escrow Items, Prepayment Charges, and Late Charges. Borrower shall pay when due the principal of, and interest on, the debt evidenced by the Note and any prepayment charges and late charges due under the Note. Borrower shall also pay funds for Escrow Items pursuant to Section 3. Payments due under the Note and this Security Instrument shall be made in U.S. currency. However, if any check or other instrument received by Lender as payment under the Note or this Security Instrument is returned to Lender unpaid, Lender may require that any or all subsequent payments due under the Note and this Security Instrument be made in one or more of the following forms, as selected by Lender: (a) cash; (b) money order; (c) certified check, bank check, treasurer's check or cashier's check, provided any such check is

TEXAS--Single Family--Fannie Mae/Freddie Mac UNIFORM INSTRUMENT Form 3044 1/01 *(page 3 of 17 pages)*

buildings or other improvements on the mortgaged property are damaged or destroyed, the value of the property might fall below the amount owed on the debt. With insurance, the buildings can be repaired or replaced, restoring the value of the borrower's collateral.

The *covenant to repair* shown at [11] requires the borrower to keep the mortgaged property in good condition and not to destroy, damage, or substantially change the property. At [12] is the condemnation clause. If all or any part

FIGURE 11.3 Deed of trust (*continued*)

drawn upon an institution whose deposits are insured by a federal agency, instrumentality, or entity; or (d) Electronic Funds Transfer.

Payments are deemed received by Lender when received at the location designated in the Note or at such other location as may be designated by Lender in accordance with the notice provisions in Section 15. Lender may return any payment or partial payment if the payment or partial payments are insufficient to bring the Loan current. Lender may accept any payment or partial payment insufficient to bring the Loan current, without waiver of any rights hereunder or prejudice to its rights to refuse such payment or partial payments in the future, but Lender is not obligated to apply such payments at the time such payments are accepted. If each Periodic Payment is applied as of its scheduled due date, then Lender need not pay interest on unapplied funds. Lender may hold such unapplied funds until Borrower makes payment to bring the Loan current. If Borrower does not do so within a reasonable period of time, Lender shall either apply such funds or return them to Borrower. If not applied earlier, such funds will be applied to the outstanding principal balance under the Note immediately prior to foreclosure. No offset or claim which Borrower might have now or in the future against Lender shall relieve Borrower from making payments due under the Note and this Security Instrument or performing the covenants and agreements secured by this Security Instrument.

2. Application of Payments or Proceeds. Except as otherwise described in this Section 2, all payments accepted and applied by Lender shall be applied in the following order of priority: (a) interest due under the Note; (b) principal due under the Note; (c) amounts due under Section 3. Such payments shall be applied to each Periodic Payment in the order in which it became due. Any remaining amounts shall be applied first to late charges, second to any other amounts due under this Security Instrument, and then to reduce the principal balance of the Note.

If Lender receives a payment from Borrower for a delinquent Periodic Payment which includes a sufficient amount to pay any late charge due, the payment may be applied to the delinquent payment and the late charge. If more than one Periodic Payment is outstanding, Lender may apply any payment received from Borrower to the repayment of the Periodic Payments if, and to the extent that, each payment can be paid in full. To the extent that any excess exists after the payment is applied to the full payment of one or more Periodic Payments, such excess may be applied to any late charges due. Voluntary prepayments shall be applied first to any prepayment charges and then as described in the Note.

Any application of payments, insurance proceeds, or Miscellaneous Proceeds to principal due under the Note shall not extend or postpone the due date, or change the amount, of the Periodic Payments.

3. Funds for Escrow Items. Borrower shall pay to Lender on the day Periodic Payments are due under the Note, until the Note is paid in full, a sum (the "Funds") to provide for payment of
[9] amounts due for: (a) taxes and assessments and other items which can attain priority over this Security Instrument as a lien or encumbrance on the Property; (b) leasehold payments or ground rents on the Property, if any; (c) premiums for any and all insurance required by Lender under Section 5; and (d) Mortgage Insurance premiums, if any, or any sums payable by Borrower to Lender in lieu of the payment of Mortgage Insurance premiums in accordance with the provisions of Section 10. These items are called "Escrow Items." At origination or at any time during the term of the Loan, Lender may require that Community Association Dues, Fees, and Assessments, if any,

of the property is taken by action of eminent domain, any money so received must be paid to the lender.

Alienation Clause

When used in a mortgage, an **alienation clause** (also called a **due-on-sale** clause) gives the lender the right to call the entire loan balance due if the mortgaged property is sold or otherwise conveyed (alienated) by the borrower. An example

FIGURE 11.3 Deed of trust (*continued*)

be escrowed by Borrower, and such dues, fees and assessments shall be an Escrow Item. Borrower shall promptly furnish to Lender all notices of amounts to be paid under this Section. Borrower shall pay Lender the Funds for Escrow Items unless Lender waives Borrower's obligation to pay the Funds for any or all Escrow Items. Lender may waive Borrower's obligation to pay to Lender Funds for any or all Escrow Items at any time. Any such waiver may only be in writing. In the event of such waiver, Borrower shall pay directly, when and where payable, the amounts due for any Escrow Items for which payment of Funds has been waived by Lender and, if Lender requires, shall furnish to Lender receipts evidencing such payment within such time period as Lender may require. Borrower's obligation to make such payments and to provide receipts shall for all purposes be deemed to be a covenant and agreement contained in this Security Instrument, as the phrase "covenant and agreement" is used in Section 9. If Borrower is obligated to pay Escrow Items directly, pursuant to a waiver, and Borrower fails to pay the amount due for an Escrow Item, Lender may exercise its rights under Section 9 and pay such amount and Borrower shall then be obligated under Section 9 to repay to Lender any such amount. Lender may revoke the waiver as to any or all Escrow Items at any time by a notice given in accordance with Section 15 and, upon such revocation, Borrower shall pay to Lender all Funds, and in such amounts, that are then required under this Section 3.

Lender may, at any time, collect and hold Funds in an amount (a) sufficient to permit Lender to apply the Funds at the time specified under RESPA, and (b) not to exceed the maximum amount a lender can require under RESPA. Lender shall estimate the amount of Funds due on the basis of current data and reasonable estimates of expenditures of future Escrow Items or otherwise in accordance with Applicable Law.

The Funds shall be held in an institution whose deposits are insured by a federal agency, instrumentality, or entity (including Lender, if Lender is an institution whose deposits are so insured) or in any Federal Home Loan Bank. Lender shall apply the Funds to pay the Escrow Items no later than the time specified under RESPA. Lender shall not charge Borrower for holding and applying the Funds, annually analyzing the escrow account, or verifying the Escrow Items, unless Lender pays Borrower interest on the Funds and Applicable Law permits Lender to make such a charge. Unless an agreement is made in writing or Applicable Law requires interest to be paid on the Funds, Lender shall not be required to pay Borrower any interest or earnings on the Funds. Borrower and Lender can agree in writing, however, that interest shall be paid on the Funds. Lender shall give to Borrower, without charge, an annual accounting of the Funds as required by RESPA.

If there is a surplus of Funds held in escrow, as defined under RESPA, Lender shall account to Borrower for the excess funds in accordance with RESPA. If there is a shortage of Funds held in escrow, as defined under RESPA, Lender shall notify Borrower as required by RESPA, and Borrower shall pay to Lender the amount necessary to make up the shortage in accordance with RESPA, but in no more than 12 monthly payments. If there is a deficiency of Funds held in escrow, as defined under RESPA, Lender shall notify Borrower as required by RESPA, and Borrower shall pay to Lender the amount necessary to make up the deficiency in accordance with RESPA, but in no more than 12 monthly payments.

Upon payment in full of all sums secured by this Security Instrument, Lender shall promptly refund to Borrower any Funds held by Lender.

TEXAS--Single Family--**Fannie Mae/Freddie Mac UNIFORM INSTRUMENT** **Form 3044 1/01** *(page 5 of 17 pages)*

is shown at **[13]**. The purpose of an alienation clause is two-fold. If the mortgaged property is put up for sale and a buyer proposes to assume the existing loan, the lender can refuse to accept that buyer as a substitute borrower if the buyer's credit is not good. But, more importantly, lenders have been using it as an opportunity to eliminate old loans with low rates of interest.

Responding to complaints by consumers, 17 states have taken the attitude that due-on-sale clauses cannot be enforced in order to raise interest rates. However, the U.S. Supreme Court has ruled that a due-on-sale clause can be enforced by

FIGURE 11.3 Deed of trust (*continued*)

4. Charges; Liens. Borrower shall pay all taxes, assessments, charges, fines, and impositions attributable to the Property which can attain priority over this Security Instrument, leasehold payments or ground rents on the Property, if any, and Community Association Dues, Fees, and Assessments, if any. To the extent that these items are Escrow Items, Borrower shall pay them in the manner provided in Section 3.

Borrower shall promptly discharge any lien which has priority over this Security Instrument unless Borrower: (a) agrees in writing to the payment of the obligation secured by the lien in a manner acceptable to Lender, but only so long as Borrower is performing such agreement; (b) contests the lien in good faith by, or defends against enforcement of the lien in, legal proceedings which in Lender's opinion operate to prevent the enforcement of the lien while those proceedings are pending, but only until such proceedings are concluded; or (c) secures from the holder of the lien an agreement satisfactory to Lender subordinating the lien to this Security Instrument. If Lender determines that any part of the Property is subject to a lien which can attain priority over this Security Instrument, Lender may give Borrower a notice identifying the lien. Within 10 days of the date on which that notice is given, Borrower shall satisfy the lien or take one or more of the actions set forth above in this Section 4.

Lender may require Borrower to pay a one-time charge for a real estate tax verification and/or reporting service used by Lender in connection with this Loan.

5. Property Insurance. Borrower shall keep the improvements now existing or hereafter erected on the Property insured against loss by fire, hazards included within the term "extended [10] coverage," and any other hazards including, but not limited to, earthquakes and floods, for which Lender requires insurance. This insurance shall be maintained in the amounts (including deductible levels) and for the periods that Lender requires. What Lender requires pursuant to the preceding sentences can change during the term of the Loan. The insurance carrier providing the insurance shall be chosen by Borrower subject to Lender's right to disapprove Borrower's choice, which right shall not be exercised unreasonably. Lender may require Borrower to pay, in connection with this Loan, either: (a) a one-time charge for flood zone determination, certification and tracking services; or (b) a one-time charge for flood zone determination and certification services and subsequent charges each time remappings or similar changes occur which reasonably might affect such determination or certification. Borrower shall also be responsible for the payment of any fees imposed by the Federal Emergency Management Agency in connection with the review of any flood zone determination resulting from an objection by Borrower.

If Borrower fails to maintain any of the coverages described above, Lender may obtain insurance coverage, at Lender's option and Borrower's expense. Lender is under no obligation to purchase any particular type or amount of coverage. Therefore, such coverage shall cover Lender, but might or might not protect Borrower, Borrower's equity in the Property, or the contents of the Property, against any risk, hazard or liability and might provide greater or lesser coverage than was previously in effect. Borrower acknowledges that the cost of the insurance coverage so obtained might significantly exceed the cost of insurance that Borrower could have obtained. Any amounts disbursed by Lender under this Section 5 shall become additional debt of Borrower secured by this Security Instrument. These amounts shall bear interest at the Note rate from the date of disbursement and shall be payable, with such interest, upon notice from Lender to Borrower requesting payment.

TEXAS--Single Family--**Fannie Mae/Freddie Mac UNIFORM INSTRUMENT** **Form 3044 1/01** *(page 6 of 17 pages)*

the lender in most circumstances. (The due-on-sale issue, from both the borrower's and lender's perspectives, is discussed more in Chapter 14.) Texas courts have tended to uphold due-on-sale clauses.

At [14] is the acceleration clause. If the borrower breaks any of the mortgage covenants or note agreements, the lender wants the right to terminate the loan. The acceleration clause permits the lender to demand the balance to be paid in full immediately. If the borrower cannot pay, foreclosure takes place and the property is sold.

FIGURE 11.3 Deed of trust (*continued*)

All insurance policies required by Lender and renewals of such policies shall be subject to Lender's right to disapprove such policies, shall include a standard mortgage clause, and shall name Lender as mortgagee and/or as an additional loss payee. Lender shall have the right to hold the policies and renewal certificates. If Lender requires, Borrower shall promptly give to Lender all receipts of paid premiums and renewal notices. If Borrower obtains any form of insurance coverage, not otherwise required by Lender, for damage to, or destruction of, the Property, such policy shall include a standard mortgage clause and shall name Lender as mortgagee and/or as an additional loss payee.

In the event of loss, Borrower shall give prompt notice to the insurance carrier and Lender. Lender may make proof of loss if not made promptly by Borrower. Unless Lender and Borrower otherwise agree in writing, any insurance proceeds, whether or not the underlying insurance was required by Lender, shall be applied to restoration or repair of the Property, if the restoration or repair is economically feasible and Lender's security is not lessened. During such repair and restoration period, Lender shall have the right to hold such insurance proceeds until Lender has had an opportunity to inspect such Property to ensure the work has been completed to Lender's satisfaction, provided that such inspection shall be undertaken promptly. Lender may disburse proceeds for the repairs and restoration in a single payment or in a series of progress payments as the work is completed. Unless an agreement is made in writing or Applicable Law requires interest to be paid on such insurance proceeds, Lender shall not be required to pay Borrower any interest or earnings on such proceeds. Fees for public adjusters, or other third parties, retained by Borrower shall not be paid out of the insurance proceeds and shall be the sole obligation of Borrower. If the restoration or repair is not economically feasible or Lender's security would be lessened, the insurance proceeds shall be applied to the sums secured by this Security Instrument, whether or not then due, with the excess, if any, paid to Borrower. Such insurance proceeds shall be applied in the order provided for in Section 2.

If Borrower abandons the Property, Lender may file, negotiate and settle any available insurance claim and related matters. If Borrower does not respond within 30 days to a notice from Lender that the insurance carrier has offered to settle a claim, then Lender may negotiate and settle the claim. The 30-day period will begin when the notice is given. In either event, or if Lender acquires the Property under Section 22 or otherwise, Borrower hereby assigns to Lender (a) Borrower's rights to any insurance proceeds in an amount not to exceed the amounts unpaid under the Note or this Security Instrument, and (b) any other of Borrower's rights (other than the right to any refund of unearned premiums paid by Borrower) under all insurance policies covering the Property, insofar as such rights are applicable to the coverage of the Property. Lender may use the insurance proceeds either to repair or restore the Property or to pay amounts unpaid under the Note or this Security Instrument, whether or not then due.

6. Occupancy. Borrower shall occupy, establish, and use the Property as Borrower's principal residence within 60 days after the execution of this Security Instrument and shall continue to occupy the Property as Borrower's principal residence for at least one year after the date of occupancy, unless Lender otherwise agrees in writing, which consent shall not be unreasonably withheld, or unless extenuating circumstances exist which are beyond Borrower's control.

7. Preservation, Maintenance and Protection of the Property; Inspections. Borrower
[11] shall not destroy, damage or impair the Property, allow the Property to deteriorate or commit waste

TEXAS--Single Family--Fannie Mae/Freddie Mac UNIFORM INSTRUMENT Form 3044 1/01 *(page 7 of 17 pages)*

At [15] we have the release clause, which provides that the lender has the obligation to release the lien upon payment in full of the note secured by the deed of trust.

At [16], the mortgagor states that he has made this mortgage. Actually, the execution statement is more a formality than a requirement; the mortgagor's signature alone indicates his execution of the mortgage and agreement to its provisions. At [17], the mortgage is acknowledged and/or witnessed as required by state law for placement in the public records. Like deeds, mortgages must be recorded if they are to be effective against any subsequent purchaser, mortgagee,

FIGURE 11.3 Deed of trust (*continued*)

on the Property. Whether or not Borrower is residing in the Property, Borrower shall maintain the Property in order to prevent the Property from deteriorating or decreasing in value due to its condition. Unless it is determined pursuant to Section 5 that repair or restoration is not economically feasible, Borrower shall promptly repair the Property if damaged to avoid further deterioration or damage. If insurance or condemnation proceeds are paid in connection with damage to, or the taking
[12] of, the Property, Borrower shall be responsible for repairing or restoring the Property only if Lender has released proceeds for such purposes. Lender may disburse proceeds for the repairs and restoration in a single payment or in a series of progress payments as the work is completed. If the insurance or condemnation proceeds are not sufficient to repair or restore the Property, Borrower is not relieved of Borrower's obligation for the completion of such repair or restoration.

Lender or its agent may make reasonable entries upon and inspections of the Property. If it has reasonable cause, Lender may inspect the interior of the improvements on the Property. Lender shall give Borrower notice at the time of or prior to such an interior inspection specifying such reasonable cause.

8. Borrower's Loan Application. Borrower shall be in default if, during the Loan application process, Borrower or any persons or entities acting at the direction of Borrower or with Borrower's knowledge or consent gave materially false, misleading, or inaccurate information or statements to Lender (or failed to provide Lender with material information) in connection with the Loan. Material representations include, but are not limited to, representations concerning Borrower's occupancy of the Property as Borrower's principal residence.

9. Protection of Lender's Interest in the Property and Rights Under this Security Instrument. If (a) Borrower fails to perform the covenants and agreements contained in this Security Instrument, (b) there is a legal proceeding that might significantly affect Lender's interest in the Property and/or rights under this Security Instrument (such as a proceeding in bankruptcy, probate, for condemnation or forfeiture, for enforcement of a lien which may attain priority over this Security Instrument or to enforce laws or regulations), or (c) Borrower has abandoned the Property, then Lender may do and pay for whatever is reasonable or appropriate to protect Lender's interest in the Property and rights under this Security Instrument, including protecting and/or assessing the value of the Property, and securing and/or repairing the Property. Lender's actions can include, but are not limited to: (a) paying any sums secured by a lien which has priority over this Security Instrument; (b) appearing in court; and (c) paying reasonable attorneys' fees to protect its interest in the Property and/or rights under this Security Instrument, including its secured position in a bankruptcy proceeding. Securing the Property includes, but is not limited to, entering the Property to make repairs, change locks, replace or board up doors and windows, drain water from pipes, eliminate building or other code violations or dangerous conditions, and have utilities turned on or off. Although Lender may take action under this Section 9, Lender does not have to do so and is not under any duty or obligation to do so. It is agreed that Lender incurs no liability for not taking any or all actions authorized under this Section 9.

Any amounts disbursed by Lender under this Section 9 shall become additional debt of Borrower secured by this Security Instrument. These amounts shall bear interest at the Note rate from the date of disbursement and shall be payable, with such interest, upon notice from Lender to Borrower requesting payment.

TEXAS--Single Family--**Fannie Mae/Freddie Mac** UNIFORM INSTRUMENT **Form 3044 1/01** *(page 8 of 17 pages)*

or lessee. The reason the mortgage is recorded, but not the promissory note, is that the mortgage deals with rights and interests in real property, whereas the note represents a personal obligation.

Partial Release

Occasionally, the situation arises wherein the borrower wants the lender to release a portion of the mortgaged property from the mortgage after part of the loan has been repaid. This is known as asking for a **partial release.** For example, a land developer purchases 40 acres of land for a total price of $500,000 and

FIGURE 11.3 Deed of trust (*continued*)

If this Security Instrument is on a leasehold, Borrower shall comply with all the provisions of the lease. If Borrower acquires fee title to the Property, the leasehold and the fee title shall not merge unless Lender agrees to the merger in writing.

10. Mortgage Insurance. If Lender required Mortgage Insurance as a condition of making the Loan, Borrower shall pay the premiums required to maintain the Mortgage Insurance in effect. If, for any reason, the Mortgage Insurance coverage required by Lender ceases to be available from the mortgage insurer that previously provided such insurance and Borrower was required to make separately designated payments toward the premiums for Mortgage Insurance, Borrower shall pay the premiums required to obtain coverage substantially equivalent to the Mortgage Insurance previously in effect, at a cost substantially equivalent to the cost to Borrower of the Mortgage Insurance previously in effect, from an alternate mortgage insurer selected by Lender. If substantially equivalent Mortgage Insurance coverage is not available, Borrower shall continue to pay to Lender the amount of the separately designated payments that were due when the insurance coverage ceased to be in effect. Lender will accept, use and retain these payments as a non-refundable loss reserve in lieu of Mortgage Insurance. Such loss reserve shall be non-refundable, notwithstanding the fact that the Loan is ultimately paid in full, and Lender shall not be required to pay Borrower any interest or earnings on such loss reserve. Lender can no longer require loss reserve payments if Mortgage Insurance coverage (in the amount and for the period that Lender requires) provided by an insurer selected by Lender again becomes available, is obtained, and Lender requires separately designated payments toward the premiums for Mortgage Insurance. If Lender required Mortgage Insurance as a condition of making the Loan and Borrower was required to make separately designated payments toward the premiums for Mortgage Insurance, Borrower shall pay the premiums required to maintain Mortgage Insurance in effect, or to provide a non-refundable loss reserve, until Lender's requirement for Mortgage Insurance ends in accordance with any written agreement between Borrower and Lender providing for such termination or until termination is required by Applicable Law. Nothing in this Section 10 affects Borrower's obligation to pay interest at the rate provided in the Note.

Mortgage Insurance reimburses Lender (or any entity that purchases the Note) for certain losses it may incur if Borrower does not repay the Loan as agreed. Borrower is not a party to the Mortgage Insurance.

Mortgage insurers evaluate their total risk on all such insurance in force from time to time, and may enter into agreements with other parties that share or modify their risk, or reduce losses. These agreements are on terms and conditions that are satisfactory to the mortgage insurer and the other party (or parties) to these agreements. These agreements may require the mortgage insurer to make payments using any source of funds that the mortgage insurer may have available (which may include funds obtained from Mortgage Insurance premiums).

As a result of these agreements, Lender, any purchaser of the Note, another insurer, any reinsurer, any other entity, or any affiliate of any of the foregoing, may receive (directly or indirectly) amounts that derive from (or might be characterized as) a portion of Borrower's payments for Mortgage Insurance, in exchange for sharing or modifying the mortgage insurer's risk, or reducing losses. If such agreement provides that an affiliate of Lender takes a share of the insurer's risk in exchange for a share of the premiums paid to the insurer, the arrangement is often termed "captive reinsurance." Further:

TEXAS--Single Family--**Fannie Mae/Freddie Mac** UNIFORM INSTRUMENT   Form 3044 1/01 *(page 9 of 17 pages)*

finances the purchase with $100,000 in cash plus a mortgage and note for $400,000 to the seller. In the mortgage agreement the developer might ask that the seller release 10 acres free and clear of the mortgage encumbrance for each $100,000 paid against the loan.

"SUBJECT TO" CLAUSE

If an existing mortgage on a property does not contain a due-on-sale clause, the seller can pass the benefits of that financing along to the buyer. (This can

FIGURE 11.3 Deed of trust (*continued*)

(a) Any such agreements will not affect the amounts that Borrower has agreed to pay for Mortgage Insurance, or any other terms of the Loan. Such agreements will not increase the amount Borrower will owe for Mortgage Insurance, and they will not entitle Borrower to any refund.

(b) Any such agreements will not affect the rights Borrower has – if any – with respect to the Mortgage Insurance under the Homeowners Protection Act of 1998 or any other law. These rights may include the right to receive certain disclosures, to request and obtain cancellation of the Mortgage Insurance, to have the Mortgage Insurance terminated automatically, and/or to receive a refund of any Mortgage Insurance premiums that were unearned at the time of such cancellation or termination.

11. Assignment of Miscellaneous Proceeds; Forfeiture. All Miscellaneous Proceeds are hereby assigned to and shall be paid to Lender.

If the Property is damaged, such Miscellaneous Proceeds shall be applied to restoration or repair of the Property, if the restoration or repair is economically feasible and Lender's security is not lessened. During such repair and restoration period, Lender shall have the right to hold such Miscellaneous Proceeds until Lender has had an opportunity to inspect such Property to ensure the work has been completed to Lender's satisfaction, provided that such inspection shall be undertaken promptly. Lender may pay for the repairs and restoration in a single disbursement or in a series of progress payments as the work is completed. Unless an agreement is made in writing or Applicable Law requires interest to be paid on such Miscellaneous Proceeds, Lender shall not be required to pay Borrower any interest or earnings on such Miscellaneous Proceeds. If the restoration or repair is not economically feasible or Lender's security would be lessened, the Miscellaneous Proceeds shall be applied to the sums secured by this Security Instrument, whether or not then due, with the excess, if any, paid to Borrower. Such Miscellaneous Proceeds shall be applied in the order provided for in Section 2.

In the event of a total taking, destruction, or loss in value of the Property, the Miscellaneous Proceeds shall be applied to the sums secured by this Security Instrument, whether or not then due, with the excess, if any, paid to Borrower.

In the event of a partial taking, destruction, or loss in value of the Property in which the fair market value of the Property immediately before the partial taking, destruction, or loss in value is equal to or greater than the amount of the sums secured by this Security Instrument immediately before the partial taking, destruction, or loss in value, unless Borrower and Lender otherwise agree in writing, the sums secured by this Security Instrument shall be reduced by the amount of the Miscellaneous Proceeds multiplied by the following fraction: (a) the total amount of the sums secured immediately before the partial taking, destruction, or loss in value divided by (b) the fair market value of the Property immediately before the partial taking, destruction, or loss in value. Any balance shall be paid to Borrower.

In the event of a partial taking, destruction, or loss in value of the Property in which the fair market value of the Property immediately before the partial taking, destruction, or loss in value is less than the amount of the sums secured immediately before the partial taking, destruction, or loss in value, unless Borrower and Lender otherwise agree in writing, the Miscellaneous Proceeds shall be applied to the sums secured by this Security Instrument whether or not the sums are then due.

If the Property is abandoned by Borrower, or if, after notice by Lender to Borrower that the Opposing Party (as defined in the next sentence) offers to make an award to settle a claim for

TEXAS--Single Family--**Fannie Mae/Freddie Mac** UNIFORM INSTRUMENT Form 3044 1/01 *(page 10 of 17 pages)*

occur when the existing loan carries a lower rate of interest than currently available on new loans.) One method of doing this is for the buyer to purchase the property **subject to the existing loan.** In the purchase contract the buyer states that he is aware of the existence of the loan and the mortgage that secures it, but takes no personal liability for it. Although the buyer may pay the remaining loan payments as they come due, the seller continues to be personally liable to the lender for the loan. As long as the buyer faithfully continues to

FIGURE 11.3 Deed of trust (*continued*)

damages, Borrower fails to respond to Lender within 30 days after the date the notice is given, Lender is authorized to collect and apply the Miscellaneous Proceeds either to restoration or repair of the Property or to the sums secured by this Security Instrument, whether or not then due. "Opposing Party" means the third party that owes Borrower Miscellaneous Proceeds or the party against whom Borrower has a right of action in regard to Miscellaneous Proceeds.

Borrower shall be in default if any action or proceeding, whether civil or criminal, is begun that, in Lender's judgment, could result in forfeiture of the Property or other material impairment of Lender's interest in the Property or rights under this Security Instrument. Borrower can cure such a default and, if acceleration has occurred, reinstate as provided in Section 19, by causing the action or proceeding to be dismissed with a ruling that, in Lender's judgment, precludes forfeiture of the Property or other material impairment of Lender's interest in the Property or rights under this Security Instrument. The proceeds of any award or claim for damages that are attributable to the impairment of Lender's interest in the Property are hereby assigned and shall be paid to Lender.

All Miscellaneous Proceeds that are not applied to restoration or repair of the Property shall be applied in the order provided for in Section 2.

12. Borrower Not Released; Forbearance By Lender Not a Waiver. Extension of the time for payment or modification of amortization of the sums secured by this Security Instrument granted by Lender to Borrower or any Successor in Interest of Borrower shall not operate to release the liability of Borrower or any Successors in Interest of Borrower. Lender shall not be required to commence proceedings against any Successor in Interest of Borrower or to refuse to extend time for payment or otherwise modify amortization of the sums secured by this Security Instrument by reason of any demand made by the original Borrower or any Successors in Interest of Borrower. Any forbearance by Lender in exercising any right or remedy including, without limitation, Lender's acceptance of payments from third persons, entities or Successors in Interest of Borrower or in amounts less than the amount then due, shall not be a waiver of or preclude the exercise of any right or remedy.

13. Joint and Several Liability; Co-signers; Successors and Assigns Bound. Borrower covenants and agrees that Borrower's obligations and liability shall be joint and several. However, any Borrower who co-signs this Security Instrument but does not execute the Note (a "co-signer"): (a) is co-signing this Security Instrument only to mortgage, grant and convey the co-signer's interest in the Property under the terms of this Security Instrument; (b) is not personally obligated to pay the sums secured by this Security Instrument; and (c) agrees that Lender and any other Borrower can agree to extend, modify, forbear or make any accommodations with regard to the terms of this Security Instrument or the Note without the co-signer's consent.

Subject to the provisions of Section 18, any Successor in Interest of Borrower who assumes Borrower's obligations under this Security Instrument in writing, and is approved by Lender, shall obtain all of Borrower's rights and benefits under this Security Instrument. Borrower shall not be released from Borrower's obligations and liability under this Security Instrument unless Lender agrees to such release in writing. The covenants and agreements of this Security Instrument shall bind (except as provided in Section 20) and benefit the successors and assigns of Lender.

14. Loan Charges. Lender may charge Borrower fees for services performed in connection with Borrower's default, for the purpose of protecting Lender's interest in the Property and rights under this Security Instrument, including, but not limited to, attorneys' fees, property inspection and valuation fees. In regard to any other fees, the absence of express authority in this Security

TEXAS--Single Family--**Fannie Mae/Freddie Mac UNIFORM INSTRUMENT** **Form 3044 1/01** *(page 11 of 17 pages)*

make the loan payments, which he would normally do as long as the property is worth more than the debts against it, this arrangement presents no problem to the seller. However, if the buyer stops making payments before the loan is fully paid, even though it may be years later, in most states the lender can require the seller to pay the balance due plus interest. This is true even though the seller thought he was free of the loan because he sold the property.

FIGURE 11.3 Deed of trust (*continued*)

Instrument to charge a specific fee to Borrower shall not be construed as a prohibition on the charging of such fee. Lender may not charge fees that are expressly prohibited by this Security Instrument or by Applicable Law.

If the Loan is subject to a law which sets maximum loan charges, and that law is finally interpreted so that the interest or other loan charges collected or to be collected in connection with the Loan exceed the permitted limits, then: (a) any such loan charge shall be reduced by the amount necessary to reduce the charge to the permitted limit; and (b) any sums already collected from Borrower which exceeded permitted limits will be refunded to Borrower. Lender may choose to make this refund by reducing the principal owed under the Note or by making a direct payment to Borrower. If a refund reduces principal, the reduction will be treated as a partial prepayment without any prepayment charge (whether or not a prepayment charge is provided for under the Note). Borrower's acceptance of any such refund made by direct payment to Borrower will constitute a waiver of any right of action Borrower might have arising out of such overcharge.

15. Notices. All notices given by Borrower or Lender in connection with this Security Instrument must be in writing. Any notice to Borrower in connection with this Security Instrument shall be deemed to have been given to Borrower when mailed by first class mail or when actually delivered to Borrower's notice address if sent by other means. Notice to any one Borrower shall constitute notice to all Borrowers unless Applicable Law expressly requires otherwise. The notice address shall be the Property Address unless Borrower has designated a substitute notice address by notice to Lender. Borrower shall promptly notify Lender of Borrower's change of address. If Lender specifies a procedure for reporting Borrower's change of address, then Borrower shall only report a change of address through that specified procedure. There may be only one designated notice address under this Security Instrument at any one time. Any notice to Lender shall be given by delivering it or by mailing it by first class mail to Lender's address stated herein unless Lender has designated another address by notice to Borrower. Any notice in connection with this Security Instrument shall not be deemed to have been given to Lender until actually received by Lender. If any notice required by this Security Instrument is also required under Applicable Law, the Applicable Law requirement will satisfy the corresponding requirement under this Security Instrument.

16. Governing Law; Severability; Rules of Construction. This Security Instrument shall be governed by federal law and the law of the jurisdiction in which the Property is located. All rights and obligations contained in this Security Instrument are subject to any requirements and limitations of Applicable Law. Applicable Law might explicitly or implicitly allow the parties to agree by contract or it might be silent, but such silence shall not be construed as a prohibition against agreement by contract. In the event that any provision or clause of this Security Instrument or the Note conflicts with Applicable Law, such conflict shall not affect other provisions of this Security Instrument or the Note which can be given effect without the conflicting provision.

As used in this Security Instrument: (a) words of the masculine gender shall mean and include corresponding neuter words or words of the feminine gender; (b) words in the singular shall mean and include the plural and vice versa; and (c) the word "may" gives sole discretion without any obligation to take any action.

17. Borrower's Copy. Borrower shall be given one copy of the Note and of this Security Instrument.

TEXAS--Single Family--**Fannie Mae/Freddie Mac UNIFORM INSTRUMENT** **Form 3044 1/01** *(page 12 of 17 pages)*

ASSUMPTION OF THE LOAN

The seller is on somewhat different ground if he requires the buyer to **assume the loan.** Under this agreement, the buyer promises in writing to the seller that he will pay the loan, thus personally obligating himself. In the event of default on the loan or a breach of the mortgage agreement, the lender will first expect the buyer to remedy the problem. If the buyer does not pay, the lender will look to the seller, because the seller is still liable on the original promissory note.

FIGURE 11.3 Deed of trust (*continued*)

18. Transfer of the Property or a Beneficial Interest in Borrower. As used in this Section 18, "Interest in the Property" means any legal or beneficial interest in the Property,
[13] including, but not limited to, those beneficial interests transferred in a bond for deed, contract for deed, installment sales contract or escrow agreement, the intent of which is the transfer of title by Borrower at a future date to a purchaser.

If all or any part of the Property or any Interest in the Property is sold or transferred (or if Borrower is not a natural person and a beneficial interest in Borrower is sold or transferred) without Lender's prior written consent, Lender may require immediate payment in full of all sums secured by this Security Instrument. However, this option shall not be exercised by Lender if such exercise is prohibited by Applicable Law.

If Lender exercises this option, Lender shall give Borrower notice of acceleration. The notice shall provide a period of not less than 30 days from the date the notice is given in accordance with Section 15 within which Borrower must pay all sums secured by this Security Instrument. If Borrower fails to pay these sums prior to the expiration of this period, Lender may invoke any remedies permitted by this Security Instrument without further notice or demand on Borrower.

19. Borrower's Right to Reinstate After Acceleration. If Borrower meets certain conditions, Borrower shall have the right to have enforcement of this Security Instrument discontinued at any time prior to the earliest of: (a) five days before sale of the Property pursuant to any power of sale contained in this Security Instrument; (b) such other period as Applicable Law might specify for the termination of Borrower's right to reinstate; or (c) entry of a judgment enforcing this Security Instrument. Those conditions are that Borrower: (a) pays Lender all sums which then would be due under this Security Instrument and the Note as if no acceleration had occurred; (b) cures any default of any other covenants or agreements; (c) pays all expenses incurred in enforcing this Security Instrument, including, but not limited to, reasonable attorneys' fees, property inspection and valuation fees, and other fees incurred for the purpose of protecting Lender's interest in the Property and rights under this Security Instrument; and (d) takes such action as Lender may reasonably require to assure that Lender's interest in the Property and rights under this Security Instrument, and Borrower's obligation to pay the sums secured by this Security Instrument, shall continue unchanged. Lender may require that Borrower pay such reinstatement sums and expenses in one or more of the following forms, as selected by Lender: (a) cash; (b) money order; (c) certified check, bank check, treasurer's check or cashier's check, provided any such check is drawn upon an institution whose deposits are insured by a federal agency, instrumentality or entity; or (d) Electronic Funds Transfer. Upon reinstatement by Borrower, this Security Instrument and obligations secured hereby shall remain fully effective as if no acceleration had occurred. However, this right to reinstate shall not apply in the case of acceleration under Section 18.

20. Sale of Note; Change of Loan Servicer; Notice of Grievance. The Note or a partial interest in the Note (together with this Security Instrument) can be sold one or more times without prior notice to Borrower. A sale might result in a change in the entity (known as the "Loan Servicer") that collects Periodic Payments due under the Note and this Security Instrument and performs other mortgage loan servicing obligations under the Note, this Security Instrument, and Applicable Law. There also might be one or more changes of the Loan Servicer unrelated to a sale of the Note. If there is a change of the Loan Servicer, Borrower will be given written notice of the change which will state the name and address of the new Loan Servicer, the address to which payments should be made and any other information RESPA requires in connection with a notice

TEXAS--Single Family--Fannie Mae/Freddie Mac UNIFORM INSTRUMENT Form 3044 1/01 (*page 13 of 17 pages*)

Deed of Trust to Secure Assumption

In the event the grantor under a deed of trust wants to sell the property and allow the purchaser to assume the obligations of that deed of trust, the TREC-promulgated forms require that the proposed purchaser execute a deed of trust in favor of the grantor to secure the assumption. An example of a deed of trust to secure an assumption is shown in Figure 11.4. In this instrument, we will assume that the parties, N. Debted and wife May B. Debted, have conveyed their

FIGURE 11.3 Deed of trust (*continued*)

of transfer of servicing. If the Note is sold and thereafter the Loan is serviced by a Loan Servicer other than the purchaser of the Note, the mortgage loan servicing obligations to Borrower will remain with the Loan Servicer or be transferred to a successor Loan Servicer and are not assumed by the Note purchaser unless otherwise provided by the Note purchaser.

Neither Borrower nor Lender may commence, join, or be joined to any judicial action (as either an individual litigant or the member of a class) that arises from the other party's actions pursuant to this Security Instrument or that alleges that the other party has breached any provision of, or any duty owed by reason of, this Security Instrument, until such Borrower or Lender has notified the other party (with such notice given in compliance with the requirements of Section 15) of such alleged breach and afforded the other party hereto a reasonable period after the giving of such notice to take corrective action. If Applicable Law provides a time period which must elapse before certain action can be taken, that time period will be deemed to be reasonable for purposes of this paragraph. The notice of acceleration and opportunity to cure given to Borrower pursuant to Section 22 and the notice of acceleration given to Borrower pursuant to Section 18 shall be deemed to satisfy the notice and opportunity to take corrective action provisions of this Section 20.

21. Hazardous Substances. As used in this Section 21: (a) "Hazardous Substances" are those substances defined as toxic or hazardous substances, pollutants, or wastes by Environmental Law and the following substances: gasoline, kerosene, other flammable or toxic petroleum products, toxic pesticides and herbicides, volatile solvents, materials containing asbestos or formaldehyde, and radioactive materials; (b) "Environmental Law" means federal laws and laws of the jurisdiction where the Property is located that relate to health, safety or environmental protection; (c) "Environmental Cleanup" includes any response action, remedial action, or removal action, as defined in Environmental Law; and (d) an "Environmental Condition" means a condition that can cause, contribute to, or otherwise trigger an Environmental Cleanup.

Borrower shall not cause or permit the presence, use, disposal, storage, or release of any Hazardous Substances, or threaten to release any Hazardous Substances, on or in the Property. Borrower shall not do, nor allow anyone else to do, anything affecting the Property (a) that is in violation of any Environmental Law, (b) which creates an Environmental Condition, or (c) which, due to the presence, use, or release of a Hazardous Substance, creates a condition that adversely affects the value of the Property. The preceding two sentences shall not apply to the presence, use, or storage on the Property of small quantities of Hazardous Substances that are generally recognized to be appropriate to normal residential uses and to maintenance of the Property (including, but not limited to, hazardous substances in consumer products).

Borrower shall promptly give Lender written notice of (a) any investigation, claim, demand, lawsuit or other action by any governmental or regulatory agency or private party involving the Property and any Hazardous Substance or Environmental Law of which Borrower has actual knowledge, (b) any Environmental Condition, including but not limited to, any spilling, leaking, discharge, release or threat of release of any Hazardous Substance, and (c) any condition caused by the presence, use or release of a Hazardous Substance which adversely affects the value of the Property. If Borrower learns, or is notified by any governmental or regulatory authority, or any private party, that any removal or other remediation of any Hazardous Substance affecting the Property is necessary, Borrower shall promptly take all necessary remedial actions in accordance with Environmental Law. Nothing herein shall create any obligation on Lender for an Environmental Cleanup.

TEXAS--Single Family--**Fannie Mae/Freddie Mac UNIFORM INSTRUMENT** **Form 3044 1/01** *(page 14 of 17 pages)*

property to Chuck Roast and wife Berna. The only significant difference between Figure 11.4 and Figure 11.3 is the obligation secured. Instead of securing a real estate lien note, Figure 11.4 secures the assumption of an existing note. The grantors, Mr. and Mrs. Debted, become the beneficiaries under this Deed of Trust to Secure Assumption.

There has been little Texas law to date regarding the use of the Deed of Trust to Secure Assumption form. In practice, if the purchaser defaults, the sellers probably are unaware of it. However, because the Texas statutes for

FIGURE 11.3 Deed of trust (*continued*)

NON-UNIFORM COVENANTS. Borrower and Lender further covenant and agree as follows:

22. Acceleration; Remedies. Lender shall give notice to Borrower prior to acceleration following Borrower's breach of any covenant or agreement in this Security Instrument (but
[14] not prior to acceleration under Section 18 unless Applicable Law provides otherwise). The notice shall specify: (a) the default; (b) the action required to cure the default; (c) a date, not less than 30 days from the date the notice is given to Borrower, by which the default must be cured; and (d) that failure to cure the default on or before the date specified in the notice will result in acceleration of the sums secured by this Security Instrument and sale of the Property. The notice shall further inform Borrower of the right to reinstate after acceleration and the right to bring a court action to assert the non-existence of a default or any other defense of Borrower to acceleration and sale. If the default is not cured on or before the date specified in the notice, Lender at its option may require immediate payment in full of all sums secured by this Security Instrument without further demand and may invoke the power of sale and any other remedies permitted by Applicable Law. Lender shall be entitled to collect all expenses incurred in pursuing the remedies provided in this Section 22, including, but not limited to, reasonable attorneys' fees and costs of title evidence. For the purposes of this Section 22, the term "Lender" includes any holder of the Note who is entitled to receive payments under the Note.

If Lender invokes the power of sale, Lender or Trustee shall give notice of the time, place and terms of sale by posting and filing the notice at least 21 days prior to sale as provided by Applicable Law. Lender shall mail a copy of the notice to Borrower in the manner prescribed by Applicable Law. Sale shall be made at public vendue. The sale must begin at the time stated in the notice of sale or not later than three hours after that time and between the hours of 10 a.m. and 4 p.m. on the first Tuesday of the month. Borrower authorizes Trustee to sell the Property to the highest bidder for cash in one or more parcels and in any order Trustee determines. Lender or its designee may purchase the Property at any sale.

Trustee shall deliver to the purchaser Trustee's deed conveying indefeasible title to the Property with covenants of general warranty from Borrower. Borrower covenants and agrees to defend generally the purchaser's title to the Property against all claims and demands. The recitals in the Trustee's deed shall be prima facie evidence of the truth of the statements made therein. Trustee shall apply the proceeds of the sale in the following order: (a) to all expenses of the sale, including, but not limited to, reasonable Trustee's and attorneys' fees; (b) to all sums secured by this Security Instrument; and (c) any excess to the person or persons legally entitled to it.

If the Property is sold pursuant to this Section 22, Borrower or any person holding possession of the Property through Borrower shall immediately surrender possession of the Property to the purchaser at that sale. If possession is not surrendered, Borrower or such person shall be a tenant at sufferance and may be removed by writ of possession or other court proceeding.

23. Release. Upon payment of all sums secured by this Security Instrument, Lender shall
[15] provide a release of this Security Instrument to Borrower or Borrower's designated agent in accordance with Applicable Law. Borrower shall pay any recordation costs. Lender may charge

TEXAS--Single Family--Fannie Mae/Freddie Mac UNIFORM INSTRUMENT Form 3044 1/01 *(page 15 of 17 pages)*

foreclosures under a deed of trust specify that "each debtor" must receive written notice of the proposed sale, it is assumed that the sellers, who are the original debtors on the deed of trust and promissory note, would be given notice of such sale. This would give them the right to pay the obligation or buy the property at the foreclosure sale.

At best, the Assumption form purports to give the seller of the property some tangible equity in the property. Note the paragraph specifying default in the payment of the note being assumed. The seller (the beneficiary) may, at his option,

FIGURE 11.3 Deed of trust (*continued*)

Borrower a fee for releasing this Security Instrument, but only if the fee is paid to a third party for services rendered and the charging of the fee is permitted under Applicable Law.

24. Substitute Trustee; Trustee Liability. All rights, remedies and duties of Trustee under this Security Instrument may be exercised or performed by one or more trustees acting alone or together. Lender, at its option and with or without cause, may from time to time, by power of attorney or otherwise, remove or substitute any trustee, add one or more trustees, or appoint a successor trustee to any Trustee without the necessity of any formality other than a designation by Lender in writing. Without any further act or conveyance of the Property the substitute, additional or successor trustee shall become vested with the title, rights, remedies, powers and duties conferred upon Trustee herein and by Applicable Law.

Trustee shall not be liable if acting upon any notice, request, consent, demand, statement or other document believed by Trustee to be correct. Trustee shall not be liable for any act or omission unless such act or omission is willful.

25. Subrogation. Any of the proceeds of the Note used to take up outstanding liens against all or any part of the Property have been advanced by Lender at Borrower's request and upon Borrower's representation that such amounts are due and are secured by valid liens against the Property. Lender shall be subrogated to any and all rights, superior titles, liens and equities owned or claimed by any owner or holder of any outstanding liens and debts, regardless of whether said liens or debts are acquired by Lender by assignment or are released by the holder thereof upon payment.

26. Partial Invalidity. In the event any portion of the sums intended to be secured by this Security Instrument cannot be lawfully secured hereby, payments in reduction of such sums shall be applied first to those portions not secured hereby.

27. Purchase Money; Owelty of Partition; Renewal and Extension of Liens Against Homestead Property; Acknowledgment of Cash Advanced Against Non-Homestead Property. Check box as applicable:

☐ **Purchase Money.**

The funds advanced to Borrower under the Note were used to pay all or part of the purchase price of the Property. The Note also is primarily secured by the vendor's lien retained in the deed of even date with this Security Instrument conveying the Property to Borrower, which vendor's lien has been assigned to Lender, this Security Instrument being additional security for such vendor's lien.

☐ **Owelty of Partition.**

The Note represents funds advanced by Lender at the special instance and request of Borrower for the purpose of acquiring the entire fee simple title to the Property and the existence of an owelty of partition imposed against the entirety of the Property by a court order or by a written agreement of the parties to the partition to secure the payment of the Note is expressly acknowledged, confessed and granted.

☐ **Renewal and Extension of Liens Against Homestead Property.**

The Note is in renewal and extension, but not in extinguishment, of the indebtedness described on the attached Renewal and Extension Exhibit which is incorporated by reference. Lender is expressly subrogated to all rights, liens and remedies securing the original holder of a note evidencing Borrower's indebtedness and the original liens securing the indebtedness are renewed and extended to the date of maturity of the Note in renewal and extension of the indebtedness.

TEXAS--Single Family--**Fannie Mae/Freddie Mac UNIFORM INSTRUMENT** **Form 3044 1/01** *(page 16 of 17 pages)*

advance and pay the sums required to cure any such default. The grantors (purchasers of the property) must reimburse the beneficiaries (sellers of the property) within five days. If this is not done, the beneficiaries may exercise their right to foreclose under the power of sale clause.

The Deed of Trust to Secure Assumption form is intended to be used in conjunction with an assumption deed. An assumption deed is similar to other deeds, except that for consideration it specifies that the grantee is to assume the obligations of the note and deed of trust signed by the grantor.

FIGURE 11.3 Deed of trust (*continued*)

☐ **Acknowledgment of Cash Advanced Against Non-Homestead Property.**
The Note represents funds advanced to Borrower on this day at Borrower's request and Borrower acknowledges receipt of such funds. Borrower states that Borrower does not now and does not intend ever to reside on, use in any manner, or claim the Property secured by this Security Instrument as a business or residential homestead. Borrower disclaims all homestead rights, interests and exemptions related to the Property.

28. Loan Not a Home Equity Loan. The Loan evidenced by the Note is not an extension of credit as defined by Section 50(a)(6) or Section 50(a)(7), Article XVI, of the Texas Constitution. If the Property is used as Borrower's residence, then Borrower agrees that Borrower will receive no cash from the Loan evidenced by the Note and that any advances not necessary to purchase the Property, extinguish an owelty lien, complete construction, or renew and extend a prior lien against the Property, will be used to reduce the balance evidenced by the Note or such Loan will be modified to evidence the correct Loan balance, at Lender's option. Borrower agrees to execute any documentation necessary to comply with this Section 28.

BY SIGNING BELOW, Borrower accepts and agrees to the terms and covenants contained
[16] in this Security Instrument and in any Rider executed by Borrower and recorded with it.

Witnesses:

__________________ __________________(Seal)
N. Debted - Borrower
Social Security Number __________

__________________ __________________(Seal)
May B. Debted - Borrower
Social Security Number __________

[Space Below This Line For Acknowledgment]

State of Texas §
County of §

[17] Before me, a Notary Public, on this day personally appeared

known to me (or proved to me through __________
(description of identity card or other document)) to be the person whose name is subscribed to the foregoing instrument and acknowledged to me that he executed the same for the purposes and consideration therein expressed.

Given under my hand and seal of office this day of , A.D.,

(Seal) __________________
Notary Public

____
Title of Officer

My Commission Expires: __________

Initials: ___ ___ ___ ___

TEXAS--Single Family--Fannie Mae/Freddie Mac UNIFORM INSTRUMENT Form 3044 1/01 *(page 17 of 17 pages)*

NOVATION

The safest arrangement for the seller is to ask the lender to substitute the buyer's liability for his. This releases the seller from the personal obligation created by his promissory note, and the lender can now require only the buyer to repay the loan. The seller is also on safe ground if the mortgage agreement or state law prohibits ***deficiency judgments***, a topic that will be explained later in this chapter.

FIGURE 11.4 Deed of trust to secure assumption

DEED OF TRUST TO SECURE ASSUMPTION

THE STATE OF TEXAS §
§ KNOW ALL MEN BY THESE PRESENTS:
COUNTY OF HARRIS §

THAT Chuck Roast and wife, Berna Roast, of County, Texas, hereinafter called Grantor (whether one or more) for the purpose of securing the indebtedness hereinafter described, and in consideration of the sum of TEN DOLLARS ($10.00) to us in hand paid by the Trustee hereinafter named, the receipt of which is hereby acknowledged, and for the further consideration of the uses, purposes and trusts hereinafter set forth, have granted, sold and conveyed, and by these presents do grant, sell and convey unto Chuck J. Jacobus, Trustee, whose address is 6800 West Loop South, Suite 1800, Bellaire, Harris County, Texas, and his substitutes or successors, all of the following described property situated in Harris County, Texas, to-wit:

TO HAVE AND TO HOLD the above described property, together with the rights, privileges and appurtenances thereto belonging, unto the said Trustee and to his substitutes or successors forever. And Grantor does hereby bind Grantor, Grantor's heirs, executors, administrators and assigns to warrant and forever defend the said premises unto the said Trustee, Trustee's substitutes or successors and assigns forever, against the claim or claims, of all persons claiming or to claim the same or any part thereof.

This conveyance, however, is made in TRUST for the following purposes:

WHEREAS, N. Debted and wife, May B. Debted, hereinafter called Beneficiary, by deed of even date herewith conveyed the above described property to Grantor named herein, who, as part of the consideration therefore assumed and promised to pay, according to the terms thereof, all principal and interest remaining unpaid upon that one certain promissory note in the original principal sum of $83,000.00 dated February 21, 2002, executed by N. Debted and May B. Debted, and payable to the order of Mort Gage's Mortgage Company, which said note is secured by a Deed of Trust recorded under Clerk's File No. H99999 of the Official Public Records of Real Property of Harris County, Texas, the obligations and covenants of the Grantor named in said Deed of Trust were also assumed by Grantor named herein, and in said Deed the superior title and a vendor's lien were expressly reserved and retained by Beneficiary until said indebtedness and obligations so assumed are fully paid and satisfied, and should Grantor do and perform all of the obligations and covenants so assumed and make prompt payment of the indebtedness evidenced by said note so assumed as the same shall become due and payable, then this conveyance shall become null and void and of no further force and effect, it being agreed that a release of such indebtedness so assumed and of the liens securing the same by the legal owner and holder thereof prior to the advancement and payment thereon by Beneficiary of any sum or sums required to cure any default, shall be sufficient to release the lien created by this instrument as well as said vendor's lien so

Source: © 2012 Cengage Learning

When a buyer is to continue making payments on an existing loan, he will want to know exactly how much is still owing. An **estoppel certificate** (also called a **mortgagee's information letter**) is prepared by the lender to show how much of the loan remains to be paid. If a recorded mortgage states that it secures a loan for $35,000, but the borrower has reduced the amount owed to $25,000, the certificate will show that $25,000 remains to be paid. This is also used when the holder of a mortgage loan sells it to another investor. In it, the borrower is asked to verify the amount still owed and the rate of interest.

FIGURE 11.4 Deed of trust to secure assumption (*continued*)

retained, without the joinder of Beneficiary. Unless, prior to the filing of a release of the indebtedness so assumed and of the liens securing the same in the office of the County Clerk of the County where said real property is situated, Beneficiary shall have filed in the office of the County Clerk of said County a sworn statement duly acknowledged and containing a legal description of the property hereinafter described and setting forth any and all sums that Beneficiary may have so advanced and paid, it shall be conclusively presumed that no sum or sums have been advanced and paid thereon by Beneficiary.

Grantor agrees that in the event of default in the payment of any installment, principal or interest, of the note so assumed by Grantors, or in the event of default in the payment of said note when due or declared due, or of a breach of any of the obligations or covenants contained in the Deed of Trust securing said note so assumed, Beneficiary may advance and pay such sum or sums as may be required to cure any such default, and that any and all such sums so advanced and paid by Beneficiary to cure such default shall be paid by Grantors to Beneficiary at Piggy National Bank in the City of Houston, Harris County, Texas, within five days after the date of such payment, without notice or demand, which are expressly waived. Grantor covenants to pay promptly to Beneficiary, without notice or demand, within the time and as provided in the foregoing paragraph, any and all sums that may, under the provisions of the foregoing paragraph, be due Beneficiary.

In the event of a breach of the foregoing covenant, it shall thereupon, or at any time thereafter, be the duty of the Trustee, or his successor or substitute as hereinafter provided, at the request of Beneficiary (which request is hereby conclusively presumed), to enforce this Trust, and after advertising the time, place and terms of the sale of the above-described and conveyed property, then subject to the lien hereof and mailing and filing notices, all as required by Section 51.002 Texas Property Code, as then amended, and otherwise complying with that statute, the Trustee shall sell the above-described property, then subject to the lien hereof, at public auction in accordance with such notices on the first Tuesday in any month between the hours of 10:00 a.m. and 4:00 p.m., to the highest bidder for cash, selling all of the property as an entirety or in such parcels as the Trustee acting may elect, and make due conveyance to the Purchaser or Purchasers, with general warranty binding Grantor, Grantor's executors, administrators, heirs, successors and assigns; and out of the money arising from such sale, the Trustee acting shall pay first, all the expenses of advertising the sale and making the conveyance, including a commission of five percent to Trustee which commission shall be due and owing in addition to the attorney's fees provided for in said note, and then to Beneficiary the full amount of principal, interest, attorney's fees and other charges due and unpaid on said note and all other indebtedness secured hereby, rendering the balance of the sales price, if any, to Grantor, Grantor's heirs, executors, administrators, successors or assigns; and the recitals in the conveyance to Purchaser or Purchasers shall be full and conclusive evidence of the truth of the matter therein stated, and all prerequisites to said sale shall be presumed to have been performed, and such sale and conveyance shall be conclusive against Grantor, Grantor's heirs, executors, administrators, successors or assigns.

Beneficiary shall have the right to purchase at any sale of the property, being the

DEBT PRIORITIES

The same property can usually be pledged as collateral for more than one mortgage. This presents no problems to the lenders involved as long as the borrower makes the required payments on each note secured by the property. The difficulty arises when a default occurs on one or more of the loans, and the price the property brings at its foreclosure sale does not cover all the loans against it. As a result, a priority system is necessary. The debt with the highest priority is satisfied first from the foreclosure sale proceeds, and then the next highest priority debt is

FIGURE 11.4 Deed of trust to secure assumption (*continued*)

highest bidder and to have the amount for which such property is sold credited on the total sums owed Beneficiary.

Beneficiary is hereby authorized to appoint a substitute trustee, or a successor trustee, to act instead of the Trustee named herein without other formality than the designation in writing of a substitute or successor trustee; and the authority hereby conferred shall extend to the appointment of other successor and substitute trustees successively until the full and final payment and satisfaction of the indebtedness and obligations so assumed by Grantor; and each substitute and successor trustee shall succeed to all of the rights and powers of the original Trustee named herein.

Beneficiary may institute suit to enforce the provisions of this Deed of Trust and for the foreclosure of this Deed of Trust lien.

The term "Grantor" used in this instrument shall also include any and all successors in interest of Grantor to all or any part of the herein described and conveyed property as well as any and all purchasers thereof at any sale made hereunder by the Trustee or Substitute Trustee, and the provisions of this Deed of Trust shall be covenants running with the land.

It is expressly stipulated that the liability of Grantor to Beneficiary, arising by virtue of the assumption by Grantor of the payment of the note herein described and of the obligations of the Deed of Trust securing said note, as well as the liability to Beneficiary of any and all persons hereafter assuming payment of said note and performance of the obligations of said Deed of Trust, shall in no way be discharged or released by this instrument or by the exercise by Beneficiary of the rights and remedies herein provided for it being agreed that this instrument and all rights and remedies herein accorded Beneficiary are cumulative of any and all other rights and remedies existing at law.

Grantor expressly represents that any indebtedness becoming due and payable under and by virtue of the terms and provisions of this Deed of Trust is in part payment of the purchase price of the herein described and conveyed property and that this Deed of Trust is cumulative and in addition to the Vendor's Lien expressly retained in deed of even date herewith executed by Beneficiary to Grantor, and it is expressly agreed that Beneficiary may foreclose under either, or both, of said liens as Beneficiary may elect, without waiving the other, said deed hereinbefore mentioned, together with its record, being here referred to and made a part of this instrument.

In the event any sale is made of the above-described property, or any portion thereof, under the terms of this Deed of Trust, Grantor, Grantor's heirs and assigns, shall forthwith upon the making of such sale surrender and deliver possession of the property so sold to the Purchase at such sale, and in the event of their failure to do so they shall thereupon from and after the making of such sale be and continue as tenants at will of such Purchaser, and in the event of their failure to surrender possession of said property upon demand, the Purchaser, his heirs or assigns, shall be entitled to institute and maintain an action for forcible detainer of said property in the Justice of Peace Court in the Justice

satisfied, then the next, until either the foreclosure sale proceeds are exhausted or all debts secured by the property are satisfied.

First Lien Mortgage

In the vast majority of foreclosures, the sale proceeds are not sufficient to pay all the outstanding debt against the property; thus, it becomes extremely important that a lender know its priority position before making a loan. Unless there is a compelling reason otherwise, a lender will want to be in the most senior position possible. This is normally accomplished by being the first lender to record a mortgage against a property that is otherwise free and clear of mortgage debt; this

FIGURE 11.4 Deed of trust to secure assumption (*continued*)

Precinct in which such property, or any part thereof, is situated.

Grantor represents and warrants and covenants and agrees that (i) Grantor has not used and will not use and, to the best of Grantor's knowledge, no prior owner or current or prior tenant, subtenant, or other occupant of all or any part of the Property has used or is using hazardous material (as that term is hereinafter defined) on, from or affecting the Property in any manner that violates any laws pertaining to hazardous materials applicable to Grantor or to the Property; (ii) to the best of Grantor's knowledge, no hazardous materials have been disposed of on the Property nor have any hazardous materials migrated onto the Property, in either event in violation of any laws pertaining to hazardous materials applicable to Grantor or to the Property; and (iii) Grantor will not permit or suffer any such violation of any laws pertaining to hazardous materials applicable to Grantor or to the Property.

In the event that any investigation, site monitoring, containment, clean-up, removal, restoration or other remedial work of any kind or nature (hereinafter referred to as the "remedial work") is required under any laws pertaining to hazardous materials applicable to Grantor or to the Property, because of, or in connection with, the current or future presence, suspected presence, release or suspected release of a hazardous material in or about the air, soil, ground water, surface water or soil vapor at, on, about, under or within the Property (or any portion thereof), Grantor shall within the time periods required by the applicable laws pertaining to hazardous materials, commence and thereafter diligently prosecute to completion, all such remedial work. All remedial work shall be performed by contractors reasonably approved in advance by Lender and under the supervision of a consulting engineer reasonably approved by Lender. All costs and expenses of such remedial work shall be paid by Grantor including, without limitation, Lender's reasonable attorneys' fees and costs incurred in connection with monitoring or review of such remedial work. In the event Grantor shall fail to timely prosecute to completion such remedial work, Lender may, but shall not be required to, cause such remedial work to be performed and all costs and expenses thereof or incurred in connection therewith, shall be immediately due and payable by Grantor to Lender and shall become part of the indebtedness.

Grantor shall provide Lender with prompt written notice (a) upon Grantor's becoming aware of any release or threat of release of any hazardous materials upon, under or from the Property in violation of any laws pertaining to hazardous materials applicable to Grantor or to the Property, (b) upon Grantor's receipt of any notice from any federal, state, municipal or other governmental agency or authority in connection with any hazardous materials located upon or under or emanating from the Property; and (c) upon Grantor's obtaining knowledge of any incurrence of expense, for which Grantor or the Property could be liable, by any governmental agency or authority in connection with the assessment, containment or removal of any hazardous materials located upon or under or emanating from the Property.

This Deed of Trust lien shall be subordinate and inferior to any purchase money lien hereafter created.

---

lender is said to hold a **first lien mortgage** on the property. If the same property is later used to secure another note before the first is fully satisfied, the new mortgage is a **second lien mortgage,** and so on. The first mortgage is also known as the **senior mortgage.** Any mortgage with a lower priority is a ***junior mortgage.*** As time passes and higher priority mortgages are satisfied, the lower priority mortgages move up in priority. Thus, if a property is secured by a first and a second mortgage and the first is paid off, the second becomes a first mortgage. Note that nothing is stamped or written on a mortgage document to indicate whether it is a first or second or third mortgage, etc. That priority can be determined only

FIGURE 11.4 Deed of trust to secure assumption (*continued*)

EXECUTED this 21st day of February, 2004.

GRANTOR:

____
Chuck Roast

____
Berna Roast

THE STATE OF TEXAS §
§
COUNTY OF HARRIS §

This instrument was acknowledged before me on this the Twenty-First day of February, 2004.

____
NOTARY PUBLIC, STATE OF TEXAS

THE STATE OF TEXAS §
§
COUNTY OF HARRIS §

This instrument was acknowledged before me on this the Twenty-First day of February, 2004.

____
NOTARY PUBLIC, STATE OF TEXAS

by searching the public records for mortgages recorded against the property that have not been released.

Subordination

Sometimes a lender will voluntarily take a lower priority position than he would otherwise be entitled to by virtue of his recording date. This is known as ***subordination*** and it allows a junior loan to move up in priority. For example, the holder of a first mortgage can volunteer to become a second mortgagee and allow the second mortgage to move into the first position. Although it seems irrational that a lender would actually volunteer to lower his priority position, it is sometimes done by landowners to encourage developers to buy their land.

Chattel Liens

An interesting situation regarding priority occurs when chattels are bought on credit and then affixed to land that is already mortgaged. If the chattels are not paid for, can the chattel lienholder come onto the land and remove them? If there is default on the mortgage loan against the land, are the chattels sold as fixtures? The solution is for the chattel lienholder to record a chattel mortgage or a **financing statement.** This protects the lienholder's interest even though the chattel becomes a fixture when it is affixed to land.

THE FORECLOSURE PROCESS

Although relatively few mortgages are foreclosed, it is important to have a basic understanding of what happens when ***foreclosure*** takes place. First, knowledge of what causes foreclosure can help in avoiding it; and, second, if foreclosure does occur, one should know the rights of the parties involved.

Although noncompliance with any part of the mortgage agreement by the borrower can result in the lender calling the entire balance immediately due, in most cases foreclosure occurs because the note is not being repaid on time. When a borrower is behind in payments, the loan is said to be **delinquent** or **nonperforming.** At this stage, rather than presume foreclosure is automatically the next step, the borrower and lender usually meet and attempt to work out an alternative payment program. Contrary to early motion picture plots in which lenders seem anxious to foreclose their mortgages, today's lender considers foreclosure to be the last resort. This is because the foreclosure process is time-consuming, expensive, and unprofitable. The lender would much rather have the borrower make regular payments. Consequently, if a borrower is behind in loan payments, the lender prefers to arrange a new, stretched-out, payment schedule rather than immediately to declare the acceleration clause in effect and move toward foreclosing the borrower's rights to the property.

If a borrower realizes that stretching out payments is not going to solve his financial problem, instead of presuming foreclosure to be inevitable, he can seek a buyer for the property who can make the payments. More than any other reason, this is why relatively few real estate mortgages are foreclosed. The borrower, realizing he is in or is about to be in financial trouble, sells his property. It is only when the borrower cannot find a buyer and when the lender sees no further sense in stretching the payments that the acceleration clause is invoked and the path toward foreclosure taken.

Foreclosure Routes

Basically there are two foreclosure routes: judicial and nonjudicial. **Judicial foreclosure** means taking the matter to a court of law in the form of a lawsuit that asks the judge to foreclose (cut off) the borrower. A **nonjudicial foreclosure** does not go to court and is not heard by a judge. It is conducted by the lender (or by a trustee) in accordance with provisions in the mortgage and in accordance with state law pertaining to nonjudicial foreclosures. Comparing the two, a judicial foreclosure is more costly and more time-consuming, but it does carry the approval of a court of law and it may give the lender rights to collect the full amount of the loan if the property sells for less than the amount owed. It is also the preferred method when the foreclosure case is complicated and involves many parties and interests. The nonjudicial route is usually faster, simpler, and cheaper, and it is preferred by lenders when the case is simple and straightforward.

Except for home equity loans, which require a judicial hearing, almost all loans in Texas are foreclosed nonjudicially because of Texas's wide use of the deed of trust as a mortgage.

NONJUDICIAL FORECLOSURE

Forty-two states, including Texas, permit the use of a power of sale as a means of simplifying and shortening the foreclosure proceeding.

The foreclosure process, as set out in the power of sale provision, is pursuant to statutory guidelines that provide for executions by sales under a deed of trust. To be enforceable, the power of sale provisions cannot be in violation of state law.

Texas law states that upon default, sale of real estate under the power conferred by the deed of trust shall be made in the county in which the real estate is located. When the real estate is situated in more than one county, the sale may be held in any of these counties, as long as all notices specify in which county the real estate will be sold. Texas statute now requires that a 20-day notice be given to each debtor to cure their default if it is the borrower's primary residence. If the default is not cured, notice of the intent to accelerate and the notice of acceleration of the indebtedness must be sent to the borrower, and notice of the proposed sale shall be given by posting written notice of the sale at least 21 days preceding the date of the sale. The notice must be posted at the courthouse door (and most courthouses provide a bulletin board located in close proximity to the courthouse door). If the real estate is situated in more than one county, the notice is to be posted at the courthouse door of each county in which the real estate is located. The notice must also be filed in the office of the county clerk. The lender must also serve written notice of the proposed sale at least 21 days preceding the date of the sale (by certified mail) on each debtor obligated to pay such debt, according to the records of the lender or note holder. Service of the notice is considered complete upon deposit of the notice in the United States Mail in a properly addressed post-paid wrapper. The sale is held open to the public at specified time intervals between the hours of 10 a.m. and 4 p.m. on the first Tuesday of the next month after proper notice has been given.

As a practical matter, the mortgagee generally gives the trustee a request to exercise the right to foreclose. The trustee gives (1) the required notice to cure,

FIGURE 11.5 Notice of trustee's sale

NOTICE OF TRUSTEE'S SALE

Pursuant to authority conferred upon me by that certain Deed of Trust executed by N. Debted and wife, Mary B. Debted, of Harris County, Texas, dated February 1, 200x, and duly recorded in Clerks file No: 2010123456 of the Real Property Records of Harris County, Texas, I will as Trustee under said Deed of Trust, in order to satisfy the indebtedness secured thereby and at the request the holder of said indebtedness, default having been made in the payment of thereof, sell on Tuesday, April 4, 19xx, at public auction to the highest bidder for cash before the courthouse door of Harris County, Texas, in Houston, Texas, between the hours of ten o'clock A.M. and four o'clock P.M. of that day, the following described property, to wit:

> *Lot 1, Block 1, Shakey Acres Subdivision, Harris County Texas, as shown of record at Volume 7, Page 3 of the Map Records of Harris County, Texas.*

EXECUTED this 4th day of March, 200x.

Charles J. Jacobus
Charles J. Jacobus, Trustee

(2) a notice of intent to accelerate, and (3) a notice of acceleration, and then posts the notice of trustee's sale (Figure 11.5) on the courthouse door 21 days prior to the first Tuesday of the following month in which the sale is to take place. The trustee also files a copy of the notice in the county clerk's office. Then, on the day and time specified by statute, a public auction is held at the courthouse door or at some other location within a reasonable proximity to the courthouse as designated by the county commissioners. If there are no other bidders, the sale is normally made to a representative of the mortgage company or the note holder. Upon finalization of the sale and execution of the trustee's deed, the trustee executes an affidavit that such notice was properly carried out in compliance with state law. By execution of the deed and signing of this affidavit, the law presumes that the sale was carried out correctly.

Deficiencies

After the foreclosure, the lender is given the right to sue under the Promissory Note for any **deficiency.** For instance, suppose there is a $300,000.00 Deed of Trust and, at the time of foreclosure, $170,000.00 is still owed on the note. If the foreclosure sale is held, and the property is sold for $50,000.00, the lender can then sue on the Promissory Note for the $120,000.00 deficiency. Texas has adopted, however, an anti-deficiency statute that allows the homeowner, upon being sued by the lender, to produce evidence in court of the fair market value of the house. If the appraised value of the house (presuming fair market value) is in excess of $50,000.00, the court must allow an offset for the entire appraised value of the house against the deficiency. In the current example, if the house appraised for $200,000.00, the court would require a complete offset against the sales price and the lender could not pursue a deficiency.

The antideficiency statute also applies to judicial foreclosures and to anyone who may have guaranteed the Note. The antideficiency statute does not apply to private mortgage insurance. The mortgage insurer can still sue the borrower if the insurer pays the deficiency. Private mortgage insurance is discussed in Chapter 12.

A new federal law has also been passed to protect consumers. The general rule is that any deficiency that is forgiven becomes taxable income to the borrower. So, while the lender may not pursue a deficiency, they may file a 1099 with the Internal Revenue Service declaring that they gave you income during the year of the foreclosure when they did not pursue a deficiency. This is often termed "phantom income." The new Mortgage Debt Relief Act of 2007, however, allows the taxpayer to exclude from income any gain on cancelled debt due on the principal residence. It applies only to the taxpayer's principal residence. It applies to all loans to buy, build, or substantially improve that residence. The act is effective from 2007 through 2012.

Redemption

Some states provide an **equitable** (arising out of fairness) or **statutory** (created by statute) **right of redemption** to redeem the property prior to sale and reinstate the borrower's right to continue to make payments. The form in Figure 11.3 contains a contractual right to redeem (note Paragraph 19). Under Texas law, however, once the notice to cure has been sent to the debtor, the only equity of redemption that the debtor has is to pay the full amount owing, or to buy the property at the foreclosure. There is also no statutory *right of redemption* in Texas to reinstate the deed of trust after the foreclosure sale has taken place. The net effect of this is that once the note has been accelerated, the mortgagor has no rights except that of paying the full amount of the note due in cash at or before the foreclosure sale, unless otherwise agreed to by the mortgagee.

The power of sale provision of a deed of trust has consistently been upheld to be constitutional. However, it is important to take into consideration that because the state allows this type of foreclosure, lenders are more ready to make loans and provide money for mortgages, knowing that in the event of default their remedy is reasonably swift and inexpensive. In states that do not allow a quick and swift remedy to foreclosure proceedings, one consistently finds that loan procedures and credit searches become much more intense to allow the mortgagee to minimize the risk of making a real estate loan. This, coupled with the fact that most mortgagees do not want to foreclose on property, means that mortgagees will generally give the mortgagor an agreed time to redeem, rather than immediately foreclose. The lender is in the business of making money on house payments, not in foreclosing and becoming a homeowner. A consistent string of foreclosures puts the lender into the real estate business, and most mortgagees wish to remain solely in the lending business.

ADVANTAGES OF THE DEED OF TRUST

The popularity of the deed of trust can be traced to the following attributes: (1) the time between default and foreclosure is relatively short, (2) the foreclosure process under the power of sale provision is far less expensive and complex than a courtordered foreclosure, and (3) once the foreclosure sale takes place, there is no statutory redemption. These are primarily advantages to the lender, but such advantages have attracted lenders and made real estate loans less expensive and easier for borrowers to obtain. Some states prohibit deficiency judgments against borrowers when a deed of trust is used.

Property can be purchased "subject to" an existing deed of trust or it can be "assumed," just as with a regular mortgage. Debt priorities are established as for mortgages: There are the first and second, senior and junior trust deeds. Deeds of trust can be subordinated and partial releases are possible.

DEED IN LIEU OF FORECLOSURE

To avoid the hassle of foreclosure proceedings, a borrower may voluntarily deed the property to the lender. In turn, the borrower should demand cancellation of the unpaid debt and a letter to that effect from the lender. This method relieves the lender of foreclosing and waiting out any required redemption periods, but it also presents the lender with a sensitive situation. With the borrower in financial distress and about to be foreclosed, it is quite easy for the lender to take advantage of the borrower. As a result, courts may side with the borrower if the borrower complains of any unfair dealings. Thus, the lender must be prepared to prove conclusively that the borrower received a fair deal by deeding the property voluntarily to the lender in return for cancellation of his debt. A deed in lieu of foreclosure is a voluntary act by both borrower and lender; if either feels they will fare better in regular foreclosure proceedings, they need not agree to it. Texas has a statute that gives renewed validity to deeds in lieu, so lenders may start using them more often.

REVIEW QUESTIONS

Answers to these questions are found in the Answer Key section at the back of the book.

1. When a deed of trust is recorded, bare title is conveyed by the
   A. lender to the borrower.
   B. borrower to the lender.
   C. borrower to the trustee.
   D. trustee to the lender.

2. When a deed of trust is foreclosed, title is conveyed by the
   A. borrower to the lender.
   B. trustee to the borrower.
   C. borrower to the trustee.
   D. trustee to the purchaser at foreclosure.

3. Which of the following clauses would be found in a deed of trust but not in a mortgage?
   A. A reconveyance clause
   B. A power of sale clause
   C. An acceleration clause
   D. A defeasance clause

4. If the trustee should die or be dissolved before the debt secured by a deed of trust is paid off, a successor may be named by the
   A. trustor.
   B. beneficiary.
   C. judge.
   D. both A and B.

5. Comparing a deed of trust to a mortgage, which of the following would be unique to the deed of trust?
   A. Reconveyance
   B. Power of sale
   C. Statutory redemption
   D. None of the above

6. The period of equitable redemption given to a borrower
   A. begins when the loan goes into default.
   B. ends when the property is sold at foreclosure.
   C. both A and B.
   D. neither A nor B.

7. When the amount received from a foreclosure sale is insufficient to pay off the mortgage loan and the other expenses of the sale, the lender may sometimes secure
   A. a deficiency judgment.
   B. a mechanic's lien.
   C. an estoppel lien.
   D. a statutory lien.

8. The period of time set by state law, during which the mortgagor may redeem the property, is known as the period of
   A. equitable redemption.
   B. legal redemption.
   C. voluntary redemption.
   D. statutory redemption.

9. A borrower who feels mistreated by a power of sale foreclosure can
   A. obtain a judicial foreclosure.
   B. appeal the issue to the courts.
   C. obtain a judgment.
   D. obtain a lien.

10. By voluntarily giving the lender a deed in lieu of foreclosure, a delinquent borrower might avoid
    A. foreclosure proceedings.
    B. possible deficiency judgments.
    C. both A and B.
    D. neither A nor B.

11. A document that for all intents and purposes is a mortgage, although not labeled one, would most likely be
    A. an installment contract.
    B. a deed of trust.
    C. an equitable mortgage.
    D. a deed as security.

12. The borrower under a deed of trust is the
    A. beneficiary.
    B. trustee.
    C. grantor.
    D. assignor.

13. The lender under a deed of trust is the
    A. beneficiary.
    B. trustee.
    C. grantor.
    D. assignee.

14. Evidence of the amount and terms of a borrower's debt to a lender is provided by means of a
    A. mortgage.
    B. promissory note.
    C. deed of trust.
    D. first mortgage.

15. A promissory note that fails to state that it is to be secured by a mortgage or deed of trust is
    A. a personal obligation of the borrower.
    B. an unsecured obligation of the borrower.
    C. both A and B.
    D. neither A nor B.

16. Should a borrower fail to make payments when due, the lender may demand immediate payment of the entire balance under the terms of the
    A. prepayment clause.
    B. defeasance clause.
    C. acceleration clause.
    D. hypothecation clause.

17. At the time of origination, a mortgage creates a lien on the mortgaged property in states that subscribe to the
    A. lien theory.
    B. title theory.
    C. intermediate theory.
    D. both A and B.
    E. both A and C.

18. The clause that gives the lender the right to call in the note if the mortgaged property is sold or otherwise conveyed by the borrower is known as the
    A. due-on-sale clause.
    B. alienation clause.
    C. both A and B.
    D. neither A nor B.

19. Who may be held responsible for mortgage loan repayment when a loan is assumed as part of a real estate sale?
    A. the purchaser
    B. the seller
    C. both A and B
    D. neither A nor B

20. When a loan is assumed, the
    A. seller can be relieved of liability by novation.
    B. the buyer should verify the loan balance with the lender.
    C. both A and B.
    D. neither A nor B.

Chapter 12

KEY TERMS

Amortized loan: a loan requiring periodic payments that include both interest and partial repayment of principal

Balloon loan: any loan in which the final payment is larger than the preceding payments

Conventional loans: real estate loans that are not insured by the FHA or guaranteed by the VA

Equity: the market value of a property less the debt against it

FHA: Federal Housing Administration

Impound or reserve account: an account into which the lender places monthly tax and insurance payments

Loan origination fee: the expenses a lender incurs in processing a mortgage loan

Loan-to-value ratio: a percentage reflecting what a lender will lend divided by the sale price or market value of the property, whichever is less

Maturity: the end of the life of a loan

PITI payment: a loan payment that combines principal, interest, taxes, and insurance

PMI: private mortgage insurance—a private mortgage insurance source to insure lenders against foreclosure loss

Point: 1% of the loan amount

Principal: the balance owing on a loan

UFMIP: up-front mortgage insurance premium—a one-time charge by the FHA for insuring a loan

VA: Department of Veterans Affairs

Lending Practices

IN THIS CHAPTER

Whereas Chapter 11 dealt with the legal aspects of notes, mortgages, and trust deeds, Chapters 12 and 13 deal with the money aspects of these instruments. We begin in this chapter with term loans, amortized loans, balloon loans, partially amortized loans, loan-to-value ratio, equity, and points. These topics are followed by the functions and importance of the FHA and VA and private mortgage insurance. Chapter 13 discusses Truth in Lending and provides a helpful and informative description of the loan application and approval process you (or your buyer) will experience when applying for a real estate loan. In Chapters 14 and 15, we look at sources and types of financing, including where to find mortgage loan money, where mortgage lenders obtain their money, and various types of financing instruments such as the adjustable rate mortgage, equity mortgage, wraparound mortgage, seller financing, and so forth. Note that from here on whatever is said about mortgages applies equally to deeds of trust.

One more thought before we start. The United States has had a longstanding commitment to individual home ownership. We have long had governmental assistance in the form of tax-deductible interest on mortgages and government-insured or guaranteed loans. Other countries require significant down payments and have short-term loans. We have standardized appraisal systems, standardized secondary mortgage markets, and a proliferation of loan originators. In the next few chapters, we will discuss how all these factors interrelate to produce this profitable system and a unique way of life.

TERM LOANS

A loan that requires only interest payments until the last day of its life, at which time the full amount borrowed is due, is called a **term loan** (or straight loan). Until 1930, the term loan was the standard method of financing real estate in the United States. These loans were typically made for a period of three to five years. The borrower signed a note or bond agreeing: (1) to pay the lender interest on the loan every six months, and (2) to repay the entire amount of the loan upon ***maturity;*** that is, at the end of the life of the loan. As security, the borrower mortgaged the property to the lender.

Loan Renewal

In practice, most real estate term loans were not paid off when they matured. Instead, the borrower asked the lender, typically a bank, to renew the loan for another three to five years. The major flaw in this approach to lending was that the borrower might never own the property free and clear of debt. This left the borrower continuously at the mercy of the lender for renewals. As long as the lender was not pressed for funds, the borrower's renewal request was granted. However, if the lender was short of funds, no renewal was granted and the borrower was expected to pay in full.

The inability to renew term loans caused hardship to hundreds of thousands of property owners during the Great Depression that began in 1930 and lasted most of the decade. Banks were unable to accommodate requests for loan renewals and at the same time satisfy unemployed depositors who needed to withdraw their savings to live. As a result, owners of homes, farms, office buildings, factories, and vacant land lost their property as foreclosures reached into the millions. The market was so glutted with properties being offered for sale to satisfy unpaid mortgage loans that real estate prices fell at a sickening pace.

AMORTIZED LOANS

In 1933, a congressionally legislated Home Owner's Loan Corporation (HOLC) was created to assist financially distressed homeowners by acquiring mortgages that were about to be foreclosed. The HOLC then offered monthly repayment plans tailored to fit the homeowner's budget that would repay the loan in full by its maturity date without the need for a balloon payment. The HOLC was terminated in 1951 after rescuing over one million mortgages in its 18-year life. However, the use of this stretched-out payment plan, known as an ***amortized loan,*** took hold in American real estate, and today it is the accepted method of loan repayment. In the United States, 66% of all mortgages are 30-year, fixed-rate, long-term loans, which is a rarity in most other countries. The United States Congress has had a long-standing commitment to home-ownership, as evidenced by the decision to create what has become a well-developed, sophisticated secondary mortgage market (discussed in detail in Chapter 14) that meets the needs of both home buyers and investors in a free enterprise society.

As a practical matter, there are a number of handheld computers that can help a student analyze loans in a variety of ways. Real estate agents are continually trained in the variety of types of loans to meet their clients' needs. As more loan products become available, it is always a new learning experience. Our purpose here is to discuss the fundamentals of how the amortization system works. As one becomes more experienced, the high tech approach to loan analysis changes from market to market, but the basics remain the same.

FIGURE 12.1 Repaying a six-year $1,000 loan

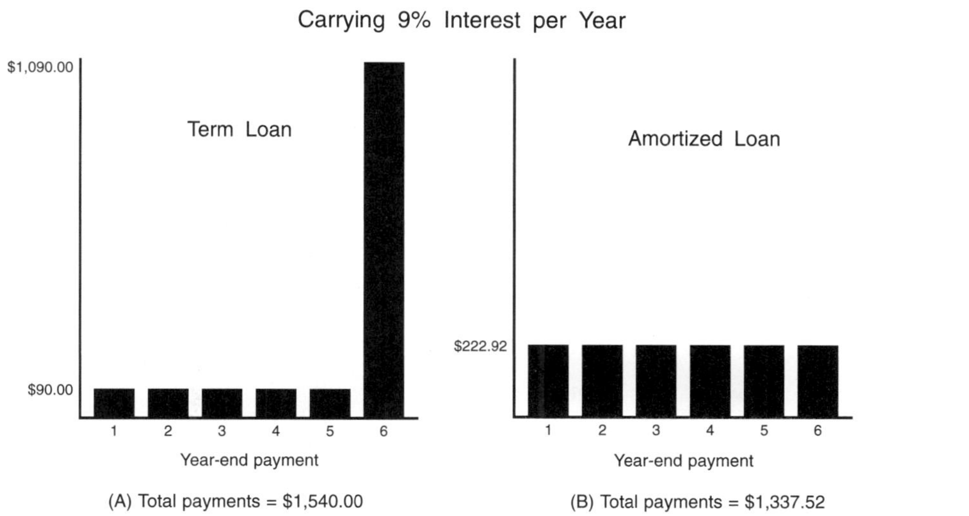

Source: © 2012 Cengage Learning

Repayment Methods

The amortized loan requires regular equal payments during the life of the loan, of sufficient size and number to pay all interest due on the loan and reduce the amount owed to zero by the loan's maturity date. Figure 12.1 illustrates the contrast between an amortized and a term loan. Figure 12.1A shows a six-year, $1,000 term loan with interest of $90 due each year of its life. At the end of the sixth year, the entire ***principal*** (the amount owed) is due in one lump sum payment along with the final interest payment. In Figure 12.1B, the same $1,000 loan is fully amortized by making six equal annual payments of $222.92. From the borrower's standpoint, $222.92 once each year is easier to budget than $90 for 5 years and $1,090 in the sixth year.

Furthermore, the amortized loan shown in Figure 12.1 actually costs the borrower less than the term loan. The total payments made under the term loan are $90 + $90 + $90 + $90 + $90 + $1,090 = $1,540. Amortizing the same loan requires total payments of 6 × $222.92 = $1,337.52. The difference is due to the fact that under the amortized loan the borrower begins to pay back part of the $1,000 principal with the first payment. In the first year, $90 of the $222.92 payment goes to interest and the remaining $132.92 reduces the principal owed. Thus, the borrower starts the second year owing only $867.08. At 9% interest per year, the interest on $867.08 is $78.04; therefore, when the borrower makes the second payment of $222.92, only $78.04 goes to interest. The remaining $144.88 is applied to reduce the loan balance, and the borrower starts the third year owing $722.20. Figure 12.2 charts this repayment program. Notice that the balance owed drops faster as the loan becomes older, that is, as it matures.

Monthly Payments

As you have just seen, calculating the payments on a term loan is relatively simple compared with calculating amortized loan payments. The widespread use of

FIGURE 12.2 Repaying a six-year $1,000 amortized loan

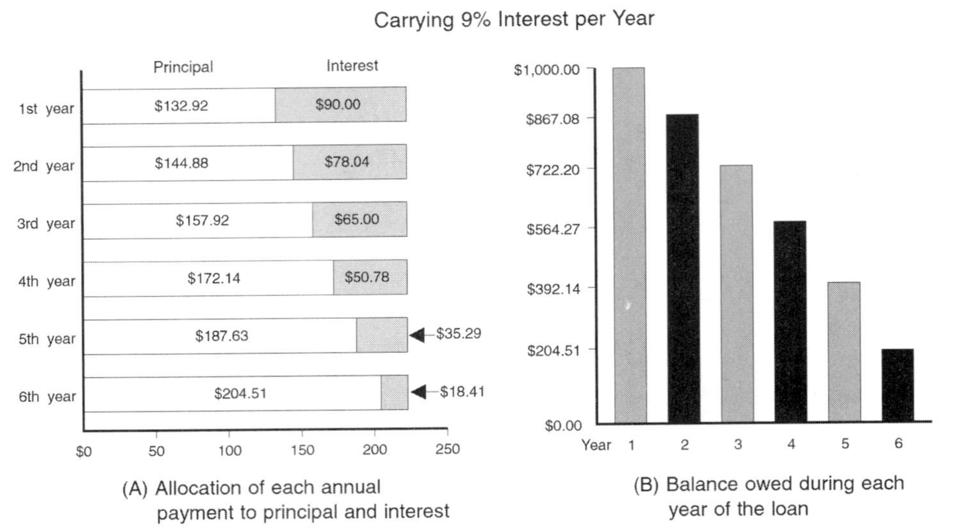

Source: © 2012 Cengage Learning

computers has greatly simplified the calculations, however. To illustrate how the amortization works, though, we should note that ***amortization tables*** are published and used throughout the real estate industry. Table 12.1 shows the monthly payments per $1,000 of loan for interest rates from 5% to 15% for periods ranging from 5 to 40 years. (Amortization tables are also published for quarterly, semiannual, and annual payments.) When you use an amortization table, notice that there are five variables: (1) frequency of payment, (2) interest rate, (3) maturity, (4) amount of the loan, and (5) amount of the periodic payment. If you know any four of these, you can obtain the fifth variable from the tables. For example, suppose that you want to know the monthly payment necessary to amortize a $60,000 loan over 30 years at 9.5% interest. The first step is to look in Table 12.1 for the 9.5% line. Then locate the 30-year column. Where they cross, you will find the necessary monthly payment per $1,000: $8.41. Next, multiply $8.41 by 60 to get the monthly payment for a $60,000 loan: $504.60. If the loan is to be $67,500, then multiply $8.41 by 67.5 to get the monthly payment: $567.68.

Continuing the foregoing example, suppose we reduce the repayment period to 15 years. First look for the 9.5% line, then go over to the 15-year column. The number there is $10.45. Next, multiply $10.45 by 60 to get the monthly payment for a $60,000 loan: $627.00. If the loan is to be $67,500, then multiply $10.45 by 67.5 to get the monthly payment: $705.38.

Loan Size

Amortization tables are also used to determine the amount of loan a borrower can support if you know how much the borrower has available to spend each

TABLE 12.1 Amortization table monthly payment per $1,000 of loan

Interest Rate per Year	Life of the Loan							
	5 years	10 years	15 years	20 years	25 years	30 years	35 years	40 years
5%	$18.88	$10.61	$ 7.91	$ 6.60	$ 5.85	$ 5.37	$5.05	$4.83
5.5	19.11	10.86	8.18	6.88	6.15	5.68	5.38	5.16
6	19.34	11.11	8.44	7.17	6.45	6.00	5.71	5.51
6.5	19.57	11.36	8.72	7.46	6.76	6.32	6.05	5.86
7	19.81	11.62	8.99	7.76	7.07	6.66	6.39	6.22
7.5	20.04	11.88	9.28	8.06	7.39	7.00	6.75	6.59
8	20.28	12.14	9.56	8.37	7.72	7.34	7.11	6.96
8.5	20.52	12.40	9.85	8.68	8.06	7.69	7.47	7.34
9	20.76	12.67	10.15	9.00	8.40	8.05	7.84	7.72
9.5	21.01	12.94	10.45	9.33	8.74	8.41	8.22	8.11
10	21.25	13.22	10.75	9.66	9.09	8.78	8.60	8.50
10.5	21.50	13.50	11.06	9.99	9.45	9.15	8.99	8.89
11	21.75	13.78	11.37	10.33	9.81	9.53	9.37	9.29
11.5	22.00	14.06	11.69	10.67	10.17	9.91	9.77	9.69
12	22.25	14.35	12.01	11.02	10.54	10.29	10.16	10.09
12.5	22.50	14.64	12.33	11.37	10.91	10.68	10.56	10.49
13	22.76	14.94	12.66	11.72	11.28	11.07	10.96	10.90
13.5	23.01	15.23	12.99	12.08	11.66	11.46	11.36	11.31
14	23.27	15.53	13.32	12.44	12.04	11.85	11.76	11.72
14.5	23.53	15.83	13.66	12.80	12.43	12.25	12.17	12.13
15	23.79	16.14	14.00	13.17	12.81	12.65	12.57	12.54

Source: © 2012 Cengage Learning

month on loan payments. Suppose that a prospective home buyer can afford monthly principal and interest payments of $650 and lenders are making 30-year loans at 10%. How large a loan can this buyer afford? In Table 12.1 find where the 10% line and the 30-year column meet. You will see 8.78 there. This means that every $8.78 of monthly payment will support $1,000 of loan. To find how many thousands of dollars $650 per month will support, just divide $650 by $8.78. The answer is 74.031 thousands or $74,031. By adding the buyer's down payment, you know what price property the buyer can afford to purchase. If interest rates are 7.5%, the number from the table is 7.00 and the loan amount is $92,857. (You can begin to see why the level of interest rates is so important to real estate prices.)

As you have noticed, everything in Table 12.1 is on a monthly payment per thousand basis. With a full book of amortization tables rather than one page, it is possible to look up monthly payments for loans from $100 to $100,000 to determine loan maturities for each year from 1 to 40 years and to calculate many more interest rates. Amortization books are available from most local bookstores.

Change in Maturity Date

An amortization table also shows the impact on the size of the monthly payment when the life of a loan is extended. For example, at 11% interest, a 10-year loan requires a monthly payment of $13.78 per thousand of loan. Increasing the life of the loan to 20 years drops the monthly payment to $10.33 per $1,000. Extending the loan payback to 30 years reduces the monthly payment to $9.53 per thousand. The smaller monthly payment is why 30 years is a popular loan term with borrowers. Note, however, that going beyond 30 years does not significantly reduce the monthly payment. Going from 30 to 35 years reduces the monthly payment by only 16¢ per thousand but adds 5 years of monthly payments. Extending the payback period from 35 to 40 years reduces the monthly payment by just 8¢ per $1,000 ($4 per month on a $50,000 loan) and adds another 60 months of payments at $464.50 per month. As a practical matter, amortized real estate loans are seldom made for more than 30 years.

BUDGET MORTGAGE

The **budget mortgage** takes the amortized loan one step further. In addition to collecting the monthly principal and interest payment (often called $P + I$), the lender collects one-twelfth of the estimated cost of the annual property taxes and hazard insurance on the mortgaged property. The money for tax and insurance payments is placed in an ***impound account*** (also called an **escrow** or ***reserve account***). When taxes and insurance payments are due, the lender pays them. Thus, the lender makes certain that the value of the mortgaged property will not be undermined by unpaid property taxes or by uninsured fire or weather damage. This form of mortgage also helps the borrower to budget for property taxes and insurance on a monthly basis. To illustrate, if insurance is $240 per year and property taxes are $1,800 per year, the lender collects an additional $20 and $150 each month along with the regular principal and interest payments. This combined principal, interest, taxes, and insurance payment is often referred to as a ***PITI payment.***

BALLOON LOAN

A ***balloon loan*** is any loan that has a final payment larger than any of the previous payments on the loan. The final payment is called a **balloon payment.** The term loan described at the beginning of this chapter is a type of balloon loan. Partially amortized loans, discussed next, are another type of balloon loan. In tight money markets, the use of balloon loans increases considerably. Balloon loans with maturities as short as three to five years are commonplace. This arrangement gives the buyer (borrower) three to five years to find cheaper and longer-term financing elsewhere. If such financing does not materialize and the loan is not repaid on time, the lender has the right to foreclose. The alternative is for the lender and borrower to agree to an extension of the loan, usually at prevailing interest rates.

PARTIALLY AMORTIZED LOAN

When the repayment schedule of a loan calls for a series of amortized payments followed by a balloon payment at maturity, it is called a **partially amortized loan.** For example, a lender might agree to a 30-year amortization schedule with a provision that at the end of the tenth year all the remaining principal be paid in a single balloon payment. The advantage to the borrower is that for 10 years the monthly payments will be smaller than if the loan was completely amortized in 10 years. (You can verify this in Table 12.1.) However, the disadvantage is that the balloon payment due at the end of the tenth year might be the borrower's financial downfall. Just how large that balloon payment will be can be determined in advance by using a **loan balance table** (also called a *remaining balance table*). Presuming an interest rate of 11.5% and a 30-year loan, at the end of 10 years the loan balance table in Table 12.2 shows that for each $1,000 originally loaned, $929 would still be owed. If the original loan was for $100,000, at the end of 10 years 100 × $929 = $92,900 would be due as one payment. This qualifies it as a balloon loan.

As you can see from this example, when an amortized loan has a long maturity, relatively little of the debt is paid off during the initial years of the loan's life. Nearly all the early payments go for interest, so that little remains for principal reduction. For example, Table 12.2 shows that even after 16 years of payments on a 30-year, 11.5% loan, 82.5% of the loan is still unpaid. Not until this loan is about six years from maturity will half of it have been repaid.

EARLIER PAYOFF

During the late 1970s when inflation rates exceeded interest rates, the popular philosophy was to borrow as much as possible for as long as possible. Then in the early 1980s inflation rates dropped below interest rates and the opposite philosophy became attractive to many borrowers. This was especially true for those who had borrowed (or were contemplating borrowing) at double-digit interest rates. Let us use as an example an $80,000 loan at 11.5% interest. If the loan has a maturity of 30 years, from Table 12.1 we can determine the monthly payments to be $792.80. (Follow this example on your own.)

15-Year Loan

Suppose the maturity of the aforementioned loan is changed from 30 to 15 years. Looking at Table 12.1, the monthly payments would now be $935.20. This is $142.40 more per month, but the loan is fully paid in 15 years, not 30 years. The total amount of interest paid on the 15-year loan is (15 × 12 × $935.20) – $80,000=$88,336. The total amount of interest paid on the 30-year loan is (30 × 12 × $792.80) – $80,000=$205,408. Thus, for an extra $142.40 per month for 180 months (which amounts to $25,632), the borrower saves the difference between $205,408 and $88,336 (which is $117,072). Many borrowers consider this a very good return on their money. (It is, in fact, an 11.5% compounded rate of return.) Lenders are also more receptive to making

TABLE 12.2 Balance owing on a $1,000 amortized loan

Age of Loan (yrs.)	9.5% Annual Interest — Original Life (years)						Age of Loan (yrs.)	11.5% Annual Interest — Original Life (years)					
	10	15	20	25	30	35		10	15	20	25	30	35
2	$868	$934	$963	$978	$987	$992	2	$880	$944	$971	$984	$991	$995
4	708	853	918	952	971	983	4	729	873	935	965	981	989
6	515	756	864	921	953	971	6	539	784	889	940	967	982
8	282	639	799	883	930	957	8	300	672	831	909	950	972
10		497	720	837	902	940	10		531	759	870	929	960
12		326	625	781	869	920	12		354	667	821	902	945
14		119	510	714	828	896	14		132	553	759	868	926
16			371	633	780	866	16			409	682	825	903
18			203	535	721	830	18			228	585	772	873
20				416	650	787	20				462	704	836
22				273	564	735	22				308	620	789
24				100	460	671	24				115	513	729
26					335	595	26					380	655
28					183	503	28					211	561
30						391	30						444
32						256	32						296
34						94	34						110

fixed-rate loans for 15 years than for 30 years. This is because the lender is locked into the loan for 15 years, not 30 years. As a result, a lender is usually willing to offer a 15-year loan at a lower rate of interest than a 30-year loan. In view of these benefits to borrower and lender alike, the 15-year loan is becoming a popular home financing tool.

Biweekly Payments

A growing number of lenders offer a biweekly repayment plan. The loan is amortized as if it were going to last 30 years. But instead of paying once a month, the borrower makes one-half the monthly payment every two weeks. This may not sound like much of a difference but the results are eye-opening. Assume you borrow $100,000 at 7% interest, paying (see Table 12.1) $666.00 per month. You will retire the loan in 30 years at a cost of $139,509 in interest. If you decide to pay half of $666.00 every two weeks, the loan will be fully paid in just 18 years and will have cost you $105,046 in interest. This happens because biweekly compounding works in your favor and because you make 26 half-size payments a year, not 24.

Existing Loans

Borrowers with existing loans who want to celebrate with an early mortgage burning can simply add a few dollars each month to the required monthly payment. This can be particularly beneficial for people who borrowed at rates of 11% or more. In effect, whatever extra amount is added to the monthly payment will "earn" interest at the loan's interest rate. Thus, if a loan has a 14% rate, early payments "earn" at 14%. If the borrower has no alternative places to invest that will yield 14%, then a few additional dollars each month will work miracles. For example, a 30-year, $100,000 loan at 14% interest requires monthly payments (see Table 12.1) of $1,185. Voluntarily adding an extra $19 per month reduces the maturity (payoff) date from 30 years to 25 years (see Table 12.1 again). If an extra $40 is added to the $19, the maturity date shrinks to 20 years. In other words, an extra $59 per month eliminates 10 years of payments.

You may be wondering why this has not been a popular idea with borrowers. When interest rates are around 6% and 7% (as they were in the 1960s and, more recently, in the 2000s), the mathematics of early payoff are not nearly as impressive.

LOAN-TO-VALUE RATIO

The relationship between the amount of money a lender is willing to loan and the lender's estimate of the market value of the property that will serve as security is called the ***loan-to-value ratio*** (often abbreviated L/V or LTV ratio). For example, a prospective home buyer wants to purchase a house priced at $200,000. A local lender appraises the house, finds it has a market value of $200,000, and agrees to make an 80% L/V loan. This means that the lender will loan up to 80% of the $200,000 and the buyer must provide at least 20% in cash. In dollars, the lender will loan up to $160,000, and the buyer must make a cash down payment of at least $40,000. If the lender appraises the home for more than $200,000, the loan will still be $160,000. If the appraisal is for less than $200,000, the loan will be 80% of the appraised value, and the buyer must pay the balance in cash. The rule is that the price or value, whichever is lower, is applied to the L/V ratio. This rule exists to prevent the lender from overlending on a property just because the borrower overpaid for it.

EQUITY

The difference between the market value of a property and the debt owed against it is called the owner's ***equity***. On a newly purchased $150,000 home with a $30,000 cash down payment, the buyer's equity is $30,000. As the value of the property rises or falls and as the mortgage loan is paid down, the equity changes. For example, if the value of the home rises to $180,000 and the loan is paid down to $115,000, the owner's equity will be $65,000. If the owner completely repays the loan so that there is no debt against the home, the owner's equity is equal to the market value of the property.

LOAN POINTS

Probably no single term in real estate finance causes as much confusion and consternation as the word *points*. In finance, the word ***point*** means 1% of the loan amount. Thus, on a $100,000 loan, one point is $1,000. On a $80,000 loan, three points is $2,400.

The use of points in real estate mortgage finance can be split into two categories: (1) loan origination fees expressed in terms of points and (2) the use of points to change the effective yield of a mortgage loan to a lender. Let us look at these two uses in more detail.

Origination Fee

When a borrower asks for a mortgage loan, the lender incurs a number of expenses, including such things as the time its loan officer spends interviewing the borrower, office overhead, the purchase and review of credit reports on the borrower, an on-site appraisal of the property to be mortgaged, title searches and review, legal and recording fees, and so forth. For these, some lenders make an itemized billing, charging so many dollars for the appraisal, credit report, title search, and so forth. The total becomes the ***loan origination fee,*** which the borrower pays to get the loan. Other lenders do not make an itemized bill, but instead simply state the origination fee in terms of a percentage of the loan amount, for example, one point. Thus, a lender quoting a loan origination fee of one point is saying that for a $95,000 loan, its fee to originate the loan will be $950.

Discount Points

Points charged to raise the lender's monetary return on a loan are known as **discount points.** A simplified example illustrates their use and effect. If you are a lender and agree to make a term loan of $100 to a borrower for one year at 10% interest, you would normally expect to give the borrower $100 now (disregard loan origination fees for a moment) and, one year later, the borrower would give you $110. In percentage terms, the **effective yield** on your loan is 10% per annum (year) because you received $10 for your one-year, $100 loan. Now suppose that instead of handing the borrower $100, you handed him $99 but still required him to repay $100 plus $10 in interest at the end of the year. This is a discount of one point ($1 in this case), and the borrower paid it out of the loan funds. The effect of this financial maneuver is to raise the effective yield (yield to maturity) to you without raising the interest rate itself. Therefore, if you loan out $99 and receive $110 at the end of the year, you effectively have a return of $11 for a $99 loan. This gives you an effective yield of $11/$99 or 11.1%, rather than 10%.

Calculating the effective yield on a discounted 20-or 30-year mortgage loan is more difficult because the amount owed drops over the life of the loan, and because the majority are paid in full ahead of schedule due to refinancing. Computers and calculators usually make these calculations; however, a useful rule of thumb states that on the typical home loan each point of discount raises the effective yield by 1/8 of 1%. Thus, four discount points would raise the effective yield by approximately 1/2 of 1% and eight points would raise it by 1%. Discount points are most often charged during periods of **tight money,** that is, when mortgage money is in short supply. During periods of **loose money,** when lenders have adequate funds to lend and are actively seeking borrowers, discount points disappear.

Real estate loans that are not insured by the FHA or guaranteed by the VA are termed ***conventional loans.*** The conventional loan market has a growing presence in the marketplace, as conventional lenders are very competitive with rates and loan processing procedures. FHA and VA loans are now only a small fraction of the single-family loan origination market. FHA handles a little over 12%; VA about 2%. Let's discuss the impact of the FHA and VA.

FHA INSURANCE PROGRAMS

The Great Depression caused a major change in the attitude of the federal government toward home financing in the United States. In 1934, one year after the Home Owners Loan Corporation was established, Congress passed the National Housing Act. The Act's most far-reaching provision was to establish the ***Federal Housing Administration (FHA)*** for the purpose of encouraging new construction as a means of creating jobs. To accomplish this goal, the FHA offered to insure lenders against losses due to nonrepayment when they made loans on both new and existing homes. In turn, the lender had to grant 20-year fully amortized loans with loan-to-value ratios of 80% rather than the three-to five-year, 50% to 60% term loans common up to that time.

The FHA did its best to keep from becoming a burden to the American taxpayer. When a prospective borrower approached a lender for an FHA-secured home loan, the FHA reviewed the borrower's income, expenses, assets, and debts. The objective was to determine whether there was adequate room in the borrower's budget for the proposed loan payments. The FHA also sent inspectors to the property to make certain that it was of acceptable construction quality and to determine its fair market value. To offset losses that would still inevitably occur, the FHA charged the borrower an annual insurance fee of approximately 1/2 of 1% of the balance owed on the loan. The FHA was immensely successful in its task. Not only did it create construction jobs, but it raised the level of housing quality in the nation and, in a pleasant surprise to taxpayers, actually returned annual profits to the U.S. Treasury. In response to its success, in 1946 Congress changed its status from temporary to permanent.

Current FHA Coverage

The FHA has had a marked influence on lending policies in the real estate industry. Foremost among these is the widespread acceptance of the high loan-to-value, fully amortized loan. In the 1930s, lenders required FHA insurance before making 80% L/V loans. By the 1960s, lenders were readily making 80% L/V loans without FHA insurance. Meanwhile, the FHA insurance program was working so well that the FHA raised the portion it was willing to insure. The maximum amount the FHA will insure varies from city to city and changes from time to time. As of 2010, the maximum loan amount in Texas was $332,500.

Any loan made before December 15, 1989 may be assumed by an investor. Effective January 1, 2009, the borrower must make a contribution (down payment) of at least 3.5%, making the maximum loan-to-value ratio for a purchase transaction 96.5%.

Assumability

Traditionally, FHA loans were popular because the 30-year fixed-rate loans could be assumed without any increase in interest. This is still true for loans that were originated prior to December 1, 1986. The assumption procedure can be one of two types, a simple assumption or a formal assumption. In the **simple assumption** procedure, the property is sold and the loan is assumed by the buyer without notification to the FHA or its agent. The seller remains fully liable to the FHA for full repayment. In the **formal assumption,** the property is not conveyed to a new buyer until the new buyer's creditworthiness has been approved by the FHA or its agent. When the creditworthy buyer assumes the loan, the seller may obtain a full release of liability from the FHA.

If the FHA loan was originated between December 1, 1986, and December 15, 1989, the owner-occupant cannot sell the property with a loan assumption during the first 12 months after execution of the mortgage without creditworthiness approval for each person who assumes the loan. If the seller is an investor, the assumption cannot be made without prior approval during the first 24 months after execution of the mortgage. Failure to comply with either requirement results in an acceleration of the loan balance. After the one- or two-year loan period, the loan can be assumed without approval. If the assumption is a simple assumption, the seller remains fully liable for five years after the new mortgage is executed. If the loan is not in default after the five years, the seller is automatically released from liability.

If the loan was originated after December 15, 1989, the FHA requires the credit-worthiness approval prior to the conveyance of title on all assumption loans. If the borrower assumes a mortgage loan, the lender cannot refuse to release the original borrower from liability on the loan.

Mortgage Insurance

The FHA charges a one-time ***up-front mortgage insurance premium (UFMIP)*** that is paid when the loan is made. Premiums are currently 1.5% of the loan amount.

The FHA now also charges an annual premium amounting to ½ of 1% of the annual loan balance (.55% for loans in excess of 90%). One-twelfth of the annual premium is added to the monthly payment and must be included in the proposed monthly housing expense to qualify the borrower for the loan. The amount is calculated each year on the unpaid principal balance without the UFMIP and excluding closing costs. The half-point annual premium will be eliminated when homeowners build a 22% equity in their homes as applied to the original value of the property. Depending on the interest rate and the down payment, a borrower could generally eliminate the annual premium by the eleventh year of the loan. This keeps the FHA insurance program in line with the 1998 federal legislation that enables homeowners to eliminate private mortgage insurance once their homeowner equity reaches 78%. Unlike the Homeowners' Protection Act (discussed later under Private Mortgage Insurance), the FHA continues to insure the mortgage. The recurring mortgage insurance premiums for the loans with a loan of 15 or fewer years is .25% if the L/V ratio exceeds 90%.

The FHA also offers an adjustable rate loan program under Section 251 which is indexed to one-year Treasury Constant Maturities. The annual cap is 1% per annum increase or decrease with a lifetime cap of 5% over the initial rate. There is also a graduated payment program available under Section 245(a) that provides mixed increases and payments over 5 to 15 years.

Floating Interest Rates

At one time, the FHA set interest rate ceilings. Fixed-rate FHA loans are now negotiable and float with the market, and the seller can choose how many points to contribute toward the borrower's loan. This can be none, some, or all the points, and the seller can even pay the borrower's mortgage insurance premium (MIP). Typical purchase contract language is, "The seller will pay *X* points and the buyer will pay not more than *Y* points and the agreed-on interest rate is *Z*%." Thus, *X* is the contribution the seller will make, and the seller is protected from having to pay more. The buyer will pay any additional points, but not more than *Y* points. Beyond that, the buyer can cancel the purchase contract. That would happen if the market rates rose quickly while the rate at *Z* is fixed.

Loan Qualification

Before leaving the topic of the FHA, it is interesting to note that much of what we take for granted as standard loan practice today is the result of FHA innovation years ago. As already noted, before 1934 standard real estate loan practice called for short-term renewable loans. Then the FHA boldly offered 20-year amortized loans. Once these were shown to be successful investments for lenders, loans without FHA insurance were made for 20 years. Later, when the FHA successfully went to 30 years, non-FHA-insured loans followed. The FHA also established loan application review techniques that have been widely accepted and copied throughout the real estate industry. The biggest step in this direction was to analyze a borrower's loan application in terms of earning power.

The U.S. Department of Housing and Urban Development (HUD) announced major revisions in its FHA single-family underwriting guidelines in January 1995, giving lenders more flexibility in considering an applicant's income and savings. The new regulations provide that FHA may now participate in state housing finance agencies and programs to use alternative qualifying methods, such as (1) the applicant's existing housing payments, (2) tax benefits of home ownership, and (3) non-housing debt history. In addition, FHA now uses a three-year test for income stability instead of the previous five-year test. Only debts extending 10 or more months are included in debt-to-income calculations and child care costs are no longer counted as a recurring debt. FHA lenders can now also use a three-repository merged credit report. HUD also gave FHA limited approval for the use of automatic underwriting systems (discussed in Chapter 14).

Construction Regulations

Since its inception, the FHA has imposed its own minimum construction requirements. Often this was essential where local building codes did not exist or were weaker than the FHA wanted. Before issuing a loan, particularly on new construction, the FHA would impose minimum requirements as to the quantity and quality of building materials to be used. Lot size, street access, landscaping, siting, and general house design also were required to fit within broad FHA guidelines. During construction, an FHA inspector would come to the property several times to check on whether or not the work was being done correctly.

The reason for such care in building standards was that the FHA recognized that if a building is defective from either a design or construction standpoint, the borrower is more likely to default on the loan and create an insurance claim against the FHA. Furthermore, the same defects will lower the price the property will bring at its foreclosure sale, thus increasing losses to the FHA. Because building codes are now becoming stricter and more standardized in states, counties, and cities, the FHA anticipates eliminating its own minimum property standards. FHA has also softened its standards for property defects. The new FHA standards, which became effective January 1, 1995, advised underwriters to delete "conditions that have little or nothing to do with the safety and soundness of the property" from repair requirements stipulated by an appraiser.

As we leave our discussion of the FHA and go to the Department of Veterans Affairs, keep in mind that the FHA is not a lender. The FHA is an insurance agency. The loan itself is obtained from a savings and loan, bank, mortgage company, or similar lender. In addition to principal and interest payments, the lender collects an insurance premium from the borrower that is forwarded to the FHA. The FHA, in turn, guarantees repayment of the loan to the lender. This arrangement makes lenders much more willing to loan to buyers who are putting only 3% to 5% cash down. Thus, when you hear the phrase "FHA loan" in real estate circles, know that it is an FHA-*insured* loan, not a loan from the FHA.

DEPARTMENT OF VETERANS AFFAIRS

In 1944, to show its appreciation to servicemen returning from World War II, Congress passed far-reaching legislation to aid veterans in education, hospitalization, employment training, and housing. In housing, the popularly named G.I. Bill of Rights empowered the Comptroller General of the United States to guarantee the repayment of a portion of first mortgage real estate loans made to veterans. For this guarantee, no fee would be charged to the veteran. Rather, the government itself would stand the losses. On March 15, 1989, the Veterans Administration was elevated to cabinet level and is now officially called the ***Department of Veterans Affairs,*** but still uses its old initials, the ***VA.***

No Down Payment

The original 1944 law provided that lenders would be guaranteed against losses up to 50% of the amount of the loan, but in no case for more than $2,000. The objective was to make it possible for a veteran to buy a home with no cash down payment. Thus, on a house offered for sale at $5,000 (houses were much cheaper in 1944), this guarantee enabled a veteran to borrow the entire $5,000. From the lender's stand-point, having the top $2,000 of the loan guaranteed by the U.S. government offered the same asset protection as a $2,000 cash down payment. If the veteran defaulted and the property went into foreclosure, the lender had to net less than $3,000 before suffering a loss.

To keep up with the increased cost of homes, the guarantee has been increased several times. The VA now uses the sliding-scale system for calculating the applicable guarantee amounts. The guarantee increases with the amount of the loan using fixed dollar amounts and percentages of loan amounts. The current limits are shown in Table 12.3.

In the original G.I. Bill of 1944, eligibility was limited to World War II veterans. However, subsequent legislation has broadened eligibility to include any veteran who served for a period of at least 90 days in the armed forces of the United States or an ally between September 16, 1940 and July 25, 1947, or between June 27, 1950 and January 31, 1955. Any veteran of the United States who has served at least 181 days of continuous active duty from January 31, 1955 to September 7, 1980 is also eligible. If service was during the Vietnam conflict period (August 5, 1964 to May 7, 1975) or the Persian Gulf War, 90 days is sufficient to qualify.

The VA requires a length of service of at least 2 years for a veteran who enlisted after September 7, 1980, or was an officer and began service after October 16, 1981. These veterans must have completed either: (1) at least 24 months, or (2) the full period ordered active duty (not less than 90 days during wartime or

TABLE 12.3 VA loan guarantee amounts

Loan Amount	Guarantee
Up to $45,000	50% of the loan amount
$45,001 to $56,250	$22,500
$56,251 to $144,000	40% of the loan amount with a maximum of $36,000
$144,001 to $417,000	25% of the FHLMC conforming loan with a maximum of $104,250
	Some lenders will go higher if the borrower makes a down payment, generally four times the guaranty ($240,000).

*This pertains to loans originally closed on or after March 1, 1988. No funding fee is required for assumption of loans closed prior to March 1, 1988.

Source: © 2012 Cengage Learning

181 days during peacetime). The benefit is also available to those who serve in the Select Reserves or National Guard at least 6 years with an honorable discharge.

The veteran's discharge must be on conditions other than dishonorable, and the guarantee entitlement is good until used. If not remarried, the spouse of a veteran who died as a result of service can also obtain a housing guarantee. Active duty personnel can also qualify. Shorter active duty periods are allowed for service-connected disabilities.

VA Certificates

To determine benefits, a veteran should make application to the Department of Veterans Affairs for a *certificate of eligibility,* which shows whether the veteran is qualified and the amount of guarantee available. This document (Form 26-1880), along with a copy of the veteran's discharge papers, is necessary to obtain a VA-guaranteed loan.

The VA works diligently to protect veterans and reduce foreclosure losses. When a veteran applies for a VA guarantee, the property is appraised and the VA issues a *certificate of reasonable value.* Often abbreviated **CRV,** it reflects the estimated value of the property as determined by the VA staff appraiser. Similarly, the VA establishes income guidelines to make certain that the veteran can comfortably meet the proposed loan payments. Also, the veteran must agree to occupy the property. Pursuant to the newly enacted Safe Drinking Water Act, if the building was constructed after June 19, 1988, the CRV must now reflect a certification that any solders or fluxes used in construction did not contain more than 0.2% lead in any pipes or that the pipe fittings used did not contain more than 8% lead.

The VA guarantees fixed-rate loans for as long as 30 years on homes, and no pre-payment penalty is charged if the borrower wishes to pay sooner. Moreover, there is no due-on-sale clause that requires the loan to be repaid if the property is sold. The VA guarantees loans for the purchase of townhouses and condominiums, to build or improve a home, and to buy a mobile home as a residence. A veteran wishing to refinance an existing home or farm can obtain a VA-guaranteed loan provided that there is existing debt that will be repaid. The VA also makes direct loans to veterans if no private lending institutions are nearby.

Financial Liability

No matter what loan guarantee program is elected, the veteran should know that in the event of default and subsequent foreclosure, he or she is required eventually to make good any losses suffered by the VA on the loan. (This is not the case with FHA-insured loans, in which the borrower pays for protection against foreclosure losses that may result from the loan.) Even if the veteran sells the property and the buyer assumes the VA loan, the veteran is still financially responsible if the buyer later defaults. To avoid this, the veteran must arrange with the VA to be released from liability. For VA loans underwritten after March 1, 1988, Congress created a new Guarantee and Indemnity Fund that allows a release from liability to the VA in the event of foreclosure, provided that the following requirements are met:

1. The loan payments must be current.
2. The prospective purchaser must meet creditworthiness standards as required by the VA.
3. The prospective purchaser must assume full liability for repayment of the loan, including indemnity liability to the VA.

In the event borrowers are unable to make their mortgage payments, the VA offers an assistance procedure that may be helpful in declining markets. If the borrower can obtain a purchase offer that is insufficient to pay off the existing loan balance, a *compromise agreement* may allow the VA to pay the difference between the sales proceeds and the mortgage balance. To effect the compromise agreement, the borrower must be willing to find a purchaser who will pay fair market value of the house, and the original borrower must agree to remain liable to the government for the amount that the VA pays to the noteholder.

A veteran is permitted a full new guarantee entitlement if complete repayment of a previous VA-guaranteed loan has been made. If a veteran has sold and let the buyer assume the VA loan, the balance of the entitlement is still available. For example, if a veteran has used $15,000 of his or her entitlement to date, the difference between $15,000 and the current VA guarantee amount is still available for use.

Funding Fee

From its inception until October 1, 1982, the VA made loan guarantees on behalf of veterans without a charge. Congress initially enacted a funding fee in 1982, increased it in 1991, and in 1993 established a funding fee with three categories of veterans, each with different fees depending on the veteran status and down payment. Note the new rates set out in Table 12.4. Funding fees for interest-rate-reduction refinancing loans were reduced to 1/2 of 1%. Funding fees on manufactured homes remain at 1% for all veterans and reservists. The fee still remains at 1/2 of 1% for assumptions by veterans or reservists. Funding fees can be added to the loan amount for calculating the loan-to-value ratio.

Interest Rates

In 1992, Congress passed an historic change that eliminated the interest rate ceilings on VA loans. The new program allows an interest rate and discount points agreed on by the veteran and the lender. Discount points cannot be financed on any loan except interest-rate-reduction refinancing loans (IRRRLs). IRRRLs are

TABLE 12.4 VA funding fees

PURCHASE AND CONSTRUCTION LOANS

Loan Type	Required Down Payment	Active Duty Personnel and Veterans	National Guard and Reservists
First Time Use of VA Loan Guaranty Benefits			
Purchase/Construction	0% down	2.15%	4%
	5% down	1.50%	1.75%
	10% down	1.25%	1.5%
Second or Subsequent Use of VA Loan Guaranty Benefits			
Purchase/Construction	0%	3.3%	3.3%
	5%	1.50%	1.75%
	10%	1.25%	1.5%

OTHER LOANS

Loan Type	Active Duty Personnel and Veterans	National Guard and Reservists
All Interest Rate Reduction Refinance Loans	0.50%	0.50%
First Loan Cash-Out Refinance	2.15%	2.4%
Subsequent Loan Cash-Out Refinance or	3.3%	3.3%
Assumptions*	0.50%	0.50%

*This pertains to loans originally closed on or after March 1, 1988. No funding fee is required for assumption of loans closed prior to March 1, 1988.

Source: © 2012 Cengage Learning

limited to two discount points. The two-point limit does not include origination fees, which are limited to one point.

Assumption Requirements

On VA loans assumed prior to March 1, 1988, approval was not required prior to loan assumption. Therefore, sellers could sell their property on assumption without obtaining any approval from the VA, but sellers remained fully liable for repayment. As stated previously, they could be released from liability if the VA approved the credit-worthiness of the new purchaser. After March 1, 1988, the VA required prior approval for transfer of the property. Federal law now requires that the mortgage or deed of trust and note for loans carry on the first page in type $2\frac{1}{2}$ times larger than the regular type the following statement:

> THIS LOAN IS NOT ASSUMABLE WITHOUT THE PRIOR APPROVAL OF THE DEPARTMENT OF VETERANS AFFAIRS OR AUTHORIZED AGENT.

Because Congress frequently changes eligibility and benefits, a person contemplating a VA or FHA loan should make inquiry to the field offices of these two agencies and to mortgage lenders to ascertain the current status and details of the law, as well as the availability of loan money. Field offices also have information on foreclosed properties that are for sale. Additionally, one should query lenders as to the availability of state veteran benefits. A number of states offer special advantages, including mortgage loan assistance, to residents who have served in the armed forces.

Adjustable-Rate Mortgages

The VA can also issue its guarantee for an adjustable-rate mortgage. The approved plan is structured the same as the FHA adjustable-rate mortgages, underwritten at an interest rate 1% above the initial rate agreed on by the veteran and the lender. Increases in the interest rate are limited to an annual adjustment of 1% and capped at 5% over the life of the loan. The index for calculating interest-rate adjustments is the weekly average yield on Treasury securities to a constant maturity of one year as reported by the Federal Reserve Board. Additional information on the VA can be obtained from the website, http://www.homeloans.va.gov.

PRIVATE MORTGAGE INSURANCE

In 1957, the Mortgage Guaranty Insurance Corporation (MGIC) was formed in Milwaukee, Wisconsin, as a privately owned business venture to insure home mortgage loans. Demand was slow but steady for the first 10 years and then grew rapidly until today when there are over a dozen private mortgage insurance companies. Like FHA insurance, the object of ***private mortgage insurance (PMI)*** is to insure lenders against foreclosure losses. But, unlike the FHA, PMI insures only the top 20% to 25% of a loan, not the whole loan. This allows a lender to make 90% and 95% L/V loans with about the same exposure to foreclosure losses as a 70% to 75% L/V loan. The borrower, meanwhile, can purchase a home with a cash down payment of either 10% or 5% rather than the 20% to 30% down required by lenders when mortgage insurance is not purchased. For this privilege the borrower pays a PMI fee of 1% or less when the loan is made plus an annual fee of a fraction of 1%. When the loan is partially repaid (e.g., to a 70% L/V), the premiums and coverage can be terminated. PMI is also available on apartment buildings, offices, stores, warehouses, and leaseholds, but at higher rates than on homes.

Under a 1997 Texas statute, a lender must now provide an annual promulgated notice to each borrower who is required to purchase mortgage guaranty insurance. The notice informs the borrower that if the principal of her loan is 80% or less of the current fair market value of her home, the borrower may have the right to cancel the insurance.

In 1999, Congress passed the Homeowner's Protection Act (HPA), which became effective in 2000. The Act requires services to automatically cancel PMI once a loan reaches 78% of the property's original value. The Act also requires notification to the borrower that they can request PMI cancellation when their loan amount is paid to 80% of the property value. Lenders are allowed to require an appraisal to prove the value at that time, so some owners may choose to wait until the automatic cancellation is triggered. The Act also allows lenders to refuse to cancel the insurance if the borrower does not have a good payment record. FHA and VA loans are exempted from this new legislation.

Approval Procedure

Private mortgage insurers work to keep their losses to a minimum by first approving the lenders with whom they do business. Particular emphasis is placed on the lender's operating policy, appraisal procedure, and degree of government regulation. Once approved, a lender simply sends the borrower's loan application, credit report, and property appraisal to the insurer. Based on these documents, the insurer either agrees or refuses to issue a policy. Although the insurer relies on the appraisal prepared by the lender, the insurer sends, on a random basis, its own appraiser to verify the quality of the information being submitted. When an insured loan goes into default, the insurer has the option of either buying the property from the lender for the balance due or letting the lender foreclose and then paying the lender's losses up to the amount of the insurance. As a rule, insurers take the first option because it is more popular with lenders and it leaves the lender with immediate cash to relend. The insurer is then responsible for foreclosing.

RURAL HOUSING SERVICES ADMINISTRATION

The *Rural Housing Services Administration* is a federal agency under the U.S. Department of Agriculture. Like the FHA, it came into existence due to the financial crises of the 1930s. The RHSA offers programs to help purchase or operate farms. The RHSA will either guarantee a portion of a loan made by a private lender or it will make the loan itself. RHSA loans can also be used to help finance the purchase of homes in rural areas.

REVIEW QUESTIONS

Answers to these questions are found in the Answer Key section at the back of the book.

1. A loan wherein the principal is all repaid in one lump sum payment at the end of the loan's life is known as a (an)
   A. straight or term loan.
   B. amortized loan.
   C. budget mortgage.
   D. conventional loan.

2. The last day of a loan's life is known as the
   A. settlement date.
   B. maturity date.
   C. sale date.
   D. contract date.

3. To determine the amount of loan payments by using an amortization table, you must know all the following EXCEPT:
   A. loan-to-value ratio.
   B. frequency of payments.
   C. interest rates.
   D. amount of loan.

4. Amortization tables can be used by real estate agents to determine which of the following?
   A. Frequency of payment
   B. Interest rate
   C. Maturity
   D. Amount of loan
   E. All of the above

5. A major negative of balloon loan financing is that the borrower may have difficulty
   A. meeting the final payment when it becomes due.
   B. refinancing when the final payment comes due.
   C. both A and B.
   D. neither A nor B.

6. Kevin wants to know what portion of a 30-year, fully amortized loan would be paid off by the fourth year of the loan's life. Kevin would consult
   A. an amortization table.
   B. a loan balance table.
   C. a partial amortization table.
   D. the loan-to-value ratio.

7. By the tenth year of a 9.5% 30-year amortization period, how much of the principal balance will have been repaid under a monthly amortization of equal installments? Use Table 12.2 in the text.
   A. One-half
   B. One-third
   C. Two-thirds
   D. None of the above

8. The FHA has been influential in bringing about acceptance of
   A. long-term amortization of loans.
   B. standardized construction techniques.
   C. both A and B.
   D. neither A nor B.

9. Regarding mortgage insurance, which of the following statements are true?
   A. PMI insures only the top 20 or 25% of the loan.
   B. FHA insures the entire loan.
   C. both A and B.
   D. neither A nor B.

Chapter 13

KEY TERMS

APR: the annual percentage rate as calculated under the federal Truth-in-Lending Act by combining the interest rate with other costs of the loan

Credit report: a report reflecting the creditworthiness of a borrower by showing past credit history

Fair Credit Reporting Act: federal law giving an individual the right to inspect his or her file with the credit bureau and correct any errors

Finance charge: the total amount the credit will cost over the life of the loan

Liquid asset: asset that is in cash or is readily convertible to cash

Redlining: a lender's refusal to make loans in certain neighborhoods

Regulation Z: federal regulations that implement the enforcement of the Truth-in-Lending Act

Truth-in-Lending Act: a federal law that requires certain disclosures when extending or advertising credit

The Loan and the Consumer

IN THIS CHAPTER

The previous chapter discussed lending practices applied to the types of payment arrangements that can be made in retiring debt. Consumer protection was enabled through the Federal Consumer Credit Protection Act, and additional protections have been created through standardized loan procedures. This chapter will discuss the federal Truth-in-Lending Act and standard loan procedures that consumers need to use in order to make application for a loan.

TRUTH-IN-LENDING ACT

The *Federal Consumer Credit Protection Act,* popularly known as the ***Truth in Lending Act,*** went into effect in 1969. The act, implemented by Federal Reserve Board ***Regulation Z,*** requires that a borrower be clearly shown, before committing to a loan, how much is being paid for credit in both dollar terms and percentage terms. The borrower is also given the right to rescind (cancel) the transaction in certain instances. The act came into being because it was not uncommon to see loans advertised for rates lower than the borrower actually wound up paying. Once the act took effect, several weaknesses and ambiguities of the act and Regulation Z became apparent. Thus, the Truth in Lending Simplification and Reform Act (TILSRA) was passed by Congress and became effective October 1, 1982. Concurrently, the Federal Reserve Board issued a *Revised Regulation Z (RRZ)* that details rules and regulations for TILSRA. For purposes of discussion we refer to all of this as the Truth-in-Lending Act or TILA.

Advertising

Whether you are a real estate practitioner or a property owner acting on your own behalf, TILA rules affect you when you advertise just about anything (including real estate) and include financing terms in the ad.

Trigger Terms

Five specific disclosures must be included in any ad that contains even one of the following trigger terms: (1) the amount of down payment (for example, only 5% down, 10% down, $4,995 down, 95% financing); (2) the amount of any payment (for example, monthly payments only $499, buy for less than $650 a month, payments only 1% per month); (3) the number of payments (for example, only 36 monthly payments and you own it, all paid up in 10 annual payments); (4) the period of repayment (for example, 30-year financing, owner will carry for 5 years, 10-year second available); and (5) the dollar amount of any finance charge (finance this for only $999) or the statement that there is no charge for credit (pay no interest for 3 years).

If any of the aforementioned trigger terms are used, then the following five disclosures must appear in the ad: (1) the cash price or the amount of the loan; (2) the amount of down payment or a statement that none is required; (3) the number, amount, and frequency of repayments; (4) the annual percentage rate; and (5) the deferred payment price or total payments. Item 5 is not a requirement in the case of the sale of a dwelling or a loan secured by a first lien on the dwelling that is being purchased.

PUTTING IT TO WORK

If an advertisement contains any item from the TIL list of financing terms, the ad must also include other required information. For example, an advertisement that reads: "Bargain! Bargain! Bargain! New 3-bedroom townhouses only $499 per month" may or may not be a bargain depending on other financing information missing from the ad.

Annual Percentage Rate

The ***annual percentage rate (APR)*** combines the interest rate with the other costs of the loan into a single figure that shows the true annual cost of borrowing. This is one of the most helpful features of the law because it gives the prospective borrower a standardized yardstick by which to compare financing from different sources.

If the annual percentage rate being offered is subject to increase after the transaction takes place (such as with an adjustable rate mortgage), that fact must be stated; for example, "9% annual percentage rate subject to increase after settlement." If the loan has interest rate changes that follow a predetermined schedule, those terms must be stated, for example, "7% first year, 9% second year, 11% third year, 13% remainder of loan, 12.5% annual percentage rate."

If you wish to say something about financing and avoid triggering full disclosure, you may use general statements. The following would be acceptable: "assumable loan," "financing available," "owner will carry," "terms to fit your budget," "easy monthly payments," or "FHA and VA financing available."

Lending Disclosures

If you are in the business of making loans, the Truth-in-Lending Act requires you to make 18 disclosures to your borrower. Of these, the four that must be most prominently displayed on the papers the borrower signs are: (1) the amount financed, (2) the finance charge, (3) the annual percentage rate, and (4) the total payments.

The **amount financed** is the amount of credit provided to the borrower. The ***finance charge*** is the total dollar amount the credit will cost the borrower over the life of the loan. This includes interest, *plus* such things as borrower-paid discount points, loan fees, loan finder's fees, loan service fees, required life insurance, and mortgage guarantee premiums. On a long-term mortgage loan, the total finance charge can easily exceed the amount of money being borrowed. For example, the total amount of interest on a 7%, 30-year, $160,000 loan is just over $223,000.

The annual percentage rate was described earlier. The total payment is the amount in dollars the borrower will have paid after making all the payments as scheduled. In the aforementioned 7%, 30-year loan it would be the interest of $223,000 plus the principal of $160,000 for a total of $383,000.

The other 14 disclosures that a lender must make are as follows: (1) the identity of the lender; (2) the payment schedule; (3) prepayment penalties and rebates; (4) late payment charges; (5) any insurance required; (6) any filing fees; (7) any collateral required; (8) any required deposits; (9) whether or not the loan can be assumed; (10) the demand feature, if the note has one; (11) the total sales price of the item being purchased if the seller is also the creditor; (12) any adjustable rate features of the loan; (13) an itemization of the amount financed; and (14) a reference to any terms not shown on the disclosure statement but that are shown on the loan contract.

These disclosures must be delivered or mailed to the credit applicant within three business days after the creditor receives the applicant's written request for credit. The applicant must have this information before the transaction can take place—for example, before the closing.]

Who Must Comply?

Any person or firm that regularly extends consumer credit subject to a finance charge (such as interest) or payable by written agreement in more than four installments must comply with the lending disclosures. This includes banks, savings and loans, credit unions, finance companies, and so forth, as well as private individuals who extend credit more than five times a year.

Whoever is named on the note as the creditor must make the lending disclosures even if the note is to be resold. A key difference between the old and the new TILA is that the new TILA does not include mortgage brokers or real estate practitioners as creditors just because they brokered a deal containing financing. This is because they do not appear as creditors on the note. But if a broker takes back a note for part of the commission on a deal, that is an extension of credit and the lending disclosures must be made.

Exempt Transactions

Certain transactions are exempt from the lending disclosure requirement. The first exemption is for credit extended primarily for business, commercial, or agricultural purposes. This exemption includes dwelling units purchased for rental purposes (unless the property contains four or fewer units and the owner occupies one of them, in which case special rules apply).

The second exemption applies to credit over $25,000 secured by personal property unless the property is the principal residence of the borrower. For example, a mobile home that secures a loan over $25,000 qualifies under this exemption if it is used as a vacation home, but is not exempt if it is used as a principal residence.

Failure to Disclose

If the Federal Trade Commission (FTC) determines that an advertiser has broken the law, it can order the advertiser to cease from further violations. Each violation of that order can result in a $10,000 civil penalty each day the violation continues.

Failure to disclose properly when credit is extended can result in a penalty of twice the amount of the finance charge with a minimum of $100 and a maximum of $1,000 plus court costs, attorney fees, and actual damages. In addition, the FTC can add a fine of up to $5,000 and/or one year of imprisonment. If the required disclosures are not made or the borrower is not given the required three days to cancel (see the following section), the borrower can cancel the transaction at any time within three years following the date of the transaction. In that event the creditor must return all money paid by the borrower, and the borrower returns the property to the creditor.

Right to Cancel

A borrower has a limited *right to rescission* (right to cancel) in a credit transaction. The borrower has three business days (which includes Saturdays) to back out after signing the loan papers. This aspect of the law was inserted primarily to protect a homeowner from unscrupulous sellers of home improvements and appliances when the credit to purchase is secured by a lien on the home. Vacant lots for sale on credit to buyers who expect to use them for principal residences are also subject to cancellation privileges.

The right to rescind does not apply to credit used for the acquisition or initial construction of one's principal dwelling.

LOAN APPLICATION AND APPROVAL

When a mortgage lender reviews a real estate loan application, the primary concern for both applicant and lender is to approve loan requests that show a high probability of being repaid in full and on time, and to disapprove requests that are likely to result in default and eventual foreclosure. How is this decision made? Loan analysis varies. However, the five major federal agencies have recently combined their requirements for credit reports. All loans intended for underwriting by Fannie Mae, Freddie Mac, HUD/FHA, or VA must comply with the new standards. Figure 13.1 shows the Uniform Residential Loan Application (a requirement for standardized loan applications) and summarizes the key terms that a loan officer considers when making a decision regarding a loan request. Let's review these items and observe how they affect the acceptance of a loan by a lender.

Note that in section [1] the borrower is requested to specify the type of mortgage and terms of the loan being sought. This greatly facilitates the lender's ability to determine the availability of the loan that the borrower may be seeking.

In section [2] the lender begins the loan analysis procedure by looking at the property and the proposed financing. Using the property address and legal description, an appraiser is assigned to prepare an appraisal of the property and a title search is ordered. These steps are taken to determine the fair market value of the property and the condition of title. In the event of default, the property is the collateral the lender must fall back on to recover the loan. If the loan request is in connection with a purchase rather than the refinancing of an existing property, the lender will know the purchase price. As a rule, loans are made on the basis of the appraised value or purchase price, whichever is lower. If the appraised value is lower than the purchase price, the usual procedure is to require the buyer to make a larger cash down payment. The lender does not want to overloan simply because the buyer overpaid for the property.

Settlement Funds

In section **VI**, the lender wants to know whether the borrower has adequate funds for settlement. Are these funds presently in a checking or savings account, or are they coming from the sale of the borrower's present property? In the latter case, the lender knows that the present loan is contingent on closing that escrow. If the down payment and settlement funds are to be borrowed, then the lender needs to be extra cautious because experience has shown that the less money a borrower personally puts into a purchase, the higher is the probability of default and foreclosure.

Purpose of Loan

The lender is also interested in the proposed use of the property. Lenders feel most comfortable when a loan is for the purchase or improvement of a property the loan applicant will actually occupy. This is because owner-occupants usually have pride of ownership in maintaining their property and even during bad economic conditions will continue to make the monthly payments. An owner-occupant also realizes that losing the home still means paying for shelter elsewhere. It is standard practice for lenders to ask loan applicants to sign a statement declaring whether they intend to occupy the property.

If the loan applicant intends to purchase a dwelling to rent out as an investment, the lender will be more cautious because, during periods of high vacancy,

FIGURE 13.1 Uniform residential loan application

FannieMae

Uniform Residential Loan Application/*Solicitud Uniforme para Préstamo Hipotecario Residencial*

This application is designed to be completed by the applicant(s) with the Lender's assistance. Applicants should complete this form as "Borrower" or "Co-Borrower," as applicable. Co-Borrower information must also be provided (and the appropriate box checked) when ☐ the income or assets of a person other than the Borrower (including the Borrower's spouse) will be used as a basis for loan qualification or ☐ the income or assets of the Borrower's spouse or other person who has community property rights pursuant to state law will not be used as a basis for loan qualification, but his or her liabilities must be considered because the spouse or other person has community property rights pursuant to applicable law and Borrower resides in a community property state, the security property is located in a community property state, or the Borrower is relying on other property located in a community property state as a basis for repayment of the loan.

Esta solicitud se diseñó para ser completada por el solicitante o solicitantes con la ayuda del prestador. Los solicitantes deben completar esta solicitud como "Prestatario" o "Co-Prestatario", según corresponda. La información sobre el Co-Prestatario también debe proporcionarse (marque el cuadro correspondiente) ☐ si el ingreso o los bienes de una persona que no sea el "Prestatario" (incluyendo el cónyugue del prestatario) se emplearán como base para calificar para el préstamo o ☐ los bienes e ingresos del cónyuge del prestatario o de otra persona con derechos de comunidad conyugal de conformidad con la ley estatal no se usarán como base para calificar para el préstamo, pero las deudas de dichas personas tienen que considerarse debido a que el cónyuge u otra persona tienen derechos de comunidad conyugal de conformidad con la ley aplicable y a que el Prestatario reside en un estado en el que rige el régimen de comunidad conyugal, la propiedad que se ofrece como garantía se encuentra en un estado en el que rige el régimen de comunidad conyugal, o el Prestatario depende de otra propiedad que se encuentra en un estado en el que rige el régimen de comunidad conyugal para el pago total del préstamo.

If this is an application for joint credit, Borrower and Co-Borrower each agree that we intend to apply for joint credit (sign below):

Si se trata de una solicitud de crédito conjunto, el Prestatario y Co-Prestatario acuerdan que pretenden solicitar un crédito conjunto (firmar a continuación):

Borrower *Prestatario*	Co-Borrower *Co-Prestatario*

I. TYPE OF MORTGAGE AND TERMS OF LOAN/*TIPO DE HIPOTECA Y CONDICIONES DEL PRÉSTAMO*

Mortgage Applied for/ *Préstamo Hipotecario Solicitado:*	☐ VA/*VA* ☐ FHA/*FHA*	☐ Conventional/*Convencional* ☐ USDA/Rural Housing Service *USDA/Servicio Rural de Vivienda*	☐ Other (explain)/ *Otro (explique):*	Agency Case Number/ *N° de Préstamo de la Agencia*	Lender Case Number/ *N° de Préstamo del Prestador*

[1]

Amount/*Cantidad Total del Préstamo* $	Interest Rate/ *Tasa de Interés* %	No. of Months/ *Plazo (Meses)*	**Amortization Type/ *Tipo de Amortización:***	☐ Fixed Rate/ *Tasa Fija* ☐ GPM/*GPM*	☐ Other (explain)/ *Otro (explique):* ☐ ARM (type)/ *ARM (tipo):*

II. PROPERTY INFORMATION AND PURPOSE OF LOAN/*INFORMACIÓN SOBRE LA PROPIEDAD Y PROPÓSITO DEL PRÉSTAMO*

[2]

Subject Property Address (street, city, state & ZIP)/ *Dirección de la Propiedad (calle, ciudad, estado y código postal)*	No. of Units/ *N° de Unidades*
Legal Description of Subject Property (attach description if necessary)/ *Descripción Legal de la Propiedad (adjunte descripción si es necesario)*	Year Built/ *Año de Construcción*

Purpose of Loan/ *Propósito del Préstamo*	☐ Purchase/*Compra* ☐ Refinance/ *Refinanciamiento*	☐ Construction/*Construcción* ☐ Construction-Permanent/ *Financiamiento Permanente de Construcción*	☐ Other (explain): *Otro (explique)*	Property will be/*La propiedad será:* ☐ Primary Residence/ *Residencia Principal*	☐ Secondary Residence/ *Residencia Secundaria*	☐ Investment/ *Inversión*

Complete this line if construction or construction-permanent loan./ Complete esta línea si es un préstamo para construcción o financiamiento permanente de construcción.

Year Lot Acquired/ *Año en que se Adquirió el Lote*	Original Cost/ *Costo Original*	Amount Existing Liens/ *Monto de los Gravámenes Actuales*	(a) Present Value of Lot/ *Valor Actual del Lote*	(b) Cost of Improvements/ *Costo de las Mejoras*	Total (a + b)/ *Total (a + b)*
	$	$	$	$	$

Complete this line if this is a refinance loan./Complete esta línea si es un préstamo de refinanciamiento.

Year Acquired/ *Año en que se Adquirió*	Original Cost/ *Costo Original*	Amount Existing Liens/ *Monto de los Gravámenes Actuales*	Purpose of Refinance/ *Propósito del Refinanciamiento*	Describe Improvements/ *Descripción de las Mejoras*	☐ made/ *realizadas*	☐ to be made/ *por realizarse*
	$	$		Cost/*Costo:* $		

Title will be held in what Name(s) /*Nombre(s) que se Registrará(n) en el Título*	Manner in which Title will be held/ *Manera en que se Registrará el Título*	Estate will be held in/ *La propiedad se mantendrá en:* ☐ Fee Simple/ *Pleno Dominio* ☐ Leasehold (show expiration date)/ *Arrendamiento (indique fecha de vencimiento)*
Source of Down Payment, Settlement Charges, and/or Subordinate Financing (explain)/ *Origen de Pago Inicial, Costos de Cierre y/o Financiamiento Subordinado (explique)*		

FIGURE 13.1 Uniform residential loan application (*continued*)

III. BORROWER INFORMATION/ *INFORMACIÓN SOBRE EL PRESTATARIO*

Borrower/*Prestatario*	Co-Borrower/*Co-Prestatario*
Borrower's Name (include Jr. or Sr. if applicable)/ *Nombre del Prestatario (indique Jr., o Sr. si aplica)* [3]	Co-Borrower's Name (include Jr. or Sr. if applicable)/ *Nombre del Co-Prestatario (indique Jr., o Sr. si aplica)* [4]
Social Security Number/ *Número de Seguro Social* · Home Phone (incl. area code)/ *Teléfono de la Casa (incluya código de área)* · DOB (mm/dd/yyyy)/ *Fecha de nacimiento (mm/dd/aaaa)* · Yrs. School/ *Años de Educación*	Social Security Number/ *Número de Seguro Social* · Home Phone (incl. area code)/ *Teléfono de la Casa (incluya código de área)* · DOB (mm/dd/yyyy)/ *Fecha de nacimiento (mm/dd/aaaa)* · Yrs. School/ *Años de Educación*
☐ Married *Casado* ☐ Unmarried (include single, divorced, widowed)/ *No está casado (incluye soltero, divorciado, viudo)* ☐ Separated *Separado* · Dependents (not listed by Co-Borrower)/ *Dependientes (no incluidos por el Co-Prestatario)* No./*N°* Ages/*Edades*	☐ Married *Casado* ☐ Unmarried (include single, divorced, widowed)/ *No está casado (incluye soltero, divorciado, viudo)* ☐ Separated *Separado* · Dependents (not listed by Borrower)/ *Dependientes (no incluidos por el Prestatario)* No./*N°* Ages/*Edades*
Present Address (street, city, state, ZIP)/ *Dirección Actual (calle, ciudad, estado, código postal)* ☐ Own/ *Propietario* ☐ Rent *Inquilino* ___No. Yrs./ *N° de Años*	Present Address (street, city, state, ZIP)/ *Dirección Actual (calle, ciudad, estado, código postal)* ☐ Own/ *Propietario* ☐ Rent *Inquilino* ___No. Yrs./ *N° de Años*
Mailing Address, if different from Present Address/ *Dirección donde recibe su correspondencia, si es diferente de su dirección actual*	Mailing Address, if different from Present Address/ *Dirección donde recibe su correspondencia, si es diferente de su dirección actual*

If residing at present address for less than two years, complete the following:/Si habita en dicha dirección hace menos de dos años, por favor complete:

Borrower	Co-Borrower
Former Address (street, city, state, ZIP) ☐ Own ☐ Rent ___No. Yrs. *Dirección Anterior (calle, ciudad, estado, código postal)* *Propietario* *Inquilino* *N° de Años*	Former Address (street, city, state, ZIP) ☐ Own ☐ Rent ___No. Yrs. *Dirección Anterior (calle, ciudad, estado, código postal)* *Propietario* *Inquilino* *N° de Años*

IV. EMPLOYMENT INFORMATION/ *INFORMACIÓN SOBRE EL EMPLEO*

Borrower/*Prestatario*	Co-Borrower/*Co-Prestatario*
Name & Address of Employer/ *Nombre y Dirección del Empleador* [5] · ☐ Self Employed/ *Empleado por Cuenta Propia* · Yrs. on this job/ *Años en este trabajo* · Yrs. employed in this line of work/profession/ *Años de empleo en este tipo de trabajo/profesión*	Name & Address of Employer/ *Nombre y Dirección del Empleador* [6] · ☐ Self Employed/ *Empleado por Cuenta Propia* · Yrs. on this job/ *Años en este trabajo* · Yrs. employed in this line of work/profession/ *Años de empleo en este tipo de trabajo/profesión*
Position/Title/Type of Business/ *Posición/Título/Tipo de Negocio* · Business Phone (incl. area code)/*Teléfono en el lugar de trabajo (incluya código de área)*	Position/Title/Type of Business/ *Posición/Título/Tipo de Negocio* · Business Phone (incl. area code)/*Teléfono en el lugar de trabajo (incluya código de área)*

If employed in current position for less than two years or if currently employed in more than one position, complete the following:/ Si ha estado trabajando en la posición actual menos de dos años o si actualmente está empleado en más de una posición, complete lo siguiente:

Borrower	Co-Borrower
Name & Address of Employer/ *Nombre y Dirección del Empleador* · ☐ Self Employed/ *Empleado por Cuenta Propia* · Dates (from – to)/ *Fechas de empleo (desde – hasta)* · Monthly Income/ *Ingreso Mensual* $	Name & Address of Employer/ *Nombre y Dirección del Empleador* · ☐ Self Employed/ *Empleado por Cuenta Propia* · Dates (from – to)/ *Fechas de empleo (desde – hasta)* · Monthly Income/ *Ingreso Mensual* $
Position/Title/Type of Business/ *Posición/Título/Tipo de Negocio* · Business Phone (incl. area code)/ *Teléfono en el lugar de trabajo (incluya código de área)*	Position/Title/Type of Business/ *Posición/Título/Tipo de Negocio* · Business Phone (incl. area code)/ *Teléfono en el lugar de trabajo (incluya código de área)*
Name & Address of Employer/ *Nombre y Dirección del Empleador* · ☐ Self Employed/ *Empleado por Cuenta Propia* · Dates (from – to)/ *Fechas de empleo (desde – hasta)* · Monthly Income/ *Ingreso Mensual* $	Name & Address of Employer/ *Nombre y Dirección del Empleador* · ☐ Self Employed/ *Empleado por Cuenta Propia* · Dates (from – to)/ *Fechas de empleo (desde – hasta)* · Monthly Income/ *Ingreso Mensual* $

Uniform Residential Loan Application
Freddie Mac Form 65s 7/05 (rev.6/09)

Page 2 of 8
Página 2 de 8

Fannie Mae Form 1003s 7/05 (rev.6/09)

FIGURE 13.1 Uniform residential loan application (*continued*)

Borrower/*Prestatario*		IV. EMPLOYMENT INFORMATION/ *INFORMACIÓN SOBRE EL EMPLEO* (cont'd)	Co-Borrower/*Co-Prestatario*
Position/Title/Type of Business/ *Posición/Título/Tipo de Negocio*	Business Phone (incl. area code)/ *Teléfono en el lugar de trabajo (incluya código de área)*	Position/Title/Type of Business/ *Posición/Título/Tipo de Negocio*	Business Phone (incl. area code)/ *Teléfono en el lugar de trabajo (incluya código de área)*

V. MONTHLY INCOME AND COMBINED HOUSING EXPENSE INFORMATION/ *INFORMACIÓN SOBRE EL INGRESO Y LOS GASTOS MENSUALES COMBINADOS DE VIVIENDA*

Gross Monthly Income *Ingreso Bruto Mensual*	Borrower *Prestatario*	Co-Borrower *Co-Prestatario*	Total	Combined Monthly Housing Expense/*Gastos Mensuales Combinados de Vivienda*	Present *Actual*	Proposed *Propuesto* [8]
[7] Base Empl. Income* *Ingreso Básico del Empleado**	$	$	$	Rent *Alquiler*	$	
Overtime *Horas extra*				First Mortgage (P&I) *Hipoteca Principal (Principal e Interés)*		$
Bonuses *Pagas Extras*				Other Financing (P&I) *Otro Financiamiento (Principal e Interés)*		
Commissions *Comisiones*				Hazard Insurance *Seguro Contra Riesgos*		
Dividends/Interest *Dividendos/Intereses*				Real Estate Taxes *Impuestos Sobre Bienes Raíces*		
Net Rental Income *Ingreso Neto por Alquiler*				Mortgage Insurance *Seguro de Hipoteca*		
Other (before completing, see the notice in "describe other income", below) *Otros (antes de llenar, vea el aviso en "describa otros ingresos", a continuación)*				Homeowner Assn. Dues *Cuotas de la Asociación de Propietarios* / Other: *Otro:*		
Total	$	$	$	**Total**	$	$

[9]

* **Self Employed Borrower(s) may be required to provide additional documentation such as tax returns and financial statements.**

* ***Se podrá requerir al Prestatario o Prestatarios que trabajan por cuenta propia que proporcionen documentos adicionales, tales como declaraciones y planillas de impuestos y estados financieros.***

Describe Other Income/ *Describa Otros Ingresos*

Notice: **Alimony, child support, or separate maintenance income need not be revealed if the Borrower (B) or Co-Borrower (C) does not choose to have it considered for repaying this loan.**

Aviso: ***La pensión conyugal, pensión para el sustento de los hijos o ingreso de mantenimiento por separación, no tienen que declararse si el Prestatario (B) o Co-Prestatario (C) no desea que se considere para el pago de este Préstamo.***

B/C		Monthly Amount *Cantidad Mensual*
		$

VI. ASSETS AND LIABILITIES/*BIENES Y PASIVOS*

This Statement and any applicable supporting schedules may be completed jointly by both married and unmarried Co-Borrowers if their assets and liabilities are sufficiently joined so that the Statement can be meaningfully and fairly presented on a combined basis; otherwise, separate Statements and Schedules are required. If the Co-Borrower section was completed about a non-applicant spouse or other person, this Statement and supporting schedules must be completed about that spouse or other person also.

Esta Declaración y cualquier anexo respaldatorio pertinente pueden llenarse conjuntamente tanto por Co-Prestatarios casados como no casados si sus bienes y deudas están suficientemente unidos de manera que la Declaración pueda presentarse con sentido sobre una base combinada y de una forma fiel; o de lo contrario, se requieren Declaraciones y Anexos por separado. Si en la sección del Co-Prestatario se completó la parte sobre el cónyuge, no solicitante u otra persona, esta Declaración y los anexos respaldatorios también deben completarse para dicho cónyuge u otra persona.

Completed/*Se completó* ☐ Jointly/*En Conjunto* ☐ Not Jointly/*Por Separado* [10]

ASSETS/*BIENES* Description/*Descripción*	Cash or Market Value/ *Valor en Efectivo o Valor en el Mercado*	**Liabilities and Pledged Assets.** List the creditor's name, address, and account number for all outstanding debts, including automobile loans, revolving charge accounts, real estate loans, alimony, child support, stock pledges, etc. Use continuation sheet, if necessary. Indicate by (*) those liabilities, which will be satisfied upon sale of real estate owned or upon refinancing of the subject property.
Cash deposit toward purchase held by:/ *Depósito en efectivo para la compra en poder de:*	$	***Deudas y Bienes Gravados.*** *Indique el nombre, la dirección y el número de cuenta de todas las deudas pendientes, incluyendo préstamos para autos, cuentas de poder de: crédito rotativo, préstamos de bienes raíces, pensión conyugal, pensión para el sustento de hijos, valores gravados, etc. Si es necesario, use una hoja adicional. Indique con un (*) aquellas deudas que se satisfarán al venderse o refinanciarse la propiedad inmobiliaria en cuestión.*

Uniform Residential Loan Application
Freddie Mac Form 65s 7/05 (rev.6/09)

Page 3 of 8
Página 3 de 8

Fannie Mae Form 1003s 7/05 (rev.6/09)

FIGURE 13.1 Uniform residential loan application (*continued*)

VI. ASSETS AND LIABILITIES/*BIENES Y PASIVOS* (cont'd)

		LIABILITIES/*PASIVOS*	Monthly Payment & Months Left to Pay/ *Pago Mensual y Nº de Pagos Mensuales que quedan por pagar*	Unpaid Balance/ *Balance Pendiente*
List checking and savings accounts below/ Indique abajo las cuentas de cheques y de ahorros Name and address of Bank, S&L, or Credit Union/ *Nombre y dirección del Banco, Asociación de Ahorro y Préstamo o Cooperativa* ***de Crédito***		Name and address of Company/ *Nombre y dirección de la Compañía* Acct. no./*Nº de Cuenta*	$ Payment/Months *$ Pagos/Meses*	$ [11]
Acct. no./*Nº de Cuenta*	$	Name and address of Company/ *Nombre y dirección de la Compañía* Acct. no./*Nº de Cuenta*	$ Payment/Months *$ Pagos/Meses*	$
Name and address of Bank, S&L, or Credit Union/ *Nombre y dirección del Banco, Asociación de Ahorro y Préstamo o Cooperativa* ***de Crédito***				
Acct. no./*Nº de Cuenta*	$	Name and address of Company/ *Nombre y dirección de la Compañía* Acct. no./*Nº de Cuenta*	$ Payment/Months *$ Pagos/Meses*	$
Name and address of Bank, S&L, or Credit Union/ *Nombre y dirección del Banco, Asociación de Ahorro y Préstamo o Cooperativa* ***de Crédito***				
Acct. no./*Nº de Cuenta*	$	Name and address of Company/ *Nombre y dirección de la Compañía* Acct. no./*Nº de Cuenta*	$ Payment/Months *$ Pagos/Meses*	$
Name and address of Bank, S&L, or Credit Union/ *Nombre y dirección del Banco, Asociación de Ahorro y Préstamo o Cooperativa* ***de Crédito***				
Acct. no./*Nº de Cuenta*	$	Name and address of Company/ *Nombre y dirección de la Compañía* Acct. no./*Nº de Cuenta*	$ Payment/Months *$ Pagos/Meses*	$
Stocks & Bonds (Company name/number and description)/ *Acciones y Bonos (Nombre de la compañía/número y descripción de los valores y bonos)*	$			
Life insurance net cash value/ *Valor en efectivo neto del seguro de vida* Face amount: *Monto de la póliza:* $	$	Name and address of Company/ *Nombre y dirección de la Compañía*	$ Payment/Months *$ Pagos/Meses*	$
Subtotal Liquid Assets/ *Subtotal de los Bienes Líquidos*	$			
Real estate owned (enter market value from schedule of real estate owned)/ *Propiedad inmobiliaria de la cual es dueño (indique el valor en el mercado según el anexo de la propiedad inmobiliaria)*	$			
Vested interest in retirement fund/ *Intereses adquiridos en el fondo de retiro*	$			
Net worth of business(es) owned (attach financial statement)/ *Valor neto de negocio(s) propio(s) (incluya estados financieros)*	$	Acct. no./*Nº de Cuenta*		
Automobiles owned (make and year) / *Automóviles de los cuales es dueño (marca y año)*	$	Alimony/Child Support/Separate Maintenance Payments Owed to:/ *Pensión Alimenticia/Pensión Para el Sustento de los Hijos/Manutención por Separación:*	$	
Other Assets (itemize)/ *Otros Bienes (detalle)*	$	Job-Related Expense (child care, union dues, etc.)/ *Gastos Relacionados con el Empleo(cuidado de los hijos, cuotas de sindicatos, etc.)*	$	
		Total Monthly Payments/ *Total de Pagos Mensuales*	$	
Total Assets a./ *Total de Bienes a.*	$	Net Worth (a minus b) ▶ Valor Neto (a menos b) $	[12] **Total Liabilities b. *Total de Pasivos b.***	$

FIGURE 13.1 Uniform residential loan application (*continued*)

VI. ASSETS AND LIABILITIES/*/BIENES Y PASIVOS* (cont'd)

Schedule of Real Estate Owned (If additional properties are owned, use continuation sheet.)
Anexo de Propiedades Inmobiliarias *(Si es dueño de más propiedades, use la hoja a continuación.)*

Property Address (enter S if sold, PS if pending sale or R if rental being held for income)/ *Dirección de la Propiedad (ponga una S por vendida, una PS por venta pendiente o una R si recibe ingreso por alquiler)*	▼	Type of Property/ *Tipo de Propiedad*	Present Market Value/ *Valor Actual en el Mercado*	Amount of Mortgages & Liens/ *Cantidad de Hipotecas y Gravámenes*	Gross Rental Income/ *Ingreso Bruto por Alquiler*	Mortgage Payments/ *Pagos Hipotecarios*	Insurance, Maintenance, Taxes & Misc./ *Seguro, Mantenimiento, Impuestos y Otros*	Net Rental Income/ *Ingreso Neto por Alquiler*
			$	$	$	$	$	$
		Totals/ *Totales*	$	$	$	$	$	$

List any additional names under which credit has previously been received and indicate appropriate creditor name(s) and account number(s):/
Indique otros nombres bajo los cuales ha recibido crédito anteriormente, así como los nombres de los acreedores y el número de las cuentas.

Alternate Name/*Otro Nombre*	Creditor Name/*Nombre del Acreedor*	Account Number/*Número de Cuenta* [13]

VII. DETAILS OF TRANSACTION/ *DETALLES DE LA TRANSACCIÓN*

a.	Purchase price/*Precio de compra*	$
b.	Alterations, improvements, repairs/ *Remodelaciones, mejoras, reparaciones*	
c.	Land (if acquired separately)/ *Terreno (si fue adquirido por separado)*	
d.	Refinance (incl. debts to be paid off)/ *Refinanciamiento (incluya deudas que se pagarán)*	
e.	Estimated prepaid items/ *Estimado de partidas prepagadas*	
f.	Estimated closing costs/ *Estimado de los costos de cierre*	
g.	PMI, MIP, Funding Fee/ *Seguro de hipoteca privado (PMI), Primas de seguro de hipoteca (MIP), Costos de Financiamiento*	
h.	Discount (if Borrower will pay)/ *Descuento (si el Prestatario lo pagará)*	
i.	Total costs (add items a through h)/ ***Total d e costos (s ume la s l íneas " a" hasta la "h")***	
j.	Subordinate financing/ *Financiamiento subordinado*	
k.	Borrower's closing costs paid by Seller/ *Costos de cierre del Prestatario pagados por el Vendedor*	
l.	Other Credits (explain)/ *Otros Créditos (explique)*	

VIII. DECLARATIONS/ *DECLARACIONES*

If you answer "Yes" to any questions a through i, please use continuation sheet for explanation. / ***Si responde "Sí" a cualquier de las preguntas de la "a" a la "i", debe utilizar una hoja adicional para dar una explicación.***	**Borrower/** *Prestatario* Yes/*Sí*	No	**Co-Borrower/** *Co-Prestatario* Yes/*Sí*	No
a. Are there any outstanding judgments against you? *¿Existe alguna sentencia o fallo judicial pendiente en contra suya?*	☐	☐	☐	☐
b. Have you been declared bankrupt within the past 7 years? *¿Se ha declarado en bancarrota durante los últimos 7 años?*	☐	☐	☐	☐
c. Have you had property foreclosed upon or given title or deed in lieu thereof in the last 7 years? *¿Se le ha entablado una ejecución hipotecaria o ha transferido el título de propiedad en sustitución de una ejecución hipotecaria en los últimos 7 años?*	☐	☐	☐	☐
d. Are you a party to a lawsuit? *¿Es usted parte en una demanda judicial?*	☐	☐	☐	☐
e. Have you directly or indirectly been obligated on any loan which resulted in foreclosure, transfer of title in lieu of foreclosure, or judgment? *¿Ha estado usted obligado, directa o indirectamente, en algún préstamo que provocó una ejecución hipotecaria, transferencia de título en sustitución de una ejecución hipotecaria, o alguna sentencia, o fallo en su contra?* (This would include such loans as home mortgage loans, SBA loans, home improvement loans, educational loans, manufactured (mobile) home loans, any mortgage, financial obligation, bond, or loan guarantee. If "Yes," provide details, including date, name, and address of Lender, FHA or VA case number, if any, and reasons for the action.) *(Esto incluye préstamos tales como préstamos hipotecarios para vivienda, préstamos SBA, préstamos para mejoras en la casa, préstamos educacionales, préstamos para casa móviles, cualquier hipoteca, obligación financiera, bono o préstamo garantizado. Si la respuesta es "Sí", incluya la fecha, el nombre y la dirección del Prestador, o el número de caso de FHA o VA, si lo hubiera, y las razones de la acción.)*	☐	☐	☐	☐
f. Are you presently delinquent or in default on any Federal debt or any other loan, mortgage, financial obligation, bond, or loan guarantee? If "Yes," give details as described in the preceding question. *¿Se encuentra atrasado, moroso o en incumplimiento con alguna deuda federal o cualquier otro préstamos, hipoteca, obligación finaciera, bono o garantía de préstamos? Si la respuesta es "Sí", provea detalles según se describe en la pregun ta anterior.*	☐	☐	☐	☐
g. Are you obligated to pay alimony, child support, or separate maintenance? *¿Está obligado a pagar por pensión alimenticia, pensión para el sustento de los hijos, o manutención por separación?*	☐	☐	☐	☐
h. Is any part of the down payment borrowed? *¿Le prestaron alguna parte del pago inicial?*	☐	☐	☐	☐

Uniform Residential Loan Application
Freddie Mac Form 65s 7/05 (rev.6/09)

Page 5 of 8
Página 5 de 8

Fannie Mae Form 1003s 7/05 (rev. 6/09)

FIGURE 13.1 Uniform residential loan application (*continued*)

VII. DETAILS OF TRANSACTION/ *DETALLES DE LA TRANSACCIÓN*			VIII. DECLARATIONS/ *DECLARACIONES*				
m.	Loan amount (exclude PMI, MIP, Funding Fee financed)/ *Cantidad del Préstamo (excluya PMI, MIP, Costos de Financiamiento financiados)*		i. Are you a co-maker or endorser on a note? *¿Es usted co–prestatario o fiador de un pagaré?*	☐	☐	☐	☐
			j. Are you a U.S. citizen? *¿Es usted ciudadano de los Estados Unidos?*	☐	☐	☐	☐
n.	PMI, MIP, Funding Fee financed/ *Seguro de hipoteca privado (PMI), Primas de seguro de hipoteca (MIP), Costos de Financiamiento financiados*		k. Are you a permanent resident alien? *¿Es usted un residente extranjero permanente de los Estados Unidos?*	☐	☐	☐	☐
o.	Loan amount (add m & n) / *Cantidad del Préstamo (sume líneas "m" y "n")*		l. Do you intend to occupy the property as your primary residence? If "Yes," complete question m below. *¿Tiene usted la intención de ocupar la propiedad como su residencia principal? Si la respuesta es "Sí" conteste la pregunta "m".*	☐	☐	☐	☐
p.	Cash from/to Borrower (subtract j, k, l & o from i)/ *Dinero del / para el Prestatario (reste j, k, l & o de i)*		m. Have you had an ownership interest in a property in the last three years? *¿Ha tenido usted participación como dueño en una propiedad en los últimos 3 años?* (1) What type of property did you own—principal residence (PR), second home (SH), or investment property (IP)? *¿De qué tipo de propiedad era usted dueño–residencia principal (PR), reisdencia secundaria (SH) o propiedad de inversion (IP)?* (2) How did you hold title to the home—solely by yourself (S), jointly with your spouse (SP), or jointly with another person (O)? *¿Cómo estaba registrado el título–a nombre suyo solamente (S), conjuntamente con su cónyuge (SP), o conjuntamente con otra persona (O)?*	☐ ____ ____	☐	☐ ____ ____	☐

IX. ACKNOWLEDGEMENT AND AGREEMENT/*RECONOCIMIENTO Y ACUERDO*

Each of the undersigned specifically represents to Lender and to Lender's actual or potential agents, brokers, processors, attorneys, insurers, servicers, successors and assigns and agrees and acknowledges that: (1) the information provided in this application is true and correct as of the date set forth opposite my signature and that any intentional or negligent misrepresentation of this information contained in this application may result in civil liability, including monetary damages, to any person who may suffer any loss due to reliance upon any misrepresentation that I have made on this application, and/or in criminal penalties including, but not limited to, fine or imprisonment or both under the provisions of Title 18, United States Code, Sec. 1001, et seq.; (2) the loan requested pursuant to this application (the "Loan") will be secured by a mortgage or deed of trust on the property described in this application; (3) the property will not be used for any illegal or prohibited purpose or use; (4) all statements made in this application are made for the purpose of obtaining a residential mortgage loan; (5) the property will be occupied as indicated in this application; (6) the Lender, its servicers, successors or assigns may retain the original and/or an electronic record of this application, whether or not the Loan is approved; (7) the Lender and its agents, brokers, insurers, servicers, successors, and assigns may continuously rely on the information contained in the application, and I am obligated to amend and/or supplement the information provided in this application if any of the material facts that I have represented herein should change prior to closing of the Loan; (8) in the event that my payments on the Loan become delinquent, the Lender, its servicers, successors or assigns may, in addition to any other rights and remedies that it may have relating to such delinquency, report my name and account information to one or more consumer reporting agencies; (9) ownership of the Loan and/or administration of the Loan account may be transferred with such notice as may be required by law; (10) neither Lender nor its agents, brokers, insurers, servicers, successors or assigns has made any representation or warranty, express or implied, to me regarding the property or the condition or value of the property; and (11) my transmission of this application as an "electronic record" containing my "electronic signature," as those terms are defined in applicable federal and/or state laws (excluding audio and video recordings), or my facsimile transmission of this application containing a facsimile of my signature, shall be as effective, enforceable and valid as if a paper version of this application were delivered containing my original written signature.

Cada uno de los suscritos representa específicamente al Prestamista y a los verdaderos o posibles agentes, corredores, procesadores, abogados, aseguradores, administradores, sucesores y cesionarios del Prestamista, y está de acuerdo y acepta que: (1) la información que se proporciona en esta solicitud es exacta y correcta a partir de la fecha expuesta en la línea opuesta a mi firma, y que toda distorsión, intencional o negligente, de esta información contenida en esta solicitud pudiera resultar en una penalidad civil, incluyendo daños monetarios, hacia cualquier persona que sufra alguna pérdida debido a la toma de decisiones hecha en base a cualquier declaración falsa que yo haya hecho en esta solicitud, o en castigos penales, incluyendo, pero sin limitar a, multa o arresto o ambos, de acuerdo con las disposiciones del Título 18, del Código de los Estados Unidos, Sec. 1001, et seq.; (2) el préstamo solicitado de acuerdo a esta solicitud (el "Préstamo") estará asegurado por una hipoteca o escritura de fideicomiso sobre la propiedad descrita en la presente solicitud; (3) la propiedad no se utilizará para ningún propósito o uso ilegal o prohibido; (4) todas las declaraciones realizadas en esta solicitud se hacen con el fin de obtener un préstamo hipotecario residencial; (5) la propiedad se ocupará de acuerdo con lo indicado en la presente solicitud; (6) el Prestamista, sus administradores, sucesores o cesionarios pudieran retener los registros originales o electrónicos contenidos en esta solicitud, se apruebe o no el Préstamo; (7) el Prestamista y sus agentes, corredores, aseguradores, administradores, sucesores y cesionarios, pueden tomar decisiones constantemente en base a la información contenida en esta solicitud, y yo estoy obligado a corregir y complementar la información proporcionada en esta solicitud si alguno de los hechos significativos que he declarado en la presente cambia antes del cierre del Préstamo; (8) en el caso de que mis pagos al Préstamo se atrasen, el Prestamista, sus administradores, sucesores o cesionarios pudiera, además de cualquier otro derecho y recurso que pueda tener relacionado a dicho atraso, reportar mi nombre e información de cuenta a una o más agencias de información de crédito del consumidor; (9) la propiedad del Préstamo o la administración de la cuenta del Préstamo pudiera transferirse otorgando la notificación que requiera la ley; (10) ningún Prestamista ni sus agentes, corredores, aseguradores, administradores, sucesores o cesionarios me han hecho alguna manifestación o garantía, expresa o implícita, respecto a la propiedad, o la condición o el valor de la propiedad; (11) mi transmisión de esta solicitud como un "registro electrónico" que contenga mi "firma electrónica", como se definen esos términos en las leyes federales y estatales correspondientes (excluyendo grabaciones de audio y video), o mi transmisión de facsímil de esta solicitud que contenga un facsímil de mi firma, deberá ser tan eficaz, acatable y válida como si se hubiera entregado una versión en papel de esta solicitud que contenga mi firma escrita original.

Acknowledgement. Each of the undersigned hereby acknowledges that any owner of the Loan, its servicers, successors and assigns, may verify or reverify any information contained in this application or obtain any information or data relating to the Loan, for any legitimate business purpose through any source, including a source named in this application or a consumer reporting agency.

Reconocimiento. Cada uno de los abajo firmantes reconocen por la presente que el titular del Préstamo, sus administradores, sucesores y cesionarios pueden verificar y reverificar cualquier información incluida en esta solicitud u obtener cualquier información o datos relacionados con el Préstamo, para cualquier propósito comercial legítimo, a través de cualquier fuente, incluida una fuente mencionada en esta solicitud o una agencia de crédito del consumidor.

THE SPANISH TRANSLATION IS FOR CONVENIENCE PURPOSES ONLY. IN THE EVENT OF AN INCONSISTENCY BETWEEN THE ENGLISH AND SPANISH LANGUAGE VERSIONS OF THIS FORM, THE ENGLISH LANGUAGE VERSION SHALL PREVAIL.
LA TRADUCCIÓN AL ESPAÑOL ES PARA SU CONVENIENCIA ÚNICAMENTE. EN CASO DE QUE EXISTA UNA INCONSISTENCIA ENTRE LA VERSIÓN EN INGLÉS Y LA VERSIÓN EN ESPAÑOL DE ESTE FORMULARIO, PREVALECERÁ LA VERSIÓN EN INGLÉS.

LEA ESTO PRIMERO: Este documento contiene una traducción al español de su texto en inglés.

Borrower's Signature/*Firma del Prestatario*	Date/*Fecha*	Co-Borrower's Signature/*Firma del Co-Prestatario*	Date/*Fecha*
X		X	

Uniform Residential Loan Application
Freddie Mac Form 65s 7/05 (rev.6/09)

Page 6 of 8
Página 6 de 8

Fannie Mae Form 1003s 7/05 (rev. 6/09)

FIGURE 13.1 Uniform residential loan application (*continued*)

X. INFORMATION FOR GOVERNMENT MONITORING PURPOSES/*INFORMACIÓN PARA FINES DE VERIFICACIÓN POR EL GOBIERNO*

The following information is requested by the Federal Government for certain types of loans related to a dwelling in order to monitor the lender's compliance with equal credit opportunity, fair housing and home mortgage disclosure laws. You are not required to furnish this information, but are encouraged to do so. The law provides that a lender may not discriminate either on the basis of this information, or on whether you choose to furnish it. If you furnish the information, please provide both ethnicity and race. For race, you may check more than one designation. If you do not furnish ethnicity, race, or sex, under Federal regulations, this lender is required to note the information on the basis of visual observation and surname if you have made this application in person. If you do not wish to furnish the information, please check the box below. (Lender must review the above material to assure that the disclosures satisfy all requirements to which the lender is subject under applicable state law for the particular type of loan applied for.)

La siguiente información la solicita el gobierno Federal para ciertos tipos de préstamos relacionados con una vivienda, con el fin de verificar el cumplimiento del Prestador con las leyes de igualdad de Oportunidades de Crédito, "fair housing" y las leyes de divulgación de hipotecas para viviendas. Usted no está obligado a proporcionar esta información, pero le instamos a hacerlo. La ley dispone que un Prestador no puede discriminar en base a esta información ni por el hecho de que decida o no proporcionarla. Si usted decide proporcionarla debe indicar grupo étnico y raza. Usted puede indicar más de una raza. Si usted no desea suministrar la información, de acuerdo a las reglamentaciones federales el Prestador debe anotar la raza y el sexo basado en una observación visual y de acuerdo a su apellido si usted preparó esta solicitud en persona. Si usted no desea proporcionar la información, sírvase marcar en el cuadro ubicado en la parte inferior. (El Prestador debe evaluar el material arriba mencionado para asegurarse de que la información proporcionada cumple con todos los requisitos a los que está sujeto el Prestador bajo la ley estatal pertinente para el tipo de préstamo en particular que se ha solicitado.)

BORROWER/*PRESTATARIO* ☐ I do not wish to furnish this information / *No deseo proporcionar esta información*	CO-BORROWER/*CO-PRESTATARIO* ☐ I do not wish to furnish this information / *No deseo proporcionar esta información*
Ethnicity: / ***Grupo étnico*** ☐ Hispanic or Latino/ *Hispano o Latino* ☐ Not Hispanic or Latino/ *No Hispano o Latino*	**Ethnicity:** / ***Grupo étnico*** ☐ Hispanic or Latino/ *Hispano o Latino* ☐ Not Hispanic or Latino/ *No Hispano o Latino*
Race/*Raza*: ☐ American Indian or Alaska Native/ *Indio Americano o Nativo de Alaska* ☐ Asian/ *Asiático* ☐ Black or African American/ *Negro o Afroamericano* ☐ Native Hawaiian or Other Pacific Islander/ *Nativo de Hawai o de otra isla del Pacífico* ☐ White/*Blanco*	**Race/*Raza*:** ☐ American Indian or Alaska Native/ *Indio Americano o Nativo de Alaska* ☐ Asian/ *Asiático* ☐ Black or African American/ *Negro o Afroamericano* ☐ Native Hawaiian or Other Pacific Islander/ *Nativo de Hawai o de otra isla del Pacífico* ☐ White/*Blanco*
Sex/*Sexo*: ☐ Female/*Femenino* ☐ Male/*Masculino*	**Sex/*Sexo*:** ☐ Female/*Femenino* ☐ Male/*Masculino*

To be Completed by Loan Originator:
A COMPLETARSE POR EL ORIGINADOR DEL PRÉSTAMO
This information was provided:
Esta información fue proporcionada a través de:
☐ In a face-to-face interview /*Entrevista en persona*
☐ In a telephone interview/*Entrevista por teléfono*
☐ By the applicant and submitted by fax or mail/*El solicitante y enviado por fax o por correo*
☐ By the applicant and submitted via e-mail or the Internet/*El solicitante y enviado por correo electrónico o por el Internet*

Loan Originator's Signature / *Firma del Originador del Préstamo* X		Date/ *Fecha*
Loan Originator's Name (print or type) / *Nombre del Originador del Préstamo (use en letra de imprenta o a máquina)*	Loan Originator Identifier / *Identificación del Originador del Préstamo*	Loan Originator's Phone Number (including area code) / *Nº de Teléfono del Originador del Préstamo (incl. código de área)*
Loan Origination Company's Name / *Nombre de la Compañía Originadora del Préstamo*	Loan Origination Company Identifier / *Identificación de la Compañía Originadora del Préstamo*	Loan Origination Company's Address / *Dirección de la Compañía Originadora del Préstamo*

Uniform Residential Loan Application
Freddie Mac Form 65s 7/05 (rev.6/09)

Page 7 of 8
Página 7 de 8

Fannie Mae Form 1003s 7/05 (rev. 6/09)

FIGURE 13.1 Uniform residential loan application (*continued*)

CONTINUATION SHEET/RESIDENTIAL LOAN APPLICATION/*HOJA DE CONTINUACIÓN/SOLICITUD PARA PRÉSTAMO HIPOTECARIO RESIDENCIAL*

Use this continuation sheet if you need more space to complete the Residential Loan Application. Mark **B** f or Borrower or **C** for Co-Borrower. *Utilice esta hoja si necesita más espacio para completar la aplicación para hipoteca residencial. Escriba **"B"** para Prestatario y **"C"** para Co–Prestatario.*	Borrower/*Prestatario*:	Agency Case Number/ *Número de Préstamo de la Agencia*:
	Co-Borrower/*Co-Prestatario*:	Lender Case Number/ *Número de Préstamo del Prestador:*

I/We fully understand that it is a Federal crime punishable by fine or imprisonment, or both, to knowingly make any false statements concerning any of the above facts as applicable under the provisions of Title 18, United States Code, Section 1001, et seq.
Entiendo/Entendemos que es un crimen federal penado con multa o encarcelamiento, o ambos, el hacer declaraciones falsas con respecto a cualquiera de los hechos arriba declarados, según sea pertinente de acuerdo con las disposiciones del Título 18 del Código de los Estados Unidos, Artículo 1001, et seq.

Borrower's Signature/*Firma del Prestatario*	Date/*Fecha*	Co-Borrower's Signature/*Firma del Co-Prestatario*	Date/*Fecha*
X		X	

the property may not generate enough income to meet the loan payments. At that point, a strapped-for-cash borrower is likely to default. Note too that lenders generally avoid loans secured by purely speculative real estate. If the value of the property drops below the amount owed, the borrower may see no further logic in making the loan payments.

Finally, the lender assesses the borrower's attitude toward the proposed loan. Someone with a casual attitude, such as "I'm buying because real estate always goes up," or an applicant who does not appear to understand the obligation being undertaken, would bring a low rating. Much more welcome is the applicant who shows a mature attitude and understanding of the loan obligation and who exhibits a strong and logical desire for ownership.

Borrower Analysis

In sections [3] and [4] the lender begins an analysis of the borrower, and, if there is one, the co-borrower. At one time age, sex, and marital status played an important role in the lender's decision to lend or not to lend. Often the young and the old had trouble getting loans, as did women and persons who were single, divorced, or widowed. Today, the federal Equal Credit Opportunity Act prohibits discrimination based on age, sex, race, and marital status. Lenders are no longer permitted to discount income earned by women because a job is part-time or the woman is of childbearing age. If the applicant chooses to disclose it, alimony, separate maintenance, and child support must be counted in full. Young adults and single persons cannot be turned down because the lender feels they have not "put down roots." Seniors cannot be turned down as long as life expectancy exceeds the early risk period of the loan and collateral is adequate. In other words, the emphasis in borrower analysis is now focused on job stability, income adequacy, net worth, and credit rating.

Thus in sections [5] and [6] we see questions directed at how long the applicants have held their present jobs and the stability of the jobs themselves. An applicant who possesses marketable job skills and has been regularly employed with a stable employer is considered the ideal risk. Persons whose income can rise and fall erratically, such as commissioned salespersons, present greater risks. Persons whose skills (or lack of skills) or lack of job seniority result in frequent unemployment are more likely to have difficulty repaying a loan. In these sections the lender also inquires as to the number of dependents the applicant must support from his or her income. This information provides some insight as to how much will be left for monthly house payments.

Monthly Income

In section [7] the lender looks at the amount and sources of the applicants' income. Quantity alone is not enough for loan approval because the income sources must be stable too. Thus a lender will look carefully at overtime, bonus, and commission income in order to estimate the levels at which these may be expected to continue. Interest, dividend, and rental income is considered in light of the stability of their sources also. Income from social security and retirement pensions is entered and added to the totals for the applicants. Alimony, child support, and separate maintenance payments received need not be revealed. However, such sums must be listed in order to be considered as a basis for repaying the loan.

In section **[8]** the lender compares what the applicants have been paying for housing with what they will be paying if the loan is approved. Included in the proposed housing expense total are principal, interest, taxes, and insurance along with any assessments or homeowner association dues (such as in a condominium). Some lenders add the monthly cost of utilities to this list.

At **[9]** proposed monthly housing expense is compared with gross monthly income. A general rule of thumb is that monthly housing expense (PITI) should not exceed 25% to 30% of gross monthly income. A second guideline is that total fixed monthly expenses should not exceed 33% to 38% of income. This includes housing payments plus automobile payments, installment loan payments, alimony, child support, and investments with negative cash flows. These are general guidelines, but lenders recognize that food, health care, clothing, transportation, entertainment, and income taxes must also come from the applicants' income. For instance, a location efficient mortgage (LEM) now being offered allows homeowners in urban areas to qualify for larger mortgages when they have significantly reduced transportation costs.

Assets and Liabilities

In section **[10]** the lender is interested in the applicants' sources of funds for closing and whether, once the loan is granted, the applicants have assets to fall back on in the event of an income decrease (a job layoff) or unexpected expenses (hospital bills). Of particular interest is the portion of those assets that are in cash or are readily convertible into cash in a few days. These are called ***liquid assets.*** If income drops, they are much more useful in meeting living expenses and loan payments than assets that may require months to sell and convert to cash—that is, assets that are **illiquid.**

Note in section **[10]** that two values are shown for life insurance. **Cash value** is the amount of money the policyholder would receive if the policy were surrendered to the insurance company or, alternatively, the amount the policyholder could borrow against the policy. **Face amount** is the amount that would be paid in the event of the insured's death. Lenders feel most comfortable if the face amount of the policy equals or exceeds the amount of the proposed loan. Obviously a borrower's death is not anticipated before the loan is repaid, but lenders recognize that its possibility increases the probability of default. The likelihood of foreclosure is lessened considerably if the survivors receive life insurance benefits.

In section [11] the lender is interested in the applicants' existing debts and liabilities for two reasons. First, each month these items compete against housing expenses for available monthly income. Thus high monthly payments in this section may lower the lender's estimate of what the applicants will be able to repay and, consequently, may influence the lender to reduce the size of the loan. The presence of monthly liabilities is not all negative: It can also show the lender that the applicants are capable of repaying their debts. Second, the applicants' total debts are subtracted from their total assets to obtain their *net worth,* reported at [12]. If the result is negative (more owed than owned), the loan request will probably be turned down as too risky. In contrast, a substantial net worth can often offset weaknesses elsewhere in the application, such as too little monthly income in relation to monthly housing expense or an income that can rise and fall erratically.

References

At number [13] lenders ask for credit references as an indicator of the future. Applicants with no previous credit experience will have more weight placed on income and employment history. Applicants with a history of collections, adverse judgments, foreclosure, or bankruptcy will have to convince the lender that this loan will be repaid on time. Additionally, the applicants may be considered poorer risks if they have guaranteed the repayment of someone else's debt by acting as a co-maker or endorser.

Redlining

In the past, it was not uncommon for lenders to refuse to make loans in certain neighborhoods regardless of the quality of the structure or the ability of the borrower to repay. This practice was known as ***redlining,*** and it effectively shut off mortgage loans in many older or so-called "bad risk" neighborhoods across the country. Today a lender cannot refuse to make a loan simply because of the age or location of a property; the neighborhood income level; or the racial, ethnic, or religious composition of the neighborhood.

A lender can refuse to lend on a structure intended for demolition; a property in a known geological hazard area; a single-family dwelling in an area devoted to industrial or commercial use; or a property that is in violation of zoning laws, deed covenants, conditions or restrictions, or significant health, safety, or building codes.

Loan-to-Value Ratios

The lender next looks at the amount of down payment the borrower proposes to make, the size of the loan being requested, and the amount of other financing the borrower plans to use. This information is then converted into loan-to-value ratios. As a rule, the larger the down payment, the safer the loan is for the lender. On an uninsured loan, the ideal loan-to-value (L/V) ratio for a lender on owner-occupied residential property is 70% or less. This means the value of the property would have to fall more than 30% before the debt owed would exceed the property's value, thus encouraging the borrower to stop making loan payments.

Loan-to-value ratios from 70% through 80% are considered acceptable but do expose the lender to more risk. Lenders sometimes compensate by charging slightly higher interest rates. Loan-to-value ratios above 80% present even more risk of default to the lender, and the lender will either increase the interest rate charged on these loans or require insurance coverage from an outside insurer, such as the FHA or a private mortgage insurer.

Credit Report

As part of the loan application, the lender will order a ***credit report*** on the applicant(s). The applicant is asked to authorize this and to pay for the report. This provides the lender with an independent means of checking the applicant's credit history. A credit report that shows active use of credit with a good repayment record and no derogatory information is most desirable. The applicant will be asked by the lender to explain any negative information. Because it is possible for inaccurate or untrue information in a credit report to unfairly damage a person's credit reputation, Congress passed the ***Fair Credit Reporting Act.*** This act gives individuals the right to inspect their file at a credit bureau, correct any errors, and make explanatory statements to supplement the file.

As previously discussed, the major federal agencies have combined their requirements for credit reports, and loans intended for underwriting by federal government agencies must comply with the new credit standards. Under these newly adopted rules, the name of the consumer reporting agency must be clearly identified, as well as who ordered the report and who is paying for it. The information must be obtained from at least two national repositories for each area in which the borrower resided in the past two years, and must be verified for the previous two years. An explanation must be provided if the information is unavailable, and all questions must be responded to, even if the answer must be "unable to verify." A history must be furnished and all missing information must be verified by the lender. The history must have been checked within 90 days of the credit report and the age of information that is not considered obsolete by the Fair Credit Reporting Act (7 years general credit date or 10 years for bankruptcy) must be indicated. If any credit information is incomplete or if undisclosed information is discovered, the lender must have a personal interview with the borrower. The lender is additionally required to warrant that the credit report complies with all of the new standards.

Real estate practitioners should be particularly aware of this law. If an applicant for rental of a property is rejected on the basis of a credit report, there are special disclosures (set out by federal law) the owner, or the owner's agent, must make. If the applicant is rejected for reasons other than a credit report, the reasons must be disclosed. All disclosures must be made even if no request is made by the applicant.

Credit Scoring

Credit scoring is used as a method of evaluating credit risk. The scoring system is applied to a list of subjective factors that are considered relevant in evaluating credit risks. Credit scores often are shown on the credit report as additional information.

More than 75% of mortgage lenders and 80% of the largest financial institutions use scores developed by Fair, Isaac & Company (called FICO scores) in their evaluations and approvals in processing credit applications. Lenders maintain that these scores provide a better assessment of how customers will perform on loan payments and allows them to better balance the credit risk they take into their loan portfolios. The scale runs from 300 to 850. A score of 720 or higher will get the borrower the most favorable interest rate on a mortgage. Because the interest rate charged by the lender may vary depending on the applicant's credit score, bad credit can result in paying significantly higher interest rates, which, over the term of the loan, can be a huge differential in payments.

How does one improve their credit score? Fair, Isaac determines five different factors, each of which are weighted differently. They include: type of credit use (10%), applications for new credit (10%), length of credit history (15%), payment history (35%), and amounts owed (30%). The most important factors in evaluating credit are payment history and amounts owed. Most creditors suggest that you check your credit score frequently and correct any blatant errors that may show up (identity theft is a major problem in this area). Other factors considered in creating the credit score include: and paying your bills on time; consistently reducing your credit card balances (and keeping them below 25% of your credit card limit); and not moving debt around, transferring debts to different credit cards or other sources of debt. What a surprise! Making your payments on time and keeping your debt within a manageable range gives you a better credit score. The simplest rules are often overlooked by many consumers. Lots of information is available on how to improve your credit score through the FICO website at http://www.myfico.com.

There is another private credit scoring company called Vantage Score. They maintain that they will provide consumers and businesses with a highly predictive, consistent score that is easy to understand and apply. Vantage Score uses score ranges from 501 to 990.

Both FNMA and Freddie Mac announced recently that they will make information about their credit scoring more available to the public. These agencies explain that they are committed to working with lenders to help borrowers understand the lending process and thus improve their ability to qualify for an affordable mortgage. Many states, too, are requiring credit scoring processes to be more open.

FHA recently released a credit scoring procedure that is open to the mortgage industry. It is called "TOTAL," an acronym for "Technology Open To All Lenders." The program assesses credit-worthiness for FHA borrowers by evaluating certain mortgage applications and credit information to accurately predict the likelihood of a borrower default. It is intended to be used along with FHA's automated underwriting system.

Subprime Loans

Subprime loans have risk-based pricing and rates are not quoted. Usually a rate is found, or negotiated, if it fits the risk profile. Interest rates are typically one to five percentage points higher than for good credit risks. With these loans, appraisals are critical and the risk profiles tend to be variable from lender to lender. The lowest risk borrowers are considered prime borrowers and are rated an "A" classification. Higher risk loans fall into lower categories from "A2" to "F." Although exact criteria vary, the "A" to "F" credit scoring has become somewhat standard in the last few years.

Predatory Lending

In the next chapter we will discuss sources of financing. Many sources of financing are readily available to most consumers, but a lot of consumers lack the knowledge to evaluate lending practices and are often preyed upon by unscrupulous lenders who take advantage of that lack of knowledge. In general terms, the industry refers to this as **predatory lending.** The Mortgage Bankers Association has identified 12 practices considered to be predatory: (1) steering borrowers/buyers to high-rate lenders; (2) intentionally structuring high-cost loans with payments the borrower cannot afford; (3) falsifying loan documents; (4) making loans to mentally incapacitated homeowners; (5) forging signatures on loan documents; (6) changing the loan terms at closing; (7) requiring credit insurance; (8) falsely identifying loans as lines of credit or open-end mortgages; (9) increasing interest charges for loan payments when loan payments are late; (10) charging excessive prepayment penalties or excessive charges for preparing releases; (11) failing to report good payment on borrowers' credit reports; and (12) failing to provide accurate loan balance and payoff amounts, which includes not responding in a timely manner to credit inquiries for payoff information.

Coupled with these lending practices are shoddy appraisals made by unscrupulous appraisers to falsely inflate the value of the house. This allows a borrower to: (1) make no down payment, or (2) resell property shortly after closing for large profits to a "strawman" who will not make any payments on the loans. This practice merely dupes their lender into making too large a loan on the property because of these false appraisal practices. Most states are curbing this practice through state legislation against predatory lending and mortgage fraud. In addition, the FBI has stepped up its investigation of these practices.

A word of caution is always in order. Whenever a real estate transaction is not "straight up" with an acceptable loan-to-value ratio and a defined down payment procedure, it is going to be suspect. If it doesn't "smell" right, or if information is being withheld from the lender during the closing, don't do it.

Mortgage Fraud

One of the hottest topics in the country today is mortgage fraud. It seems to be caused by aggressive lender tactics by lenders who want to increase their base of loans, servicing fees, and origination fees. This has led to abuse by mortgage brokers, appraisers, and home purchasers who have determined that they can dupe the lender into making a loan far in excess of the home's value, while pocketing the excess proceeds. In most cases the buyer of the house never makes a payment and the lender has a nonperforming loan almost from the first day of origination. There are a number of tactics that people use to engage in this kind of misconduct. The scandal almost always involves buying a house at the low end of the neighborhood (e.g., it is neglected, bought from an estate, there's a pending divorce and the house hasn't been maintained, has been on the market a long time, or may have some stigma associated with it). In such circumstances, the house can appraise at a high per square foot value when compared to higher-end homes in the same neighborhood.

The Flip

One of the most common methods of maintaining this scam is "B" buying from home seller "A" at a below market price. B knows that the house can appraise at a much higher price because of his knowledge of the marketplace (the buyer may be a loan broker!). B then can "flip" the sale of the property to an unsuspecting "C," who may be an innocent purchaser whom B can assist in getting a loan. C doesn't realize he's paying above market for this particular house. For example, B could buy the property from A for $100,000, then help C with "easy financing" at an inflated price of $200,000. C borrows 80% ($160,000) to finance the loan, which goes to the new seller B. B simply pockets the difference ($60,000). C paid too much for the house and probably doesn't know it ... yet.

The Inflated Price

In this scenario, the loan broker or real estate agent finds a house for sale at below market value. He has good connections with an aggressive lender and/or a loan broker. In some cases, the buyer's broker or the listing broker may also be a loan broker who has a double incentive to see that the transaction closes because he gets both loan fees and a real estate commission. Not surprisingly, the house appraises far in excess of the list price. If we use the prior example, we have a list price of $100,000, yet the house appraises for $200,000. The buyer then goes back to the seller and asks that she increase the sales price under the contract to $200,000 so that he can get a loan on the larger amount. In this scam, the buyer ends up putting $60,000 in his pocket and the seller gets the original, agreed-upon $100,000 sales price. This scam is easy to do, because the seller and the listing broker are getting exactly what they bargained for (the original sales price and the commission). They conveniently look the other way. There has always been an issue, however, as to whether or not the listing broker and seller (and maybe the title company) aided and abetted the federal fraud perpetrated on the lender.

The Contractor

In this scenario, similar to the previous situation, a contractor is willing to do improvements to the property for $100,000. Assume a sales price of $100,000 and home improvements of $100,000. The lender funds all of the construction proceeds to the borrower at the closing. The borrower then never makes the improvements and pockets the difference and once again, the lender has over-funded. In many cases the borrower is the contractor, using a fictitious name or business entity as a front for the scam. The loan broker and appraiser are also parties to the fraud.

The Ultimate Lie

This transaction is similar to the flip, but involves fraud in obtaining loans through false financial information. An aggressive loan broker (who may also be the buyer's real estate broker!) has a very high credit loan package, which has already been approved by a lender for another loan. It contains all the proper information (social security number, driver's license number, work history, credit history, IRS returns, pay check stubs, and other useful information for obtaining a loan). The aggressive loan broker then simply pays an unsuspecting person $50 to show up at the closing, using the same loan information but changing the name and social security number. The loan broker may even set up a fake phone number of an employer that goes to the his own office. The ultimate buyer who signs the loan documents has a false ID, buys from the middleman (possibly the company owned by the loan broker), and all the proceeds from the flip go to the loan broker. The ultimate purchaser is never seen again and never makes a payment. From the loan broker's perspective this is $50 well spent; he made a lot of money and can do the transaction again by simply changing the name on the original loan application.

Although these scams may seem incredible, they are all too common in today's real estate market. It is fraud on federally insured lenders, which has serious criminal repercussions. Texas has recently enacted new laws to prevent this type of misconduct. Lenders must now provide a notice at closing that warns borrowers of the consequences of fraud. Another new law requires a party to be a "whistleblower" and report suspected fraud to the appropriate government authority. Title companies and real estate agencies now have a duty to police closings.

REVIEW QUESTIONS

Answers to these questions are found in the Answer Key section at the back of the book.

1. All of the following are exempt from the provisions of the Federal Truth-in-Lending Act EXCEPT:
   A. commercial loans.
   B. personal property loans in excess of $25,000.
   C. financing extended to corporations.
   D. consumer loans to natural persons.

2. Which of the following loans would be exempt from the disclosure requirements of the truth in lending laws?
   A. An unsecured personal loan of $3,000
   B. An educational loan from a commercial bank
   C. A second mortgage loan on a residence
   D. A $30,000 loan for the purchase of a $40,000 automobile

3. Penalties for violation of the truth in lending laws include
   A. a fine of up to $5,000 and/or imprisonment for up to one year.
   B. civil penalties up to twice the amount of the finance charge up to a maximum of $1,000.
   C. court costs, attorney fees, and actual damages.
   D. all of the above.

4. A borrower does not have the right, under the truth in lending laws, to rescind a credit transaction
   A. for a consumer loan on personal property.
   B. for the acquisition of the borrower's principal dwelling.
   C. both A and B.
   D. neither A nor B.

5. Generally, before a lender will approve a loan, the borrower must
   A. have sufficient funds for the down payment.
   B. sign a statement if the borrower intends to occupy the property.
   C. both A and B.
   D. neither A nor B.

6. Which of the following is given consideration in evaluation of a loan application?
   A. Race
   B. Marital status
   C. Sex
   D. Income adequacy

7. A lender can legally discriminate in loan terms based on the applicant's
   A. religion.
   B. marital status.
   C. race or skin color.
   D. intention to occupy (or not occupy) the mortgaged property.

8. The right of an individual to inspect his or her file at a credit bureau is found in the
   A. Truth-in-Lending Act.
   B. Fair Credit Reporting Act.
   C. Regulation Z.
   D. Federal Consumer Credit Protection Act.

9. The abbreviation APR stands for
   A. average percentage rate.
   B. allotted percentage rate.
   C. approximate percentage rate.
   D. annual percentage rate.

10. The annual percentage rate is
    A. usually lower than the interest rate.
    B. made up of the interest rate combined with the other costs of the loan.
    C. both A and B.
    D. neither A nor B.

Chapter 14

KEY TERMS

Alienation clause: requires immediate repayment of the loan if ownership transfers; also called a due-on-sale clause

Automated underwriting systems: computerized systems for loan approval communication between a loan originator and the investor

Computerized loan origination: originating loans through the use of a networked computer system

Disintermediation: the result created when lenders are required to pay high rates of interest for deposits while receiving long-term income from low-interest-rate mortgage loans

Fannie Mae: a real estate industry nickname for the Federal National Mortgage Association

Federal National Mortgage Association: a company organized initially by the Federal government to buy FHA loans

Freddie Mac: a real estate industry nickname for the Federal Home Loan Mortgage Corporation

Mortgage broker: one who brings together borrowers and lenders

Mortgage company: a firm that makes mortgage loans and then sells them to investors

Participation certificates: a certificate representing an undivided interest in a Freddie Mac pool

Primary market: the market in which lenders originate loans and make funds available to borrowers

Secondary mortgage market: a market in which mortgage loans can be sold to investors

Usury: charging an interest rate that is in excess of the legal rate

Sources of Financing

IN THIS CHAPTER

After reading this chapter, you will be able to (1) identify various mortgage lenders (the primary market), (2) describe where these lenders get much of their money (the secondary market), and (3) explain provisions of mortgage loan instruments that have an impact on the cost of funds. Many people feel that understanding the financing market is the most important of all real estate topics because, without financing, real estate profits and commissions would be difficult to achieve.

PRIMARY MARKET

The ***primary market*** (also called the *primary mortgage market*) is where lenders originate loans—that is, where lenders make funds available to borrowers. The primary market is what the borrower sees as the source of mortgage loan money, the institution with which the borrower has direct and personal contact. It's the place where the loan application is taken, where the loan officer interviews the loan applicant, where the loan check comes from, and the place to which loan payments are sent by the borrower.

These sources of funds can generally be divided into two markets: (1) those markets regulated by the federal government and (2) those markets that are not regulated by the government. The regulated lenders are commercial banks, savings and loan (S&L) associations, and savings banks. The nonregulated lenders are investment bankers, life insurance companies, and finance companies. Nonregulated sources of funds are not subject to the same restrictive regulations that are designed to protect the lender with deposits insured by the federal government. The regulated lenders are subject to examinations by federal regulators, pay risk-based premiums on their deposit insurance, and are restricted to certain loan-to-value ratios. In today's markets, a purchaser is wise to contact both regulated and nonregulated lenders to make an adequate comparison of available loan money. Markets differ widely within states and even within certain urban areas.

Most borrowers assume that the loan they receive comes from depositors who visit the same bank or S&L to leave their excess funds. This is partly true. But this, by itself, is an inadequate source of loan funds in today's market. Thus, primary lenders often sell their loans in what is called the secondary market. Insurance companies, pension funds, and individual investors, as well as other primary lenders with excess deposits, buy these loans for cash. This makes more money available to a primary lender who, in turn, can loan these additional funds to borrowers. The secondary market is so huge that it rivals the entire U.S. corporate bond market in size of annual offerings. We discuss the secondary market later in this chapter. Let's discuss the various lenders a borrower will encounter when looking for a real estate loan.

SAVINGS AND LOAN ASSOCIATIONS

Historically, the origin of *savings and loan associations* can be traced to early building societies in England and Germany and to the first American building society, the Oxford Provident Building Association, started in 1831 in Pennsylvania. These early building societies were cooperatives whose savers were also borrowers. As times progressed, savings and loan associations became a primary source of residential real estate loans. To encourage residential lending, the federally chartered savings and loans were required by federal regulation to hold at least 80% of their assets in residential loans. In addition, they were subjected to special tax laws that permitted a savings and loan association to defer payment of income taxes on profits, so long as those profits were held in surplus accounts and not distributed to the savings and loan association's owners. During this same period, there were also limits on the interest rates that could be paid on savings accounts. This provided the savings and loan associations with a dependable source of funds at a fixed interest rate, which gave them the potential for making long-term loans at reasonable rates. For instance, if the passbook savings account was limited to 5.25% per annum, home loans in the vicinity of 7.5% to 8.5% would still allow for reasonable profit margins. Unfortunately, the nature of the finance markets began to change in the late 1970s when an inflationary economy caused interest rates to skyrocket. This created problems that were unforeseen by the savings and loan industry.

Disintermediation

To attract depositors, savings and loans offer, in addition to passbook accounts, **certificates of deposit (CDs)** at rates higher than passbook rates. These are necessary to compete with higher yields offered by U.S. Treasury bills, notes, and bonds and to prevent disintermediation. ***Disintermediation*** results when depositors take money out of their savings accounts and invest directly in government securities, corporate bonds, and money market funds. A major problem, and one that nearly brought the S&L industry to its knees in the late 1970s and early 1980s, was that S&Ls traditionally relied heavily on short-term deposits from savers and then loaned that money on long-term (often 30-year) loans to borrowers. When interest rates rose sharply in the 1970s, S&Ls had to either raise the interest paid to their depositors or watch depositors withdraw their savings and take the money elsewhere for higher returns. Meanwhile, the S&Ls were holding long-term, fixed-rate mortgage loans, and, with interest rates rising, borrowers were not anxious to repay those loans early.

Restructuring the System

Disintermediation was only the beginning of the problems. Loan demand at S&Ls was declining. In 1976, 57% of the residential mortgage loans were held by savings and loan institutions. By 2000, the percentage fell to 13%. There are many reasons for this flow of funds out of the S&L industry. One of the primary reasons, however, appears to be the deregulation of the lending industry. This, coupled with bad investments, inadequately trained executives, and loose government controls on S&L risks and investments, resulted in an industry that could not remain solvent.

In August 1989, President Bush signed into law a sweeping revision of the regulatory authorities governing savings and loans. This law is referred to as the *Financial Institutions Reform, Recovery, and Enforcement Act of 1989,* commonly called *FIRREA*. The law redefined or created seven new regulatory authorities and initiated a system of federally designated real property appraisers, discussed in greater detail in Chapter 19. Because federal regulations of commercial banks and savings and loans are virtually the same, the difference between savings and loans and commercial banks as a primary source of funds is indistinguishable to the average borrower.

COMMERCIAL BANKS

The nation's 15,000 *commercial banks* store far more of the country's money than the S&Ls. However, only one bank dollar in six goes to real estate lending. Of the loans made by banks for real estate, the tendency is to emphasize short-term maturities and adjustable rate mortgages because the bulk of a bank's deposit money comes from demand deposits (checking accounts) and a much smaller portion from savings and time deposits.

Oddly enough, the same factors that have plagued the S&Ls helped the commercial banks. During the Deregulation Acts of 1980 and 1982, banks began making more home loans, but they were short-term, with adjustable rates. These types of loans prevent the problem of disintermediation, because the loan rates can rise with the rates that are required by the source of funds. Commercial banks, too, have realized that first-lien residential loans are very secure, low-risk loans. Banks have also determined that maintaining all of a customer's loan accounts, including a home loan, in the bank's portfolio provides a market advantage. "One-stop banking" has become a very successful marketing tool. The merger of many banks into large multistate national banks has created a larger source of funds to lend. To accommodate higher demand and facilitate the organization of sources of funds for the bank's lending purposes, many banks have organized their own mortgage departments to assist customers in making home loans, even through sources other than bank deposits.

In 1999, Congress passed the Financial Services Modernization (FSM) bill, which lifted banking restrictions imposed by legislation dating back to 1933. The new legislation allows banks to become one-stop financial conglomerates marketing a range of financial products such as annuities, certificates of deposits, stocks, and bonds, creating a tremendous potential for cross-marketing in very large banks. This diversification may have a far-reaching impact on future banking practices, including the availability of mortgage money and other financial services to homeowners.

LIFE INSURANCE COMPANIES

As a group, the nation's 2,200 *life insurance companies* have long been active investors in real estate as developers, owners, and long-term lenders. Although not federally regulated, life insurance companies are subject to state regulations. Their source of money is the premiums paid by policyholders. These premiums are invested and ultimately returned to the policyholders. Because premiums are collected in regular amounts on regular dates and because policy payoffs can be calculated from actuarial tables, life insurers are in ideal positions to commit money to long-term investments. Life insurance companies channel their funds primarily into government and corporate bonds and real estate. The dollars allocated to real estate go to buy land and buildings, which are leased to users, and to make loans on commercial, industrial, and residential property. Generally, life insurers specialize in large-scale investments such as shopping centers, office and apartment buildings, and million-dollar blocks of home loans purchased in the ***secondary mortgage market***, which is discussed later in this chapter.

Repayment terms on loans made by insurance companies for shopping centers, office buildings, and apartment complexes sometimes call for interest and a percentage of any profits from rentals over a certain level. These **participation loans,** which provide a "piece of the action" for the insurance company, also provide the insurance company with more inflation protection than a fixed rate of interest.

MORTGAGE COMPANIES

A ***mortgage company*** makes a mortgage loan and then sells it to a long-term investor. The process begins with locating borrowers, qualifying them, preparing the necessary loan papers, and, finally, making the loans. Once a loan is made, it is sold for cash on the secondary market. The mortgage company will usually continue to *service the loan*—that is, collect the monthly payments and handle such matters as insurance and property tax impounds, delinquencies, early payoffs, and mortgage releases.

Mortgage companies, also known as **mortgage bankers,** vary in size from one or two persons to several dozen. As a rule, they close loans in their own names and are locally oriented, finding and making loans within 25 or 50 miles of their offices. This gives them a feel for their market, greatly aids in identifying sound loans, and makes loan servicing much easier. For their efforts, mortgage bankers typically receive 1% to 3% of the amount of the loan when it is originated, and from ¼ to ½ of 1% of the outstanding balance each year thereafter for servicing. Mortgage banking, as this business is called, is not limited to mortgage companies. Commercial banks, savings and loan associations, and mutual savings banks in active real estate areas often originate more real estate loans than they can hold themselves, and these are sold on the secondary market. As the shift in mortgage origination continues, it is important to note that the mortgage brokers' share of originations, which increased more than 30% from 1980 to 2000, will probably continue to increase.

MORTGAGE BROKERS

Mortgage brokers, in contrast to mortgage bankers, specialize in bringing together borrowers and lenders, just as real estate brokers bring together buyers and sellers. The mortgage broker does not lend money and usually does not service loans. The mortgage broker's fee is expressed in points and is usually paid by the borrower. Mortgage brokers are locally oriented, often small firms of 1 to 10 persons. They seldom make loans in their own names as lender.

The mortgage brokering businesses actually felt an explosion during the late 1980s and early 1990s. The secondary market (discussed later in this chapter) has made investors' funds more readily available, and virtually anyone with some expertise in loan qualifications can originate loans and sell to secondary market purchasers. As a result, the field has become crowded with new loan originators such as home builders, finance companies, commercial credit companies, insurance agents, attorneys, and real estate brokers. These have generally been considered nontraditional lenders, but they can originate mortgage loans with their own resources or, through various networks, have the loan funded directly through to the secondary market purchaser. These new loan originators have offered substantial competition to regulated lenders. The proliferation of mortgage brokers has also led to an increase in the number of cases of abuse, fraud, and predatory lending practices, discussed in the prior chapter.

PUTTING IT TO WORK

Whether or not a real estate broker may operate as a mortgage broker and collect a fee for placing a loan has been a "gray" area of the law. The concern expressed by some is that the fee retained by the broker (which is in addition to the real estate broker's fee) may be an undisclosed kickback, which violates the Real Estate Settlement Procedures Act (RESPA; see Chapter 17). Agency law also comes into play because a real estate broker may be representing the buyer on a loan while also representing the seller in the sale of the home. This may result in a duty for the listing broker to disclose everything the practitioner knows (including borrower financial information) to the principal (seller). Lenders also have some concern that the real estate agent may "fudge" mortgage qualification criteria to facilitate a lucrative sale. However, changes in RESPA now allow the involvement of a broker in the mortgage process on a limited basis, provided proper disclosures are made to the borrower.

Congress responded to these abuses by passing the Federal Secure and Fair Enforcement of Mortgage Licensing Act of 2008 (SAFE). Under SAFE, a residential mortgage loan originator who is an employee or subsidiary of a depository institution must be registered with a federal banking agency having jurisdiction over that institution and will be included in the Nationwide Mortgage Licensing System. A residential loan originator is defined as an individual who, for compensation or gain or any expectation of compensation or gain, takes a residential mortgage loan application or offers to negotiate the terms of a residential mortgage loan. This federal law is very broad, and some have interpreted it to mean that seller financing is no longer legal if the seller is not a licensed residential mortgage loan originator. All states have passed very similar state laws to assure compliance with the federal SAFE Act; Texas amended its Finance Code in 2008. In effect, this is a federal licensing of mortgage loan originators.

COMPUTERIZED LOAN ORIGINATION

The growth of computer networks has also enabled many independent loan processors to work under the guidance of large lending institutions and mortgage companies. Using a ***computerized loan origination (CLO)***, real estate brokers, attorneys, insurance agents, or mortgage companies can arrange to have a computer link installed in their offices, connected to lenders' mainframe computers. By using a series of questions, borrowers can obtain preliminary loan approval immediately from the loan originator with a firm acceptance or rejection from the lending institution within a few days.

A full-featured CLO has three basic functions: (1) it provides information on current mortgage loan terms and loan types available on the market, (2) it conveys loan application information electronically, and (3) it monitors the loan approval process so that the practitioner can check on the progress of the loan application at any time. From the home buyer's perspective, the CLO provides the convenience of seeking home financing alternatives without calling and visiting a large number of local lenders, and in many cases it can increase the number of choices available. A broker should exercise caution, however, because conflicts can exist.

PUTTING IT TO WORK

New RESPA regulations greatly limit the use of CLOs by real estate agents, so legal counsel should be consulted before a practitioner attempts to use a CLO as a second source of income.

MUNICIPAL BONDS

In some cities, **municipal bonds** provide a source of mortgage money for home buyers. The special advantage to borrowers is that municipal bonds pay interest that is tax-free from federal income taxes. Knowing this, bond investors will accept a lower rate of interest than they would if the interests were taxable—as it normally is on mortgage loans. This saving is passed on to the home buyer. Those who qualify will typically pay about 2% less than if they had borrowed through conventional channels.

The objective of such programs is to make home ownership more affordable for low-and middle-income households. Also, a city may stipulate that loans be used in neighborhoods the city wants to revitalize. The loans are made by local lenders who are paid a fee for originating and servicing these loans. Although popular with the real estate industry, the U.S. Treasury has been less than enthusiastic about the concept because it bears the cost in lost tax revenues. As a result, federal legislation has been passed to limit the future use of this source of money.

OTHER LENDERS

Pension funds and *trust funds* traditionally have channeled their money to high-grade government and corporate bonds and stocks. However, the trend now is to place more money into real estate loans. Already active buyers on the secondary market, pension and trust funds will likely become a still larger source of real estate financing in the future. In some localities, pension fund members can tap their own pension funds for home mortgages at very reasonable rates. Pension funds are an often overlooked source of primary market financing.

Finance companies that specialize in making business and consumer loans also provide limited financing for real estate. As a rule, finance companies seek second mortgages at interest rates 2% to 5% higher than the rates prevailing on first mortgages. First mortgages are also taken as collateral; however, the lenders already discussed usually charge lower interest rates for these loans and thus are more competitive.

Credit unions normally specialize in consumer loans. However, real estate loans are becoming more and more important because many of the country's 16,000 credit unions have branched out into first and second mortgage loans. Credit unions are an often overlooked but excellent source of home loan money.

Commercial finance companies also have entered the mortgage lending fields. These are private companies, such as General Electric Capital Mortgage Corporation, General Motors Acceptance Corporation, and Ford Motor Company, which are subject to neither banking restrictions nor deposit insurance regulations. They are becoming a more widely used source of finance money, particularly in affordable housing loans, discussed in the next chapter.

Individuals are sometimes a source of cash loans for real estate, with the bulk of these loans made between relatives or friends, often as investments with their IRAs or private pension plans that require a low-risk investment with attractive rates. Generally, loan maturities are shorter than those obtainable from the institutional lenders already described. In some cities, persons can be found who specialize in making or buying second and third mortgage loans of up to 10-year maturities. Individuals are also beginning to invest substantial amounts of money in secondary mortgage market securities. Ironically, these investments are often made with money that would have otherwise been deposited in a savings and loan.

TEXAS LOAN PROGRAMS

Texas has made its own loan programs available for veterans and low- to middle-income borrowers. All of them have had a very beneficial impact on the Texas housing industry and deserve more detailed discussion.

Texas Veterans Land Fund

The Texas Veterans Land Board has made a program available by which an eligible veteran may buy land from the Veterans Land Board (VLB) by a contract of sale, installment land contract, or contract for deed at very favorable interest rates determined by the Texas Veterans Land Board. The contract cannot exceed 30 years and the purchase price of the property cannot exceed the least of the following options: (1) $80,000, or (2) 95% of the final agreed purchase price, or (3) 95% of the appraised value of the land.

There must be a minimum down payment of 5%. The land must be at least 1 acre. The veteran may either purchase land owned by the Board, or designate certain land that the Board may purchase in his or her behalf and then resell to him or her under the installment land contract.

Veterans' Housing Assistance Program

Another program that the Texas Veterans Land Board has made available is the Veterans' Housing Assistance Program (VHAP). You will note that the TREC-promulgated contracted forms have special provisions under the "Financing Conditions" section to provide for the Veterans' Housing Assistance Program. The program is made available to eligible veterans who wish to purchase a new or existing home, which must be the primary residence of the veteran for at least three years. The VHAP loan is used in conjunction with any other type of financing, and enables the veteran to borrow up to $45,000 as a first or second lien mortgage. There is a maximum amount of $45,000 on the loan, so if there is going to be a single mortgage of less than $45,000, the Veterans Land Board will be the only note holder on the loan. If more than $45,000 is borrowed, the Veterans Land Board and the first lien lender share the first lien position, and the first lien lender services and originates the loan. All VLB-originated loans are subject to an 85% loan-to-value ratio. The VLB will lend only 85% of the home's appraised value up to $45,000. The VHAP does not guarantee an interest rate on any loan. The interest rate on the VHAP loan is determined at the time the lender secures a rate lock.

If the VHAP loan is used in conjunction with another conventional first lien, it is a **Lender-Originated Loan,** and the Veterans Land Board will lend the amount of the home's purchase price up to $325,000. The down payment, if any, will be determined by the approved lender. There is a 1% origination fee and a 1% participation fee payable by the seller or buyer. If the loan is used in conjunction with a VA loan, no down payment is required if the veteran has full VA eligibility. As with other veteran loans, the veteran can transfer the loan to another veteran or nonveteran as long as the original veteran has lived in the house for a minimum of three years.

In addition, veterans can borrow as much as $60,000 from VLB to buy tracts of land as small as one acre.

Additional information on both of these Veterans Land Board approved loans can be obtained by calling the Texas Veterans Land Board at their toll-free number, 1 (800) 252-VETS, or by visiting their website, www.texasveterans.com.

Veterans Home Improvement Program

The Texas Veterans Home Improvement Program (VHIP) provides for allowance to eligible Texas veterans up to $25,000 on a fixed rate note to make substantial repairs to their existing primary residence. The loans can be for as long as 20 years; no down payment is required. However, if the loan is less than $10,000, the maximum term of the loan will be for 10 years. The loan is funded after the improvements are complete to the homeowner's satisfaction and an inspection is completed by the Veterans Land Board Representative.

There is also an emergency loan program for eligible Texas veterans, who, for self-help or safety reasons, need immediate home repairs. This "rapid response home improvement loan" can get same day approval and next day final approval for a loan up to $25,000.

Texas Department of Housing and Community Affairs

By periodically selling tax-exempt mortgage revenue bonds (MRBs), the Texas Department of Housing and Community Affairs (TDHCA) raises money in financial markets at the lower interest rates available to state and municipal bonds (the interest paid on such bonds is exempt from federal income tax). By passing the lower rates on to home buyers, mortgage loans can be made at less than conventional market rates.

There are also the Texas governmental agencies administrating several significant programs under the American Recovery and Reinvestment Act of 2009.

They oversee roughly 17 housing programs, including the First Time Homebuyer Program, the "Boot-strap" Homebuilder Loan Program, the Down Payment Assistance Program, and the HOME Investment Partnerships Program (HOME). To qualify for the First Time Homebuyer Program, the applicant must not have owned a principal residence in the past three years, must have an annual income in the low to moderate range, must be considered creditworthy, and must agree to buy a residence within the State of Texas. Income limits vary depending upon the area, the number of people in the family, and whether or not the property is within a targeted or nontargeted area. (Targeted areas are federally designated regions defined as being economically depressed. Some program restrictions are waived or reduced to encourage development and housing in these areas).

"Bootstrap" Homebuilder Loan Program

The "Bootstrap" Homebuilder Loan Program provides low-interest home mortgage loans of up to $30,000 to low-income Texas families that agree to help build their own home. Two-thirds of the total funds are used to help residents of impoverished border colonies and communities build new, better homes. The remaining one-third will be available statewide to low-income families. Funds for the initiative come from the Department's Housing Trust Fund and other sources. The program is administered through TDHCA's Colonia Self-help Centers and other nonprofit organizations across the state.

Home Investment Partnerships Program (HOME)

The HOME Investment Partnerships Program (HOME) provides grants and loans to help local governments, nonprofit agencies, for-profit entities, and public housing agencies provide safe, decent, affordable housing to extremely low-, very low-, and low-income families. HOME allocates funds through four basic activities: Homebuyer Assistance, Rental Housing Development, Owner-Occupied Housing Assistance, and Tenant-Based Rental Assistance. The program has a 15% set-aside for community housing development organizations, and a 10% set-aside for special needs, including the homeless, the elderly, persons with disabilities, and persons with AIDS.

HOME reserves funds for people at or below 80% of Average Medium Family Income (AMFI) for an area. TDHCA receives a statewide block grant of home funds for participating jurisdictions made on an annual basis according to a formula based on several HUD criteria. The home regulations allow for a variety of housing activities all aimed at providing safe, affordable housing to low-income families. These programs change from time to time. The Department can be accessed on the Internet at http://www.tdhca.state.tx.us.

Housing Finance Corporation

Texas also provides a mechanism whereby a local governmental unit can authorize the creation of a Housing Finance Corporation within that governmental unit. This is a nonprofit corporation that can sell bonds and use other methods of incurring income to provide financing to local lending institutions for low- and middle-income housing, similar to a state-sponsored program administered by the Texas Department of Housing and Community Affairs. There are also similar criteria for providing housing for the elderly. These corporations can be enabled only by the local governing body such as a city council. The determination must be made from town to town as to whether or not a housing financing corporation is available as a source for these types of funds.

Fannie Mae REALTOR® Programs

Fannie Mae partnered with the Texas Association of REALTORS® (TAR) to create the "Borrow With Confidence" program, teaching agents how to use Fannie Mae products. A similar program was created with the Texas Department of Housing and Community Affairs termed "United Texas: Housing Initiatives That Work" offered around the state through the local Associations of

REALTORS®. You can obtain more information on this growing number of realtor efforts by contacting their website: http://www.texasrealtors.com and click on the "Affordable Housing" link.

Texas State Affordable Housing Corporation

The Texas State Affordable Housing Corporation provides home ownership opportunities to Texans who may not qualify for financing through conventional channels. To be eligible for a loan the person must, at the time he or she files the application, be a firefighter, correction officer, county jailer, public security officer, or peace officer. A number of loans are available at a very low (5.99%) fixed interest rate and a 5% grant is available for down payment assistance. Programs include a professional educators help home loan program, "The Homes For Heroes" home loan program, the nursing facility home loan program, multifamily bond programs, and multifamily direct lending program. Their information can be accessed through http://www.tsahc.org/programs.

SECONDARY MARKET

The *secondary market* (also called the *secondary mortgage market*) provides a way for a lender to sell a loan. It also permits investment in real estate loans without the need for loan origination and servicing facilities. Although not directly encountered by real estate buyers, sellers, and agents, the secondary market plays an important role in getting money from those who want to lend to those who want to borrow. In other words, think of the secondary market as a pipeline for loan money. Visualize that pipeline running via the Wall Street financial district in New York City, because Wall Street is now a major participant in residential mortgage lending. Figure 14.1 illustrates this pipeline and diagrams key differences between the traditional mortgage delivery system and the secondary market system.

FIGURE 14.1 Mortgage loan delivery system

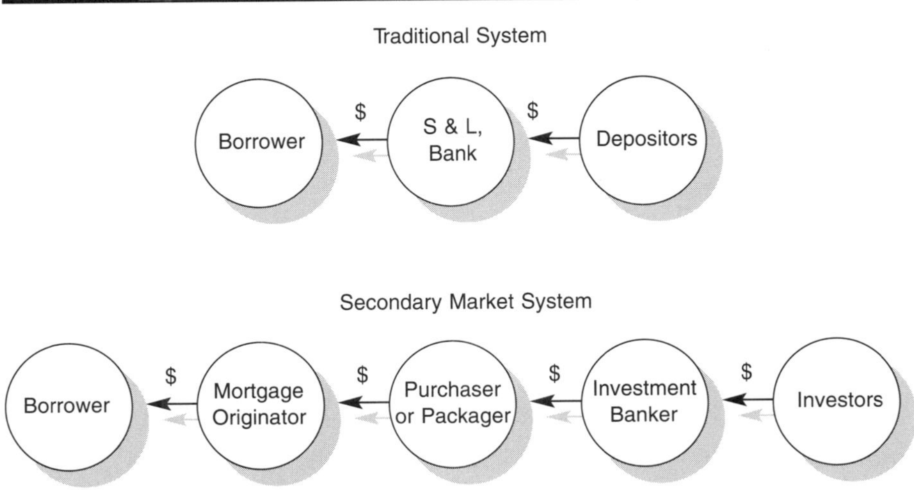

Source: © 2012 Cengage Learning

Traditional Delivery System

Notice in Figure 14.1 that, in the traditional system, the lender is a local institution gathering deposits from the community and then lending that money as real estate loans in the same community. Traditionally, each lender (S&L, bank, commercial bank, credit union) was an independent unit that developed its own appraisal technique, loan application form, loan approval criteria, note and mortgage forms, servicing method, and foreclosure policy. Nonetheless, three major problems needed solving. The first occurred when an institution had an imbalance of depositors and borrowers. Rapidly growing areas of the United States often needed more loan money than their savers were capable of depositing. Stable regions had more depositors than loan opportunities. Thus it was common to see correspondent relationships between lenders; for example, a lender in Los Angeles would sell some of its mortgage loans to a savings bank in Brooklyn. This provided loans for borrowers and interest for savers. The system worked well, but required individual correspondent relationships.

The second problem occurred when depositors wanted to withdraw their money from their accounts and invest it in other sources. Lenders, seeking to attract these depositors, raised their interest rates, which increases the loan rates. The third problem was timing. Lenders must borrow "short" (from their deposit relationships) and lend "long" (30-year mortgages). Savers, then, are encouraged to leave their money on deposit for longer periods of time.

The answer to these three problems is relatively simple: Find a market to sell your loans to investors who will pay cash for them and reimburse the primary lender. The result, then, is that there is an investor who is willing to hold the loan long-term for its guaranteed rate of return. The primary lender continues to make loans, gambling that he will find another investor in the secondary market to buy that loan for a long term. In effect, the primary lenders can make loans from the secondary market funds instead of their own deposits.

Secondary Market Delivery Systems

As shown in Figure 14.1, with the secondary market system the borrower obtains a loan from a mortgage originator. This includes mortgage companies, banks, CLOs, and thrifts that originate loans they intend to sell. The mortgage originator packages the loan with other loans and then either sells the package as a whole or keeps the package and sells securities that are backed by the loans in the package. If the originator is not large enough to package its own mortgages, it will sell the loans to someone who can.

There are now two sources for this secondary market. The first is private investors such as commercial banks, savings and loans, pension plans, trust funds, and other investors looking for low-risk, long-term returns on their investments. The second group of investors, relatively new in the investment business, is the investment "pools" or "poolers" looking for more security in their investments. This results in two primary investors in the secondary market: (1) the pure portfolio purchasers looking for the initial investments with an attractive return, and (2) the "poolers" looking for the longer term, more stable return.

Standardized Loan Procedures

A major stumbling block to a highly organized and efficient secondary market has been the uniqueness of both lenders and loans. Traditionally, each primary lender developed its own special loan forms and procedures. Moreover, each loan is a unique combination of real estate and borrower. No two are exactly alike. How do you package such diversity into an attractive package for investors? A large part of the answer has come through standardized loan application forms; standardized appraisal forms; standardized credit report forms; standardized closing statements; standardized loan approval criteria; and standardized promissory notes, mortgages, and trust deeds. Loan terms have been standardized into categories, for example, fixed-rate, 30-year loans; fixed-rate, 15-year loans; and various adjustable rate combinations. Additionally, nearly all loans must be insured. This can take the form of FHA or private mortgage insurance, or a VA guarantee on each loan in the package. Additionally, there will be some form of assurance of timely repayment of the mortgage package as a whole. The net result is a mortgage security that is attractive to investors that in the past have not been interested in investing in mortgages.

Let's now look at some of the key secondary market participants including the giants of the industry: the Federal National Mortgage Association, the Government National Mortgage Association, the Federal Home Loan Mortgage Corporation, and Farmer Mac.

OFHEO

First, let's discuss oversight of these giants. In the early 1990s, there was a growing concern about the liquidity and self-regulation of the government-sponsored entities in the secondary market. In 1992, the Office of Federal Housing Enterprise Oversight (OFHEO) was established as an independent entity within the Department of Housing and Urban Development. Its purpose is to ensure the capital adequacy and financial soundness of Fannie Mae and Freddie Mac, to ensure that both comply with the public purposes set forth in their charters, and to exercise regulatory authority over them. It examines them using a risk-based capital standard and makes quarterly findings of capital adequacy. In exchange for carrying out their public purposes, Fannie Mae and Freddie Mac are given various privileges that provide them with some benefits not available to other private corporations. These benefits include an exemption from state and local taxes (except property taxes) and conditional access to a $2.2 billion line of credit from the U.S. Treasury Department. With these benefits, they are able to fund their operations at lower costs than other private firms with similar financial characteristics. OFHEO also requires Fannie Mae and Freddie Mac to meet certain affordable housing goals set annually by the Secretary of HUD to purchase low-income, moderate-income, and central-city homes.

The credit profile of FNMA and FHLMC fell in 2006 and 2007. In the first half of 2007, roughly one-third of their new loans were composed of mortgages that had less than standard documentation, interest-only, or Option ARM products, and mortgages with multiple risk characteristics.

As a result of the perceived increase in risk for investors in FNMA and FHLMC, the Federal Housing Financing Agency (FHFA) was created by merging the Federal Housing Finance Board (FHFB) with OFHEO. This created an expanded legal and regulatory authority as part of the Federal Housing Finance Regulatory Reform Act of 2008.

Investors who had traditionally bought FNMA and FHLMC certificates ceased doing so. On September 7, 2008, the FHFA director put FNMA and FHLMC under the conservatorship of the FHFA, and FHFA is now managing both FNMA and FHLMC until they are stabilized. Congress has appropriated funds up to $700 billion to purchase these securities to prop up the liquidity of both Fannie Mae and Freddie Mac. What follows is a discussion of Fannie Mae and Freddie Mac's traditional roles in the secondary and investment markets. There may be big changes ahead.

FNMA

The ***Federal National Mortgage Association (FNMA)*** was organized by the federal government in 1938 to buy FHA mortgage loans from lenders. This made it possible for lenders to grant more loans to consumers. Ten years later it began purchasing VA loans. FNMA (fondly known in the real estate business and to itself as ***Fannie Mae***) was successful in its mission.

In 1968, Congress divided the FNMA into two organizations: the Government National Mortgage Association (to be discussed in the next section) and the FNMA, as we know it today. As part of that division, the FNMA changed from a government agency to a private profit-making corporation, chartered by Congress but owned by its shareholders and managed independently of the government. Some 60 million shares of Fannie Mae stock are in existence, and it is one of the most actively traded issues on the New York Stock Exchange. Fannie Mae buys FHA, VA, and conventional whole loans from lenders across the United States. Money to buy these loans comes from the sale of FNMA stock plus the sale of FNMA bonds and notes. FNMA bond and note holders look to Fannie Mae for timely payment of principal and interest on these bonds and notes, and Fannie Mae looks to its mortgagors for principal and interest payments on the loans it owns. Thus, Fannie Mae stands in the middle and, although it is very careful to match interest rates and maturities between the loans it buys and the bonds and notes it sells, it still takes the risk of the middleman. In this respect, it is like a giant thrift institution.

Commitments

Fannie Mae's method of operation is to sell commitments to lenders pledging to buy specified dollar amounts of mortgage loans within a fixed period of time and usually at a specified yield. Lenders are not obligated to sell loans to Fannie Mae if they can find better terms elsewhere. However, Fannie Mae must purchase all loans delivered to it under the terms of the commitments. Loans must be made using FNMA-approved forms and loan approval criteria. The largest loan Fannie Mae would buy in 2006 was $417,000 for a single-family unit. This limit is adjusted each year as housing prices change. Fannie Mae also buys loans on duplexes, triplexes, and fourplexes all at larger loan limits. Although the FNMA loan limit may seem inadequate for some houses and neighborhoods, the intention of Congress is that Fannie Mae cater to the mid-range of housing prices and leave the upper end of the market to others.

In addition to purchasing first mortgages, Fannie Mae also purchases second mortgages from lenders. The loan limit for second mortgages as of 2006 was $208,500. FNMA forms and criteria must be followed and the loan-to-value ratio of the combined first and second mortgages cannot exceed 80% if owner-occupied and 70% if not owner-occupied. This is a very helpful program for those who have watched the value of their homes increase and want to borrow against that increase without first having to repay the existing mortgage loan. Updated information is available at http://www.fanniemae.com, tab to FAQ.

FNMA Pooling

The demand for loans in the primary market could not match the demand that investors required in the secondary market, so Fannie Mae began purchasing large blocks of mortgage loans, and then assigned them to specified pools with an "agency guarantee" certificate that guaranteed long-term return to the pool investors. Fannie Mae guarantees to pass through to the certificate holders whatever principal, interest, and prepayments of principal are generated by the loans into the underlying pool of mortgage investors. Fannie Mae's pooling arrangements undertook the issuance of **mortgage-backed securities (MBS).** Using this system of issuing securities that are backed by mortgages, the securities markets could then be used as a source for investment funds. In the first quarter of 2005, Fannie Mae held $2,526 billion dollars of loans in portfolio investments. At the same time, however, Fannie Mae had underwritten $513.2 billion in mortgage pools. This is also a strong indication that the government-guaranteed loan pools provide a much better procedure for making funds available in the secondary market. This, in turn, assures that funds are available for the primary market and long-term mortgage loans for individual home purchasers.

Home Seller Program

Another innovation of Fannie Mae to help real estate is the **home seller program.** This is a secondary market for sellers who carry back mortgages. To qualify, the note and mortgage must be prepared by a FNMA-approved lender using standard FNMA loan qualification procedures. The note and mortgage may be kept by the home seller as an investment or sold to a FNMA-approved lender for possible resale to the FNMA.

In other developments, Fannie Mae has standardized the terms of adjustable rate mortgages it will purchase. This is a major step forward in reducing the proliferation of variety in these loans. Fannie Mae is also test marketing mortgage-backed securities in $1,000 increments to appeal to individuals, particularly for Individual Retirement Accounts. Additionally, Fannie Mae has started a collateralized mortgage obligation program and begun a mortgage pass-through program, both of which will be defined momentarily.

Revised Lending Practices

In 1992, as pressure increased from both Congress and the U.S. Department of Housing and Urban Development to become more socially responsible in lending practices, Congress passed legislation requiring stricter supervision of Fannie Mae by a HUD-appointed oversight committee. In March 1994, Fannie Mae announced a plan to provide one trillion dollars in financing over the rest of the decade to poor families, rural communities, and disabled people. Fannie Mae now cooperates with others to facilitate loans for low- to moderate-income borrowers in the purchase of 97% of conventional loans and flexible mortgages, working with local housing authorities, nonprofit associations, nonprofit housing groups, and private mortgage insurance, to spread the risk of some other loans. Fannie Mae has also aggressively adopted practices to provide affordable housing and prevent fraud in real estate loan transactions, discussed in the next chapter under Affordable Housing Loans.

FHLMC

The **Federal Home Loan Mortgage Corporation (FHLMC,** also known to the industry and to itself as ***"Freddie Mac"*** or the "Mortgage Corporation") was created by Congress in 1970. Its goal, like that of the FNMA and GNMA, is to increase the availability of financing for residential mortgages. Where FHLMC differs is that Freddie Mac deals primarily in conventional mortgages.

Freddie Mac was initially established to serve as a secondary market for S&L members of the Federal Home Loan Bank System. The ownership of Freddie Mac was originally held by more than 3,000 savings associations. In 1988, the shares were released and sold publicly by the savings associations. Unlike Ginnie Mae, which guarantees securities issued by others, Freddie Mac issues its own securities against its own mortgage pools. These securities are its participation certificates and collateralized mortgage obligations. By the first quarter of 2002, Freddie Mac held nearly $60 billion in its own loan portfolio, accounting for almost 18% (including FHLMC pools) of all outstanding loans in residential lending.

Participation Certificates

Participation certificates (PCs) allow a mortgage originator to deliver to Freddie Mac either whole mortgages or part interest in a pool of whole mortgages. In return, Freddie Mac gives the mortgage originator a PC representing an undivided interest in a pool of investment-quality conventional mortgages created from mortgages and mortgage interests purchased by Freddie Mac. Freddie Mac guarantees that the interest and principal on these PCs will be repaid in full and on time, even if the underlying mortgages are in default. (Freddie Mac reduces its losses by setting strict loan qualification criteria and requiring mortgage insurance on high loan-to-value loans.) The PCs can be kept as investments, sold for cash, or used as collateral for loans. PCs are popular investments for S&Ls, pension funds, and other institutional investors looking for high-yield investments. Individuals who can meet the $25,000 minimum also find PCs attractive. Freddie Mac also has a collateralized mortgage obligation program and plans to offer a trust for investments in mortgages. Both of these programs are designed to deal with the unpredictability of mortgage maturities caused by early repayment by dividing the cash flows from a mortgage pool into separate securities with separate maturities, which are then sold to investors.

As with Fannie Mae, Congress and HUD provide the oversight committee to Freddie Mac. New guidelines provided by HUD call for both Freddie Mac and Fannie Mae to purchase about 30% of their mortgages in inner-city areas and from lower-income home buyers.

GNMA

The **Government National Mortgage Association (GNMA,** popularly known to the industry and to itself as **"Ginnie Mae"**) was created in 1968 when the FNMA was partitioned into two separate corporations. Ginnie Mae is a federal agency entirely within the HUD. Although Ginnie Mae has some low-income housing functions, it is best known for its mortgage-backed securities (MBS) program. Previously discussed, the MBS program attracts additional sources of credit to FHA, VA, and RHSA mortgages. Ginnie Mae does this by guaranteeing timely repayment of privately issued securities backed by pools of these mortgages. Remember that the FNMA MBS program offers "agency guarantees" for their investors. GNMA offers a government guarantee of repayment, backed by the full faith and credit of the U.S. government.

Ginnie Mae Procedures

Ginnie Mae is limited to underwriting only HUD/FHA, VA, and certain other loans. It is not possible to purchase loans as both FNMA and FHLMC (discussed next). Ginnie Mae sets its own requirements for loans that can be accepted into their mortgage pool, then it subsequently approves loan poolers who are committed to comply with those requirements. Ginnie Mae must examine the loans and the loan poolers before it can determine its ability to guarantee those loans into the loan pooler source of funds. The result is that Ginnie Mae issues guarantee certificates, popularly known as "Ginnie Maes." A Ginnie Mae certificate carries the equivalent of a U.S. government bond guarantee and pays the holder of those certificates, the loan pooler, an interest rate of 1% to 1.5% higher than that of a government bond.

Farmer MAC

The newest agency created by Congress to underwrite loan pools is the *Federal Agricultural Mortgage Corporation,* known as *Farmer Mac.* The Agricultural Credit Act of 1987 established Farmer Mac as a separate agency within the Farm Credit System to establish the secondary market needed for farm real estate loans. Farmer Mac started actual operations in 1989.

Originally, Farmer Mac functioned similarly to Ginnie Mae in that it certified loan poolers rather than purchase loans. Farmer Mac guaranteed timely repayment of principal and interest in the loan pool, but did not guarantee any individual loans within that pool.

In 1996, Congress passed the *Farm Credit System Reform Act* allowing Farmer Mac to act as a pooler for qualified loans. Farmer Mac is now permitted to purchase loans directly from originators and to issue its own 100% guaranteed securities backed by the loans. For the first time, Farmer Mac became a true secondary market.

Loan Qualification

To qualify for a pool, a loan must be collateralized by agricultural real estate located in the United States. The real estate can include a home, which can cost no more than $100,000, and must be located in a rural community with a population of 2,500 or less. The maximum loan is $2.5 million or the amount secured by no more than 1,000 acres, whichever is larger. The loan-to-value ratio must be less than 80%, and the borrower must be a United States citizen engaged in agriculture and must demonstrate a capability to repay the loan.

Private Conduits

The financial success of the three giants of the secondary mortgage market (FNMA, GNMA, and FHLMC) has brought private mortgage packagers into the marketplace. The 1990s saw substantial growth in commercial loan fundings for the sale of mortgage bank securities, called **Commercial Mortgage-Backed Securities (CMBS)**.

Organizations that handle CMBS are called conduits, who originate commercial and multifamily housing loans for purposes of pooling them as collateral for the issuance of Commercial Mortgage Back Securities, rather than holding them in the lender's own portfolio. Conduits are often subsidiaries of commercial banks and security firms who participate loans out to other banks or private investment sources. It is effectively a commercial secondary market without governmental support and has been very successful in generating fund availability for commercial projects.

These are organizations such as MGIC Investment Corporation (a subsidiary of Mortgage Guaranty Investment Corporation); Residential Funding Corporation (a subsidiary of Norwest Mortgage Corp.); financial subsidiaries of such household-name companies as General Electric, Lockheed Aircraft, and Sears, Roebuck; and mortgage packaging subsidiaries of state REALTOR® associations. These organizations both compete with the big three and specialize in markets not served by them, including commercial lending markets. For example, Residential Funding Corp. will package mortgage loans as large as $500,000, well above the limits imposed by FNMA and FHLMC and on FHA and VA loans. All of these organizations will buy from loan originators that are not large enough to create their own pools.

The entry of these private investment sources into the single-family residential market was initially met with the great success as it created an entirely new secondary market for first-lien purchase money home loans and a tremendous source of new investment funds. It encouraged substantial growth in the housing market with easy to obtain attractive loans for homeowners, particularly first-time homeowners. The new source of funds enabled more funds to be available at lower cost, and enabled many homeowners to move into a home with mortgage payments cheaper than the rent they were paying in their existing apartment. By the third quarter of 2007, the private mortgage conduits held $2,179 billion, or 19.76% of the one- to four-family loans. This is an increase of 192% from 2003.

There is a downside to the market, however. Many loans were made to borrowers who couldn't really qualify for the loans. In many cases, encouraging new home loans also led to predatory lending practices and mortgage fraud, as a lot of these private conduits didn't properly monitor the quality of the loans that were being made in the primary market and didn't exercise proper due diligence in managing the loan portfolio. This is a major factor in our "credit crisis" or "mortgage crisis" that the government is now dealing with.

Computerization

Before leaving the topic of the secondary market, it is important to note that, without electronic data transmission and computers, the programs just described would be severely handicapped. There are currently thousands of mortgage pools, each containing from $1 million to $500 million (and more) in mortgage loans. Each loan in a pool has its own monthly payment schedule, and each payment must be broken down into its principal and interest components and any property tax and insurance impounds. Computers do this work as well as issue receipts and late notices. The pool, in turn, will be owned by several dozen to a hundred or more investors, each with a different fractional interest in the pool. Once a month, incoming mortgage payments are tallied, a small fee is deducted for the operation of the pool, and the balance is allotted among the investors—all by computer. A computer also prints and mails checks to investors and provides them with an accounting of the pool's asset level.

AUTOMATED UNDERWRITING SYSTEMS

The computer age has introduced a whole new system in underwriting procedures as they apply to the relationship between the loan originator and the investor (secondary market). In the "old days," underwriting guidelines would be published and circulated to the primary lenders weekly. As interest rates began to fluctuate wildly in the 1970s, the sheet was updated and circulated more often. In some real estate offices, one person was given the job of calling lenders daily for quotes on loan availability and interest rates.

The entire process is being overhauled by a computerized mortgage loan underwriting system with the introduction of Freddie Mac's Loan Prospector program, which was made available on the Internet in 1999. At this time, the program is limited to Freddie Mac's approved sellers and servicers. This process is very streamlined. The regular uniform residential loan application is submitted to the lender and the lender then verifies the applicant's employment, income, and assets. This information is fed into the computer and is promptly analyzed by the computer program. If the borrower is accepted and the loan-to-value ratio is greater than 80%, the application is then forwarded to a private mortgage insurer. Those that are not accepted are considered as "refer" or "caution." Those classified as "refer" are sent to the underwriting department with at least four reasons stating why the loan is referred. The "caution" category indicates that there are serious issues preventing the loan's purchase. The real estate can be appraised and a loan completely processed in as little as two hours if the lender requests an "expedited" appraisal. A nonexpedited appraisal can take less than 72 hours. Freddie Mac reports that about 60% of all applicants can be accepted in four minutes. It is anticipated that by using this streamlined program, the cost of processing the loan is cut in half.

FNMA now has its own software program, also available on the Internet, called Desktop Originator/Desktop Underwriter Government Underwriting Service (Do/Du) (used by a broker or lender to submit the application directly to FNMA). As with the Freddie Mac program, responses can be confirmed in seconds.

Fannie Mae and Freddie Mac have agreed to an open standard that would encompass automatic underwriting. The standards are set by the Mortgage Bankers Association's *Mortgage Industry Standards Maintenance Organization,* commonly referred to as "MISMO," and were implemented in July of 2002. The ***automated underwriting*** system's specifications consist of a dated dictionary and a document-type definition, plus a set of rules used to build a file for underwriting requests. This is a common automated underwriting standard that will simplify the electronic mortgage application process and reduce its cost.

In October 2004, Fannie Mae introduced several enhancements to the Desktop Originator/Desktop Underwriter service to help lenders identify and stop fraud in mortgage transactions before the loan is closed. The new program includes a standardized property address implementation to determine if there are matches to addresses or similar addresses for potential loan applicants, which helps develop a potential "red flag." Red flags consist of inconsistent or contradictory loan data (usually fraudulent appraisals) in a given neighborhood. This new program also, in an attempt to prevent identity theft, determines matches for social security numbers.

Commercial Loans in the Secondary Market

As previously discussed, the primary sources of financing for commercial and multi-family mortgages are pension funds, life insurance companies, and commercial banks. The 1990s saw substantial growth in commercial loan fundings for the sale of mortgage bank securities, called **Commercial Mortgage-Backed Securities (CMBS).**

Organizations that handle CMBS are called **conduits,** that originate commercial and multifamily housing loans to pool them as collateral for the issuance of Commercial Mortgage-Backed Securities, rather than hold them in the lender's own portfolio. Conduits are often subsidiaries of commercial banks and security firms that participate loans to other banks or private investment sources.

It is effectively a commercial secondary market without government support, and has been very successful in generating fund availability for commercial projects.

AVAILABILITY AND PRICE OF MORTGAGE MONEY

Thus far we have been concerned with the money pipelines between lenders and borrowers. Ultimately, though, money must have a source. These sources are savings generated by individuals and businesses as a result of their spending less than they earn **(real savings)** and government-created money, called **fiat money** or "printing press money." This second source does not represent unconsumed labor and materials; instead it competes for available goods and services alongside the savings of individuals and businesses.

In the arena of money and capital, real estate borrowers must compete with the needs of government, business, and consumers. Governments, particularly the federal government, compete the hardest when they borrow to finance a deficit. Not to borrow would mean bankruptcy and the inability to pay government employees and provide government programs and services. Strong competition also comes from business and consumer credit sectors. In the face of such strong competition for loan funds, home buyers must either pay higher interest or be outbid.

One "solution" to this problem is for the federal government to create more money, thus making competition for funds easier and interest rates lower. Unfortunately, the net result is often too much money chasing too few goods, and prices are pulled upward by the demand caused by the newly created money. This is followed by rising interest rates as savers demand higher returns to compensate for losses in purchasing power. Many economists feel that the higher price levels and interest rates of the 1970s resulted from applying too much of this "solution" to the economy since 1965.

The alternative solution, from the standpoint of residential loans, is to increase real savings or decrease competing demands for available money. A number of plans and ideas have been put forth by civic, business, and political leaders. They include proposals to simplify income taxes and balance the federal budget, incentives to increase productive output, and incentives to save money in retirement accounts.

USURY

An old idea that has been tried, but is of dubious value for holding down interest rates, is legislation to impose interest rate ceilings. Known as ***usury*** laws and found in nearly all states, these laws were originally enacted to prohibit lenders from overcharging interest on loans to individuals. Most states raised usury limits in response to higher interest rates. Additionally, the U.S. Congress passed legislation in 1980 that exempts from state usury limits most first-lien home loans made by institutional lenders. Low interest rates and the availability of funds for loans has been so competitive that usury is not much of an issue anymore.

PRICE TO THE BORROWER

Ultimately, the rate of interest the borrower must pay to obtain a loan is dependent on the cost of money to the lender, reserves for default, loan servicing costs, and available investment alternatives. For example, go to a savings institution and see what they are paying depositors on various accounts. To this add 2% for the cost of maintaining cash in the tills, office space, personnel, advertising, free gifts for depositors, deposit insurance, loan servicing, loan reserves for defaults, and a ½% profit margin. This gives you an idea of how much borrowers must be charged.

Life insurance companies, pension funds, and trust funds do not have to "pay" for their money as do thrift institutions. Nonetheless, they do want to earn the highest possible yields, with safety, on the money in their custody. Thus, if a real estate buyer wants to borrow to buy a home, the buyer must compete successfully with the other investment opportunities available on the open market. To determine the rate for yourself, look at the yields on newly issued corporate bonds as shown in the financial section of your daily newspaper. Add ½ of 1% to this for the extra work in packaging and servicing mortgage loans and you will have the interest rate home borrowers must pay to attract lenders.

DUE-ON-SALE

From an investment risk standpoint, when a lender makes a loan with a fixed interest rate, the lender recognizes that during the life of the loan interest rates may rise or fall. When they rise, the lender remains locked into a lower rate. Most loans contain a *due-on-sale clause* (also called an ***alienation clause*** or a **call clause**). In the past, these were inserted by lenders so that if the borrower sold the property to someone considered uncreditworthy by the lender, the lender could call the loan balance due. When interest rates increase, though, lenders can use these clauses to increase the rate of interest on the loan when the property changes hands by threatening to accelerate the balance of the loan unless the new owner accepts a higher rate of interest.

PREPAYMENT

If loan rates drop, it becomes worthwhile for a borrower to shop for a new loan and repay the existing one in full. To compensate, loan contracts sometimes call for a **prepayment penalty** in return for giving the borrower the right to repay the loan early. A typical prepayment penalty amounts to the equivalent of six months interest on the amount that is being paid early. However, the penalty varies from loan to loan and from state to state. Some loan contracts permit up to 20% of the unpaid balance to be paid in any one year without penalty. Other contracts make the penalty stiffest when the loan is young. In certain states, laws do not permit prepayment penalties on loans more than five years old. By federal law, prepayment penalties are not allowed on FHA and VA loans.

REVIEW QUESTIONS

Answers to these questions are found in the Answer Key section at the back of the book.

1. The place where a real estate borrower makes a loan application, receives a loan, and makes loan payments describes the
   A. primary mortgage market.
   B. secondary mortgage market.
   C. first loan market.
   D. second loan market.

2. Historically, the foremost single source of funds for residential mortgage loans in this country has been
   A. commercial banks.
   B. insurance companies.
   C. mortgage companies.
   D. savings and loan associations.

3. When savings are removed from thrift institutions in large amounts for investment in Treasury securities,
   A. the real estate market enjoys an increase in activity.
   B. disintermediation occurs.
   C. both A and B.
   D. neither A nor B.

4. Reasons for the decline in residential loans made by the S&Ls include all but the following:
   A. deregulation of the lending industry.
   B. proliferation of savings and loan organizations.
   C. new laws that allowed higher risk loans.
   D. placing the Federal Savings and Loan Insurance Corporation under the Federal Depositors Insurance Corporation.

5. A real estate loan that calls for the lender to receive interest plus a percentage of the rental income from a property is
   A. designed to protect the lender from inflation.
   B. known as a participation loan.
   C. both A and B.
   D. neither A nor B.

6. Mortgage companies
   A. originate loans.
   B. service loans that they have sold on the secondary mortgage market.
   C. both A and B.
   D. neither A nor B.

7. The secondary mortgage market provides
   A. a means for investors to acquire real estate loans with origination and servicing facilities.
   B. a way for a lender to sell real estate loans.
   C. both A and B.
   D. neither A nor B.

8. All of the following are true of the Federal National Mortgage Association EXCEPT that it is
   A. a privately owned corporation.
   B. managed by the federal government.
   C. active in buying FHA and VA mortgage loans.
   D. known as Fannie Mae.

9. Participation certificates issued by Freddie Mac can be
   A. sold for cash.
   B. used as collateral for loans.
   C. both A and B.
   D. neither A nor B.

10. Collateralized mortgage obligations issued by the FHLMC provide an investor with investments of
    A. predictable maturity.
    B. guaranteed yields.
    C. both A and B.
    D. neither A nor B.

Chapter 15

KEY TERMS

Adjustable rate mortgage (ARM): a mortgage on which the interest rate rises and falls with changes in prevailing interest rates

Affordable Housing Loan: loans targeted to first-time home buyers or low to medium income borrowers

Asset Blanket mortgage: a mortgage secured by two or more properties

Construction loan: short-term loan for new construction or remodeling of an existing structure

Equity sharing: an arrangement whereby a party providing financing gets a portion of the ownership

Graduated payment mortgage: a mortgage with an interest rate and maturity that are fixed, but the monthly payment gradually rises, because the initial monthly payments are insufficient to fully amortize the loan

Negative amortization: accrual of interest on a loan balance so that, as loan payments are made, the loan balance rises

Option: a right, for a given period of time, to buy, sell, or lease property at specified price and terms

Package mortgage: a mortgage that secures personal property in addition to real property

Reverse mortgage: a mortgage wherein the lender pays the homeowner instead of the homeowner paying the lender

Seller financing: a note accepted by a seller instead of cash

Wraparound mortgage: a mortgage that encompasses any existing mortgages and is subordinate to them

Types of Financing

IN THIS CHAPTER

An "alphabet soup" of mortgaging alternatives are now available to a borrower. With computerized loan origination, the expanded secondary market, and the availability of mortgage funds from nonregulated lending sources, a vast array of available mortgaging techniques and types of financing have been created. Loan brokers are now using computer programs to customize mortgages for individual homebuyers, usually on the Internet. "Customized mortgages" are now part of an individualized pricing trend sweeping through the U.S. economy. What was once a "prime" or "subprime" generalized loan is now replaced by an almost endless array of mortgage rates, and accompanying fees. The documents (discussed in Chapter 11) and the sources of funds (discussed in Chapter 14) still remain the same, but the number of alternative types of financing continues to expand. Only the most fundamental concepts will be discussed in this chapter, including types of financing, such as adjustable rate mortgages, other generally accepted types of loans often encountered by a broker in real estate lending, and the newest concepts of the affordable housing programs.

ADJUSTABLE RATE MORTGAGES

As we have already seen, a major problem for savings institutions is that they are locked into long-term loans while being dependent on short-term savings deposits. As a result, savings institutions now prefer to make mortgage loans that allow the interest rate to rise and fall during the life of the loan. To make this arrangement more attractive to borrowers, these loans are offered at a lower rate of interest than a fixed-rate loan of similar maturity.

The first step toward mortgage loans with adjustable interest rates came in the late 1970s. The loan was called a **variable rate mortgage** and the interest rate could be adjusted up or down by the lender during the 30-year life of the loan to reflect the rise and fall in interest rates paid to savers by the lender.

Current Format

The Office of Thrift Supervision (OTS) authorizes institutions to make the type of adjustable mortgage loan you are most likely to encounter in today's loan marketplace. This loan format is called an ***adjustable rate mortgage (ARM).*** Other federal agencies followed, but used differing guidelines. The main ARM requirement is that the interest rate on these loans be tied to some publicly available index that is mutually acceptable to the lender and the borrower. As interest rates rise and fall in the open market, the interest rate the lender is entitled to receive from the borrower rises and falls (Figure 15.1). The purpose is to match more closely what the savings institution receives from borrowers to what it must pay savers to attract funds.

The benefit of an ARM to a borrower is that ARMs carry an initial interest rate that is lower than the rate on a fixed-rate mortgage of similar maturity. This often makes the difference between being able to qualify for a desired home and not qualifying for it. Other advantages to the borrower are that if market interest rates fall, the borrower's monthly payments fall. (This happens without incurring prepayment penalties or new loan origination costs, which could be the case with a fixed-rate loan.) Most ARMs allow assumption by a new buyer at the terms in the ARM, and most allow total prepayment without penalty, particularly if there has been an upward adjustment in the interest rate.

For the borrower, the disadvantage of an ARM is that if interest rates rise, the borrower is going to pay more. During periods of rising interest rates, property values and wages presumably will also rise. But the possibility of progressively larger monthly payments for the family home is still not attractive. As a result, various compromises have been worked out between lenders and borrowers whereby rates can rise on loans, but not by too much. In view of the fact that about one-half of all mortgage loans being originated by thrifts, banks, and mortgage companies are now adjustable, let's take a closer look at what a borrower gets with this loan format.

FIGURE 15.1 Adjustable Rate Mortgage

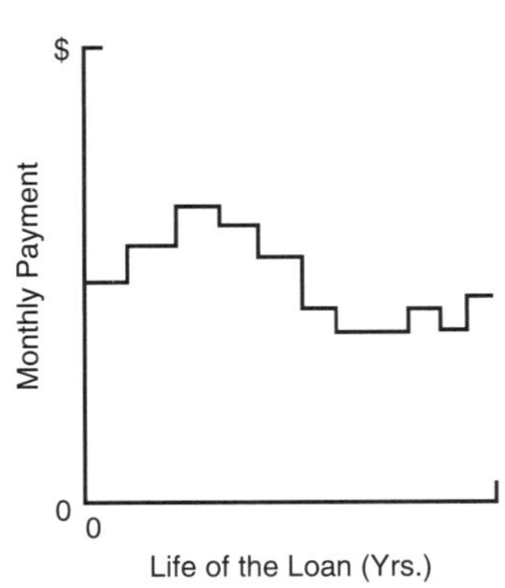

Source: © 2012 Cengage Learning

Interest Rate

The interest rate on an ARM is tied to an **index rate.** As the index rate moves up or down, so do the borrower's payments when adjustment time arrives. Lenders and borrowers alike want a rate that genuinely reflects current market conditions for interest rates and that can be easily verified. The most popular index is based on an index that includes interest rates of all treasuries and securities, from 3-month bills to 30-year bonds. This index, called a one-year constant maturity treasury, is published by the Federal Reserve based on daily calculations.

Margin

To the index rate is added the margin. The **margin** is for the lender's cost of doing business, risk of loss on the loan, and profit. Currently this runs from 2% to 3%, depending on the characteristics of the loan. The margin is a useful comparison device because if two lenders are offering the same loan terms and the same index, but one loan has a margin of 2% and the other 3%, then the one with the 2% margin will have lower loan payments. As a rule, the margin stays constant during the life of the loan. At each adjustment point in the loan's life, the lender takes the index rate and adds the margin. The total becomes the interest the borrower will pay until the next adjustment occurs.

Adjustment Period

The amount of time that elapses between adjustments is called the *adjustment period*. By far the most common adjustment period is one year. Less commonly used are six-month, three-year, and five-year adjustment periods. When market rates are rising, the longer adjustment periods benefit the borrower. When market rates are falling, the shorter periods benefit the borrower because index decreases will show up sooner in their monthly payments.

Interest Rate Cap

Lenders are now required by federal law to disclose an **interest rate cap** or ceiling on how much the interest rate can increase for any one adjustment period during the life of the loan. If the cap is very low, say 0.5% per year, the lender does not have much more flexibility than if holding a fixed-rate loan. Thus, there would be little reduction of the initial rate on the loan compared with a fixed-rate loan. Compromises have prevailed, and the two most popular caps are 1% and 2% per year. In other words, the index rate may rise by 3%, but the cap limits the borrower's rate increase to 1% or 2%. Any unused difference may be added the next year, assuming the index rate has not fallen in the meantime. Because federal law now requires the ceiling, many lenders simply impose a very high ceiling (e.g., 18%) if they choose not to negotiate with the borrower.

Payment Cap

What if a loan's index rate rises so fast that the annual rate cap is reached each year and the lifetime cap is reached soon in the life of the loan? A borrower might be able to handle a modest increase in payments each year, but not big jumps in quick succession. To counteract this possibility, a **payment cap** sets a limit on how much the borrower's monthly payment can increase in any one year. A popular figure now in use is 7.5%. In other words, no matter how high a payment is called for by the index rate, the borrower's monthly payment can rise, at the most, 7.5% per year. For example, given an initial rate of 10% on a 30-year ARM for $100,000, the monthly payment of interest and principal is $878 (see Table 12.1). If the index rate calls for a 2% upward adjustment at the end of one year, the payment on the loan would be $1,029. This is an increase of $151 or 17.2%. A 7.5% payment cap would limit the increase to 107.5% $878 = $943.85.

Negative Amortization

Although the 7.5% payment cap in the foregoing example protects the borrower against a monthly payment that rises too fast, it does not make the difference between what's called for ($1,029) and what's paid ($943.85) go away. The difference ($85.15) is added to the balance owed on the loan and earns interest just like the original amount borrowed. This is called ***negative amortization***: instead of the loan balance dropping each month as loan payments are made, the balance owed rises. This can bring concern to the lender who can visualize the day the loan balance exceeds the value of the property. A popular arrangement is to set a limit of 125% of the original loan balance. At that point, either the lender accrues no more negative amortization or the loan is reamortized depending on the wording of the loan contract. *Reamortized* in this situation means the monthly payments will be adjusted upward by enough to stop the negative amortization.

Disclosures

In response to consumers' concern over adjustable rate mortgages, Regulation Z requires creditors to provide consumers with more extensive information about the variable rate feature of ARMs. The amendments apply only to closed-end credit transactions secured by the consumer's principal dwelling. Transactions secured by the consumer's principal dwelling with a term of one year or less are exempt from the new disclosure. To comply with the amendment, lenders must provide consumers with a historical example that shows how actual changes in index values would have affected payments on a $10,000 loan, as well as provide a statement of initial and maximum interest rates. Lenders must also provide prospective borrowers with an educational brochure about ARMs called "The Consumer Handbook on Adjustable Rate and Mortgages" or a suitable substitute. All the information must be given to the consumer at the time the loan application form is provided or before a nonrefundable fee is paid, whichever is earlier. The maximum interest rate must be stated as a specified amount or stated in a manner in which the consumer may easily ascertain the maximum interest rate at the time of entering the obligation.

Choosing Wisely

When a lender makes an ARM loan, the lender must explain to the borrower, in writing, the *worst case scenario*. In other words, the lender must explain what will happen to the borrower's payments if the index rises the maximum amount each period up to the lifetime interest cap. If there is a payment cap, that and any possibility of negative amortization must also be explained. If the borrower is uneasy with these possibilities, then a fixed-rate loan should be considered. Most lenders offer fixed-rate loans as well as adjustable rate loans. VA loans are fixed-rate loans, but FHA now provides an adjustable rate loan program.

"Teaser rate" adjustables have been offered from time to time by a few lenders and are best avoided. This type of loan is an ARM with an enticingly attractive, below-market initial rate. For example, the teaser rate may be offered at 2% below market. A borrower who cannot qualify at the market rate might be able to do so at the teaser rate. However, in a year the loan contract calls for a 2% jump followed by additional annual increases. This overwhelms the borrower who, unable to pay, allows foreclosure to take place. This practice creates similar concerns for both mortgage insurers and secondary markets, which are always concerned about predatory lending practices.

GRADUATED PAYMENT MORTGAGE

The objective of a ***graduated payment mortgage*** is to help borrowers qualify for loans by basing repayment schedules on salary expectations. With this type of mortgage, the interest rate and maturity are fixed but the monthly payment gradually rises. For example, a 10%, $60,000, 30-year loan normally requires monthly payments of $527 for complete amortization. Under the graduated payment mortgage, payments could start out as low as $437 per month the first year, then gradually increase to $590 in the eleventh year and then remain at that level until the thirtieth year. Because the interest alone on this $60,000 loan is $500 per month, the amount owed on the loan actually increases during its early years. Only when the monthly payment exceeds the monthly interest does the balance owed on the loan decrease. These loans were very common during periods of high inflation. They are seldom used now that inflation and interest rates remain low.

EQUITY SHARING

Giving the party that provides the financing a "piece of the action in the deal" is not an innovation. Insurance companies financing shopping centers and office buildings have long used the idea of requiring part of the rental income and/or part of the profits plus interest on the loan itself. In other words, in return for providing financing, the lender wants to share in some of the benefits normally reserved for the equity holder, called ***equity sharing.*** The equity holder would agree to this either to get a lower rate of interest or to get financing when financing was scarce or where the equity holder was not big enough to handle the deal alone. For example, on a

$5 million project, the lender might agree to make a loan of $4 million at a very attractive rate if it can buy a half-interest in the equity for $500,000.

"RICH UNCLE" FINANCING

A second variation of equity sharing is often called *"rich uncle" financing.* The investor may be a parent helping a son or daughter buy a home or a son or daughter buying a parent's present home while giving the parent(s) the right to occupy it. A third variation is for an investor to provide most of the down payment for a home buyer, collect rent from the home buyer, pay the mortgage payments and property taxes, and claim depreciation. Each party has a right to a portion of any appreciation and the right to buy out the other. The FHLMC will buy mortgage loans on shared-equity properties. The FHLMC requires that the owner-occupant contribute at least 5% of the equity, that the owner-occupant and the owner-investor sign the mortgage and note, that both be individuals, and that there be no agreement requiring sale or buy-out within seven years of the loan date. Equity sharing can provide attractive tax benefits; however, you must seek competent tax advice before involving yourself or someone else in such a plan.

PACKAGE MORTGAGE

Normally, we think of real estate mortgage loans as being secured solely by real estate. However, it is possible to include items classed as personal property in a real estate mortgage, thus creating a ***package mortgage.*** In residential loans (particularly in new construction or remodeling), such items as the refrigerator, clothes washer, and dryer can be pledged along with the house and land in a single mortgage. The purpose is to raise the value of the collateral to raise the amount a lender is willing to loan. For the borrower, it offers the opportunity of financing major appliances at the same rate of interest as the real estate itself. This rate is usually lower than if the borrower finances the appliances separately. Once an item of personal property is included in a package mortgage, selling it without the prior consent of the lender is a violation of the mortgage.

BLANKET MORTGAGE

A mortgage secured by two or more properties is called a ***blanket mortgage.*** Suppose you want to buy a house plus the vacant lot next door, financing the purchase with a single mortgage that covers both properties. The cost of preparing one mortgage instead of two is a savings. Also, by combining the house and the lot, the lot can be financed on better terms than if it were financed separately, because lenders more readily loan on a house and land than on land alone. Note, however, that if the vacant lot is later sold separately from the house before the mortgage loan is fully repaid, it will be necessary to have it released from the blanket mortgage. This is usually accomplished by including in the original mortgage agreement a partial release clause that specifies how much of the loan must be repaid before the lot can be released.

REVERSE MORTGAGE

Lender Pays You

With a regular mortgage, the lender makes a lump-sum payment to the borrower, who, in turn, repays it through monthly payments to the lender. With a ***reverse mortgage***, the lender has two alternatives: (1) payment to the homeowner in a lump sum, or (2) monthly payments to the homeowner as an annuity for the reverse term of the loan. The reverse mortgage can be particularly valuable for an elderly homeowner who does not want to sell, but whose retirement income is not quite enough for comfortable living. The home-owner receives a monthly check, has full use of the property, and is not required to repay until he or she sells or dies. If the home is sold, money from the sale is taken to repay the loan. If the borrower dies first, the property is sold through the estate and the loan repaid.

You Make No Payments

Fannie Mae introduced a type of reverse annuity mortgage aimed at senior citizens, which is activated at the time the house is purchased. It allows all owners and their spouses (who must be 62 years or older) to obtain a mortgage against the equity in a house if a substantial down payment is made. Repayment of the mortgage is deferred until the borrower no longer occupies the principal residence. If the loan balance exceeds the value of the property, the borrower, or the estate, will never owe more than the value of the property. For instance, if a homeowner sells an existing home for $100,000 and chooses to purchase a retirement home, also costing $100,000, the homeowner would immediately qualify for a $52,000 loan, with a $48,000 down payment. There would be no monthly payments, and the homeowner would have $52,000 in cash!

Texas Requirements

Texas has passed a constitutional amendment allowing reverse mortgages on Texas homesteads. As with home equity loans (discussed later), the requirements are extensive. A reverse mortgage is valid only under the following conditions (Note the bolded provisions):

1. It is secured by a voluntary lien with the consent of each owner and each owner's spouse.
2. It is made to a person **who is or whose spouse is 62 years or older.**
3. It is made **without recourse** for personal liability.
4. Advances are provided to a borrower **based on the equity** in the borrower's homestead.
5. It cannot permit the lender to reduce the amount or number of advances because of adjustment in the interest, if periodic advances are made.
6. It **requires no payment of principal or interest** until the homestead is sold or all borrowers have died or ceased to occupy the homestead property for

more than 12 consecutive months without prior written approval from the lender; the borrower defaults on the loan.

7. Documents provide that if the lender fails to make the loan advances as required by the loan documents, and if the lender fails to secure the default as required in the loan documents, the lender forfeits all principal and interest of the reverse mortgage.
8. The loan cannot be made unless the owner of the home attests in writing that the **owner received counseling** on the advisability and availability of reverse mortgages and other alternatives.
9. The lender discloses to the borrower a written notice concerning the lack of required payments of principal and interest.
10. The lender cannot commence foreclosure until the lender gives special notice to the borrower as provided in the constitution.
11. The lien can be foreclosed upon only by a court order unless it is for reasons stated in paragraph 6 above.

A reverse mortgage can provide for an interest rate that is fixed or adjustable, as well as provide for interest that is contingent on appreciation and fair market value of the homestead property. The reverse mortgage can also be established as a line of credit, allowing the homeowner to pull loan proceeds down (up to the loan limit) and pay it back at the will of the homeowner.

Who makes these loans? Private lenders are the primary source of these loans, although there are two government programs that purchase these loans in the secondary market. The Home Equity Conversion Mortgage (HECM) is insured by the Federal Housing Administration. The FHA ensures that the lender will be able to recover the full amount of principal when that loan is terminated, and that the borrower will receive the contract of loan proceeds no matter what becomes of the lender. The borrower is required to pay an insurance premium, which is normally made out of loan proceeds. The cost is currently 2% of the origination fee and ½% per year on the unpaid balance, unless the borrower owns the loan amount as insurance premiums for the FHA coverage for this FHA protection.

The second loan program is Fannie Mae's HomeKeeper. These loans also carry an origination fee and a monthly processing fee, both of which are paid from loan proceeds. Loan products such as these are always being updated and revised. You can find FHA information available at http://www.hud.gov/buying/rvrsmort.cfm. Fannie Mae information is available at http://www.fanniemae.com/global/pdf/homebuyers/moneyfromhome.pdf.

CONSTRUCTION LOAN

Under a ***construction loan***, also called an **interim loan,** money is advanced as construction takes place. For example, a vacant lot owner arranges to borrow $60,000 to build a house. The lender does not advance all $60,000 at once because the value of the collateral is insufficient to warrant that amount until the house is finished. Instead, the lender will parcel out the loan as the building is being constructed, always holding a portion until the property is ready for occupancy or, in some cases, actually occupied. Some lenders specialize only in construction loans and do not want to wait 20 or 30 years to be repaid. In this case, the buyer will have to obtain a permanent long-term mortgage from another source for the purpose of repaying the construction loan. This is known as a *permanent commitment* or a *take-out loan* because it takes the construction lender out of the financial picture when construction is completed and allows the lender to recycle its money into new construction projects.

BLENDED-RATE LOAN

Many real estate lenders still hold long-term loans that were made at interest rates below the current market rate. One way of raising the return on these loans is to offer borrowers who have them a **blended-rate loan.** Suppose you owe $150,000 on your home loan and the interest rate on it is 7%. Suppose further that the current rate on home loans is 12%. Your lender might offer to refinance your home for $170,000 at 9%, presuming the property will appraise high enough and you have the income to qualify. The $170,000 refinance offer would put $20,000 in your pocket (less loan fees), but would increase the interest you pay from 7% to 9% on the original $150,000. This makes the cost of the $20,000 24% per year. The arithmetic is as follows: You will now be paying 9% × $70,000 = $15,300 in interest. Before, you paid 7% × $150,000 = $10,500 in interest. The difference, $4,800, is what you pay to borrow the additional $20,000. This equates to $2,800/$20,000 = 24% interest. This is the figure you should use in comparing other sources of financing (such as a second mortgage) or deciding whether or not you even want to borrow.

A blended-rate loan can be very attractive in a situation in which you want to sell your home and do not want to help finance the buyer. Suppose your home is worth $187,500 and you have the aforementioned $150,000, 7% loan. A buyer would normally expect to make a down payment of $37,500 and pay 12% interest on a new $150,000 loan. But, with a blended loan, your lender could offer the buyer the needed $150,000 financing at 9%, a far more attractive rate and one that requires less income to qualify. Blended loans are available on FHA, VA, and conventional loans held by the FNMA. Other lenders also offer them on fixed-rate assumable loans they hold.

EQUITY MORTGAGE

An **equity mortgage** is a loan arrangement wherein the lender agrees to make a loan based on the amount of equity in a borrower's home. The maximum amount of the loan is 80% of the home value, less any first mortgage or other liens against the property.

It is typically a second mortgage that is used to tap the increase in equity resulting from rising home prices and first loan principal reductions. It's all done without having to refinance the first loan and uses the home as an asset against which the homeowner can borrow and repay as needed. Equity mortgages are very popular as a source of money for college expenses, money to start a business, money for a major vacation, and money to buy more real estate. Because the Internal Revenue Code of 1986 limited personal interest deductions to home mortgages, these loans have become one of the fastest growing areas of real estate lending.

The Texas Rules on home equity loans, however, are unbelievably complex. They are not the typical home equity loan that you find in other states. In addition to the 80% loan-to-value limitations, lenders are not allowed to charge more than 3% of the loan amount for loan fees. They cannot have any prepayment penalties, and they must be nonrecourse loans (the lender can't sue the borrower for a deficiency). In addition, there must be a judicial hearing before foreclosure. There can be only one home equity loan per year, and there must be a 12-day "cooling off" period after the loan application before the loan can be closed. A loan can't be funded for at least 3 full business days after the closing. The closing must take place at the office of a lender, title company, or attorney-at-law. All lenders can't make home equity loans; it must either be an "authorized lender" as specified in the Texas Constitution or a close relative (parent, grandparent, grandchild, aunt or uncle). There are additional requirements for special home equity documentation, and the borrower and lender must have a written agreement as to the home's value. In all, there are about 36 very specific requirements to be met, or these loans may be unenforceable.

New legislation has recently made **home equity line of credit** loans available for consumers. These loans are limited to 50% of the fair market value of the house but can be "drawn down" in increments of $4,000 each, and paid back in accordance with the terms of the borrower's agreement. These loans can also be blended with a regular home equity loan, so that the line of credit loan could total 50% of the fair market value of the property and the regular home equity loan could go up to a total of 80% of the value of the property. New constitutional amendments are also now allowing home equity loans to be refinanced by a reverse mortgage.

All of these are new concepts to Texas where home equity loans and reverse mortgage loans were constitutionally prohibited until 1997. Homeowners must be cautioned, however, that if they default on these loans, they lose their homestead. They must constantly reevaluate the risk they are taking when they make a loan and have the potential of losing their home. This is a new concept for Texas and there will be a lot of new products available in the coming years.

AFFORDABLE HOUSING LOAN

An ***affordable housing loan*** is an umbrella term that covers many slightly different loans that target first-time home buyers and low- to moderate-income borrowers. Although there are no fixed standards for measurement, the generally accepted definition of a *low-income borrower* is a person or family with an income of not more than 80% of the median income for the local area. *Moderate income* is 115% of the median income for the area. *Median* means an equal number of people of incomes above or below the number. Funding for the programs is obtained through a commitment from an investor to buy the loans. Freddie Mac and Fannie Mae cooperate with local community, labor union, or trade associations by committing to buy a large block of mortgage loans provided they meet the agreed-on standards. Affordable housing loans can be privately insured through the Mortgage Guaranty Insurance Company or GE Capital Mortgage Insurance Corporation.

Freddie Mac now offers two programs supporting construction of affordable single-family homes in urban centers. One allows builders to cover up to 3% of a borrower's down payment, and borrowers are allowed to pay for closing costs with cash in combination with gifts, grants, affordable second loans, or other flexible options. The second mortgage product benefits builders by reducing some of the economic risks associated with building homes in urban centers. The program extends flexible underwriting and low down payments to buyers and provides builders with access to a cash reserve fund as a financial safety net. The reserve fund will cover principal, interest, taxes, and insurance payments during construction for a period of up to six months. The program will be tested in five cities, including San Antonio, Texas.

Fannie Mae has also introduced its "Home Style Construction-to-Permanent Mortgage," which enables a borrower to cover the construction loan and a permanent mortgage with one loan. One interest rate can be locked in for both phases of the loan, which is sold to Fannie Mae as soon as it is closed.

The Department of Housing and Urban Development is also encouraging affordable housing loans. It is currently promoting the "Officer Next Door" (OND) housing program, which allows police officers to buy FHA-foreclosed properties at half price, if the officers live in the cities in which they work. The program has been highly successful. HUD plans to offer a "Teacher Next Door" program patterned after the Officer Next Door program. HUD also has a program to sell foreclosed single-family homes to local governments for $1.00 each. The houses are FHA foreclosures that have remained unsold for six months. The program is designed to create housing for families in need and to revitalize neighborhoods. HUD also sets goals for FNMA and Freddie Mac for the purchase of mortgages made to low- and moderate-income persons, African Americans, Hispanics, and other minorities in underserved areas.

Fannie Mae also promotes their **Community Solutions Program** of flexible mortgages for school employees, police officers, firefighters, and healthcare workers. It provides greater flexibility with credit scores and their credit histories, allows for a greater portion of income to go toward mortgage payment, and gives credit for overtime or part-time income. It offers 97% and 100% loan programs.

Fannie Mae also produces the **MyCommunityMortgage Program,** which provides mortgage options for borrowers of one- to four-family homes. It includes extra flexibilities for rural residents and may offer additional incentives for buyers of energy-efficient homes. It has a $300,700 loan limit on single-family homes and allows for a $500 or 1% down payment, greater flexibility on credit histories, and income limits up to 115% in rural areas.

As part of the MyCommunityMortgage Program, **Fannie Neighbors** is a nationwide, neighborhood-based mortgage program designed to increase home ownership and revitalization in areas underserved by HUD, in low- to moderate-income minorities census tracts or central cities. Lenders and other Houston professionals can use the Fannie Mae Property GeoCoder, a free, online application, to determine whether a property qualifies for the Fannie Neighbors option.

Credit Criteria

Underwriting standards for affordable housing loans are modified to recognize different forms of credit responsibility. Many low- and moderate-income families do not have checking accounts. Recognizing the lack of payment records, most affordable housing programs accept timely payment of rent and utility bills as credit criteria. Initial cash down payments can be reduced by allowing borrowing or acceptance of grants from housing agencies or local communities, which sometimes offer cash assistance. Studies indicate that lower-income families pay a higher percentage of their income for housing than others, so an affordable housing program allows a higher ratio of income to be applied to housing (33% of gross income instead of 28% found in similar loans; you may recall that the FHA housing guideline is 29%).

Consumer Education

One of the requirements to qualify for an affordable housing loan is for the borrower to take a prepurchase home buyer education course. Many of these first-time home buyers are unaware of real estate brokers, title insurance, or appraisals. These subjects, plus the care and maintenance of a home, are included in the variety of courses now available through community colleges, banks, and mortgage companies. The four major supporting entities of these programs are Fannie Mae, Freddie Mac, MGIC, and GE Capital Mortgage Insurance Corporation. All of these entities provide videotapes and course outlines that are available for these educational purposes.

Licensees should be aware that these programs are most effective if presented to a group of applicants. If there is not a program in your area, one could be started. An agent may want to contact local lenders, because many are still not fully aware of the opportunities available, and some tend to overlook the lower income market for economic reasons. Participation in the program, however, greatly benefits their Community Reinvestment Act rating. Effectively marketing these programs can be very profitable and provide a great amount of personal satisfaction.

97% Conventional Loan

One of the most significant developments in mortgage lending has been the introduction of a 3%-down-payment conventional loan. FIRREA and the Community Reinvestment Act (discussed in Chapter 19) provided strong incentives for private lenders to engage in affordable housing loans to help lower-middle-income home-owners. To encourage homeownership among lower- and middle-income people, General Electric Capital Mortgage Insurance Corporation experimented with affordable housing loans, which it calls "community home buyer's program" loans. Results show that the rates of default among their borrowers prove to be as good or better than those of its regular loan portfolio. GE introduced a 97% conventional loan in February of 1994. Fannie Mae agreed to purchase 97% loans as long as the applicant met Fannie Mae guidelines, which include an income limit not to exceed 100% of the local area median income. Another conduit has been established by the investment banker Goldman Sachs to purchase these loans for buyers with up to 115% of area median income.

The Nehemiah Program

The Nehemiah Program contributes a portion of the down payment (usually 1% to 6% of the loan) and the lender or developer commits to a contribution to the Nehemiah Pool. The Nehemiah Program has become the largest down payment assistance program in the United States, having provided over 300 million dollars in assistance so far. It is administered by the Nehemiah Corporation and now operates in 4,900 cities in every state except Hawaii. It has provided down payment assistance to nearly 100,000 families. The candidate must meet Nehemiah's qualifying criteria, which may include taking a free home ownership education course.

The Nehemiah Program has provided a larger pool to eligible buyers because builders' inventory moves more quickly, its holding costs are lower for builders, and it increases loan volume for the lenders. The program can be accessed online at http://www.nehemiahcorp.org.

SELLER FINANCING

When a seller is willing to accept part of the property's purchase price in the form of the buyer's promissory note accompanied by a mortgage or deed of trust, it is called ***seller financing.*** This allows the buyer to substitute a promissory note for cash, and the seller is said to be "taking back paper." Seller financing is popular for land sales (where lenders rarely loan), on property where an existing mortgage is being assumed by the buyer, and on property where the seller prefers to receive the money spread out over a period of time with interest instead of lump-sum cash. For example, a retired couple sells a rental home they own. The home is worth $120,000, and they owe $20,000. If they need only $60,000 in cash, they might be more than happy to take $60,000 down, let the buyer assume the existing mortgage, and accept the remaining $40,000 in monthly payments at current interest rates. Alternatively, the buyer and seller can agree to structure the $40,000 as an adjustable, graduated, partially amortized, or interest-only loan.

If the seller receives the sales price spread out over two or more years, income taxes are calculated using the installment reporting method discussed in Chapter 16. Being able to spread out the taxes on a gain may be an incentive to use seller financing. The seller should be aware, however, that the "paper" may not be convertible to cash without a long wait or without having to sell it at a substantial discount to an investor (although this can be remedied by a "balloon" provision). Additionally, the seller is responsible for servicing the loan and is subject to losses due to default and foreclosure.

Note that some real estate agents and lenders refer to a loan that is carried back by a seller as a **purchase money** loan. Others define a purchase money loan as any loan, carryback or institutional, that is used to finance the purchase of real property.

WRAPAROUND MORTGAGE

An alternative method of financing a real estate sale such as the one just reviewed is to use a ***wraparound mortgage*** or *wraparound deed of trust.* A wraparound encompasses existing mortgages and is subordinate (junior) to them. The existing mortgages stay on the property and the new mortgage wraps around them. Note Figure 15.2.

To illustrate, presume the existing $20,000 loan in the previous example carries an interest rate of 7% and that 10 years remain on the loan. Presume further that current interest rates are 12%, and the current seller chooses to sell for $100,000. This is done by taking the buyer's $40,000 down payment and then creating a new junior mortgage (for $60,000) that includes not only the $20,000 owed on the existing first mortgage but also the $40,000 the buyer owes the seller. The seller continues to remain liable for payment of the first mortgage. If the interest rate on the wrap-around is set at 10%, the buyer saves by not having to pay 12% as he would on an entirely new loan. The advantage to the seller is that she is earning 10%, not only on her $40,000 equity, but also on the $20,000 loan for which she is paying 7% interest. This gives the seller an actual yield of 11.5% on her $40,000. (The calculation is as follows. The seller receives 10% on $60,000, which amounts to $6,000. She pays 7% on $20,000, which is $1,400. The difference, $4,600, is divided by

FIGURE 15.2 The wraparound mortgage

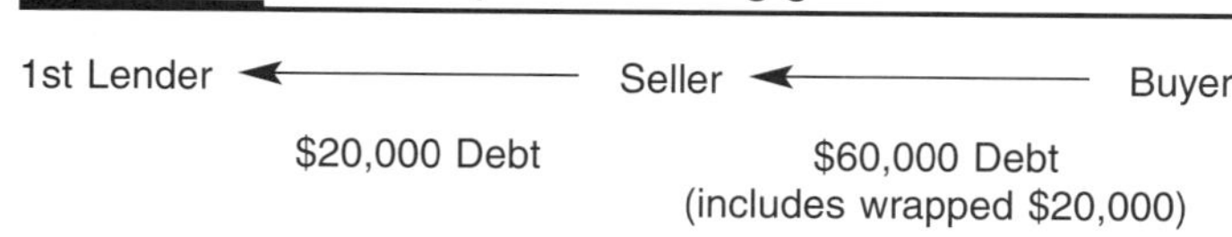

$40,000 to get the seller's actual yield of 11.5%.) There is an additional point of concern. If the monthly payment on the underlying $20,000 debt includes taxes and insurance (PITI payment), the wraparound mortgage payment amount should also include taxes and insurance so that the monthly payment is sufficient to meet *all* of the underlying debt.

Wraparounds are not limited to seller financing. If the seller in the foregoing example did not want to finance the sale, a third-party lender could provide the needed $40,000 and take a wraparound mortgage. The wraparound concept does not work when the underlying mortgage debt to be "wrapped" contains a due-on-sale clause. One other word of caution. If the seller defaults (and doesn't tell the buyer), the buyer may have an unwelcome surprise.

SUBORDINATION

Another financing technique is *subordination*. For example, a person owns a $200,000 vacant lot suitable for building, and a builder wants to build an $800,000 building on the lot. The builder has only $100,000 cash and the largest construction loan available is $800,000. If the builder can convince the lot owner to take $100,000 in cash and $100,000 later, the buyer would have the $1 million total. However, the lender making the $800,000 loan will want to be the first mortgagee to protect its position in the event of foreclosure. The lot owner must be willing to take a subordinate position, in this case a second mortgage. If the project is successful, the lot owner will receive $100,000, plus interest, either in cash after the building is built and sold, or as monthly payments. If the project goes into foreclosure, the lot owner can be paid only if the $800,000 first mortgage claim is satisfied in full from the sale proceeds. As you can surmise here, the lot owner must be very careful that the money loaned by the lender actually goes into construction and that whatever is built is worth at least $800,000 in addition to the land.

CONTRACT FOR DEED

A *contract for deed*, also called an *installment contract*, *land contract*, or *executory contract*, enables the seller to finance a buyer by permitting him to make a down payment followed by monthly payments. However, title remains in the name of the seller. In addition to its wide use in financing land sales, it has also been a very effective financing tool in several states as a means of selling homes. For example, a homeowner owes $25,000 on his home and wants to sell it for $85,000. A buyer is found but does not have the $60,000 down payment necessary to assume the existing loan. The buyer does have $8,000, but for one reason or another cannot or chooses not to borrow from an institutional lender. If the seller is agreeable, the buyer can pay the seller $8,000 and enter into an installment contract with the seller for the remaining $77,000. The contract calls for monthly payments by the buyer to the seller that are large enough to allow the seller to meet the payments on the $25,000 loan plus repay the $52,000 owed to the seller, with interest. Unless property taxes and insurance are billed to the buyer, the seller will also collect for these and pay them. When the final payment is made to the seller (or the property refinanced through an institutional lender), title is conveyed to the buyer. Meanwhile, the seller continues to hold title and is responsible for paying the mortgage. In addition to wrapping around a mortgage, an installment contract can also be used to wrap around another installment contract, provided it does not contain an enforceable due-on-sale clause. Recent legislation in Texas has made the use of this type of financing very risky for most sellers. (Please see Chapter 10 for more about the contractual side of installment contracts.)

OPTION

When viewed as a financing tool, an ***option*** provides a method by which the need to finance the full price of a property immediately can be postponed. For example, a developer is offered 100 acres of land for a house subdivision but is not sure that the market will absorb that many houses. The solution is to buy 25 acres outright and take three 25-acre options at present prices on the remainder. If the houses on the first 25 acres sell promptly, the builder can exercise the options to buy the remaining land. If sales are not good, the builder can let the remaining options expire and avoid being stuck with unwanted acreage.

A popular variation on the option idea is the *lease with option to buy* combination. Under it, an owner leases to a tenant who, in addition to paying rent and using the property, also obtains the right to purchase it at a present price for a fixed period of time. Homes are often sold this way, particularly when the resale market is sluggish. (Please see Chapter 10 for more about these topics.)

Options can provide speculative opportunities to persons with limited amounts of capital. If prices do not rise, the optionee loses only the cost of the option; if prices do rise, the optionee exercises the option and realizes a profit.

OVERLY CREATIVE FINANCING?

One seller-financing arrangement that deserves special attention because of its traps for the unwary is the **overencumbered property.** Institutional lenders are closely regulated regarding the amount of money they can loan against the appraised value of the property. Individuals are not regulated. The following illustrates the potential problem. Suppose a seller owns a house that is realistically worth \$100,000 and the mortgage balance is \$10,000. A buyer offers to purchase the property, with the condition that she be allowed to obtain an \$80,000 loan on the property from a lender. The \$80,000 is used to pay off the existing \$10,000 loan and to pay the broker's commission, loan fees, and closing costs.

The remaining $62,000 is split $30,000 to the seller and $32,000 to the buyer. The buyer also gives the seller a note, secured by a second mortgage against the property, for $80,000. The seller may feel good about getting $30,000 in cash and an $80,000 mortgage, because this is more than the property is worth, or so it seems.

But the $80,000 second mortgage stands junior to the $80,000 first mortgage. That's $160,000 of debt against a $100,000 property. The buyer might be trying to resell the property for $160,000 or more, but the chances of this are slim. More likely the buyer will wind up walking away from the property. This leaves the seller the choice of taking over the payments on the first mortgage or losing the property completely to the holder of the first.

Although such a scheme sounds crazy when viewed from a distance, the reason it can be performed is that the seller wants more for the property than it's worth. Someone then offers a deal showing that price, and the seller looks the other way from the possible consequences. Real estate practitioners who participate in such transactions are likely to find their licenses suspended. State licensing authorities take the position that a real estate practitioner is a professional who should know enough not to take part in a deal that leaves the seller holding a junior lien on an overencumbered property. This, too, seems logical when viewed from a distance. But when sales are slow and commissions thin, it is sometimes easy to put commission income ahead of fiduciary responsibility. If in doubt about the propriety of a transaction, the Golden Rule of doing unto others as you would have them do unto you still applies. (Or, as some restate it: "What goes around, comes around.")

INVESTING IN MORTGAGES

Individuals can invest in mortgages in two ways. One is to invest in mortgage loan pools through certificates guaranteed by Ginnie Mae and Freddie Mac and available from stockbrokers. These yield about 0.5 of 1% below what FHA and VA borrowers are paying. In 1997, for example, this was approximately 7%, and the certificates are readily convertible to cash at current market prices on the open market if the investor does not want to hold them through maturity.

Individuals can also buy junior mortgages at yields above Ginnie Mae and Freddie Mac certificates. These junior mortgages are seconds, thirds, and fourths offered by mortgage brokers. They yield more because they are riskier as to repayment and much more difficult to convert to cash before maturity. "There is," as the wise old adage says, "no such thing as a free lunch." Thus, it is important to recognize that when an investment of any kind promises above-market returns, some kind of added risk is attached. With junior mortgages, it is important to realize that when a borrower offers to pay a premium above the best loan rates available from banks and thrift institutions, it is because the borrower and/or the property does not qualify for the best rates.

Before buying a mortgage as an investment, one should have the title to the property searched. This is the only way to know for certain what priority the mortgage will have in the event of foreclosure. There have been cases where investors have purchased what they were told to be first and second mortgages only to find in foreclosure that they were actually holding third and fourth mortgages and the amount of debt exceeded the value of the property.

And how does one find the value of a property? By having it appraised by a professional appraiser who is independent of the party making or selling the mortgage investment. This value is compared to the existing and proposed debt against the property. The investor should also run a credit check on the borrower. The investor's final protection is, however, in making certain that the market value of the property is well in excess of the loans against it and that the property is well constructed, well located, and functional.

RENTAL

Even though tenants do not acquire fee ownership, *rentals* and **leases** are means of financing real estate. Whether the tenant is a bachelor receiving the use of a $30,000 apartment for which he pays $350 rent per month or a large corporation leasing a warehouse for 20 years, leasing is an ideal method of financing when the tenant does not want to buy, cannot raise the funds to buy, or prefers to invest available funds elsewhere. Similarly, *farming leases* provide for the use of land without the need to purchase it. Some farm leases call for fixed rental payment. Other leases require the farmer to pay the landowner a share of the value of the crop that is actually produced—say 25%—and the landowner shares with the farmer the risks of weather, crop output, and prices.

Under a **sale and leaseback** arrangement, an owner-occupant sells the property and then remains as a tenant. Thus, the buyer acquires an investment and the seller obtains capital for other purposes while retaining the use of the property. A variation is for the tenant to construct a building, sell it to a prearranged buyer, and immediately lease it back.

LAND LEASES

Although *leased land* arrangements are common throughout the United States for both commercial and industrial users and for farmers, anything other than fee ownership of residential land is unthinkable in many areas. Yet in some parts of the United States (e.g., Baltimore, Maryland; Orange County, California; throughout Hawaii; and parts of Florida) homes built on leased land are commonplace. Typically, these leases are at least 55 years in length and, barring an agreement to the contrary, the improvements to the land become the property of the fee owner at the end of the lease. Rents may be fixed in advance for the life of the lease, renegotiated at present points during the life of the lease, or a combination of both.

To hedge against inflation, when fixed rents are used in a long-term lease, it is common practice to use **step-up rentals.** For example, under a 55-year house-lot lease, the rent may be set at $400 per year for the first 15 years, $600 per year for the next 10 years, $800 for the next 10 years, and so forth. An alternative is to renegotiate the rent at various points during the life of a lease so that the effects of land value changes are more closely equalized between the lessor and the lessee. For example, a 60-year lease may contain renegotiation points at the fifteenth, thirtieth, and forty-fifth years. At those points, the property would be reappraised and the lease rent adjusted to reflect any changes in the value of the property. Property taxes and any increases in property taxes are paid by the lessee.

FINANCING OVERVIEW

If people always paid cash for real estate, the last several chapters would not have been necessary. But 95% of the time they don't; thus means have been devised to finance their purchases. This has been true since the beginning of recorded history and will continue into the future. The financing methods that evolve will depend on the problems to be solved. For example, long-term fixed-rate amortized loans were the solution to foreclosures in the 1930s, and they worked well as long as interest rates did not fluctuate greatly. Graduated payment loans were devised when housing prices rose faster than buyer's incomes. Adjustable rate loans were developed so that lenders could more closely align the interest they receive from borrowers with the interest they pay their savers. Extensive use of loan assumptions, wraparounds, and seller financing became necessary in the early 1980s because borrowers could not qualify for 16% and 18% loans and sellers were unwilling to drop prices.

With regard to the future, if mortgage money is expensive or in short supply, seller financing will play a large role. With the experience of rapidly fluctuating interest rates fresh in people's minds, loans with adjustable rates will continue to be widely offered. Fixed-rate loans will either have short maturities or carry a premium to compensate the lender for being locked into a fixed rate for a long period. When interest rates are low, borrowers with adjustable loans will benefit from lower monthly payments. If rates stay down long enough, fixed-rate loans will become more popular again.

REVIEW QUESTIONS

Answers to these questions are found in the Answer Key section at the back of the book.

1. To make adjustable rate mortgage loans more attractive to borrowers, lenders offer
   A. lower initial interest rates.
   B. gifts such as appliances, trips, etc.
   C. lower insurance rates.
   D. lower down payments.

2. When considering an ARM loan, the lender must explain to the borrower, in writing, the
   A. initial interest rate.
   B. maximum interest rate.
   C. actual changes in index value.
   D. all of the above.

3. Equity sharing is based on the concept of someone who has assets sharing those assets in exchange for
   A. a share of the ownership.
   B. tax benefits.
   C. both A and B.
   D. neither A nor B.

4. When an existing loan at a low interest rate is refinanced by a new loan at an interest rate between the current market rate and the rate on the old loan, the result is a
   A. combined loan.
   B. blended loan.
   C. wraparound loan.
   D. merged loan.

5. An individual who is contemplating the purchase of a mortgage as an investment should have
   A. the property appraised.
   B. a credit check made on the borrower.
   C. the title searched.
   D. all of the above.

6. Under the terms of a shared appreciation mortgage
   A. the loan is made at a below-market interest rate.
   B. the lender received a portion of the property's appreciation.
   C. both A and B.
   D. neither A nor B.

7. ARM loans with teaser rates are avoided by
   A. mortgage insurers.
   B. secondary market buyers.
   C. both A and B.
   D. neither A nor B.

8. All of the following statements are true of seller financing EXCEPT:
   A. The seller of the property is the mortgagee under the mortgage.
   B. Mortgage terms and interest rates are negotiable between the seller and buyer.
   C. If repayment is spread over two or more years, income taxes are calculated on the installment reporting method.
   D. Carryback mortgages are usually salable to investors without discount.

9. Which of the following is NOT true of wrap-around mortgages?
   A. They are junior mortgages, subordinate to an existing first mortgage.
   B. The interest rate on the buyer's note is usually the same as the market rate.
   C. They are useless when the first mortgage carries a due-on-sale clause.
   D. The yield to the seller (mortgagee) is usually greater than the interest rate specified on the note.

10. A sale may be made and financed under a contract for deed
    A. only when the seller owns the property free and clear.
    B. by combining wraparound financing with an existing mortgage loan on the property, provided the existing mortgage does not contain a due-on-sale clause.
    C. both A and B.
    D. neither A nor B.

Chapter 16

KEY TERMS

Adjusted sales price: the sales price of a property less commissions, fix-up, and closing costs

Ad valorem taxes: taxes charged according to the value of a property

Appraisal Review Board: local governmental body that hears and rules on property owner complaints of overassessment

Assessed value: a value placed on a property for the purpose of taxation

Basis: the price paid for property; used in calculating income taxes

Gain: the profit on the sale of an appreciated asset

Installment method: sale of real estate in which the proceeds of the sale are deferred beyond the year of sale

Mill rate: property tax rate that is expressed in tenths of a cent per dollar of assessed valuation

Tax lien: a charge or hold by the government against property to insure the payment of taxes

Taxes and Assessments

IN THIS CHAPTER

In this chapter, we are primarily concerned with ad valorem taxes and various types of property assessments. Determining how much tax the property owner must pay involves these basic steps: appropriation, assessment, and tax rate calculation. The chapter also covers unpaid property taxes, assessment appeal, property tax exemptions and variations, tax limitation measures, and special assessments. In the latter half of the chapter, income taxes on the sale of a residence, including the lifetime exclusion, taxable gain, and installment sales, are covered. The chapter concludes with coverage of property tax and interest deductions and the agent's liability for tax advice.

PROPERTY TAXES

The largest single source of income in America for local government programs and services is the property tax. Schools (from kindergarten through two-year colleges), fire and police departments, local welfare programs, public libraries, street maintenance, parks, and public hospital facilities are mainly supported by property taxes. Some state governments also obtain a portion of their revenues from this source.

Property taxes are ***ad valorem taxes.*** This means that they are levied according to the value of one's property; the more valuable the property, the higher the tax, and vice versa. The underlying theory of ad valorem taxation is that those owning the more valuable properties are wealthier and hence able to pay more taxes.

Determining how much tax a property owner will be charged involves three basic steps: (1) local government budget determination and appropriation, (2) appraisal of all taxable property within the taxation district, and (3) allocation among individual property owners of the revenue that needs to be collected.

Appropriation

Each taxing body with the authority to tax prepares its budget for the coming year. Taxing bodies include the State of Texas, counties, cities, towns and villages, school districts, utility districts, water districts, and, in some counties, levee districts, sanitation districts, and other improvement districts. Each budget, along with a list of sources from which the money will be derived, is enacted into law. This is the **appropriation process.** Then estimated sales taxes, state and federal revenue sharing, business licenses, and city income taxes are subtracted from the budget. The balance must come from property taxes.

Assessment

Next, the valuation of the taxable property within each taxing body's district must be determined. To assure uniformity in appraisals, the Texas Property Tax Code provides for an *appraisal district* in each county. All taxing districts are required to use the appraisal district's value in determining the taxes to be paid. The county appraisal district appraises each taxable parcel of land and the improvements thereon. Since 1989, the market value of the land and the total market value of the improvements must be listed separately. The appraised value is the estimated fair market cash value of the property. This is the cash price one would expect a buyer and a seller to agree upon in a normal open market transaction.

The appraised value is converted into an assessed value upon which taxes are based. In Texas, the ***assessed value*** is set equal to the fair market value; in some other states, it is a percentage of the appraised value. Mathematically, the percentage selected makes no difference as long as each property is treated equally. Consider two houses with appraised values of $160,000 and $320,000, respectively. Whether the assessed values are set equal to appraised values or at a percentage of appraised values, the second house will still bear twice the property tax burden of the first.

Tax Rate Calculation

Certain types of property are exempt from taxation. The assessed values of the remaining taxable properties are then added together in order to calculate the **tax rate** that must be determined by the appropriate elected governing body. To explain this process, suppose that a building lies within the taxation districts of the Westside School District, the city of Rostin, and the county of Pearl River. The school district's budget for the coming year requires $800,000 from property taxes, and the assessed value of taxable property within the district is $20,000,000. By dividing $800,000 by $20,000,000, we see that the school district must collect a tax of 4 cents for every dollar of assessed valuation. This levy can be expressed three ways: (1) as a ***mill rate,*** (2) as dollars per hundred, or (3) as dollars per thousand. All three rating methods are found in the United States. The State of Texas uses dollars per hundred. For instance, a rate would be $4 per hundred of assessed valuation. As *dollars per thousand,* it would be $40 per thousand.

A city calculates its tax rate by dividing its property tax requirements by the assessed value of the property within its boundaries. Suppose that its needs are

TABLE 16.1 Expressing property tax rates

	Dollars per Hundred	Dollars per Thousand
School district	$4.00	$40.00
City	3.00	30.00
County	1.00	10.00
Total	$8.00	$80.00

$300,000 and the city limits enclose property totaling $10,000,000 in assessed valuation. (In this example, the city covers a smaller geographical area than the school district.) Thus, the city must collect 3 cents for each dollar of assessed valuation in order to balance its budget.

The county government's budget requires $2,000,000 from property taxes and the county contains $200,000,000 in assessed valuation. This makes the county tax rate 1 cent per dollar of assessed valuation. Table 16.1 shows the school district, city, and county tax rates expressed as dollars per hundred and dollars per thousand.

The final step is to apply the tax rate to each property. Applying the rate on a dollars per hundred basis, divide the $20,000 assessed valuation by $100 and multiply by $8. The result is $1,600. To ensure collection, a lien for this amount is placed by the taxing authority against the property. It is removed when the tax is paid. Property tax liens are superior to other types of liens. Also, a mortgage foreclosure does not clear property tax liens; they still must be paid.

To avoid duplicate tax bill mailings, it is a common practice for all taxing bodies in a given county to have the county collect for them at the same time that the county collects on its own behalf.

The property tax year in Texas for state and county taxes is the calendar year. County and state taxes are billed once a year, are payable on October 1, and become delinquent on February 1 of the following year. Other taxing jurisdictions vary. A small discount is allowed for early payment of state and county taxes. Penalties are charged for late payment in all taxing jurisdictions.

UNPAID PROPERTY TAXES

All ***tax liens*** in Texas are, by law, superior to any other liens on real estate. When an owner fails to pay property taxes, the property is sold at a public tax auction; this extinguishes all other liens. However, unlike most liens in Texas, if foreclosure is due to unpaid taxes, the tax statutes provide a redemption period for the taxpayer to pay the taxes and have the property returned to him.

If the property is used as the residence homestead of the owner, or the land was designated for agricultural use when the suit to collect the taxes was filed, Texas statute provides that the period of redemption for suits brought under the authority of the tax foreclosure statute for the taxpayer's residence homestead or land designated for agricultural use shall be within *two years* from the date of the filing for record of the purchaser's deed, on the following basis:

1. Within the first year of the redemption period, upon the payment of the amount of the bid for the property by the purchaser at such sale, including a $1 tax deed recording fee and all taxes, penalties, interest, and costs thereafter paid thereon, plus 25% of the aggregate total.
2. Within the last year of the redemption period, upon the payment of the amount bid for the property at such sale, including a $1 tax deed recording fee and all taxes, penalties, interest, and costs thereafter paid thereon, plus 50% of the aggregate total; and no further or additional amount than herein specified shall be required to be paid to effect any such redemption.

All other property must be redeemed on the same basis, but within *six months,* rather than two years.

If the property is not the taxpayer's residence homestead or designated for agricultural use, the redemption period is six months, and the owner must pay a 25% penalty to redeem. Texas does not allow the former owner to retain possession or receive the benefits of the property during the redemption period. There are other provisions for redemption if the land is sold under a decree and judgment of a court. Title does not pass to the purchaser until the deed is confirmed after the redemption period.

The right of government to foreclose on a property owner for nonpayment of property taxes is well established by law. However, if the sale procedure is not properly followed, the purchaser may later find the property's title successfully challenged in court. Thus, it behooves the purchaser to obtain a title search and title insurance and, if necessary, to conduct a quiet title suit or file a suit to foreclose the rights of anyone previously having a right to the property. Tax liens are barred from enforcement if they are over 20 years old (the statute of limitations).

ASSESSMENT APPEAL

By law, assessment procedures must be uniformly applied to all properties within a taxing jurisdiction. To this end, the values of all lands and buildings, as determined by the tax assessors, are made available for public inspection. These are the **assessment rolls.** They permit property owners to compare the assessed valuation on their property with assessed valuations on similar properties. If an owner feels overassessed, an appeal can be filed before the ***Appraisal Review Board.*** Texas also permits appeal to a court of law or to professional arbitration if the property owner remains dissatisfied with the assessment. Note that the appeal process deals only with the method of assessment and taxation, not with the tax rate or the amount of tax.

PROPERTY TAX EXEMPTIONS

More than half the land in many cities and counties is exempt from real property taxation. This is because governments and their agencies do not tax themselves or each other. Thus, government-owned offices of all types, public roads and parks, schools, military bases, and government-owned utilities are exempt from property taxes. Also exempted are properties owned by religious and charitable organizations (so long as they are used for religious or charitable purposes), hospitals, and cemeteries. In rural areas of Texas, large tracts of land are owned by federal and state governments, and these too are exempt from taxation. Texas also exempts from taxation poorhouses, public libraries, art galleries, property of Boy and Girl Scouts, prison farms, veterans' organizations, fraternal organizations, public charities, certain nonprofit organizations, and volunteer fire departments. There are certain additional property tax exemptions for veterans of the armed forces.

Property tax exemptions are also used to attract industries and to appease voters. In the first instance, a local government agency can buy industrial land and buildings and lease them to industries at a price lower than would be possible if they were privately owned and hence taxed. Alternatively, outright property tax reductions can be granted for a certain length of time to newly established or relocating firms. The rationale is that the cost to the public is outweighed by the economic boost that the new industry brings to the community. In the second instance, a number of states, including Texas, grant assessment reductions to resident homeowners for homestead property. This increases the tax burden for owners of rented houses and property used for commercial purposes.

PROPERTY TAX VARIATIONS

Property taxes on similarly priced homes within a city or county can vary widely when prices change faster than the assessor's office can reappraise. As a result, a home worth \$90,000 in one neighborhood may receive a tax bill of \$1,800 per year, while a \$90,000 home in another neighborhood will be billed \$2,400. When the appraisal district conducts a reappraisal, taxes in the first neighborhood will suddenly rise 33%, undoubtedly provoking complaints from property owners who were unaware that they were previously underassessed. In times of slow-changing real estate prices, reappraisals were made only once every 10 years. Today, appraisal districts are developing computerized assessment systems that can adjust assessments to the market annually.

As an aid to keeping current on property value changes, some states are enacting laws that require a real estate buyer to advise the assessor's office of the price and terms of his purchase within 90 days after taking title. This information, coupled with building permit records and on-site visits by assessor's office employees, provides the data necessary to regularly update assessments. Such laws have not yet been enacted in Texas.

The amount of property taxes a property owner may expect to pay varies quite widely across the United States. On a home worth \$90,000, for example, property taxes range from less than \$900 per year to more than \$3,600 per year. Why do differences exist and why are they so great? The answers fall into four basic categories: level of services offered, other sources of revenue, type of property, and government efficiency. Generally, cities with low property taxes offer fewer services to their residents. This may be by choice, such as smaller welfare payments, lower school expenditures per student, no subsidized public transportation, fewer parks and libraries, or because the city does not include the cost of some services in the property tax. For example, sewer fees may be added to the water bill and trash may be hauled by private firms. Lower rates can also be due to location. Wage rates are lower in some regions of the country, and a city not subject to ice and snow will have lower street maintenance expenses. Finally, a city may have other sources of revenue, such as oil royalties from wells on city property.

Supplemental Funding

Property tax levels are also influenced by the ability of local tax districts to obtain federal revenue sharing funds and money from state revenues (especially for schools) and to share in collections from sales taxes, license fees, liquor and tobacco taxes, and fines.

The amount and type of taxable property in a community greatly affects local tax rates. Taxable property must bear the burden avoided by tax-exempt property, whereas privately owned vacant land, stores, factories, and high-priced homes generally produce more taxes than they consume in local government services thereby helping to keep rates lower. Finally, one must look at the efficiency of the city under review. Has it managed its affairs in prior years so that the current budget is not burdened with large interest payments on debts caused by deficits in previous years? Is the city or county itself laid out in a compact and efficient manner, or does its sheer size make administration expensive? How many employees are required to perform a given service?

TAX LIMITATION MEASURES

Texas restricts increases in property taxes by local taxing units. The statute basically provides that the governing body may not adopt a tax rate that exceeds the rate for the previous year by more than 3% until the governing body has (1) given public notice of its intention to adopt a higher rate and (2) held a public hearing on the proposed increase. Homestead property is limited to 10% per year increases. The hearing must be on a weekday that is not a public holiday and must begin after 5:00 P.M. and before 9:00 P.M. There are also provisions for notice to the property owners if the property value has been increased over the preceding tax year. The governing body of the taxing unit may decrease the official tax rate for the current year at any time.

SPECIAL ASSESSMENTS

Often the need arises to make local municipal improvements that will benefit property owners within a limited area, such as the paving of a street, the installation of street lights, curbs, storm drains, and sanitary sewer lines, or the construction of irrigation and drainage ditches. Such improvements can be provided through special assessments on property.

The theory underlying special assessments is that the improvements must benefit the land against which the cost will be charged, and the value of the benefits must exceed the cost. The area receiving the benefit of an improvement is the *improvement district* or **assessment district,** and the property within that district bears the cost of the improvement. This is different from a **public improvement.** A public improvement, such as reconstruction of the city's sewage plant, benefits the public at large and is financed through the general (ad valorem) property tax. A local improvement, such as extending a sewer line into a street of homes presently using septic tanks or cesspools, does not benefit the public at large and should properly be charged only to those who directly benefit. Similarly, when streets are widened, owners of homes lining a 20-foot-wide street in a strictly residential neighborhood would be expected to bear the cost of widening it to 30 or 40 feet and to donate the needed land from their front yards. But a street widening from two lanes to four to accommodate traffic not generated by the homes on the street is a different situation, because the widening benefits the public at large. In this case, the street widening is funded from public monies and the homeowners are compensated for any land taken from them.

Forming an Improvement District

An improvement district can be formed by the action of a group of concerned citizens who want and are willing to pay for an improvement. Property owners desiring the improvement take their proposal to the state legislature, city council, or other similar public body in charge of levying assessments. A public notice showing the proposed improvements, the extent of the improvement district, and the anticipated costs is prepared by the board. This notice is mailed to landowners in the proposed improvement district, posted conspicuously in the district, and published in a local newspaper. The notice also contains the date and place of public hearings on the matter at which property owners within the proposed district are invited to voice their comments and objections.

Texas Homestead Exemption

Special assessments pose a particular problem in Texas because of the constitutional nature of the homestead laws. Therefore, assessments for water districts, street improvements, or any special assessments district may not necessarily operate as a lien on a homestead to force a sale of the home to satisfy the amounts due. In an effort to make these liens more enforceable, lenders often put requirements for maintenance fees, homeowners' association dues, and special district assessments in the homeowner's mortgage. Defaulting in the payment of such special assessments might then be considered to be a default in the payment of the purchase money mortgage. This theory has been successfully enforced in Texas.

Confirmation

If the hearings result in a decision to proceed, then under the authority granted by Texas law regarding special improvements, a local government ordinance is passed that describes the project and its costs and the improvement district boundaries. An assessment roll is also prepared that shows the cost to each parcel in the district. Hearings are held regarding the assessment roll. When everything is in order, the roll is **confirmed** (approved). Then the contract to construct the improvements is awarded and work is started.

The proposal to create an improvement district can also come from a city council, board of trustees, or board of supervisors. Whenever this happens, notices are distributed and hearings held to hear objections from affected parties. Objections are ruled upon by a court of law and if found to have merit, the assessment plans must be revised or dropped. Once approved, assessment rolls are prepared, more hearings are held, the roll is confirmed, and the contract is awarded.

Bond Issues

Upon completion of the improvement, each landowner receives a bill for his portion of the cost. If the cost to a landowner is less than $100, the landowner either pays the amount in full to the contractor directly or to a designated public official who, in turn, pays the contractor. If the assessment is larger, the landowner can immediately pay it in full or let it *go to bond.* If let go to bond, local government officials prepare a bond issue that totals all the unpaid assessments in the improvement district. These bonds are either given to the contractor as payment for the work or sold to the public through a securities dealer and the proceeds are used to pay the contractor. The collateral for the bonds is the land in the district upon which assessments have not been paid.

The bonds spread the cost of the improvements over a period of 5 to 10 years and are payable in equal annual (or semiannual) installments plus accumulated interest. Thus, a $2,000 sewer and street-widening assessment on a 10-year bond would be charged to a property owner at the rate of $200 per year (or $100 each 6 months) plus interest. As the bond is gradually retired, the amount of interest added to the regular principal payment declines.

Apportionment

Special assessments are apportioned according to benefits received, rather than by the value of the land and buildings being assessed. In fact, the presence of buildings in an improvement district is not usually considered in preparing the assessment roll; the theory is that the land receives all the benefit of the improvement. Several illustrations can best explain how assessments are apportioned. In a residential neighborhood, the assessment for installation of storm drains, curbs, and gutters is made on a **front-foot basis.** A property owner is charged for each foot of lot that abuts the street being improved.

In the case of a sanitary sewer line assessment, the charge per lot can either be based on front footage or on a simple count of the lots in the district. In the latter case, if there are 100 lots on the new sewer line, each would pay 1% of the cost. In the case of a park or playground, lots nearest the new facility are deemed to benefit more and thus are assessed more than lots located farther away. This form of allocation is very subjective and usually results in spirited objections at public hearings from those who do not feel they will use the facility in proportion to the assessment that their lots will bear.

INCOME TAXES ON THE SALE OF A RESIDENCE

We now turn to the income taxes that are due if a home is sold for more than it cost. Income taxes are levied by the federal government, by 44 states (the exceptions are Florida, Nevada, South Dakota, Texas, Washington, and Wyoming), and by 48 cities, including New York City, Baltimore, Pittsburgh, Philadelphia, Cincinnati, Cleveland, and Detroit. The discussion here centers on the federal income tax and includes key provisions of the Internal Revenue Code as it applies to owner occupied residences. Aspects of this code that apply to real estate investments are explained in Chapter 25.

Calculating a Home's Basis

The first step in determining the amount of taxable gain upon the sale of an owner-occupied residence is to calculate the home's ***basis.*** This is the price originally paid for the home plus any fees paid for closing services and legal counsel and any fee or commission paid to help find the property. If the home was built rather than purchased, the basis is the cost of the land plus the cost of construction, such as the cost of materials and construction labor, architect's fees, building permit fees, planning and zoning commission approval costs, utility connection charges, and legal fees. The value of labor contributed by the homeowner and free labor from friends and relatives cannot be added. If the home was received as compensation, a gift, an inheritance, or in a trade, or if a portion of the home was depreciated for business purposes, special rules apply that will not be covered here, and the seller should consult the Internal Revenue Service (IRS).

Assessments for local improvements and any improvements made by the seller during occupancy are added to the original cost of the home. An improvement is a permanent betterment that materially adds to the value of a home, prolongs its life, or changes it use. For example, finishing an unfinished basement or upper floor, building a swimming pool, adding a bedroom or bathroom, installing new plumbing or wiring, installing a new roof, erecting a new fence, and paving a new driveway are classed as improvements and are added to the home's basis. Maintenance and repairs are not added because they merely maintain the property in ordinary operating condition. Fixing gutters, mending leaks in plumbing, replacing broken windowpanes, and painting the inside or outside of the home are considered maintenance and repair items. However, repairs, when done as part of an extensive remodeling or restoration job, may be added to the basis.

Calculating the Amount Realized

The next step in determining taxable gain is to calculate the **amount realized** from the sale. This is the selling price of the home less selling expenses, which is the ***adjusted sales price.*** Selling expenses include brokerage commissions, advertising, legal fees, title services, escrow or closing fees, and mortgage points paid by the seller. If the sale includes furnishings, the value of those furnishings is deducted from the selling price and reported separately as personal property. If the seller takes back a note and mortgage that is immediately sold at a discount, the discounted value of the note is used, not its face amount.

TABLE 16.2 Calculation of gain

May 1, 1992	Buy home for $90,000; closing costs are $500	Basis is	$90,500
July 1, 1993	Add landscaping and fencing for $3,500	Basis is	$94,000
Dec. 1, 1999	Add extra bedroom and bath-room for $15,000	Basis is	$109,000
June 1, 2006	Sell home for $150,000; sales commissions and closing costs are $9,000	Amount realized is	$141,000
	Calculation of gain:	Amount realized is	$141,000
		Less basis	−109,000
		Equals gain	$32,000

Source: © 2012 Cengage Learning

Calculating Gain on the Sale

The ***gain*** on the sale is the difference between the amount realized and the basis. Table 16.2 illustrates this with an example. Unless the seller qualifies for tax post-ponement or tax exclusion as discussed next, this is the amount he reports as gain on his annual income tax forms.

Income Tax Exclusion

A taxpayer can exclude $250,000 of gain from the sale of the taxpayer's principal residence. If the taxpayer is married, there is a $500,000 exclusion for married individuals filing jointly, if: (1) either spouse meets the ownership test, (2) both spouses meet the use test and the taxpayer has resided there for at least two of the past five years, (3) a husband and wife file a joint return in the year of sale or exchange, and (4) neither spouse is ineligible for exclusion by virtue of sale or exchange of the residence within the last two years. This new rule *eliminates* taxable gain on the sale of the residence up to these limits.

This exclusion is allowable each time the homeowner meets the eligibility requirement but no more frequently than once every two years.

There is still a need to keep records for home improvements, however. The gain is calculated as the sales price, less the home's basis, or adjusted basis, whichever is applicable. If one owns a house that will *never* exceed the allowable gain, then there is no need to keep a record of improvements.

The IRS does not even receive notification of any home sales of $250,000 or under ($500,000 for married taxpayers) provided that the homebuyer provides to the escrow agent assurances that (1) the home was a "principal residence," (2) there was no federally subsidized mortgage financing assistance, and (3) the final gain is excludable from gross income *(Internal Revenue Code 6045(e)(5))*.

Exceptions to the two-year use rule include (1) if a uniformed or foreign service personnel is called away to active duty, (2) there's a change in the taxpayer's place of employment, (3) the taxpayer is forced to move for health reasons, or

(4) other unforeseen circumstances recognized by the IRS. In most circumstances, the taxpayer can prorate his tax exclusion.

CAPITAL GAINS

Capital gains tax is a tax on the profits from the sale of a capital asset. For years, Congress has recognized the benefit of investment in capital assets. When a person buys or builds shopping centers, homes, office buildings, and other substantial improvements, they are investing in the future. This type of improvement provides jobs for people in businesses and also provides employment for real estate brokers, title companies, contractors, and other elements of society, creating a ripple effect that benefits virtually all levels of a community. As an incentive of the development of capital assets, Congress has traditionally taxed gains on the sale of capital assets at a much lower rate than normal income rates. Capital gains tax benefits were virtually wiped out in 1987 when Congress raised capital gain rates to the same level as normal income tax rates while, at the same time, lowering the overall income tax rate. It seemed like a fair trade-off at the time. What we discovered, however, was that when people don't sell their capital assets and develop new parcels of real estate (there is no incentive to do so without a tax benefit), the economy tends to stagnate. In an effort to improve the economy, the Taxpayer Relief Act of 1997 lowered capital gains tax rates for properties sold after May 6, 1997. Not surprisingly, that area of the economy improved. In a continuing effort to benefit the economy, Congress again lowered the capital gains rate in 2003 for property sold on or after May 6, 2003.

The Jobs and Growth Tax Relief Reconciliation Act of 2003 reduced the 10% rate on the adjusted net capital gain to 5% for individuals in the 10% or 15% tax bracket and reduced the 20% rates on the adjusted net capital gain to 15% for individuals in the 25%-35% tax brackets. This created the lower rates to capital assets sold or exchanged (and installment payments received) on or after May 6, 2003, that were held for more than 12 months. In addition, the 5% tax rate is reduced to 0% (as in "tax free") for taxable years beginning after December 31, 2007 and before January 1, 2009. The 5%/15% rates revert to the 10%/20% rates for tax years beginning after December 31, 2008. Table 16.3 illustrates these reductions.

There are interesting economic philosophies about capital gains tax. It is supposed to stimulate capital investments (good for a growing economy) by providing tax breaks on profit when the capital asset is resold. Capital gains have a secondary effect, however.

When the asset is sold, brokers, lawyers, title companies, and various service providers all make their fees. These fees are taxed at normal income rates. The

TABLE 16.3 Long-term capital gain rates

Tax Bracket	1/1/01-5/5/03	5/6/03-12/31/07	2008	2009
10% and 15%	8% / 10%	5%	0%	10%
25% and above	20%	15%	15%	20%

Source: © 2012 Cengage Learning

result: more total tax income to the government. If there are no tax incentives, and the capital asset is not sold (because the investor prefers to keep the income), no fees are generated. History has shown us that when capital gains tax is reduced, the economy tends to strengthen. The latest capital gains tax cuts have shown that history has repeated itself. Déjà vu, all over again.

INSTALLMENT SALES

When a gain cannot be postponed by purchasing a more expensive home, or excluded using the lifetime exclusion, the seller can spread out the payment of taxes on the gain by selling on the ***installment method.*** This means the seller accepts a note or an installment contract for part (or all) of the purchase price, and receives one or more payments in later taxable years. When this occurs, the seller reports that proportion of the gain that is received in each year as it is received. We will not go through the calculations (which are different for homes versus investment property) because these are available on IRS forms should you be involved in an installment sale. The point to know for now is that a seller can postpone some of the taxes due on a gain by agreeing with the buyer to accept some of the purchase price in subsequent taxable years. If a taxpayer is classed as a "dealer" in real property, however, the taxpayer must report all of the income in the first year, regardless of when it is received.

PROPERTY TAX AND INTEREST DEDUCTIONS

The Internal Revenue Code of 1986 retains the deductibility of state and local real estate taxes. A homeowner can deduct real property taxes and personal property taxes from other income when calculating income taxes. This applies to single-family residences, condominiums, and cooperatives. The deduction does not extend to special assessment taxes for improvement districts.

The Internal Revenue Code of 1986 also retains the deductibility of interest on debt not to exceed $1,000,000, but subject to two limitations. The basic rule is that interest paid to finance the purchase of a home is deductible against a homeowner's other income. Also deductible are interest paid on improvement district bonds, loan prepayment penalties, and the deduction of points on new loans that are clearly distinguishable as interest and not service fees for making the loan. Loan points paid by a seller to help a buyer obtain an FHA or VA loan are not deductible as interest (it is not the seller's debt), but can be deducted from the home's selling price in computing a gain or loss on the sale. FHA mortgage insurance premiums are not deductible, nor are those paid to private mortgage insurers.

From an individual taxpayer's standpoint, the ability to deduct property taxes and mortgage interest on a personal residence becomes more valuable in successively higher tax brackets. At the 28% bracket, every dollar spent for something tax-deductible costs the taxpayer only 72¢ in after-tax money. Or seen from another viewpoint, the taxpayer obtains the full enjoyment of the money he spends on interest and property taxes without having to first pay income taxes on it. Although progressively less dramatic, the same argument applies to persons in the 15% tax bracket. As viewed from a national standpoint, the deductibility of interest and property taxes encourages widespread ownership of the country's land and buildings.

BELOW-MARKET INTEREST

Many homeowners were trying to avoid a taxable event on sales to relatives or loved ones. One could charge a higher price for the sale of a home, but require no interest on the loan. This will allow all of the income to be taxed at a capital gains rate, much cheaper than the normal income rate for people of high-income levels.

In 1984 and 1985, Congress enacted legislation requiring sellers to charge market rates of interest or be taxed as if they had. This legislation requires minimum rates tied to prevailing rates on federal securities, that is, U.S. Treasury notes and bonds. The seller must charge no less than applicable federal rate (AFR). This rule applied to home sellers as well as investors. Investing in real estate and its tax implications are discussed in Chapter 25.

Because tax rules for real estate are continually changing, only the major rules are reported and discussed here and in Chapter 25. As a real estate owner or agent you need a source of more frequent and more detailed information such as the annual income tax guide published by the Internal Revenue Service (free) or the privately published guides available in most bookstores. Additionally, you may wish to subscribe to a tax newsletter for up-to-the-minute tax information.

AGENT'S LIABILITY FOR TAX ADVICE

The real estate industry's desire for professional recognition coupled with the results of several key court cases strongly suggests that a real estate practitioner ought to be reasonably knowledgeable about taxes. This does not mean the practitioner must have knowledge of tax laws at the level of an accountant or tax attorney. Neither does it mean a practitioner can plead ignorance of tax laws. Rather it means a real estate practitioner is now liable for tax advice (or lack of it) if the advice is material to the transaction—and giving such advice is common in the brokerage business. What this means is that a practitioner should have enough general knowledge of real estate tax laws to be able to answer basic questions accurately and to warn clients and recommend tax counsel if the questions posed by the transaction are beyond the agent's knowledge. Note that the obligation to inform exists even when a client fails to ask about tax consequences. This is to avoid situations where after the deed has been recorded the client says, "Gee, I didn't know I'd have to pay all these taxes, my agent should have warned me," and then sues the agent. Lastly, if the agent tries to fill the role of accountant or tax attorney for the client, then the agent will be held liable to the standards of an accountant or tax attorney.

To summarize, a real estate practitioner must be aware of tax laws that affect the properties the practitioner is handling. A real estate agent has a responsibility to alert clients to potential tax consequences, liabilities, and advantages whether they ask for it or not. Lastly, an agent is responsible for the quality and accuracy of tax information given out by the agent.

REVIEW QUESTIONS

Answers to these questions are found in the Answer Key section at the back of the book.

1. Local government programs and services are financed primarily through
   A. property taxes.
   B. federal income taxes.
   C. state income taxes.
   D. states sales taxes.

2. Taxes on real property are levied
   A. on an ad valorem basis.
   B. according to the value of the property.
   C. both A and B.
   D. neither A nor B.

3. The assessment ratio of real property in a community may be
   A. 100% of its appraised value.
   B. more than its fair market value.
   C. more than its appraised value.
   D. all of the above.

4. Which of the following properties has the highest assessed value?
   A. Market value $75,000, assessed at 75% of value.
   B. Market value $50,000, assessed at 100% of value.
   C. Market value $90,000, assessed at 50% of value.
   D. Market value $130,000, assessed at 35% of value.

5. Tax rates may be expressed as
   A. a millage rate.
   B. dollars of tax per hundred dollars of valuation.
   C. dollars of tax per thousand dollars of valuation.
   D. all of the above.

6. Which of the following would be the highest tax rate?
   A. 38 mills
   B. $3.80/$100
   C. $38/$1,000
   D. No difference

7. Jeff plans to bid on real estate being offered at a tax auction. Before bidding on a parcel he would be wise to
   A. conduct a title search.
   B. purchase title insurance.
   C. sign a contract.
   D. obtain a tax receipt.

8. Which of the following liens holds the highest degree of lien priority?
   A. Federal income tax liens
   B. Mechanics' liens
   C. Ad valorem tax liens
   D. First mortgage liens

9. Records of the assessed valuations of all properties within a jurisdiction are known as
   A. appraisal rolls.
   B. allocation rolls.
   C. appropriation rolls.
   D. assessment rolls.

10. In Texas, the assessed value of real property is set
    A. equal to its fair market value.
    B. greater than its fair market value.
    C. at a percentage of its appraised value.
    D. less than its appraised value.

11. Land and buildings may be exempted from property taxation
    A. as a means of attracting industry to a community.
    B. if they are used for religious or educational purposes.
    C. both A and B.
    D. neither A nor B.

12. All of the following types of property are usually exempt from taxation EXCEPT:
    A. government-owned utilities.
    B. residences owned by elderly homeowners.
    C. property owned by charitable organizations.
    D. hospitals.

13. Real property taxes are sometimes limited by laws that limit
    A. the amount of taxes that can be collected.
    B. how much a government can spend.
    C. both A and B.
    D. neither A nor B.

14. An improvement district may be created as a result of action originated by
    A. a group of concerned citizens.
    B. local governing bodies.
    C. both A and B.
    D. neither A nor B.

15. Which of the following statements is correct?
    A. There is no redemption period in Texas when foreclosure due to taxes has occurred.
    B. All tax liens in Texas are superior to any other liens.
    C. The redemption period in Texas is one year when foreclosure due to taxes has occurred.
    D. Properties in Texas, when tax foreclosure has occurred, may not be sold at public auction.

16. When a person sells land for more than she paid for it
    A. there is no federal tax applicable to the gain.
    B. the gain is taxed by all state governments.
    C. both A and B.
    D. neither A nor B.

17. Which of the following would NOT be considered an improvement to a home in determining its cost basis?
    A. Repairs to a leaky roof.
    B. Construction of a new fence.
    C. Repairs done as part of an extensive remodeling project.
    D. None of the above.

18. Sources of information on income tax laws and rules include
    A. tax guides published by the Internal Revenue Service.
    B. privately published tax guides sold in book-stores.
    C. privately published tax newsletters.
    D. all of the above.

19. In 1979, the Texas legislature voted to restrict increases in property tax rates by local taxing units. An increase, without public hearing, may not exceed the previous year by more than
    A. 3%
    B. 2%
    C. 5%
    D. 10%

Chapter 17

KEY TERMS

Closing meeting: a meeting at which the buyer pays for the property and receives a deed to it, and all other matters pertaining to the sale are concluded

Escrow agent: the person placed in charge of an escrow

Escrow closing: the deposit of documents and funds with a neutral third party along with instructions as to how to conduct the closing

Prorating: the division of ongoing expenses and income items between the buyer and the seller

Real Estate Settlement Procedures Act (RESPA): a federal law that deals with procedures to be followed in certain types of real estate closings

Settlement statement: an accounting of funds to the buyer and the seller at the completion of a real estate transaction

Title closing: the process of completing a real estate transaction

Walk-through: a final inspection of the property just prior to settlement

Title Closing and Escrow

IN THIS CHAPTER

Once the title has been searched, a decision should have been made as to how to take title, prepare a deed, make loan arrangements, check property tax records, and begin the final steps in the process. In this chapter you learn how the process evolves from the buyer's walk-through to the closing meeting or escrow. You will also become familiar with the calculations and procedures to determine prorations and complete the final settlement statement.

Numerous details must be handled between the time a buyer and seller sign a sales contract and the day title is conveyed to the buyer. Title must be searched (Chapter 8), a decision made as to how to take title (Chapter 6), a deed prepared (Chapter 7), loan arrangements made (Chapters 11 through 15), property tax records checked (Chapter 16), and so forth. In this chapter we look at the final steps in the process, in particular the buyer's walk-through, the closing meeting or escrow, prorations, and the settlement statement.

BUYER'S WALK-THROUGH

You may recall that Paragraph 7.A of the TREC-promulgated one- to four-family contract allows the buyer access to the property at reasonable times. To protect both the buyer and the seller, it is good practice for a buyer to make a ***walk-through***. This is a final inspection of the property just prior to the settlement date. It is quite possible the buyer has not been on the parcel or inside the structure since the initial offer and acceptance. Now, several weeks later, the buyer wants to make certain that the premises have been vacated, no damage has occurred, the seller has left behind personal property agreed upon, and the seller has not removed and taken any real property. If the sales contract requires all mechanical items to be in normal working order, then the buyer may want to test the heating and air-conditioning systems, dishwasher, disposal, stove, garage door opener, etc., as well as the refrigerator, washer, and dryer if included. The buyer may also want to test all the plumbing to be certain the hot water heater works, faucets and showers run, toilets flush, and sinks drain. A final inspection of the structure is made, including walls, roof, gutters, driveway, decks, patios, etc., as well as the land and landscaping.

Note that a walk-through is not the time for the buyer to make the initial inspection of the property. That is done before the contract is signed, and if there are questions in the buyer's mind regarding the structural soundness of the property, a thorough inspection (possibly with the aid of a professional real estate inspector) should be conducted within ten days of signing the purchase contract. The walk-through is for the purpose of giving the buyer the opportunity to make certain that agreements regarding the condition of the premises have been kept. If during the walk-through the buyer notes the walls were damaged when the seller moved out, or the furnace does not function, the buyer (or the buyer's agent) notes these items and asks that funds be withheld at the closing to pay for repairs.

TITLE CLOSING

Title closing refers to the completion of a real estate transaction. This is when the buyer pays for the property and the seller delivers the deed. The day on which this occurs is called the **closing date.** Depending on where one resides in the United States, the title closing process is referred to as a **closing, settlement,** or *escrow*. All accomplish the same basic goal, but the method of reaching that goal can follow one of two paths.

In some parts of the United States, particularly in the East, and to a certain extent in the Mountain states, the Midwest, and the South, the title closing process is concluded at a meeting at which each party to the transaction, or his/her representative, is present. Elsewhere, title closing is conducted by an escrow agent, who is a neutral third party mutually selected by the buyer and seller to carry out the closing. With an escrow, there is no necessity for a ***closing meeting***; in fact, most of the closing process is conducted by mail. In Texas, the ***escrow closing*** is the fastest, safest, and most convenient method of carrying out the title closing process. The escrow agent is usually a title company. It is customary for everyone to meet. Let's look at common Texas-style closings.

CLOSING OR SETTLEMENT MEETING

When a meeting is used to close a real estate transaction, the seller (or the seller's representative) meets in person with the buyer and delivers the deed. At the same time, the buyer pays the seller for the property. To ascertain that everything promised in the sales contract has been properly carried out, the buyer and seller may choose to each have an attorney present. The real estate practitioners who brought the buyer and seller together are also usually present. An escrow officer from the title company coordinates the closing. If a new loan is being made or an existing one is being paid off at the closing, a representative of the lender may be present.

The location of the meeting and the selection of the person responsible for conducting the closing will depend on local custom and the nature of the closing.

In Texas, the title company responsible for the title search and title policy conducts the closing at its office. In smaller counties, the closing may be at an attorney's office or lender's office.

Seller's Responsibilities at Closing

To ensure a smooth closing, each person attending a closing is responsible for providing certain documents. As a practical matter, it doesn't have to be complicated. Although the seller is required to provide the deed, the title company usually has its attorney prepare the deeds and other documents required by the contract if the seller does not have an attorney or does not prepare the documents himself. The title company will also prepare affidavits for the seller to sign (i.e., no liens, identity affidavits, marital status or heirship) and obtain pertinent ad valorem tax information. They will also contact the seller concerning any title curative information that may be needed (releases of liens, existing lender's loan information, estate matters).

The seller is usually required by the contract for sale to (1) provide a deed transferring title to the buyer, (2) provide proof that ad valorem taxes have been paid, and (3) provide the insurance policy for the property. The seller should also provide documents showing the removal of unacceptable liens and encumbrances, a bill of sale for personal property, and a statement showing the remaining balance of any existing mortgage. The seller should also bring the keys to the property, garage door openers, satellite dish controls, and similar items. If the property is income producing, the seller will usually provide the original leases, rent schedules, and letters advising the tenants of the new owner. In a nutshell, the seller delivers documents that prove he can deliver clear title so that the title company can insure it for the buyer in accordance with the terms of the contract.

Buyer's Responsibilities at Closing

The buyer's responsibilities primarily include having adequate settlement funds ready. If a new loan is required, the lender will usually also require a survey, termite reports, flood-prone area information, and insurance (including flood insurance, if required).

When a new loan is involved, it is a little more complicated. The lender wants absolute assurance of the condition of the house and clear title. They will provide lengthy escrow instructions to the escrow officer, along with a large pile of closing documents to ensure the priority of the lien and quality of the security (the house), and a plethora of disclosures required by federal law. The lender seldom shows up at the closing.

Real Estate Agent's Duties

The seller and the seller's attorney may be unaware of all the things expected of them at the closing. Therefore, it is the duty of the agent who listed the property to make certain that they are prepared. Similarly, it is the duty of the agent who found the buyer to make certain that the buyer and the buyer's attorney are prepared for the closing. If the agent both lists and sells the property, he or she assists both the buyer and seller. If more than one agent is involved in the transaction, each should keep the other(s) fully informed so the transaction will go as smoothly as possible. At all times the buyer and seller are to be kept informed as to the status of the closing. An agent should provide them with a preview of all actions that will take place, explain the amounts of money involved and the purpose served by each payment or receipt, and in general prepare the parties for informed participation at the closing.

The Transaction

When everyone concerned has arrived for the closing, the closing begins. The various documents called for by the sales contract are provided for inspection. The buyer or his attorney may inspect the deed the seller is offering, the title search and/or title policy, the mortgage papers, survey, leases, removals of encumbrances, and proration calculations. The seller usually reviews the closing statement and confirms payoffs and fees are correct. This continues until each party has a chance to inspect each document of interest.

The title search will have been prepared before the closing, but the buyer and lender both want protection against any changes in title condition since then. A common solution is for the seller to sign a **seller's affidavit.** In this affidavit, the seller states that he is the true owner of the property, that there are no liens or proceedings currently against him, and that he has done nothing to damage the quality of title since the title search. If a defect caused by the seller later appears, he may be sued for damages. Furthermore, he may be liable for criminal charges if it can be shown that he was attempting to obtain money under false pretenses by signing the affidavit. Another solution is to require the person in charge of the closing to hold the money being paid to the seller until a final title search is made and the new deed recorded.

A settlement statement (discussed later in this chapter) is prepared by the escrow officer and given to the buyer and seller to summarize the financial aspects of their transaction. It is prepared by the person in charge of the closing either just before or at the meeting. It provides a clear picture of where the buyer's and seller's money is going at the closing by identifying each party to whom money is being paid.

If everyone involved in the closing has done his or her homework and comes to the meeting prepared, the closing usually goes smoothly. After the parties have reviewed the documents in their respective closing statements, all documents are then executed and handed to the escrow officer, along with any checks (usually from the buyer) that need to be tendered to complete the closing. Due to new RESPA regulations, virtually every dime that passes through the closing must be shown on the closing statement. Those closing costs that are paid outside of the closing may be marked "POC," but must be shown on the closing statement. The escrow officer then sends those documents that need to be recorded to the courthouse, makes copies of other documents, and gives the originals to the parties that are entitled to them. The escrow officer will usually send a copy of the note and closing statement to the buyer's lender to confirm regulatory compliance, then receives a funding number from the lender so that the proceeds can be disbursed to the parties. The escrow officer disburses funds out of the closing in accordance with the terms of the closing statement. A few days (or weeks, depending on the county) later, the original documents are returned to the title company, which forwards them to the party entitled to them. The original deed and owner's title policy are delivered to the purchaser. The recorded deed of trust and original note are delivered to the lender.

Closing into Escrow

Occasionally an unavoidable circumstance can cause delays in a closing. Perhaps an important document, known to be in the mail, has not arrived. Yet it will be difficult to reschedule the meeting. In such a situation, the parties concerned may agree to **close into escrow.** In such a closing, all parties sign their documents and entrust them to the escrow agent for safekeeping. No money is disbursed and the deed is not delivered until the missing paperwork has arrived. When it does, the escrow agent completes the transaction and delivers the money and documents by mail or messenger. The use of escrow to close a real estate transaction involves a neutral third party, called an ***escrow agent***, escrow holder, or escrowee, who acts as a trusted stakeholder for all the parties to the transaction. Instead of delivering the deed directly to the buyer at a closing meeting, the seller gives the deed to the escrow agent with instructions that it be delivered only after the buyer has completed all his promises in the sales contract. Similarly, the buyer hands the escrow agent the money for the purchase price plus instructions that it be given to the seller only after fulfillment of the seller's promises. Let's look more closely at this arrangement.

A typical real estate escrow closing starts when a sales contract is signed by the buyer and seller. They select a neutral escrow agent to handle the closing. This may be the escrow department of a bank or savings and loan or other lending agency, an attorney, or a title insurance company. Sometimes real estate brokers offer escrow services. However, if the broker is earning a sales commission in the transaction, the broker cannot be neutral and disinterested.

Escrow Agent's Duties

The escrow agent's task begins with the deposit of the buyer's earnest money in a special bank trust account. In most commercial closings and almost all residential closings in Texas, the escrow agent's duties are very seldom written out as formal escrow instructions. An exception to this is the lender who furnishes a *mortgagee's information letter (MIL)* to direct the escrow agent as to how to disburse the funds for the loan proceeds.

When the title search is completed, the escrow agent forwards it to the buyer or his attorney for approval. The property insurance and tax papers the seller would otherwise bring to the closing meeting are sent to the escrow agent for proration. Leases, service contracts, and notices to tenants are also sent to the escrow agent for proration and delivery to the buyer. The deed conveying title to the buyer is prepared, signed by the seller, and given to the escrow agent. Once delivered into escrow, even if the seller dies, marries, or is declared legally incompetent before the close of escrow, the deed will still pass title to the buyer.

In Texas, most escrows are handled by title companies. Although all escrow agents are bonded and heavily regulated by the Texas Department of Insurance, it is a complicated business and closings are not to be taken lightly. It is not a party; it is the final consummation of a business transaction.

The Closing

As the closing date draws near, if all the instructions are otherwise complete, the escrow agent requests any additional money the buyer and lender must deposit in order to close. The day before closing the escrow agent orders a last-minute check on the title. If no changes have occurred since the first (preliminary) title search, the deed, mortgage, mortgage release, and other documents to be recorded as part of the transaction are recorded first thing the following morning. As soon as *good funds* (cash, wired funds, cashier check) have been deposited in the escrow agent's trust account, the escrow agent hands or mails a check to every party to whom funds are due from the escrow (usually the seller, real estate broker, and previous lender), along with any papers or documents that must be delivered through escrow (such as the fire insurance policy, copy of the property tax bill, and tenant leases). Several days later the buyer and lender will receive a title insurance policy through mail from the title company. The county clerk's office mails the documents it recorded to each party or back to the title company, who will forward the documents to the proper parties. The deed is sent to the buyer, the mortgage release to the seller, and the new mortgage to the lender.

In the escrow closing method, the closing, delivery of title, and recordation are considered to take place at the same moment. Technically, the seller does not physically hand a deed to the buyer on the closing day. However, once all the conditions of the escrow are met, the escrow agent, as a disinterested third party, represents neither party but fulfills the escrow requirements as set out by both parties. Thus, a buyer, through the escrow agent, receives the deed, and the law regarding delivery is fulfilled. Even though cash is considered good funds, taking cash to a closing is not a particularly good idea. The cash transaction must be reported to the Internal Revenue Service (IRS Form 8300) with an explanation from the bank collecting the deposit why the deposit was in cash. Banks also have to report cash deposits in excess of $10,000.

PUTTING IT TO WORK

With an escrow closing, it is not necessary for the buyer and seller to meet face-to-face during the escrow period or at the closing. This can eliminate personality conflicts that might be detrimental to an otherwise sound transaction. The escrow agent, having previously accumulated all the documents, approvals, deeds, and monies prior to the closing date, does the closing alone.

In a brokered transaction, the real estate agent may be the only person who actually meets the escrow agent. All communication can be handled through the broker, by mail, or by telephone. If a real estate agent is not involved, the buyer and/or seller can open the escrow, either in person or by mail. The use of an escrow agent does not eliminate the need for an attorney. Although there might be no closing meeting for the attorneys to attend, they play a vital role in advising the buyer and seller on each document sent by the escrow agent for approval and signature.

DELAYS AND FAILURE TO CLOSE

When a real estate purchase contract is written, a closing date is also negotiated and placed in the contract. The choice of closing date will depend on when the buyer wants possession, when the seller wants to move out, and how long it will take to obtain a loan, title search, and termite report, and otherwise fulfill the contract requirements. In a typical residential sale this is 30 to 60 days, with 45 days being a popular choice when new financing is involved. The Texas Real Estate Commission (TREC)-promulgated earnest money form simply states that the closing will be "on or before" a specified date.

Delays along the way are sometimes encountered and may cause a delay in the closing. This is usually not a problem as long as the buyer still intends to buy, the seller still intends to sell, and the delay is for a reasonable cause and a justifiable length of time. Note that the TREC form provides for extensions beyond the specified closing date to cure title objections or to complete loan requirements. These are common delays that are often beyond the control of either the buyer or seller. This allows for some reasonable flexibility when these problems occur without requiring extensive or stress-filled renegotiation.

The delay might be quite lengthy, however. For example, there may be a previously undisclosed title defect that will take months to clear, or perhaps there are unusual problems in financing, or there has been a major damage to the premises. In such cases, relieving all parties from further obligation to each other may be the wisest choice for all involved. This is one of the remedies provided for in Paragraph 15 of the TREC-promulgated form. If so, it is essential that the buyer and seller sign mutual release papers. These are necessary to rescind the purchase contract and cancel the escrow if one has been opened. The buyer's deposit is also returned. Without release papers, the buyer still has a vaguely defined liability to buy and the seller can still be required to convey the property, so the escrow agent will refuse to disburse to either party. A mutual release gives the buyer the freedom to choose another property and the seller the chance to fix the problem and remarket the property later.

A stickier problem occurs when one party wants out of the contract and attempts to use any delay in closing as grounds for contract termination. (For example, the buyer may have found a preferable property for less money and better terms. Or, the seller may have received a higher offer since signing the purchase contract.) Although the party wishing to cancel may threaten with a lawsuit, courts might not enforce cancellation of valuable contract rights because of reasonable delays that are not the fault of the other party. Conversely, courts might not go along with a reluctant buyer or seller who manufactures delays so as to delay the closing and then claims default and cancellation of the contract. If the reluctance continues and negotiations to end it fail, the performing party may choose to complete its requirements and then ask the courts to force the reluctant party to the closing table.

LOAN ESCROWS

Escrows can be used for purposes other than real estate or sales transactions. For example, a homeowner who is refinancing his property could enter into an escrow with the lender. The conditions of the escrow would be that the homeowner deliver a properly executed note and mortgage to the escrow agent and that the lender deposit the loan money. Upon closing, the escrow agent delivers the documents to the lender and the money to the homeowner. Or, in reverse, an escrow could be used to pay off the balance of a loan. The conditions would be the borrower's deposit of the balance due and the lender's deposit of the mortgage release and note. Even the weekly office sports pool is an escrow—with the person holding the pool money acting as escrow agent for the participants.

REPORTING REQUIREMENTS

The Internal Revenue Code now requires that the seller's proceeds from all sales of real estate be reported to the Internal Revenue Service on their Form 1099-S. The responsibility for filing Form 1099-S goes in the following order: the person responsible for the closing, the mortgage lender, the seller's broker, the buyer's broker, and any person designated by the U.S. Treasury. It is important to determine at the closing who needs to file the Form 1099-S. This forms must be filed at no charge to the taxpayer.

The Taxpayer Relief Act of 1997 provides that real estate reporting persons generally do not need to file Form 1099-S for sales or exchanges of a principal residence with a sales price at or below $250,000 for a single individual or $500,000 for a married couple, so long as the reporting person obtains a certification from the seller in a form that is satisfactory to the Secretary of the Treasury. The form must be in writing and signed by the seller, and it must confirm that:

1. the seller has owned and used the principal residence for two of the last five years.
2. the seller has not owned or exchanged another principal residence during this two-year period.
3. no portion of the residence has been used for business or rental purposes.
4. the sales price, capital gains, and marital status filing requirements are met.

The form must be sworn to, under penalty of perjury. It must be obtained any time on or before January 31 of the year following the sale or exchange, and retained in the title company's files for four years.

PRORATING AT THE CLOSING

Ongoing expenses and income items must be prorated between the seller and buyer when property ownership changes hands. Items subject to ***proration*** include property insurance premiums, property taxes, accrued interest on assumed loans, and rents and operating expenses if the property produces income. If heating is done by oil and the oil tank is partially filled when title transfers, that oil can be prorated, as can utility bills when service is not shut off between owners. The TREC-promulgated forms state that all prorations are made "through the closing date," indicating that for the day of closing, the seller is responsible for payments, and is entitled to income prorations also. The prorating process has long been a source of considerable mystery to real estate newcomers. Several sample prorations common to most closings are set out below to help clarify the process.

Please note as we start this discussion, prorations can be done two ways. The first is by dividing the entire amount due for the year by 365 or 366 days and prorating accordingly. The second way of calculating prorations is to divide by twelve months and then the number of days in that month. Both are considered to be acceptable methods of calculation when taking an exam. Make sure you know which method is specified.

Hazard Insurance

Hazard insurance policies for such things as fire, wind, storm, and flood damage are paid for in advance. At the beginning of each year of the policy's life, the premium for that year's coverage must be paid. When real estate is sold, the buyer may ask the seller to transfer the remaining coverage to him. The seller usually agrees if the buyer reimburses him for the value of the remaining coverage on a prorated basis.

The first step in prorating hazard insurance is to find out how often the premium is paid, how much it is, and what period of time it covers. Suppose that the seller has a one-year policy that costs $180 and started on January 1 of the current year. If the property is sold and the closing date is June 30, the policy is half used up. Therefore, if the buyer wants the policy transferred to him, he must pay the seller $90 for the remaining six months of coverage.

Because closing dates do not always occur on neat, evenly divided portions of the year, nor do most items that need prorating, it is usually necessary to break the year into months and the months into days to make proration calculations. Suppose, in the previous hazard insurance example, that prorations are to be made on June 29 instead of June 30. This would give the buyer six months and one day of coverage. How much does he owe the seller? The first step is to calculate the monthly and daily rates for the policy: $180 divided by 12 is $15 per month. Dividing the monthly rate of $15 by 30 days gives a daily rate of 50¢. The second step is to add 6 months at $15 and 1 day at 50¢. Thus, the buyer owes the seller $90.50 for the unused portion of the policy.

Loan Interest

When a buyer agrees to assume an existing loan from the seller, an interest proration is necessary. For example, a sales contract calls for the buyer to assume a 9% mortgage loan with a principal balance of $31,111 at the time of closing. Loan payments are due the tenth of each month, and the sales contract calls for a July 3 closing date, with interest on the loan to be prorated through the closing date. How much is to be prorated and to whom?

First, we must recognize that interest is normally paid in arrears. On a loan that is payable monthly, the borrower pays interest for the use of the loan at the end of each month of the loan. Thus, the July 10 monthly loan payment includes the interest due for the use of $31,111 from June 10 through July 9. However, the seller owned the property through July 3, and from June 10 through July 3 is 24 days. At the closing the seller must give the buyer enough money to pay for 24 days interest on the $31,111. If the annual interest rate is 9%, one month's interest is $31,111 times 9% divided by 12, which is $233.33. Divide this by 30 days to get a daily interest rate of $7.7777. Multiply the daily rate by 24 to obtain the interest for 24 days, $186.66.

Rents

It is the custom in Texas to prorate rents on the basis of the actual number of days in the month. Using the July 3 closing date again, if the property is currently rented for $1,450 per month, paid in advance on the first of each month, what would the proration be? If the seller has already collected the rent for the month of July, he is obligated to hand over to the buyer that portion of the rent earned between July 4 and July 31, inclusive, a period of 28 days. To determine how many dollars this is, divide $1,450 by the number of days in July. This gives $46.77 as the rent per day. Then multiply the daily rate by 28 days to get $1,309.56, the portion of the July rent that the seller must hand over to the buyer. If the renter has not paid the July rent by the July 3 closing date, no proration is made. If the buyer later collects the July rent, he must return three days rent to the seller.

Property Taxes

Prorated property taxes are common to nearly all real estate transactions. The amount of proration depends on when the property taxes are due, what portion has already been paid, and what period of time they cover. Property taxes are levied on an annual basis, but depending on the locality, they may be due at the beginning, middle, or end of the tax year. In Texas, property owners are permitted to pay half their property taxes during the first six months of the tax year and the other half during the second six months, although this is seldom done. Prorations are usually made on an annual basis. The state and county tax year is concurrent with the calendar year. Property tax bills are sent out in early October and are due January 1 of the following year, but are not delinquent until February 1 of that year. If a transaction calls for property taxes to be prorated to September 4, how is the calculation made?

Our problem is complicated by the fact that the new property tax bill will not have been issued by the September 4 closing date. The solution is to use the previous year's tax bill as the best estimate available. Suppose that it was $1,080 for the year. The proration would be from January 1 through September 4, a period of 246 days. Dividing $1,080 by 365 gives a daily rate of $2.96. If you take 246 days at $2.96 each, the total is $728.16. The seller pays the buyer $728.16 because he owned the property through September 4; yet the buyer will later receive a property tax bill for the period starting January 1. If there is a possibility that the October property tax bill will change substantially from the previous year, the buyer and seller can agree to make another adjustment between themselves when the new bill is available.

In the event there is a miscalculation of the taxes, most title companies and escrow agents require the buyer and seller to settle their differences between themselves.

Let us work one more property tax proration example. Presume that the annual property tax is $1,350, the tax year runs from January 1 through the following December 31, the closing and proration date is December 28, and the day of closing belongs to the seller. First, determine how much of the annual property tax bill has been paid by the seller. If the seller has paid the taxes for January 1 through December 31, the buyer must reimburse the seller for the taxes from December 29 through December 31, a period of 3 days. The amount is calculated by dividing $1,350 by 365 to find the daily tax rate of $3.70. Then by multiplying the daily rate by 3 days we get $11.10, the amount that the buyer must give the seller.

Homeowners' Association

If the property being sold is a condominium unit or in a cooperative or planned unit development, there will be a monthly homeowners' association payment to be prorated. Suppose the monthly fee is $120 and is paid in advance on the first of the month. If the closing takes place two-thirds of the way through the month, the buyer owes the seller $40 for the unused portion of the month.

Proration Date

Prorations need not be calculated as of the closing date. In the sales contract, the buyer and seller can mutually agree to a different proration date if they wish. If nothing is said, local law and custom will prevail. As stated previously, this means the seller pays for the day of closing in Texas.

Special assessments for such things as street improvements, water mains, and sewer lines are not usually prorated. As a rule, the selling price of the property reflects the added value of the improvements, and the seller pays any assessments in full before closing. This is not an ironclad rule, however; the buyer and seller in their sales contract can agree to do whatever they want about the assessment.

PRORATION SUMMARY

Figure 17.1 summarizes the most common proration situations found in real estate closings. The figure also shows who is to be charged and who is to be

FIGURE 17.1 Common prorations

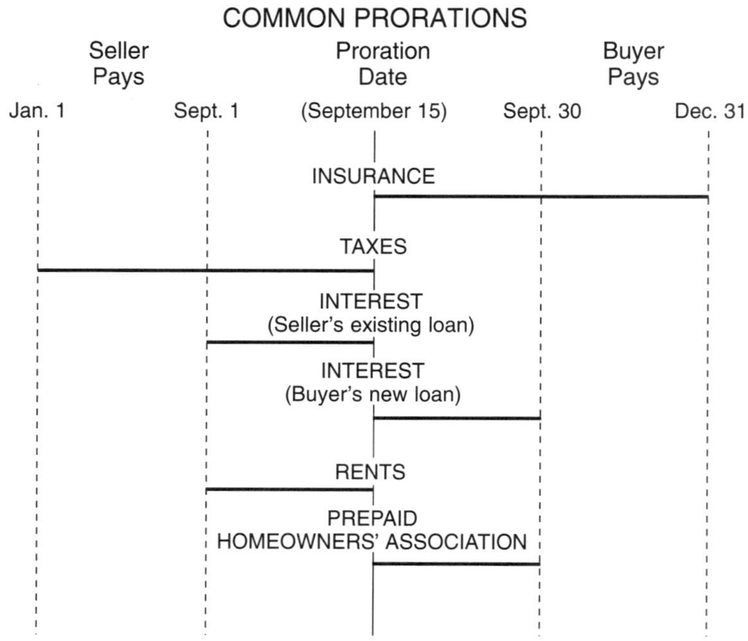

Source: © 2012 Cengage Learning

credited and whether the proration is to be worked forward from the closing date or backward. As a rule, items that are paid in advance by the seller are prorated forward from the closing date; for example, prepaid fire insurance. Items that are paid in arrears, such as interest on an existing loan, are prorated backward from the closing date.

SAMPLE CLOSING

To illustrate the arithmetic involved, let's work through a residential closing situation.

Homer Leavitt has listed his home for sale with List-Rite Realty for \$420,000, and the sales commission is to be 6% of the selling price. A salesperson from Quick-Sale Realty learns about the property through the multiple listing service and produces a buyer willing to pay \$410,000 with \$82,000 down. The offer is conditioned on the seller paying off the existing \$215,325.02 loan, and the buyer obtaining a new loan for \$328,000. Property taxes are to be prorated between the buyer and seller as of the closing date. The buyer also asks the seller to pay for a termite inspection and repairs if necessary, a title search, an owner's title insurance policy, and one-half of the closing fee. The seller accepts this offer on February 15, and they agree to close on March 23.

The property-tax year for this home runs from January 1 through December 31. Mr. Leavitt has paid the taxes for last year, but not for the current year. Newly issued tax bills show that \$3,000 will be due on October 1 for the current year's County taxes, and \$3,500 for school taxes. The hazard insurance policy that the buyer wishes to purchase was $2,369. Charter Title Company will charge the seller $2,503 for an owner's title policy.

The buyer obtains a loan commitment from the Best Mortgage Company for $328,000. To make this loan, the bank will charge an adjusted origination fee of $1,683 and a flood certification fee of $9. The bank also requires a loan title policy for the amount of the loan (added cost of $433.05), 6 months of property tax reserves, and 3 months of hazard insurance reserves. The loan is to be repaid in equal monthly installments beginning May 1. The termite inspection by Dead-Bug Pest Company costs $70, and recording fees are $140. The title company charges the buyer and the seller $250 each to conduct the closing and an attorney charges $90 to prepare a deed for the seller, although this may be prepared by one of the party's attorneys and included in their fees for representation.

List-Rite Realty and Quick-Sale Realty have advised the closing agent that they are splitting the $24,600 sales commission equally.

Finally, the $4,500 earnest money deposit that the buyer made with the offer is to be credited toward the down payment. Using this information, which is summarized in Figure 17.2 for your convenience, let us see exactly how a settlement statement is prepared.

FIGURE 17.2 Transaction summary

	Amount	Comments
Sale Price	$410,000.00	
Down Payment	$ 82,000.00	
Deposit (Earnest Money)	$ 4,500.00	Credit to buyer's down payment
Existing Loan	$215,325.02	Seller to pay off through settlement
New Loan	$328,000.00	Monthly payments begin Nov. 1
Adjusted Origination Charge	$ 1,683.04	
Owner's Title Policy	$ 2,503.00	Seller pays Charter Title Co.
Lender's Title Policy	$ 433.05	Buyer pays Charter Title Co..
County Property Taxes	$ 3000/yr	Not yet paid
Hazard Insurance	$ 2,369.00	New policy
Pest Inspection	$ 70.00	Seller pays Dead-Bug Pest Co.
Property Tax Reserves	$ 3,250.02	6 months
Hazard Insurance Reserves	$ 592.26	3 months
Closing Fee	$ 250.00	Charter Title Company; buyer & seller each pay $250
Record Mortgage		
Brokerage Commission	$ 24,600.00	Seller pays; to be split equally between List-Rite Realty and Quick-Sale Realty.
County Tax Proration	$ 673.97	
School Tax Proration	$ 786.30	
HOA Assessment	$ 389.04	
Tax Certificates	$	
Policy Guaranty	$ 5.00	Per side
HOA Transfer Fee	$ 100.00	Paid by Seller

Settlement and Proration date is March 23.

Source: © 2012 Cengage Learning

RESIDENTIAL SETTLEMENT STATEMENT

Figure 17.3 shows the required HUD-a residential settlement form and it is filled out to reflect the transaction outlined in Figure 17.2. Let us work through this sample transaction in order to see where each item is placed on the ***settlement statement***. (You will notice that the buyer is referred to as the borrower throughout Figure 17.3. This is not important for the moment and will be explained at the end of the chapter.)

Buyer's Side

Lines 101 (Section J) and 401 (Section K) of the settlement statement show identically the price the buyer is paying and the seller is receiving for the property. On line 103 is the $11,468.16 total of the borrower's (buyer's) settlement charges from the reverse side of this form. (The reverse side will be discussed in a moment.) On lines 108 and 408 we see the prorations for the annual HOA assessment. The gross amount of $421,857.20 that is due from the buyer is tallied on line 120.

On line 201 the buyer is credited with the $4,500 earnest money paid at the time the purchase contract was written. On the next line, the buyer is credited with the principal amount of the new $328,000 loan. On line 211 there is a county property tax proration credit for the borrower; on lines 511 and 513, the same proration is shown as a charge to the seller. This is because $6,500 in property taxes are due on October 1 for the period January 1 through December 31. Not yet paid for the year, these taxes must be paid by the buyer on October 1. However, the seller owned the property from January 1 to March 23, a period of 8 months. At the rate of $63.49 per day, this means the seller must give the buyer $1,460.27 for taxes as part of the closing costs.

On line 220 we see the $336,463.27 total of the borrower's credits. Line 301 shows the gross amount that is due from the borrower for this transaction. The difference, on line 303, is the cash that is needed from the buyer (borrower) to close the transaction.

Seller's Side

On the seller's side of the settlement statement (Section K) on line 420 we have the gross amount due to the seller from the sales price and proration credits. On line 502 is the $25,007.12 total of the seller's settlement costs from the reverse side of the form (line 1400). Continuing, on line 504 the seller is charged for the existing mortgage loan that is being paid off as part of the closing. On line 520 the $245,524.19 total is what must come out of the seller's funds at the closing. This is subtracted from the gross amount due to the seller on line 601. The difference, on line 603, is the $164,774.35 cash the seller will receive at the closing.

Settlement Charges

Continuing on the next page of Figure 17.3 (reverse side of the actual form), the real estate commission is detailed on lines 700, 701, and 702. Note that an

FIGURE 17.3 HUD settlement statement

OMB No. 2502-0265

A. Settlement Statement (HUD-1)

B. Type of Loan

1. ☐ FHA 2. ☐ RHS 3. ☒ Conv Unins 4. ☐ VA 5. ☐ Conv Ins. 6. ☐ Seller Fin 7. ☐ Cash Sale.	6. File Number **1015000000X**	7. Loan Number	8. Mortgage Ins Case Number

C. Note: This form is furnished to give you a statement of actual settlement costs. Amounts paid to and by the settlement agent are shown. Items marked "(p.o.c.)" were paid outside the closing; they are shown here for informational purposes and are not included in the totals.

D. Name & Address of Borrower	E. Name & Address of Seller	F. Name & Address of Lender
JOHN Q. BUYER **123 PROPERTY LANE** **HOUSTON, TX**	**JANE SELLER and JOE SELLER** ,	**Lender2** **777 Second Lender Lane** **Anytown, TX 12345**
G. Property Location **123 PROPERTY LANE HOUSTON, TX** **123 PROPERTY LANE** **HOUSTON, TX**	H. Settlement Agent Name **Charter Title Company** **4265 San Felipe, Suite 350** **Houston, TX 77027** **713-871-9700** **Underwritten By: Lawyers**	I. Settlement Date **3/23/2010** **Fund: 3/23/2010**
	Place of Settlement **Charter Title Company** **4265 San Felipe, Suite 350** **Houston, TX 77027**	

J. Summary of Borrower's Transaction

100. Gross Amount Due from Borrower	
101. Contract sales price	$410,000.00
102. Personal property	
103. Settlement charges to borrower	$11,468.16
104.	
105.	
Adjustments for items paid by seller in advance	
106. City property taxes	
107. County property taxes	
108. Annual assessments 03/23/10 thru 12/31/10	$389.04
109. School property taxes	
110. MUD taxes	
111. Other	
112.	
113.	
114.	
115.	
116.	
120. Gross Amount Due From Borrower	$421,857.20
200. Amounts Paid By Or In Behalf Of Borrower	
201. Deposit or earnest money	$4,500.00
202. Principal amount of new loan(s)	$328,000.00
203. Existing loan(s) taken subject to	
204.	
205.	
206.	
207.	
208. Portion of Owner's Policy Paid by Seller	$2,503.00
209.	
Adjustments for items unpaid by seller	
210. City property taxes	
211. County property taxes 01/01/10 thru 03/23/10	$673.97
212. Annual assessments	
213. School property taxes 01/01/10 thru 03/23/10	$786.30
214. MUD taxes	
215. Other	
216.	
217.	
218.	
219.	
220. Total Paid By/For Borrower	$336,463.27
300. Cash At Settlement From/To Borrower	
301. Gross Amount due from borrower (line 120)	$421,857.20
302. Less amounts paid by/for borrower (line 220)	$336,463.27
303. Cash From Borrower	$85,393.93

K. Summary of Seller's Transaction

400. Gross Amount Due to Seller	
401. Contract sales price	$410,000.00
402. Personal property	
403.	
404.	
405.	
Adjustments for items paid by seller in advance	
406. City property taxes	
407. County property taxes	
408. Annual assessments 03/23/10 thru 12/31/10	$389.04
409. School property taxes	
410. MUD taxes	
411. Other	
412.	
413.	
414.	
415.	
416.	
420. Gross Amount Due to Seller	$410,389.04
500. Reductions in Amount Due to Seller	
501. Excess deposit (see instructions)	
502. Settlement charges to seller (line 1400)	$25,007.12
503. Existing loan(s) taken subject to	
504. Payoff of first mortgage loan	$215,325.02
505. Payoff of second mortgage loan	
506.	
507. (EMD $4,500 Disbursed as Proceeds)	
508. Portion of Owner's Policy Paid by Seller	$2,503.00
509.	
Adjustments for items unpaid by seller	
510. City property taxes	
511. County property taxes 01/01/10 thru 03/23/10	$673.97
512. Annual assessments	
513. School property taxes 01/01/10 thru 03/23/10	$786.30
514. MUD taxes	
515. Other	
516.	
517.	
518.	
519.	
520. Total Reduction Amount Due Seller	$244,295.41
600. Cash At Settlement To/From Seller	
601. Gross Amount due to seller (line 420)	$410,389.04
602. Less reductions in amt. due seller (line 520)	$244,295.41
603. Cash To Seller	$166,093.63

The Public Reporting Burden for this collection of information is estimated at 35 minutes per response for collecting, reviewing, and reporting the data. This agency

escrow agent makes the commission split shown here, that escrow agent must have written instructions to do so from the real estate broker who is being paid by the seller. Otherwise, all the commission goes to the seller's broker, who pays the cooperating broker according to whatever agreement they have.

FIGURE 17.3 HUD settlement statement (*continued*)

L. Settlement Charges		Paid From Borrower's Funds at Settlement	Paid From Seller's Funds at Settlement
700. Total Real Estate Broker Fees	**$24,600.00**		
Division of Commission (line 700) as follows:			
701. **$12,300.00** to **Listing Broker Name**			
702. **$12,300.00** to **SELLING AGENT**			
703. **Commission Paid at Settlement**		$0.00	$24,600.00
800. Items Payable in Connection with Loan			
801. Our origination charge	$6,134.00 (from GFE #1)		
802. Your credit or charge (points) for the specific rate chosen	$-4,450.96 (from GFE #2)		
803. Your adjusted origination charges to	(from GFE A)	$1,683.04	
804. Appraisal Fee to **Appraiser**	POC (B) $360.00 (from GFE #3)		
805. Credit report to	(from GFE #3)		
806. Tax service to	(from GFE #3)		
807. Flood certification to **BEST MORTGAGE COMPANY**	(from GFE #3)	$9.00	
900. Items Required by Lender To Be Paid in Advance			
901. Daily interest charges from **3/23/2010** to **4/1/2010** @ **$38.191781**/day	(from GFE #10)	$343.73	
902. Mortgage Insurance Premium for months to	(from GFE #3)		
903. Homeowner's insurance for years to **Insurance Company**	(from GFE #11)	$2,369.00	
1000. Reserves Deposited With Lender			
1001. Initial Deposit for your escrow account	(from GFE #9)	$3,257.28	
1002. Homeowner's insurance 3 months @ **$197.42** per month	$592.26		
1003. Mortgage insurance months @ per month	$0.00		
1004. City property taxes months @ per month	$0.00		
1005. County property taxes 6 months @ **$250.00** per month	$1,500.00		
1006. Annual assessments months @ **$41.67** per month	$0.00		
1007. School property taxes 6 months @ **$291.67** per month	$1,750.02		
1008. MUD taxes months @ per month	$0.00		
1009. Other 0 months @			
1010. Flood Insurance 0 months @			
1011. Aggregate Adjustment	$-585.00		
1100. Title Charges			
1101. Title services and lender's title insurance to **Charter Title Company**	(from GFE #4)	$533.05	
1102. Settlement or closing fee to **Charter Title Company**	$250.00		$250.00
1103. Owner's title insurance to **Center Street Plaza, CAI**	(from GFE #5)	$2,503.00	
1104. Lender's title insurance to **Charter Title Company**	$278.05		
1105. Lender's title policy limit $ **$328,000.00/$278.05** .			
1106. Owner's title policy limit $ **$410,000.00/$2,498.00**			
1107. Agent's portion of the total title insurance premium to	$2,359.64		
1108. Underwriter's portion of the total title insurance premium to	$416.41		
1109. State of Texas Policy Guaranty Fee to **Texas Title Insurance Guaranty Association**	$5.00 (from GFE #4)		$0.00
1110. State of Texas Policy Guaranty Fee to **Texas Title Insurance Guaranty Association**	$5.00 (from GFE #5)		$0.00
1111. to			
1112. E File Fee to	(from GFE #4)		$0.00
1113. TAX CERTIFICATE to			$67.12
1114. to	(from GFE #4)		$0.00
1115. DOCUMENT PREP to ATTORNEY AT LAW			$90.00
1200. Government Recording and Transfer Charges			
1201. Government recording charges	(from GFE #7)	$140.00	
1202. Deed **$24.00** ; Mortgage **$116.00** , Release $0.00 to **Charter Title Company**			
1203. Transfer taxes	(from GFE #8)		
1204. City/County tax/stamps Deed **$0.00** ; Mortgage **$0.00**			
1205. State tax/stamps Deed **$0.00** ; Mortgage **$0.00**			
1300. Additional Settlement Charges			
1301. Required services you can shop for	(from GFE #6)	$530.06	
1302. SURVEY to **Survey Express**	$460.06 (from GFE #6)		$0.00
1303. HOA TRANSFER FEE to **HOA**		$100.00	
1304. PEST INSPECTION to **INSPECTOR**	$70.00 (from GFE #6)		$0.00
1400. Total Settlement Charges (enter on lines 103, Section J and 502, Section K)		$11,468.16	$25,007.12

POC (B) – Paid Outside of Closing by Borrower. POC (S) – Paid Outside of Closing by Seller. POC (L) – Paid Outside of Closing by Lender.

Lines 801-807 show the charges incurred by the buyer in connection with obtaining the new $328,000 loan. Line 901 carries the interest on the $328,000 loan as it is calculated from the date of closing to March's end. This charge brings the loan up to the first day of the next month and simplifies future bookkeeping for the monthly loan payments. At 5% the interest on $328,000 is $38.19 a day, and the buyer is charged $343.73 for 9 days.

FIGURE 17.3 HUD settlement statement (*continued*)

Comparison of Good Faith Estimate (GFE) and HUD-1 Charges		Good Faith Estimate	HUD-1
Charges That Cannot Increase	**HUD-1 Line Number**		
Our origination charge	# 801	$6,134.00	$6,134.00
Your credit or charge (points) for the specific rate chosen	# 802	$-4,450.96	$-4,450.96
Your adjusted origination charges	# 803	$1,683.04	$1,683.04
Transfer taxes	# 1203	$0.00	$0.00

Charges That In Total Cannot Increase More Than 10%		Good Faith Estimate	HUD-1
Government recording charges	# 1201	$178.00	$140.00
Appraisal Fee	# 804	$425.00	$360.00
Flood certification	# 807	$0.00	$9.00
Title services and lender's title insurance	# 1101	$825.00	$533.05
Owner's title insurance	# 1103	$2,250.00	$2,503.00
	Total	$3,678.00	$3,545.05
	Increase between GFE and HUD-1 Charges	$-132.95 or	-3.61%

Charges That Can Change		Good Faith Estimate	HUD-1
Initial deposit for your escrow account	# 1001	$5,000.00	$3,257.28
Daily interest charges	# 901 $38.191781/day	$39.00	$343.73
Homeowner's insurance	# 903	$2,400.00	$2,369.00

Loan Terms

Your initial loan amount is	$328,000.00
Your loan term is	15 years
Your initial interest rate is	4.25%
Your initial monthly amount owed for principal, interest, and any mortgage insurance is	$2,467.47 includes ☒ Principal ☒ Interest ☐ Mortgage Insurance
Can your interest rate rise?	☒ No. ☐ Yes, it can rise to a maximum of 0%. The first change will be on and can change again every after. Every change date, your interest rate can increase or decrease by 0%. Over the life of the loan, your interest rate is guaranteed to never be lower than 0% or higher than 0%.
Even if you make payments on time, can your loan balance rise?	☒ No. ☐ Yes, it can rise to a maximum of $0.00
Even if you make payments on time, can your monthly amount owed for principal, interest, and mortgage insurance rise?	☒ No. ☐ Yes, the first increase can be on and the monthly amount owed can rise to $0.00 The maximum it can ever rise to is $0.00
Does your loan have a prepayment penalty?	☒ No. ☐ Yes, your maximum prepayment penalty is $0.00
Does your loan have a balloon payment?	☒ No. ☐ Yes, you have a balloon payment of $0.00 due in 0 years on
Total monthly amount owed including escrow account payments	☐ You do not have a monthly escrow payment for items, such as property taxes and homeowner's insurance. You must pay these items directly yourself. ☒ You have an additional monthly escrow payment of $681.59 that results in a total initial monthly amount owed of $3,149.06. This includes principal, interest, any mortgage insurance and any items checked below: ☒ Property taxes ☒ Homeowner's Insurance ☐ Flood insurance ☐ ☐ ☐

Note: If you have any questions about the Settlement Charges and Loan Terms listed on this form, please contact your lender.

As a condition for the loan, the lender requires impound accounts for hazard insurance and property taxes. In order to have enough on hand to make the property tax payment on October 1, the lender requires an immediate reserve of $3,257.28 (line 1001). Beginning April 1, one-twelfth of the estimated taxes for next year will be added to the buyer's monthly payment so as to have money in the impound account from which to pay taxes next year. The same concept applies to the hazard insurance. It comes due in 12 months; therefore, the lender requires four months worth of reserves in advance (line 1002).

Lines 1101-1104 show the settlement (closing fee), and the document preparation fee associated with this closing. Title insurance charges of $2,503 to the borrower for the owner's policy (it is charged to the seller and credited to the borrower on page one, so the seller is actually paying for it) and $533.05 to the borrower for the loan policy are itemized on line 1105. Lines 1109 and 1110 show the Texas title insurance guaranty fee. Outside of the closing (POC) or

FIGURE 17.3 HUD settlement statement (*continued*)

File No. 1015000000X

I have carefully reviewed the HUD-1 Settlement Statement and to the best of my knowledge and belief, it is a true and accurate statement of all receipts and disbursements made on my account or by me in this transaction. I further certify that I have received a completed copy of pages 1, 2 and 3 of this HUD-1 Settlement Statement.

JOHN Q. BUYER

JANE SELLER

SETTLEMENT AGENT CERTIFICATION

The HUD-1 Settlement Statement which I have prepared is a true and accurate account of this transaction. I have caused the funds to be disbursed in accordance with this statement.

JOE SELLER

Settlement Agent Date

Warning: It is a crime to knowingly make false statements to the United States on this or any other similar form. Penalties upon conviction can include a fine and imprisonment. For details see: Title 18 U.S. Code Section 1001 and Section 1010.

outside of escrow means a party to the closing has paid someone directly and not through the closing agent.

Government recording fees and conveyance taxes necessary to complete this transaction are itemized on line 1201 and are charged to the buyer and seller as shown. On line 1304 the settlement agent pays the pest inspection company $70 on behalf of the seller. This is another item that is sometimes paid outside of the closing; that is, the seller can write a check directly to the termite company once the inspection has been made. On line 1400, the totals for both the buyer (borrower) and seller are entered. The same totals ($11,468.16 and $25,007.12) are transferred to page 1 or obverse of the settlement statement on lines 103 and 502, respectively.

Note that Figure 17.3 shows both the buyer's side of the transaction and the seller's side. In actual practice, the seller will receive this settlement statement with lines 101 through 303 (Section J) blacked out, and the buyer will receive this statement with lines 401 through 603 (Section K) blacked out.

REAL ESTATE SETTLEMENT PROCEDURES ACT

In response to consumer complaints regarding real estate closing costs and procedures, Congress passed the ***Real Estate Settlement Procedures Act (RESPA)***. The purpose of RESPA, which is administered by the U.S. Department of Housing and Urban Development (HUD), is to regulate and standardize real estate settlement practices when "federally related" first mortgage loans are made on one- to four-family residences, condominiums, and cooperatives. Now, RESPA also applies to closings involving subordinate liens and refinancings. Federally related is defined to include FHA or VA or other government-backed or government-assisted loans; loans from lenders with federally insured deposits; loans that are to be purchased by FNMA, GNMA, FHLMC, or other federally controlled secondary mortgage market institutions; and loans made by lenders who make or invest more than $1 million per year in residential loans. Because the bulk of all home loans now made fall into one of these categories, the impact of this law is far-reaching.

Restrictions

RESPA prohibits kickbacks and fees for services not performed during the closing process. For example, in some regions of the United States prior to this act, it was common practice for attorneys and closing agents to channel title business to certain title companies in return for a fee. This increased settlement costs without adding services. Now a justifiable service must be rendered for each closing fee charge. The act also prohibits the seller from requiring that the buyer purchase title insurance from a particular title company. RESPA underwent major revisions in 1996. You might recall the discussion in Chapter 13 as to how disclosures must now be made for business referrals and origination fees.

The RESPA also contains restrictions on the amount of advance property tax and insurance payments a lender can collect and place in an impound or reserve account. The amount is limited to the property owner's share of taxes and insurance accrued prior to settlement, plus one-sixth of the estimated amount that will come due for these items in the 12-month period beginning at settlement. This requirement assures that the lender has an adequate but not excessive amount of money impounded when taxes and insurance payments fall due. If the amount in the reserve account is not sufficient to pay an item when it comes due, the lender must temporarily use his own funds to make up the difference. Then the lender bills the borrower or increases the monthly reserve payment. If there is a drop in the amount the lender must pay out, then the monthly reserve requirement can be reduced.

Considerable criticism and debate have raged over the topic of reserves. Traditionally, lenders have not been required to pay interest to borrowers on money held as reserves, effectively creating an interest-free loan to themselves. This, in turn, tempted many lenders to require overly adequate reserves. HUD's RESPA sets a reasonable limit on reserve requirements, and some states now require that interest be paid on reserves. Although not always required to do so, some lenders now voluntarily pay interest on reserves.

RESPA underwent extensive changes in 2009 in an attempt to clarify mortgaging procedures and make them simpler for the consumer. Disclosure requirements were broadened and now must match the disclosures given to the consumer under their Good Faith Estimate, discussed later. Fundamentally, it has complicated closing procedures and loan processing. The result has been lengthy delays in closing which will probably shorten somewhat after the new procedures become more common for lenders and title companies.

Benefits

To the typical home buyer who is applying for a first mortgage loan the most obvious benefits of RESPA are that (1) the borrower will receive from the lender a special HUD information booklet explaining RESPA, (2) the borrower will receive a good faith estimate of closing costs from the lender, (3) the lender will use the HUD Uniform Settlement Statement, and (4) the buyer as borrower has the right to inspect the Uniform Settlement Statement one business day before the day of closing.

The primary reason lenders are required to promptly give loan applicants an estimate of closing costs is to allow the loan applicant an opportunity to compare prices for the various services the transaction will require. Additionally, these estimates help the borrower calculate how much the total closing costs will be. Figure 17.4 illustrates a good faith estimate form. Note that it is primarily concerned with settlement services.

RESPA does not require estimates of escrow impounds for property taxes and insurance, although the lender can voluntarily add these items to the form. Note also that RESPA allows lenders to make estimates in terms of ranges. For example, escrow fees may be stated as $150 to $175 to reflect the range of rates being charged by local escrow companies for that service.

HUD SETTLEMENT STATEMENT

The HUD Settlement Statement you saw in Figure 17.3 is required of all federally related real estate lenders. There is also another form, HUD-1A, that is widely used. Because it is actually a lender requirement, it uses the word *borrower* instead of *buyer*. However, if the loan is in connection with a sale, and most are, the buyer and the borrower are one and the same person. This is not true when an owner is refinancing a property, however.

The HUD Settlement Statement has become so widely accepted that it is now used even when it is not required. Closing agents who handle high volumes of closings use computers with special HUD Settlement Statement programs to fill out these forms. Typically, the closing agent types the numbers onto a video screen and a tractor-fed printer with continuous-feed HUD forms takes over the rest of the typing task.

Texas Restrictions on Closing Practices

Texas recently stepped into the arena of actively prohibiting title company kickbacks. Section 8 of RESPA, previously discussed, does not allow referral fees to be paid to anyone who is a closing service provider. They can charge fees only for services performed. A referral fee, by definition, involves only the referral of business and no services performed. The federal government has taken the position that this increases the cost to consumers, and therefore, referral fees are prohibited. Texas has a similar theory. This is particularly important because the state, through the Texas Department of Insurance, sets the insurance rates that consumers pay for title insurance premiums. The Department reviews the income and expenses of title companies annually in order to determine the proper title insurance premium rates, based on risk and losses in the industry (similar to any other type of regulated insurance). If the title company's expenses include paying, for example, for an agent's open houses, dinners, tickets to baseball games, preparing advertising brochures for real estate agents, the insurer ends up paying that through increased title insurance companies. Again, this is an additional cost that consumers bear

FIGURE 17.4 Good faith estimate

OMB Approval No. 2502-0265

Good Faith Estimate (GFE)

Name of Originator	Borrower
Originator Address	Property Address
Originator Phone Number	
Originator Email	Date of GFE

Purpose

This GFE gives you an estimate of your settlement charges and loan terms if you are approved for this loan. For more information, see HUD's *Special Information Booklet* on settlement charges, your *Truth-in-Lending Disclosures,* and other consumer information at www.hud.gov/respa. If you decide you would like to proceed with this loan, contact us.

Shopping for your loan

Only you can shop for the best loan for you. Compare this GFE with other loan offers, so you can find the best loan. Use the shopping chart on page 3 to compare all the offers you receive.

Important dates

1. The interest rate for this GFE is available through ☐. After this time, the interest rate, some of your loan Origination Charges, and the monthly payment shown below can change until you lock your interest rate.
2. This estimate for all other settlement charges is available through ☐.
3. After you lock your interest rate, you must go to settlement within ☐ days (your rate lock period) to receive the locked interest rate.
4. You must lock the interest rate at least ☐ days before settlement.

Summary of your loan

Your initial loan amount is	$
Your loan term is	years
Your initial interest rate is	%
Your initial monthly amount owed for principal, interest, and any mortgage insurance is	$ per month
Can your interest rate rise?	☐ No ☐ Yes, it can rise to a maximum of %. The first change will be in .
Even if you make payments on time, can your loan balance rise?	☐ No ☐ Yes, it can rise to a maximum of $
Even if you make payments on time, can your monthly amount owed for principal, interest, and any mortgage insurance rise?	☐ No ☐ Yes, the first increase can be in and the monthly amount owed can rise to $. The maximum it can ever rise to is $.
Does your loan have a prepayment penalty?	☐ No ☐ Yes, your maximum prepayment penalty is $.
Does your loan have a balloon payment?	☐ No ☐ Yes, you have a balloon payment of $ due in years.

Escrow account information

Some lenders require an escrow account to hold funds for paying property taxes or other property-related charges in addition to your monthly amount owed of $☐.
Do we require you to have an escrow account for your loan?
☐ No, you do not have an escrow account. You must pay these charges directly when due.
☐ Yes, you have an escrow account. It may or may not cover all of these charges. Ask us.

Summary of your settlement charges

A	Your Adjusted Origination Charges *(See page 2.)*	$
B	Your Charges for All Other Settlement Services *(See page 2.)*	$
A+B	Total Estimated Settlement Charges	$

Good Faith Estimate (HUD-GFE) 1

when they pay their premiums. The Texas Department of Insurance has recently published rules that strictly prohibit what titles companies can pay for outside of their normal business activities. Although the Texas Department of Insurance will allow traditional marketing, anything that can be construed

FIGURE 17.4 Good faith estimate (*continued*)

Understanding your estimated settlement charges

Your Adjusted Origination Charges	
1. **Our origination charge** This charge is for getting this loan for you.	
2. **Your credit or charge (points) for the specific interest rate chosen** ☐ The credit or charge for the interest rate of [ ] % is included in "Our origination charge." (See item 1 above.) ☐ You receive a credit of $[ ] for this interest rate of [ ] %. This credit **reduces** your settlement charges. ☐ You pay a charge of $[ ] for this interest rate of [ ] %. This charge (points) **increases** your total settlement charges. The tradeoff table on page 3 shows that you can change your total settlement charges by choosing a different interest rate for this loan.	
A Your Adjusted Origination Charges	$

Some of these charges can change at settlement. See the top of page 3 for more information.

Your Charges for All Other Settlement Services	
3. **Required services that we select** These charges are for services we require to complete your settlement. We will choose the providers of these services. *Service* *Charge*	
4. **Title services and lender's title insurance** This charge includes the services of a title or settlement agent, for example, and title insurance to protect the lender, if required.	
5. **Owner's title insurance** You may purchase an owner's title insurance policy to protect your interest in the property.	
6. **Required services that you can shop for** These charges are for other services that are required to complete your settlement. We can identify providers of these services or you can shop for them yourself. Our estimates for providing these services are below. *Service* *Charge*	
7. **Government recording charges** These charges are for state and local fees to record your loan and title documents.	
8. **Transfer taxes** These charges are for state and local fees on mortgages and home sales.	
9. **Initial deposit for your escrow account** This charge is held in an escrow account to pay future recurring charges on your property and includes ☐ all property taxes, ☐ all insurance, and ☐ other [ ].	
10. **Daily interest charges** This charge is for the daily interest on your loan from the day of your settlement until the first day of the next month or the first day of your normal mortgage payment cycle. This amount is $[ ] per day for [ ] days (if your settlement is [ ]).	
11. **Homeowner's insurance** This charge is for the insurance you must buy for the property to protect from a loss, such as fire. *Policy* *Charge*	
B Your Charges for All Other Settlement Services	$
A + B Total Estimated Settlement Charges	$

Good Faith Estimate (HUD-GFE) 2

as extravagant entertainment—trips such as tickets to baseball games, and expensive dinners—have "nothing to do with the title insurance business" and should therefore not be listed as accepted title insurance expenses. The Texas legislature clarified certain issues by amending the insurance code to allow title companies to engage in certain legal, promotional, and educational

FIGURE 17.4 Good faith estimate (*continued*)

Understanding your estimated settlement charges

Your Adjusted Origination Charges	
1. **Our origination charge** This charge is for getting this loan for you.	
2. **Your credit or charge (points) for the specific interest rate chosen** ☐ The credit or charge for the interest rate of [ ] % is included in "Our origination charge." (See item 1 above.) ☐ You receive a credit of $[ ] for this interest rate of [ ] %. This credit **reduces** your settlement charges. ☐ You pay a charge of $[ ] for this interest rate of [ ] %. This charge (points) **increases** your total settlement charges. The tradeoff table on page 3 shows that you can change your total settlement charges by choosing a different interest rate for this loan.	
A Your Adjusted Origination Charges	$

Some of these charges can change at settlement. See the top of page 3 for more information.

Your Charges for All Other Settlement Services	
3. **Required services that we select** These charges are for services we require to complete your settlement. We will choose the providers of these services. *Service* — *Charge*	
4. **Title services and lender's title insurance** This charge includes the services of a title or settlement agent, for example, and title insurance to protect the lender, if required.	
5. **Owner's title insurance** You may purchase an owner's title insurance policy to protect your interest in the property.	
6. **Required services that you can shop for** These charges are for other services that are required to complete your settlement. We can identify providers of these services or you can shop for them yourself. Our estimates for providing these services are below. *Service* — *Charge*	
7. **Government recording charges** These charges are for state and local fees to record your loan and title documents.	
8. **Transfer taxes** These charges are for state and local fees on mortgages and home sales.	
9. **Initial deposit for your escrow account** This charge is held in an escrow account to pay future recurring charges on your property and includes ☐ all property taxes, ☐ all insurance, and ☐ other [ ].	
10. **Daily interest charges** This charge is for the daily interest on your loan from the day of your settlement until the first day of the next month or the first day of your normal mortgage payment cycle. This amount is $[ ] per day for [ ] days (if your settlement is [ ]).	
11. **Homeowner's insurance** This charge is for the insurance you must buy for the property to protect from a loss, such as fire. *Policy* — *Charge*	
B Your Charges for All Other Settlement Services	$
A + B Total Estimated Settlement Charges	$

Good Faith Estimate (HUD-GFE) 2

activities that are not conditioned on a referral title insurance business. Title companies can also participate in associations of real estate practitioners, attorneys, builders, and developers, and deliver documents or funds to the parties of a closing, so long as they pay a market rate for participating.

REVIEW QUESTIONS

Answers to these questions are found in the Answer Key section at the back of the book.

1. Details that must be handled between the time a purchase contract is signed and the closing typically include
   A. title search.
   B. deed preparation.
   C. loan arrangements.
   D. checking the property taxes.
   E. all of the above.

2. A buyer's walk-through is conducted for the purpose of
   A. appraising the property in order to get a loan on it.
   B. inspecting the property for major structural defects.
   C. meeting the seller and obtaining the keys to the property.
   D. making a final inspection just prior to closing.

3. At which of the following are the buyer and seller more likely to shake hands upon completing the real estate transaction?
   A. Escrow closing
   B. Settlement meeting

4. A settlement meeting may take place in the offices of
   A. the real estate agent.
   B. an attorney.
   C. a title company.
   D. a lender's office.
   E. all of the above.

5. When a real estate settlement is held in escrow,
   A. there is no closing meeting.
   B. the closing process may be conducted by mail.
   C. both A and B.
   D. neither A nor B.

6. The purpose of a settlement statement is to
   A. provide an accounting of all funds involved in the transaction.
   B. identify all parties who receive funds from the transaction.
   C. both A and B.
   D. neither A nor B.

7. Taxes in Texas are customarily prorated on the basis of
   A. 30-day months.
   B. the actual number of days in the year.
   C. a 360-day year.
   D. none of the above.

8. Which of the following may serve as an escrow agent?
   A. A title company
   B. A bank
   C. An independent escrow company
   D. All of the above

9. Barnes sold his home to Hyatt through broker Quinn. The sale is to be settled through escrow. The escrow agent would be selected by
   A. Barnes.
   B. Hyatt.
   C. Quinn.
   D. Mutual agreement between Barnes and Hyatt.

10. In Texas, when title transfers are handled in escrow by a title company, the escrow agent must be
    A. bonded.
    B. licensed.
    C. both A and B.
    D. neither A nor B.

11. In an escrow closing, funds are disbursed
    A. when all escrow papers have been signed.
    B. as soon as the buyer brings his money in.
    C. after necessary recordings take place.
    D. none of the above.

12. In an escrow closing, the escrow agent serves as agent for
    A. the buyer.
    B. the seller.
    C. both A and B.
    D. neither A nor B.

13. One advantage of the escrow closing method is that it can eliminate
    A. personal confrontation between buyer and seller.
    B. the need for an attorney.
    C. both A and B.
    D. neither A nor B.

14. In addition to the closing of sales of real property through standard purchase agreements, escrows can be used when a
    A. property is being refinanced.
    B. mortgage loan is being paid off.
    C. property is being sold under an installment contract.
    D. all of the above.

15. RESPA
    A. prohibits the seller from requiring that the buyer purchase title insurance from a particular title company.
    B. requires that each settlement fee charged be for a justifiable service rendered.
    C. both A and B.
    D. neither A nor B.

16. When a home is sold and a new loan by an institutional lender is required to complete the transaction, the typical time between purchase contract signing and settlement will most likely be
    A. 0-29 days.
    B. 30-60 days.
    C. 61-120 days.
    D. over 120 days.

17. Which of the following statements is true?
    A. The buyer always pays for the day of closing in Texas.
    B. Local law prohibits negotiation of the proration date.
    C. Special assessments are part of the tax proration in Texas.
    D. In Texas, the seller usually pays for the day of closing.

18. Prorations of items in a real estate closing are made usually as of the date of
    A. signing of the sales contract.
    B. title transfer.
    C. buyers' walk-through.
    D. the mortgage payment.

19. In a typical closing, insurance prorations will usually be
    A. a credit to the seller and an expense to the buyer.
    B. a credit to the buyer and an expense to the seller.
    C. a credit to the seller and a credit to the buyer.
    D. an expense to the buyer and an expense to the seller.

20. Under the provisions of RESPA,
    A. the buyer must be given an estimate of closing charges and costs in advance of closing.
    B. payments outside of escrow are prohibited.
    C. both A and B.
    D. neither A nor B.

Chapter 18

KEY TERMS

Escalation clause: provision in a lease for upward and downward rent adjustments

Ground rent: rent paid to occupy a plot of land

Lessee: the tenant

Lessor: the landlord

Option clause: the right at some future time to purchase or lease a property at a predetermined price

Quiet enjoyment: the right of possession and use of property without undue disturbance by others

Reversionary interest: the right to retake possession of a leased property at some future time

Sublease: a lease that is given by a lessee

Sublessee: a lessee who rents from another lessee

Sublessor: a lessee who rents to another lessee

Real Estate Leases

IN THIS CHAPTER

In this chapter you will look at leases from the standpoint of the tenant, owner, and property manager. First, we will cover some of the important terminology used and explain a sample lease. Landlord-tenant laws, Statute of Frauds, setting rents, ground leases, lease termination, fair housing laws, and rent controls are also covered in this chapter. Specific terminology and concepts covered include assignment and subletting.

Earlier chapters of this book discussed leases as estates in land (Chapter 4) and as a means of financing (Chapter 15). This chapter looks at leases from the standpoint of the tenant, the property owner, and the property manager. (During your lifetime you may be in any one of these roles, and perhaps all three.) Our discussion begins with some important terminology. Then comes a sample lease form with explanation; information on locating, qualifying, and keeping tenants; and finally, some information on job opportunities available in professional property management. Emphasis is on residential property, although a number of key points regarding commercial property leases are also included.

THE LEASEHOLD ESTATE

A lease conveys to the ***lessee*** (tenant) the right to possess and use another's property for a period of time. During this time, the ***lessor*** (the landlord or fee owner) possesses a *reversion* that entitles the landlord to retake possession at the end of the lease period. This is also called a *reversionary right* or ***reversionary interest.***

The tenant's right to occupy land is called a leasehold estate. There are four categories of leasehold estates: estate for years, periodic estate, estate at will, and tenancy at sufferance. An *estate for years* must have a specific starting time and a specific ending time. It can be for any length of time, and it does not automatically renew itself. A *periodic estate* has an original lease period of fixed length that continually renews itself for like periods of time until the tenant or landlord acts to terminate it. A month-to-month lease is an example. In an *estate at will* all the normal landlord-tenant rights and duties exist except that the estate can be terminated by either party at any time. A *tenancy at sufferance* occurs when a tenant stays beyond the legal tenancy without the consent of the landlord. The tenant is commonly called a *holdover tenant* and no advance notice is required for eviction. The holdover tenant differs from a trespasser in that his original entry onto the property was legal.

CREATING A VALID LEASE

A lease is both a conveyance and a contract. As a conveyance it transfers or conveys rights of possession to the tenant in the form of a leasehold estate. As a contract it establishes legally enforceable provisions for the payment of rent and any other obligations the landlord and tenant have to each other.

For a valid lease to exist, it must meet the usual requirements of a contract as described in Chapter 9. That is to say, the parties involved must be legally competent, and there must be mutual agreement, lawful objective, and sufficient consideration. The main elements of a lease are (1) the names of the lessee and lessor, (2) a description of the premises, (3) an agreement to convey (let) the premises by the lessor and to accept possession by the lessee, (4) provisions for the payment of rent, (5) the starting date and duration of the lease, and (6) signatures of the parties to the lease.

Statute of Frauds

The Statute of Frauds in Texas provides that a lease of real estate for a term that cannot be performed within one year must be in writing. A lease of one year or less need not be in writing to be enforceable.

PUTTING IT TO WORK

A lease for one year or less or a month-to-month lease could be oral and still be valid, but as a matter of good business practice, all leases should be written and signed. This gives all parties a written reminder of their obligations under the lease and reduces chances for dispute. A real estate practitioner should remember, however, that there are no promulgated forms for leases. Except for the TREC temporary lease forms, the agent should not use a lease form without seeking legal assistance.

THE LEASE DOCUMENT

Figure 18.1 illustrates a lease document that contains provisions typically found in a residential lease. These provisions are presented in simplified language to help you more easily grasp the rights and responsibilities created by a lease.

FIGURE 18.1 Lease document

LEASE

This lease agreement is entered into the 10th day of April, 200x between John and Sally Landlord **[1]** *(hereinafter called the Lessor) and Gary and Barbara Tenant* **[2]** *(hereinafter called the Lessee). The Lessor hereby leases to the Lessee* **[3]** *and the Lessee hereby leases from the Lessor the premises known as Apartment 24, 1234 Maple St., City, State* **[4]** *for the term of one* **[5]** *year beginning 12:00 noon on April 15, 200x and ending 12:00 noon on April 15, 200x unless sooner terminated as herein set forth.*

The rent for the term of this lease is $ 6,000.00 **[6]** *payable in equal monthly installments of $ 500.00* **[7]** *on the 15th day of each month beginning on April 15, 200x . Receipt of the first monthly installment and $ 500.00* **[8]** *as a security, damage, and clean-up deposit is hereby acknowledged. It is furthermore agreed that:*

[9] *The use of the premises shall be as a residential dwelling for the above named Lessee only.*

[10] *The Lessee may not assign this lease or sublet any portion of the premises without written permission from the Lessor.*

[11] *The Lessee agrees to abide by the house rules as posted. A current copy is attached to this lease.*

[12] *The Lessor shall furnish water, sewer, and heat as part of the rent. Electricity and telephone shall be paid for by the Lessee.*

[13] *The Lessor agrees to keep the premises structure maintained and in habitable condition.*

[14] *The Lessee agrees to maintain the interior of said premises and at the termination of this lease to return said premises to the Lessor in as good condition as it is now except for ordinary wear and tear.*

[15] *The Lessee shall not make any alterations or improvements to the premises without the Lessor's prior written consent. Any alterations or improvements become the property of the Lessor at the end of this lease.*

[16] *If the premises are not ready for occupancy on the date herein provided, the Lessee may cancel this agreement and the Lessor shall return in full all money paid by the Lessee.*

[17] *If the Lessee defaults on this lease agreement, the Lessor may give the Lessee three days notice of intention to terminate the lease. At the end of those three days the lease shall terminate and the Lessee shall vacate and surrender the premises to the Lessor.*

[18] *If the Lessee holds over after the expiration of this lease without the Lessor's consent, the tenancy shall be month to month at twice the monthly rate indicated herein.*

[19] *If the premises are destroyed or rendered uninhabitable by fire or other cause, this lease shall terminate as of the date of the casualty.*

[20] *The Lessor shall have access to the premises for the purpose of inspecting for damage, making repairs, and showing to prospective tenants or buyers.*

[21] John Landlord *Lessor*	**[22]** Gary Tenant *Lessee*
Sally Landlord *Lessor*	Barbara Tenant *Lessee*

Source: © 2012 Cengage Learning

Conveyance

The first paragraph is the conveyance portion of the lease. At **[1]** and **[2]** the lessor and lessee are identified. At **[3]**, the lessor conveys to the lessee and the lessee accepts the property. A description of the property follows at **[4]**, and the *term* of the conveyance at **[5]**. The property must be described so that there is no question as to the extent of the premises the lessee is renting. If the lease illustrated here were a month-to-month lease instead, the term of the lease would be changed to read, "commencing April 15, 20xx and continuing on a month-to-month basis until terminated by either the lessee or the lessor." During the tenancy the lessee is entitled to ***quiet enjoyment*** of the property. This means uninterrupted use of the property without interference from the owner, lessor, or other third party.

A month-to-month rental is the most flexible arrangement. It allows the owner to recover possession of the property on one-month notice and the tenant to leave on one-month notice with no further obligation to the owner. In rental agreements for longer periods of time, each party gives up some flexibility to gain commitment from the other. Under a one-year lease, a tenant has the property committed to him for a year. This also means that the tenant is committed to paying rent for a full year, even though the tenant may want to move out before the year is over. Similarly, the owner has the tenant's commitment to pay rent for a year, but loses the flexibility of being able to regain possession of the property until the year is over.

The balance of the lease document is concerned with contract aspects of the lease. At number **[6]**, the amount of rent that the lessee will pay for the use of the property is set forth. In a lease for years it is the usual practice to state the total rent for the entire lease period. This is the total number of dollars the lessee is obligated to pay to the lessor. If the lessee wants to leave the premises before the lease period expires, there is still liability for the full amount of the contract. The method of payment of the obligation is shown at number **[7]**. Unless the contract calls for rent to be paid in advance, under common law it is not due until the end of the rental period. At number **[8]**, the lessor has taken a deposit in the form of the first monthly installment and acknowledges receipt of it. The lessor has also taken additional money as security against the possibility of uncollected rent or damage to the premises and for clean-up expenses. (The tenant is supposed to leave the premises clean.) The deposit is refunded, less legitimate charges, when the tenant leaves.

Items **[9]** through **[20]** summarize commonly found lease clauses. At **[9]** and **[10]**, the lessor wants to maintain control over the use and occupancy of the premises. Without this the lessor might find the premises used for an entirely different purpose by people to whom the lessor did not rent. At **[11]**, the tenant agrees to abide by the house rules. These normally cover such things as use of laundry and trash facilities, swimming pool rules, noise rules, etc. Number **[12]** states the responsibility of the lessee and lessor with regard to the payment of utilities.

The strict legal interpretation of a lease as a conveyance means the lessee is responsible for upkeep and repairs during the tenancy unless the lessor promises to do so in the lease contract. The paragraph at number [13] is that promise. Note however that with regard to residential properties, Texas courts and the Texas legislature now take the position that the landlord is obligated to keep a residential property repaired and habitable even if this is not specifically stated in the contract. Commercial property still goes by the traditional lease interpretation.

Number [14] is the lessee's promise to maintain the interior of the dwelling. If the lessee damages the property, that individual is to repair it. Normal wear and tear are considered to be part of the rent. At paragraph [15], the lessor protects against unauthorized alterations and improvements and then goes on to point out that anything the tenant affixes to the building becomes realty. As realty it remains a part of the building when the tenant leaves.

Paragraphs [16] through [19] deal with the rights of both parties if the premises are not ready for occupancy, if the lessee defaults after moving in, if the lessee holds over, or if the premises are destroyed. The lessor also retains the right (paragraph [20]) to enter the leased premises from time to time for business purposes.

Finally, at [21] and [22], the lessor and lessee sign. It is not necessary to have these signatures notarized. That is done only if the lease is to be recorded. The purpose of recording is to give constructive notice that the lessee has an estate in the property. Recording is usually done only when the lessee's rights are not apparent from inspection of the property for actual notice, where the lease has an option to purchase, or is to run many years. From the property owner's standpoint, the lease is an encumbrance on the property. If the owner should subsequently sell the property or mortgage it, the lessee's tenancy remains undisturbed. The buyer or lender must accept the property subject to the lease.

If one of the lessors dies, the lease is still binding on the remaining lessor(s) and upon the estate of the deceased lessor. Similarly, if one of the lessees dies, the lease is still binding on the remaining lessee(s) and upon the estate of the deceased lessee. This is based on common law doctrine that applies to contracts in general. The lessee and lessor can, however, agree to do otherwise. The lessee could ask the lessor to *waive* (give up) the right to hold the lessee's estate to the lease in the event of the lessee's death. For example, an elderly tenant about to sign a lease might want to add wording to the lease whereby the tenant's death would allow the estate to terminate the lease early.

LANDLORD-TENANT LAWS

Traditionally, a lease was enforceable in court based solely on what it contained. However, with regard to residential rental property, the trend today is for the legislature to establish special landlord-tenant laws. The intent is to strike a reasonable balance between the responsibilities of landlords to tenants and vice versa. Typically, these laws limit the amount of security deposit a landlord can require, tell the tenant how many days' notice need to be given before vacating a periodic tenancy, and require the landlord to deliver possession on the date agreed. The landlord must maintain the premises in a fit condition for living, and the tenant is to keep the unit clean and not damage it. The tenant is to obey the house rules and the landlord must give advance notice before entering an apartment except in legitimate emergencies. Additionally the laws set forth such things as the procedure for accounting for any deposit money not returned, the right of the tenant to make needed repairs and bill the landlord, the right of the landlord to file court actions for unpaid rent, and the proper procedure for evicting a tenant.

A number of Texas statutes have been passed to provide protection to the tenant in residential leasehold situations. These laws, very generally summarized, specify:

1. **Notice must be provided before a tenancy may be terminated.** This is generally 30 days on a month-to-month tenancy. This does not apply to eviction proceedings, but rather to termination of tenancies.
2. **Interruption and exclusion by the landlord of the tenant's right to the premises.** This basically provides that the landlord may not exclude the tenant from the premises, but may only change the door locks to the tenant's premises, after proper notice is given. If the landlord does change the door locks to the tenant's premises, a written notice must be posted on the tenant's door indicating that the tenant may pick up the new key to the premises at any time upon request, 24 hours a day. The tenant can also exercise a right to re-enter, under certain circumstances, by filing a sworn affidavit. In a commercial tenancy, the landlord has the right to demand rent prior to providing the key.
3. **Landlord's lien for rent.** The exemptions provided under this statute are very extensive and ultimately allow very little of the furniture and household goods as those on which the landlord may obtain a lien as security for his rent.
4. **Security deposits.** There are very strict provisions now for the landlord's retaining security deposits. Basically, the landlord must return the security deposit within 30 days (60 days for a commercial lease) or give the tenant an explanation of why the security deposit was not returned and what the funds were used to repair. There are some strict provisions for the landlord's failure to comply with the statute.
5. **Habitable premises.** The landlord must provide habitable premises and may not evict a tenant for the purposes of retaliation for tenant's notice to repair the premises. The term habitable is determined by the facts in any given situation and varies from case to case.
6. **Installation of security devices.** The landlord has an obligation, upon request of tenant, to install security devices. The law defines security devices as window latches, deadbolt locks, pen locks, and night latches. The initial installation of these devices must be at the landlord's expense. Any installation of additional security devices will be at the tenant's expense. There is also a time limit for the landlord's responses for repairs to the security devices.

7. **Disclosure of ownership and management of dwelling unit.** The landlord has the duty to disclose to the tenant the name and address of the owner of the dwelling unit in the manner specified in the statute. The same is true of the name and address of any property management company that is currently managing the dwelling unit.
8. **Smoke detectors in dwelling units.** At least one smoke detector must be installed in dwelling units by the landlord outside of each separate bedroom in the immediate vicinity of the bedroom, with certain specified exceptions. If the tenant is deaf, different types of smoke alarms are required.
9. **Occupying limits.** There is now a maximum limit of three adults per bedroom.
10. **Duty to mitigate.** Texas imposes on commercial and residential landlords a duty to mitigate damages if a tenant abandons leased premises in violation of a lease. This requires a landlord to use diligent efforts to lease the premises to another tenant, in order to lower his damages. A provision of a commercial or residential lease that purports to have the tenant waive this right is void.
11. **Family Violence.** A tenant has the right to terminate his obligations under a lease if the tenant provides the landlord a copy of the court order protecting the tenant pursuant to specific provisions of the Texas Family Code.
12. **Service Member.** A tenant who is a service member, or the dependent of a service member, has the right to terminate her obligations under a lease by providing the landlord written notice of the termination and a copy of the government document providing evidence of the tenant's entry into military service.

Note that these statutes apply to *all* landlord-tenant residential situations. Even when the TREC-promulgated "temporary" leases are used, these rights (except for the security device requirements) exist, *regardless of the term of the tenancy.*

Fewer statutory provisions apply to commercial landlord and tenant relationships. Texas does recognize, however, an *implied warranty of suitability* for commercial tenants, which means that the landlord must provide suitable premises for the tenant's intended business. In most cases, this involves health and safety matters such as regarding doctors' offices and clinics. The law generally provides that if the premises are not kept to a suitable standard (e.g., clean conditions and adequate maintenance), courts may allow an offset of rents or a forgiveness of rental payments all together.

The Texas Supreme Court, too, recently addressed a major change in landlord and tenant relationships. Texas law now requires a landlord to mitigate (lessen) his damages when a tenant defaults and leaves the premises. This means that when a tenant is in default, the landlord must use some effort to relet the premises in an effort to lower his damages, rather than just suing the tenant for the remainder of the rents due under the lease. In response to the Supreme Court's holding, the Texas Legislature passed a new statute (no.10 above) that created a statutory duty for the landlord to mitigate damages in both residential and commercial premises. Any provision of a commercial or residential lease that purports to have a tenant waive his right or exempt a landlord from his duty to mitigate damages is void under the terms of the statute. This basically reversed 150 years of Texas law (which used to uphold the lease as written). The law is very broadly written, so certainly there will be litigation on this subject in the future.

METHODS FOR SETTING RENTS

There are several methods for setting rents. The first is the *fixed rental fee,* also called a *flat rent* or **gross lease.** The tenant agrees to pay a specified amount of money for the use of the premises. A tenant paying $600 per month on a month-to-month apartment lease or a dentist paying $13,000 per year for office space are both examples of fixed rents. A second method of setting rents is called the **step-up** or **graduated rental.** For example, a five-year office lease might call for monthly rents of $1.00 per square foot of floor space the first year, $1.25 the second year, $1.75 the third year, $2.00 the fourth year, and $2.10 the fifth. The first year's rental often serves as a "teaser" rate to attract tenants. The tenant can better absorb costs of moving and initial occupancy.

Because of inflation, most lessors (particularly in office buildings) add an ***escalation clause.*** This allows the landlord to pass along to the tenant increases in uncontrollable costs, such as property taxes, utility charges, or insurance costs.

Another variation is to have the tenant pay for all property taxes, insurance, repairs, utilities, etc., in addition to the base rent. This arrangement is called a **net lease** (because the tenant pays all expenses, the rent is *net* to the landlord), and it is commonly used when an entire building is being leased.

Another system for setting rents is the **percentage rents** wherein the owner receives a percentage of the tenant's gross receipts as rent. For example, a farmer who leases land may give the landowner 20% of the value of the crop when it is sold. The monthly rent for a small hardware store might be $600 plus 6% of gross sales above $10,000. A supermarket may pay $7,500 plus 1.5% of gross above $50,000 per month. By setting rents this way, the tenant shares some of the business risk with the property owner. Also, there is a built-in inflation hedge to the extent that inflation causes the tenant's receipts to increase.

OPTION CLAUSES

Option clauses give the tenant the right at some future time to lease the property at a predetermined price. This gives a tenant flexibility. For example, suppose that a prospective tenant is starting a new business and is not certain how successful it will be. Thus, in looking for space to rent, the prospective tenant will want a lease that allows an "out" if the new venture does not succeed but will permit staying if the venture is successful. The solution is a lease with options. The landlord could offer a one-year lease, plus an option to stay for two more years at a higher rent plus a second option for an additional five years at a still higher rent. If the venture is not successful, the tenant is obligated for only one year. But if successful, he has the option of staying two more years, and if still successful, for five years after that.

Another option possibility offers the tenant a lease that also contains an option to buy the property for a fixed period of time at a preset price. This is called a *lease with option to buy* and is discussed in Chapter 10.

ASSIGNMENT AND SUBLETTING

In Texas, the tenant may not assign the lease or sublet the premises without the landlord's consent unless provision was made in the lease contract. An **assignment** is the total transfer of the tenant's rights to another person. These parties are referred to as the **assignor** and the **assignee** respectively. The assignee acquires all the right, title, and interest of the assignor, no more and no less. However, the assignor remains liable for the performance of the contract unless release is given by the landlord. To *sublet* means to transfer only a portion of the rights held under a lease. The ***sublease*** thereby created may be for a portion of the premises or for part of the lease term. The party acquiring those rights is called the ***sublessee.*** The original lessee is the ***sublessor*** with respect to the sublessee. The sublessee pays rent to the sublessor who in turn remains liable to the landlord for rent on the entire premises.

GROUND LEASE

A **ground lease** is a lease of land alone. The lessor is the fee simple owner of the land and conveys to the lessee an estate for years, typically lasting from 25 to 99 years. The lessee pays for and owns the improvements. Thus a ground lease separates the ownership of land from the ownership of buildings on that land. The lease rent, called the ***ground rent,*** is on a net lease basis. As a hedge against inflation, the rent is usually increased every 5 to 10 years. This is done either by a graduated lease or by requiring a reappraisal of the land and then charging a new rent based on that valuation.

A lease need not be restricted to the use of the earth's surface. In Chapter 3 it was shown that land extends from the center of the earth skyward. Consequently, it is possible for one person to own the mineral rights, another the surface rights, and a third the air rights. This can also be done with leases. A landowner can lease to an oil company the right to explore and extract minerals, oil, and gas below the land and, at the same time, lease the surface rights to a farmer. In Chicago and New York City, railroads have leased surface and air rights above their downtown tracks for the purpose of constructing office buildings.

CONTRACT RENT, ECONOMIC RENT

The amount specified in the lease is the rent that the tenant must pay the landlord for the use of the premises and is called the **contract rent.** The rent that the same property can command in the competitive open market is called the **economic rent.** When a lease contract is negotiated, the contract rent and economic rent are nearly always the same. However, as time passes the market value of the right to use the premises may increase while the contract rent stays the same. When this occurs the lease itself becomes valuable. That value is determined by the difference between the contract rent and the economic rent, and how long the lease has to run. An example would be a five-year lease with three years left at a contract rent of $1,200 per month where the current rental value of the premises is now $1,500 per month. If the lease is assignable, the fact that it offers a $300 per month savings for three years makes it valuable. Similarly, an oil lease obtained for $50 per acre before oil was discovered might be worth millions after its discovery. Conversely, when contract rent exceeds economic rent, the lease takes on a negative value.

LEASE TERMINATION

Most leases terminate because of the expiration of the term of the lease. The tenant has received the use of the premises and the landlord has received rent in return. However, a lease can be terminated if the landlord and the tenant mutually agree. The tenant surrenders the premises and the landlord releases him from the contract. Under certain conditions, destruction of the premises is cause for lease termination. Abandonment of the premises by the tenant can be grounds for lease termination provided the tenant's intention to do so is clear.

If either the tenant or the landlord fails to live up to the lease contract, termination can occur. Where the tenant is at fault, the landlord can evict him and recover possession of the premises. If the premises are unfit for occupancy, the tenant can claim constructive eviction as the reason for leaving. The government, under its right of eminent domain, can also terminate a lease, but must provide just compensation. An example of this would be construction of a new highway that requires the demolition of a building rented to tenants. The property owner and the tenants would both be entitled to compensation.

A mortgage foreclosure can also bring about lease termination. It all depends on priority. If the mortgage was recorded before the lease was signed, then foreclosure of the mortgage also forecloses the lease. If the lease was recorded first, then the lease still stands. Because a lease can cloud a lender's title, wording is sometimes inserted in leases that makes them subordinate to any future financing of the property. This is a highly technical, but nonetheless very significant, matter for long-term shopping center, office building, and industrial leases.

Eviction

Under Texas law, the Forcible Entry and Detainer statutes provide for eviction proceedings. "Forcible Entry and Detainer" is a legal term referring to a tenant who takes possession of the premises without the consent of the landlord and then refuses to give up possession after demand is made by the landlord. According to the statutes, the landlord must give the tenant a minimum of three days' written notice to vacate the premises before filing an action for Forcible Entry and Detainer. A person cannot be guilty of Forcible Entry and Detainer until he has been so adjudged by the Justice of the Peace Court in the precinct where the real estate is situated. The lawsuit must be heard within ten days after the filing. As in all other legal proceedings, there are additional procedural laws pertaining to the Forcible Entry and Detainer statutes, which could provide for quite a lengthy tenancy while eviction proceedings are in process. If the landlord doesn't provide habitable premises, or there is a situation where the premises cannot be used (road construction that prohibits entry or refusing to repair the premises) it can be deemed to be a **constructive eviction** and the tenant can abandon the premises and not have to pay rent. This situation is a rare occurrence.

TEXAS ASSOCIATION OF REALTORS®

RESIDENTIAL LEASE

1. **PARTIES:** The parties to this lease are:

   the owner of the Property, Landlord,: ______________________________
   ______________________________; and

   Tenant(s): ______________________________
   ______________________________.

2. **PROPERTY:** Landlord leases to Tenant the following real property:

   Address: ______________________________
   legally described as: ______________________________
   ____
   in ______________ County, Texas, together with the following non-real-property items: ______________________________
   ______________________________.
   The real property and the non-real-property are collectively called the "Property".

3. **TERM:**

   A. Primary Term: The primary term of this lease begins and ends as follows:

   Commencement Date: ______________ Expiration Date: ______________.

   B. Delay of Occupancy: Tenant must occupy the Property within 5 days after the Commencement Date. If Tenant is unable to occupy the Property by the 5th day after the Commencement Date because of construction on the Property or a prior tenant's holding over of the Property, Tenant may terminate this lease by giving written notice to Landlord before the Property becomes available to be occupied by Tenant, and Landlord will refund to Tenant the security deposit and any rent paid. Landlord will abate rent on a daily basis for a delay caused by construction or a prior tenant's holding over. This paragraph does not apply to any delay in occupancy caused by cleaning, repairs, or make-ready items.

4. **AUTOMATIC RENEWAL AND NOTICE OF TERMINATION:**

   A. This lease automatically renews on a month-to-month basis unless Landlord or Tenant provides the other party written notice of termination not less than: *(Check only one box.)*
   ❑ (1) 30 days before the Expiration Date.
   ❑ (2) ______________ days before the Expiration Date.

   B. If this lease automatically renews on a month-to-month basis, it will continue to renew on a month-to-month basis until either party provides written notice of termination to the other party and the notice of termination will be effective: *(Check only one box.)*
   ❑ (1) on the last day of the month following the month in which the notice is given. Landlord is not obligated to prorate rent even if Tenant surrenders the Property before the termination date.
   ❑ (2) on the date designated in the notice but not sooner than 30 days after the notice is given and, if necessary, rent will be prorated on a daily basis.

Residential Lease concerning: ____

C. Oral notice of termination is not sufficient under any circumstances. Time is of the essence for providing notice of termination (strict compliance with dates by which notice must be provided is required). The date on which rent is due does not apply to the requirement for providing written notice of termination. If a box is not checked under Paragraph 4A, Paragraph 4A(1) will apply. If a box is not checked under Paragraph 4B, Paragraph 4B(1) will apply.

5. RENT:

A. Monthly Rent: Tenant will pay Landlord monthly rent in the amount of $__________ for each full month during this lease. The first full month's rent is due and payable not later than ________________. Thereafter, Tenant will pay the monthly rent so that Landlord receives the monthly rent on or before:

❑ (1) the first day of each month during this lease.

❑ (2) ____.

Weekends, holidays, and mail delays do not excuse Tenant's obligation to timely pay rent.

B. Prorated Rent: On or before ________________ Tenant will pay Landlord $________ as prorated rent from the Commencement Date through the last day of the month in which this lease begins.

C. Place of Payment: Unless this lease provides otherwise, Tenant will remit all amounts due to Landlord under this lease to the following person or entity at the place stated and make all payments payable to the named person or entity. Landlord may later designate, in writing, another person or place to which Tenant must remit amounts due under this lease.

Name: ____

Address: ____

____

Notice: Place the Property address and Tenant's name on all payments.

D. Method of Payment:

(1) Tenant must pay all rent timely and without demand, deduction, or offset, except as permitted by law or this lease.

(2) Time is of the essence for the payment of rent (strict compliance with rental due dates is required).

(3) Unless the parties agree otherwise, Tenant may not pay rent in cash and will pay all rent by check, cashier's check, money order, or other means acceptable to Landlord.

(4) Landlord ❑ requires ❑ does not require Tenant(s) to pay monthly rents by one payment.

(5) If Tenant fails to timely pay any amounts due under this lease or if any check of Tenant is not honored by the institution on which it was drawn, Landlord may require Tenant to pay such amount and any subsequent amounts under this lease in certified funds. This paragraph does not limit Landlord from seeking other remedies under this lease for Tenant's failure to make timely payments with good funds.

E. Rent Increases: There will be no rent increases through the primary term. Landlord may increase the rent that will be paid during any month-to-month renewal period by providing at least 30 days written notice to Tenant.

6. LATE CHARGES:

A. If Landlord does not actually receive a rent payment in the full amount at the designated place of payment by the ________ day of each month at 11:59pm, Tenant will pay Landlord for each late payment:

(1) an initial late charge equal to *(check one box only)*: ❑ (a) $_______; or ❑ (b)________% of one month's rent; **and**

(2) additional late charges of $_______ per day thereafter until rent and late charges are paid in full. Additional late charges for any one payment may not exceed more than 30 days.

Notice: §92.019, Property Code prohibits assessing a late fee until rent has remained unpaid for at least one full day after the date on which the rent is due.

Residential Lease concerning: ____________________

B. For the purposes of paying rent and any late charges, the mailbox is not the agent for receipt for Landlord (the postmark date is not the date Landlord receives the payment). The parties agree that the late charge is based on a reasonable estimate of uncertain damages to the Landlord that are incapable of precise calculation and result from late payment of rent. Landlord's acceptance of a late charge does not waive Landlord's right to exercise remedies under Paragraph 27.

7. **RETURNED PAYMENT:** Tenant will pay Landlord $________ for each payment Tenant tenders to Landlord which is returned or not honored by the institution on which it is drawn for any reason, plus any late charges until Landlord receives payment. Tenant must make any returned payment good by paying such amount(s) plus any associated charges in certified funds.

8. **APPLICATION OF FUNDS:** Regardless of any notation on a payment, Landlord may apply funds received from Tenant first to any non-rent obligations of Tenant, including but not limited to, late charges, returned payment charges, repairs, brokerage fees, periodic utilities, pet charges, and then to rent.

9. **PETS:**

A. Unless the parties agree otherwise in writing, Tenant may not permit, even temporarily, any pet on the Property (including but not limited to any mammal, reptile, bird, fish, rodent, or insect).

B. If Tenant violates this Paragraph 9 or any agreement to keep a pet on the Property, Landlord may take all or any of the following action:
(1) declare Tenant to be in default of this lease and exercise Landlord's remedies under Paragraph 27;
(2) charge Tenant, as additional rent, an initial amount of $________ and $_______ per day thereafter per pet for each day Tenant violates the pet restrictions;
(3) remove or cause to be removed any unauthorized pet and deliver it to appropriate local authorities by providing at least 24-hour written notice to Tenant of Landlord's intention to remove the unauthorized pet; and
(4) charge to Tenant the Landlord's cost to:
(a) remove any unauthorized pet;
(b) exterminate the Property for fleas and other insects;
(c) clean and deodorize the Property's carpets and drapes; and
(d) repair any damage to the Property caused by the unauthorized pet.

C. When taking any action under Paragraph 9B Landlord will not be liable for any harm, injury, death, or sickness to any pet.

10. **SECURITY DEPOSIT:**

A. Security Deposit: On or before execution of this lease, Tenant will pay a security deposit to Landlord in the amount of $______________. "Security deposit" has the meaning assigned to that term in §92.102, Property Code.

B. Interest: No interest or income will be paid to Tenant on the security deposit. Landlord may place the security deposit in an interest-bearing or income-producing account and any interest or income earned will be paid to Landlord or Landlord's representative.

C. Refund: Tenant must give Landlord at least thirty (30) days written notice of surrender before Landlord is obligated to refund or account for the security deposit.

Notices about Security Deposits:
(1) §92.108, Property Code provides that a tenant may not withhold payment of any portion of the last month's rent on grounds that the security deposit is security for unpaid rent.

Residential Lease concerning: ______________________________

(2) Bad faith violations of §92.108 may subject a tenant to liability up to 3 times the rent wrongfully withheld and the landlord's reasonable attorney's fees.

(3) The Property Code does not obligate a landlord to return or account for the security deposit until the tenant surrenders the Property and gives the landlord a written statement of the tenant's forwarding address, after which the landlord has 30 days in which to account.

(4) "Surrender" is defined in Paragraph 16 of this lease.

(5) One may view the Texas Property Code at the Texas Legislature's website which, as of the date shown in the lower left-hand corner of this form, is http://www.statutes.legis.state.tx.us/.

D. Deductions:

(1) Landlord may deduct reasonable charges from the security deposit for:

(a) damages to the Property, excluding normal wear and tear, and all reasonable costs associated to repair the Property;
(b) costs for which Tenant is responsible to clean, deodorize, exterminate, and maintain the Property;
(c) unpaid or accelerated rent;
(d) unpaid late charges;
(e) unpaid utilities and utility expenses Landlord incurs to maintain utilities to the Property as required by this Lease;
(f) unpaid pet charges;
(g) replacing unreturned keys, garage door openers, security devices, or other components;
(h) the removal of unauthorized locks or fixtures installed by Tenant;
(i) Landlord's cost to access the Property if made inaccessible by Tenant;
(j) missing or burned-out light bulbs and fluorescent tubes (at the same location and of the same type and quality that are in the Property on the Commencement Date);
(k) packing, removing, and storing abandoned property;
(l) removing abandoned or illegally parked vehicles;
(m) costs of reletting (as defined in Paragraph 27), if Tenant is in default;
(n) attorney's fees, costs of court, costs of service, and other reasonable costs incurred in any legal proceeding against Tenant;
(o) mailing costs associated with sending notices to Tenant for any violations of this lease;
(p) any other unpaid charges or fees or other items for which Tenant is responsible under this lease; and
(q) cost to restore walls, flooring, landscaping or any alteration to the Property not approved in writing by Landlord.

(2) If deductions exceed the security deposit, Tenant will pay to Landlord the excess within 10 days after Landlord makes written demand.

11. UTILITIES:

A. Tenant will pay all connection fees, service fees, usage fees, and all other costs and fees for all utilities to the Property (for example, electricity, gas, water, wastewater, garbage, telephone, alarm monitoring systems, cable, and Internet connections) except the following which Landlord will pay: ______________
____
____.
Unless otherwise agreed, amounts under this paragraph are payable directly to the service providers.

B. Unless provided by Landlord, Tenant must, at a minimum, keep the following utilities on, if available, at all times this lease is in effect: gas; electricity; water; wastewater; and garbage services.

Notice: Before signing this lease, Tenant should determine if all necessary utilities are available to the Property and are adequate for Tenant's use.

Residential Lease concerning: ______________________________

12. USE AND OCCUPANCY:

A. Occupants: Tenant may use the Property as a private residence only. The only persons Tenant may permit to reside on the Property during the term of this lease are (*include names and ages of all occupants*): ______________________________
____
______________________________.

B. Phone Numbers and E-mail: Tenant must promptly inform Landlord of any changes in Tenant's phone numbers (home, work, and mobile) and e-mail not later than 5 days after a change.

C. HOA Rules: Tenant must comply with any owners' association rules or restrictive covenants affecting the Property. Tenant will reimburse Landlord for any fines or other charges assessed against Landlord for violations by Tenant of any owners' association rule or restrictive covenant.

D. Prohibitions: Unless otherwise authorized by this lease, Tenant may not install or permit any of the following on the Property, even temporarily: a spa, hot tub, above-ground pool, trampoline, or any item which causes a suspension or cancellation of insurance coverage or an increase in insurance premiums. Tenant may not permit any part of the Property to be used for: (1) any activity which is a nuisance, offensive, noisy, or dangerous; (2) the repair of any vehicle; (3) any business of any type, including but not limited to child care; (4) any activity which violates any zoning ordinance, owners' association rule, or restrictive covenant; (5) any illegal or unlawful activity; or (6) activity that obstructs, interferes with, or infringes on the rights of other persons near the Property.

E. Guests: Tenant may not permit any guest to stay on the Property longer the amount of time permitted by any owners' association rule or restrictive covenant or ___________ days without Landlord's written permission, whichever is less.

F. Common Areas: Landlord is not obligated to pay any non-mandatory or user fees for Tenant's use of any common areas or facilities (for example, pool or tennis courts).

13. PARKING RULES: Tenant may not permit more than ___________ vehicles, including but not limited to automobiles, trucks, recreational vehicles, trailers, motorcycles, all-terrain vehicles, jet skis, and boats, on the Property unless authorized by Landlord in writing. Tenant may not park or permit any person to park any vehicles in the yard. Tenant may permit vehicles to be parked only in drives, garages, designated common parking areas, or in the street if not prohibited by law or an owners' association. Tenant may not store or permit any person to store any vehicles on or adjacent to the Property or on the street in front of the Property. In accordance with applicable state and local laws, Landlord may have towed, at Tenant's expense: (a) any inoperative vehicle on or adjacent to the Property; (b) any vehicle parked in violation of this paragraph or any additional parking rules made part of this lease; or (c) any vehicle parked in violation of any law, local ordinance, or owners' association rule.

14. ACCESS BY LANDLORD:

A. Advertising: Landlord may prominently display a "For Sale" or "For Lease" or similarly worded sign on the Property during the term of this lease or any renewal period. Landlord or Landlord's contractor may take interior or exterior photographs or images of the Property and use the photographs or images in any advertisements to lease or sell the Property.

B. Access: Before accessing the Property, Landlord or anyone authorized by Landlord will attempt to first contact Tenant, but may enter the Property at reasonable times without notice to make repairs or to show the Property to prospective tenants or buyers, inspectors, fire marshals, lenders, appraisers, or insurance agents. Additionally, Landlord or anyone authorized by Landlord may peacefully enter the

Property at reasonable times without first attempting to contact Tenant and without notice to: (1) survey or review the Property's condition and take photographs to document the condition; (2) make emergency repairs; (3) exercise a contractual or statutory lien; (4) leave written notices; or (5) seize nonexempt property if Tenant is in default.

C. Trip Charges: If Landlord or Landlord's agents have made prior arrangements with Tenant to access the Property and are denied or are not able to access the Property because of Tenant's failure to make the Property accessible, Landlord may charge Tenant a trip charge of $________.

D. Keybox: **A keybox is a locked container placed on the Property holding a key to the Property. The keybox is opened by a special combination, key, or programmed access device so that persons with the access device may enter the Property, even in Tenant's absence. The keybox is a convenience but involves risk (such as unauthorized entry, theft, property damage, or personal injury). Neither the Association of REALTORS® nor MLS requires the use of a keybox.**

(1) Tenant authorizes Landlord, Landlord's property manager, and Landlord's broker to place on the Property a keybox containing a key to the Property:
(a) during the last ______ days of this lease or any renewal or extension; and
(b) at any time Landlord lists the Property for sale with a Texas licensed broker.

(2) Tenant may withdraw Tenant's authorization to place a keybox on the Property by providing written notice to Landlord and paying Landlord a fee of $___________ as consideration for the withdrawal. Landlord will remove the keybox within a reasonable time after receipt of the notice of withdrawal and payment of the required fee. Removal of the keybox does not alleviate Tenant's obligation to make the Property available for showings as indicated in Paragraph 14B.

(3) If Landlord or Landlord's agents have notified Tenant of their intent to access the Property to show it to prospects and are denied or are not able to access the Property because of Tenant's failure to make the Property accessible, Landlord may charge Tenant a trip charge of $___________.

(4) Landlord, the property manager, and Landlord's broker are not responsible to Tenant, Tenant's guests, family, or occupants for any damages, injuries, or losses arising from use of the keybox unless caused by Landlord, the property manager, or Landlord's broker.

15. MOVE-IN CONDITION:

A. Landlord makes no express or implied warranties as to the Property's condition. Tenant has inspected the Property and accepts it **AS-IS** provided that Landlord:______________________________
____
____.

B. Tenant will complete an Inventory and Condition Form, noting any damages to the Property, and deliver it to Landlord within ________ days after the Commencement Date. If Tenant fails to timely deliver the Inventory and Condition Form, the Property will be deemed to be free of damages, unless otherwise expressed in this lease. The Inventory and Condition Form is not a request for repairs. Tenant must direct all requests for repairs in compliance with Paragraph 18.

16. MOVE-OUT:

A. Move-Out Condition: When this lease ends, Tenant will surrender the Property in the same condition as when received, normal wear and tear excepted. Tenant will leave the Property in a clean condition free of all trash, debris, and any personal property. Tenant may not abandon the Property.

Residential Lease concerning: ______________________________

B. Definitions:

(1) "*Normal wear and tear*" means deterioration that occurs without negligence, carelessness, accident, or abuse.

(2) "*Surrender*" occurs when all occupants have vacated the Property, in Landlord's reasonable judgment, and one of the following events occurs:
(a) the date Tenant specifies as the move-out or termination date in a written notice to Landlord has passed; or
(b) Tenant returns keys and access devices that Landlord provided to Tenant under this lease.

(3) "*Abandonment*" occurs when all of the following occur:
(a) all occupants have vacated the Property, in Landlord's reasonable judgment;
(b) Tenant is in breach of this lease by not timely paying rent; and
(c) Landlord has delivered written notice to Tenant, by affixing it to the inside of the main entry door or if the Landlord is prevented from entering the Property by affixing it to the outside of the main entry door, stating that Landlord considers the Property abandoned, and Tenant fails to respond to the affixed notice by the time required in the notice, which will not be less than 2 days from the date the notice is affixed to the main entry door.

C. Personal Property Left After Move-Out:

(1) If Tenant leaves any personal property in the Property after surrendering or abandoning the Property Landlord may:
(a) dispose of such personal property in the trash or a landfill;
(b) give such personal property to a charitable organization; or
(c) store and sell such personal property by following procedures in §54.045(b)-(e), Property Code.
(2) Tenant must reimburse Landlord all Landlord's reasonable costs under Paragraph 16C(1) for packing, removing, storing, and selling the personal property left in the Property after surrender or abandonment.

17. PROPERTY MAINTENANCE:

A. Tenant's General Responsibilities: Tenant, at Tenant's expense, must:
(1) keep the Property clean and sanitary;
(2) promptly dispose of all garbage in appropriate receptacles;
(3) supply and change heating and air conditioning filters at least once a month;
(4) supply and replace all light bulbs, fluorescent tubes, and batteries for smoke detectors, carbon monoxide detectors, garage door openers, ceiling fan remotes, and other devices (of the same type and quality that are in the Property on the Commencement Date);
(5) maintain appropriate levels of necessary chemicals or matter in any water softener;
(6) take action to promptly eliminate any dangerous condition on the Property;
(7) take all necessary precautions to prevent broken water pipes due to freezing or other causes;
(8) replace any lost or misplaced keys;
(9) pay any periodic, preventive, or additional extermination costs desired by Tenant;
(10) remove any standing water;
(11) know the location and operation of the main water cut-off valve and all electric breakers and how to switch the valve or breakers off at appropriate times to mitigate any potential damage;
(12) water the foundation of the Property at reasonable and appropriate times; and
(13) promptly notify Landlord, in writing, of all needed repairs.

Residential Lease concerning: ______________________________

B. Yard Maintenance:

(1) *"Yard"* means all lawns, shrubbery, bushes, flowers, gardens, trees, rock or other landscaping, and other foliage on or encroaching on the Property or on any easement appurtenant to the Property, and does not include common areas maintained by an owners' association.

(2) *"Maintain the yard"* means to perform activities such as, but not limited to: (a) mowing, fertilizing, and trimming the yard; (b) controlling pests in the yard; and (c) removing debris from the yard.

(3) Unless prohibited by ordinance or other law, Tenant will water the yard at reasonable and appropriate times including but not limited to the following times: ______________________________ ______________________________. Other than watering, the yard will be maintained as follows:

❒ (a) Landlord, at Landlord's expense, will maintain the yard. Tenant will permit Landlord and Landlord's contractors reasonable access to the yard and will remove any pet from the yard at appropriate times.

❒ (b) Tenant, at Tenant's expense, will maintain the yard.

❒ (c) Tenant will maintain in effect a scheduled yard maintenance contract with: ❑ a contractor who regularly provides such service; ❑ ______________________________.

C. Pool/Spa Maintenance: Any pool or spa on the Property will be maintained according to a Pool/Spa Maintenance Addendum.

D. Prohibitions: If Tenant installs any fixtures on the Property, authorized or unauthorized, such as additional smoke detectors, locks, alarm systems, cables, satellite dishes, or other fixtures, such fixtures will become the property of the Landlord. Except as otherwise permitted by law, this lease, or in writing by Landlord, Tenant may not:

(1) remove any part of the Property or any of Landlord's personal property from the Property;
(2) remove, change, add, or rekey any lock;
(3) make holes in the woodwork, floors, or walls, except that a reasonable number of small nails may be used to hang pictures in sheetrock and grooves in paneling;
(4) permit any water furniture on the Property;
(5) install additional phone or video cables, outlets, antennas, satellite receivers, or alarm systems;
(6) alter, replace or remove flooring material, paint, or wallpaper;
(7) install, change, or remove any: fixture, appliance, or non-real-property item listed in Paragraph 2;
(8) keep or permit any hazardous material on the Property such as flammable or explosive materials;
(9) keep or permit any material or item which causes any liability or fire and extended insurance coverage to be suspended or canceled or any premiums to be increased;
(10) dispose of any environmentally detrimental substance (for example, motor oil or radiator fluid) on the Property; or
(11) cause or allow any lien to be filed against any portion of the Property.

E. Failure to Maintain: If Tenant fails to comply with this Paragraph 17 or any Pool/Spa Maintenance Addendum, Landlord may, in addition to exercising Landlord's remedies under Paragraph 27, perform whatever action Tenant is obligated to perform and Tenant must immediately reimburse Landlord the reasonable expenses that Landlord incurs.

18. REPAIRS: (Notice: Subchapter B, Chapter 92, Property Code governs repair obligations).

A. Repair Requests: All requests for repairs must be in writing and delivered to Landlord. If Tenant is delinquent in rent at the time a repair notice is given, Landlord is not obligated to make the repair. In the event of an emergency related to the condition of the Property that materially affects the physical health or safety of an ordinary tenant, call:__________________. Ordinarily, a repair to the heating and air conditioning system is not an emergency.

Residential Lease concerning: ____________________

B. NOTICE: If Landlord fails to repair a condition that materially affects the physical health or safety of an ordinary tenant as required by this lease or the Property Code, Tenant may be entitled to exercise remedies under §92.056 and §92.0561 of the Property Code. If Tenant follows the procedures under those sections, the following remedies may be available to Tenant: (1) terminate the lease and obtain an appropriate refund under §92.056(f); (2) have the condition repaired or remedied according to §92.0561; (3) deduct from the rent the cost of the repair or remedy according to §92.0561; and (4) obtain judicial remedies according to §92.0563. Do not exercise these remedies without consulting an attorney or carefully reviewing the procedures under the applicable sections. The Property Code presumes that 7 days is a reasonable period of time for the Landlord to make a diligent effort to repair a condition unless there are circumstances which establish that a different period of time is appropriate (such as the severity and nature of the condition and the availability of materials, labor, and utilities). Failure to strictly follow the procedures in the applicable sections may cause Tenant to be in default of the lease.

C. Completion of Repairs:

(1) Tenant may not repair or cause to be repaired any condition, regardless of the cause, without Landlord's permission. All decisions regarding repairs, including the completion of any repair, whether to repair or replace the item, and the selection of contractors, will be at Landlord's sole discretion.

(2) Landlord is not obligated to complete a repair on a day other than a business day unless required to do so by the Property Code.

D. Payment of Repair Costs: Except as otherwise specified in this lease, Landlord will pay to repair or remedy conditions in the Property in need of repair if Tenant complies with the procedures for requesting repairs as described in this Paragraph 18.

(1) Landlord will pay the entire cost to repair the following items not caused by Tenant or Tenant's negligence:
  (a) heating and air conditioning systems;
  (b) water heaters; or
  (c) water penetration from structural defects.

(2) Landlord will NOT pay to repair the following items unless caused by Landlord's negligence:
  (a) conditions caused by Tenant, an Occupant, or any guest or invitee of Tenant;
  (b) damage to doors, windows, and screens;
  (c) damage from windows or doors left open;
  (d) damage from wastewater stoppages caused by foreign or improper objects in lines that exclusively serve the Property;
  (e) items that are cosmetic in nature with no impact on the functionality or use of the item; and
  (f) the following specific items or appliances: ____________________
  ____
  ____________________.

E. Trip Charges: If a repair person is unable to access the Property after making arrangements with Tenant to complete the repair, Tenant will pay any trip charge the repair person may charge, which amount may be different from the amount stated in Paragraph 14C.

F. Advance Payments and Reimbursements: Landlord may require advance payment of repairs or payments under this Paragraph 18 for which Tenant is responsible. Tenant must promptly reimburse Landlord the amounts under this Paragraph 18 for which Tenant is responsible.

Residential Lease concerning: ______________________________

19. SECURITY DEVICES AND EXTERIOR DOOR LOCKS:

A. Subchapter D, Chapter 92, Property Code requires the Property to be equipped with certain types of locks and security devices. Landlord has rekeyed the security devices since the last occupant vacated the Property or will rekey the security devices within 7 days after Tenant moves in. "Security device" has the meaning assigned to that term in §92.151, Property Code.

B. All notices or requests by Tenant for rekeying, changing, installing, repairing, or replacing security devices must be in writing. Installation of additional security devices or additional rekeying or replacement of security devices desired by Tenant will be paid by Tenant in advance and may be installed only by contractors authorized by Landlord.

20. SMOKE DETECTORS: Subchapter F, Chapter 92, Property Code requires the Property to be equipped with smoke detectors in certain locations. Requests for additional installation, inspection, or repair of smoke detectors must be in writing. Disconnecting or intentionally damaging a smoke detector or removing a battery without immediately replacing it with a working battery may subject Tenant to civil penalties and liability for damages and attorney fees under §92.2611, Property Code.

21. LIABILITY: Unless caused by Landlord, Landlord is not responsible to Tenant, Tenant's guests, family, or occupants for any damages, injuries, or losses to person or property caused by fire, flood, water leaks, ice, snow, hail, winds, explosion, smoke, interruption of utilities, theft, burglary, robbery, assault, vandalism, other persons, condition of the Property, environmental contaminants (for example, carbon monoxide, asbestos, radon, lead-based paint, mold, fungus, etc.), or other occurrences or casualty losses. Tenant will promptly reimburse Landlord for any loss, property damage, or cost of repairs or service to the Property caused by Tenant, Tenant's guests, any occupants, or any pets.

22. HOLDOVER: If Tenant fails to vacate the Property at the time this lease ends Tenant will pay Landlord rent for the holdover period and indemnify Landlord and prospective tenants for damages, including but not limited to lost rent, lodging expenses, costs of eviction, and attorneys' fees. Rent for any holdover period will be three (3) times the monthly rent, calculated on a daily basis, and will be immediately due and payable daily without notice or demand.

23. RESIDENTIAL LANDLORD'S LIEN: Landlord will have a lien for unpaid rent against all of Tenant's nonexempt personal property that is in the Property and may seize such nonexempt property if Tenant fails to pay rent. Subchapter C, Chapter 54, Property Code governs the rights and obligations of the parties regarding Landlord's lien. Landlord may collect a charge for packing, removing, or storing property seized in addition to any other amounts Landlord is entitled to receive. Landlord may sell or dispose of any seized property in accordance with the provisions of §54.045, Property Code.

24. SUBORDINATION: This lease and Tenant's leasehold interest are and will be subject, subordinate, and inferior to: (i) any lien or encumbrance now or later placed on the Property by Landlord; (ii) all advances made under any such lien or encumbrance; (iii) the interest payable on any such lien or encumbrance; (iv) any and all renewals and extensions of any such lien or encumbrance; (v) any restrictive covenant; and (vi) the rights of any owners' association affecting the Property.

25. CASUALTY LOSS OR CONDEMNATION: Section 92.054, Property Code governs the rights and obligations of the parties regarding a casualty loss to the Property. Any proceeds, payment for damages, settlements, awards, or other sums paid because of a casualty loss to the Property will be Landlord's sole property. For the purpose of this lease, any condemnation of all or a part of the Property is a casualty loss.

Residential Lease concerning: ______________________________

26. SPECIAL PROVISIONS: *(Do not insert a lease-option or lease-purchase clause without the assistance of legal counsel. Special obligations and liabilities under statute apply to such transactions.)*

27. DEFAULT:

A. If Landlord fails to comply with this lease, Tenant may seek any relief provided by law.

B. If Tenant fails to timely pay all amounts due under this lease or otherwise fails to comply with this lease, Tenant will be in default and:
   (1) Landlord may terminate Tenant's right to occupy the Property by providing Tenant with at least one day written notice to vacate;
   (2) all unpaid rents which are payable during the remainder of this lease or any renewal period will be accelerated without notice or demand;
   (3) Landlord may exercise Landlord's lien under Paragraph 23 and any other rights under this lease or the Property Code; and
   (4) Tenant will be liable for:
      (a) any lost rent;
      (b) Landlord's cost of reletting the Property including but not limited to leasing fees, advertising fees, utility charges, and other fees reasonably necessary to relet the Property;
      (c) repairs to the Property for use beyond normal wear and tear;
      (d) all Landlord's costs associated with eviction of Tenant, including but not limited to attorney's fees, court costs, costs of service, witness fees, and prejudgment interest;
      (e) all Landlord's costs associated with collection of amounts due under this lease, including but not limited to collection fees, late charges, and returned check charges; and
      (f) any other recovery to which Landlord may be entitled by law.

C. Notice to vacate under Paragraph 27B(1) may be by any means permitted by §24.005, Property Code.

D. Landlord will attempt to mitigate any damage or loss caused by Tenant's breach by attempting to relet the Property to acceptable tenants and reducing Tenant's liability accordingly.

28. EARLY TERMINATION: This lease begins on the Commencement Date and ends on the Expiration date unless: (i) renewed under Paragraph 4; (ii) extended by written agreement of the parties; or (iii) terminated earlier under Paragraph 27, by agreement of the parties, applicable law, or this Paragraph 28.

A. Special Statutory Rights Tenants may have special statutory rights to terminate the lease early in certain situations involving family violence, military deployment or transfer, or certain sex offenses.

   (1) Military: If Tenant is or becomes a servicemember or a dependent of a servicemember, Tenant may terminate this lease by delivering to Landlord a written notice of termination and a copy of an appropriate government document providing evidence of: (a) entrance into military service; (b) military orders for a permanent change of station (PCS); or (c) military orders to deploy with a military unit for not less than 90 days. Termination is effective on the 30th day after the first date on which the next rental payment is due after the date on which the notice is delivered. §92.017, Property Code governs the rights and obligations of the parties under this paragraph.

Residential Lease concerning: ______________________________

(2) Family Violence: Tenant may terminate this lease if Tenant provides Landlord with a copy of a court order described under §92.016, Property Code protecting Tenant or an occupant from family violence committed by a cotenant or occupant of the Property. §92.016, Property Code governs the rights and obligations of the parties under this paragraph. If the family violence is committed by someone other than a cotenant or co-occupant of the Property, Tenant must give written notice of termination 30 days prior to the effective date of the notice.

(3) Sex Offenses: Tenant may have special statutory rights to terminate this lease in certain situations involving sexual assault or sexual abuse. For more information about the types of abuse and assault covered by this provision, Tenant is advised to review §92.0161, Property Code.

B. Assignment, Subletting and Replacement Tenants:

(1) Tenant may not assign this lease or sublet the Property without Landlord's written consent.

(2) If Tenant requests an early termination of this lease under this Paragraph 28B, Tenant may attempt to find a replacement tenant and may request Landlord to do the same. Landlord may, but is not obligated to, attempt to find a replacement tenant under this paragraph.

(3) Any assignee, subtenant, or replacement tenant must, in Landlord's discretion, be acceptable as a tenant and must sign: (a) a new lease with terms not less favorable to Landlord than this lease or otherwise acceptable to Landlord; (b) a sublease with terms approved by Landlord; or (c) an assignment of this lease in a form approved by Landlord.

(4) At the time Landlord agrees to permit an assignee, subtenant, or replacement tenant to occupy the Property, Tenant will pay Landlord:

(a) if Tenant procures the assignee, subtenant, or replacement tenant:
❑ (i) $__________________.
❑ (ii) ______% of one's month rent that the assignee, subtenant, or replacement tenant is to pay.

(b) if Landlord procures the assignee, subtenant, or replacement tenant:
❑ (i) $__________________.
❑ (ii) ______% of one's month rent that the assignee, subtenant, or replacement tenant is to pay.

(5) Unless expressly stated otherwise in an assignment or sublease, Tenant will not be released from Tenant's obligations under this lease because of an assignment or sublease. An assignment of this lease or a sublease of this lease without Landlord's written consent is voidable by Landlord.

29. **ATTORNEY'S FEES**: Any person who is a prevailing party in any legal proceeding brought under or related to the transaction described in this lease is entitled to recover prejudgment interest, attorney's fees, costs of service, and all other costs of the legal proceeding from the non-prevailing party.

30. **REPRESENTATIONS**: Tenant's statements in this lease and any application for rental are material representations. Each party to this lease represents that he or she is of legal age to enter into a contract. If Tenant makes a misrepresentation in this lease or in an application for rental, Tenant is in default.

31. **ADDENDA**: Incorporated into this lease are the following addenda, exhibits and other information. If Landlord's Rules and Regulations are made part of this lease, Tenant agrees to comply with the Rules and Regulations as Landlord may, at Landlord's discretion, amend from time to time.

❑ Addendum Regarding Lead-Based Paint
❑ Inventory & Condition Form
❑ Landlord's Additional Parking Rules
❑ Pet Agreement
❑ Protecting Your Home from Mold
❑ Agreement for Application Deposit & Hold
❑ ______________________________
❑ ______________________________
❑ Agreement Between Brokers
❑ Landlord's Rules & Regulations
❑ Owners' Association Rules
❑ Pool/Spa Maintenance Addendum
❑ Residential Lease Application
❑ Residential Lease Guaranty
❑ ______________________________
❑ ______________________________

Residential Lease concerning: ______________________________

32. NOTICES: All notices under this lease must be in writing and are effective when hand-delivered, sent by mail, or sent by electronic transmission to *(Do not insert an e-mail address or a fax number unless the party consents to receive notices under this lease at the e-mail address or fax number specified.)*:

Tenant at the Property and a copy to:	Landlord c/o:
______________________	______________________
______________________	______________________
______________________	______________________
E-mail: ______________	E-mail: ______________
Fax: ________________	Fax: ________________

33. AGREEMENT OF PARTIES:

A. Entire Agreement: There are no oral agreements between Landlord and Tenant. This lease contains the entire agreement between Landlord and Tenant and may not be changed except by written agreement.

B. Binding Effect: This lease is binding upon and inures to the benefit of the parties to this lease and their respective heirs, executors, administrators, successors, and permitted assigns.

C. Joint and Several: All Tenants are jointly and severally liable for all provisions of this lease. Any act or notice to, refund to, or signature of, any one or more of the Tenants regarding any term of this lease, its extension, its renewal, or its termination is binding on all Tenants executing this lease.

D. Waiver: Landlord's past delay, waiver, or non-enforcement of a rental due date or any other right will not be deemed to be a waiver of any other breach by Tenant or any other right in this lease.

E. Severable Clauses: Should a court find any clause in this lease unenforceable, the remainder of this lease will not be affected and all other provisions in this lease will remain enforceable.

F. Controlling Law: The laws of the State of Texas govern the interpretation, validity, performance, and enforcement of this lease.

G. Copyright: If an active REALTOR® member of the Texas Association of REALTORS® or an active member of the State Bar of Texas does not negotiate this lease as a party or for one of the parties, either as a party's broker or attorney, this lease is voidable at will by Tenant.

34. INFORMATION:

A. Future inquiries about this lease, rental payments, and security deposits should be directed to the person listed for receipt of notices for Landlord under Paragraph 32.

B. It is Tenant's responsibility to determine, before signing this lease, if: (i) all services (e.g., utilities, connections, schools, and transportation) are accessible to or from the Property; (ii) such services are sufficient for Tenant's needs and wishes; and (iii) Tenant is satisfied with the Property's condition.

C. The brokers to this lease have no knowledge of whether Landlord is delinquent in the payment of any lien against the Property.

Residential Lease concerning: ______________________________

D. Unpaid rent and any unpaid amount under this lease are reportable to credit reporting agencies.

E. Landlord is not obligated to respond to any requests for Tenant's rental and payment history from a mortgage company or other prospective landlord until Tenant has given notice of termination of this lease and Tenant is not in breach of this lease. (*Notice: Landlord or Landlord's agent may charge a reasonable fee for processing such information.)*

F. If all occupants over 18 years of age die during this lease, Landlord may: (i) permit the person named below to access the Property at reasonable times in Landlord's or Landlord's agent's presence; (ii) permit the named person to remove Tenant's personal property; and (iii) refund the security deposit, less deductions, to the named person. Section 92.014, Property Code governs procedures to follow in the event of a tenant's death.

Name: ______________________ Phone: ______________
Address: ______________________________
E-mail: ______________________________

G. The Texas Department of Public Safety maintains a database that the public may search, at no cost, to determine if registered sex offenders are located in certain areas (see www.txdps.state.tx.us under on-line services). For information concerning past criminal activity in certain areas, contact the local police department.

H. Landlord's insurance does not cover Tenant from loss of personal property. Landlord recommends that Tenant obtain insurance for casualties such as fire, flood, water damage, and theft. Tenant represents that Tenant ❑ intends ❑ does not intend to purchase such insurance.

I. Landlord's broker, ______________________________,
❑ will ❑ will not act as the property manager for landlord.

J. This lease is negotiable between the parties. This lease is binding upon final acceptance. READ IT CAREFULLY. If you do not understand the effect of this lease, consult your attorney BEFORE signing.

K. This lease should not be used in conjunction with executory contracts of any type, such as contracts for deed, leases with options to purchase, or lease options, without the advice of an attorney.

Landlord Date	Tenant Date
Landlord Date	Tenant Date
Or signed for Landlord under written property management agreement or power of attorney:	Tenant Date
By: ______________ Date	Tenant Date

Printed Name: ______________
Firm Name: ______________
Broker's License No.: ______________

TEXAS ASSOCIATION OF REALTORS®

RESIDENTIAL LEASE FOR A MULTI-FAMILY PROPERTY UNIT

1. **PARTIES:** The parties to this lease are:

   the owner of the Unit, Landlord,: ____
   ____; and

   Tenant(s): ____
   ____.

2. **PROPERTY:** Landlord leases to Tenant the following Unit Number ________ located at:

   Address: ____
   in ______________________________ County, Texas, together with the following non-real-property items: ____
   ____.

   The Unit and the non-real-property are collectively called the "Unit". "Property" refers to the real property on which the Unit is located including, but not limited to, the building and common areas.

3. **TERM:**

   A. Primary Term: The primary term of this lease begins and ends as follows:

   Commencement Date: ________________________ Expiration Date: ______________________

   B. Delay of Occupancy: Tenant must occupy the Unit within 5 days after the Commencement Date. If Tenant is unable to occupy the Unit by the 5th day after the Commencement Date because of construction in the Unit or a prior tenant's holding over of the Unit, Tenant may terminate this lease by giving written notice to Landlord before the Unit becomes available to be occupied by Tenant, and Landlord will refund to Tenant the security deposit and any rent paid. Landlord will abate rent on a daily basis for a delay caused by construction or a prior tenant's holding over. This paragraph does not apply to any delay in occupancy caused by cleaning, repairs, or make-ready items.

4. **AUTOMATIC RENEWAL AND NOTICE OF TERMINATION:**

   A. This lease automatically renews on a month-to-month basis unless Landlord or Tenant provides the other party written notice of termination not less than: *(Check only one box.)*
   ❑ (1) 30 days before the Expiration Date.
   ❑ (2) ______________ days before the Expiration Date.

   B. If this lease automatically renews on a month-to month basis, it will continue to renew on a month-to-month basis until either party provides written notice of termination to the other party and the notice of termination will be effective: *(Check only one box.)*
   ❑ (1) on the last day of the month following the month in which the notice is given. Landlord is not obligated to prorate rent even if Tenant surrenders the Unit before the termination date.
   ❑ (2) on the date designated in the notice but not sooner than 30 days after the notice is given and, if necessary, rent will be prorated on a daily basis.

   C. Oral notice of termination is not sufficient under any circumstances. Time is of the essence for providing notice of termination (strict compliance with dates by which notice must be provided is required). The date on which rent is due or on which late charges may be assessed does not apply to the date on which the written notice of termination is required to be given. If a box is not checked under Paragraph 4A, Paragraph 4A(1) will apply. If a box is not checked under Paragraph 4B, Paragraph 4B(1) will apply.

Residential Lease concerning: ____

5. RENT:

A. Monthly Rent: Tenant will pay Landlord monthly rent in the amount of $__________ for each full month during this lease. The first full month's rent is due and payable not later than ____________________. Thereafter, Tenant will pay the monthly rent so that Landlord receives the monthly rent on or before:

❑ (1) the first day of each month during this lease.

❑ (2) ____.

Weekends, holidays, and mail delays do not excuse Tenant's obligation to timely pay rent.

B. Prorated Rent: On or before ____________________ Tenant will pay Landlord $________ as prorated rent from the Commencement Date through the last day of the month in which this lease begins.

C. Place of Payment: Unless this lease provides otherwise, Tenant will remit all amounts due to Landlord under this lease to the following person or entity at the place stated and make all payments payable to the named person or entity. Landlord may later designate, in writing, another person or place to which Tenant must remit amounts due under this lease.

Name: ____

Address: ____

____

Notice: Place the address, Unit number and Tenant's name on all payments.

D. Method of Payment:

(1) Tenant must pay all rent timely and without demand, deduction, or offset, except as permitted by law or this lease.

(2) Time is of the essence for the payment of rent (strict compliance with rental due dates is required).

(3) Unless the parties agree otherwise, Tenant may not pay rent in cash and will pay all rent by check, cashier's check, money order, or other means acceptable to Landlord.

(4) Landlord ❑ requires ❑ does not require Tenant(s) to pay monthly rents by one payment.

(5) If Tenant fails to timely pay any amounts due under this lease or if any check of Tenant is not honored by the institution on which it was drawn, Landlord may require Tenant to pay such amount and any subsequent amounts under this lease in certified funds. This paragraph does not limit Landlord from seeking other remedies under this lease for Tenant's failure to make timely payments with good funds.

E. Rent Increases: There will be no rent increases through the primary term. Landlord may increase the rent that will be paid during any month-to-month renewal period by providing at least 30 days written notice to Tenant.

6. LATE CHARGES:

A. If Landlord does not actually receive a rent payment in the full amount at the designated place of payment by the ________ day of each month at 11:59p, Tenant will pay Landlord for each late payment:

(1) an initial late charge equal to *(check one box only)*: ❑ (a) $_________; or ❑ (b)_______% of one month's rent; **and**

(2) additional late charges of $________ per day thereafter until rent and late charges are paid in full. Additional late charges for any one payment may not exceed more than 30 days.

§92.019, Property Code prohibits assessing a late fee until rent has remained unpaid for at least one full day after the date on which the rent is due.

B. For the purposes of paying rent and any late charges, the mailbox is not the agent for receipt for Landlord (the postmark date is not the date Landlord receives the payment). The parties agree that the late charge is based on a reasonable estimate of uncertain damages to the Landlord that are incapable of precise calculation and result from late payment of rent. Landlord's acceptance of a late charge does not waive Landlord's right to exercise remedies under Paragraph 27.

Residential Lease concerning: ______________________________

7. **RETURNED PAYMENT:** Tenant will pay Landlord $________ for each payment Tenant tenders to Landlord which is returned or not honored by the institution on which it is drawn for any reason, plus any late charges until Landlord receives payment. Tenant must make any returned payment good by paying such amount(s) plus any associated charges in certified funds.

8. **APPLICATION OF FUNDS:** Regardless of any notation on a check, Landlord may apply funds received from Tenant first to any non-rent obligations of Tenant, including but not limited to, late charges, returned payment charges, repairs, brokerage fees, periodic utilities, pet charges, and then to rent.

9. **PETS:**

A. Unless the parties agree otherwise in writing, Tenant may not permit, even temporarily, any pet in the Unit (including but not limited to any mammal, reptile, bird, fish, rodent, or insect).

B. If Tenant violates this Paragraph 9 or any agreement to keep a pet in the Unit, Landlord may take all or any of the following action:
(1) declare Tenant to be in default of this lease and exercise Landlord's remedies under Paragraph 27;
(2) charge Tenant, as additional rent, an initial amount of $___ and $_______ per day thereafter per pet for each day Tenant violates the pet restrictions;
(3) remove or cause to be removed any unauthorized pet and deliver it to appropriate local authorities by providing at least 24-hour written notice to Tenant of Landlord's intention to remove the unauthorized pet; and
(4) charge to Tenant the Landlord's cost to:
(a) remove any unauthorized pet;
(b) exterminate the Unit for fleas and other insects;
(c) clean and deodorize the Unit's carpets and drapes; and
(d) repair any damage to the Unit caused by the unauthorized pet.

C. When taking any action under Paragraph 9B Landlord will not be liable for any harm, injury, death, or sickness to any pet.

10. **SECURITY DEPOSIT:**

A. Security Deposit: On or before execution of this lease, Tenant will pay a security deposit to Landlord in the amount of $______________. "Security deposit" has the meaning assigned to that term in §92.102, Property Code.

B. Interest: No interest or income will be paid to Tenant on the security deposit. Landlord may place the security deposit in an interest-bearing or income-producing account and any interest or income earned will be paid to Landlord or Landlord's representative.

C. Refund: Tenant must give Landlord at least thirty (30) days written notice of surrender before Landlord is obligated to refund or account for the security deposit.

Notices about Security Deposits:
(1) §92.108, Property Code provides that a tenant may not withhold payment of any portion of the last month's rent on grounds that the security deposit is security for unpaid rent.
(2) Bad faith violations of §92.108 may subject a tenant to liability up to 3 times the rent wrongfully withheld and the landlord's reasonable attorney's fees.
(3) The Property Code does not obligate a landlord to return or account for the security deposit until the tenant surrenders the Unit and gives the landlord a written statement of the tenant's forwarding address, after which the landlord has 30 days in which to account.
(4) "Surrender" is defined in Paragraph 16 of this lease.
(5) One may view the Texas Property Code at the Texas Legislature's website which, as of the date shown in the lower left-hand corner of this form, is http://www.statutes.legis.state.tx.us/.

D. Deductions:

(1) Landlord may deduct reasonable charges from the security deposit for:
  (a) damages to the Unit and Property, excluding normal wear and tear, and all reasonable costs associated to repair the Unit and Property;
  (b) costs for which Tenant is responsible to clean, deodorize, exterminate, and maintain the Unit;
  (c) unpaid or accelerated rent;
  (d) unpaid late charges;
  (e) unpaid utilities and utility expenses Landlord incurs to maintain utilities to the Unit as required by this Lease;
  (f) unpaid pet charges;
  (g) replacing unreturned keys, garage door openers, security devices, or other components;
  (h) the removal of unauthorized locks or fixtures installed by Tenant;
  (i) Landlord's cost to access the Unit if made inaccessible by Tenant;
  (j) missing or burned-out light bulbs and fluorescent tubes (at the same location and of the same type and quality that are in the Unit on the Commencement Date);
  (k) packing, removing, and storing abandoned property;
  (l) removing abandoned or illegally parked vehicles;
  (m) costs of reletting (as defined in Paragraph 27), if Tenant is in default;
  (n) attorney's fees, costs of court, costs of service, and other reasonable costs incurred in any legal proceeding against Tenant;
  (o) mailing costs associated with sending notices to Tenant for any violations of this lease;
  (p) any other unpaid charges or fees or other items for which Tenant is responsible under this lease; and
  (q) cost to restore walls, flooring, landscaping or any alteration to the Property not approved in writing by Landlord.

(2) If deductions exceed the security deposit, Tenant will pay to Landlord the excess within 10 days after Landlord makes written demand.

11. UTILITIES:

A. Tenant will pay all connection fees, service fees, usage fees, and all other costs and fees for all utilities to the Unit (for example, electricity, gas, water, wastewater, garbage, telephone, alarm monitoring systems, cable, and Internet connections) except the following which Landlord will pay:____________
____
____.
Unless otherwise agreed, amounts under this paragraph are payable directly to the service providers.

B. Unless provided by Landlord, Tenant must, at a minimum, keep the following utilities on, if available, at all times this lease is in effect: gas; electricity; water; wastewater; and garbage services.

C. Tenant authorizes all utility service providers to release to Landlord information concerning connections, disconnections, and charges.

Notice: Before signing this lease, Tenant should determine if all necessary utilities are available to the Unit and are adequate for Tenant's use.

12. USE AND OCCUPANCY:

A. Occupants: Tenant may use the Unit as a private residence only. The only persons Tenant may permit to reside in the Unit during the term of this lease are (*include names and ages of all occupants*): ______
____
____.

Residential Lease concerning: ____________________

B. Phone Numbers: Tenant must promptly inform Landlord of any changes in Tenant's phone numbers (home, work, and mobile) not later than 5 days after a change.

C. HOA Rules: Tenant must comply with any owners' association rules or restrictive covenants affecting the Property. Tenant will reimburse Landlord for any fines or other charges assessed against Landlord for violations by Tenant of any owners' association rule or restrictive covenant.

D. Prohibitions: Unless otherwise authorized by this lease, Tenant may not install or permit any of the following in the Unit, even temporarily: a spa, hot tub, above-ground pool, trampoline, or any item which causes a suspension or cancellation of insurance coverage or an increase in insurance premiums. Tenant may not permit any part of the Unit to be used for: (1) any activity which is a nuisance, offensive, noisy, or dangerous; (2) the repair of any vehicle; (3) any business of any type, including but not limited to child care; (4) any activity which violates any zoning ordinance, owners' association rule, or restrictive covenant; (5) any illegal or unlawful activity; or (6) activity that obstructs, interferes with, or infringes on the rights of other persons near the Unit.

E. Guests: Tenant may not permit any guest to stay in the Unit longer than the amount of time permitted by any owners' association rule or restrictive covenant or ________ days without Landlord's written permission, whichever is less.

F. Common Areas: Landlord is not obligated to pay any non-mandatory or user fees for Tenant's use of any common areas or facilities (for example, pool or tennis courts). If Tenant uses any of the common areas, Tenant shall exercise reasonable care, not damage the common areas, and keep the common areas clean and sanitary.

G. Property Rules: Landlord may adopt rules to maintain and enhance the safety and appearance of the Property. From time to time Landlord, at its discretion, may amend the rules. Tenant agrees to comply with the rules as they may be amended. Exceptions or waivers must be authorized by Landlord in writing.

13. PARKING RULES:

A. Parking Type:

❑ (1) Common Parking: Tenant may park no more than _________ vehicles (cars, motorcycles, and passenger trucks) on the Property in the common parking areas located on the Property.

❑ (2) Assigned Parking: Tenant's assigned parking areas are identified as follows: ______________
____
____.
Only one vehicle may be parked in each assigned parking space. Each month, on or before the date rent is due under the Lease, Tenant will pay additional rent of $ _______________ for the assigned parking. Tenant may not assign, sublet, or trade any assigned parking space or area.

B. Tenant may not use any parking spaces or areas on the Property for any boat, trailer, recreational vehicle, all terrain vehicle, jet ski, or any other type of personal property.

C. Tenant's guests, patrons or invitees may park only in those area designated by Landlord for Tenant's guests, patrons, or invitees.

D Landlord may, but is not obligated to, institute controlled-access systems to the parking areas, including but not limited to systems such as vehicle identification stickers, license numbers, or controlled-access devices. At the time the lease ends, Tenant must return all access devices to Landlord.

E In accordance with applicable state and local laws, the Landlord may tow, at Tenant's expense: (a) any inoperative vehicle on or adjacent to the Property; (b) any vehicle parked in violation of this paragraph

Residential Lease concerning: ____________________

or any additional parking rules made part of this lease; or (c) any vehicle parked in violation of any law, local ordinance, or owners' association rule.

14. ACCESS BY LANDLORD:

A. Advertising: Landlord may prominently display a "For Sale" or "For Lease" or similarly worded sign in the Unit during the term of this lease or any renewal period. Landlord or Landlord's contractor may take interior and exterior photographs or images of the Unit and use the photographs or images in any advertisements to lease or sell the Unit or Property.

B. Access: Before accessing the Unit, Landlord or anyone authorized by Landlord will attempt to first contact Tenant, but may enter the Unit at reasonable times without notice to make repairs or to show the Unit to prospective tenants or buyers, inspectors, fire marshals, lenders, appraisers, or insurance agents. Additionally, Landlord or anyone authorized by Landlord may peacefully enter the Unit at reasonable times without first attempting to contact Tenant and without notice to: (1) survey or review the Unit's condition and take photographs to document the condition; (2) make emergency repairs; (3) exercise a contractual or statutory lien; (4) leave written notices; or (5) seize nonexempt property if Tenant is in default.

C. Trip Charges: If Landlord or Landlord's agents have made prior arrangements with Tenant to access the Unit and are denied or are not able to access the Unit because of Tenant's failure to make the Unit accessible, Landlord may charge Tenant a trip charge of $_______.

D. Keybox: **A keybox is a locked container placed on the Unit holding a key to the Unit. The keybox is opened by a special combination, key, or programmed access device so that persons with the access device may enter the Unit, even in Tenant's absence. The keybox is a convenience but involves risk (such as unauthorized entry, theft, property damage, or personal injury). Neither the Association of REALTORS® nor MLS requires the use of a keybox.**

(1) Tenant authorizes Landlord, Landlord's property manager, and Landlord's broker to place a keybox near the Unit containing a key to the Unit:
(a) during the last ______ days of this lease or any renewal or extension; and
(b) at any time Landlord lists the Unit for sale with a Texas licensed broker.

(2) Tenant may withdraw Tenant's authorization to place a keybox near the Unit by providing written notice to Landlord and paying Landlord a fee of $___________ as consideration for the withdrawal. Landlord will remove the keybox within a reasonable time after receipt of the notice of withdrawal and payment of the required fee. Removal of the keybox does not alleviate Tenant's obligation to make the Unit available for showings as stated in Paragraph 14B.

(3) If Landlord or Landlord's agents have notified Tenant of their intent to access the Unit to show it to prospects and are denied or are not able to access the Unit because of Tenant's failure to make the Unit accessible, Landlord may charge Tenant a trip charge of:$___________.

(4) Landlord, the property manager, and Landlord's broker are not responsible to Tenant, Tenant's guests, family, or occupants for any damages, injuries, or losses arising from use of the keybox unless caused by Landlord, the property manager, or Landlord's broker.

15. MOVE-IN CONDITION:

A. Landlord makes no express or implied warranties as to the Unit's or Property's condition. Tenant has inspected the Unit and Property and accepts the unit **AS-IS** provided that Landlord:________________
____
____

B. Tenant will complete an Inventory and Condition Form, noting any damages to the Unit, and deliver it to Landlord within ___________ days after the Commencement Date. If Tenant fails to timely deliver the Inventory and Condition Form, the Unit will be deemed to be free of damages, unless otherwise

Residential Lease concerning: ____________________

expressed in this lease. The Inventory and Condition Form is not a request for repairs. Tenant must direct all requests for repairs in compliance with Paragraph 18.

16. MOVE-OUT:

A. Move-Out Condition: When this lease ends, Tenant will surrender the Unit in the same condition as when received, normal wear and tear excepted. Tenant will leave the Unit in a clean condition free of all trash, debris, and any personal property. Tenant may not abandon the Unit.

B. Definitions:

(1) "*Normal wear and tear*" means deterioration that occurs without negligence, carelessness, accident, or abuse.

(2) "*Surrender*" occurs when all occupants have vacated the Unit, in Landlord's reasonable judgment, and one of the following events occurs:
(a) the date Tenant specifies as the move-out or termination date in a written notice to Landlord has passed; or
(b) Tenant returns keys and access devices that Landlord provided to Tenant under this lease.

(3) "*Abandonment*" occurs when all of the following occur:
(a) all occupants have vacated the Unit, in Landlord's reasonable judgment;
(b) Tenant is in breach of this lease by not timely paying rent; and
(c) Landlord has delivered written notice to Tenant, by affixing it to the inside of the main entry door or if the Landlord is prevented from entering the Unit by affixing it to the outside of the main entry door, stating that Landlord considers the Unit abandoned, and Tenant fails to respond to the affixed notice by the time required in the notice, which will not be less than 2 days from the date the notice is affixed to the main entry door.

C. Personal Property Left After Move-Out:
(1) If Tenant leaves any personal property in the Unit of Property after surrendering or abandoning the Unit Landlord may:
(a) dispose of such personal property in the trash or a landfill;
(b) give such personal property to a charitable organization; or
(c) store and sell such personal property by following procedures in §54.045(b)-(e), Property Code.
(2) Tenant must reimburse Landlord all Landlord's reasonable costs under Paragraph 16C(1) for packing, removing, storing, and selling the personal property left in the Unit after surrender or abandonment.

17. UNIT AND PROPERTY MAINTENANCE:

A. Tenant's General Responsibilities: Tenant, at Tenant's expense, must:
(1) keep the Unit clean and sanitary and use the Property only in ways that are sanitary, clean and non-disruptive;
(2) promptly dispose of all garbage in appropriate receptacles;
(3) supply and change heating and air conditioning filters at least once a month;
(4) supply and replace all light bulbs, fluorescent tubes, and batteries for smoke detectors, carbon monoxide detectors, garage door openers, ceiling fan remotes, and other devices (of the same type and quality that are in the Unit on the Commencement Date);
(5) maintain appropriate levels of necessary chemicals or matter in any water softener;
(6) take action to promptly eliminate any dangerous condition in the Unit;
(7) take all necessary precautions to prevent broken water pipes due to freezing or other causes;
(8) replace any lost or misplaced keys;
(9) pay any periodic, preventive, or additional extermination costs desired by Tenant;
(10) remove any standing water;

Residential Lease concerning: ____________________

(11) know the location and operation of the main water cut-off valve and all electric breakers to the Unit and how to switch the valve or breakers off at appropriate times to mitigate any potential damage; and
(12) promptly notify Landlord, in writing, of all needed repairs.

B. Prohibitions: If Tenant installs any fixtures in the Unit, authorized or unauthorized, such as additional smoke detectors, locks, alarm systems, cables, satellite dishes, or other fixtures, such fixtures will become the property of the Landlord. Except as otherwise permitted by law, this lease, or in writing by Landlord, Tenant may not:
(1) remove any part of the Property or Unit or any of Landlord's personal property from the Unit or Property;
(2) remove, change, add, or rekey any lock;
(3) make holes in the woodwork, floors, or walls, except that a reasonable number of small nails may be used to hang pictures in sheetrock and grooves in paneling;
(4) permit any water furniture in the Unit;
(5) install additional phone or video cables, outlets, antennas, satellite receivers, or alarm systems;
(6) alter, replace or remove flooring material, paint, or wallpaper;
(7) install, change, or remove any: fixture, appliance, or non-real-property item listed in Paragraph 2;
(8) keep or permit any hazardous material on the Property or in the Unit such as flammable or explosive materials;
(9) keep or permit any material or item which causes any liability or fire and extended insurance coverage to be suspended or canceled or any premiums to be increased;
(10) dispose of any environmentally detrimental substance (for example, motor oil or radiator fluid) on the Property or in the Unit; or
(11) cause or allow any lien to be filed against any portion of the Property.

C. Failure to Maintain: If Tenant fails to comply with this Paragraph 17 Landlord may, in addition to exercising Landlord's remedies under Paragraph 27, perform whatever action Tenant is obligated to perform and Tenant must immediately reimburse Landlord the reasonable expenses that Landlord incurs.

18. REPAIRS: (Notice: Subchapter B, Chapter 92, Property Code governs repair obligations).

A. Repair Requests: **All requests for repairs must be in writing and delivered to Landlord. If Tenant is delinquent in rent at the time a repair notice is given, Landlord is not obligated to make the repair. In the event of an emergency related to the condition of the Unit that materially affects the physical health or safety of an ordinary tenant, call:____________________. Ordinarily a repair to the heating and air conditioning system is not an emergency.**

B. **NOTICE: If Landlord fails to repair a condition that materially affects the physical health or safety of an ordinary tenant as required by this lease or the Property Code, Tenant may be entitled to exercise remedies under §92.056 and §92.0561 of the Property Code. If Tenant follows the procedures under those sections, the following remedies may be available to Tenant: (1) terminate the lease and obtain an appropriate refund under §92.056(f); (2) have the condition repaired or remedied according to §92.0561; (3) deduct from the rent the cost of the repair or remedy according to §92.0561; and (4) obtain judicial remedies according to §92.0563. Do not exercise these remedies without consulting an attorney or carefully reviewing the procedures under the applicable sections. The Property Code presumes that 7 days is a reasonable period of time for the Landlord to repair a condition unless there are circumstances which establish that a different period of time is appropriate (such as the severity and nature of the condition and the availability of materials, labor, and materials). Failure to strictly follow the procedures in the applicable sections may cause Tenant to be in default of the lease.**

Residential Lease concerning: ____________________

C. <u>Completion of Repairs</u>:

(1) Tenant may not repair or cause to be repaired any condition, regardless of the cause, without Landlord's permission. All decisions regarding repairs, including the completion of any repair, whether to repair or replace the item, and the selection of contractors, will be at Landlord's sole discretion.

(2) Landlord is not obligated to complete a repair on a day other than a business day unless required to do so by the Property Code.

D. <u>Payment of Repair Costs</u>: Except as otherwise specified in this lease, Landlord will pay to repair or remedy conditions in the Unit in need of repair if Tenant complies with the procedures for requesting repairs as described in this Paragraph 18.

(1) Landlord will pay the entire cost to repair the following items not caused by Tenant or Tenant's negligence:
(a) heating and air conditioning systems;
(b) water heaters; or
(c) water penetration from structural defects.

(2) Landlord will NOT pay to repair the following items unless caused by Landlord's negligence:
(a) conditions caused by Tenant, an Occupant, or any guest or invitee of Tenant;
(b) damage to doors, windows, and screens;
(c) damage from windows or doors left open;
(d) damage from wastewater stoppages caused by foreign or improper objects in lines that exclusively serve the Unit;
(e) items that are cosmetic in nature with no impact on the functionality or use of the item; and
(f) the following specific items or appliances: ____________________
____
____________________.

E. <u>Trip Charges</u>: If a repair person is unable to access the Unit after making arrangements with Tenant to complete the repair, Tenant will pay any trip charge the repair person may charge, which amount may be different from the amount stated in Paragraph 14C.

F. <u>Advance Payments and Reimbursements</u>: Landlord may require advance payment of repairs or payments under this Paragraph 18 for which Tenant is responsible. Tenant must promptly reimburse Landlord the amounts under this Paragraph 18 for which Tenant is responsible.

19. SECURITY DEVICES AND EXTERIOR DOOR LOCKS:

A. Subchapter D, Chapter 92, Property Code requires the Unit to be equipped with certain types of locks and security devices. Landlord has rekeyed the security devices since the last occupant vacated the Unit or will rekey the security devices within 7 days after Tenant moves in. "Security device" has the meaning assigned to that term in §92.151, Property Code.

B. <u>All notices or requests by Tenant for rekeying, changing, installing, repairing, or replacing security devices must be in writing. Installation of additional security devices or additional rekeying or replacement of security devices desired by Tenant will be paid by Tenant in advance and may be installed only by contractors authorized by Landlord.</u>

20. SMOKE DETECTORS: Subchapter F, Chapter 92, Property Code requires the Unit to be equipped with smoke detectors in certain locations. <u>Requests for additional installation, inspection, or repair of smoke detectors must be in writing</u>. Disconnecting or intentionally damaging a smoke detector or removing a battery without immediately replacing it with a working battery may subject Tenant to civil penalties and liability for damages and attorney fees under §92.2611, Property Code.

Residential Lease concerning: ______________________________

21. LIABILITY: Unless caused by Landlord, Landlord is not responsible to Tenant, Tenant's guests, family, or occupants for any damages, injuries, or losses to person or property caused by fire, flood, water leaks, ice, snow, hail, winds, explosion, smoke, interruption of utilities, theft, burglary, robbery, assault, vandalism, other persons, condition of the Property or Unit, environmental contaminants (for example, carbon monoxide, asbestos, radon, lead-based paint, mold, fungus, etc.), or other occurrences or casualty losses. Tenant will promptly reimburse Landlord for any loss, property damage, or cost of repairs or service to the Property or Unit caused by Tenant, Tenant's guests, any occupants, or any pets.

22. HOLDOVER: If Tenant fails to vacate the Unit at the time this lease ends Tenant will pay Landlord rent for the holdover period and indemnify Landlord and prospective tenants for damages, including but not limited to lost rent, lodging expenses, costs of eviction, and attorneys' fees. Rent for any holdover period will be three (3) times the monthly rent, calculated on a daily basis, and will be immediately due and payable daily without notice or demand.

23. RESIDENTIAL LANDLORD'S LIEN: Landlord will have a lien for unpaid rent against all of Tenant's nonexempt personal property that is in the Unit or on the Property and may seize such nonexempt property if Tenant fails to pay rent. Subchapter C, Chapter 54, Property Code governs the rights and obligations of the parties regarding Landlord's lien. Landlord may collect a charge for packing, removing, or storing property seized in addition to any other amounts Landlord is entitled to receive. Landlord may sell or dispose of any seized property in accordance with the provisions of §54.045, Property Code.

24. SUBORDINATION: This lease and Tenant's leasehold interest are and will be subject, subordinate, and inferior to: (i) any lien or encumbrance now or later placed on the Unit or Property by Landlord; (ii) all advances made under any such lien or encumbrance; (iii) the interest payable on any such lien or encumbrance; (iv) any and all renewals and extensions of any such lien or encumbrance; (v) any restrictive covenant; and (vi) the rights of any owners' association affecting the Unit or Property.

25. CASUALTY LOSS OR CONDEMNATION: Section 92.054, Property Code governs the rights and obligations of the parties regarding a casualty loss to the Unit and Property. Any proceeds, payment for damages, settlements, awards, or other sums paid because of a casualty loss to the Unit or Property will be Landlord's sole property. For the purpose of this lease, any condemnation of all or a part of the Unit is a casualty loss.

26. SPECIAL PROVISIONS: *(Do not insert a lease-option or lease-purchase clause without the assistance of legal counsel. Special obligations and liabilities under statute apply to such transactions.)*

27. DEFAULT:

A. If Landlord fails to comply with this lease, Tenant may seek any relief provided by law.

B. If Tenant fails to timely pay all amounts due under this lease or otherwise fails to comply with this lease, Tenant will be in default and:

Residential Lease concerning: ______________________________

(1) Landlord may terminate Tenant's right to occupy the Unit by providing Tenant with at least one day written notice to vacate;
(2) all unpaid rents which are payable during the remainder of this lease or any renewal period will be accelerated without notice or demand;
(3) Landlord may exercise Landlord's lien under Paragraph 23 and any other rights under this lease or the Property Code; and
(4) Tenant will be liable for:
  (a) any lost rent;
  (b) Landlord's cost of reletting the Unit including but not limited to leasing fees, advertising fees, utility charges, and other fees reasonably necessary to relet the Unit;
  (c) repairs to the Unit for use beyond normal wear and tear;
  (d) all Landlord's costs associated with eviction of Tenant, including but not limited to attorney's fees, court costs, costs of service, witness fees, and prejudgment interest;
  (e) all Landlord's costs associated with collection of amounts due under this lease, including but not limited to collection fees, late charges, and returned check charges; and
  (f) any other recovery to which Landlord may be entitled by law.

C. Notice to vacate under Paragraph 27B(1) may be by any means permitted by §24.005, Property Code.

D. Landlord will attempt to mitigate any damage or loss caused by Tenant's breach by attempting to relet the Unit to acceptable tenants and reducing Tenant's liability accordingly.

28. EARLY TERMINATION: This lease begins on the Commencement Date and ends on the Expiration date unless: (i) renewed under Paragraph 4; (ii) extended by written agreement of the parties; or (iii) terminated earlier under Paragraph 27, by agreement of the parties, applicable law, or this Paragraph 28.

A. Special Statutory Rights: Tenants may have special statutory rights to terminate the lease early in certain situations involving family violence, military deployment or transfer, or certain sex offenses..

(1) Military: If Tenant is or becomes a servicemember or a dependent of a servicemember, Tenant may terminate this lease by delivering to Landlord a written notice of termination and a copy of an appropriate government document providing evidence of: (a) entrance into military service; (b) military orders for a permanent change of station (PCS); or (c) military orders to deploy with a military unit for not less than 90 days. Termination is effective on the 30th day after the first date on which the next rental payment is due after the date on which the notice is delivered. Section 92.017, Property Code governs the rights and obligations of the parties under this paragraph.

(2) Family Violence: Tenant may terminate this lease if Tenant provides Landlord with a copy of a court order described under §92.016, Property Code protecting Tenant or an occupant from family violence committed by a cotenant or occupant of the Unit. Section 92.016, Property Code governs the rights and obligations of the parties under this paragraph. If the family violence is committee by someone other than a cotenant or co-occupant of the Property, Tenant must give written notice of termination 30 days prior to the effective date of the notice.

(3) Sex Offenses: Tenant may have special statutory rights to terminate this lease in certain situations involving sexual assault or sexual abuse. For more information about the types of abuse and assault covered by this provision, Tenant is advised to review §92.0161, Property Code

B. Assignment, Subletting and Replacement Tenants:

(1) Tenant may not assign this lease or sublet the Unit without Landlord's written consent.

(2) If Tenant requests an early termination of this lease under this Paragraph 28B, Tenant may attempt to find a replacement tenant and may request Landlord to do the same. Landlord may, but is not obligated to, attempt to find a replacement tenant under this paragraph.

(3) Any assignee, subtenant, or replacement tenant must, in Landlord's discretion, be acceptable as a tenant and must sign: (a) a new lease with terms not less favorable to Landlord than this lease or otherwise acceptable to Landlord; (b) a sublease with terms approved by Landlord; or (c) an assignment of this lease in a form approved by Landlord.

(4) At the time Landlord agrees to permit an assignee, subtenant, or replacement tenant to occupy the Unit, Tenant will pay Landlord:

(a) if Tenant procures the assignee, subtenant, or replacement tenant:

❑ (i) $____________________.

❑ (ii) ______% of one's month rent that the assignee, subtenant, or replacement tenant is to pay.

(b) if Landlord procures the assignee, subtenant, or replacement tenant:

❑ (i) $____________________.

❑ (ii) ______% of one's month rent that the assignee, subtenant, or replacement tenant is to pay.

(5) Unless expressly stated otherwise in an assignment or sublease, Tenant will not be released from Tenant's obligations under this lease because of an assignment or sublease. An assignment of this lease or a sublease of this lease without Landlord's written consent is voidable by Landlord.

29. ATTORNEY'S FEES: Any person who is a prevailing party in any legal proceeding brought under or related to the transaction described in this lease is entitled to recover prejudgment interest, attorney's fees, costs of service, and all other costs of the legal proceeding from the non-prevailing party.

30. REPRESENTATIONS: Tenant's statements in this lease and any application for rental are material representations. Each party to this lease represents that he or she is of legal age to enter into a contract. If Tenant makes a misrepresentation in this lease or in an application for rental, Tenant is in default.

31. ADDENDA: Incorporated into this lease are the following addenda, exhibits and other information. If Landlord's Rules and Regulations are made part of this lease, Tenant agrees to comply with the Rules and Regulations as Landlord may, at Landlord's discretion, amend from time to time.

❑ Addendum Regarding Lead-Based Paint
❑ Inventory & Condition Form
❑ Landlord's Additional Parking Rules
❑ Pet Agreement
❑ Protecting Your Home from Mold
❑ Agreement for Application Deposit & Hold
❑ Residential Lease Guaranty
❑ Landlord's Rules
❑ Owners' Association Rules
❑ Agreement Between Brokers
❑ Residential Lease Application
❑ ____________________

32. NOTICES: All notices under this lease must be in writing and are effective when hand-delivered, sent by mail, or sent by electronic transmission to *(Do not insert an e-mail address or a fax number unless the party consents to receive notices under this lease at the e-mail address or fax number specified.)*:

Tenant at the Unit and a copy to:
____
____
____
E-mail:____________________
Fax: ____________________

Landlord c/o:
____
____
____
E-mail:____________________
Fax: ____________________

33. AGREEMENT OF PARTIES:

A. Entire Agreement: There are no oral agreements between Landlord and Tenant. This lease contains the entire agreement between Landlord and Tenant and may not be changed except by written agreement.

Residential Lease concerning: ______________________________

B. Binding Effect: This lease is binding upon and inures to the benefit of the parties to this lease and their respective heirs, executors, administrators, successors, and permitted assigns.

C. Joint and Several: All Tenants are jointly and severally liable for all provisions of this lease. Any act or notice to, refund to, or signature of, any one or more of the Tenants regarding any term of this lease, its extension, its renewal, or its termination is binding on all Tenants executing this lease.

D. Waiver: Landlord's past delay, waiver, or non-enforcement of a rental due date or any other right will not be deemed to be a waiver of any other breach by Tenant or any other right in this lease.

E. Severable Clauses: Should a court find any clause in this lease unenforceable, the remainder of this lease will not be affected and all other provisions in this lease will remain enforceable.

F. Controlling Law: The laws of the State of Texas govern the interpretation, validity, performance, and enforcement of this lease.

G. Copyright: If an active REALTOR® member of the Texas Association of REALTORS® or an active member of the State Bar of Texas does not negotiate this lease as a party or for one of the parties, either as a party's broker or attorney, this lease is voidable at will by Tenant.

34. INFORMATION:

A. Future inquires about this lease, rental payments, and security deposits should be directed to the person listed for receipt of notices for Landlord under Paragraph 32.

B. It is Tenant's responsibility to determine, before signing this lease, if: (i) all services (e.g., utilities, connections, schools, and transportation) are accessible to or from the Unit; (ii) such services are sufficient for Tenant's needs and wishes; and (iii) Tenant is satisfied with the Unit's and Property's condition.

C. The brokers to this lease have no knowledge of whether Landlord is delinquent in the payment of any lien against the Unit or Property.

D. Unpaid rent and any unpaid amount under this lease are reportable to credit reporting agencies.

E. Landlord is not obligated to respond to any request for Tenant's rental and payment history from a mortgage company or other prospective landlord until Tenant has given notice of termination of this lease and Tenant is not in breach of this lease. (*Notice: Landlord or Landlord's agent may charge a reasonable fee for processing such information.*) Tenant authorizes Landlord to disclose personal information about Tenant and Tenant's rental history for law enforcement and governmental purposes.

F. If all occupants over 18 years of age die during this lease, Landlord may: (i) permit the person named below to access the Unit at reasonable times in Landlord's or Landlord's agent's presence; (ii) permit the named person to remove Tenant's personal property; and (iii) refund the security deposit, less deductions, to the named person. Section 92.014, Property Code governs procedures to follow in the event of a tenant's death.

Name: ______________________________ Phone: ______________
Address: ______________________________
E-mail: ______________________________

Residential Lease concerning: ______________________________

G. The Texas Department of Public Safety maintains a database that the public may search, at no cost, to determine if registered sex offenders are located in certain areas (see www.txdps.state.tx.us under on-line services). For information concerning past criminal activity in certain areas, contact the local police department.

H. Landlord's insurance does not cover Tenant from loss of personal property. Landlord recommends that Tenant obtain insurance for casualties such as fire, flood, water damage, and theft. Tenant represents that Tenant ❑ intends ❑ does not intend to purchase such insurance.

I. Landlord's broker, ______________________________,
❑ will ❑ will not act as the property manager for landlord.

J. This lease is negotiable between the parties. This lease is binding upon final acceptance. READ IT CAREFULLY. If you do not understand the effect of this lease, consult your attorney BEFORE signing.

Landlord Date	Tenant Date
Landlord Date	Tenant Date
Or signed for Landlord under written property management agreement or power of attorney:	Tenant Date
By: ______________ Date	Tenant Date

Printed Name: ______________

Firm Name: ______________

Broker's License No.: ______________

REVIEW QUESTIONS

Answers to these questions are found in the Answer Key section at the back of the book.

1. A lease for a definite period of time, which terminates when that time has expired, is an estate
   A. for years.
   B. periodic estate.
   C. at will.
   D. at sufferance.

2. A lease of fixed length that continually renews itself for like periods of time until the lessor or lessee acts to terminate it is
   A. a holdover estate.
   B. a periodic estate.
   C. an estate at will.
   D. an estate at sufferance.

3. A lease is a
   A. conveyance.
   B. contract.
   C. both A and B.
   D. neither A nor B.

4. To be valid, which of the following must be in writing and signed?
   A. A month-to-month lease
   B. A 14-month lease
   C. A three-month lease
   D. All of the above

5. The right of the lessee to uninterrupted use of the leased premises is called
   A. quiet possession.
   B. quiet enjoyment.
   C. quiet rights.
   D. tenant rights.

6. A written lease agreement is still legal even though it fails to include
   A. the terms of the lease.
   B. a property description.
   C. both A and B.
   D. neither A not B.

7. As compared to a lease for years, a month-to-month lease gives flexibility to the
   A. landlord.
   B. tenant.
   C. both A and B.
   D. neither A nor B.

8. Bob Short and Bill Tall rent an apartment unit from owner Haf High. Bill dies during the lease term. The lease is still binding upon
   A. Bob.
   B. Haf.
   C. Bill's estate.
   D. all of the above.

9. The word "waive" means to
   A. say "goodbye."
   B. demand.
   C. relinquish.
   D. die naturally.

10. A lease that calls for specified rental increases at predetermined intervals is known as a
    A. step-up lease.
    B. graduated lease.
    C. both A and B.
    D. neither A nor B.

11. The clause in a lease that allows the landlord to pass along to the tenant certain increases in operating expenses is called
    A. an escalator clause.
    B. a participation clause.
    C. both A and B.
    D. neither A nor B.

12. When the tenant pays a base rent plus some or all of the operating expenses of a property, the result is a
    A. gross lease.
    B. net lease.
    C. percentage lease.
    D. graduated lease.

13. A lease in which the tenant pays a rent based upon the gross sales made from the rented premises is known as a
    A. percentage lease.
    B. participation lease.
    C. net lease.
    D. gross lease.

14. Which of the following is NOT specifically designed to protect against rising operating costs?
    A. A net lease
    B. An escalator clause
    C. An index clause
    D. A gross lease

15. A lease for years may be terminated by
    A. constructive eviction.
    B. eminent domain.
    C. mutual agreement.
    D. actual eviction.
    E. all of the above.

16. A written lease agreement is still legal even though it fails to include
    A. the amount of rent to be paid.
    B. a security deposit.
    C. both A and B.
    D. neither A nor B.

17. Flint leased a building to Newton under an agreement that gave Newton the right to occupy the premises for two years, with an option to renew for an additional one-year period. In order to be enforceable, must this lease be in writing and signed by both Flint and Newton?
    A. Yes, because all contracts dealing with real property must be in writing in order to be enforceable.
    B. Yes, because the lease is for a period of time in excess of one year.
    C. No, because oral leases for five years or less are enforceable.
    D. No, because a two-year oral lease is enforceable.

18. Under the Forcible Entry and Detainer statutes in Texas, the landlord must give the tenant
    A. 3 days written notice to vacate the premises.
    B. 3 days notice to vacate the premises.
    C. 10 days written notice to vacate the premises.
    D. 10 days written or oral notice to vacate the premises.

19. The best defense against losses from uncollected rent is
    A. a threat of legal action against the delinquent tenant.
    B. careful tenant selection, good service, and a businesslike policy on rent collections.

20. Regarding residential rentals, Texas courts and the Texas legislature now take the position that
    A. the landlord and tenant are jointly responsible for all repairs.
    B. without a contract, the tenant is responsible for repairs.
    C. without a contract, the landlord is obligated to keep the property repaired.
    D. without a contract, the cost of repairs must be negotiated.

Chapter 19

KEY TERMS

Appraise: to estimate the value of something

Capitalize: to convert future income to current value

Comparables: properties similar to the subject property that have sold recently

Cost approach: land value plus current construction costs minus depreciation

Depreciation: loss in value due to deterioration and obsolescence

FIRREA: the Financial Institution's Reform, Recovery, and Enforcement Act of 1989

Gross rent multiplier (GRM): a number that is multiplied by a property's gross rents to produce an estimate of the property's worth

Highest and best use: the use of a parcel of land that will produce the greatest current value

Income approach: a method of valuing a property based on the monetary returns it can be expected to produce

Market approach: a method of valuing property based on recent sales of similar properties

Market value: the cash price that a willing buyer and a willing seller would agree upon, given reasonable exposure of the property to the marketplace, full information as to the potential uses of the property, and no undue compulsion to act

Operating expenses: expenditures necessary to maintain the production of income

Scheduled gross, Projected gross: the estimated rent that a fully occupied property can be expected to produce on an annual basis

Real Estate Appraisal

IN THIS CHAPTER

This chapter deals with the three approaches to estimating value—the market approach, the cost approach, and the income approach. The market approach is sometimes referred to as the market comparison approach, which provides an estimate of the market or fair market value. The market approach is also used in estimating values of the condominiums and townhouses. Other topics covered include competitive market analysis and gross rent multipliers. The cost and income approaches lead into a discussion of income forecasting, depreciation, construction costs, operating expense ratio, and capitalizing income. The chapter concludes with coverage of the appraisal report, principles of value, and the multiple meanings of the word "value."

To ***appraise*** real estate, in general terms, means to estimate its value. An **appraisal** is defined under federal law as "a written statement used in connection with a federally related transaction that is independent and impartially prepared by a licensed, certified appraiser that states an opinion of the defined value of an adequately described property as of a specific date that is supported by the presentation, and analysis of relevant market information." In more generic terms, an appraisal is defined in applying the Uniform Standard of Professional Appraisal Practice as "the act or process of estimating the value."

There are three approaches to making this estimate. The first is to locate similar properties that have sold recently and use them as benchmarks in estimating the value of the property you are appraising. This is the ***market approach***, also called the market-data approach or market comparison approach. The second approach is to add together the cost of the individual components that make up the property being appraised. This is the ***cost approach***; it starts with the cost of a similar parcel of vacant land and adds the cost of the lumber, concrete, plumbing, wiring, labor, etc., necessary to build a similar building. Depreciation is then subtracted. The third approach is to consider only the amount of net income that the property can reasonably be expected to produce for its owner plus any anticipated price increase or decrease. This is the ***income approach***.

PUTTING IT TO WORK

For the person who owns or plans to own real estate, knowing how much a property is worth is a crucial part of the buying or selling decision. For the real estate practitioner, being able to estimate the value of a property is an essential part of taking a listing and conducting negotiations.

MARKET VALUE

In this chapter you will see demonstrations of the market, cost, and income approaches and how they are used in determining market value. ***Market value***, also called *fair market value*, is the highest price in terms of money that a property will bring if (1) payment is made in cash or its equivalent, (2) the property is exposed on the open market for a reasonable length of time, (3) the buyer and seller are fully informed as to market conditions and the uses to which the property may be put, (4) neither is under abnormal pressure to conclude a transaction, and (5) the seller is capable of conveying marketable title. Market value is at the heart of nearly all real estate transactions.

MARKET COMPARISON APPROACH

Let's begin by demonstrating the application of the *market comparison approach* to a single-family residence. The residence to be appraised is called the **subject property** and is described as follows:

> The subject property is a one-story, wood-frame house of 1,520 square feet containing three bedrooms, two bathrooms, a living room, dining room, kitchen, and utility room. There is a two-car garage with concrete driveway to the street, a 300-square-foot concrete patio in the backyard, and an average amount of landscaping. The house is located on a 10,200-square-foot, level lot that measures 85 by 120 feet. The house is 12 years old, in good repair, and located in a well-maintained neighborhood of houses of similar construction and age.

Comparables

After becoming familiar with the physical features and amenities of the subject property, the next step in the market approach is to locate houses with similar physical features and amenities that have sold recently under market value conditions. These are known as ***comparables*** or "comps." The more similar they are to the subject property, the fewer and smaller the adjustments that must be made in the comparison process, and hence the less room for error. As a rule it is best to use comparable sales no more than six months old. During periods of relatively stable prices, this can be extended to one year. However, during periods of rapidly changing prices even a sale six months old may be out of date.

Sales Records

To apply the market comparison approach, the following information must be collected for each comparable sale: date of sale, sales price, financing terms, location of the property, and a description of its physical characteristics and amenities. Recorded deeds at public records offices can provide dates and locations of recent sales. Although a deed seldom states the purchase price, nearly all states (not Texas, however) levy a deed transfer fee or conveyance tax, the amount of which is shown on the recorded deed. This tax can sometimes provide a clue as to the purchase price.

Records of past sales can often be obtained from real estate trade associations. Property tax assessors keep records on changes in ownership as well as property values. Where these records are kept up-to-date and are available to the public, they can provide information on what has sold recently and for how much. Assessors also keep detailed records of improvements made to land. This can be quite helpful in making adjustments between the subject property and the comparables. For real estate salespeople, locally operated multiple listing services provide asking prices and descriptions of properties currently offered for sale by member brokers along with descriptions, sales prices, and dates for properties that have been sold. In some cities, commercially operated financial services publish information on local real estate transactions and sell it on a subscription basis.

Verification

To produce the most accurate appraisal possible, each sale used as a comparable should be inspected and the price and terms verified. An agent who specializes in a given neighborhood will have already visited the comparables when they were still for sale. The agent can verify price and terms with the selling broker or from multiple listing service sales records.

Number of Comparables

Three to five comparables usually provide enough basis for reliable comparison. To use more than five, the additional accuracy must be weighed against the extra effort involved. When the supply of comparable sales is more than adequate, one should choose the sales that require the fewest adjustments.

It is also important that the comparables selected represent current market conditions. Sales between relatives or close friends may result in an advantageous price to the buyer or seller, and sales prices that for some other reason appear to be out of line with the general market should not be used. Listings and offers to buy should not be used in place of actual sales. They do not represent a meeting of minds between a buyer and a seller. Listing prices do indicate the upper limit of prices, whereas offers to buy indicate lower limits. Thus, if a property is listed for sale at $180,000 and there have been offers as high as $172,000, it is reasonable to presume the market price lies somewhere between $172,000 and $180,000.

Adjustment Process

Let us now work through the example shown in Table 19.1 to demonstrate the application of the market comparison approach to a house. We begin at lines 1 and 2 by entering the address and sale price of each comparable property. For convenience, we shall refer to these as comparables A, B, and C. On lines 3 through 10, we make time adjustments to the sale price of each comparable to make it equivalent to the subject property today. *Adjustments* are made for price changes since each comparable was sold, as well as for differences in physical features, amenities, and financial terms. The result indicates the market value of the subject property.

Time Adjustments

Returning to line 3 in Table 19.1, let us assume that house prices in the neighborhood where the subject property and comparables are located have risen 3%

TABLE 19.1 Valuing a house by the market comparison approach

Line	Item	Comparable Sale A		Comparable Sale B		Comparable Sale C	
1	Address	1702 Brookside Ave.		1912 Brookside Ave.		1501 18th Street	
2	Sales price		$191,800		$188,000		$189,000
3	Time adjustment	sold 6 mos. ago, add 3%	+5,754	sold 3 mos. ago, add 1.5%	+2,820	just sold	0
4	House size	160 sq ft larger at $60/sq ft	−9,600	20 sq ft smaller at $60/sq ft	+1,200	same size	0
5	Garage/carport	carport	+$4,000	3-car garage	−2,000	2-car garage	0
6	Other	larger patio	−300	no patio	+900	built-in bookcases	−700
7	Age, upkeep, and overall quality of house	superior	−3,000	inferior	+800	equal	0
8	Landscaping	inferior	+2,000	equal	0	superior	−900
9	Lot size, features, and location	superior	−3,890	inferior	+900	equal	0
10	Terms and conditions of sale	equal	0	special financing	−1,500	equal	0
11	Total adjustments		−5,036		+3,120		−1,600
12	Adjusted Market Price		$186,764		$191,120		$187,400
13	Correlation process:						
	Comparable A	$186,764 × 20% = $37,353					
	Comparable B	$191,120 × 30% = $57,336					
	Comparable C	$187,400 × 50% = $93,700					
14	Indicated Value	$188,389					
		Round to $188,000					

during the six months that have elapsed since comparable A was sold. If it were for sale today, comparable A would bring 3% or $5,754 more. Therefore, we must add $5,754 to bring it up to the present. Comparable B was sold three months ago, and to bring it up to the present we need to add 1.5% or $2,820 to its sales price. Comparable C was just sold and needs no time correction because its price reflects today's market.

When using the market comparison approach, all adjustments are made to the comparable properties, not to the subject property. This is because we cannot adjust the value of something for which we do not yet know the value.

House Size

Because house A is 160 square feet larger than the subject house, it is logical to expect that the subject property would sell for less money. Hence, a deduction is made from the sales price of comparable A on line 4. The amount of this deduction is based on the difference in floor area and the current cost of similar construction, minus an allowance for depreciation. If we value the extra 160 square feet at $60 per square foot, we must subtract $9,600. For comparable B, the house is 20 square feet smaller than the subject house. At $60 per square foot, we add $1,200 to comparable B, because it is reasonable to expect that the subject property would sell for that much more because it is that much larger. Comparable C is the same-sized house as the subject property, so no adjustment is needed.

Garage and Patio Adjustments

Next, the parking facilities (line 5) are adjusted. We first look at the current cost of garage and carport construction and the condition of these structures. Assume that the value of a carport is $3,000; a one-car garage, $5,000; a two-car garage, $7,000; and a three-car garage, $9,000. Adjustments would be made as follows. The subject property has a two-car garage worth $7,000 and comparable A has a carport worth $3,000. Therefore, based on the difference in garage facilities, we can reasonably expect the subject property to command $4,000 more than comparable A. By adding $4,000 to comparable A, we effectively equalize this difference. Comparable B has a garage worth $2,000 more than the subject property's garage. Therefore, $2,000 must be subtracted from comparable B to equalize it with the subject property. For comparable C, no adjustment is required, as comparable C and the subject property have similar garage facilities.

At line 6, the subject property has a 300-square-foot patio in the backyard worth $900. Comparable A has a patio worth $1,200; therefore, $300 is deducted from comparable A's selling price. Comparable B has no patio. Because it would have sold for $900 more if it had one, a +$900 adjustment is required. The patio at comparable C is the same as the subject property's. However, comparable C has $700 worth of custom built-in living room bookcases that the subject property does not have. Therefore, $700 is subtracted from comparable C's sales price. Any other differences between the comparables and the subject property such as swimming pools, fireplaces, carpeting, drapes, roofing materials, and kitchen appliances would be adjusted in a similar manner.

Building Age, Condition, and Quality

On line 7 we recognize differences in building age, wear and tear, construction quality, and design usefulness. Where the difference between the subject property and a comparable can be measured in terms of material and labor, the adjustment is the cost of that material and labor. For example, the $800 adjustment for comparable B reflects the cost of needed roof repair at the time B was sold. The adjustment of $3,000 for comparable A reflects the fact it has better-quality plumbing and electrical fixtures than the subject property. Differences that cannot be quantified in terms of labor and materials are usually dealt with as lump-sum judgments. Thus, one might allow $1,500 for each year of age difference between the subject and a comparable, or make a lumpsum adjustment of $3,000 for an inconvenient kitchen design.

Keep in mind that adjustments are made on the basis of what each comparable property was like on the day it was sold. Thus, if an extra bedroom was added or the house was painted after its sale date, these items are not included in the adjustment process.

Landscaping

Line 8 shows the landscaping at comparable A to be inferior to the subject property. A positive correction is necessary here to equalize it with the subject. The landscaping at comparable B is similar and requires no correction; that at comparable C is better and thus requires a negative adjustment. The dollar amount of each adjustment is based on the market value of lawn, bushes, trees, and the like.

Lot Features and Location

Line 9 deals with any differences in lot size, slope, view, and neighborhood. In this example, all comparables are in the same neighborhood as the subject property, thus eliminating the need to judge, in dollar terms, the relative merit of one neighborhood over another. However, comparable A has a slightly larger lot and a better view than the subject property. Based on recent lot sales in the area, the difference is judged to be $890 for the larger lot and $3,000 for the better view. Comparable B has a slightly smaller lot judged to be worth $900 less, and comparable C is similar in all respects.

Terms and Conditions of Sale

Line 10 in Table 19.1 accounts for differences in financing. As a rule, the more accommodating the terms of the sale to the buyer, the higher the sales price, and vice versa. We are looking for the highest cash price the subject property may reasonably be expected to bring, given adequate exposure to the marketplace and a knowledgeable buyer and seller not under undue pressure. If the comparables were sold under these conditions, no corrections would be needed in this category. However, if it can be determined that a comparable was sold under different conditions, an adjustment is necessary. For example, if the going rate of interest on home mortgages is 10% per year and the seller offers to finance the buyer at 7% interest, it is reasonable to expect that the seller can charge a higher selling price. Similarly, the seller can get a higher price if he has a low-interest loan that can be assumed by the buyer. Favorable financing terms offered by the seller of comparable B enabled him to obtain an extra $1,500 in selling price. Therefore, we must subtract $1,500 from comparable B. Another situation that requires an adjustment on line 10 is if a comparable was sold on a rush basis. If a seller is in a hurry to sell, a lower selling price usually must be accepted than if the property can be given more time in the marketplace.

Adjusted Market Price

Adjustments for each comparable are totaled and either added or subtracted from its sale price. The result is the *adjusted market price* shown at line 12. This is the dollar value of each comparable sale after it has gone through an adjustment process to make it the same as the subject property. If it were possible to precisely evaluate every adjustment, and if the buyers of comparables A, B, and C had paid exactly what their properties were worth at the time they purchased them, the three prices shown on line 12 would be the same. However, buyers are not that precise, particularly in purchasing a home where amenity value influences price and varies considerably from one person to the next.

Correlation Process

While comparing the properties, it will usually become apparent that some comparables are more like the subject property than others. The **correlation** step gives the appraiser the opportunity to assign more weight to the more similar comparables and less to the others. At line 13, comparable C is given a weight of 50% because it is more like the subject and required fewer adjustments. Moreover, this sameness is in areas where adjustments tend to be the hardest to estimate accurately: time, age, quality, location, view, and financial conditions. Of the remaining two comparables, comparable B is weighted slightly higher than comparable A because it is a more recent sale and required fewer adjustments overall.

In the correlation process, the adjusted market price of each comparable is multiplied by its weighting factor and totaled at line 14. The result is the **indicated value** of the subject property. It is customary to round off to the nearest $50 or $100 for properties under $10,000, to the nearest $250 or $500 for properties between $10,000 and $100,000, to the nearest $1,000 or $2,500 for properties between $100,000 and $250,000, and to the nearest $2,500 or $5,000 above that.

Unique Issues

Condominium, Townhouse, and Cooperative Appraisal

The process for estimating the market value of a condominium, townhouse, or cooperative living unit by the market approach is similar to the process for houses except that fewer steps are involved. For example, in a condominium complex with a large number of two-bedroom units of identical floor plan, data on a sufficient number of comparable sales may be available within the building. This would eliminate adjustments for differences in unit floor plan, neighborhood, lot size and features, age and upkeep of the building, and landscaping. The only corrections needed would be those that make one unit different from another. This would include the location of the individual unit within the building (end units and units with better views sell for more), the upkeep and interior decoration of the unit, a time adjustment, and an adjustment for terms and conditions of the sale.

When there are not enough comparable sales of the same floor plan within the same building and it is necessary to use different-sized units, an adjustment must be made for floor area. If the number of comparables is still inadequate and units in different condominium buildings must be used, adjustments will be necessary for neighborhood, lot features, management, upkeep, age, and overall condition of the building.

Vacant Land Valuation

Subdivided lots zoned for commercial, industrial, or apartment buildings are usually appraised and sold on a square foot basis. Thus, if apartment land is currently selling for $30.00 per square foot, a 100,000-square-foot parcel of comparable zoning and usefulness would be appraised at $3,000,000. Another method is to value on a frontfoot basis. For example, if a lot has 70 feet of street frontage and if similar lots are selling for $1,000 per front foot, that lot would be appraised at $70,000. Storefront land is often sold this way. House lots can be valued either by the square foot, front foot, or lot method. The lot method is useful when one is comparing lots of similar size and zoning in the same neighborhood. For example, recent sales of 100-foot by 100-foot house lots in the $180,000 to $200,000 range would establish the value of similar lots in the same neighborhood.

Rural land and large parcels that have not been subdivided are usually valued and sold by the acre. For example, how would you value 21 acres of vacant land when the only comparables available are 16-acre and 25-acre sales? The method is to establish a per acre value from comparables and apply it to the subject land. Thus, if 16- and 25- acre parcels sold for $32,000 and $50,000, respectively, and are similar in all other respects to the 21-acre subject property, it would be reasonable to conclude that land is selling for $2,000 per acre. Therefore, the subject property is worth $42,000.

4-3-2-1 Rule

The *4-3-2-1 rule* is a depth adjustment that appraisers sometimes use when valuing vacant lots. It states that the land at the back of the lot is worth less than the land at the front. To illustrate, consider a single-family residential lot that has 75 feet of frontage on a street and is 200 feet deep. Across the street and in an equally desirable location are two lots for sale that are each 75 feet on the street and 100 feet deep. Would you pay as much for the single 75' x 200' lot as you would for two 75' x 100' lots? Let us omit the arithmetic and just remember the principle: The land at the back of a lot is worth less than the land at the front.

Competitive Market Analysis

A variation of the market comparison approach and one that is very popular with agents who list and sell residential property is the **competitive market analysis (CMA).** This method is based on the principle that value can be estimated not only by looking at similar homes that have sold recently but also by taking into account homes presently on the market plus homes that were listed for sale but did not sell. The CMA is a listing tool that a sales agent prepares in order to show a seller what the home is likely to sell for, and the CMA helps the agent decide whether or not to accept the listing.

Figure 19.1 shows a competitive market analysis form published by the National Association of REALTORS®. The procedure in preparing a CMA is to select homes that are comparable to the subject property. The greater the similarity, the more accurate the appraisal will be and the more likely it is that the client will accept the agent's estimate of value and counsel. It is usually best to use only properties in the same neighborhood; this is easier for the seller to relate to and removes the need to compensate for neighborhood differences. The comparables should also be similar in size, age, and quality. Although a CMA does not require that individual adjustments be shown as in Table 19.1, it does depend on the agent's understanding of the process that takes place in that table. That is why Table 19.1 and its explanation are important. A residential agent may not be called upon to make a presentation as is done in Table 19.1; nonetheless, all those steps are considered and consolidated in the practitioner's mind before entering a probable final sales price on the CMA.

Homes for sale. In section [1] of the CMA shown in Figure 19.1, similar homes presently offered for sale are listed. This information is usually taken directly from the practitioner's multiple listing service (MLS) book, and ideally the agent will already have toured these properties and have first-hand knowledge of their condition. These are the homes the seller's property will compete against in the marketplace.

In section [2] the agent lists similar properties that have sold in the past several months. Ideally, the agent will have toured the properties when they were for sale. Sale prices are usually available through MLS sales records. Section [3] is for listing homes that were offered for sale but did not sell. In other words, buyers were unwilling to take these homes at the prices offered.

In section [4] recent FHA and VA appraisals of comparable homes can be included if it is felt that they will be useful in determining the price at which to list. Two words of caution are in order here. First, using someone else's opinion of value is risky. It is better to determine your own opinion based on actual facts. Second, FHA and VA appraisals often tend to lag behind the market. This means in a rising market they will be too low; in a declining market they will be too high.

Buyer appeal. In section [5], buyer appeal, and in section [6], market position, the agent evaluates the subject property from the standpoint of whether or not it will sell if placed on the market. It is important to make the right decision to take or not to take a listing. Once taken, the agent knows that valuable time and

FIGURE 19.1 Competitive market analysis

COMPETITIVE MARKET ANALYSIS

Property Address ______ Date ______

For Sale Now: [1]	Bed-rms.	Baths	Den	Sq. Ft.	1st Loan	List Price	Days on Market	Terms

Sold Past 12 Mos. [2]	Bed-rms.	Baths	Den	Sq. Ft.	1st Loan	List Price	Days on Market	Date Sold	Sale Price	Terms

Expired Past 12 Mos. [3]	Bed-rms.	Baths	Den	Sq. Ft.	1st Loan	List Price	Days on Market	Terms

[4] **F.H.A. – V.A. Appraisals**

Address	Appraisal	Address	Appraisal

[5] **Buyer Appeal** [6] **Marketing Position**

(Grade each item 0 to 20% on the basis of desirability or urgency)

1 Fine Location ______ %
2 Exciting Extras ______ %
3 Extra Special Financing ______ %
4 Exceptional Appeal ______ %
5 Under Market Price ______ Yes ______ No ______ %

Rating Total ______ %

1 Why Are They Selling ______ %
2 How Soon Must They Sell ______ %
3 Will They Help Finance .... Yes ______ No ______ %
4 Will They List at Competitive Market Value .... Yes ______ No ______ %
5 Will They Pay for Appraisal .... Yes ______ No ______ %

Rating Total ______ %

[7]

Assets ______
Drawbacks ______
Area Market Conditions ______

Recommended Terms ______

[8] **Selling Costs**

Brokerage	$
Loan Payoff	$
Prepayment Privilege	$
FHA – VA Points	$
Title and Escrow Fees: IRS Stamps Recons Recording	$
Termite Clearance	$
Misc. Payoffs: 2nd T.D., Pool, Patio, Water Softener, Fence, Improvement Bond.	$
	$
	$
Total	$

Top Competitive Market Value $ ______

[9]

Probable Final Sales Price $ ______

Total Selling Costs $ ______

Net Proceeds $ ______ Plus or Minus $ ______

BY PERMISSION

The statements and figures presented herein, while not guaranteed, are secured from sources we believe authoritative

Prepared by ______

money must be committed to get a property sold. Factors that make a property more appealing to a buyer include good location, extra features, small down payment, low interest, meticulous maintenance, and a price below market. Similarly, a property is more saleable if the sellers are motivated to sell, want to sell soon, will help with financing, and will list at or below market. A busy practitioner will want to avoid spending time on overpriced listings, listings for which no financing is available, and listings where the sellers have no motivation to sell. Under the rating systems in sections [5] and [6], the closer the total is to zero, the less desirable the listing; the closer to 100%, the more desirable the listing.

Section [7] provides space to list the property's high and low points, current market conditions, and recommended terms of sale. Section [8] shows the seller how much to expect in selling costs. Section [9] shows the seller what to expect in the way of a sales price and the amount of cash that can be expected from the sale.

The emphasis in CMA is on a visual inspection of the data on the form in order to arrive at market value directly. No pencil and paper adjustments are made. Instead, adjustments are made in a generalized fashion in the minds of the agent and the seller. In addition to its application to single-family houses, CMA can also be used on condominiums, cooperative apartments, townhouses, and vacant lots—provided sufficient comparables are available.

Gross Rent Multipliers

A popular market comparison method that is used when a property produces income is the ***gross rent multiplier***, or ***GRM***. The GRM is an economic comparison factor that relates the gross rent a property can produce to its purchase price. For apartment buildings and commercial and industrial properties, the GRM is computed by dividing the sales price of the property by its gross annual rent. For example, if an apartment building grosses $100,000 per year in rents and has just sold for $700,000, it is said to have a GRM of 7. The use of a GRM to value single-family houses is questionable because they are usually sold as owner-occupied residences rather than as income properties. Note that if you do work a GRM for a house, it is customary to use the monthly (not yearly) rent.

Where comparable properties have been sold at fairly consistent gross rent multiples, the GRM technique presumes the subject property can be valued by multiplying its gross rent by that multiplier. To illustrate, suppose that apartment buildings were recently sold in your community as shown in Table 19.2. These sales indicate that the market is currently paying seven times gross. Therefore, to find the value of a similar apartment building grossing $24,000 per year, multiply by 7.00 to get an indicated value of $168,000.

The GRM method is popular because it is simple to apply. Having once established what multiplier the market is paying, one need only know the gross

TABLE 19.2 Calculating gross rent multipliers

Building	Sales Price		Gross Annual Rents		Gross Rent Multiplier
No. 1	$245,000	÷	$34,900	=	7.02
No. 2	$160,000	÷	$22,988	=	6.96
No. 3	$204,000	÷	$29,352	=	6.95
No. 4	$196,000	÷	$27,762	=	7.06
As a Group:	$805,000	÷	$115,002	=	7.00

Source: © 2012 Cengage Learning

rents of a building to set a value. However, this simplicity is also the weakness of the GRM method because the GRM takes into account only the gross rent a property produces. Gross rent does not allow for variations in vacancies, uncollectible rents, property taxes, maintenance, management, insurance, utilities, or reserves for replacements.

Weakness of GRM. To illustrate the problem, suppose that two apartment buildings each gross $100,000 per year. However, the first has expenses amounting to $40,000 per year and the second, expenses of $50,000 per year. Using the same GRM, the buildings would be valued the same, yet the first produces $10,000 more in net income for its owner. The GRM also overlooks the expected economic life span of a property. For example, a building with an expected remaining life span of 30 years would be valued exactly the same as one expected to last 20 years, if both currently produce the same rents. One method of partially offsetting these errors is to use different GRMs under different circumstances. Thus, a property with low operating expenses and a long expected economic life span might call for a GRM of 7 or more, whereas a property with high operating expenses or a shorter expected life span would be valued using a GRM of 6 or 5 or even less.

COST APPROACH

There are times when the market approach is an inappropriate valuation tool. For example, the market approach is of limited usefulness in valuing a fire station, school building, courthouse, or highway bridge. These properties are rarely placed on the market and comparables are rarely found. Even with properties that are well-suited to the market approach, there may be times when it is valuable to apply another valuation approach. For example, a real estate agent may find that comparables indicate a certain style and size of house is selling in a particular neighborhood for $150,000. Yet the astute agent discovers through the cost approach that the same house can be built from scratch, including land, for $125,000. The agent builds and sells ten of these and concludes that, yes, there really is money to be made in real estate. Let us take a closer look at the cost approach.

Table 19.3 demonstrates the cost approach. Step 1 is to estimate the value of the land upon which the building is located. The land is valued as though vacant using the market comparison approach described earlier. In Step 2, the cost of constructing a similar building at today's costs is estimated. These costs include the current prices of building materials, construction wages, architect's fees, contractor's services, building permits, utility hookups, etc., plus the cost of financing during the construction stage and the cost of construction equipment used at the project site. Step 3 is the calculation of the amount of money that represents the subject building's wear and tear, lack of usefulness, and obsolescence when compared to the new building of Step 2. In Step 4, depreciation is subtracted from today's construction cost to give the current value of the subject building on a used basis. Step 5 is to add this amount to the land value. Let us work through these steps.

Estimating New Construction Costs

In order to choose a method of estimating construction costs, one must decide whether cost will be approached on a reproduction or on a replacement basis. **Reproduction cost** is the cost at today's prices of constructing an *exact replica* of the subject improvements using the same or very similar materials. **Replacement cost** is the cost, at today's prices and using today's methods of construction, for an improvement having the same or *equivalent usefulness* as the subject property. Replacement cost is the more practical choice of the two because it eliminates nonessential or obsolete features and takes full advantage of current construction materials and techniques. It is the approach that will be described here.

Square-Foot Method

The most widely used approach for estimating construction costs is the **square-foot method.** It provides reasonably accurate estimates that are fast and simple to prepare.

The square-foot method is based on finding a newly constructed building that is similar to the subject building in size, type of occupancy, design, materials, and construction quality. The cost of this building is converted to cost per square foot by dividing its current construction cost by the number of square feet in the building.

Cost Handbooks

Cost information is also available from construction cost handbooks. Using a **cost handbook** starts with selecting a handbook appropriate to the type of building being appraised. From photographs of houses included in the handbook along with brief descriptions of the buildings' features, the appraiser finds a house that most nearly fits the description of the subject house. Next to pictures of the house is the current cost per square foot to construct it. If the subject house has a better quality roof, floor covering, or heating system; greater or fewer built-in appliances, or plumbing fixtures; or a garage, basement, porch, or

TABLE 19.3 Cost approach to value

Step 1:	Estimate land as vacant		$30,000
Step 2:	Estimate new construction cost of similar building	$120,000	
Step 3:	Less estimated depreciation	−12,000	
Step 4:	Indicated value of building		$108,000
Step 5:	Appraised property value by the cost approach		$138,000

Source: © 2012 Cengage Learning

swimming pool, the handbook provides costs for each of these. Figure 19.2 illustrates the calculations involved in the square-foot method.

Estimating Depreciation

Having estimated the current cost of constructing the subject improvements, the next step in the cost approach is to estimate the loss in value due to depreciation since they were built. In making this estimate we look for three kinds of ***depreciation***: physical deterioration, functional obsolescence, and economic obsolescence.

Physical deterioration results from wear and tear through use, such as wall-to-wall carpet that has been worn thin or a dishwasher, garbage disposal, or water heater that must be replaced. Physical deterioration also results from the action of

FIGURE 19.2 Square-foot method of cost estimating

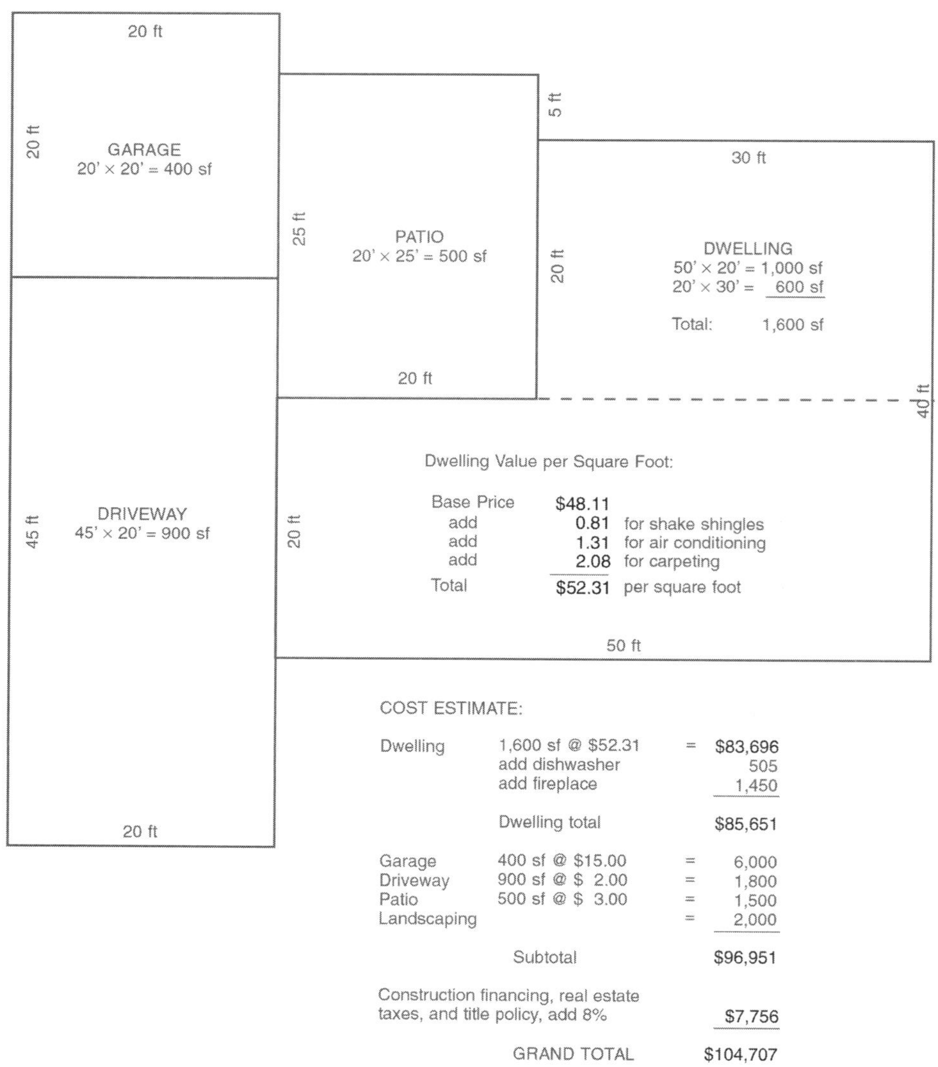

Source: © 2012 Cengage Learning

nature in the form of sun, rain, heat, cold, and wind, and from damage due to plants and animal life such as tree roots breaking sidewalks and termites eating wood. Physical deterioration can also result from neglect (an overflowing bathtub) and from vandalism.

Functional obsolescence results from outmoded equipment (old-fashioned plumbing fixtures in the bathrooms and kitchen), faulty or outdated design (a single bathroom in a three- or four-bedroom house or an illogical room layout), inadequate structural facilities (inadequate wiring to handle today's household appliance loads), and overadequate structural facilities (high ceilings in a home). Functional and physical obsolescence can be separated into curable and incurable components. **Curable** is something that can be fixed at reasonable cost such as worn carpeting, a leaky roof, or outdated faucets in bathrooms. **Incurable** is something that cannot be reasonably fixed and must simply be lived with, for example, an illogical room layout.

Economic obsolescence is the loss of value due to external forces or events. For example, a once-popular neighborhood becomes undesirable because of air or noise pollution or because surrounding property owners fail to maintain their properties. Or, a city that is dependent on a military base finds the base closed and with it a big drop in demand for real estate. Or, the motel district in town loses customers because a new interstate highway has been built several miles away. Far more often, however, properties experience economic appreciation and not economic obsolescence. The appreciation can come from new industries moving into town, city growth in a new direction, a shortage of land in beach or waterfront areas, etc. Thus it is quite possible for the economic appreciation of a property to more than offset the depreciation it experiences. The result is a building that is physically and functionally depreciating and at the same time appreciating in value. Consequently, while the chronological age of a building is important to value, what is more important is the remaining economic life of the building and whether or not it is functionally adequate for use in the future. This is what real estate investors look for.

Final Steps in the Cost Approach

After calculating the current construction cost of the subject improvements and estimating the amount of depreciation, the next step is to subtract the amount of depreciation from the current construction cost to get the depreciated value of the improvements. This is added to the value of the land upon which the subject improvements rest. The total is the value of the property by the cost approach.

INCOME APPROACH

The market approach is very useful in connection with the sale or purchase of a home. The cost approach is very useful for someone planning to build. But what about someone planning to invest? For investors the income approach is the most popular method of valuing a property. The income approach considers the monetary returns a property can be expected to produce and converts that into a value the property should sell for if placed on the market today. This is called capitalizing the income stream. To ***capitalize*** means to convert future income to current value. To illustrate, suppose that an available apartment building is expected to return, after expenses, \$18,000 per year. How much would you, as an investor, pay for the building? The answer depends on the return you require on each dollar you invest. Suppose you will accept a return of 9% per year. In that case you will pay \$200,000 for this building. The calculation is as follows:

$$\frac{\text{Income}}{\text{Rate}} = \text{Value} \qquad \frac{\$18{,}000}{0.09} = \$200{,}000$$

This is the basic principle of capitalization. The appraisal work comes in estimating the net income a property will produce and looking at recent sales of similar properties to see what capitalization rates are currently acceptable to investors. Let us look at the techniques one would use in estimating a property's income. Pay close attention because each \$1 error in projected annual income or expenses can make a difference of from \$8 to \$15 in the market value of the property.

Income and Expense Forecasting

The best starting point is to look at the actual record of income and expenses for the subject property over the past three to five years. Although the future will not be an exact repetition of the past, the past record of a property is usually the best guide to future performance. These historical data are blended with the current operating experience of similar buildings in order to estimate what the future will bring. The result is a projected operating statement, such as the one shown in Table 19.4, which begins with the estimated rents that the property can be expected to produce on an annual basis. This is the ***projected gross***, or ***scheduled gross***, and represents expected rentals from the subject property on a fully occupied basis. From this, vacancy and collection losses are subtracted. These are based partly on the building's past experience and partly on the operating experience of similar buildings.

Operating Expenses

The next step is to itemize anticipated ***operating expenses*** for the subject property. These are expenses necessary to maintain the production of income. For an apartment building without recreational facilities or an elevator, the list in Table 19.4 is typical. Again, we must consider both the property's past operating expenses and what we expect those expenses to be in the future. For example, even though a property is currently being managed by its owner and no management fee is being paid, a typical management fee, say 6% of the gross rents, is included.

Not included as operating expenses are outlays for capital improvements, such as the construction of a new swimming pool, the expansion of parking

TABLE 19.4 Projected annual operating statement (also called a pro forma statement)

Scheduled gross annual income	$84,000	
Vacancy allowance and collection losses	4,200	
Effective Gross Income		$79,800
Operating Expenses		
Property taxes	9,600	
Hazard and liability insurance	1,240	
Property management	5,040	
Janitorial services	1,500	
Gardener	1,200	
Utilities	3,940	
Trash pickup	600	
Repairs and maintenance	5,000	
Other	1,330	
Reserves for replacement		
Furniture and furnishings	1,200	
Stoves and refrigerators	600	
Furnace and/or air-conditioning	700	
Plumbing and electrical	800	
Roof	750	
Exterior painting	900	
Total Operating Expenses		$34,400
Net Operating Income		$45,400
Operating Expense Ratio: $34,400 / $79,800 = 43.1%		

facilities, and assessments for street improvements. Improvements are not classified as expenses because they increase the usefulness of the property, which increases the rent the property will generate and therefore the property's value.

Reserves

Reserves for replacement are established for items that do not require an expenditure of cash each year. To illustrate, lobby furniture (and furniture in apartments rented as "furnished") wears out a little each year, eventually requiring replacement. Suppose that these items cost $7,200 and are expected to last six years, at which time they must be replaced. An annual $1,200 reserve for replacement not only reflects wear and tear of the furniture during the year, but also reminds us that to avoid having to meet the entire furniture and furnishings replacement cost out of one year's income, money should be set aside for this purpose each year. In a similar manner, reserves are established for other items that must be replaced or repaired more than once during the life of the building, but not yearly.

Net Operating Income

The operating expense total is then subtracted from the effective gross income. The balance that remains is the **net operating income.** From the net operating income the property owner receives both a return *on* and a return *of* investment. The return *on* investment is the interest received for investing money in the property. The return *of* investment is compensation for the fact that the building is wearing out.

Operating Expense Ratio

At this point, the **operating expense ratio** can be calculated. It is obtained by dividing the total operating expenses by the effective gross income. The resulting ratio provides a handy yardstick against which similar properties can be compared. If the operating expense ratio is out of step compared to similar properties, it signals the need for further investigation. A range of 25% to 45% is typical for apartment buildings. The Institute of Real Estate Management of the National Association of REALTORS® publishes books and articles that give typical operating ratios for various types of income properties across the United States. Local inquiry to appraisers and brokers who specialize in income properties will also provide typical ratios for buildings in a community.

Capitalizing Income

The final step in the income approach is to capitalize the net operating income. In other words, what price should an investor offer to pay for a property that produces a given net income per year? The solution is: income / rate = value. If the annual net operating income is $45,400 and if the investor intends to pay all cash, expects to receive a 10% return on this investment, and anticipates no change in the value of the property while owning it, the solution is to divide $45,400 by 10%. However, most investors today borrow much of the purchase price and usually expect an increase in property value. Under these conditions, how much should the investor pay?

The best known method for solving this type of investment question involves using the Ellwood Tables, published in 1959 by L. W. Ellwood, MAI. However, for the person who does not use these tables regularly, the arithmetic involved can prove confusing. As a result *mortgage-equity tables* are now available from bookstores. These allow the user to look up a single number, called an **overall rate,** and divide it into the net operating income to find a value for the property.

For example, suppose an investor who is interested in buying the above property can obtain a 9%, fully amortized 25-year mortgage loan for 75% of the purchase price. He wants a 10% return on his equity in the property, plans to hold it 10 years, and expects it will increase 50% in value (after selling costs) during that time. How much should he offer to pay the seller? In Table 19.5, we look for an interest rate of 9% and for appreciation of 50%. This gives an overall rate of 0.09376 and the solution is:

$$\frac{\text{Income}}{\text{Overall rate}} = \text{Value} \qquad \frac{\$45{,}400}{0.09376} = \$484{,}215$$

TABLE 19.5 Overall rates—10-year holding period, 25-year loan for 75% of the purchase price, 10% investor return

Appreciation, Depreciation	Loan Interest Rate			
	9%	10%	11%	12%
+100%	0.07251	0.07935	0.08631	0.09338
+ 50%	**0.09376**	0.10060	0.10756	0.11463
+ 25%	0.10439	0.11123	0.11819	0.12526
+ 15%	0.10864	0.11548	0.12244	0.12951
+ 10%	0.11077	0.11761	0.12457	0.13164
+ 5%	0.11289	0.11973	0.12669	0.13376
0	0.11502	0.12186	0.12882	0.13589
− 5%	0.11715	0.12399	0.13095	0.13802
− 10%	0.11927	0.12611	0.13307	0.14014
− 15%	0.12140	0.12824	0.13520	0.14227
− 25%	0.12565	0.13249	0.13945	0.14652
− 50%	0.13628	0.14312	0.15008	0.15715
−100%	0.15753	0.16437	0.17133	0.17840

Source: © 2012 Cengage Learning

Further exploration of the numbers in Table 19.5 shows that as loan money becomes more costly, the overall rate rises, and as interest rates fall, so does the overall rate. If the investor can anticipate appreciation in value, the overall rate drops; if she can't, the overall rate climbs. You can experiment by dividing some of the other overall rates in this table into $45,400 to see how the value of this property changes under different circumstances.

Depreciation

The pro forma in Table 19.4 provides reserves for replacement of such items as the roof, furnace, air conditioning, plumbing, electrical and exterior paint, and so forth. Nonetheless, as the building ages the style of the building will become dated, the neighborhood will change, and the structure will experience physical deterioration. Allowance for this is usually accounted for in the selection of the capitalization rate. The less functional, economic, and physical obsolescence that is expected to take place, the lower the acceptable "cap" rate and vice versa.

Fictional Depreciation

In contrast to actual depreciation, there is the **fictional depreciation** that the U.S. Treasury allows income property owners to deduct as an expense when calculating income taxes. The Internal Revenue Service allows a purchaser of a commercial building to completely depreciate the structure over a period of 27.5 years regardless of the age or condition of the structure. This figure may be an understatement of the remaining life of the structure, but it was chosen by

Congress to create an incentive to invest in real estate, not as an accurate gauge of a property's life. Thus it is quite common to see depreciation claimed on buildings that are in reality appreciating because of rising income from rents and/or falling capitalization rates.

CHOICE OF APPROACHES

For certain types of real property, some approaches are more suitable than others. This is especially true for single-family residences. Here you must rely almost entirely on the market and cost approaches because very few houses are sold on their ability to generate cash rent. Unless you can develop a measure of the "psychic income" in home ownership, relying heavily on rental value will lead to a property value below the market and cost approaches. Applying all three approaches to special-purpose buildings may also prove to be impractical. For example, in valuing a college or university campus or a state capitol building, the income and market approaches have only limited applicability.

When appraising a property that is bought for investment purposes such as an apartment building, shopping center, office building, or warehouse, the income approach is the primary method of valuation. As a cross-check on the income approach, an apartment building should be compared to other apartment buildings on a price per apartment unit basis or price per square foot basis. Similarly, an office, store, or warehouse can be compared to other recent office, store, or warehouse sales on a price per square foot basis. Additionally, the cost approach can be used to determine whether or not it would be cheaper to buy land and build rather than to buy an existing building.

APPRAISER'S BEST ESTIMATE

It is important to realize that the appraised value is the appraiser's best *estimate* of the subject property's worth. Thus, no matter how painstakingly it is done, property valuation requires the appraiser to make many subjective judgments. Because of this, it is not unusual for three highly qualified appraisers to look at the same property and produce three different appraised values. It is also important to recognize that an appraisal is made as of a specific date. It is not a certificate of value, good forever until used. If a property was valued at $115,000 on January 5th of this year, the more time that has elapsed since that date, the less accurate that value is as an indication of the property's current worth.

An appraisal does not take into consideration the financial condition of the owner, the owner's health, sentimental attachment, or any other personal matter. An appraisal does not guarantee that the property will sell for the appraised market value. (The buyer and the seller determine the actual selling price.) Nor does buying at the appraised market value guarantee a future profit for the purchaser. (The real estate market can change.) An appraisal is not a guarantee that the roof will not leak, that there are no termites, or that everything in the building works. An appraisal is not an offer to buy, although a buyer can order one made so as to know how much to offer. An appraisal is not a loan commitment, although a lender can order one made so as to apply a loan-to-value ratio when making a loan.

APPRAISAL REGULATION

The Appraisal Foundation

When the country was suffering from harsh economic times, standards of appraisals came under extremely close scrutiny by many lenders. For instance, two appraisers may appraise the same property for significantly different values while using the same data, both acting in good faith. It is hard to draw a distinction, however, between an error in judgment and a fraudulent appraisal. The more difficult question is: How can a lender, in reviewing an appraisal, distinguish between good and bad appraisals? At least part of the answer is being addressed by an organization called the Appraisal Foundation. It is a private organization whose purpose is (1) to establish and approve uniform appraisal standards, (2) to set appropriate criteria for the certification and recertification of qualified appraisers, and (3) to maintain appropriate systems for the certification and recertification of qualified appraisers.

To effect this result, the Appraisal Foundation has established two subcommittees, the Appraiser Qualifications Board and the Appraisal Standards Board. The first establishes criteria for appraisers. The second sets standards for the appraisal to be performed. The Foundation's aim is to disseminate such qualification criteria to the various states, governmental entities, and others to assist them in establishing and maintaining an appropriate system for the certification and recertification of qualified appraisers.

Federal Regulation

Congress addressed the appraisal issue by enacting Title XI of the ***Financial Institutions Reform, Recovery, and Enforcement Act of 1989 (FIRREA)***. The Act, for the first time in history, established standards that will have a far-reaching impact on the appraisal industry.

Congress also created the Appraisal Subcommittee of the Federal Financial Institution's Examination Council to establish standards. The Subcommittee looks exclusively to the Appraisal Foundation for establishing standards under FIRREA for both appraiser qualifications as well as appraisal standards and has proven to be an excellent effort by leaders in the appraisal industry, coupled with the governmental enforcement powers, to establish standards that ultimately benefit the lenders and public in general.

Developing the Appraisal

FIRREA created mandatory requirements for real estate appraisals. These requirements are known as the *Uniform Standards of Professional Appraisal Practice*, commonly referred to as the *USPAP standards.*

In developing an appraisal, the Act requires that the appraiser must be aware of, understand, and correctly use those recognized methods and techniques that are necessary to produce a credible appraisal. There are specific requirements for an appraiser's analysis, requiring consideration of current sales, options, or listings within certain time periods prior to the date of the appraisal. Specifically, this analysis of market data must consider all sales, options, or listings: (1) within one year for a one- to four-family residential property and (2) within three years for all other property types. The Act further requires that the appraiser must consider and reconcile the quality and quantity of data available and analyze within the approaches used, the applicability or suitability of the approaches used as it pertains to the subject parcel of real estate.

Appraisal Standards

Recent revisions to the appraisal standards now provide that all appraisals must meet the following standards:

1. The appraisal must conform to generally accepted appraisal standards as evidenced by the USPAP standards, unless principles of safe and sound banking require compliance with stricter standards.
2. Be written and contain sufficient information analysis to support the institute's decision to make the loan.
3. Analyze and report appropriate deductions and discounts for proposed construction or renovation (partially leased buildings, non-market lease terms, and tract developments with unsold units).
4. Be based upon the definition of market value as defined under law.
5. The appraisal must be performed by a State licensed or State certified appraiser in accordance with the appraisal regulations.

Market value under the statute is defined as the most probable price which a property should bring in a competitive and open market under all conditions requisite to a fair sale, the buyer and seller each acting prudently and knowledgably, and assuming the price is not affected by undue stimulus. Implicit in this definition is the consummation of the sale as of a specified date and the passing of title from seller to buyer under conditions whereby:

1. Buyer and seller are typically motivated.
2. Both parties are well informed or well advised, and acting in what they consider their own best interests.
3. A reasonable time is allowed for exposure in the open market.
4. Payment is made in terms of cash in U.S. dollars or in terms of financial arrangements comparable thereto.
5. The price represents the normal consideration for the property sold unaffected by special or creative financing or sales concession granted by anyone associated with the sale.

Appraisals Required

The revised standards provide that an appraisal performed by a State certified or a licensed appraiser is required for all real estate related financial transactions. A State certified appraiser is required in all transactions, (1) of $1,000,000.00 or more; (2) nonresidential transactions of $250,000.00 or more, other than those involving appraisals of one- to four-family residential properties; (3) complex residential transactions of $250,000.00 or more. All appraisals of related transactions not requiring the services of a State certified appraiser should be prepared by either a State certified appraiser or a State licensed appraiser.

There are a number of other exceptions. For instance, an appraisal is not required for a transaction value of $250,00.00 or less, a lien on real estate which have been taken as collateral in an abundance of caution, a transaction secured by a lien on real estate that has been taken for purposes other than a real estate's value (i.e., additional collateral), and certain business loans.

Reporting Standards

USPAP also sets forth required standards for the appraisal report. Each self-contained appraisal report must (1) identify and describe the real estate being appraised; (2) state the real property interest being appraised; (3) state the purpose and intended use of the appraisal; (4) define the value to be estimated; (5) state the effective date of the appraisal and the date of the report; (6) state the extent of the process of collecting, confirming, and reporting data; (7) state all assumptions and limiting conditions that affect the analyses, opinions, and conclusions; (8) describe the information considered, the appraisal procedures followed, and the reasoning that supports the analyses, opinions, and conclusions; (9) describe the appraiser's opinion of the highest and best use of the real estate, when such an opinion is necessary and appropriate; (10) explain and support the exclusion of any of the usual valuation approaches; (11) describe any additional information that may be appropriate to show compliance with, or clearly identify and explain permitted departures from the specific guidelines of Standard 1 (on developing an appraisal); and (12) include a signed certification.

Each appraisal report must also (1) clearly and accurately set forth the appraisal in a manner that will not be misleading; (2) contain sufficient information to enable person(s) who are expected to receive or rely on the report to understand it properly; and (3) clearly and accurately disclose any extraordinary assumption or limiting condition that directly affects the appraisal and indicate its impact on value.

USPAP requires that each written real property appraisal report include a signed certification similar in content to the following form:

I certify that, to the best of my knowledge and belief:

- The statements of fact contained in this report are true and correct.
- The reported analyses, opinions, and conclusions are limited only by the reported assumptions and limiting conditions and are my personal, unbiased professional analyses, opinions, and conclusions.
- I have no (or the specified) present or prospective interest in the property that is the subject of this report, and I have no (or the specified) personal interest or bias with respect to the parties involved.
- My compensation is not contingent upon the reporting of a predetermined value or direction in value that favors the cause of the client, the amount of the value estimate, the attainment of a stipulated result, or the occurrence of a subsequent event.

- My analyses, opinions, and conclusions were developed, and this report has been prepared, in conformity with the Uniform Standards of Professional Appraisal Practice.
- I have (or have not) made a personal inspection of the property that is the subject of this report. (If more than one person signs the report, this certification must clearly specify which individuals did and which individuals did not make a personal inspection of the appraised property.)
- No one provided significant professional assistance to the person signing this report. (If there are exceptions, the name of each individual providing significant professional assistance must be stated.)

FORMATS OF APPRAISAL REPORTS

Written reports have three traditional formats. The choice depends on the amount of detail required by the client, the intended use of the report, and the appraisal standards to be met. The format to be used also depends on the reporting option (self-contained, summary, or restricted). A brief description of reporting formats follows.

Letter Report

The least formal letter report is usually only one to five pages long. It contains the conditions of the assignment, a summary of the nature and scope of the appraiser's investigation, and an opinion of value. Although brief, the letter report must describe the extent of the appraisal process performed and clearly state its detail. Whether reporting a complete or limited appraisal, the letter format is most suited to the restricted appraisal report. It is used most often when the client is familiar with the property and appraisal details are not needed.

Form Report

The form report is an appraisal made on a preprinted form. A checklist is often used for describing and rating property characteristics. This makes the appraisal form a logical choice for the summary report option.

Institutions and government agencies use forms designed to suit their special needs. Standard forms are usually available for single-family residential, multifamily residential, commercial, and industrial properties. This is the most common type of report used for real estate loan appraisals.

Narrative Report

The narrative appraisal is the longest and most formal of the appraisal reports. It is a step-by-step presentation of the facts used by the appraiser to arrive at a value. This report also contains a detailed discussion of the methods used to interpret the data presented. Narrative appraisal reports are used when the client needs to review each logical step taken by the appraiser. They are the preferred format for self-contained appraisal reports.

Review Appraisal

FIRREA also developed standards for reviewing appraisals and reporting their adequacy and appropriateness. In reviewing the appraisal, the appraiser must observe specific guidelines that identify the report being reviewed and the real property being appraised, the effective date of the report, and the date of the review. The review appraiser must also identify the scope of the review process to be conducted and form an opinion as to the adequacy and relevance of the data and propriety of any adjustments to the data. The opinion must also reflect the appropriateness of the appraisal and the methods and techniques used to develop the reasons for any disagreement with the appraiser.

Real Estate Analysis

An *analysis* is the act or process of providing information, recommendations, and/or conclusions on diversified problems in real estate other than estimating the value and can include a number of different forms of analysis, such as cash flow analysis, feasibility analysis, investment analysis, or market analysis. This differs from an *appraisal,* which, under USPAP standards, is defined as the act or process of estimating value.

In developing the real estate analysis, the analyst must be aware of, understand, and correctly use those recognized methods and techniques that are necessary to produce a credible analysis. The analyst must not commit a substantial error of omission or commission that significantly affects the analysis and must not render services in a careless or negligent manner that, when considering the results of the analysis, would be considered to be misleading. The analyst must also observe the following specific guidelines: (1) clearly identify the client's objective; (2) define the problem to be considered and the purpose and intended use of the analysis, consider the scope of the assignment, adequately identify the real estate under consideration, and describe any special limiting condition; (3) collect, verify, and reconcile such data as may be required to complete the assignment and withhold no pertinent information; (4) apply the appropriate tools and techniques of analysis to data collected; and (5) base all projections of the analysis on reasonably clear and appropriate evidence. Each type of analysis has additional requirements established and separate criteria being used by the analyst.

In reporting the results of the real estate analysis, the analyst must communicate each analysis, opinion, and conclusion in a manner that is not misleading, and the report must contain sufficient information to enable the persons who receive it to understand it properly, and clearly and accurately disclose any extraordinary assumptions that would indicate any impact on the final conclusions or recommendation of the analysis.

The analysis report must contain a certification that is similar in content to that of the appraisal certification.

APPRAISER QUALIFICATIONS

To comply with federal regulations established by the Appraisal Subcommittee, the Appraiser Qualifications Board of the Appraisal Foundation has established federal standards for certification and licensing of appraisers. Texas has adopted these standards in their entirety and has established five categories of appraisers: (1) a certified general real estate appraiser, (2) a certified residential real estate appraiser, (3) a state licensed real estate appraiser, (4) provisional licensed real estate appraiser, and (5) an appraiser trainee. The respective qualifications are described in Table 19.6.

Texas Regulations

In Texas, the Appraiser Licensing and Certification Board (TALCB) was created to recommend education, experience, and continuing education requirements for applications for certification and renewal of certification, specifications of any examination to be required, standards for the development of communication of real estate appraisal by certified appraisers, and a code of professional responsibility for certified real estate appraisers. The Governor appoints eight of the members, four of which must be appraiser members and four of which must be public members. The ninth member will be the executive secretary of the Texas Veterans Land Board. The TALCB is an "independent subdivision of the Texas Real Estate Commission."

The Texas Real Estate Commission has responded to the Appraisal Foundation's USPAP by passing rules and regulations governing appraisals and property analyses to be made by all licensees and to bring Texas into compliance with the new federal rules.

There are two major exceptions. The new regulations do not apply to: (1) a statement of opinion of value of real property (commonly known as a broker's opinion of value) given by a licensee in connection with seeking or obtaining a listing contract; or (2) a price comparison of similar properties (commonly known as a comparative market analysis) provided as part of other brokerage business for the purpose of determining a listing, selling, or rental price for a specific property. These exceptions provide that a real estate licensee can provide information and determine an estimate of value without having to comply with all the technical regulations required for formal real estate appraisals if the licensee provides the person for whom the opinion or analysis is prepared with a written statement containing the following language:

> THIS IS AN OPINION OF VALUE OR COMPARATIVE MARKET ANALYSIS AND SHOULD NOT BE CONSIDERED AN APPRAISAL. In making any decision that relies upon my work, you should know that I

TABLE 19.6 Texas appraiser licensing and certification board requirements

Classification	Education	Experience	Examination
Certified General Real Estate Appraiser	180 classroom hours of acceptable real estate appraisal-related courses, including at least 90 hours of fundamental real estate appraisal courses, with 30 hours of "nonresidential" appraisal, and 15 hours of the Uniform Standards of Professional Appraisal Practice (USPAP). After October 31, 2007, applicants must meet all requirements set forth by the Appraiser Qualifications Board	3,000 hours of acceptable real estate appraisal experience with a minimum of 30 months and may be acquired any time during one's career. A minimum of 1,500 hours must be in nonresidential appraising.	Appraiser Qualifications Board (AQB)-approved TALCB general certification examination.
Certified Residential Real Estate Appraiser	120 classroom hours of acceptable real estate appraisal-related courses, including at least 60 hours of fundamental real estate appraisal courses, and 15 hours of USPAP. After October 31, 2007, applicants must meet all requirements set forth by the Appraiser Qualifications Board	2,500 hours of acceptable real estate appraisal experience with a minimum of 24 months and may be acquired any time during one's career.	AQB-approved TALCB residential certification examination.
State Licensed Real Estate Appraiser	90 classroom hours of acceptable real estate appraisal-related courses, including at least 40 hours of fundamental real estate appraisal courses, and 15 hours of USPAP. After October 31, 2007, applicants must meet all requirements set forth by the Appraiser Qualifications Board	2,000 hours of acceptable real estate appraisal experience acquired over a minimum of 12 months.	AQB-approved TALCB state licensed exam.
Provisional Licensed Real Estate Appraiser	After October 31, 2007, applicants must meet all requirements set forth by the Appraiser Qualifications Board	None. A provisional licensed person has 60 months after receiving the provisional license in which to acquire 2,000 hours of acceptable real estate appraisal experience or the provisional license will be revoked.	AQB-approved state licensed exam.
Appraiser Trainee	None	None	None

Source: 2006 requirements. Updates can be obtained online at http://www.talcb.state.tx.us

have not followed the guidelines for development of an appraisal or analysis contained in the Uniform Standards of Professional Appraisal Practice of the Appraisal Foundation.

CHARACTERISTICS OF VALUE

Up to this point we have been concerned primarily with value based on evidence found in the marketplace and how to report it. Before concluding this chapter, let us briefly touch on what creates value, the principles of real property valuation, and appraisal for purposes other than market value.

For a good or service to have value in the marketplace it must possess four characteristics: demand, utility, scarcity, and transferability. **Demand** is a need or desire coupled with the purchasing power to fill it, whereas **utility** is the ability of a good or service to fill that need. **Scarcity** means there must be a short supply relative to demand. Air, for example, has utility and is in demand, but it is not scarce. Finally, a good or service must be **transferable** to have value to anyone other than the person possessing it.

PRINCIPLES OF VALUE

The **principle of anticipation** reflects the fact that what a person will pay for a property depends on the expected benefits from the property in the future. Thus, the buyer of a home anticipates receiving shelter plus the investment and psychic benefits of home ownership. The investor buys property in anticipation of future income.

The **principle of substitution** states that the maximum value of a property in the marketplace tends to be set by the cost of purchasing an equally desirable substitute property provided no costly delay is encountered in making the substitution. In other words, substitution sets an upper limit on price. Thus, if there are two similar houses for sale, or two similar apartments for rent, the lower-priced one will generally be purchased or rented first. In the same manner, the cost of buying land and constructing a new building sets a limit on the value of existing buildings.

Highest and Best Use

The ***highest and best use*** of a property is that use that will give the property its greatest current value. This means you must be alert to the possibility that the present use of a parcel of land may not be the one that makes the land the most valuable. Consider a 30-year-old house located at a busy intersection in a shopping area. To place a value on that property based on its continued use as a residence would be misleading if the property would be worth more with the house removed and shopping or commercial facilities built on the land instead.

The *principle of competition* recognizes that where substantial profits are being made, competition will be encouraged. For example, if apartment rents increase to the point where owners of existing apartment buildings are making substantial profits, builders and investors will be encouraged to build more apartment buildings.

Supply and Demand

Applied to real estate, the *principle of supply and demand* refers to the ability of people to pay for land coupled with the relative scarcity of land. This means that attention must be given to such matters on the demand side as population growth, personal income, and preferences of people. On the supply side, you must look at the available supply of land and its relative scarcity. When the supply of land is limited and demand is great, the result is rising land prices. Conversely, where land is abundant and there are relatively few buyers, supply and demand will be in balance at only a few cents per square foot.

The *principle of change* reminds us that real property uses are always in a state of change. Although it may be imperceptible on a day-to-day basis, change can easily be seen over longer periods of time. Because the present value of a property is related to its future uses, the more potential changes that can be identified, the more accurate the estimate of its present worth will be.

Diminishing Marginal Returns

The *principle of diminishing marginal returns,* also called the *principle of contribution,* refers to the relationship between added cost and the value it returns. It tells us that we should invest dollars whenever they will return to us more than $1 of value and we should stop when each dollar invested returns less than $1 in value.

The *principle of conformity* holds that maximum value is realized when there is a reasonable degree of homogeneity in a neighborhood. This is the basis for zoning laws across the country; certain tracts in a community are zoned for single-family houses, others for apartment buildings, stores, and industry. Within a tract there should also be a reasonable amount of homogeneity. For example, a $200,000 house would be out of place in a neighborhood of $90,000 houses.

MULTIPLE MEANINGS OF THE WORD "VALUE"

When we hear the word *value,* we tend to think of market value. However, at any given moment in time, a single property can have other values too. This is because value or worth is very much affected by the purpose for which the valuation was performed. For example, **assessed value** is the value given a property by the county tax assessor for purposes of property taxation. *Estate tax value* is the value that federal and state taxation authorities establish for a deceased person's property; it is used to calculate the amount of estate taxes that must be paid. *Insurance value* is concerned with the cost of replacing damaged property. It differs from market value in two major respects: (1) the value of the land is not included, as it is presumed that only the structures are destructible; and (2) the amount of coverage is based on the replacement cost of the structures. **Loan value** is the value set on a property for the purpose of making a loan.

Plottage Value

When two or more adjoining parcels are combined into one large parcel it is called **assemblage.** The increased value of the large parcel over and above the sum of the smaller parcels is called **plottage value.** For example, local zoning laws may permit a six-unit apartment building on a single 10,000-square-foot lot. However, if two of these lots can be combined, zoning laws permit 15 units. This makes the lots more valuable if sold together.

Rental Value

Rental value is the value of a property expressed in terms of the right to its use for a specific period of time. The fee simple interest in a house may have a market value of $80,000, whereas the market value of one month's occupancy might be $600.

Replacement Value

Replacement value is the value as measured by the current cost of building a structure of equivalent utility. **Salvage value** is what a structure is worth if it has to be removed and taken elsewhere, either in whole or dismantled for parts. Because salvage operations require much labor, the salvage value of most buildings is usually very low.

This list of values is not exhaustive, but it points out that the word *value* has many meanings. When reading an appraisal report, always read the first paragraph to see why the appraisal was prepared. Before preparing an appraisal, make certain you know its purpose and then state it at the beginning of your report.

BUYER'S AND SELLER'S MARKETS

Whenever supply and demand are unbalanced because of excess supply, a **buyer's market** exists. This means a buyer can negotiate prices and terms more to his liking, and a seller who wants to sell must accept them. When the imbalance occurs because demand exceeds supply it is a **seller's market;** sellers are able to negotiate prices and terms more to their liking as buyers compete for the available merchandise.

A **broad market** means that many buyers and sellers are in the market at the same time. This makes it relatively easy to establish the price of a property and for a seller to find a buyer quickly, and vice versa. A **thin market** is said to exist when there are only a few buyers and a few sellers in the market at the same time. It is oftentimes difficult to appraise a property in a thin market because there are so few sales to use as comparables.

REVIEW QUESTIONS

Answers to these questions are found in the Answer Key section at the back of the book.

1. Which of the following is NOT one of the three standard approaches to the appraisal of real property?
   A. Income approach
   B. Cost approach
   C. Assessment approach
   D. Market approach

2. To apply the market data approach, a real estate appraiser must collect all the following data on each comparable sale EXCEPT:
   A. date of sale.
   B. marketability of title.
   C. financing terms.
   D. sale price.

3. Adjustments for advantageous financing would be made in the
   A. market comparison approach to appraisal.
   B. cost approach to appraisal.
   C. income approach to appraisal.
   D. capitalization approach to appraisal.

4. After all adjustments are made to a comparable property, its comparative value for appraisal purposes is known as its
   A. adjusted market price.
   B. indicated market value.
   C. amended market price.
   D. revised market price.

5. The value of vacant land is commonly stated in any of the following terms EXCEPT value per
   A. square foot.
   B. acre.
   C. front foot.
   D. square yard.

6. To evaluate a home in order to list it for sale, a real estate agent could use the
   A. standard market comparison method.
   B. competitive market analysis method.
   C. both A and B.
   D. neither A nor B.

7. Seller motivation is considered most in the
   A. income approach.
   B. cost approach.
   C. gross rent multiplier method.
   D. competitive market analysis.

8. Which of the following approaches is most likely to provide only a rough estimate of the value of a rental property?
   A. Cost approach
   B. Income approach
   C. Market comparison approach
   D. Gross rent multiplier

9. In appraising an historically significant residence built in the Victorian era using the cost approach, an appraiser will probably appraise it on the basis of its
   A. reproduction cost.
   B. restoration cost.
   C. replacement cost.
   D. reconstruction cost.

10. Which of the following results from factors outside the property?
   A. Functional obsolescence
   B. Physical deterioration
   C. Economic obsolescence
   D. None of the above

11. The conversion of future income into present value is known as
   A. capitalization.
   B. amortization.
   C. hypothecation.
   D. appreciation.

12. The rents that a property can be expected to produce on an annual basis may be referred to as the
   A. projected gross.
   B. scheduled gross.
   C. both A and B.
   D. neither A nor B.

13. The operating expense ratio of a building is determined by dividing the total operating expenses by the
   A. effective net income.
   B. net operating income.
   C. effective gross income.
   D. actual gross income.

14. From the viewpoint of a qualified real estate appraiser, the value of the subject property is NOT affected by
   A. demand.
   B. scarcity.
   C. highest and best use.
   D. transferability.

15. The use of a property that will give it its greatest current value is its
   A. highest use.
   B. best use.
   C. highest and best use.
   D. maximum use.

16. The relationship between added cost and the value it returns is known as the principle of
   A. diminishing marginal returns.
   B. contribution.
   C. both A and B.
   D. neither A nor B.

17. The principle that holds that maximum value is realized when a reasonable degree of homogeneity is present in a neighborhood is known as the principle of
   A. harmony.
   B. homogeneity.
   C. similarity.
   D. conformity.

18. The process of combining two or more parcels of land into one larger parcel is called
   A. assemblage.
   B. plottage.
   C. salvage.
   D. reproduction.

19. A market where there is an excess of supply over demand is known as a
    A. buyer's market.
    B. broad market.
    C. seller's market.
    D. thin market.

20. Which of the following is not a classification of an appraiser in Texas?
    A. State licensed real estate appraiser
    B. Certified general real estate appraiser
    C. Certified licensed real estate appraiser
    D. Certified residential real estate appraiser

Chapter 20

PERCENT

Percent (%) means part per hundred. For example, 10% means 10 parts per hundred; 25% means 25 parts per hundred. Percentages are related to common and decimal fractions as follows:

$5\% = 0.05 = \frac{1}{20}$
$10\% = 0.10 = \frac{1}{10}$
$25\% = 0.25 = \frac{1}{4}$
$75\% = 0.75 = \frac{3}{4}$
$99\% = 0.99 = \frac{99}{100}$

A percentage greater than 100% is greater than 1. For example:

$110\% = 1.10 = 1\frac{1}{10}$
$150\% = 1.50 = 1\frac{1}{2}$
$200\% = 2.00 = 2$
$1,100\% = 11.00 = 11$

To change a decimal fraction to a percentage, move the decimal point two places to the right and add the % sign. For example:

$0.001 = 0.1\%$
$0.01 = 1\%$
$0.06 = 6\%$
$0.35 = 35\%$
$0.356 = 35.6\%$

A percentage can be changed to a common fraction by writing it as hundredths and then reducing it to its lowest common denominator. For example:

$20\% = 20/100 = \frac{1}{5}$
$90\% = 90/100 = \frac{9}{5}$
$225\% = 225/100 = 2\frac{1}{4}$

Real Estate Math

ADDING AND SUBTRACTING DECIMALS

To add decimals, place the decimal points directly over one another. Then place the decimal point for the solutions in the same column and add. For example:

$$\begin{array}{r} 6.25 \\ 1.10 \\ \underline{10.277} \\ 17.627 \end{array}$$

If you are working with percentages, there is no need to convert to decimal fractions; just line up the decimal points and add. For example:

$$\begin{array}{r} 68.8\% \\ 6.0\% \\ \underline{25.2\%} \\ 100.0\% \end{array}$$

When subtracting, the same methods apply. For example:

$$\begin{array}{r} 1.00 \\ \underline{-0.80} \\ 0.20 \end{array} \qquad \begin{array}{r} 100\% \\ \underline{-80\%} \\ 20\% \end{array}$$

When there is a mixture of decimal fractions and percentages, first convert them all either to percentage or to decimal fractions.

MULTIPLYING AND DIVIDING DECIMALS

Multiplying decimals is like multiplying whole numbers except that the decimal point must be correctly placed. This is done by counting the total number of places to the right of the decimal point in the numbers to be multiplied. Then count off the same number of places in the answer. The following examples illustrate this:

$$\begin{array}{r} 0.6 \\ \underline{\times\ 0.3} \\ 0.18 \end{array} \quad \begin{array}{r} 0.2 \\ \underline{\times\ 0.2} \\ 0.04 \end{array} \quad \begin{array}{r} 1.01 \\ \underline{\times\ 2} \\ 2.02 \end{array} \quad \begin{array}{r} 6 \\ \underline{\times\ 0.1} \\ 0.6 \end{array} \quad \begin{array}{r} 6 \\ \underline{\times\ 0.11} \\ 0.66 \end{array} \quad \begin{array}{r} 0.03 \\ \underline{\times\ 0.02} \\ 0.0006 \end{array}$$

When dividing, the process starts with properly placing the decimal point. A normal division then follows. When a decimal number is divided by a whole number, place the decimal point in the answer directly above the decimal point in the problem. For example:

$$\begin{array}{r} 1.03 \\ 3\overline{)3.09} \end{array} \qquad \begin{array}{r} 0.033 \\ 3\overline{)0.099} \end{array}$$

To divide by a decimal number, you must first change the divisor to a whole number. Then you must make a corresponding change in the dividend. This is done by simply moving both decimal points the same number of places to the right. For example, to divide 0.06 by 0.02, move the decimal point of each to the right two places.

$$\begin{array}{ll} 0.02 \div 0.06 & \text{becomes } 2 \div 6 \\ 0.5 \div 3 & \text{becomes } 5 \div 30 \\ 0.05 \div 30 & \text{becomes } 5 \div 3{,}000 \end{array}$$

When multiplying or dividing with percentages, first convert them to decimal form. Thus 6% of 200 is

$$\begin{array}{r} 200 \\ \times 0.06 \\ \hline 12.00 \end{array}$$

PROBLEMS INVOLVING RATES

The basic equation for solving rate problems is: **Percent** times **Base amount** equals **Result**

$$P \times B = R$$

If you know the result and the percent and you want the base amount, then divide both sides of the equation by P to get:

$$B = \frac{R}{P}$$

If you know the result and the base amount and you want to know the percentage, divide both sides of the equation by B to get:

$$P = \frac{R}{B}$$

An equation will remain an equation as long as you make the same change on both sides of the equal sign. If you add the same number to both sides, it is still an equation. If you subtract the same amount from each side, it is still equal. If you multiply both sides by the same number, it remains equal. If you divide both sides by the same number, it remains equal.

One way to remember the basic equation for solving rate problems is to think of a campaign button that looks like this:

$$R = P \times B \quad P = \frac{R}{B} \quad B = \frac{R}{P}$$

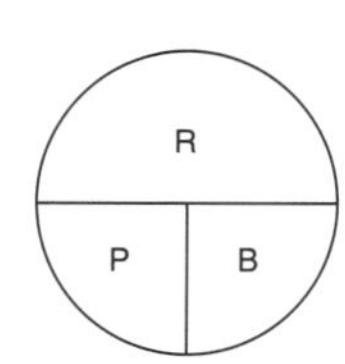

A simple way to solve rate problems is to think of

the word **is** as = (an equal sign).
the word **of** as × (a multiplication sign).
the word **per** as ÷ (a division sign).

For example:

"7% of $50,000 is 3,500"

translates:

"7% × $50,000 = 3,500"

Problem 1

Beverly Broker sells a house for $260,000. Her share of the commission is to be 2.5% of the sales price. How much does she earn?

Her commission is 2.5% of $260,000
Her commission = 0.025 × $260,000
Her commission = $6,500

This is an example of Result = Percent × Base.

Problem 2

Sam Salesman works in an office that will pay him 70% of the commission on each home he lists and sells. With a 6% commission, how much would he earn on a $250,000 sale?

His commission is 70% of 6% of $250,000
His commission = 0.70 × 0.06 × $250,000
His commission = $10,500

This is an example of Result = Percent ×Base.

Problem 3

Newt Newcomer wants to earn $21,000 during his first 12 months as a salesman. He feels he can average 3% on each sale. How much property must he sell?

3% of sales is $21,000
0.03 × sales = $21,000
sales = $21,000 ÷ 0.03
sales = $700,000

This is an example of Base=Result × Percent.

Problem 4

An apartment building nets the owners $12,000 per year on their investment of $100,000. What percent return are they receiving on their investment?

$12,000 is _____ % of $100,000
$12,000 = _____ % × $100,000
$12,000 ÷ $100,000 = 12%

This is an example of Percent = Result × Base.

Problem 5

Smith wants to sell his property and have \$47,000 after paying a 6% brokerage commission on the sales price. What price must Smith get?

$\$47{,}000$ is 94% of selling price

$$\$47{,}000 = 0.94 \times \text{selling price}$$

$$\frac{\$47{,}000}{0.94} = \text{selling price}$$

$$\$50{,}000 = \text{selling price}$$

Problem 6

Miller sold his home for \$275,000, paid off an existing loan of \$35,000, and paid closing costs of \$500. The brokerage commission was 6% of the sales price. How much money did Miller receive?

The amount he received is 94% of \$275,000 less \$35,500.

$$\text{amount} = 0.94 \times \$275{,}000 - \$35{,}500$$

$$\text{amount} = \$258{,}500 - \$35{,}500$$

$$\text{amount} = \$223{,}000$$

Problem 7

The assessed valuation of the Kelly home is \$100,000. If the property tax rate is \$12.50 per \$100 of assessed valuation, what is the tax?

$$\text{The tax is } \frac{\$12.50}{\$100} \text{ of } \$100{,}000$$

$$\text{tax} = \frac{\$12.50}{\$100} \times \$100{,}000$$

$$\text{tax} = \$12{,}500.00$$

Problem 8

Property in Clark County is assessed at 75% of market value. What should the assessed valuation of a \$40,000 property be?

Assessed valuation is 75% of market value

$$\text{Assessed valuation} = 0.75 \times \$40{,}000$$

$$\text{Assessed valuation} = \$30{,}000$$

Problem 9

An insurance company charges \$0.24 per \$100 of coverage for a one-year fire insurance policy. How much would a \$40,000 policy cost?

$$\text{Cost is } \frac{\$0.24}{\$100} \text{ of } \$40{,}000$$

$$\text{Cost} = \frac{\$0.24}{\$100} \times \$40{,}000$$

$$\text{Cost} = \$96$$

AREA MEASUREMENT

The measurement of the distance from one point to another is called *linear* measurement. Usually this is along a straight line, but it can also be along a curved line. Distance is measured in inches, feet, yards, and miles. Less commonly used are chains (66 feet) and rods ($16\frac{1}{2}$). Surface areas are measured in square feet, square yards, acres (43,560 square feet), and square miles. In the metric system, the standard unit of linear measurement is the meter (39.37 inches). Land area is measured in square meters and hectares. A hectare contains 10,000 square meters or 2.471 acres.

To determine the area of a square or rectangle, multiply its length times its width. The formula is:

$$\text{Area} = \text{Length} \times \text{Width}$$
$$A = L \times W$$

Problem 10

A parcel of land measures 660 feet by 330 feet. How many square feet is this?

$$\text{Area} = 660 \text{ feet} \times 330 \text{ feet}$$
$$\text{Area} = 217{,}800 \text{ square feet}$$

How many acres does this parcel contain?

$$\text{Acres} = 217{,}800 \div 43{,}560$$
$$\text{Acres} = 5$$

If a buyer offers $42,500 for this parcel, how much is the offering per acre?

$$\$42{,}500 \div 5 = \$8{,}500$$

To determine the area of a right triangle, multiply one-half of the base times the height:

$$A = \tfrac{1}{2} \times B \times H$$
$$A = \tfrac{1}{2} \times 25 \times 50$$
$$A = 625 \text{ square feet}$$

$$A = \tfrac{1}{2} \times B \times H$$
$$A = \tfrac{1}{2} \times 40 \times 20$$
$$A = 400 \text{ square feet}$$

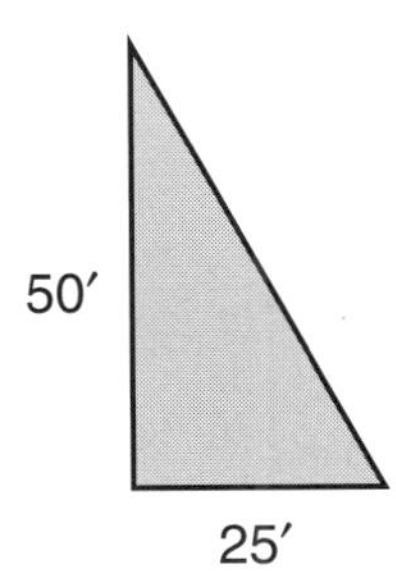

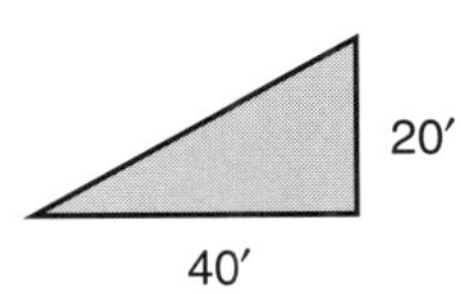

To determine the area of a circle, multiply 3.14 (π) times the square of the radius:

$$A = \pi \times r^2$$
$$A = 3.14 \times 40^2$$
$$A = 3.14 \times 1{,}600$$
$$A = 5{,}024 \text{ sq ft}$$

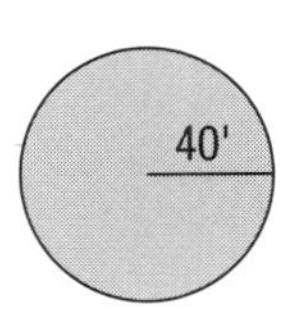

Note: Where the diameter of a circle is given, divide by two to get the radius.

To determine the area of composite figures, separate them into their various components. Thus:

$20' \times 60' = 1{,}200$ sq ft
$10' \times 50' = 500$ sq ft
$1{,}700$ sq ft

$20' \times 70' = 1{,}400$ sq ft
$10' \times 30' = 300$ sq ft
$1{,}700$ sq ft

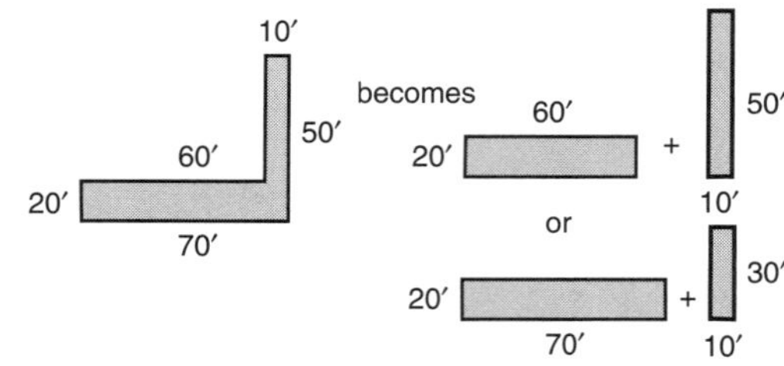

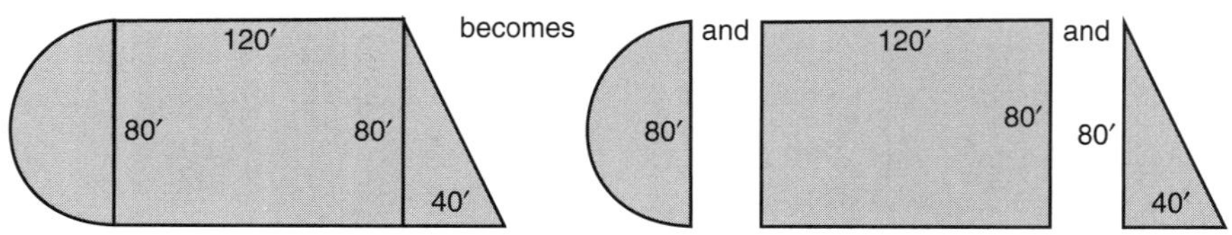

$$(3.14 \times 40'^2 \times \tfrac{1}{2}) + (80' \times 120') + (\tfrac{1}{2} \times 40' \times 80') = 13{,}712 \text{ sq ft}$$

VOLUME MEASUREMENT

Volume is measured in cubic units. The formula is:

Volume = Length × Width × Height
$V = L \times W \times H$

For example, what is the volume of a room that is 10 ft by 15 ft with an 8-ft ceiling?

$V = 10' \times 15' \times 8'$
$V = 1{,}200$ cu ft

Caution: When solving area and volume problems, make certain that all the units are the same. For example, if a parcel of land is one-half mile long and 200 ft wide, convert one measurement so that both are expressed in the same unit; thus the answer will be either in square feet or in square miles. There is no such area measurement as a mile-foot. If a building is 100 yards long by 100 feet wide by 16' 6" high, convert to 300 ft by 100 ft by 16.5 ft before multiplying.

RATIOS AND PROPORTIONS

If the label on a five-gallon can of paint says it will cover 2,000 square feet, how many gallons are necessary to cover 3,600 sq ft?

A problem like this can be solved two ways:

One way is to find out what area one gallon will cover. In this case 2,000 sq ft ÷ 5 gallons = 400 sq ft per gallon. Then divide 400 sq ft/gal into 3,600 sq ft and the result is 9 gallons.

The other method is to set up a proportion:

$$\frac{5 \text{ gal}}{2{,}000 \text{ sq ft}} = \frac{Y \text{ gal}}{3{,}600 \text{ sq ft}}$$

This reads, "5 gallons is to 2,000 sq ft as 'Y' gallons is to 3,600 sq ft." To solve for "Y," multiply both sides of the proportion by 3,600 sq ft. Thus:

$$\frac{5 \text{ gal} \times 3,600 \text{ sq ft}}{2,000 \text{ sq ft}} = \text{Y gal}$$

Divide 2,000 sq ft into 3,600 sq ft and multiply the result by 5 gallons to get the answer.

FRONT-FOOT CALCULATIONS

When land is sold on a front-foot basis, the price is the number of feet fronting on the street times the price per front foot.

Price = front footage × rate per front foot

Thus a 50 ft × 150 ft lot priced at $1,000 per front foot would sell for $50,000. Note that in giving the dimensions of a lot, the first dimension given is the street frontage. The second dimension is the depth of the lot.

REVIEW QUESTIONS

Answers to these questions are found in the Answer Key section at the back of the book.

1. Jennifer Rand is purchasing a $158,000 townhome. The lender has agreed to make her a 95% loan. How much cash will she need at closing in addition to her $1,200 earnest deposit?
   A. $7,900.00
   B. $ 5,000.00
   C. $6,700.00
   D. $9,210.00

2. John Dalton paid annual property taxes of $3,657in 2005. If the tax rate in the area is $2.65 per $100 of valuation, what was the appraised value of the property?
   A. $231,000.00
   B. $138,000.00
   C. $969,105.00
   D. $158,000.00

3. Betty sold a duplex for $189,500. Her broker charged a 6% commission. Betty is on a 60/40 split. Another agent in the office listed the property. How much will Betty earn from the sale?
   A. $6,822.00
   B. $2,274.00
   C. $4,471.00
   D. $3,411.00

4. Mrs. Waters wants to net $90,500 from the sale of her home. If she pays her broker a 7% commission and he estimates her closing costs will an additional $2,300, at what price must she list the property? Round to the nearest $100.00.
   A. $99,800.00
   B. $92,800.00
   C. $99,300.00
   D. $95,900.00

5. The appraiser has estimated the annual net income from a commercial building to be $235,875. When capitalized at a rate of 12.75%, what is the estimated property value?
   A. $1,650.000.00
   B. $1,850,000.00
   C. $2,000,000.00
   D. $998,750.00

6. Mr. Wilson's percentage lease calls for a minimum monthly fee of $1450, plus 6% of gross annual sales in excess of $100,000 per year. His gross sales for the year were $275,000. What was his total rent for the year?
   A. $25,600.00
   B. $27,900.00
   C. $17,400.00
   D. $36,900.00

7. You borrow $63,000 at 11.3/4% simple interest. How much will you repay at the end of 21 months?
   A. $74,200.60
   B. $63,000.01
   C. $61,687.52
   D. $75,954.38

8. How much is applied to interest on a payment of $868.90 when the interest rate is 8.5% and the loan balance is $88,483.77?
   A. $626.76
   B. $524.82
   C. $752.12
   D. $456.98

9. You sell a property for $162,150, which is 15% over what you paid for it. What did you pay for it originally?
   A. $122,979.00
   B. $134,300.00
   C. $141,000.00
   D. $722,060.00

10. A parcel of land 500 feet long and 400 feet wide has been subdivided into 20 lots that are 60 feet by 130 feet. The remainder of square footage is reserved for roads. What percent of the parcel is reserved for roads?
    A. 25%
    B. 31%
    C. 28%
    D. 22%

11. A rectangular warehouse has outside dimensions of 100' wide and 200' long. The walls are one foot thick. Based on this information, how much useable square footage space remains?
    A. 27,200 square feet
    B. 25,789 square yards
    C. 17,395 square yards
    D. 19,404 square feet

12. Sam Smith purchased a home. The selling price is $107,000. He is acquiring a new conventional loan and decided to put 10% down payment. The interest rate is 8%. He is closing September 10. Use a 30 day month. How much interest would the buyer pay at closing?
    A. $531.00
    B. $449.40
    C. $344.00
    D. $416.67

13. A Banker's or Statutory year is often used in prorations and assumes a 360-day year with each month having 30 days. Use a Banker's year in the following proration. Prorate taxes for a closing date of March 30,2007, in which the assessed value of the property is $141,000 and the combined tax rate is $2.40 per $100 valuation Taxes for 2006 are paid.
    A. $846.00 Debit the seller/Credit the buyer
    B. $846.00 Debit the buyer/Credit the seller
    C. $940.00 Debit the seller/Credit the buyer
    D. $940.00 Debit the buyer/Credit the seller

14. For a closing scheduled October 22, 2001, the parties want the insurance policy to transfer for consideration. The 1 year policy was purchased August 10, 2001. The annual premium of $1385 was paid on that date. How much will the buyer owe the seller at closing?
    A. $1401.15 Debit the buyer/Credit the seller
    B. $1104.15 Debit the buyer/Credit the seller
    C. $1401.15 Debit the seller/Credit the buyer
    D. $1104.15 Debit the seller/Credit the buyer

Chapter 21

KEY TERMS

Exclusive authority to purchase: listing used by buyer's brokers

Exclusive right to sell: a listing that gives the broker the right to collect a commission no matter who sells the property during the listing period

Listing: a contract wherein a broker is employed to find a buyer or tenant

Multiple listing service: organization of member brokers agreeing to share listing information and share commissions

Net listing: a listing agreement that pays the broker an uncertain amount of commission, generating the principal net proceeds from the sale

Ready, willing, and able buyer: a buyer who is ready to buy at the seller's price and terms and who has the financial capability to do so

The Principal–Broker Relationship: Employment

IN THIS CHAPTER

This chapter covers the employment relationship between a broker and his principal. The main topics of the chapter include the listing agreement, the exclusive right to sell the listing, the exclusive agency listing, open listing, net listing, and the listing period. The chapter also covers the multiple listing service and broker compensation. A discussion of procuring cause, listing contract termination, and bargain brokers is also included.

Chapter 2 discussed licensure requirements and professional affiliations. This chapter will discuss the principal-broker relationship as it relates to employment, listing agreements, buyer representation agreements, and compensation of real estate brokers. Chapter 22 will then expand into theories of agency relationships and duties of care that result from the laws of agency. Note that the formalities of employment are not necessarily required to establish an agency relationship, so the licensee may be responsible as an agent without the benefits of formal employment!

LISTING AGREEMENT

A real estate ***listing*** is an *employment contract* between a property owner (the seller) and a real estate broker. Through it the property owner appoints the broker as the owner's agent for the specific purpose of finding a buyer or tenant who is willing to meet the conditions set forth in the listing. It does not authorize the broker to sell or convey title to the property or to sign contracts.

Although persons licensed as real estate salespersons perform listing and sales functions, they are actually extensions of the broker. A seller may conduct all aspects of a listing and sale through a salesperson licensee, but it is the broker behind the salesperson with whom the seller has the listing contract and who is legally liable for its proper execution. If you plan to be a salesperson for a broker, be aware of what is legally and ethically required of a broker because you are the broker's eyes, ears, hands, and mouth. If your interest is in listing your property with a broker, know that it is the broker with whom you have the listing contract even though your day-to-day contact is with the broker's sales associates. *Sales associates* are the licensed salespersons or brokers who work for a broker.

When a property owner signs a listing, all the essential elements of a valid contract must be present. The owner and broker must be legally capable of contracting, there must be mutual assent, and the agreement must be for a lawful purpose. Texas requires that a listing be in writing and signed to be valid and thereby enforceable against a principal in a court of law.

Figure 21.1 illustrates a simplified ***exclusive right to sell*** listing agreement. Actual listing contracts tend to be longer and more complex and vary in detail from one contract to the next. The listing in Figure 21.1 is an educational introduction to listings that provides in plain English commonly found listing contract provisions. Beginning at **[1]**, there is a description of the property plus the price and terms at which the broker is instructed to find a buyer. At **[2]**, the broker promises to make a reasonable effort to find a buyer. The period of time that the listing is to be in effect is shown at **[3]**. It is usually to the broker's advantage to make the listing period for as long as possible because this provides more time to find a buyer. Sometimes even an overpriced property will become salable if the listing period is long enough and prices rise fast enough. However, most owners want a balance between their flexibility and the amount of time necessary for a broker to conduct a sales campaign. In residential sales, three to four months is a popular compromise; farm, ranch, commercial, and industrial listings are usually made for six months to one year.

At **[4]**, the owner agrees not to list the property with any other brokers, permit other brokers to have a sign on the property, or advertise it during the listing period. Also, the owner agrees not to revoke the broker's exclusive right to find a buyer as set forth by this contract.

The broker recognizes that the owner may later accept a price and terms that are different from those in the listing. The wording at **[5]** states that the broker will earn a commission no matter what price and terms the owner ultimately accepts.

Brokerage Commission

At **[6]**, the amount of compensation the owner agrees to pay the broker is established. The usual arrangement is to express the amount as a percentage of the sale or exchange price, although a stated dollar amount could be used if the owner and broker agreed. In any event, the amount of the fee is negotiable between the owner and the broker. An owner who feels the fee is too high can list with someone who charges less or sell the property himself. The broker recognizes that if the fee is too low it will not be worthwhile spending time and effort finding a buyer. The typical commission fee in the United States at present is 5% to 7% of the selling price for houses, condominiums, and small apartment buildings, and 6% to 10% on farms, ranches, and vacant land. On multimillion-dollar improved properties, commissions usually drop to the 1% to 4% range. Brokerage

FIGURE 21.1 Exclusive right to sell listing contract

EXCLUSIVE RIGHT TO SELL
LISTING CONTRACT

Property Description: A single-family house at 2424 E. Main Street, City, State, Legally described as Lot 17, Tract 191, County, State [1]

Price: $105,000

Terms: Cash

[2] *In consideration of the services of* ABC Realty Company *(herein called the "Broker"), to be rendered to* Roger Leeving and Mary Leeving *(herein called the "Owner"), and the promise of said Broker to make reasonable efforts to obtain a*

[3] *purchaser, therefore, the Owner hereby grants to the Broker for the period of time*

[4] *from noon on* April 1, 200x *to noon on* July 1, 200x *(herein called the "listing period") the exclusive and irrevocable right to advertise and find a purchaser for the above described property at the price and terms shown or for such sum and*

[5] *terms or exchange as the owner later agrees to accept.*

[6] *The Owner hereby agrees to pay Broker a cash fee of* 6% *of the selling or exchange price:*

[7] *(A) in case of any sale or exchange of the above property within the listing period either by the Broker, the Owner, or any other person, or*

[8] *(B) upon the Broker finding a purchase who is ready, willing, and about to complete the purchase as proposed by the owner, or*

[9] *(C) in the event of a sale or exchange within 60 days of the expiration of the listing period to any party shown the above property during the listing period by the Broker or his representative and where the name was disclosed to the Owner.*

[10] *The Owner agrees to give the Broker access to the buildings on the property for the purposes of showing them at reasonable hours, and allows the Broker to post a "For Sale" sign on the premises.*

[11] *The Owner agrees to allow the Broker to place this listing information in any multiple listing organization of which he is a member and to engage the cooperation of other brokers as subagents to bring about a sale.*

[12] *The Owner agrees to refer to the Broker all inquiries regarding this property during the listing period.*

Accepted: ABC Realty Company

[13] By: Kurt Kwiklister Owner: Roger Leeving

Date: April 1, 200x Owner: Mary Leeving

Source: © 2012 Cengage Learning

commissions are not set by a state regulatory agency or by local real estate boards. In fact, any effort by brokers to set commission rates among themselves is a violation of federal and state anti-trust laws. The penalty can be as much as triple damages and criminal liability.

The conditions under which a commission must be paid by the owner to the broker appear next. At [7], a commission is deemed to be earned if the owner agrees to a sale or exchange of the property no matter who finds the buyer. In other words, even if the owner finds a buyer, or a friend of the owner finds a buyer, the broker is entitled to a full commission fee. If the owner disregards the promise at [4] and lists with another broker who then sells the property, the owner is liable for two full commissions.

Protecting the Broker

The wording at [8] is included to protect the broker against the possibility that the owner may refuse to sell after the broker has expended time and effort to find a buyer at the price and terms of the listing contract. The listing itself is not an offer to sell property. It is strictly a contract whereby the owner employs the broker to find a buyer. Thus, even though a buyer offers to pay the exact price and terms shown in the listing, the buyer does not have a binding sales contract until the offer is accepted in writing by the owner. However, if the owner refuses to sell at the listed price and terms, the broker is still entitled to a commission. If the owner does not pay the broker voluntarily, the broker can file a lawsuit against the owner to collect.

Protecting the Owner

At [9], the broker is protected against the possibility that the listing period will expire while still working with a prospective purchaser. In fairness to the owner, however, two limitations are placed on the broker. First, a sales contract must be concluded within a reasonable time after the listing expires, and second, the name of the purchaser must have been given to the owner before the listing period expires.

Continuing at [10], the owner agrees to let the broker enter the property at reasonable hours to show it and put a "For Sale" sign on the property. At [11], the property owner gives the broker specific permission to enter the property into a multiple listing service and to engage the cooperation of other brokers as subagents to bring about a sale.

At [12], the owner agrees to refer all inquiries regarding the availability of the property to the broker. The purpose is to discourage the owner from thinking that she might be able to save a commission by personally selling it during the listing period and to provide sales leads for the broker. Finally, at [13], the owner and the broker (or the broker's sales associate if authorized to do so) sign and date the agreement.

Types of Listing

Exclusive Right to Sell Listing

The listing illustrated in Figure 21.1 is called an *exclusive right to sell* or *exclusive authorization to sell* the listing. Its distinguishing characteristic is that no matter who sells the property during the listing period, the listing broker is entitled to a commission. This is the most widely used type of listing in the United States. Once signed by the owner and accepted by the broker, the primary advantage to the broker is that the money and effort the broker expends on advertising and showing the property will be to the broker's benefit. The advantage to the owner is that the broker will usually put more effort into selling a property if the broker holds an exclusive right to sell than if the broker has an exclusive agency or an open listing.

Exclusive Agency Listing

The **exclusive agency listing** is similar to the listing shown in Figure 21.1, except that the owner may sell the property himself during the listing period and not owe a commission to the broker. The broker, however, is the only broker who can act as an agent during the listing period; hence the term *exclusive agency*. For an owner, this type of listing may seem like the best of two worlds: The owner has a broker looking for a buyer, but if the owner finds a buyer first, the owner can save a commission fee. The broker is less enthusiastic because the broker's efforts can too easily be undermined by the owner. Consequently, the broker may not expend as much effort on advertising and showing the property as with an exclusive right to sell.

Open Listing

Open listings carry no exclusive rights. An owner can give an open listing to any number of brokers at the same time, and the owner can still find a buyer and avoid a commission. This gives the owner the greatest freedom of any listing form, but there is little incentive for the broker to expend time and money showing the property because the broker has little control over who will be compensated if the property is sold. The broker's only protection is that if the broker does find a buyer at the listing price and terms, the broker is entitled to a commission. This reluctance to develop a sales effort usually means that few, if any, offers will be received and the result may be no sale or a sale below market price. Yet, if a broker does find a buyer, the commission earned may be the same as with an exclusive right to sell.

Net Listing

A ***net listing*** is created when an owner states the price she wants for her property and then agrees to pay the broker anything above that price as the commission. It can be written in the form of an exclusive right to sell, an exclusive agency, or an open listing. If a homeowner asks for a "net $60,000" and the broker sells the home for $75,000, the commission would be $15,000, less the costs of the sale.

Calculating the net amount can be tricky. The easiest method to calculate the commission is by dividing the net price by the difference in the commission amount. For instance, if you want a commission to be 5%, you would take the net asking price ($60,000), add in the closing costs (roughly 3% of the sales price, $1,800), and divide it by .95, which equals $65,052.63. The total price, then, to net the seller $60,000, would be $1,800 in closing costs, plus 3,252.63 (65,052.63 × .05), rounded up to $65,053.

By using the net listing method, many owners feel that they are forcing the broker to look to the buyer for the commission by marking up the price of the property. In reality though, would a buyer pay over $65,000 for a home that is worth $60,000? Because of widespread misunderstanding regarding net listings, some states prohibit them outright (Texas does not), and most brokers strenuously avoid them even when requested by property owners. There is no law that says a broker must accept a listing; a broker is free to accept only those listings for which the broker can perform a valuable service and earn an honest profit.

Exclusive Authority to Purchase

Previous portions of this chapter have presumed the general rule that the real estate broker represents the seller. Historically, it has been the seller who has hired brokers to assist in marketing property. Consumers, though, are far more sophisticated and informed today. They are aware of the complexities of the market, property condition, and consumer protection laws. They need, and want, advice from a real estate professional. The Real Estate Buyer Agent Council (REBAC), a division of the National Association of REALTORS®, has increased its membership dramatically, reflecting buyers' requests for an agent to help them to locate property, or to assist them in negotiating the acquisition of a specified property.

In such cases, the broker's primary responsibility is to the purchaser rather than to the seller. In this circumstance, the purchaser can reveal confidential information to the broker and rely on the broker's expertise and competence. This may be particularly helpful in situations where a real estate transaction is complex, or there are peculiar concerns unique to certain regions of the country (termites in Houston, radon in Maine, soil conditions in California) about which a buyer wants to be adequately advised before buying real estate in that area.

In these situations, the principal (the buyer) needs to be assured as to the scope of employment of the broker (i.e., locating the property) and, similar to a listing contract, the broker needs to be assured that he is protected, and that the buyer does not "go around" the broker and cut the broker out of a commission once the property has been identified. This is a major concern for buyer's brokers, because an agent can educate the buyer, then have the buyer cut out the broker in hope of a better sales price (with a lower commission paid). Buyers, then, need to be committed to their agent, and building that level of trust and confidence is not easy. A good employment contract, coupled with good service, develops this trust.

Figure 21.2 shows a simplified version of an ***exclusive authority to purchase*** contract. Note at [1] the parties are named. The real difference in this

FIGURE 21.2 Exclusive authority to purchase contract

EXCLUSIVE AUTHORITY TO PURCHASE CONTRACT

This Agreement is made in ________________ on this _______ day of __________, 20__, whereby ____________________________ (hereinafter referred to as "Buyer") hereby appoints Buyer's Broker (hereinafter referred to as "Broker") as Buyer's exclusive agent for the purposes set forth in Section 2 hereof and under the terms specified herein. [1]

Section 1. Buyer agrees to conduct all negotiations for property of the type described in Section 2 hereof through Broker, and to refer to Broker all inquiries received in any form from real estate brokers, salespersons, prospective sellers, or any other source, during the time this Agreement is in effect. [5]

Section 2. Buyer desires to purchase or lease real property (which may include items of personal property described as follows:

Type: ____ Residential ____ Residential Income ____ Other
____ Commercial ____ Industrial ____ Vacant Land [2]

General Description: ____

Approximate price range: $______________ to $_________, or any other amount which Buyer ultimately decides to spend.

Preferred Terms:____

Section 3. Broker's authority as Buyer's exclusive agent shall begin upon Buyer's signing this Agreement, and shall continue until _______________, 20__, unless sooner terminated or by completion for the purpose(s) of the agency as set forth in Section 2 hereof. [4]

Section 4. Broker represents that Broker is duly licenses as a real estate broker, and agrees that Broker will use Broker's best efforts as Buyer's agent to locate property as described in Section 2 hereof, and to negotiate acceptance of any offer to purchase or lease such property. Broker shall submit to Buyer for the Buyer's consideration, properties appearing to Broker to substantially meet the criteria set forth in Section 2.

Section 5. In consideration of the services to be performed by Broker, Buyer agrees to pay Broker an amount equal to the greater of:

(a) (__) Retainer Fee. Buyer will pay Broker a non-refundable retainer fee of $____________ due and payable upon signing of this Agreement. (__) Retainer fee shall be credited against commission, IF ANY as set forth in Sub Section 5(c) herein or Retainer Fee shall be retained by Broker in addition to commission; or [3]

(b) (__) Hourly Fee. Buyer will pay Broker at the rate of $_______ per hour for the time spent by Broker pursuant to this Agreement, to be paid to Broker when billed to Buyer. (__) Fee shall be credited against commission, IF ANY or (__) Fee shall be considered full payment of Broker's compensation; or

(c) (__) Commission. Parties hereby agree that Broker shall first seek compensation out of the transaction. Should the fee so obtained be greater than that listed in subsection (c)(1) or (2) below, Broker shall pay Buyer the difference at closing. Should the fee so obtained be less than that listed in subsection (1) or (2) hereof, Buyer shall pay Broker the difference at closing.

Section 6. If a seller in an agreement made on behalf of Buyer fails to close such agreement, with no fault on the part of Buyer, the commission provided in Section 5, subsection (c), shall be waived. If such transaction fails to close because of any fault on the part of the Buyer, such commission will not be waived, but will be due and payable immediately in an amount no less than that referred to in Section 5, said amount to be agreed upon by the parties to be liquidated damages. In no case shall Broker be obligated to advance funds for the benefit of Buyer in order to complete a closing.

Section 7. (__) Broker does (__) Does Not have Buyer's permission to disclose Buyer's identity to third parties without prior written consent of Buyer.

Section 8. Buyer understands that other potential buyers may consider, make offers on, or purchase through, Broker the same or similar properties as Buyer is seeking to acquire. Buyer consents to Broker's representation of such other potential buyers before, during and after the expiration of this Agreement.

Section 9. The parties agree not to discriminate against any prospective seller or lessor because of the race, creed, color, sex, marital status, national origin, familial or handicapped status of such person.

Accepted:

[6]

______________________________ ______________________________
Buyer's Broker Buyer

By:___________________________ ______________________________
Title Buyer

Source: © 2012 Cengage Learning

contract, versus the Listing Agreement, occurs at [2], designating the property to be required in general terms, so that the broker has guidance as to what type of property to be looking for. Compensation is different also. Most buyer's brokers would anticipate being able to access commission splits through the traditional MLS system. If, however, a seller or listing broker refuses to split a commission, there must be an alternative for compensation at [3] for that buyer's broker. Note at [4], there is an expiration date for the term of the agreement, at [5] a requirement by the buyer to refer inquiries to the broker, and at [6] a signature provision for both the buyer's broker and the purchaser.

MULTIPLE LISTING SERVICE

Multiple listing service (MLS) organizations enable a broker with a listing to make a blanket offering of subagency and/or compensation to other member brokers, thus broadening the market exposure for a given property. Member brokers are authorized to show each other's properties to their prospects. If a sale results, the commission is divided between the broker who found the buyer and the broker who obtained the listing.

Market Exposure

A property listed with a broker who is a multiple listing service member receives the advantage of greater sales exposure which, in turn, means a better price and a quicker sale. For the buyer it means learning about what is for sale at many offices without having to visit each individually. For a broker or salesperson with a prospect but not a suitable property listed in that office, the opportunity to make a sale is not lost because the prospect can be shown the listings of other brokers.

To give a property the widest possible market exposure and to maintain fairness among its members, most multiple listing organizations obligate each member broker to provide information to the organization on each new listing within three to seven days after the listing is taken. To facilitate the exchange of information, multiple listing organizations have developed customized listing forms. These forms are a combination of an exclusive right-to-sell listing agreement (with authority to place the listing into multiple) plus a data sheet on the property. The latest MLS systems are extremely hi tech. The information on the property is fed into a computer at the broker's office. A photograph of the home is scanned in or electronically loaded with the data, and the listing is officially on MLS. Then, if Broker B has a prospect interested in a property listed by Broker A, Broker B telephones Broker A and arranges to show the property. If Broker B's prospect makes an offer on the property, Broker B contacts Broker A and together they can present the offer.

In looking for a new property on behalf of the buyer, Broker B can scan the MLS listings and sort elements to locate homes by zone area, square footage, number of bedrooms and baths, price range, and any number of other criteria for which the buyer may be looking. Obviously, this computerized system eliminates combing through the old MLS books of the past. Because the MLS computer data is updated as the information is posted, the system always stays current.

MLS organizations have been taken to court for being open only to members of local real estate boards. The role that multiple listing services play directly or indirectly in commission splitting is also being tested in the courts. Another idea that has been tested in courts is that an MLS be open to anyone who wants to list a property, broker or owner. It is generally held, though, that owners lacking real estate sophistication would place much inaccurate information in the MLS and this would do considerable harm to MLS members who must rely on that information when describing and showing properties. It is also important to note that the sharing of MLS information to nonmembers may violate federal copyright and/or trademark laws.

Electronic Marketing

A prospective buyer can now take a visual tour through a neighborhood without leaving the broker's office via video or the web. Using computerized access to MLS files, the salesperson can show a prospect a color picture of each property for sale along with pictures of the street and neighborhood, plus nearby schools and shopping facilities.

Most MLS systems allow up to eight photographs to be loaded into the data bank so that the buyer can see several pictures of the property prior to a personal inspection. "Virtual tours" or "visual tours" are also available on most MLS data systems. It is up to the listing broker whether or not these additional marketing tools will be used. Both the multiple photographs and virtual tour system can be very effective marketing devices.

The web now dominates the market for both practitioners and individual buyers and sellers. Not only can individual sellers post on many Internet services (alternate sources are available for buyers and buyer's brokers), but the MLS is also on the Internet in all locations. In addition, most real estate offices have their own websites (both buyers' brokers and sellers' brokers) and a few real estate companies have been developed solely to market to the Internet customer and client. Some of these companies offer fewer services and, as a result, offer lower fees, or rebates, to their principal. These new companies frequently take the position that they are providing fewer man hours for their services, so they can charge lower fees.

Free enterprise and competition are wonderful things! In just a few short years the web and the Internet have made a huge impact on the way real estate agents handle their business.

BROKER COMPENSATION

Listing Brokers

In order to legally pursue a cause of action for a commission against a principal, the listing broker must be able to clearly show that he was employed. Usually, this requirement is fulfilled by using a preprinted listing form approved for use by the local multiple listing service. The broker fills in the blank spaces with the information that applies to the property he is listing. If listings come in letter form from property owners, the broker must make certain that all the essential requirements of a valid listing are present and clearly stated. If they are not, the broker may expend time and money finding a buyer only to be denied a commission because he was not properly employed. To guard against this, the broker should transfer the owner's request to the preprinted listing form he uses and then have the owner sign it.

"Ready, Willing, and Able"

There is considerable authority in Texas for the view that once a real estate broker has met the foregoing statutory requirements and produces a ***ready, willing, and able buyer***, the broker, at that time, has earned his commission and is owed that commission even if the listing agreement says that the commission is contingent upon the closing of the transaction. The theory is that a listing is usually a unilateral contract (I'll pay you if you perform the agency objective). Once the broker has produced a ready, willing, and able buyer, the broker has performed as required in the contract; if the seller chooses not to close the transaction, the seller still owes the broker the commission. There is further authority that in the event a broker must sue for his commission, he may also recover his attorney's fees in pursuing this cause of action against his principal.

The difference between the two arrangements becomes important when a buyer is found at the price and terms acceptable to the owner, but no sale results. The "ready, willing, and able" contract provides more protection for the broker because his commission does not depend on the deal reaching settlement. The no sale, no commission approach is to the owner's advantage, because he is not required to pay a commission unless there is a completed sale. However, with the passage of time, court decisions have tended to blur the clear-cut distinction between the two. For example, if the owner has a no sale, no commission agreement, it would appear that if the broker brought a ready, willing, and able buyer at the listing price and terms and the owner refused to sell, the owner would owe no commission, because there was no sale. However, a court of law likely would find in favor of the broker for the full amount of the commission if the refusal to sell was arbitrary and without reasonable cause or in bad faith.

Buyers' Brokers

Buyer's broker issues are a little more complicated. As previously stated, buyers might have an incentive to "go around" the broker to achieve a lower sales price. In addition, the buyer's broker's agreement cannot specify the property to be purchased, because it hasn't been identified yet. Most agreements provide that the buyer's broker will be compensated by the seller's broker, but should contain provisions that if the seller or seller's broker refuses to pay the buyer's agent, the buyer is obligated to pay.

License Act Requirements

In Texas, the Real Estate License Act sets specific requirements that a person must comply with to maintain an action for a commission. A person may not file a lawsuit for the collection of compensation for performance without alleging and proving that the person is a duly licensed real estate broker or salesperson. In addition, an action may not be brought in a court of this state for recovery of a commission unless the promise for such commission is in writing and signed by the party to be charged, or by a person lawfully authorized to sign the commission agreement. This provision does *not,* however, apply to an agreement to share compensation between licensees. These agreements can be verbal. The License Act also requires that the licensee shall advise the purchaser, in writing, that the purchaser should have the abstract examined by an attorney of the purchaser selection, or that the purchaser should be furnished with or obtain a policy of title insurance. The Act also allows brokers to sue each other for commissions (or tortious interference) even if nothing is in writing. This "opens the gate" for cooperating brokers and buyer's brokers to sue listing agents. So licensees need to be very careful when casually involving other licensees. It may result in a lawsuit!

PUTTING IT TO WORK

Under a ready, willing, and able listing, traditionally, if a broker produced a buyer, it was up to the owner to decide if the buyer was, in fact, financially able to buy. If the owner accepted the buyer's offer and subsequently the buyer did not have the money to complete the deal, the owner still owed the broker a commission. The legal thinking today is that the broker should be responsible, being in a much better position to analyze the buyer's financial ability than the owner.

In today's marketplace, buyers are usually prequalified for financial ability. Increased competition among lenders has made this quick, inexpensive, and easy. Licensees should be careful to only pass on information, though, and not make representations about a buyer's financial ability.

PROCURING CAUSE

In general terms, a **procuring cause** is the cause originating in a series of events that, without a break in their continuity, results in the accomplishment of the agency objective (closing the transaction). In the past, real estate agents have often felt that if they were the first person to introduce the buyer to a transaction, they were the procuring cause. In fact, this is just not the case. The facts surrounding any broker's involvement vary widely. On the one hand, the buyer's representative may provide very valuable advice and counsel to a prospective purchaser, and, regardless of the facts, the buyer would not submit an offer without this broker's involvement. On the other hand, there is always the buyer who suddenly remembers, upon the listing broker preparing an offer, that his third cousin's dentist is a broker and wants to earn a commission on this transaction.

A broker who possesses an employment agreement (either with the seller or the buyer) is entitled to a commission if he can prove that the resulting sale was primarily due to his efforts. That is, the broker has to have been the procuring cause, the one whose efforts originated procurement of the sale. Suppose that a broker with an exclusive right to sell a listing shows a property to a prospect and, during the listing period or an extension, that prospect goes directly to the owner and concludes a deal. Even though the owner negotiates her own transaction and prepares her own sales contract, the broker is entitled to a full commission for finding the buyer. This would also be true if the owner and the buyer used a subterfuge or strawman to purchase the property to avoid paying a commission. Texas law protects the broker who has in good faith produced a buyer at the request of an owner.

When an open listing is given to two or more brokers, the first one who produces a buyer is entitled to the commission. For example, Broker 1 shows a property to Prospect P but no sale is made. Later P goes to Broker 2 and makes an offer, which is accepted by the owner. Although two brokers have attempted to sell the property, only one has succeeded, and that one is entitled to the commission. The fact that Broker 1 receives nothing, even though he may have expended considerable effort, is an important reason why brokers dislike open listings.

Buyer's brokers create a much more complicated issue involving procuring cause, one that has caused considerable unrest in the real estate brokerage community. At times a prospect may visit a property one or more times and spend a great deal of the listing broker's time asking questions and getting information. Before submitting an offer, however, the prospect may request the assistance and advice of a buyer's broker and requests their assistance and advice in preparing a contract for presentation to the owner's agent. Who was the procuring cause? Although the listing agent may feel that she was the procuring cause, the buyer is likely to support the buyer's broker's position because he chose to retain the services of that agent in presenting the offer. In the age of email, the Internet, and highly informed consumers, there is an argument that buyers want and need representation. Once a consumer has sought and obtained a buyer's broker's advice, technically the buyer's broker may become the procuring cause when the contract is signed and presented to the listing broker.

How do brokers resolve this dispute? An easy resolution to this is for brokers who are REALTORS® to seek arbitration. The National Association of REALTORS®, code of ethics encourages arbitration and you can provide the guidelines for determining what procuring cause might mean. The factors they outline include (1) the nature and status of the transaction, (2) the nature and status in terms of the listing agreement or offer to compensate, (3) the roles and relationships of the parties, (4) the initial contact with the purchaser, (5) the conduct of the brokers, (6) the continuity and abandonment in effecting the final sales agreement, (7) the conduct of the buyer, and (8) the conduct of the seller. In turn, each of these factors has several questions to determine how it should be considered in light of the existing circumstances. It is probably obvious by now, but there is no easy answer to "who is the procuring cause?"

TERMINATING THE EMPLOYMENT CONTRACT

The usual situation in an employment contract is that the broker produces a buyer acceptable to the owner. Thus, in most employment contracts the agency terminates because the objective of the contract has been completed. In the bulk of the transactions in which a buyer is not produced, the agency is terminated because the employment period expires. Remember that if no termination date is specified in the listing agreement, the Texas Real Estate License Act provides that the agent's license can be suspended or revoked, and courts are in conflict over whether the agreement is unenforceable.

Even when an employment contract calls for mutual consideration and has a specific termination date, it is still possible to revoke the agency aspect of the listing before the termination date. If the agent's employment is terminated for cause, the principal can terminate without paying compensation. Agents should be cautioned to remove their signs immediately if the employment contract is terminated. The Texas Real Estate License Act prohibits offering property for sale without the owner's written approval. However, if there is no cause for the termination, liability for breach of contract still remains, and money damages may result. Thus, an owner who has listed his property may tell the broker not to bring any more offers, but the owner still remains liable to the broker for payment for the effort expended by the broker up to that time. Depending on how far advanced the broker is at that point, the amount could be as much as a full commission.

Similarly, if a buyer's agent finds the product that meets the buyer's criteria and the buyer refuses to purchase, the broker is entitled to be compensated. However, there is very little legal precedent for pursuing buyer broker compensation through the courts. In this regard, buyer brokerage is riskier than traditional agency.

Mutual Agreement

An employment agreement can be terminated by mutual agreement of both the owner and broker without money damage. Because these agreements are the stock in trade of the brokerage business, brokers do not like to lose them, but sometimes this is the only logical alternative because the time and effort in setting and collecting damages can be very expensive. Suppose, however, that a broker has an employment agreement and suspects that the owner (or buyer) wants to cancel because he wants to avoid the commission. The listing broker can stop showing the property, but the owner is still obligated to pay a commission if the property is sold before the listing period expires. Whatever the broker and seller decide, it is best to put the agreement into writing and sign it.

With regard to open listings, once the property is sold by anyone, broker or owner, all listing agreements pertaining to the property are automatically terminated; the objective has been completed, there is no further need for the agency to exist. Similarly, with an exclusive agency listing, if the owner sells the property himself, the agency with the exclusive broker is terminated.

Abandonment, Etc.

Agency can also be terminated by improper performance or abandonment by the agent. Thus, if a broker acts counter to the principal's best financial interests, the agency is terminated, no commission is payable, and the broker may be subject to a lawsuit for any damages suffered by the principal. If a broker accepts an employment opportunity and then does nothing to promote it, the principal can assume that the broker abandoned it and has grounds for revocation. The principal should keep written documentation in the event the matter ever goes to court.

An agency is automatically terminated by the death of either the principal or the agent, or if either is judged legally incompetent by virtue of insanity, and might also be terminated if the principal becomes bankrupt (it depends on the bankruptcy court action).

BARGAIN BROKERS

The full-service real estate broker who takes a listing and places it in multiple listing, advertises the property at his expense, holds an open house, qualifies prospects, shows property, obtains offers, negotiates, opens escrow, and follows through until closing is the mainstay of the real estate selling industry. The vast majority of all open-market sales are handled that way. The remainder are sold by owners, some handling everything themselves and some using flat-fee brokers who oversee the transaction but do not do the actual showing and selling.

Flat-Fee Brokers

For a fee that typically ranges from $400 to $1,500, a **flat-fee broker** will list a property, suggest a market price, write advertising, assist with negotiations, draw up a sales contract, and turn the signed papers over to an escrow company for closing. The homeowner is responsible for paying for advertising, answering inquiries, setting appointments with prospects, showing the property, and applying whatever salesmanship is necessary to induce the prospect to make an offer. Under the flat-fee arrangement, also called self-help brokerage, the homeowner is effectively buying real estate services on an à la carte basis. Some brokerage firms have been very successful in this—offering sellers a choice of à la carte or full service.

Discount Broker

A **discount broker** is a full-service broker who charges less than the prevailing commission rates in the community. In a seller's market a real estate agent's major problem is finding salable property to list, not finding buyers. The discount broker attracts sellers by offering to do the job for less money, for example, 3% or 4% instead of 5% to 7%. Charging less means a discount broker must sell more properties to be successful. Consequently, most discount brokers may be careful to take listings only on property that will sell quickly, and to reject those that won't.

Variable Rate Commissions

Another variation bargain brokers have used is the **variable rate commission.** This commission structure retains the lower commission for the bargain broker but allows the commission to increase (i.e., to a full 3%) to the other broker in order to give other brokers an incentive to help market their properties. It still gives the seller a lower commission structure. It can create conflict, however, when a seller doesn't want to pay the increased commission and chooses to favor contracts without cooperating brokers. The buyer's broker (or cooperating broker) can do a significant amount of work and be cut out at the last minute because of the seller's preference to accept a lower price in order to pay a lower commission rate.

REVIEW QUESTIONS

Answers to these questions are found in the Answer Key section at the back of the book.

1. A real estate listing
   A. is an employment contract between a property owner and a real estate broker.
   B. authorizes a real estate broker to sell and convey title to an owner's real property.
   C. both A and B.
   D. neither A nor B.

2. All of the following statements are true EXCEPT:
   A. a listing is a contract between an owner and the listing salesperson.
   B. the broker is legally liable for the proper execution of a listing contract.
   C. sales associates are licensed salespersons or brokers who work for a broker.
   D. sales associates operate under the authority of an employing broker's license.

3. A listing to find a buyer for each of the following types of properties will usually be for a period of time ranging from six months to one year EXCEPT:
   A. farms.
   B. commercial properties.
   C. residential properties.
   D. industrial properties.

4. A typical exclusive right to sell listing requires the owner to
   A. exclude other brokers from advertising or placing a sign on the property.
   B. pay a commission if a purchaser is found who agrees to buy at the price and terms stipulated in the listing.
   C. both A and B.
   D. neither A nor B.

5. The amount of commission to be paid the broker for selling a property is
   A. set by state law.
   B. negotiated at the time a buyer is found.
   C. set forth in the rules of the state real estate commission.
   D. stated in the listing contract.

6. Under the terms of an exclusive right to sell listing, a commission is due the listing broker if a buyer is found by
   A. the listing broker.
   B. a sales associate employed by the listing broker.
   C. the owner, through his own efforts.
   D. another broker.
   E. all of the above.

7. Broker Kim secured a written listing on a property. Kim later located a buyer who was ready, willing, and able to buy at the price and terms stated in the listing contract, but the owner refused to sign a sales agreement because of animosity toward the buyer. Is Kim entitled to a commission even though no sale was consummated?
   A. Yes, because a commission was earned when the listing was signed.
   B. Yes, because Kim produced a ready, willing, and able buyer at the price and terms requested in the listing.
   C. No, because no sales contract was signed by the owner.
   D. No, because there was not an offer and acceptance.

8. An exclusive agency listing
   A. permits the owner to sell of his own efforts without liability to pay a commission to the listing broker.
   B. allows the owner to list concurrently with other brokers.
   C. both A and B.
   D. neither A nor B.

9. All of the following are true of net listings EXCEPT:
   A. many states prohibit a broker from accepting a net listing.
   B. most brokers are reluctant to accept them, even when permitted to do so.
   C. all net listings are open listings.
   D. the commission is the excess above the seller's net price.

10. In regard to net listings,
    A. Texas prohibits them.
    B. most brokers avoid them.
    C. both A and B.
    D. neither A nor B.

11. To be valid in Texas, a listing contract must be
    A. written.
    B. signed.
    C. both A and B.
    D. neither A nor B.

12. Multiple listing services are open
    A. only to members of real estate boards.
    B. to any licensed broker.
    C. to anyone who wants to join.
    D. to sales agents belonging to the Texas Association of REALTORS® (TAR).

13. Under the terms of a multiple listing agreement, if a broker other than the listing broker sells the property, the owner
    A. may be liable for two commissions on the sale.
    B. may sell of his own efforts without any obligation to pay a commission.
    C. both A and B.
    D. neither A nor B.

14. The advantages of a multiple listing arrangement include
    A. greater market exposure of the property.
    B. the possibility of a higher sales price.
    C. quicker sale.
    D. all of the above.

15. Recent innovations for marketing properties through multiple listing services include
    A. computerized listings.
    B. videodisc display of listings.
    C. both A and B.
    D. neither A nor B.

16. When a property under an open listing is shown to a prospect by two different brokers and a sale results, the commission is
    A. payable to the broker who first showed the property to the buyer.
    B. divided between the two brokers.
    C. payable to the broker who made the sale.
    D. payable in full to each broker.

17. An exclusive listing contract with a definite termination date is NOT terminable by
    A. sale of the property.
    B. death of the listing salesperson.
    C. expiration.
    D. mutual agreement.

18. An open listing may be terminated by which of the following means?
    A. Sale of the property
    B. Abandonment by the broker
    C. Destruction of the property by casualty
    D. Death of the owner
    E. All of the above

19. If a purchaser arbitrarily defaults on a purchase contract, any earnest money previously paid, in the absence of an agreement to the contrary, will be
    A. owed to the broker as compensation for his efforts.
    B. divided between the broker and the owner/seller.
    C. returned to the purchaser.
    D. owed to the owner/seller.

20. Which of the following is most likely to accept only listings that he thinks will sell quickly?
    A. Flat-fee brokers
    B. Full-service brokers
    C. Discount brokers
    D. Self-help brokers

21. A real estate listing is a contract between
    A. the owner and the listing broker.
    B. the owner, the broker, and the listing sales-person.
    C. the owner and the listing salesperson.
    D. the broker and the listing salesperson.

Chapter 22

KEY TERMS

Agent: the person empowered to act by and on behalf of the principal

Boycotting: two or more people conspiring to restrain competition

Commingling: the mixing of clients' or customers' funds with an agent's personal funds

Dual agency: representation of two or more principals in a transaction by the same agent

Intermediary: a broker who is employed to negotiate a transaction between the parties

Middleman: a person who brings two or more parties together but does not represent either party

Ostensible authority: an agency relationship created by the conduct of the principal

Price fixing: two or more people conspiring to charge a fixed fee, having an anticompetitive effect

Principal: a person who authorizes another to act

Puffing: statements a reasonable person would recognize as nonfactual or extravagant

Third parties: persons who are not parties to a contract but who may be affected by it

The Principal–Broker Relationship: Agency

IN THIS CHAPTER

This chapter covers the principal and agent relationship, and the law of agency in general. Creation of the agency relationship and obligations of the broker to his or her principal and to third parties are discussed. The new concepts of owner disclosure statements and buyer agency are also discussed. The final portions of the chapter deal with dual agency and antitrust laws.

The previous chapter has stressed the mechanics of real estate listings. Let's now take a close look at the agency aspects of the principal-broker relationship, that is, the legal responsibilities of the broker toward the principal and vice versa.

AGENCY

When a property owner gives a real estate broker a listing authorizing the broker to find a buyer or a tenant and promising compensation if he does, an *agency relationship* is created. The same agency relationship arises when a buyer authorizes a buyer's agent to find the appropriate property. For an agency to exist, there must be a principal and an agent. The ***principal*** is the person who empowers another to act as their representative; the ***agent*** is the person who is empowered to act. When people speak about the laws of agency, they refer to those laws that govern the rights and duties of the principal, agent, and the persons (called third parties) with whom they deal.

Agencies are divided into three categories: universal, general, and special. A **universal agency** is very broad in scope, as the principal gives the agent the legal power to transact matters of all types. A **general agency** gives the agent the power to bind the principal in a particular trade or business. For example, the relationship between a real estate broker (principal) and the salesperson (agent) is considered a general agency, as is a person with a power of attorney. A **special agency** empowers the agent to perform only specific acts and no others. The special agent may not bind the principal by his actions. Applications of special agency include real estate listings, in which the agent represents the principal, but cannot sign for or bind the principal.

The principal in an agency relationship can be either a natural person or a business entity such as a corporation. Likewise, an agent can be either a natural person or a corporation such as a real estate brokerage company. The persons and firms with whom the principal and agent negotiate are called ***third parties***. You will also hear these third parties referred to as the broker's **customers** and the principal referred to as the broker's **client.** Sometimes you will see the phrase "principals only" in real estate advertisements where property is offered for sale by its owner without the aid of a broker. This means the owner wants to be contacted by persons who want to buy and not by real estate agents who want to list the property.

Establishing the Agent's Authority

Discussed in the previous chapter, a written employment agreement outlines the broker's authority to act on behalf of the principal and the principal's obligations to the agent. A written agreement is the preferred method of creating an agency because it provides a document to readily establish the existence of the agency relationship.

Agency authority may also arise from custom in the industry, common usage, and conduct of the parties involved. For example, the right of an agent to advertise the listed property in a particular publication may not be expressly stated in the listing. However, if it is the custom in the industry to do so, and presuming there are no prohibitions in the agent's agreement, the agent has **implied authority** to advertise any place they wish. A similar situation exists with regard to showing a listed property to prospects. The seller of a home can expect to have it shown on weekends and evenings, whereas a commercial property owner might expect showings only during business hours.

Ostensible authority is conferred when a principal gives a third party reason to believe that another person is his agent even though that person is unaware of the appointment. If the third party accepts this as true, the principal may well be bound by the acts of his agent. For example, as a seller's agent, one may show a home one time, with the seller's permission, to a potential buyer. Even though there may not be an enforceable listing agreement, the agent (with the principal's approval) gives the impression that he represents the seller. The buyer could communicate with the agent, relying on that agent's *apparent authority*. Similarly, if a buyer and a buyer's agent spend weeks looking for a property and have established communication with various seller's agents concerning properties available, the seller's agent can rely on the buyer's agent's apparent authority to act on behalf of the buyer.

An **agency by ratification** is one established after the fact. For example, if an agent secures a contract on behalf of a principal and the principal subsequently ratifies or agrees to it, a court may hold that an agency was created at the time the initial negotiations started. An **agency by estoppel** can result when a principal fails to maintain due diligence over the agent and the agent exercises powers not granted to him. If this causes a third party to believe the agent has these powers, an agency by estoppel has been created. An *agency coupled with an interest* exists when an agent holds an interest in the property he is representing. For example, a broker is given an ownership interest (5% or 6%) in a property he has listed for sale.

Remember, all these methods of establishing an agent's authority work for the buyer's agent as well as the seller's agent.

Broker's Obligations to the Principal

When a real estate broker accepts a listing, a *fiduciary relationship* is created. This requires that the agent exhibit trust and honesty and exercise good business judgment when working on behalf of the principal. Specifically, the broker must faithfully perform the agency agreement, be loyal to the principal, exercise competence, and account for all funds handled in performing the agency. The broker also has certain obligations toward the third parties involved. Broker responsibility in the State of Texas is also guided by the Canons of Professional Ethics and Conduct for Brokers and Salespersons as established by the Texas Real Estate Commission, the Texas Real Estate Licensing Act, and by regulations adopted by the Texas Real Estate Commission.

The Legislature has created a minimum level of services for licensees. Some licensees are hired because they charge very low fees, and, by agreement, provide no services. This often left principals at a loss on technical issues (many really don't understand the expertise a real estate agent provides), and often left the other broker to do twice as much work. The Real Estate License Act now provides that a broker who represents a party in real estate transactions, or who has real estate for sale under an exclusive agreement for a party, is that party's agent. Broker's duties are also defined; a broker: (1) may not instruct another broker to directly or indirectly violate the License Act by contacting a broker's principal either directly or indirectly; (2) must inform his principal if a broker receives material information related to the transaction to list, buy, sell, or lease the party's real estate, including the receipt of an offer by the broker; and (3) shall, at a minimum, answer their principal's questions and present any offer to or from that principal. There's one exception: If a licensee delivers an offer to another party and that party's broker consents to the delivery, and a copy is sent to the party's broker, it does *not* violate the Act's restrictions on contacting the other party directly.

Faithful Performance

Faithful performance (also referred to as **obedience**) means that the agent is to obey all legal instructions given by the principal and to apply best efforts and diligence to carry out the objectives of the agency. For a real estate broker this means performance as promised in the broker's employment contract. A broker who promises to make a "reasonable effort" or apply "diligence" in finding a buyer and then does nothing to promote the listing gives the owner legal grounds for terminating the listing. Similarly, a broker who represents a buyer but makes no efforts to pursue an acquisition, or to take heed of the buyer's requirements, may also give the buyer grounds to terminate the buyer's representation agreement. Faithful performance also means not departing from the principal's instructions. If the agent does so (except in extreme emergencies not foreseen by the principal), it is at the agent's own risk. If the principal thereby suffers a loss, the agent is responsible for that loss. For example, a broker accepts a personal note from a buyer as an earnest money deposit, but fails to tell the seller that the deposit is not in cash. If the seller accepts the offer and the note is later found to be worthless, the broker may be liable for the amount of the note.

Another aspect of faithful performance is that the agent must personally perform the tasks delegated to that agent. This protects the principal who has selected an agent on the basis of trust and confidence from finding that the agent has delegated that responsibility to another person. However, a major question arises on this point in real estate brokerage, as a large part of the success in finding a buyer for a property results from the cooperative efforts of other brokers and their salespeople. Therefore, employment agreements usually include a statement that the listing broker is authorized to secure the cooperation of other brokers and pay them part of the commission from the sale.

A genuine concern arises over how much information a real estate broker is free to disclose to other real estate brokers or other industry members who rely on this information in determining statistical data, market values, and other pertinent real estate related information. For instance, can a real estate agent maintain a confidential relationship with the principal, yet disclose pertinent details of sales prices and financing terms related to the principal's business? The Texas Real Estate License Act (Section 1101.804) specifically relieves a broker from liability for providing information about real property sales prices or terms for the purposes of facilitating the listing, selling, leasing, financing, or appraisal of real property unless this disclosure is specifically prohibited by statute or written contract. Any licensee would be well advised to make this provision clear to the principal so that the principal can make an informed decision as to whether or not to disclose this information.

Loyalty to Principal

Probably no other area of agency is as fertile ground for lawsuits as the requirement that, once an agency is created, the agent must be loyal to the principal. The law is clear in all states that in an employment agreement the broker (and the broker's sales staff) occupy a position of trust, confidence, and responsibility. As such, the agent is legally bound to keep their principal (buyer *or* seller) fully informed as to all matters that might affect the sale of the listed property and to promote and protect the owner's interests.

Unfortunately, greed and expediency sometimes get in the way. As a result, numerous laws have been enacted for the purpose of protecting the principal and threatening the agent with court action for misplaced loyalty. For example, an out-of-town landowner who is not fully up-to-date on the value of his land visits a local broker and wants to list it for $130,000. The broker is much more knowledgeable of local land prices and is aware of a recent city council decision to extend roads and utilities to the area of this property. As a result, the broker knows the land is now worth $250,000. The broker remains silent on the matter, and the property is listed for sale at $130,000. At this price the broker can find a buyer before the day is over and have a commission on the sale. However, the opportunity for a quick $120,000 is too tempting to let pass. The broker buys the property (or to cover up, buys in the name of a spouse or a friend) and shortly thereafter resells it for $250,000. Whether he sold the property to a buyer for $130,000 or bought it and resold it for $250,000, the broker did not exhibit loyalty to the principal. A similar breach can occur if a buyer's agent knows that the buyer will pay up to $100,000 for a property, and the agent finds a similar property for $50,000, buys it himself, and sells it to the buyer for $100,000. Laws and penalties for breach of loyalty are stiff: The broker can be sued for recovery of the price difference and the commission paid, his real estate license can be suspended or revoked, and he may be required to pay additional fines and money damages.

If a licensee intends to purchase a property listed for sale by his agency or through a cooperating broker, he is under both a moral and a legal obligation to make certain that the price paid is the fair market value and that the seller knows who the buyer is, and that the buyer is a licensee.

Protecting the Owner's Interest Loyalty to the principal also means that when seeking a buyer or negotiating a sale, the broker must continue to protect the owner's financial interests, putting the principal's interest above that of the agent. Suppose that an owner lists her home at $182,000 but confides in the broker, "If I cannot get $182,000, anything over $170,000 will be fine." The broker shows the home to a prospect who says, "One hundred eighty-two thousand is too much. What will the owner really take?" or "Will he take $175,000?" Loyalty to the principal requires the broker to say that the owner will take $182,000, for that is the price in the listing agreement. If the buyer balks, the broker can suggest that the buyer submit an offer for the seller's consideration. State laws require that all offers be submitted to the owner, no matter what the offering price and terms. This prevents the agent from rejecting an offer that the owner might have accepted if she had known about it. If the seller really intends for the broker to quote $170,000 as an acceptable price, the listing price should be changed; then the broker can say, "The property was previously listed for $182,000, but is now priced at $170,000." When representing a buyer, an agent can have the same conflict. The buyer acknowledges that she will pay up to $100,000, and the agent knows it could be purchased for $80,000, but the commission would be *less.* The buyer's broker has the duty to obtain the cheaper price.

A broker's loyalty to his principal also includes keeping the principal informed of changes in market conditions during the listing period. If after an adjacent landowner is successful in rezoning his land to a higher use and the listed property becomes more valuable, the broker's responsibility is to inform the seller. Similarly, if a buyer is looking at a property and the adjacent property is purchased for a nuclear waste disposal site, it is the duty of the broker to report this to the buyer. If the broker does not keep the principal fully informed, he is not properly fulfilling his duties as the principal's agent.

The Texas Real Estate Licensing Act specifically prohibits certain misplaced loyalties, such as:

1. *"... conduct which constitutes dishonest dealings, bad faith, or untrustworthiness [Section 1101.652(b)(2)]."*
2. *"... the offering of real property for sale or lease without the knowledge and consent of the owner, or on terms other than those authorized by the owner or his agent [Section 1101.652(b)(19)]."*
3. *"... accepting, receiving, or charging an undisclosed commission rebate or making a direct profit on expenditures made for the principal [Section 1101.652(b)(13)]."*
4. *"... failing to make clear to all parties to a transaction which party the agent is acting for, or receiving compensation from more than one party, except with the full knowledge and consent of all parties [Section 1101.652(b)(7),(8)]."*

Many licensees take fiduciary duty somewhat lightly, not understanding how consumers truly rely on them and trust their judgment. These principals feel truly cheated when they get less than complete loyalty from their real estate agent.

Reasonable Care

The duty of **reasonable care** implies competence and expertise on the part of the broker. It is the broker's responsibility to disclose all knowledge and material facts concerning a property to the principal. Also, the broker must not become a party to any fraud or misrepresentation likely to affect the sound judgment of the principal.

Although the broker has a duty to disclose all material facts of a transaction, legal interpretations are to be avoided. Giving legal interpretations of documents involved in a transaction can be construed as practicing law without a license, an act specifically prohibited by the Texas Real Estate License Act. Moreover, the broker can be held financially responsible for any wrong legal information given to a client.

The duty of reasonable care also requires an agent to take proper care of property entrusted to him by the principal. For example, if a broker is entrusted with a key to an owner's building to show it to prospects, it is the broker's responsibility to see that it is used for only that purpose and that the building is locked upon leaving. Similarly, if a broker receives a check as an earnest money deposit, it must be properly deposited in a bank and not carried around for several weeks.

Accounting for Funds Received

The earnest money that accompanies an offer on a property does not belong to the broker, even if the broker's name is on the check. For the purpose of holding clients' and customers' money, the law requires a broker to maintain a **trust account.** All monies received by a broker as agent for the principal are to be promptly deposited in this account or in the trust account of the attorney, escrow, or title company handling the transaction. Texas requires that a trust account be a demand deposit (checking account) at a bank or a trust account at a trust company. The broker's trust account must be separate from the broker's personal bank account, and the broker is required by law to accurately account for all funds received into and paid out of the trust account. As a rule, a broker will have one trust account for properties listed for sale and another trust account for rental properties managed by the broker. Failure to comply with trust fund requirements can result in the loss of one's real estate license.

Several provisions in the Texas Real Estate Licensing Act specifically address the broker's obligations to account for funds received. Section 1101.652(b)(9),(10) of the Act states that the broker could have his license revoked or suspended for:

> "... failing within a reasonable time to properly account for or remit money coming into his possession that belongs to others, or commingling money belonging to others with his own funds."

Section 1101.652(b)(30) of the act provides the same penalties for:

> "... failing within a reasonable time to deposit money received as escrow agent in a real estate transaction, either in trust with a title company authorized to do business in this state, or in a custodial, trust, or escrow account maintained for that purpose."

Section 1101.652(b)(31) of the act further specifies the same penalties for:

> "... disbursing money deposited in the custodial, trust, or escrow account ... before the transaction has been consummated or finally otherwise terminated."

Commingling If a broker places money belonging to a client or customer in a personal account, it is called ***commingling*** and is grounds for suspension or revocation of the broker's real estate license. The reason for such severe action is that from commingling, it is a very short step to *conversion,* that is, the agent's personal use of money belonging to others. Also, clients' and customers' money placed in a personal bank account can be attached by a court of law to pay personal claims against the broker.

If a broker receives a check as an earnest money deposit, along with instructions from the buyer that it remain uncashed, the broker may comply with the buyer's request as long as the seller is informed of this fact when the offer is presented. Similarly, the broker can accept a promissory note if he informs the seller. The objective is to disclose all material facts to the seller that might influence the decision to accept or reject the offer. The fact that the deposit accompanying the offer is not cash is a material fact. If the broker withholds this information, there is a violation of the agent's duty of care.

Broker's Obligations to Third Parties

A broker's fiduciary obligations are to the principal who has employed him. State law nonetheless makes certain demands on the broker in relation to the third parties the broker deals with on behalf of the principal. Foremost among these are honesty, integrity, and fair business dealing. This includes the proper care of deposit money and offers, as well as responsibility for written or verbal statements. Misrepresenting a property by omitting vital information is as wrong as giving false information. Disclosure of such misconduct usually results in a broker losing the right to a commission. Also possible are loss of the broker's real estate license and a lawsuit by any party to the transaction who suffered a financial loss because of the misrepresentation.

In guarding against misrepresentation, a broker must also be careful not to make misleading statements. For example, a potential buyer looks at a house listed for sale and asks if it is connected to the city sewer system. The broker does not know the answer, but sensing it is important to making a sale, says, yes. If the prospect relies on this statement, purchases the house and finds out that there is no sewer connection, the broker may be at the center of litigation regarding sale cancellation, commission loss, money damages, and license revocation or suspension. The answer should be, "I don't know, but I will find out for you."

Suppose the seller has told the broker that the house is connected to the city sewer system, and the broker, having no reason to doubt the statement, accepts it in good faith and gives that information to prospective buyers. If this statement is not true, the owner is at fault, owes the broker a commission, and both the owner *and* the broker may be subject to legal action for sale cancellation and money damages. When a broker must rely on information supplied by their principal (buyer *or* seller), it is best to have it in writing and verify its accuracy. However, relying on the principal for information may not completely relieve the broker's responsibility to third parties. If a seller says her house is connected to the city sewer system and the broker knows that is impossible because there is no sewer line on that street, it is the broker's responsibility to correct the erroneous statement. Although the licensee owes a duty of confidence and loyalty to his principal, he cannot be a part of any fraud on the principal's behalf. If his principal should request that he make any misrepresentations, the licensee should terminate his employment and refuse to engage in any such acts.

Disclosure to Third Parties—License Act Requirements

In addition to fair and honest business dealings, Texas law requires real estate licensees to disclose any interest in the real estate held by the licensee, to disclose any additional commissions received from someone other than the principal, and to advise the purchaser, in writing, to obtain title insurance or have an abstract examined. In addition, there are other required disclosures in contracts, such as municipal utility districts, lead-based paint, annexation, mandatory homeowner association membership, and tax rollbacks (discussed in Chapter 10).

In addition to these contract disclosure requirements, §§1101.652(b)(3),(4) of the Texas Real Estate License Act states that a licensee may have his license revoked or suspended for failing to disclose to a potential purchaser any latent structural defect that would be a significant factor to a reasonable and prudent purchaser in making a decision to purchase. This may seem to conflict with the licensee's fiduciary obligation to his principal not to disclose information entrusted to him. However, the licensee must remember that if the principal requires him to do anything that is in violation of the Licensing Act, it would be illegal. Therefore, it is assumed that the prudent licensee, when in doubt, would prefer to disclose a potential defect rather than risk the chance of performing an illegal act.

Section 1101.652(b)(7),(8) of the License Act subjects the licensee to penalties for failing to make clear whom he represents. It is not uncommon for a purchaser who has asked a licensee to help him in locating a house to think that the licensee is working for him. The purchaser should be informed that the licensee is working for the seller and the listing agent. Thus, the purchaser remains a third party and the agent should treat him as such. (Note: If a buyer employs a broker, the arrangement should be in writing and disclosed to the seller.)

Section 1101.652(b)(13) subjects a licensee to penalties for accepting, receiving, or charging an undisclosed commission, rebate, or direct profit on expenditures made for a principal. Section 1101.652(b)(16) creates liability for acting in the dual capacity of broker and undisclosed principal in a transaction. Section 1101.652(b)(28) requires the licensee to furnish copies of a document pertaining to a transaction dealing with real estate to a person whose signatures are affixed to the document.

Section 1101.652(b)(29) subjects a licensee to penalties for failing to advise the purchaser in writing before the closing of a transaction that she should (1) have the property abstract examined by an attorney of her own choosing or (2) be furnished with or obtain a policy of title insurance.

The foregoing obligations to third parties are a part of a constantly growing list in this age of consumerism. When coupled with the provisions of the Deceptive Trade Practices-Consumer Protection Act and Texas statutes relating to real estate fraud, they illustrate the increasing concern for Texas real estate brokers and salespeople regarding their obligations to those they serve.

Because a broker is a special agent of the principal rather than a general agent, there is no power to bind this principal. Therefore, if there is an aggrieved third party who feels damaged because of a material misrepresentation, the third party may not be able to sue the principal and recover. The third party can, however, sue the broker.

At least one court case typifies current legal thinking that facts not known by the buyer must be disclosed to him by the seller, or the broker representing him, if they materially affect the desirability of the property. Even the use of an *"as is" clause* in the purchase contract does not excuse a broker from disclosing material facts regarding a property. The court went on to say that a buyer of real estate has every right to rescind a contract when the agent by his silence has allowed the transaction to proceed without informing the buyer of all facts relevant to the property.

Puffing

Puffing refers to nonfactual or extravagant statements that a reasonable person would recognize as exaggeration. Thus, a buyer may have no legal complaint against a broker who told him that a certain hillside lot had the most beautiful view in the world or that a listed property had the finest landscaping in the county. Usually a reasonable buyer can see these things and make up his own mind. However, if a broker in showing a rural property says it has the world's purest well water, there had better be plenty of good water when the buyer moves in. If a consumer believes the broker and relies on the representation, the broker may have a potential liability. The line between puffing and misrepresentation is subjective. Avoid puffing.

Nondisclosures

Section 1101.556 of the Real Estate License Act makes a significant exception to the disclosure presumption. A licensee has no duty to inquire about, make a disclosure related to, or release information related to whether a previous or current occupant had, may have had, has or may have AIDS or an HIV-related illness. Such persons are considered "handicapped" and as such are protected by federal law (see Chapter 5).

Similar to the HIV-related illnesses, the Act now provides that a licensee has no duty to inquire about, or make disclosure related to, or release information related to whether a death occurred on a property by: (1) natural causes, (2) suicide, or (3) accident unrelated to the condition of the property. There is also no duty to disclose information about registered sex offenders.

PUTTING IT TO WORK

Today, courts look upon real estate licensees as professionals who possess superior knowledge or special information regarding real property to which their clients are legally entitled. (This is especially significant in that professional status is what the real estate industry has been working hard to achieve in recent years.)

OWNER DISCLOSURE STATEMENT

Seller disclosure statements are a detailed disclosure of house defects (or lack thereof) on a form. A disclosure form is provided in the statutes, but others are produced by real estate trade associations. The seller is required to fill out the forms, which are then presented to the buyer as a representation of the seller's statement of condition of the property. The seller is the most likely person to fill out the disclosure because the seller simply knows more about the property than anybody else.

In the last 15 years, there has been extensive litigation on the sales of real property based on misrepresentations and material omissions. When the buyer sues, the broker has often found himself as a defendant, because the seller is gone, and the broker marketed the property. This creates a burden on a broker who may have no knowledge of the defect, nor the expertise to investigate the potential for defects.

For the seller's benefit, the seller disclosure form gives the opportunity for the seller to reinvestigate the house. None of us have perfect homes. Many sellers simply overlook the defects (we all learn to live with them or forget about them, particularly when it's our house). This failure to disclose, however, results in misrepresentation on the part of seller because of negligence or perhaps because he innocently overlooked it. In the worst case scenario, he may intentionally misrepresent, or intentionally fail to mention, a defect in order to induce the buyer to purchase. In all circumstances, the seller's disclosure form yields these benefits: (1) it informs the buyer as to which defects exist, (2) it provides a basis from which the buyer can conduct further investigation on the property, (3) it allows the buyer to make an informed decision as to whether or not to purchase, and (4) it may provide a more concrete basis for litigation if the buyer can determine that the seller filled out the disclosure statement incorrectly or failed to disclose a defect that the seller knew was material.

Similarly, brokers can find the disclosure statement beneficial because they now have written proof as to what disclosures were made to them (which should be compared with their listing agreement and the MLS disclosures) to ensure consistency in marketing their product. In addition, knowing that there is a defect allows the broker to effectively market the property, disclosing the defects and therefore limiting liability for both the seller (they sometimes overlook potential liability in their eagerness to sell) and the broker.

Texas Disclosure Forms

The Property Code requires the seller of residential real property, comprising not more than one dwelling unit, to give the purchaser of the property a written notice on a form substantially similar to the one set out in Figure 22.1.

The notice is to be completed with the best of the seller's knowledge and belief as of the date the notice is completed and signed. If the information required is unknown to the seller, the seller should indicate that fact on the notice to stay in compliance with the statute.

The statute does not apply to any transfers: (1) pursuant to a court order; (2) by a trustee in bankruptcy; (3) to a mortgage by a mortgagor or successor in interest; (4) by a mortgagee or a beneficiary under a deed of trust who has acquired the real property of sale conducted pursuant to a power of sale under a deed of trust or a sale pursuant to a court ordered foreclosure or has acquired the real property by deed in lieu of foreclosure; (5) by a fiduciary in the course of the administration of a decedent's estate, guardianship, conservatorship, or trust; (6) from one co-owner to one or more other co-owners; (7) made to a spouse or to a person or persons in the initial line of consanguinity of one or more of the transferrers; (8) between the spouses resulting from a decree of dissolution of marriage or a decree of legal separation or from a property settlement agreement incident to such a decree; (9) to or from any governmental entity; (10) transfers of new residences of not more than one dwelling unit that have not previously been occupied for essential purposes; or (11) transfers of real property where the value of any dwelling does not exceed 5% of the value of the property.

The notice must be delivered by the seller to the purchaser on or before the effective date of an executory contract (signing the earnest money contract) binding the purchaser to purchase the property. If the contract is entered into without the seller providing this required notice, the purchaser may terminate the contract for any reason within seven days after receiving the notice.

FIGURE 22.1 Disclosure notice

01-01-2010

EQUAL HOUSING OPPORTUNITY

APPROVED BY THE TEXAS REAL ESTATE COMMISSION (TREC)

SELLER'S DISCLOSURE OF PROPERTY CONDITION

CONCERNING THE PROPERTY AT____
(Street Address and City)

THIS NOTICE IS A DISCLOSURE OF SELLER'S KNOWLEDGE OF THE CONDITION OF THE PROPERTY AS OF THE DATE SIGNED BY SELLER AND IS NOT A SUBSTITUTE FOR ANY INSPECTIONS OR WARRANTIES THE PURCHASER MAY WISH TO OBTAIN. IT IS NOT A WARRANTY OF ANY KIND BY SELLER OR SELLER'S AGENTS.

Seller ❑ is ❑is not occupying the Property. If unoccupied, how long since Seller has occupied the Property? ________________________________

1. The Property has the items checked below [Write Yes (Y), No (N), or Unknown (U)]:

__ Range	__ Oven	__ Microwave
__ Dishwasher	__ Trash Compactor	__ Disposal
__ Washer/Dryer Hookups	__ Window Screens	__ Rain Gutters
__ Security System	__ Fire Detection Equipment	__ Intercom System
__ TV Antenna	__ Smoke Detector	__ Satellite Dish
__ Ceiling Fan(s)	__ Smoke Detector-Hearing Impaired	__ Exhaust Fan(s)
__ Central A/C	__ Carbon Monoxide Alarm	__ Wall/Window Air Conditioning
__ Plumbing System	__ Emergency Escape Ladder(s)	__ Public Sewer System
__ Patio/Decking	__ Cable TV Wiring	__ Fences
__ Pool	__ Attic Fan(s)	__ Spa __ Hot Tub
__ Pool Equipment	__ Central Heating	__ Automatic Lawn Sprinkler System
__ Fireplace(s) & Chimney (Woodburning)	__ Septic System	__ Fireplace(s) & Chimney (Mock)
__ Gas Lines (Nat./LP)	__ Outdoor Grill	__ Carport
__ Garage: __ Attached __ Not Attached	__ Sauna	__ Water Supply __ City __ Well __ MUD __ Co-op
	__ Pool Heater	
__ Garage Door Opener(s): __ Electronic __ Controls	__ Water Heater: __ Gas __ Electric	

Roof Type: ________________________________ Age: ____________ (approx)

Are you (Seller) aware of any of the above items that are not in working condition, that have known defects or that are in need of repair? ❑ Yes ❑ No ❑ Unknown If yes, then describe. (Attach additional sheets if necessary): ________________________________

____

2. Does the property have working smoke detectors installed in accordance with the smoke detector requirements of Chapter 766, Health and Safety Code? ❑ Yes ❑ No ❑ Unknown

If the answer to the question above is no or unknown, explain. (Attach additional sheets if necessary): ____

____

____

____

TREC No. OP-H

FIGURE 22.1 Disclosure notice (*continued*)

Seller's Disclosure Notice Concerning the Property at________________________________ Page 2 01-01-2010
(Street Address and City)

* Chapter 766 of the Health and Safety Code requires one-family or two-family dwellings to have working smoke detectors installed in accordance with the requirements of the building code in effect in the area in which the dwelling is located, including performance, location, and power source requirements. If you do not know the building code requirements in effect in your area, you may check unknown above or contact your local building official for more information. A buyer may require a seller to install smoke detectors for the hearing impaired if: (1) the buyer or a member of the buyer's family who will reside in the dwelling is hearing impaired; (2) the buyer gives the seller written evidence of the hearing impairment from a licensed physician; and (3) within 10 days after the effective date, the buyer makes a written request for the seller to install smoke detectors for the hearing impaired and specifies the locations for the installation. The parties may agree who will bear the cost of installing the smoke detectors and which brand of smoke detectors to install.

3. Are you (Seller) aware of any known defects/malfunctions in any of the following?

Write Yes (Y) if you are aware, write No (N) if you are not aware.

__ Interior Walls	__ Ceilings	__ Floors
__ Exterior Walls	__ Doors	__ Windows
__ Roof	__ Foundation/Slab(s)	__ Basement
__ Walls/Fences	__ Driveways	__ Sidewalks
__ Plumbing Sewers/Septics	__ Electrical Systems	__ Lighting Fixtures

__ Other Structural Components (Describe) ____

____

____

If the answer to any of the above is yes, explain. (Attach additional sheets if necessary): __________

____

____

4. Are you (Seller) aware of any of the following conditions?

Write Yes (Y) if you are aware, write No (N) if you are not aware.

__ Active Termites (includes wood destroying insects)	__ Termite or Wood Rot Damage Needing Repair	__ Previous Termite Damage
__ Previous Termite Treatment	__ Previous Flooding	__ Improper Drainage
__ Water Penetration	__ Located in 100-Year Floodplain	__ Present Flood Insurance Coverage
__ Previous Structural or Roof Repair	__ Hazardous or Toxic Waste	__ Asbestos Components
__ Urea-formaldehyde Insulation	__ Radon Gas	__ Lead Based Paint
__ Aluminum Wiring	__ Previous Fires	__ Unplatted Easements
__ Landfill, Settling, Soil Movement, Fault Lines		__ Subsurface Structure or Pits

__ Previous Use of Premises for Manufacture of Methamphetamine

If the answer to any of the above is yes, explain. (attach additional sheets if necessary): __________

____

____

5. Are you (Seller) aware of any item, equipment, or system in or on the Property that is in need of repair? ☐ Yes (if you are aware) ☐ No (if you are not aware). If yes, then describe. (Attach additional sheets if necessary). ________________________________

____

____

____

TREC No. OP-H

FIGURE 22.1 Disclosure notice (*continued*)

Seller's Disclosure Notice Concerning the Property at__________________________________ Page 3 01-01-2010
(Street Address and City)

6. Are you (Seller) aware of any of the following? Write Yes (Y) if you are aware, write No (N) if you are not aware.

__ Room additions, structural modifications, or other alterations or repairs made without necessary permits or not in compliance with building codes in effect at that time.

__ Homeowners' Association or maintenance fees or assessments.

__ Any "common area" (facilities such as pools, tennis courts, walkways, or other areas) co-owned in undivided interest with others.

__ Any notices of violations of deed restrictions or governmental ordinances affecting the condition or use of the Property.

__ Any lawsuits directly or indirectly affecting the Property.

__ Any condition on the Property which materially affects the physical health or safety of an individual.

If the answer to any of the above is yes explain. (Attach additional sheets if necessary):______________

____

____

____

7. If the property is located in a coastal area that is seaward of the Gulf Intracoastal Waterway or within 1,000 feet of the mean high tide bordering the Gulf of Mexico, the property may be subject to the Open Beaches Act or the Dune Protection Act (Chapter 61 or 63, Natural Resources Code, respectively) and a beachfront construction certificate or dune protection permit may be required for repairs or improvements. Contact the local government with ordinance authority over construction adjacent to public beaches for more information.

Date	Signature of Seller	Date	Signature of Seller

The undersigned purchaser hereby acknowledges receipt of the foregoing notice.

Date	Signature of Purchaser	Date	Signature of Purchaser

TREC No. OP-H

Source: Texas Real Estate Commission

BUYER REPRESENTATION

It has long been recognized under Texas law that a real estate agent can represent the purchaser. Buyer's brokerage is a common topic in real estate seminars and is often touted as the solution to the dual agency/intermediary conflict of interest (discussed next). It gives the buyer representation, which some people feel the buyer is entitled to, or needs, in many circumstances. Buyer brokerage may even ease the duty of a listing broker because some duties to the buyer may be performed by the buyer's broker. In cases of office building leasing and more sophisticated commercial property acquisitions, parties frequently seek the assistance of a real estate broker to represent them in making prudent purchases when they lack the expertise to do their own investigations. This has now become more common in residential real estate.

Buyer representation shifts the entire agency theory in the opposite direction of our traditional seller representation. When representing a seller, a real estate agent (and the resulting fiduciary duty) focuses on the marketing of the product for the benefit of the owner. This involves "getting the highest price in the marketplace," maintaining the confidentiality of information, and trying to effect a sale within the shortest period of time for the benefit of the seller. This is the same focus of our traditional MLS subagency concept for cooperating brokers. Historically, the MLS system and most state laws on agency encouraged agents to be trained as seller's brokers or cooperating brokers, so few agents have training as a buyer's broker. Today, however, buyer's brokerage courses are available in virtually every real estate market, and the courses are well attended, reflecting a need for this type of expanded education. Let's talk about buyer's brokers in more detail.

The buyer's broker has a different focus. The emphasis in buyer's brokerage is to help the buyer make informed decisions and obtain the desired product at a fair price, giving the buyer's interests the highest priority. This emphasis would apparently include getting the lowest price in the market place, or at least a "good deal" for the buyer, to facilitate resale or investment potential (a main reason why relocation companies use buyer's brokers), and finding a "safe" purchase of a product without latent defects. There is also a shift of focus away from affecting the sale of the property, because the buyer's broker is more concerned with a satisfactory purchase for the buyer, not just making a sale.

What are the duties of a buyer's broker? There is little case law to guide us at this point. It is presumed that the same care of agency duties that apply to sellers as principals also apply to buyers as principals. However, the situations do differ dramatically. The buyer may request assistance in finding out certain information, or the buyer may need help in pursuing certain issues (homeowners' associations, deed restrictions, financing, and final walk-through) in which the buyer's agent may take on additional duties (remember, the agent isn't trying to market the property, but is trying to obtain the requested product). If this is the case, most state license acts, including Texas, impose a duty of diligence and competence in undertaking those additional duties. Most buyers who hire a buyer's broker want advice, or they wouldn't hire them.

This situation may create a conflict between the seller's and the buyer's brokers. The result may end up being the same, but the means to achieve the sale may vary from the "typical" transaction in the past. The buyer's broker is expected to be more protective of the buyer (the primary focus) than focused on affecting the sale (the main focus of the listing broker). Buyer brokerage is gaining wide acceptance. A growing niche in the agency marketplace has been created by consumers moving into a new area and relocation companies that may want to use the services of a buyer's broker. Brokers may perceive buyer representation and/or cooperation with buyer brokers as both beneficial and cost-effective given that a home buyer may be a home seller in a few years.

DUAL AGENCY

If a broker represents a seller, it is the broker's duty to obtain the highest price and the best terms possible for the seller. If a broker represents a buyer, the broker's duty may be to obtain the lowest price (or at least a fair price) and best terms for the buyer. When the same broker represents two or more principals in the same transaction, it is a ***dual agency*** and a conflict of interest results. If the broker represents both principals in the same transaction, to whom is the broker loyal? Does she work equally hard for each principal? This is a difficult question; therefore, the law requires that each principal be told not to expect the broker's full allegiance and thus each principal is responsible for looking after his own interest. If a broker represents more than one principal and does not obtain their consent, the broker cannot claim a commission and the defrauded principal(s) may be able to rescind the transaction. Moreover, the broker's real estate license may be suspended or revoked. This is true even though the broker does her best to be equally fair to each principal.

A dual agency also develops when a buyer agrees to pay a broker a fee for finding a property and the broker finds one, lists it, and earns a fee from the seller as well as the buyer. Again, both the buyer and seller must be informed of the dual agency in advance of negotiations. If either principal does not approve of the dual agency, he can refuse to participate. Texas recognized dual agency in the License Act for a few years, then it was removed in favor of intermediary status (discussed next). Texas still recognizes common law dual agency, though.

The Texas Real Estate Licensing Act provides that a license may be revoked if the broker or salesperson fails to make clear to all parties to a transaction which party he is acting for, or if he receives compensation from more than one party, except with the full knowledge and consent of all parties [Section 1101.652(b)(7),(8)]. If he acts in the dual capacity of broker and undisclosed principal in a transaction [Section 1101.652(b)(15)] (for instance, if the broker is also the purchaser, and takes advantage of a client by making a purchase below market value), he would violate this provision of the Act.

INTERMEDIARIES

The Texas legislature introduced a new concept of agency representation into Texas real estate brokerage law called an ***intermediary***. An intermediary is defined under the License Act as a "broker who is employed to negotiate a transaction between the parties ... and for that purpose may be an agent to the parties to the transaction." In most circumstances, the sponsoring broker acts as the intermediary.

The statute provides that a real estate broker may act as an intermediary between the parties if: (1) the real estate broker obtains written consent from each party to the transaction for the real estate broker to act as an intermediary in the transaction, and (2) the written consent of the parties states the source of any expected compensation to the real estate broker. A written employment agreement, which also authorizes the real estate broker to act as an intermediary, is sufficient to establish that written consent if the written agreement sets forth the real estate broker's obligations in conspicuous bold or underlined print.

A real estate broker who acts as an intermediary between the parties:

1. May not disclose to the buyer or tenant that the seller or landlord will accept a price less than the asking price unless otherwise instructed in a separate writing by the seller or landlord.
2. May not disclose to the seller or landlord that the buyer or tenant will pay a price greater than the price submitted in a written offer to the seller or landlord unless otherwise instructed in a separate writing by the buyer or tenant.
3. May not disclose any confidential information or any other information a party specifically instructs the real estate broker in writing not to disclose unless otherwise instructed in a separate writing by the prospective party, or is required to disclose such information by this Act [the Real Estate License Act] or a court order, or if the information materially relates to the condition of the property.
4. Shall treat all parties to the transaction honestly and "Act fairly so as not to favor one party over the other." See § 1101.551; 1101.559.

The Procedure

If a real estate broker obtains the consent of the parties to act as an intermediary, the broker may appoint, by providing written notice to the parties, one or more licensees associated with the broker to communicate with and carry out instructions of one party and one or more other licensees associated with the broker to communicate with and carry out instructions of the other party or parties.

One might explain it this way:

The Real Estate License Act has created three "window periods" that a licensee will go through to create intermediary status:

The first window period is the exclusive agency wherein the licensee has an exclusive right to sell and an exclusive buyer's representation agreement. During

FIGURE 22.2 Window periods to create intermediary status

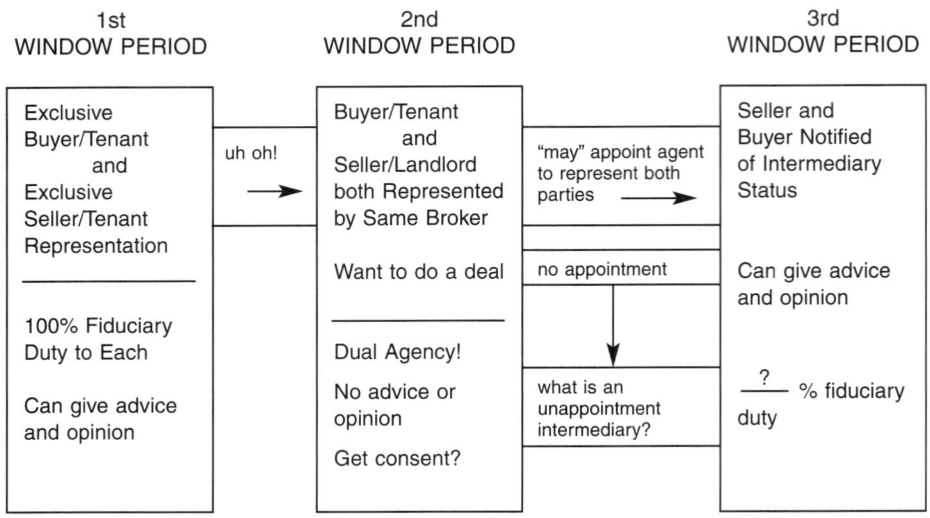

Source: © 2012 Cengage Learning

this phase there is a 100% fiduciary duty and a 100% disclosure to the principal that the agent represents.

The second window period is that time when the buyer and the seller, both represented by the same broker, are going into the same transaction. When this potential conflict arises, the licensee is a dual agent (or an unappointed intermediary, whatever that is) until the intermediary process has been completed.

The third window period is when the buyer and seller have been notified and have accepted the notification that they now have an agent who represents them. At that point, the appointed agent can give advice and opinion. Presumably, during the second window period, the agent (as a dual agent) cannot give advice and opinion. Is it a 100% fiduciary to both? Probably not. What percentage would you fill in? Is a whole fee being charged for less than 100% fiduciary duty? Hmm.

From a liability standpoint, the trick seems to be to keep the second window period as narrow as possible (i.e., as soon as the potential for conflict arises, the agent diligently pursues the intermediary appointments).

Figure 22.2 may help visualize this issue.

It does leave the lingering question. "If the broker is defined as an 'intermediary,' but doesn't go through the appointment process, what is that broker's status?" An intermediary without appointment? A dual agent? Is there a difference?

In effect, one may say that the intermediary status is nothing more than the old dual agency. The duties and responsibilities of an intermediary are very similar, if not the same, as the dual agent under the old dual agency statute. If the sponsoring broker is an intermediary, however, an appointed licensee *can give advice and opinions,* which is more than can be provided as a dual agent. To properly create intermediary status, the intermediary "check list" should work as follows:

1. Provide the required written information to any party you are working with (or to a party that is not represented) at your first substantive dialogue (it would be prudent to have it executed to acknowledge receipt).
2. When engaging employment either as a buyer's representative or as a listing broker, the listing broker should be sure that the possibility for intermediary status is disclosed and authorized by the principal.
3. Inform everyone else in the transaction (parties and licensees) who you represent at first contact (while the statute doesn't require this disclosure to be in writing, it is good business practice).
4. If the real estate firm (and your employment contract) authorizes an intermediary relationship, the agent should:
   a. remind parties that the firm will act as an intermediary when an in-house sale is apparent.
   b. the firm should choose whether or not to make appointments of its associated licensees at the time the in-house sale becomes apparent.
   c. if appointments are made, provide written notice to the parties. Should the sponsoring broker inform the parties that the intermediary appointments are not made, so that the parties shouldn't expect advice? It may be prudent to do so, but does it then create a dual agency? In the intermediary situation, the complications of presentation that we have under the single agency concept don't arise because both parties have agreed and consented to the intermediary status.

If the foregoing steps are not complied with exactly, does it result in an undisclosed dual agency? Questions still abound, with few answers. The Texas Real Estate License Act provide that a broker *must* agree to act as an intermediary if the broker agrees to represent a buyer or tenant in the transaction and the seller or landlord represents both parties. Most agree that this wipes out common law dual agency. Does it require brokers representing buyers and sellers to now go through all of the procedures, or would failure to do so create a violation of the Texas Real Estate License Act? For instance, if a broker finds that he is representing both sides, must he now get written consent, as an intermediary, or otherwise it constitutes a violation of the License Act? Another issue for the courts!

AGENCY DISCLOSURE RULES

How do we sort out all of these agency relationships? The 1995 legislation created a disclosure process in the Texas Real Estate License Act. The disclosure is made in two stages: (1) when meeting a party for the first time, and (2) while representing a party. When meeting the party for the first time, the licensee is required to furnish a party in a real estate transaction at the time of the first substantive dialogue with a party with the written statement shown in Figure 22.3.

What is a "substantive dialogue"? A meeting or written communication at which a substantive discussion occurs with respect to specific real property. It

FIGURE 22.3 Agency disclosure statement

Before working with a real estate broker, you should know that the duties of a broker depend on whom the broker represents. If you are a prospective seller or landlord (owner) or a prospective buyer or tenant (buyer), you should know that the broker who lists the property for sale or lease is the owner's agent. A broker who acts as a subagent represents the owner in cooperation with the listing broker. A broker who acts as a buyer's agent represents the buyer. A broker may act as an intermediary between the parties if the parties consent in writing. A broker can assist you in locating a property, preparing a contract or lease, or obtaining financing without representing you. A broker is obligated by law to treat you honestly.

IF THE BROKER REPRESENTS THE OWNER: The broker becomes the owner's agent by entering into an agreement with the owner, usually through a written listing agreement, or by agreeing to act as a subagent by accepting an offer of subagency from the listing broker. A subagent may work in a different real estate office. A listing broker or subagent can assist the buyer but does not represent the buyer and must place the interests of the owner first. The buyer should not tell the owner's agent anything the buyer would not want the owner to know because an owner's agent must disclose to the owner any material information known to the agent.

IF THE BROKER REPRESENTS THE BUYER: The broker becomes the buyer's agent by entering into an agreement to represent the buyer, usually through a written buyer representation agreement. A buyer's agent can assist the owner but does not represent the owner and must place the interests of the buyer first. The owner should not tell a buyer's agent anything the owner would not want the buyer to know because the buyer's agent must disclose to the buyer any material information known to the agent.

IF THE BROKER ACTS AS AN INTERMEDIARY: A broker may act as an intermediary between the parties if the broker complies with The Texas Real Estate License Act. The broker must obtain intermediary. The written consent must state who will pay the broker and, in conspicuous bold or underlined print, set forth the broker's obligations as an intermediary. The broker is required to treat each party honestly and fairly and to comply with the Texas Real Estate License Act. A broker who acts as an intermediary in a transaction: (1) shall treat all parties honestly; (2) may not disclose that the owner will accept a price less than the asking price unless authorized in writing to do so by the owner; (3) may not disclose that the buyer will pay a price greater than the price submitted in a written offer unless authorized in writing to do so by the buyer; and (4) may not disclose any confidential information or any information that a party specifically instructs the broker in writing not to disclose unless authorized in writing to disclose the information or is required to do so by the Texas Real Estate License Act or a court order or if the information materially relates to the condition of the property. With the parties' consent, a broker acting as an intermediary between the parties may appoint a person who is licensed under the Texas Real Estate License Act and associated with the broker to communicate with and carry out instructions of one party and another person who is licensed under that Act and associated with the broker to communicate with and carry out instructions of the other party.

If you choose to have a broker represent you, you should enter into a written agreement with the broker that clearly establishes the broker's obligations and your obligations. The agreement should state how and by whom the broker will be paid. You have the right to choose the type of representation, if any, you wish to receive. Your payment of a fee to a broker does not necessarily establish that the broker represents you. If you have any questions regarding the duties and responsibilities of the broker, you should resolve those questions before proceeding.

Source: © 2012 Cengage Learning

does not include a meeting that occurs at a property held open for prospective purchasers or tenants or a meeting or written communication that occurs after the parties of the transaction have signed the contract to sell, buy, rent, or lease the real property concerned.

Exemptions

A licensee is not required to provide this written information if (1) the proposed transaction for a residential lease is not more than one year and no sale is being considered, or (2) the licensee meets with the party who is represented by another licensee.

If the Licensee Represents a Party

The Texas Real Estate License Act now provides that a licensee who represents a party in a proposed real estate transaction must disclose that representation at the time of the licensee's first contact with (1) another party to the transaction, or (2) another licensee who represents another party to the transaction. The disclosure may be oral or in writing. It would seem to be a prudent business practice, however, to do it in writing so that the agent could confirm that the disclosure was properly made.

MIDDLEMAN PRINCIPLE

The broker may also operate as a ***middleman*** who represents neither party. He simply brings the parties together and neither party expects the middleman's loyalty. This middleman principle can work in some sophisticated real estate transactions. The problem with this theory though is that if either party thinks that the broker represents him, an agency relationship could be created and fiduciary duties established, resulting in potential liability for the broker. It is very difficult, in most situations, to represent neither party, yet still be an effective agent.

PRINCIPAL'S OBLIGATIONS

The principal also has certain obligations to the agent. Although these do not receive much statutory attention in most states, they are important when the principal fails to live up to those obligations. The principal's primary obligation is **compensation.** Additionally, the agent is eligible for *reimbursement* for expenses not related to the sale itself. For example, if an agent had to pay a plumber to fix a broken pipe for the owner, the agent could expect reimbursement from the owner over and above the sales commission.

The other two obligations of the principal are indemnification and performance. An agent is entitled to *indemnification* upon suffering a loss through no fault of her own, such as when a misrepresentation by the principal to the agent was passed on in good faith to the buyer. The duty of **performance** means the principal is expected to do whatever he reasonably can to accomplish the purpose of the agency such as referring inquiries by prospective buyers to the broker.

ANTITRUST LAWS

Federal antitrust laws, particularly the Sherman Antitrust Act, have had a major impact on the real estate brokerage industry. The purpose of federal antitrust laws is to promote competition in an open marketplace. To some people not familiar with the real estate business, it could appear that all real estate brokers charge the same fee (i.e., 6%). In fact and in practice, nothing is further from the truth. Real estate brokers establish their fees from a complex integration of market factors, and all real estate brokerage fees are a result of a negotiated agreement between the owner and the broker. In tougher markets, a broker may charge a much higher fee (10% to 12% of the gross sales price). Very expensive property, in a good market, may be listed by a broker for an amount that is substantially less (2% to 5% of the gross sales price).

Price Fixing

Price fixing in any industry is so grossly anticompetitive and contrary to the free enterprise form of government, that price fixing is construed to be "per se" illegal. This means that the conduct of price fixing is, in itself, so illegal that no circumstances can correct it. Although a brokerage company can establish a policy on fees, they should be acutely aware that any hint, or any perceived hint, of price fixing between brokers can result in both civil and criminal penalties. That is, if the court determines that a broker has engaged in price fixing with another broker or group of brokers, the licensee could serve time in the federal penitentiary in addition to paying a substantial fine. Consequently, brokers are well advised *never* to discuss their fees, under *any* circumstances, except with the owner of the property.

Boycotting

Another aspect of antitrust laws that has affected brokers has been ***boycotting*** of other brokers in the marketplace. This, too, is a violation of the Sherman Antitrust Act. In some circumstances, REALTOR® trade associations have established rules for membership that have resulted in some brokers being unfairly excluded (unreasonably high fees, part-time employment, "discount" brokers, etc.). Standards for membership are usually an attempt to upgrade the professionalism of the industry and maintain high standards. The difficulty that is encountered, however, is that when high-quality real estate brokers are excluded from competing with members of broker trade associations an unfair market advantage results. Antitrust cases involving boycotting have tended to recognize the procompetitive efforts of Boards of REALTORS®, MLS systems, and other similar trade associations, however. Therefore, Boards of REALTORS® and other trade associations can establish reasonable fees, residency requirements, and other pertinent requirements for membership. However, no membership requirements can be established that may arbitrarily exclude licensed real estate brokers from participation.

Most Boards or Associations of REALTORS® have opened their memberships to eliminate arbitrary exclusion of licensees from other boards who may

Approved by the Texas Real Estate Commission for Voluntary Use

Texas law requires all real estate licensees to give the following information about brokerage services to prospective buyers, tenants, sellers and landlords.

Information About Brokerage Services

Before working with a real estate broker, you should know that the duties of a broker depend on whom the broker represents. If you are a prospective seller or landlord (owner) or a prospective buyer or tenant (buyer), you should know that the broker who lists the property for sale or lease is the owner's agent. A broker who acts as a subagent represents the owner in cooperation with the listing broker. A broker who acts as a buyer's agent represents the buyer. A broker may act as an intermediary between the parties if the parties consent in writing. A broker can assist you in locating a property, preparing a contract or lease, or obtaining financing without representing you. A broker is obligated by law to treat you honestly.

IF THE BROKER REPRESENTS THE OWNER:
The broker becomes the owner's agent by entering into an agreement with the owner, usually through a written - listing agreement, or by agreeing to act as a subagent by accepting an offer of subagency from the listing broker. A subagent may work in a different real estate office. A listing broker or subagent can assist the buyer but does not represent the buyer and must place the interests of the owner first. The buyer should not tell the owner's agent anything the buyer would not want the owner to know because an owner's agent must disclose to the owner any material information known to the agent.

IF THE BROKER REPRESENTS THE BUYER:
The broker becomes the buyer's agent by entering into an agreement to represent the buyer, usually through a written buyer representation agreement. A buyer's agent can assist the owner but does not represent the owner and must place the interests of the buyer first. The owner should not tell a buyer's agent anything the owner would not want the buyer to know because a buyer's agent must disclose to the buyer any material information known to the agent.

IF THE BROKER ACTS AS AN INTERMEDIARY:
A broker may act as an intermediary between the parties if the broker complies with The Texas Real Estate License Act. The broker must obtain the written consent of each party to the transaction to act as an intermediary. The written consent must state who will pay the broker and, in conspicuous bold or underlined print, set forth the broker's obligations as an intermediary. The broker is required to treat each party honestly and fairly and to comply with The Texas Real Estate License Act. A broker who acts as an intermediary in a transaction:

(1) shall treat all parties honestly;
(2) may not disclose that the owner will accept a price less than the asking price unless authorized in writing to do so by the owner;
(3) may not disclose that the buyer will pay a price greater than the price submitted in a written offer unless authorized in writing to do so by the buyer; and
(4) may not disclose any confidential information or any information that a party specifically instructs the broker in writing not to disclose unless authorized in writing to disclose the information or required to do so by The Texas Real Estate License Act or a court order or if the information materially relates to the condition of the property.

With the parties' consent, a broker acting as an intermediary between the parties may appoint a person who is licensed under The Texas Real Estate License Act and associated with the broker to communicate with and carry out instructions of one party and another person who is licensed under that Act and associated with the broker to communicate with and carry out instructions of the other party.

If you choose to have a broker represent you,
you should enter into a written agreement with the broker that clearly establishes the broker's obligations and your obligations. The agreement should state how and by whom the broker will be paid. You have the right to choose the type of representation, if any, you wish to receive. Your payment of a fee to a broker does not necessarily establish that the broker represents you. If you have any questions regarding the duties and responsibilities of the broker, you should resolve those questions before proceeding.

Real estate licensee asks that you acknowledge receipt of this information about brokerage services for the licensee's records.

Buyer, Seller, Landlord or Tenant Date

Texas Real Estate Brokers and Salespersons are licensed and regulated by the Texas Real Estate Commission (TREC). If you have a question or complaint regarding a real estate licensee, you should contact TREC at P.O. Box 12188, Austin, Texas 78711-2188 or 512-465-3960.

01A TREC No. OP-K

(TAR-2501) 1/1/96

wish to access pertinent information. This area of law is constantly changing because REALTORS® are concerned with protecting their rights, but also want to accommodate the needs of consumers. Real estate is still a service business!

ERRORS AND OMISSION INSURANCE

Because of the trend in recent years to a more consumer-oriented and litigious society, the possibility of a broker being sued has risen to the point that *errors and omission insurance (E&O)* has become very popular. The broker pays an annual fee to an insurance company that in turn will defend the broker and pay legal costs and judgments. Most "E&O" policies, as they are sometimes called, do not cover intentional acts of a broker to deceive, punitive damages or fraud, and do not cover negligence or misrepresentation when buying or selling for one's own account. Other than that, E&O offers quite broad coverage. This includes defending so-called "nuisance cases" in which the broker may not be at fault but must defend anyway. Moreover, E&O covers not only courtroom costs and judgments, but pretrial conferences and negotiations and out-of-court settlements. Today E&O is simply a cost of the real estate business just like rent, telephone, and automobile expenses.

REVIEW QUESTIONS

Answers to these questions are found in the Answer Key section at the back of the book.

1. All of the following statements are true EXCEPT:
   A. the Statute of Frauds requires all agency agreements to be made in writing in order to be enforceable.
   B. a real estate listing is an agency contract.
   C. in a real estate listing, the property owner is the principal.
   D. a real estate broker is the agent under a real estate listing.

2. When an agent is given the right to transact all types of matters on behalf of the principal, the agent serves as a
   A. notary public.
   B. third party.
   C. universal agent.
   D. special agent.

3. An agent who is authorized to bind an employer in a trade or business is
   A. a special agent.
   B. a general agent.
   C. an exclusive agent.
   D. a principal agent.

4. The relationship of a real estate broker to the owner of property listed for sale with the broker is that of a(n)
   A. general agent.
   B. universal agent.
   C. limited agent.
   D. special agent.

5. Which of the following is NOT true of a listing contract?
   A. A corporation may be a principal.
   B. A natural person may be an agent.
   C. A sales associate may be an agent.
   D. Purchasers are third parties to the contract.

6. An agent's authority may be granted by
   A. written agreement.
   B. custom in the industry.
   C. both A and B.
   D. neither A nor B.

7. When an agent's authority arises from custom in the industry, it is identified as
   A. implied authority.
   B. ostensible authority.
   C. customary authority.
   D. conventional authority.

8. An agency may be created by
   A. ratification.
   B. estoppel.
   C. both A and B.
   D. neither A nor B.

9. Broker Gomez was part owner of an apartment building along with two co-owners. When they decided to sell the building, broker Gomez was named as the agent in the listing agreement. Broker Gomez thus held an agency
   A. by ratification.
   B. coupled with an interest.
   C. by estoppel.
   D. by implication.

10. A broker has fiduciary responsibilities to
    A. the owner of property listed by the broker.
    B. third parties with whom the broker deals.
    C. both A and B.
    D. neither A nor B.

11. Fiduciary responsibilities of an agent to the principal include all of the following EXCEPT:
    A. faithful performance.
    B. loyalty.
    C. accounting for funds or property received.
    D. provision of legal advice.

12. When a broker acts as an agent for both purchaser and seller in a transaction, this is identified as
    A. an agency by estoppel.
    B. a dual agency.
    C. an agency coupled with an interest.
    D. an agency by ratification.

13. A broker may act as an agent for both parties in a transaction only with the permission of
    A. the property owner.
    B. the real estate commission.
    C. both parties.
    D. the purchaser.

14. Isaacs introduced owner DiVita to prospect Park. DiVita and Park conducted negotiations among themselves without assistance from Isaacs. The role of Isaacs was that of a
    A. dual agent.
    B. middleman.
    C. single agent.
    D. cooperating broker.

15. Any earnest money deposits paid by the purchaser
    A. belong to the broker.
    B. must be placed in a proper trust account.
    C. both A and B.
    D. neither A nor B.

16. The placing of funds belonging to others in a broker's personal bank account constitutes
    A. commingling.
    B. grounds for revocation of the broker's license.
    C. both A and B.
    D. neither A nor B.

17. A broker who misrepresents a property to a prospect may be subject to all of the following EXCEPT:
    A. loss of rights to the commission.
    B. revocation of broker's license.
    C. criminal prosecution.
    D. civil action for damages.

18. The Texas Real Estate License Act provides that a license may be revoked if, without consent of all parties,
    A. the broker fails to make it clear for which party he is acting.
    B. the broker receives compensation from more than one party.
    C. both A and B.
    D. neither A nor B.

19. A broker who intentionally misleads a prospect by making an incorrect statement that is knowingly untrue is
    A. guilty of fraud.
    B. subject to license revocation.
    C. subject to litigation.
    D. all of the above.
    E. none of the above.

20. An agent who fails to investigate the cause of an apparent underlying defect in a property that he is selling may be found
    A. criminally liable.
    B. liable for civil damages.
    C. guilty of a felony.
    D. both A and C.

21. When an agent engages someone to look into a question raised by a purchaser, the agent
    A. should make certain of the competency of the person so engaged.
    B. may be liable for civil damages if the person is not professionally competent.
    C. both A and B.
    D. neither A nor B.

22. Can an agent protect himself from liability to disclose defects in a property by stating in writing that the property is being sold "as is"?
    A. Yes, because the statement makes it clear that the purchaser is aware of all problems that might arise.
    B. Yes, because of the rule of caveat emptor.
    C. No, because he may still be liable for having withheld material facts about the property.
    D. No, because the purchaser waives any right to future claims by accepting the property "as is."

23. If a principal asks an agent to participate in an illegal or unethical act in selling a property, the agent should do all the following EXCEPT:
    A. advise against it.
    B. have no part of it.
    C. discourage the principal from doing it.
    D. report the principal to the real estate department.

24. A broker can indemnify herself against legal actions by those with whom she deals by purchasing
    A. errors and omissions insurance.
    B. middleman insurance.
    C. property insurance.
    D. employee insurance.

Chapter 23

KEY TERMS

Bylaws: rules that govern how an owners' association will be run

CC&Rs: covenants, conditions, and restrictions by which a property owner agrees to abide

Common elements: those parts of a condominium that are owned by all the unit owners

Condominium: individual ownership of a space of air plus undivided ownership of the common elements

Condominium declaration: a document that converts a given parcel of land into a condominium subdivision

Cooperative: land and building owned or leased by a corporation which, in turn, leases space to its share holders

Limited common elements: common elements whose use is limited to certain owners

Planned unit development (PUD): individually owned lots and houses with community ownership of common areas

Proprietary lease: a lease issued by a cooperative corporation to its shareholders

Timesharing: the exclusive use of a property for a specified number of days each year

Condominiums, Cooperatives, PUDs, and Timeshares

IN THIS CHAPTER

This chapter covers methods of dividing the land. The condominium declaration is covered in some detail. Other topics include management, maintenance fees, taxes, insurance, and financing. The advantages and disadvantages of condominium living are listed along with a list of things to check before buying. Other condo topics include a discussion of legislation, condo conversions, and physical appearance. Cooperative apartments, PUDs, and timesharing are also covered.

Puerto Rican laws and experience became the basis for the passage by the U.S. Congress in 1961 of Section 234 of the National Housing Act. This section provides a legal model for condominium ownership and makes available FHA mortgage loan insurance on condominium units. Currently, one in four new residences being built in the United States is a condominium. Additionally, many existing apartment buildings are being converted to condominium ownership.

Condominium ownership is not the only legal framework available that combines community living with community ownership, although it is currently the best known. Prior to the enactment of condominium legislation, cooperative ownership of multifamily residential buildings was popular in the United States, particularly in the states of Florida, New York, and Hawaii. A more recent variation is the individually owned house combined with community ownership of common areas in what is called a planned unit development or PUD.

THE DESIRE FOR LAND-USE EFFICIENCY

Of the forces responsible for creating the need for condominiums, cooperatives, and PUDs, the most important are land scarcity in desirable areas, continuing escalation in construction costs, disenchantment with the work of maintaining the grounds around a house, and the desire to own rather than rent.

When constructing single-family houses on separate lots, a builder can usually average four to five houses per acre of land. In a growing number of cities, the sheer physical space necessary to continue building detached houses either does not exist or, if it does, it is a long distance from employment centers or is so expensive as to eliminate all but a small portion of the population from building there. As in ancient Roman times, the solution is to build more dwellings on the same parcel of land. Instead of four or five dwellings, build 25 or 100 on an acre of land. That way not only is the land more efficiently used, but the cost is divided among more owners. From the standpoint of construction costs, the builder does not have the miles of streets, sewers, or utility lines that would be necessary to reach every house in a subdivision. Furthermore, the fact that there are shared walls, that one dwelling unit's ceiling is often another's floor, and that one roof can cover many vertically stacked units can produce savings in construction materials and labor.

The Amenities of Multifamily Living

For some householders, the lure of "carefree living," wherein such chores as lawn mowing, watering, weeding, snow shoveling, and building maintenance are provided, is the major attraction. For others, it is the security often associated with clustered dwellings or the extensive recreational and social facilities that are not economically possible on a single-dwelling-unit basis. It is commonplace to find swimming pools, recreation halls, tennis and volleyball courts, gymnasiums, and even social directors at some condominium, cooperative, and PUD projects.

A large rental apartment project can also produce the same advantages of land and construction economy and amenities. Nevertheless, we cannot overlook the preference of most American households to own rather than rent their dwellings. This preference is typically based on a desire for a savings program, observation of inflation in real estate prices, and advantageous income tax laws that allow owners, but not renters, to deduct property taxes and mortgage interest.

DIVIDING THE LAND OF AN ESTATE

Figure 23.1 illustrates the estate in land created by a condominium, cooperative, and planned unit development and compares each with the estate held by the owner of a house. Notice in Figure 23.1 that the ownership of house A extends from lot line B across to lot line C. Except where limited by zoning or other legal restrictions, the owner of house A has full control over and full right to use the land between the lot lines from the center of the earth to the limits of the sky. Within the law, the owner can choose how to use the land, what to build on it or add to it, what color to paint the house and garage, how many people and animals will live there, what type of landscaping to have, from whom to purchase property insurance, and so on. The owner of house D has the same control over the land between lot lines C and E.

The owner of A cannot dictate to a neighbor what color to paint the neighbor's house, what kind of shrubs and trees to grow, or from whom to buy hazard insurance if any at all. (Occasionally, one will find deed restrictions in housing subdivisions that give the owners a limited amount of control over each other's land uses in the subdivision.)

Condominium

In a ***condominium***, each dwelling unit owner owns as his fee estate the cubicle of air space that his unit occupies. This is the space lying between the interior surfaces of the unit sides and between the floor and the ceiling. The remainder of the building and the land are called the ***common elements*** or common areas. Each unit owner holds an undivided interest in the common elements.

In Figure 23.1, the owner of dwelling unit F owns as her fee property the air space enclosed by the lines. Except for the individual unit owners' air spaces, F, G, H, I, and J each owns an undivided interest in everything between lot lines K and L. This includes the land and the shell of the building, plus such things as the manager's apartment, lobby, hallways, stairways, elevators, and recreation facilities. In Texas, the Condominium Act also recognizes ***limited common elements***. These are common elements reserved for the use of a certain number of apartments to the exclusion of other apartments, such as special corridors, stairways, elevators, and services common to apartments of a particular floor.

FIGURE 23.1 Comparison of estates

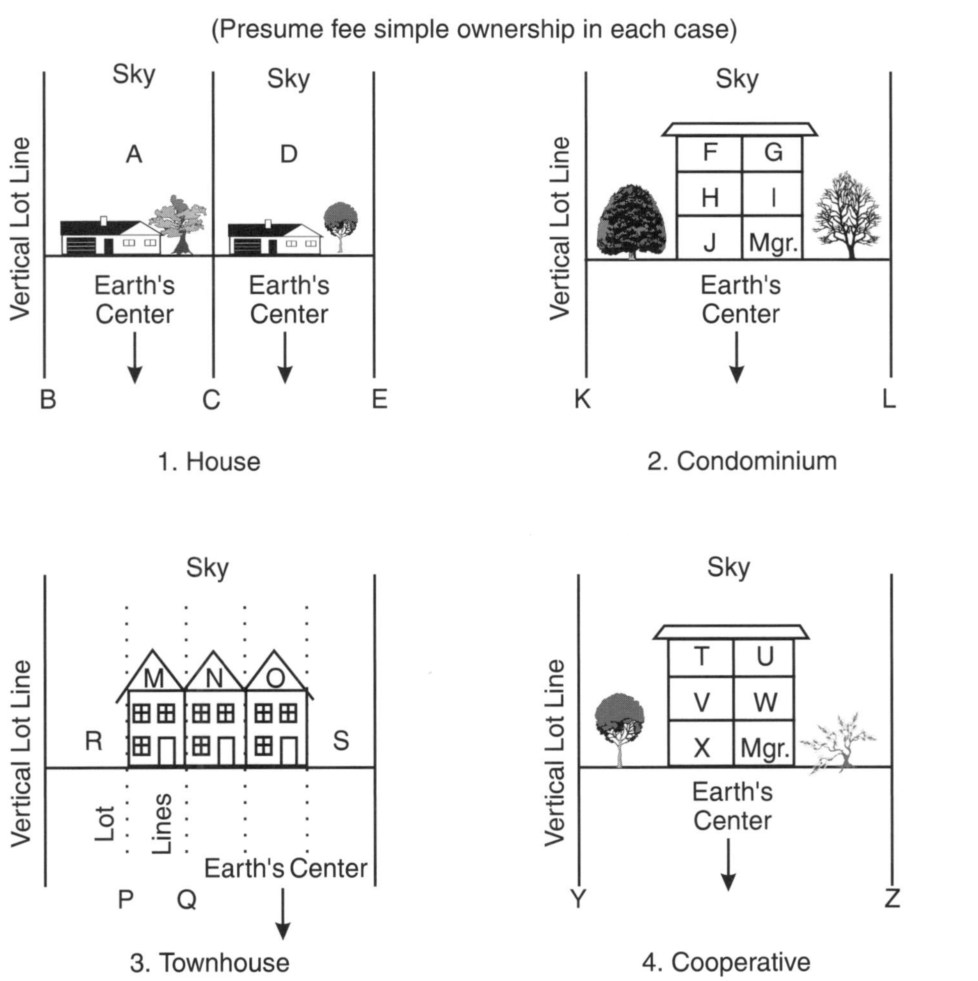

Source: © 2012 Cengage Learning

Planned Unit Development Estate

In a ***planned unit development*** each owner owns as his individual property the land that his dwelling unit occupies. For example, the owner of house M in Figure 23.1 owns the land between lot lines P and Q from the center of the earth skyward. A homeowners' association consisting of M, N, and O owns the land at R and S and any improvements thereon, such as recreation facilities or parking lots. The most distinguishing feature of a PUD is the ownership of land by the unit owner, and the PUD concept is often used for townhouse development. In both condominiums and cooperatives, there is no land attributable to the unit owner.

Cooperative Estate

In a ***cooperative estate*** there is no individually owned property at all. Rather, the owners hold shares of stock in a cooperative corporation, which, in turn, owns the land and building and issues proprietary leases to the owners to use specific apartments. A ***proprietary lease*** differs from the usual landlord-tenant lease in that the "tenant" is also an owner of the building. In the cooperative in Figure 23.1, all the land and the building lying between lot lines Y and Z are owned by a corporation that is owned by shareholders T, U, V, W, and X. Ownership of the corporation's shares carries the right to occupy apartment units in the building.

Having now briefly illustrated the estates created by the condominium, cooperative, and PUD forms of real estate ownership, let us take a closer look at their organization, financing, and management.

OVERVIEW OF CONDOMINIUMS

The Condominium Declaration

In Texas, a condominium is created when a person, usually a real estate developer, files a ***condominium declaration*** with the county clerk that converts a parcel of land held under a single deed into a number of individual condominium estates, plus an estate that includes the common elements. Included in the declaration is a description of the location of each individual unit with respect to the land, identification of the common elements to be shared, and the percentage interest each unit owner will have in the common elements. If the condominium is to be on leasehold land, the declaration converts the single leasehold interest into individual leases or subleases. The right of a person to file a condominium declaration is outlined in the Texas Uniform Condominium Act. As a general rule, the declaration can be amended only at a meeting of the unit owners, and at least 67% of the ownership must approve the change, although there are exceptions.

Owners' Association

In addition to filing the condominium declaration, also known as the **master deed,** the developer must provide a legal framework by which the unit owners can govern themselves. Often, a nonprofit condominium *unit owners' association* is incorporated, and each unit purchaser automatically becomes a member. The association can also be organized as a trust or unincorporated association. However, in the event of a lawsuit against the association, these may not offer the members the legal protection normally provided by a corporation. The main purpose of the owners' association is to control, regulate, and maintain the common elements.

Finally, the developer must file in the declaration a list of regulations by which anyone purchasing a unit in the condominium must abide. These are known as ***covenants, conditions, and restrictions (CC&Rs)*** in the declaration and tell a unit owner such things as the color of the exterior or the living room drapes, or the size of pets that can live in the apartment. Typically, these also govern such things as when the swimming pool and other recreation facilities will be open for use and when quiet hours will be observed in the building.

Bylaws

Bylaws may also be enacted to set out the rules and regulations for how the unit owner's association will function. They provide the rules by which the association's board of directors or executive committee is elected from among the association members and set the standards by which the board must rule. They also set forth how association dues (maintenance fees) will be established and collected, how contracts will be let for maintenance, management, and repair work, and how personnel will be hired.

Unit Deed

Each purchaser of a condominium unit receives a deed to the unit from the developer. The deed describes the size and location of the unit, both in terms of the unit number in the building and its surveyed airspace. Usually this is done by referring to the parcel map that was filed with the declaration. The deed will also recite the percentage interest in the common elements that the grantee is receiving. The deed is recorded upon closing just as one would record a deed to a house.

Condominium Management

For condominium owners to enjoy maintenance free living, the association usually employs the services of a building manager. If the project contains only a few units, the association may elect to employ one of its members on a part time basis. The manager takes care of the landscaping, hallways, trash, and the like and keeps records of expenses needed to do this. For major maintenance items such as painting, roof repairs, and pool refurbishing, independent contractors are hired.

The resident manager is also usually responsible for enforcing the house rules, handling complaints or problems regarding maintenance, and supervising such matters as the handling of the mail and the use of the swimming pool and recreation areas. The extent of the manager's duties and responsibilities is set by the owners' association. The association should also retain the right to fire the resident manager and the management firm if their services are not satisfactory.

Maintenance Fees

The costs of maintaining the common elements in a condominium are allocated among the unit owners in accordance with percentages set forth in the enabling declaration. These **maintenance fees** or **association dues** are collected monthly. Failure to pay creates a lien against the delinquent owner's unit. The amount collected is based on the association's budget. This in turn is based on the association's estimate of the cost of month-to-month maintenance, insurance, legal counsel, and accounting services, plus reserves for expenses that do not occur monthly.

Property Taxes and Insurance

Because condominium law recognizes each condominium dwelling unit as a separate legal ownership, property taxes are assessed on each unit separately. Property taxes are based on the assessed value of the unit, which is based on its market value. It is not necessary for the taxing authority to assess and tax the common elements separately. The reason is that the market value of each unit reflects not only the value of the unit itself, but also the value of the fractional ownership in the common elements that accompany the unit.

The association is responsible for purchasing hazard and liability insurance covering the common elements. Each dwelling unit owner is responsible for purchasing hazard and liability insurance for the interior of his or her dwelling. Owners should be cautioned to be sure that the association has insurance in force and in sufficient amounts. If damages exceed the policy coverage in Texas, the unit owners are proportionally liable for the damage.

Thus, if a visitor slips on a banana peel in the lobby or a hallway of the building, the association is responsible. If the accident occurs in an individual's unit, the unit owner is responsible. In a high-rise condominium, if the roof breaks during a heavy rainstorm and floods several apartments below, the association is responsible. If an apartment owner's dishwasher overflows and soaks the apartments below, that owner is responsible.

If the condominium unit is being rented, the owner will want to have landlord insurance, and the tenant, for protection, will want a tenant's hazard and liability policy.

Condominium Financing

Because each condominium unit can be separately owned, each can be separately financed. Thus, a condominium purchaser can choose whether or not to borrow against his unit. If he borrows, he can choose a large or small down payment and a long or short amortization period. Once in his unit, if he wants to repay early or refinance, this is his option too. When he sells, the buyer can elect to assume the loan, pay it off, or obtain new financing. In other words, although association bylaws, restrictions, and house rules may regulate how an owner may use his unit, in no way does the association control how a unit may be financed.

Because each unit is a separate ownership, if a lender needs to foreclose against a delinquent borrower in the building, the remaining unit owners are not involved. They are neither responsible for the delinquent borrower's mortgage debt, nor are they parties to the foreclosure.

Legislation Against Abuses

The legal documents involved in purchasing a house are few in comparison to those involved in purchasing a condominium. Because the master deed, bylaws, and restrictions often total 100 or more pages of legal language, unit purchasers who are not concerned with "details" often do not read them. As a result, in numerous cases developers have buried in these documents the fact that they are retaining substantial rights and title in their projects, even after all the units have been sold. The Texas legislature added meeting notice requirements, in addition to general notice and rights for a unit owner who may be assessed a fine.

Two specific areas of abuse have been recreation and management. Some developers retain title to recreation areas and then charge unit owners escalating monthly use fees that are far more than actual costs. The developer then keeps the difference. If a unit owner protests by refusing to pay, the developer can place a lien against the unit and ultimately have it sold at foreclosure. In the second area of abuse, the fine print appoints the developer as manager of the project for 25 years. When the unit owners find their management fees out of proportion to the level of services received, the developer points out the clause appointing her manager and reminds them that she cannot be fired.

In adopting the Uniform Condominium Act, Texas created a Purchaser's Right To Cancel. In the event a purchaser buys a unit from a unit owner other than the declarant, and has not received from the seller the declaration, bylaws, and association rules before the purchaser executes the contract for sale, or if the contract does not contain an underlined or bold-printed provision acknowledging the person's receipt of those documents and recommending that the purchaser read those documents before executing the contract, the purchaser may cancel the contract before the sixth day after the date the purchaser receives those documents. If the purchaser has not received a resale certificate before executing a contract of sale, the purchaser may cancel the contract before the sixth day after the date the purchaser receives a retail certificate. Similar safeguards are allowed if the purchaser purchases the condominium unit from the original developer and has not received the condominium information. In the event an existing building is converted to condominium use (discussed next), the original declarant of the condominium must give each residential tenant or a subtenant in possession of a portion of the conversion building notice of the conversion at least 60 days before the date the declarant will require the tenant or subtenant in possession to vacate.

Federal law has also addressed the subject when Congress passed the Condominium and Cooperative Abuse Relief Act, which applies to all condominium and cooperative projects where the real estate has five or more residential units in each residential structure. The Condominium and Cooperative Abuse Relief Act allows unit owners to terminate certain management contracts or portions thereof that were created while the developer was in control of the project.

The statute has a very limited impact, however, because it provides protection only for condominiums that are conversion projects.

Condominium Conversions

Enterprising developers have found that existing apartment buildings can be converted to condominiums. Compared to new construction, a condominium conversion is often simpler, faster, and more profitable for the developer. The procedure involves finding an attractively built existing building that is well located and has good floor plans. The developer does a facelift on the outside, adds more landscaping, paints the interior, and replaces carpets and appliances. The developer also files the necessary legal paperwork to convert the building and land into condominium units and common elements.

However, some significant problems have surfaced. One of these is the plight of the tenants who are forced to move out when a building is converted. In a few cities, there have been moratoriums on conversions.

Another potential problem area with condominium conversions, and one that a prospective buyer should be aware of, is that converted buildings are used buildings that were not intended as condominiums when built. As used buildings, there may be considerable deferred maintenance, and the building may have thermal insulation suitable to a time when energy costs were lower. If the building was originally built for rental purposes, sound-deadening insulation in the walls, floors, and ceilings may be inadequate. Fire protection between units may also be less than satisfactory. In contrast, newly built condominiums must meet current building code requirements regarding thermal and sound insulation, fire-wall construction, and so forth.

Last, it is worth noting that not all condominium conversions are carried out by developers. Enterprising tenants have successfully converted their own buildings and saved considerable sums of money. It is not uncommon for the value of a building to double when it is converted to a condominium. Tenants who are willing to hire the legal, architectural, and construction help they need can create valuable condominium homes for themselves in the same building where they were previously renters.

Physical Appearance of Condominiums

Before we turn our attention from condominiums, let it be reemphasized that a condominium is first and foremost a legal concept. It tells how a title to real property is owned. It does not, by itself, tell us what a condominium looks like. Physically, a condominium can take the shape of a two-story garden apartment building, a 20-story tower, row houses, or clustered houses. You will hear them called low-rise and high-rise condominiums, townhomes, garden-rises, walled garden apartments, villas, and cluster housing.

Condominiums are not restricted to residential uses. In recent years, a number of developers across the nation have built office buildings and sold individual suites to doctors, dentists, and lawyers. The same idea has been applied to shopping centers and industrial space. A condominium does not have to be a new building. Many existing apartment houses have been converted from rental status to condominium ownership with only a few physical changes to the building.

COOPERATIVE APARTMENTS

Prior to the availability of condominium-enabling legislation in the United States, owner-occupied community housing took the form of the cooperative housing corporation. Although the condominium is dominant today, there are still substantial numbers of cooperative apartments in New York City, Miami, Chicago, San Francisco, and Honolulu. They are rarely found in Texas.

A *cooperative apartment* is organized by forming a nonprofit corporation. This is usually done by a developer who is either planning to convert an existing rental building to cooperative ownership or to build a new structure. Sometimes, the tenants in a rental building will organize a cooperative corporation to buy their building from the owner. To raise the funds necessary to pay for the building, the corporation borrows as much as it can by mortgaging the building. The balance is raised by selling shares of stock in the corporation.

The Cooperator

The shareholder, or *cooperator,* receives a proprietary lease from the corporation to occupy a certain apartment in the building. The more desirable apartments require the purchase of more shares than the less desirable ones.

In return for this lease, the cooperator does not pay rent; instead, she agrees to pay to the corporation her share of the cost of maintaining the building and her share of the monthly mortgage payments and annual property taxes. This sharing of expenses is a unique and crucial feature of this form of ownership. If one or more cooperators fail to pay their pro rata share, the remaining cooperators must make up the difference. Suppose that the monthly loan payment on a 10-unit cooperative building is $20,000 and it is shared equally by its 10 cooperators, each contributing $2,000 per month. If one shareholder fails to contribute his $2,000, only $18,000 is available for the required payment. If the lender is paid $18,000 rather than $20,000, the loan is delinquent and subject to foreclosure. The lender does not take the position that because 9 of the 10 cooperators made their payments, nine-tenths of the building is free from foreclosure threat. Therefore, it is the responsibility of the remaining nine to continue making the $20,000 monthly payments or lose the building. They can seek voluntary reimbursement by the tardy cooperator, or, if that does not work, terminate him as a shareholder.

Refinancing Methods

Because the entire building serves as collateral for the loan, it is impossible to obtain new financing on an individual apartment unit in a cooperative building. So, if there is to be new mortgage financing, it must be on the entire building. When the original mortgage loan on the project is substantially reduced and/or apartment prices have risen, as evidenced by a rise in the value of shares, this can be a severe handicap if a cooperator wants to sell. To illustrate, suppose that a family buys into a cooperative for $15,000. Several years later the family wants to sell, and is offered $80,000 for its shares. Unlike the purchaser of a house or a condominium who can obtain most of the money he needs by mortgaging the dwelling he is buying, the cooperative purchaser cannot mortgage his unit. Consequently, if the buyer does not have $80,000 in cash, he would be forced to mortgage other assets, obtain a loan secured by the purchasers shares, or seek an unsecured personal loan at an interest rate higher than for regular home mortgage loans.

Board of Directors

How a cooperative will be run is set forth in its articles of incorporation, bylaws, covenants and restrictions, and house rules. The governing body is a board of directors elected by a vote of the cooperators, and voting can be based either on shares held or on a one-vote-per-apartment basis. The board hires the services needed to maintain and operate the building and decides on how cooperative facilities will be used by shareholders. The annual budget and other matters of importance are submitted to all shareholders for a vote. Between shareholder meetings, normally scheduled annually, unhappy cooperators can approach board members and ask that a desired change be made. Or, at election time, they can vote for more sympathetic contenders for board membership or can run for board positions themselves.

Owners' Association

In two very significant areas, the authority of a cooperative owners' association and its board differs from that found in a condominium. First, because the interior of a cooperator's apartment is not her separate property, the association can control how she uses it. This right is based on the principle that the entire building is owned jointly by all cooperators for their mutual benefit. Thus, if a cooperator damages her apartment or is a constant nuisance, her lease can be terminated. As a rule, this requires at least a two-thirds vote of the shareholders and a return of the cooperator's investment.

Second, in a cooperative, the owners' association has the right to accept or reject new shareholders and sublessees. (The latter occurs when a shareholder rents his apartment to another.) If there is much turnover in the building, the association will delegate this right to the board. Thus, whenever a shareholder wishes to sell or rent, the transaction is subject to approval by the board. Except in cases of unlawful discrimination, this feature has been upheld by the courts. The legal basis is that cooperators share not only mutual ownership in their building, but also a joint financial responsibility. However, the board cannot be capricious or inconsistent.

Other Cooperative Forms

Most cooperatives are organized as corporations. It is a practical way to take title, select and control management, administer the day-to-day affairs of the cooperative, and at the same time insulate the individual members from direct liability for the obligations of the corporation. It is also possible to form a cooperative as a general or limited partnership, as a trust arrangement with the cooperators as trust beneficiaries, or as a tenancy in common. None of these has been widely used, primarily because partnerships and trusts do not provide the legal protection of a corporation, and because the tenancy in common idea has now been replaced by the condominium concept.

Low-cost cooperatives can be found in a number of United States cities. Sponsored by the FHA or by the city itself, these cooperatives are subsidized by public tax revenues and provide low- and moderate-income families with an opportunity for home ownership. Leases in these buildings are usually written for only one to three years and are not automatically renewable by the cooperator. This feature reflects the possibility that public funds may be cut back in the future. Also, when a cooperator sells, she is not permitted to retain any profits made upon resale. Rather, she is restricted to recovering only the money actually invested (i.e., down payment, mortgage amortization, and improvements).

PLANNED UNIT DEVELOPMENT

As illustrated in Figure 23.1, each owner in a planned unit development (PUD) owns as separate property the land beneath his dwelling. In addition, each unit owner is a shareholder in a nonprofit, incorporated owners' association that holds title to the common areas surrounding the dwelling units. The common areas can be as minimal as a few green spaces or might include parks, pools, golf courses, clubhouses, and jogging trails.

Because each owner in a planned unit development owns his land and dwelling as separate property, presumably he may use and maintain it as he wishes. However, there may be mutual restrictions upon all separately owned lots and dwellings. The right to establish and enforce these restrictions is usually vested in the owners' association. The association can dictate what color an owner can paint his window shutters, how he can landscape the front of his lot, and how many children and pets can reside in his dwelling. Additionally, the association maintains the common areas and governs how these areas shall be used by the residents and their guests.

Such thoughtful planning is not limited to single-family PUDs. Some of the most attractive planned residential developments in the United States combine natural surroundings with detached houses, row houses, clustered houses, apartment buildings, condominiums, and stores for shopping. So skillfully has this been done that residents are far more aware of the project's green vistas and lakes than they are of neighboring buildings. Reston in Virginia and the Woodlands in Texas are city-sized examples of the planned unit development concept. A PUD can also consist of just one or two dozen homes on six acres in suburbia.

RESORT TIMESHARING

Resort ***timesharing*** is a method of dividing up and selling private occupancy of a living unit at a vacation facility for specified lengths of time each year. The idea started in Europe in the 1960s when groups of people jointly purchased ski resort lodgings and summer vacation villas so each individual owner could enjoy a week or two of exclusive occupancy. U.S. resort developers quickly recognized the market potential of the idea, and in 1969 the first resort timeshare opened in the United States. Since then hotels, motels, condominiums, townhouses, lodges, villas, recreational vehicle parks, campgrounds, houseboats, and even a cruise ship have been timeshared.

Benefits of Timesharing

The appeal of timesharing to developers is that a resort or condominium complex that can be bought and furnished for $100,000 per unit can, typically, be resold in 50 timeshare slices of $6,000 each; that is, $300,000 a unit. The primary appeal of timesharing to consumers is they have a resort to go to every year at a prepaid price. This is particularly appealing during inflationary times, although the annual maintenance fee can change. There may be certain tax benefits if the timeshare is financed and for property taxes on fee simple timeshares. There may also be appreciation of the timeshare unit if it is in a particularly popular and well-run resort.

Then again, some or all of these benefits may not materialize. First, the lump sum paid for a timeshare week is usually much lower than hotel bills added up year after year. However, the timeshare buyer must pay in full in advance (or finance at interest), whereas the vacationer at a hotel pays only for what is used each year. Also, for timesharing there is a maintenance fee of approximately $20 to $40 per day that goes for clerk and maid service, linen laundry and replacement, structural maintenance and repairs, swimming pool service, hazard and liability insurance, reservations, collections and accounting services, general management, etc.

Second, going to the same resort for the same week every year for the next 30 or 40 years may become wearisome for some people. Yet that is what a timeshare buyer is agreeing to do. And, if the week is unused because of schedule problems, the maintenance fee must still be paid. To offset this, two large resort exchange services and several smaller ones and some of the larger timeshare developers help their buyers exchange weeks among their various projects. There is a cost, however, to exchanging. There may be as many as three fees to pay: an initial fee, an annual membership fee, and a fee when an exchange is made. These can amount to $200 or more for each exchange. Moreover, someone else with an unwanted timeshare week that you do want must also be in the exchange bank at the right time of the year. Satisfaction is usually achieved in exchanging by being flexible in accepting an exchange. Note too that if you own an off-season week at Lake Conroe, do not count on exchanging it for a peakseason vacation in Hawaii. Exchange banks usually require members to accept periods of equal or lesser popularity.

Third, tax laws allow deductions for interest expense on financed timeshares and for property taxes on fee timeshares. Timeshares have occasionally been touted as tax shelter vehicles because the current rules allow for these deductions if the timeshare qualifies as a dwelling unit and is used as a secondary residence. However, this has already aroused the ire of the Internal Revenue Service.

Fourth, although there have been several reported instances of timeshare appreciation, it is generally agreed in the timeshare industry and by consumer groups that the primary reason to purchase a resort timeshare is to obtain a vacation, not price appreciation. In fact, a timeshare industry rule-of-thumb is that one-third of the retail price of a timeshare unit goes to marketing costs. This acts as a damper on timeshare resale prices and even suggests that a prospective buyer might be able to purchase a timeshare on the resale market for less than from a developer.

TEXAS TIMESHARE ACT

All transaction interests under the Texas Timeshare Act are defined as an interest in land within the meaning of the Texas Real Estate License Act. Therefore, all brokers and sales people who market timeshares must be licensed, unless they are otherwise exempt from licensure under the Real Estate License Act. The Timeshare Act further requires that all timeshare properties must be registered with the Texas Real Estate Commission before they can be offered for sale, although a developer can accept a reservation request from a prospective purchaser if the reservation deposit is placed in an escrow account that is fully refundable at any time at the request of the purchaser. A timeshare registration requires extensive disclosures to the Commission. The Commission has the power to investigate all aspects of the development and to suspend the registration (stopping sales) for any violation of the Timeshare Act. There was a major revision to the Timeshare Act in 2005 to provide for guidelines for development in multiple states and their exchange systems.

The Timeshare Act now provides different types of timeshares, those deeded and those that have an **"incidental use right."** An incidental use right is the right to use accommodations and amenities at one or more timeshare properties that is not guaranteed. It is administered by a managing entity that makes vacant accommodations accessible to timeshare owners.

Contracts to Purchase

The contract to purchase the timeshare must include the following: (1) the name and address of the seller and the address of the timeshare unit; (2) an agreement by the seller that the purchaser exercises the right of cancellation; (3) the name of the person or persons actively involved in the sales presentation on behalf of the developer; (4) a statement disclosing the amount of periodic assessments currently assessed against the timeshare interest, followed by a statement providing that the assessments will be used to pay for expense charges i.e., relating to the operation of the timeshare plan; (5) a warranty that the timeshare common properties are not mortgaged, unless the mortgage contains a nondisturbance clause that protects the timeshare owner in the event of foreclosure; and (6) in the event that such timeshare interests are sold under a lease, right to use, or membership agreement where free and clear title to the timeshare unit is not passed to the buyer, then the contract must contain a warranty that the timeshare is free and clear, or if subject to a mortgage, the mortgage must contain a nondisturbance clause that protects the timeshare owner in the event of foreclosure. The developer is required to keep a copy of each purchase contract in its records.

Annual Timeshare Fee and Expense Statement

The Timeshare Act also provides that the managing entity of a timeshare must make available to each owner a written annual accounting of the operation of the timeshare property or timeshare system not later than the 60th day after the last day of each fiscal year. The managing entity must also post prominently in the registration area of each timeshare property a notice that the timeshare owner has the right to request a written annual timeshare fee and expense statement. The new Act also provides that the managing entity that manages two or more timeshare properties that are not participants in the same timeshare system may not commingle the timeshare fees. Upon request of the owner, the managing entity must make available for examination his registered office or principal place of business at any reasonable time or times and relevant books and records relating to the collection of expenditure and timeshare fees.

Promotion and Advertising

The Timeshare Act requires that a specific promotional disclosure statement be given before the use of any promotion in connection with the offering of a timeshare interest. The person who intends to use the promotion has to include the following information in its advertisements to the prospective purchaser: (1) a statement to the effect that the promotion is intended to solicit purchasers of timeshare interests; (2) if applicable, a statement to the effect that any person whose name is obtained during the promotion may be solicited to purchase a timeshare interest; (3) the full name of the developer and seller of the timeshare property; (4) if applicable, the full name and address of any marketing company involved in the promotion of the timeshare property; (5) the complete rules of the promotion; and (6) the method of awarding, the odds of winning, and a statement of the retail value of prizes, gifts, or other benefits under the promotion as set forth. At any time, the commission may request a copy of the developer's advertisement to determine if it violates any state law. TREC now also has expanded powers to conduct hearings and administer penalties for all aspects of the timeshare sales process.

In addition to the disclosures listed above, the developer has a new emphasis on its awards. The developer must also give a statement of the retail value of the gift, prize, or award. The retail value of the items is the price at which substantial sales of the exact item have been made to members of the general public by at least two principal retail outlets of the state of Texas during the six months immediately preceding the offering of the prize or gift described in the promotion. If a substantial number of sales of the particular prize have not occurred in the state of Texas in the six months immediately preceding the offering of the prize or gift in the promotion, or if the developer elects, then the retail value of the prize or gift is the actual unit cost, net of any discounts or rebates to the developer, plus 200%. This new regulation may at least limit some of the "come ons" that have occurred in Texas such as the 12-inch "solid oak" grandfather clocks, "recliners" made of canvas and sticks, and similar phony scams. Some of these developers are pretty crafty characters, however. We will have to wait and see.

Exchange Programs

Prior to the signing of any agreement or contract to acquire a timeshare interest in which a prospective purchaser is also offered participation in any exchange program, the developer shall also deliver to the prospective purchaser the exchange disclosure statement of any exchange company whose service is advertised or offered by the developer or other person in connection with the disposition. If participation in an exchange program is offered for the first time after a disposition has occurred, any person offering such participation shall also deliver an exchange disclosure statement to the purchaser prior to the execution by the purchaser of any instrument relating to participation in the exchange program. In all cases, the person offering such participation shall obtain from the purchaser a written acknowledgment of receipt of the exchange disclosure statement. The exchange disclosure statement shall include the following information:

1. The name and address of the exchange company.
2. If the exchange company is not the developer, a statement describing the legal relationship, if any, between the exchange company and the developer.
3. A statement indicating the conditions under which the exchange program might terminate or become unavailable.
4. Whether membership or participation or both in the exchange program is voluntary or mandatory.
5. A complete description of the required procedure for executing an exchange of timeshare periods.
6. The fee required for membership or participation or both in the program and whether such fee is subject to change.
7. A statement to the effect that participation in the exchange program is conditioned upon compliance with the terms of a contract between the exchange company and the purchaser.
8. A statement in conspicuous and bold-faced print to the effect that all exchanges are arranged on a space-available basis and that neither the developer nor the exchange company guarantees that a particular timeshare period can be exchanged.
9. A description of seasonal demand and unit occupancy restrictions used in the exchange program.

All disclosure statements require that the developer obtain written acknowledgment of their receipt from the purchaser.

Right to Cancel

Any purchaser can cancel her contract to purchase a timeshare interest before the sixth day after the date her contract is signed. The purchaser may not waive the right of cancellation. Any contract containing such a waiver is voidable at the option of the purchaser. The following statement must be provided to each purchaser at the time her contract is signed and must be on a separate page, attached to the contract as Exhibit A, and must contain the following language.

PURCHASER'S RIGHT TO CANCEL

"(1) BY SIGNING THIS CONTRACT YOU ARE INCURRING AN OBLIGATION TO PURCHASE A TIMESHARE INTEREST. YOU MAY, HOWEVER, CANCEL THIS CONTRACT WITHOUT PENALTY OR OBLIGATION BEFORE THE SIXTH DAY AFTER THE DATE YOU SIGN AND RECEIVE A COPY OF THE PURCHASE CONTRACT, OR RECEIVE THE REQUIRED TIMESHARE DISCLOSURE STATEMENT, WHICHEVER IS LATER.

(2) IF YOU DECIDE TO CANCEL THIS CONTRACT, YOU MAY DO SO BY EITHER HAND-DELIVERING NOTICE OF CANCELLATION TO THE DEVELOPER BY MAILING NOTICE BY PREPAID UNITED STATES MAIL TO THE DEVELOPER OR THE DEVELOPER'S AGENT FOR SERVICE OF PROCESS, OR BY PROVIDING NOTICE BY OVERNIGHT COMMON DELIVERY SERVICE TO THE DEVELOPER OR DEVELOPER'S AGENT FOR SERVICE OF PROCESS. YOUR NOTICE OF CANCELLATION IS EFFECTIVE ON THE DATE SENT, OR DELIVERED TO, (INSERT NAME OF DEVELOPER) AT (INSERT ADDRESS OF DEVELOPER). FOR YOUR PROTECTION, SHOULD YOU DECIDE TO CANCEL YOU SHOULD EITHER SEND YOUR NOTICE OF CANCELLATION BY CERTIFIED MAIL WITH A RETURN RECEIPT REQUESTED OR OBTAIN A SIGNED AND DATED RECEIPT IF DELIVERING IT IN PERSON OR BY OVERNIGHT COMMON CARRIER.

(3) A PURCHASER SHOULD NOT RELY ON STATEMENTS OTHER THAN THOSE INCLUDED IN THIS CONTRACT AND THE DISCLOSURE STATEMENT."

"AS A TIMESHARE OWNER, YOU HAVE A RIGHT TO REQUEST A WRITTEN ANNUAL TIMESHARE FEE AND EXPENSE STATEMENT. THIS STATEMENT IS PREPARED ANNUALLY BY THE MANAGING ENTITY AND WILL BE AVAILABLE NO LATER THAN FIVE MONTHS AFTER (INSERT THE DATE OF THE LAST DAY OF THE FISCAL YEAR). YOU MAY REQUEST THE STATEMENT BY WRITING TO (INSERT ADDRESS OF THE MANAGING ENTITY)."

The seller must obtain the purchaser's signature on Exhibit A at the time the contract is signed.

A developer who violates the Timeshare Act is now guilty of a Class A misdemeanor.

If the managing entity is late in filing their statements concerning timeshare fees and expense statements, they are subject to civil penalty up to $1,000.00 per day.

PROMULGATED BY THE TEXAS REAL ESTATE COMMISSION (TREC) 02-14-2011

NOTICE: Not For Use Where Seller Owns Fee Simple Title To Land Beneath Unit

RESIDENTIAL CONDOMINIUM CONTRACT (RESALE)

1. **PARTIES:** The parties to this contract are ______________________________ (Seller) and ______________________________ (Buyer). Seller agrees to sell and convey to Buyer and Buyer agrees to buy from Seller the Property defined below.

2. **PROPERTY AND CONDOMINIUM DOCUMENTS:**
   A. The Condominium Unit, improvements and accessories described below are collectively referred to as the "Property".
   (1) CONDOMINIUM UNIT: Unit __________, in Building ______________________, of ______________________________, a condominium project, located at ______________________________(address/zip code), City of ______________________________,County of ______________________, Texas, described in the Condominium Declaration and Plat and any amendments thereto of record in said County; together with such Unit's undivided interest in the Common Elements designated by the Declaration, including those areas reserved as Limited Common Elements appurtenant to the Unit and such other rights to use the Common Elements which have been specifically assigned to the Unit in any other manner. Parking areas assigned to the Unit are:______________________________.
   (2) IMPROVEMENTS: All fixtures and improvements attached to the above described real property including without limitation, the following **permanently installed and built-in items**, if any: all equipment and appliances, valances, screens, shutters, awnings, wall-to-wall carpeting, mirrors, ceiling fans, attic fans, mail boxes, television antennas and satellite dish system and equipment, mounts and brackets for televisions and speakers, heating and air conditioning units, security and fire detection equipment, wiring, plumbing and lighting fixtures, chandeliers, shrubbery, landscaping, outdoor cooking equipment, and all other property owned by Seller and attached to the above described Condominium Unit.
   (3) ACCESSORIES: The following described related accessories, if any: window air conditioning units, stove, fireplace screens, curtains and rods, blinds, window shades, draperies and rods, door keys, mailbox keys, above ground pool, swimming pool equipment and maintenance accessories, artificial fireplace logs, and controls for: (i) satellite dish system, (ii) garage doors, (iii) entry gates, and (iv) other improvements and accessories.
   (4) EXCLUSIONS: The following improvements and accessories will be retained by Seller and must be removed prior to delivery of possession: ______________________________ ______________________________.

   B. The Declaration, Bylaws and any Rules of the Association are called "Documents". (Check one box only):
   ☐ (1) Buyer has received a copy of the Documents. Buyer is advised to read the Documents before signing the contract.
   ☐ (2) Buyer has not received a copy of the Documents. Seller shall deliver the Documents to Buyer within _______ days after the effective date of the contract. Buyer may cancel the contract before the sixth day after Buyer receives the Documents by hand-delivering or mailing written notice of cancellation to Seller by certified United States mail, return receipt requested. If Buyer cancels the contract pursuant to this paragraph, the contract will terminate and the earnest money will be refunded to Buyer.
   ☐ (3) Buyer has received Seller's affidavit that Seller requested information

   C. The Resale Certificate from the condominium owners association (the Association) is called the "Certificate". The Certificate must be in a form promulgated by TREC or required by the parties. The Certificate must have been prepared no more than 3 months before the date it is delivered to Buyer and must contain at a minimum the information required by Section 82.157, Texas Property Code.
   (Check one box only):
   ☐ (1) Buyer has received the Certificate.
   ☐ (2) Buyer has not received the Certificate. Seller shall deliver the Certificate to Buyer within_____days after the effective date of the contract. Buyer may cancel the contract before the sixth day after the date Buyer receives the Certificate by hand-delivering or mailing written notice of cancellation to Seller by certified United States mail, return receipt requested. If Buyer cancels the contract pursuant to this paragraph, the contract will terminate and the earnest money will be refunded to Buyer.
   ☐ (3) Buyer has received Seller's affidavit that Seller requested information from the Association concerning its financial condition as required by the Texas Property Code, and that the Association did not provide a Certificate or information required in the Certificate. Buyer and Seller agree to waive the requirement to furnish the Certificate.

3. **SALES PRICE:**
   A. Cash portion of Sales Price payable by Buyer at closing .... $____________________
   B. Sum of all financing described below (excluding any loan funding

Initialed for identification by Buyer______ ______ and Seller _______ ______ TREC NO. 30-9

Contract Concerning____Page 2 of 8 02-14-2011
(Address of Property)

fee or mortgage insurance premium)...$____________________
C. Sales Price (Sum of A and B) ....$____________________

4. FINANCING: The portion of Sales Price not payable in cash will be paid as follows: (Check applicable boxes below)

❑ A. THIRD PARTY FINANCING: One or more third party mortgage loans in the total amount of $_______________ (excluding any loan funding fee or mortgage insurance premium).

(1) Property Approval: If the Property does not satisfy the lenders' underwriting requirements for the loan(s), (including, but not limited to appraisal, insurability and lender required repairs), Buyer may terminate this contract by giving notice to Seller prior to closing and the earnest money will be refunded to Buyer.

(2) Credit Approval: (Check one box only)

❑ (a) This contract is subject to Buyer being approved for the financing described in the attached Third Party Financing Addendum for Credit Approval.

❑ (b) This contract is not subject to Buyer being approved for financing and does not involve FHA or VA financing.

❑ B. ASSUMPTION: The assumption of the unpaid principal balance of one or more promissory notes described in the attached TREC Loan Assumption Addendum.

❑ C. SELLER FINANCING: A promissory note from Buyer to Seller of $__________________, secured by vendor's and deed of trust liens, and containing the terms and conditions described in the attached TREC Seller Financing Addendum. If an owner policy of title insurance is furnished, Buyer shall furnish Seller with a mortgagee policy of title insurance.

5. EARNEST MONEY: Upon execution of this contract by all parties, Buyer shall deposit $_________ as earnest money with ____, as escrow agent, at ____(address). Buyer shall deposit additional earnest money of $__________________ with escrow agent within _______days after the effective date of this contract. If Buyer fails to deposit the earnest money as required by this contract, Buyer will be in default.

6. TITLE POLICY:

A. TITLE POLICY: Seller shall furnish to Buyer at ❑Seller's ❑Buyer's expense an owner policy of title insurance (Title Policy) issued by ____ (Title Company) in the amount of the Sales Price, dated at or after closing, insuring Buyer against loss under the provisions of the Title Policy, subject to the promulgated exclusions (including existing building and zoning ordinances) and the following exceptions:

(1) Restrictive covenants common to the platted subdivision in which the Property is located.
(2) The standard printed exception for standby fees, taxes and assessments.
(3) Liens created as part of the financing described in Paragraph 4.
(4) Terms and provisions of the Documents including the assessments and platted easements.
(5) Reservations or exceptions otherwise permitted by this contract or as may be approved by Buyer in writing.
(6) The standard printed exception as to marital rights.
(7) The standard printed exception as to waters, tidelands, beaches, streams, and related matters.
(8) The standard printed exception as to discrepancies, conflicts, shortages in area or boundary lines, encroachments or protrusions, or overlapping improvements.

B. COMMITMENT: Within 20 days after the Title Company receives a copy of this contract, Seller shall furnish to Buyer a commitment for title insurance (Commitment) and, at Buyer's expense, legible copies of restrictive covenants and documents evidencing exceptions in the Commitment (Exception Documents) other than the standard printed exceptions. Seller authorizes the Title Company to deliver the Commitment and Exception Documents to Buyer at Buyer's address shown in Paragraph 21. If the Commitment and Exception Documents are not delivered to Buyer within the specified time, the time for delivery will be automatically extended up to 15 days or the Closing Date, whichever is earlier.

C. OBJECTIONS: Buyer may object in writing to defects, exceptions, or encumbrances to title: disclosed in the Commitment other than items 6A(1) through (8) above; or which prohibit the following use or activity: ____. Buyer must object the earlier of (i) the Closing Date or (ii) _____ days after Buyer receives the Commitment and Exception Documents. Buyer's failure to object within the time allowed will constitute a waiver of Buyer's right to object; except that the requirements in Schedule C of the Commitment are not waived. Provided Seller is not obligated to incur any expense, Seller shall cure the timely objections of Buyer or any third party lender within 15 days after Seller receives the objections and the Closing Date will be extended as necessary. If objections are not cured within such 15 day period, this contract will terminate and the earnest money will be refunded to Buyer unless Buyer waives the objections.

D. TITLE NOTICES:

(1) ABSTRACT OR TITLE POLICY: Broker advises Buyer to have an abstract of title covering the Property examined by an attorney of Buyer's selection, or Buyer should be furnished with or obtain a Title Policy. If a Title Policy is furnished, the Commitment should be promptly reviewed by an attorney of Buyer's choice due to the time limitations on Buyer's right to object.

Initialed for identification by Buyer______ ______ and Seller _______ ______ TREC NO. 30-9

(2) STATUTORY TAX DISTRICTS: If the Property is situated in a utility or other statutorily created district providing water, sewer, drainage, or flood control facilities and services, Chapter 49, Texas Water Code, requires Seller to deliver and Buyer to sign the statutory notice relating to the tax rate, bonded indebtedness, or standby fee of the district prior to final execution of this contract.

(3) TIDE WATERS: If the Property abuts the tidally influenced waters of the state, §33.135, Texas Natural Resources Code, requires a notice regarding coastal area property to be included in the contract. An addendum containing the notice promulgated by TREC or required by the parties must be used.

(4) ANNEXATION: If the Property is located outside the limits of a municipality, Seller notifies Buyer under §5.011, Texas Property Code, that the Property may now or later be included in the extraterritorial jurisdiction of a municipality and may now or later be subject to annexation by the municipality. Each municipality maintains a map that depicts its boundaries and extraterritorial jurisdiction. To determine if the Property is located within a municipality's extraterritorial jurisdiction or is likely to be located within a municipality's extraterritorial jurisdiction, contact all municipalities located in the general proximity of the Property for further information.

(5) PROPERTY LOCATED IN A CERTIFICATED SERVICE AREA OF A UTILITY SERVICE PROVIDER: Notice required by §13.257, Water Code: The real property, described in Paragraph 2, that you are about to purchase may be located in a certificated water or sewer service area, which is authorized by law to provide water or sewer service to the properties in the certificated area. If your property is located in a certificated area there may be special costs or charges that you will be required to pay before you can receive water or sewer service. There may be a period required to construct lines or other facilities necessary to provide water or sewer service to your property. You are advised to determine if the property is in a certificated area and contact the utility service provider to determine the cost that you will be required to pay and the period, if any, that is required to provide water or sewer service to your property. The undersigned Buyer hereby acknowledges receipt of the foregoing notice at or before the execution of a binding contract for the purchase of the real property described in Paragraph 2 or at closing of purchase of the real property.

7. PROPERTY CONDITION:

A. ACCESS, INSPECTIONS AND UTILITIES: Seller shall permit Buyer and Buyer's agents access to the Property at reasonable times. Buyer may have the Property inspected by inspectors selected by Buyer and licensed by TREC or otherwise permitted by law to make inspections. Seller at Seller's expense shall turn on existing utilities for inspections.

B. SELLER'S DISCLOSURE NOTICE PURSUANT TO §5.008, TEXAS PROPERTY CODE (Notice): (Check one box only)

❑ (1) Buyer has received the Notice.

❑ (2) Buyer has not received the Notice. Within _______ days after the effective date of this contract, Seller shall deliver the Notice to Buyer. If Buyer does not receive the Notice, Buyer may terminate this contract at any time prior to the closing and the earnest money will be refunded to Buyer. If Seller delivers the Notice, Buyer may terminate this contract for any reason within 7 days after Buyer receives the Notice or prior to the closing, whichever first occurs, and the earnest money will be refunded to Buyer.

❑ (3) The Texas Property Code does not require this Seller to furnish the Notice.

C. SELLER'S DISCLOSURE OF LEAD-BASED PAINT AND LEAD-BASED PAINT HAZARDS is required by Federal law for a residential dwelling constructed prior to 1978.

D. ACCEPTANCE OF PROPERTY CONDITION: (Check one box only)

❑ (1) Buyer accepts the Property in its present condition.

❑ (2) Buyer accepts the Property in its present condition provided Seller, at Seller's expense, shall complete the following specific repairs and treatments:________________________
____.
(Do not insert general phrases, such as "subject to inspections" that do not identify specific repairs.)

NOTICE TO BUYER AND SELLER: Buyer's agreement to accept the Property in its present condition under Paragraph 7D(1) or (2) does not preclude Buyer from inspecting the Property under Paragraph 7A, from negotiating repairs or treatments in a subsequent amendment, or from terminating this contract during the Option Period, if any.

E. LENDER REQUIRED REPAIRS AND TREATMENTS: Unless otherwise agreed in writing, neither party is obligated to pay for lender required repairs, which includes treatment for wood destroying insects. If the parties do not agree to pay for the lender required repairs or treatments, this contract will terminate and the earnest money will be refunded to Buyer. If the cost of lender required repairs and treatments exceeds 5% of the Sales Price, Buyer may terminate this contract and the earnest money will be refunded to Buyer.

F. COMPLETION OF REPAIRS AND TREATMENTS: Unless otherwise agreed in writing, Seller shall complete all agreed repairs and treatments prior to the Closing Date. All required permits must be obtained, and repairs and treatments must be performed by persons who are licensed or otherwise authorized by law to provide such repairs or treatments. At Buyer's election, any transferable warranties received by Seller with respect to the repairs and treatments will be transferred to Buyer at Buyer's expense. If Seller fails to complete any agreed repairs and treatments prior to the Closing Date, Buyer may do so and receive reimbursement from Seller at closing. The Closing Date will be extended up to 15 days, if necessary, to complete repairs and treatments.

G. ENVIRONMENTAL MATTERS: Buyer is advised that the presence of wetlands, toxic substances, including asbestos and wastes or other environmental hazards or the presence of a threatened or endangered species or its habitat may affect Buyer's intended use of the Property. If Buyer is concerned about these matters, an addendum promulgated by TREC or required by the parties should be used.

H. RESIDENTIAL SERVICE CONTRACTS: Buyer may purchase a residential service contract from a residential service company licensed by TREC. If Buyer purchases a residential service contract, Seller shall reimburse Buyer at closing for the cost of the residential service contract in an amount not exceeding $_______________. Buyer should review any residential service contract for the scope of coverage, exclusions and limitations. **The purchase of a residential service contract is optional. Similar coverage may be purchased from various companies authorized to do business in Texas.**

8. BROKERS' FEES: All obligations of the parties for payment of brokers' fees are contained in separate written agreements.

9. CLOSING:

A. The closing of the sale will be on or before _____________________, 20____, or within 7 days after objections to matters disclosed in the Commitment have been cured, whichever date is later (Closing Date). If either party fails to close the sale by the Closing Date, the non-defaulting party may exercise the remedies contained in Paragraph 15.

B. At closing:

(1) Seller shall execute and deliver a general warranty deed conveying title to the Property to Buyer and showing no additional exceptions to those permitted in Paragraph 6 and furnish tax statements or certificates showing no delinquent taxes on the Property.

(2) Buyer shall pay the Sales Price in good funds acceptable to the escrow agent.

(3) Seller and Buyer shall execute and deliver any notices, statements, certificates, affidavits, releases, loan documents and other documents reasonably required for the closing of the sale and the issuance of the Title Policy.

(4) There will be no liens, assessments, or security interests against the Property which will not be satisfied out of the sales proceeds unless securing the payment of any loans assumed by Buyer and assumed loans will not be in default.

(5) If the Property is subject to a lease, Seller shall (i) deliver to Buyer the lease(s) and the move-in condition form signed by the tenant, if any, and (ii) transfer security deposits (as defined under §92.102, Property Code), if any, to Buyer. In such an event, Buyer shall deliver to the tenant a signed statement acknowledging that the Buyer has received the security deposit and is responsible for the return of the security deposit, and specifying the exact dollar amount of the security deposit.

10. POSSESSION: Seller shall deliver to Buyer possession of the Property in its present or required condition, ordinary wear and tear excepted: ❑ upon closing and funding ❑ according to a temporary residential lease form promulgated by TREC or other written lease required by the parties. Any possession by Buyer prior to closing or by Seller after closing which is not authorized by a written lease will establish a tenancy at sufferance relationship between the parties. **Consult your insurance agent prior to change of ownership and possession because insurance coverage may be limited or terminated. The absence of a written lease or appropriate insurance coverage may expose the parties to economic loss.**

11. SPECIAL PROVISIONS: (Insert only factual statements and business details applicable to the sale. TREC rules prohibit licensees from adding factual statements or business details for which a contract addendum, lease or other form has been promulgated by TREC for mandatory use.)

Contract Concerning____Page 5 of 8 02-14-2011
(Address of Property)

12. SETTLEMENT AND OTHER EXPENSES:

A. The following expenses must be paid at or prior to closing:

(1) Expenses payable by Seller (Seller's Expenses):

(a) Releases of existing liens, including prepayment penalties and recording fees; lender, FHA, or VA completion requirements; tax statements or certificates; preparation of deed; one-half of escrow fee; and other expenses payable by Seller under this contract.

(b) Seller shall also pay an amount not to exceed $ ____________ to be applied in the following order: Buyer's Expenses which Buyer is prohibited from paying by FHA, VA, Texas Veterans Land Board or other governmental loan programs, and then to other Buyer's Expenses as allowed by the lender.

(2) Expenses payable by Buyer (Buyer's Expenses): Appraisal fees; loan application fees; adjusted origination charges; credit reports; preparation of loan documents; interest on the notes from date of disbursement to one month prior to dates of first monthly payments; recording fees; copies of easements and restrictions; loan title policy with endorsements required by lender; loan-related inspection fees; photos; amortization schedules; one-half of escrow fee; all prepaid items, including required premiums for flood and hazard insurance, reserve deposits for insurance, ad valorem taxes and special governmental assessments; final compliance inspection; courier fee; repair inspection; underwriting fee; wire transfer fee; expenses incident to any loan; Private Mortgage Insurance Premium (PMI), VA Loan Funding Fee, or FHA Mortgage Insurance Premium (MIP) as required by the lender; and other expenses payable by Buyer under this contract.

(3) Except as provided by 12(A)(4) below, Buyer shall pay any and all Association fees or other charges resulting from the transfer of the Property not to exceed $____________ and Seller shall pay any excess.

(4) Buyer shall pay any deposits for reserves required at closing by the Association.

B. If any expense exceeds an amount expressly stated in this contract for such expense to be paid by a party, that party may terminate this contract unless the other party agrees to pay such excess. Buyer may not pay charges and fees expressly prohibited by FHA, VA, Texas Veterans Land Board or other governmental loan program regulations.

13. PRORATIONS: Taxes for the current year, interest, maintenance fees, regular condominium assessments, dues and rents will be prorated through the Closing Date. The tax proration may be calculated taking into consideration any change in exemptions that will affect the current year's taxes. If taxes for the current year vary from the amount prorated at closing, the parties shall adjust the prorations when tax statements for the current year are available. If taxes are not paid at or prior to closing, Buyer shall pay taxes for the current year. Cash reserves from regular condominium assessments for deferred maintenance or capital improvements established by the Association will not be credited to Seller. Any special condominium assessment due and unpaid at closing will be the obligation of Seller.

14. CASUALTY LOSS: If any part of the Unit which Seller is solely obligated to maintain and repair under the terms of the Declaration is damaged or destroyed by fire or other casualty, Seller shall restore the same to its previous condition as soon as reasonably possible, but in any event by the Closing Date. If Seller fails to do so due to factors beyond Seller's control, Buyer may (a) terminate this contract and the earnest money will be refunded to Buyer, (b) extend the time for performance up to 15 days and the Closing Date will be extended as necessary or (c) accept the Property in its damaged condition with an assignment of insurance proceeds and receive credit from Seller at closing in the amount of the deductible under the insurance policy. If any part of the Common Elements or Limited Common Elements appurtenant to the Unit is damaged or destroyed by fire or other casualty loss, Buyer will have 7 days from receipt of notice of such casualty loss within which to notify Seller in writing that the contract will be terminated unless Buyer receives written confirmation from the Association that the damaged condition will be restored to its previous condition within a reasonable time at no cost to Buyer. Unless Buyer gives such notice within such time, Buyer will be deemed to have accepted the Property without confirmation of such restoration. Seller will have 7 days from the date of receipt of Buyer's notice within which to cause to be delivered to Buyer such confirmation. If written confirmation is not delivered to Buyer as required above, Buyer may terminate this contract and the earnest money will be refunded to Buyer. Seller's obligations under this paragraph are independent of any other obligations of Seller under this contract.

15. DEFAULT: If Buyer fails to comply with this contract, Buyer will be in default, and Seller may (a) enforce specific performance, seek such other relief as may be provided by law, or both, or (b) terminate this contract and receive the earnest money as liquidated damages, thereby releasing both parties from this contract. If, due to factors beyond Seller's control, Seller fails within the time allowed to make any non-casualty repairs or deliver the Commitment, or survey, if required of Seller, Buyer may (a) extend the time for performance up to 15 days and the Closing Date will be extended as necessary or (b) terminate this contract as the sole remedy and receive the earnest money. If Seller fails to comply with this contract for any other reason, Seller will be in default and Buyer may (a) enforce specific performance, seek such other relief as may be provided by law, or both, or (b) terminate this contract and receive the earnest money, thereby releasing both parties from this contract.

Initialed for identification by Buyer______ ______ and Seller _______ ______ TREC NO. 30-9

Contract Concerning____ Page 6 of 8 02-14-2011
(Address of Property)

16. MEDIATION: It is the policy of the State of Texas to encourage resolution of disputes through alternative dispute resolution procedures such as mediation. Any dispute between Seller and Buyer related to this contract which is not resolved through informal discussion ☐will ☐will not be submitted to a mutually acceptable mediation service or provider. The parties to the mediation shall bear the mediation costs equally. This paragraph does not preclude a party from seeking equitable relief from a court of competent jurisdiction.

17. ATTORNEY'S FEES: A Buyer, Seller, Listing Broker, Other Broker, or escrow agent who prevails in any legal proceeding related to this contract is entitled to recover reasonable attorney's fees and all costs of such proceeding.

18. ESCROW:

A. ESCROW: The escrow agent is not (i) a party to this contract and does not have liability for the performance or nonperformance of any party to this contract, (ii) liable for interest on the earnest money and (iii) liable for the loss of any earnest money caused by the failure of any financial institution in which the earnest money has been deposited unless the financial institution is acting as escrow agent.

B. EXPENSES: At closing, the earnest money must be applied first to any cash down payment, then to Buyer's Expenses and any excess refunded to Buyer. If no closing occurs, escrow agent may: (i) require a written release of liability of the escrow agent from all parties, (ii) require payment of unpaid expenses incurred on behalf of a party, and (iii) only deduct from the earnest money the amount of unpaid expenses incurred on behalf of the party receiving the earnest money.

C. DEMAND: Upon termination of this contract, either party or the escrow agent may send a release of earnest money to each party and the parties shall execute counterparts of the release and deliver same to the escrow agent. If either party fails to execute the release, either party may make a written demand to the escrow agent for the earnest money. If only one party makes written demand for the earnest money, escrow agent shall promptly provide a copy of the demand to the other party. If escrow agent does not receive written objection to the demand from the other party within 15 days, escrow agent may disburse the earnest money to the party making demand reduced by the amount of unpaid expenses incurred on behalf of the party receiving the earnest money and escrow agent may pay the same to the creditors. If escrow agent complies with the provisions of this paragraph, each party hereby releases escrow agent from all adverse claims related to the disbursal of the earnest money.

D. DAMAGES: Any party who wrongfully fails or refuses to sign a release acceptable to the escrow agent within 7 days of receipt of the request will be liable to the other party for liquidated damages in an amount equal to the sum of: (i) three times the amount of the earnest money; (ii) the earnest money; (iii) reasonable attorney's fees; and (iv) all costs of suit.

E. NOTICES: Escrow agent's notices will be effective when sent in compliance with Paragraph 21. Notice of objection to the demand will be deemed effective upon receipt by escrow agent.

19. REPRESENTATIONS: All covenants, representations and warranties in this contract survive closing. If any representation of Seller in this contract is untrue on the Closing Date, Seller will be in default. Unless expressly prohibited by written agreement, Seller may continue to show the Property and receive, negotiate and accept back up offers.

20. FEDERAL TAX REQUIREMENTS: If Seller is a "foreign person," as defined by applicable law, or if Seller fails to deliver an affidavit to Buyer that Seller is not a "foreign person," then Buyer shall withhold from the sales proceeds an amount sufficient to comply with applicable tax law and deliver the same to the Internal Revenue Service together with appropriate tax forms. Internal Revenue Service regulations require filing written reports if currency in excess of specified amounts is received in the transaction.

21. NOTICES: All notices from one party to the other must be in writing and are effective when mailed to, hand-delivered at, or transmitted by facsimile or electronic transmission as follows:

To Buyer at:	**To Seller at:**
______________________	______________________
______________________	______________________
______________________	______________________
Telephone: ( ) ____________	Telephone: ( ) ____________
Facsimile: ( ) ____________	Facsimile: ( ) ____________
E-mail: ____________	E-mail: ____________

Initialed for identification by Buyer______ ______ and Seller ______ ______ TREC NO. 30-9

Contract Concerning____Page 7 of 8 02-14-2011
(Address of Property)

22. AGREEMENT OF PARTIES: This contract contains the entire agreement of the parties and cannot be changed except by their written agreement. Addenda which are a part of this contract are (check all applicable boxes):

- ❑ Third Party Financing Addendum for Credit Approval
- ❑ Loan Assumption Addendum
- ❑ Buyer's Temporary Residential Lease
- ❑ Seller's Temporary Residential Lease
- ❑ Addendum for Sale of Other Property by Buyer
- ❑ Addendum for "Back-Up" Contract
- ❑ Seller Financing Addendum
- ❑ Addendum for Coastal Area Property
- ❑ Short Sale Addendum
- ❑ Addendum for Seller's Disclosure of Information on Lead-based Paint and Lead-based Paint Hazards as Required by Federal Law
- ❑ Environmental Assessment, Threatened or Endangered Species and Wetlands Addendum
- ❑ Addendum for Property Located Seaward of the Gulf Intracoastal Waterway
- ❑ Addendum for Release of Liability on Assumption of FHA, VA, or Conventional Loan Restoration of Seller's Entitlement for VA Guaranteed Loan
- ❑ Other (list): ____

23. TERMINATION OPTION: For nominal consideration, the receipt of which is hereby acknowledged by Seller, and Buyer's agreement to pay Seller $______________ (Option Fee) within 2 days after the effective date of this contract, Seller grants Buyer the unrestricted right to terminate this contract by giving notice of termination to Seller within ________ days after the effective date of this contract (Option Period). If no dollar amount is stated as the Option Fee or if Buyer fails to pay the Option Fee to Seller within the time prescribed, this paragraph will not be a part of this contract and Buyer shall not have the unrestricted right to terminate this contract. If Buyer gives notice of termination within the time prescribed, the Option Fee will not be refunded; however, any earnest money will be refunded to Buyer. The Option Fee ❑will ❑will not be credited to the Sales Price at closing. **Time is of the essence for this paragraph and strict compliance with the time for performance is required.**

24. CONSULT AN ATTORNEY: TREC rules prohibit real estate licensees from giving legal advice. READ THIS CONTRACT CAREFULLY. If you do not understand the effect of this contract, consult an attorney BEFORE signing.

Buyer's	Seller's
Attorney is: ______________________	Attorney is: ______________________
______________________	______________________
Telephone: ( ) ______________	Telephone: ( ) ______________
Facsimile: ( ) ______________	Facsimile: ( ) ______________
E-mail: ______________________	E-mail: ______________________

EXECUTED the ______day of ____________________________, 20_____ (EFFECTIVE DATE). (BROKER: FILL IN THE DATE OF FINAL ACCEPTANCE.)

______________________	______________________
Buyer	Seller
______________________	______________________
Buyer	Seller

The form of this contract has been approved by the Texas Real Estate Commission. TREC forms are intended for use only by trained real estate licensees. No representation is made as to the legal validity or adequacy of any provision in any specific transactions. It is not intended for complex transactions. Texas Real Estate Commission, P.O. Box 12188, Austin, TX 78711-2188, (512) 459-6544 (http://www.trec.state.tx.us) TREC NO. 30-9. This form replaces TREC NO. 30-7.

Contract Concerning____ Page 8 of 8 02-14-2011
(Address of Property)

BROKER INFORMATION

Other Broker Firm — License No.	Listing Broker Firm — License No.
represents ❑ Buyer only as Buyer's agent ❑ Seller as Listing Broker's subagent	represents ❑ Seller and Buyer as an intermediary ❑ Seller only as Seller's agent
Licensed Supervisor of Associate — Telephone	Licensed Supervisor of Associate — Telephone
Associate — Telephone	Listing Associate — Telephone
Other Broker's Address — Facsimile	Listing Broker's Office Address — Facsimile
City — State — Zip	City — State — Zip
Associate Email Address	Listing Associate's Email Address
	Selling Associate — Telephone
	Selling Associate's Office Address — Facsimile
	City — State — Zip
	Selling Associate's Email Address

Listing Broker has agreed to pay Other Broker____________of the total sales price when the Listing Broker's fee is received. Escrow agent is authorized and directed to pay other Broker from Listing Broker's fee at closing.

OPTION FEE RECEIPT

Receipt of $________________ (Option Fee) in the form of ______________________ is acknowledged.

Seller or Listing Broker — Date

CONTRACT AND EARNEST MONEY RECEIPT

Receipt of ❑Contract and ❑$__________________ Earnest Money in the form of ____________________ is acknowledged.

Escrow Agent: ______________________________________ Date: ________________________

By: ____ Email Address

Address — Telephone (______) ________________

City — State — Zip — Facsimile: (______) ________________

TREC NO. 30-9

Source: Texas Real Estate Commission

PROMULGATED BY THE TEXAS REAL ESTATE COMMISSION (TREC) 06-30-08

EQUAL HOUSING OPPORTUNITY

CONDOMINIUM RESALE CERTIFICATE

(Section 82.157, Texas Property Code)

Condominium Certificate concerning Condominium Unit _____, in Building _______, of _______________ __________________________________,a condominium project, located at ____________________ ______________________________________(Address), City of ________________________, County of __________________________, Texas, on behalf of the condominium owners' association (the Association) by the Association's governing body (the Board).

A. The Declaration ❑does ❑does not contain a right of first refusal or other restraint that restricts the right to transfer the Unit. If a right of first refusal or other restraint exists, see Section _______of the Declaration.

B. The periodic common expense assessment for the Unit is $___________ per ________________.

C. There ❑ is ❑is not a common expense or special assessment due and unpaid by the Seller to the Association. The total unpaid amount is $____________ and is for _________________________.

D. Other amounts ❑are ❑are not payable by Seller to the Association. The total unpaid amount is $________________and is for ____.

E. Capital expenditures approved by the Association for the next 12 months are $______________.

F. Reserves for capital expenditures are $______________;of this amount $___________________ has been designated for____.

G. The current operating budget of the Association is attached.

H. The amount of unsatisfied judgments against the Association is $ _________________________.

I. There ❑are ❑are not any suits pending against the Association. The nature of the suits is ____.

J. The Association ❑does ❑does not provide insurance coverage for the benefit of unit owners as per the attached summary from the Association's insurance agent.

K. The Board ❑has ❑has no knowledge of alterations or improvements to the Unit or to the limited common elements assigned to the Unit or any portion of the project that violate any provision of the Declaration, by-laws or rules of the Association. Known violations are:_____________________ ____.

L. The Board ❑has ❑has not received notice from a governmental authority concerning violations of health or building codes with respect to the Unit, the limited common elements assigned to the Unit, or any other portion of the condominium project. Notices received are: _____ ____.

M. The remaining term of any leasehold estate that affects the condominium is ________________ and the provisions governing an extension or a renewal of the lease are: __________________ ____ ____.

N. The Association's managing agent is ____
(Name of Agent)

____
(Mailing Address)

______________________________ ______________________________
(Telephone Number) (Fax Number)

____
E-mail Address

____
(Address of Property)

O. Association fees resulting from the transfer of the unit described above $ ______________.

P. Required contribution, if any, to the capital reserves account $ ______________.

REQUIRED ATTACHMENTS:
1. Operating Budget
2. Insurance Summary

NOTICE: The Certificate must be prepared no more than three months before the date it is delivered to Buyer.

____
Name of Association

By: ______________________________

Name: ______________________________

Title: ______________________________

Date: ______________________________

Mailing Address: ______________________________

E-mail: ______________________________

This form has been approved by the Texas Real Estate Commission for use with similarly approved or promulgated contract forms. Such approval relates to this form only. TREC forms are intended for use only by trained real estate licensees. No representation is made as to the legal validity or adequacy of any provision in any specific transactions. It is not suitable for complex transactions. Texas Real Estate Commission, P.O. Box 12188, Austin, TX 78711-2188, 1-800-250-8732 or (512) 459-6544 (http://www.trec.state.tx.us) TREC No. 32-2. This form replaces TREC No. 32-1.

Source: Texas Real Estate Commission

REVIEW QUESTIONS

Answers to these questions are found in the Answer Key section at the back of the book.

1. Condominium developments are restricted to
   A. residential dwelling units.
   B. multiple unit buildings.
   C. both A and B.
   D. neither A nor B.

2. In order to create a condominium development, a developer may
   A. construct a new building.
   B. convert an existing building.
   C. both A and B.
   D. neither A nor B.

3. Individual units in a condominium development are
   A. individually owned.
   B. common elements.
   C. cooperative elements.
   D. limited common elements.

4. Within a condominium development, common elements are owned by
   A. the owners' association.
   B. all unit owners, who hold undivided interests in the elements.
   C. the condominium developer.
   D. individual unit owners as community property.

5. Which of the following would be classified as limited common elements in a condominium development?
   A. Elevators
   B. Hallways
   C. Assigned parking spaces
   D. The manager's apartment

6. The plan for a condominium development that converts a single parcel of land into individual separate property estates and an estate composed of all common elements may be referred to as
   A. an enabling declaration.
   B. a master deed.
   C. both A and B.
   D. neither A nor B.

7. The rules by which an owner's association operates are known as
   A. bylaws.
   B. covenants, conditions, and restrictions.
   C. house rules.
   D. ordinances.

8. If the purchaser of a condominium has not received a resale certificate before executing a contract for sale in Texas, the purchaser may
   A. request a certificate from the Texas Association of Realtors.
   B. take possession and then cancel the contract within 30 days.
   C. cancel the contract within 15 days of the date of purchase.
   D. cancel the contract before the sixth day after the date the purchaser receives a resale certificate.

9. In a condominium, the authority to raise homeowner fees (association dues) rests with the
   A. board of directors.
   B. management company.
   C. condominium act.
   D. city and county.

10. The guest of a unit owner was injured by stepping on broken glass in the swimming pool at the Sunset Hills condominium. Liability for this injury would probably initially fall upon
    A. the unit owner.
    B. the condominium association.
    C. the management company.
    D. the developers.

11. The purchaser of a condominium unit
    A. surrenders personal freedoms to community rule.
    B. exchanges freedom of choice for freedom from responsibility.
    C. both A and B.
    D. neither A nor B.

12. Ownership of the interior space of your home and garage and an undivided interest in the building structures, common areas, and land area of the entire project describes a
    A. condominium.
    B. cooperative.
    C. PUD.
    D. corporate form of ownership.

13. Traditionally, the resale of cooperative shares have been financed by means of
    A. installment sales agreements.
    B. second mortgages on the seller's unit.
    C. bonds.
    D. government securities.

14. The 1985 Timeshare Act passed by the Texas Legislature required disclosure to the purchaser
    A. prior to the use of any promotion and advertising.
    B. prior to the signing of any agreement or contract.
    C. prior to the signing of any agreement or contract to participate in an exchange program.
    D. All of the above.

15. The owner of a unit in a planned unit development holds title to all of the following EXCEPT:
    A. the air above his unit.
    B. the land beneath his unit.
    C. a share of the common area.
    D. fee simple title to his unit.

16. In a planned unit development, the owners' association can dictate all the following EXCEPT:
    A. exterior paint colors.
    B. exterior landscaping.
    C. use of common areas.
    D. interior paint colors.

17. Under the incidental use right plan of timesharing, the purchaser
    A. holds title to real property.
    B. is a tenant in common with other users of the unit.
    C. both A and B.
    D. neither A nor B.

18. In Texas, all timeshare properties must be registered with
    A. the State legislature.
    B. the county clerk.
    C. the Texas Real Estate Commission.
    D. the Veterans Land Board.

Chapter 24

KEY TERMS

Building codes: local and state laws that set minimum construction standards

Certificate of occupancy: a government-issued document that states a structure meets local zoning and building code requirements and is ready for use

Downzoning: rezoning of land from a higher-density use to a lower-density use

Environmental impact statement: a report that contains information regarding the effect of a proposed project on the environment of an area

Land-use control: a broad term that describes any legal restriction that controls how a parcel of land may be used

Nonconforming use: an improvement that is inconsistent with current zoning regulations

Restrictive covenants: clauses placed in deeds and leases to control how future owners and lessees may or may not use the property

Variance: allows an individual landowner to vary from zoning requirements

Zoning: public regulations that control the specific use of land

Land-Use Control

IN THIS CHAPTER

Land-use control describes any legal restriction that controls how a parcel of land may be used. There are both public controls and private controls. Public controls include zoning, building codes, subdivision regulations, and master plans. Private controls come in the form of deed restrictions. This chapter covers all those topics and concludes with a brief discussion of environmental impact statements.

ZONING

Zoning is based on the principal of use separation, that some land uses are incompatible with others, and should not be permitted in the same area. *Zoning* laws divide land into zones (districts) and within each zone regulate the purpose for which buildings may be constructed, the height and bulk of the buildings, the area of the lot that they may occupy, and the number of persons that they can accommodate. To establish zoning, the community to be zoned *must have a comprehensive plan* to provide the basis for the zoning ordinance. Through zoning, a community can protect existing land users from encroachment by undesirable uses; ensure that future land uses in the community will be compatible with each other; and control development so that each parcel of land will be adequately serviced by streets, sanitary and storm sewers, schools, parks, and utilities.

The authority to control land use is derived from the basic police power each state has in order to protect the public health, safety, morals, and general welfare of its citizens. Through an enabling act passed by the Texas legislature, the authority to control land use is also given to individual towns, cities, and counties. These local government units then pass zoning ordinances that establish the boundaries of the various land-use zones and determine the type of development that will be permitted in each of them according to a comprehensive plan. By going to his local government offices, a landowner can see on a map how his land is zoned. Once he knows the zoning for his land, he can consult the zoning ordinance to see how he will be allowed to use it.

In Texas it has often been said that the planning and zoning commission does not zone, but only plans. The local governing body or city council does the actual zoning because of the procedures that the zoning statutes and enabling acts have established.

Zoning Symbols

For convenience, zones are usually identified by code abbreviations such as R (residential), C (commercial), I or M (industrial-manufacturing), and A (agriculture). Within each general category there are subcategories, such as R-1 (single-family residence), R-2 (two-family residence), R-3 (low-density, garden-type apartments), R-4 (high-density, high-rise apartments), PUD (multi-use, planned use development), and RPD (residential planned development). Similarly, there are usually three or four manufacturing zones ranging from light, smoke-free industry (I-1 or M-1) to heavy industry (I-4 or M-4). However, there is no mandatory uniformity in zoning classifications in the United States. One city may use R-4 to designate high-rise apartments, whereas another uses R-4 to designate single-family homes on 4,000-square-foot lots and the letter A to designate apartments.

Land-Use Restrictions

Besides specifying how landowners may use their land, the zoning ordinance includes additional rules. For example, land zoned for low-density apartments may require 1,500 square feet of land per living unit, a minimum of 600 square feet of living space per unit for one bedroom, 800 square feet for two bedrooms, and 1,000 square feet for three bedrooms. The zoning ordinance may also contain a setback requirement that states that a building must be placed at least 25 feet back from the street, 10 feet from the sides of the lot, and 15 feet from the rear lot line. The ordinance may also limit the building's height to two stories and require that the lot be a minimum of 10,000 square feet in size. As can be seen, zoning encourages uniformity.

Enforcement of Zoning Laws

Zoning laws are enforced by virtue of the fact that in order to build upon his land a person must obtain a building permit from his city or county government. Before a permit is issued, the proposed structure must conform with government-imposed structural standards and comply with the zoning on the land. If a landowner builds without a permit, he can be forced to tear down his building.

Nonconforming Use

When an existing structure does not conform with a new zoning law, it is "grandfathered-in" as a ***nonconforming use***. Thus, the owner can continue to use the structure even though it does not conform to the new zoning. However, the owner is not permitted to enlarge or remodel the structure or to extend its life. When the structure is ultimately demolished, any new use of the land must be then in accordance with the zoning law. If you are driving through a residential neighborhood and see an old store or service station that looks very much out of place, it is probably a nonconforming use that was allowed to stay because it was built before the current zoning on the property went into effect.

Zoning Changes

Once an area has been zoned for a specific land use, changes are made by *amending the zoning ordinance* or by obtaining a variance. The amendment approach is taken when a change in zoning is necessary. An amendment can be initiated by a property owner in the area to be rezoned or by the local government. Either way, if there is a proposed change in the zoning ordinance, the zoning commission, after giving proper public notice, holds a public hearing to provide a forum for public input and response. After the public hearing, the zoning commission makes a recommendation to the city council. The city council, after posting proper public notices, holds its own public hearing. After the city council's public hearing, the city council does the actual enactment of the zoning ordinance or zoning change legislation, which ultimately becomes of record in the municipal ordinances. The city council has the right to accept or reject any recommendation of the planning and zoning commission.

Variances

By comparison, ***variances*** allow an individual landowner to deviate somewhat from zoning code requirements and do not involve a zoning change. For example, a variance might be granted to the owner of an odd-shaped lot to reduce the setback requirements slightly so that he can fit a building on it. Variances usually are granted where strict compliance with the zoning ordinance or code would cause undue hardship. However, the variance must not change the basic character of the neighborhood, and it must be consistent with the general objectives of zoning as they apply to that neighborhood.

Conditional-Use Permit

A **conditional-use permit** allows a land use that may not conform with existing zoning, provided the use is within imposed limitations contained in the city ordinance. A conditional use permit is usually quite restrictive, and if the conditions of the permit are violated the permit is no longer valid. For example, a neighborhood day-care center operating under a conditional use permit in a residential environment cannot be converted to a more intense use under any circumstances.

Spot Zoning

Spot zoning refers to the rezoning of a small area of land in an existing neighborhood. For example, a neighborhood convenience center (grocery, laundry, barbershop) might be zoned into a residential neighborhood. Spot zoning, by definition, is not according to the comprehensive plan of the city. If it does not conform to the comprehensive plan, courts are unlikely to uphold the spot zoning.

Downzoning

Downzoning means that land previously zoned for higher-density uses (or more active uses) is rezoned for lower-density uses (or less active uses). Examples are downzoning from high-rise commercial to low-rise commercial, apartment zoning to single-family, and single-family to agriculture. Although a landowner's property value may fall as a result of downzoning, there is no compensation to the landowner because there is no taking of land (discussed next) as with eminent domain.

Taking

Taking is a concept wherein the municipality regulates the property to where it has no value or, in some cases, has no remaining economic value. The U.S. Supreme Court, in several cases, has determined that if a municipality regulates land use so that it has no value, it becomes a "taking" and results in condemnation. In those instances, the municipality must pay the fair market value of the property to the landowner. Texas even has legislation that requires certain governmental entities (cities are excluded) to pay the landowner in the event the land is regulated to a less intense use, such as if the fair market value of the land is decreased by 25%, that governmental entity must pay the landowner for the reduction in value. This area of the law is clearly becoming more protective of the private landowner's rights.

Buffer Zone

A **buffer zone** is a strip of land that separates one land use from another. Thus, between a large shopping center and a neighborhood of single-family homes, there may be a row of garden apartments. Alternatively, between an industrial park and a residential subdivision, a developer may leave a strip of land in grass and trees rather than build homes immediately adjacent to the industrial buildings. Note that *buffer zone* is a generic term and not necessarily a zoning law category.

A zoning law can be changed or struck down if it can be proved in court that it is unclear; discriminatory; unreasonable; not for the protection of the public health, safety, and general welfare; or not applied to all property in a similar manner.

It must be recognized that zoning alone does not create land value. For example, zoning a hundred square miles of lonely desert or mountain land for stores and offices would not appreciably change its value. Value is created by the concerted effort of a number of people who want to use a particular parcel of land for a specific purpose. To the extent that zoning channels demand to certain parcels of land and away from others, zoning does have an important impact on property value.

PRECAUTIONS

Because zoning can greatly influence the value of a property, it is absolutely essential that you be aware of the zoning for that parcel when you purchase any real estate. You will need to know what the zoning will allow and what it will not, whether the parcel is under a restrictive or temporary permit, and what the zoning and planning departments might allow on the property in the future. Where there is any uncertainty or where a zone change or variance will be necessary in order to use the property the way you want to, a conservative approach is to make the offer to buy contingent on obtaining planning and zoning approval before going to settlement.

If you are a real estate agent (particularly as a buyer's agent), you should stay abreast of zoning and planning and building matters regarding the properties you deal with. A particularly sensitive issue that occurs regularly is a property listed for sale that does not meet zoning and/or building code requirements. For example, suppose the current (or previous) owner of a house has converted the garage to a den or bedroom without obtaining building permits and without providing space for parking elsewhere on the parcel. Legally this makes the property less marketable. If you, as agent, market this property without telling the buyer about the lack of permits, you've given the buyer grounds to sue you for misrepresentation and the seller for rescission. When faced with a situation like this you should ask the seller to obtain the necessary permits. If the seller refuses, and the buyer still wants to buy, make the problem very clear to the buyer and have the buyer sign a statement indicating acceptance of title under these conditions. You can also refuse to accept the listing if it looks as though it will create more trouble than it's worth.

Professional Obligations Toward Property Zoning

The point here is that the public has a right to expect real estate agents to be professionals in their field. Thus, the agent should be fully aware of the permitted uses for a property and whether or not current uses comply. This is necessary to properly value the property for listing and to provide accurate information to prospective buyers. Note too that even if the seller in the above example was unaware of the zoning and building violations, the agent should recognize the problem and inform the seller. Recent court decisions clearly indicate that the agent has a responsibility to inform the seller of a problem to the agent knows about so that the seller cannot later complain to the agent, "You should have told me about that when I listed the property with you and certainly before I accepted the buyer's offer."

SUBDIVISION REGULATIONS

Before a building lot can be sold, a subdivider must comply with local government regulations concerning street construction, curbs, sidewalks, street lighting, fire hydrants, storm and sanitary sewers, grading and compacting of soil, water and utility lines, minimum lot size, and so on. In addition, the subdivider may be required to either set aside land for schools and parks or provide money so that land can be purchased nearby for that purpose. Until he has complied with all state and local regulations, the subdivider cannot receive his subdivision approval. Without approval he cannot record his plat map, which in turn means he cannot sell his lots to the public. If he tries to sell his lots without approval, he can be stopped by a court order and in some states fined. Moreover, permits to build will be refused to lot owners, and anyone who bought from the subdivider is entitled to a refund.

Building Codes

Recognizing the need to protect public health and safety against slipshod construction practices, state and local governments have enacted ***building codes***. These establish minimum acceptable material and construction standards for such things as structural load and stress, windows and ventilation, size and location of rooms, fire protection, exits, electrical installation, plumbing, heating, lighting, and so forth.

Before a building permit is granted, the design of a proposed structure must meet the building-code requirements. During construction, local building department inspectors visit the construction site to make certain that the codes are being observed. Finally, when the building is completed, a ***certificate of occupancy*** is issued to the building owner to show that the structure meets the code. Without this certificate, the building cannot be legally occupied.

Deed Restrictions

Although property owners tend to think of land-use controls as being strictly a product of government, it is possible to achieve land-use control through private means. In fact, Houston, Texas, with a population of more than 4 million persons, operates without zoning and relies almost entirely upon private land-use controls and building permits to achieve a similar effect.

Private land-use controls take the form of deed and lease restrictions. In the United States, it has long been recognized that the ownership of land includes the right to sell or lease it on whatever legally acceptable conditions the owner establishes, including the right to dictate to the buyer or lessee how he shall or shall not use it. For example, a developer can sell the lots in his subdivision subject to a restriction written into each deed that the land cannot be used for anything but a single-family residence containing at least 1,200 square feet of living area. The legal theory is that, if the buyer or lessee agrees to the restrictions, he is bound by them. If they are not obeyed, any lot owner in the subdivision can obtain a court order to enforce compliance. The only limit to the number of restrictions that an owner may place on his land is economic. If there are too many restrictions, the landowner may find that no one wants his land.

Deed restrictions, also known as ***restrictive covenants***, can be used to dictate such matters as the purpose of the structure to be built, architectural requirements, setbacks, size of the structure, and aesthetics. In neighborhoods with view lots, they are often used to limit the height to which trees may be permitted to grow. In Texas, and particularly Houston, **deed restrictions** have been one of the mainstays of land-use control. Deed restrictions cannot be used to discriminate on the basis of sex, race, color, or creed; if they do these provisions are unenforceable by the courts.

Because deed restrictions are enforced pursuant to contract law, only those who benefit from that contract (i.e., previous owners who may have reserved restrictions or subsequent purchasers in the property affected by the deed restrictions) have the right to enforce these deed restrictions. They must be enforced judicially because judicial interpretation is generally required for proper construction of the deed restrictions and it normally involves lawsuits and expensive litigation. To help facilitate the enforcement of deed restrictions, the Texas legislature passed a statute that enabled some incorporated cities, towns, or villages that do not have zoning ordinances to enforce deed restrictions on behalf of the people affected by those deed restrictions.

Restrictive covenants normally carry a time limit so that they can be subject to periodic review. However, there has been a judicial interpretation that deed restrictions can run forever, providing that the limitation on the use is not unreasonable. Once the deed restrictions have been filed and are of record, they may not be subsequently modified without the consent of a high percentage of the property owners, unless the power to amend the restrictions has been reserved or some other procedure for amending the property restrictions is contained in those restrictions.

Deed restrictions can be more functional than zoning restrictions because there is no control over what provisions can be contained in deed restrictions. Virtually anything, providing that it is not unconstitutional or illegal, can be in deed restrictions, and can provide a very tight land-use control. Zoning ordinances, on the other hand, generally have to promote the public health, safety, and welfare and cannot deal with more detailed aspects of land-use control, such as paint colors, types of shingles and wood fences, or other aspects of architectural style that could be paint colors enforced through the deed restriction mechanism of land-use control.

HOA Foreclosures

The deed restrictions generally allow HOAs to collect fees to fund its ability to enforce the restrictions. If you don't pay the HOA can foreclose on the homeowner. Obviously, this power can be abusive. The Texas Legislature enacted the Texas Residential Property Owners Protection Act (the Blevins Bill), which applies to all residential subdivisions requiring membership in a property owners' association that may impose mandatory assessments. The Bill is lengthy and has built in a number of consumer protections for homeowners. The major provisions are as follows: (1) the property owners' association must record a management certificate providing subdivision recording data and the name and mailing address of the property owners' association. The property owners' officers, directors, employees, and agents are personally liable or willfully or grossly negligent in any delay of recording or failing to record a management certificate (see Section 209.004); (2) the property owners' association must make all of the books and records of the association available, including financial records, to an owner in accordance with the Texas Non-Profit Corporation Act (attorneys' files and records are excluded from that disclosure); (3) before a property owners' association can suspend an owner's right to use a common area, file a suit against the owner other than a suit to collect a regular or special assessment or foreclose under an association's lien, charge an owner for property damage, or levy a fine for violation of the restrictions or bylaws by rules of the association, the association or its agent must give written notice to the owner by certified mail, return receipt requested. The notice must describe the violation, and then inform the owner that the owner is entitled to a reasonable period to cure the violation and that the owner may request a hearing within 30 days after the owner receives the notice. The statute even sets out procedures for the hearing before the board, but also enables the association to collect reasonable attorney's fees provided the proper notice has been given to the owner.

The property owners' association is authorized to conduct nonjudicial foreclosures, just as in the past. However, the attorney's fees are limited to the greater of one-third of the actual costs and assessments or $2,500. The property owners' association may not foreclose on an assessment lien consisting solely of fines or attorney's fees associated with those fines. After the foreclosure sale, the property owner's association must send the owner a written notice stating the date and time the sale occurred and informing the property owner of the owner's right to redeem his property within 30 days. Those must be sent by certified mail, return receipt requested, to the property owner's last known address. After the foreclosure, the property owner has the right to redeem the property after paying to the association: (1) all of the amounts due to the association at the time of the foreclosure sale; (2) interest from the date of the foreclosure sale to the date of redemption and all amounts owed to the association at an annual interest rate of 10%; (3) costs incurred by the association in foreclosing the lien, including reasonable attorney's fees for an assessment levied against the property by the association after the date of the foreclosure sale; (4) any reasonable costs incurred by the association including mortgage payments and the cost of repair, maintenance, and leasing of the property; and (5) the purchase price paid by the association's foreclosure sale less any amounts due the association that were satisfied out of the foreclosure sale proceeds. The right to redeem must be exercised within 180 days after the association mails the written notice of the sale to the owner. The lender has the right to redeem for 90 days after the sale.

ENVIRONMENTAL IMPACT STATEMENTS

The purpose of an ***environmental impact statement (EIS)***, also called an *environmental impact report (EIR)*, is to gather into one document enough information about the effect of a proposed project on the total environment so that a neutral decision maker can judge the environmental benefits and costs of the project. For example, a city zoning commission that has been asked to approve a zone change can request an EIS that will show the expected impact of the change on such things as population density, automobile traffic, noise, air quality, water and sewage facilities, drainage, energy consumption, school enrollments, employment, public health and safety, recreation facilities, wildlife, and vegetation. The idea is that with this information at hand better decisions can be made about land uses. When problems can be anticipated in advance, it is easier to make modifications or explore alternatives.

The EIS requirement has the greatest effect on private development at the city and county level. Usually the EIS accompanies the development application that is submitted to the planning or zoning commission. Where applicable, copies are also sent to affected school districts, water and sanitation districts, and highway and flood control departments. The EIS is then made available for public inspection as part of the hearing process on the development application. This gives concerned civic groups and the public at large an opportunity to voice their opinions regarding the anticipated benefits and costs of the proposed development. If the proposed development is partially or wholly funded by state or federal funds, state or federal hearings are also held.

Content of an EIS

Typically, an EIS will contain a description of present conditions at the proposed development site, plus information on the following five points: (1) the probable impact of the proposed project on the physical, economic, and social environment of the area; (2) any unavoidable adverse environmental effects; (3) any alternatives to the proposed project; (4) the short-term versus long-term effects of the proposed project on the environment; and (5) a listing of any irreversible commitment of resources if the project is implemented. For a government-initiated project, the EIS is prepared by a government agency, sometimes with the help of private consultants. In the case of a private development, it may be prepared by the developer, a local government agency for a fee, or by a private firm specializing in the preparation of impact statements.

Environmental Laws

Since 1982, the number of environmental laws that have affected real estate development has expanded tremendously and has had a definite and profound effect on land-use control. The *Comprehensive Environmental Response, Compensation, and Liability Act* (commonly referred to as *CERCLA*) imposes upon (1) the owners; (2) operators of facilities; and (3) any person who, at the time of disposal of any hazardous substance, owned or operated the facility at which such hazardous substances were disposed of, and any person who arranged for disposal; or (4) any persons who have accepted hazardous substances for transport to disposal or treatment sites, joint and several, 100% liability for damages resulting from that disposal. Subsequent legislation involved changes in the Clean Water Act that provide for a prohibition against storm water discharges.

Wetlands, once considered a source of neglected development and mosquitoes, have now been determined to help control flooding, filter out pollution, and provide habitat for fish and other wildlife. Wetlands regulations enforced by the U.S. Army Corps of Engineers include the assessment of administrative, civil, and/or criminal penalties. Wetlands are defined as "areas inundated or saturated by surface or groundwater at a frequency and duration sufficient to support, and that under normal circumstances do support, a prevalence of vegetation typically adapted for life in saturated soil conditions." The definition is broad and its enforcement can vary, depending on location and the country and developers' use of mitigation technique to "bank" wetland areas while developing others. The only way to be certain whether an area comes under the wetlands definition is to request the Corps to make an inspection and issue its own determination.

Federal statutes have been passed affecting asbestos, radon gas, lead-based paint, endangered species, and underground storage tanks. This has resulted in purchasers being required to exercise a level of "due diligence" in investigating sites prior to acquisition. A licensee should also note, and be particularly careful, that pertinent questions concerning environmental hazards may be directed to the broker and the broker may be on a "should have known" duty of care to know whether or not any of these incidents may have occurred.

The net result of all this federal legislation has resulted in *environmental site assessments.* Environmental site assessments have basically been divided into Phase I, Phase II, or Phase III Assessments. Although none of these terms are specifically defined by statute or common law, the consensus among environmental consultants seems to be that the principal elements of a Phase I Assessment include an on-site visual inspection of the property, interviews with owners and area residents as to the use and possession of the property, and review of historical aerial photographs and public records to determine past use and possession of the property. A Phase II Assessment typically involves sampling of the soil and water for the presence of hazardous substances. A Phase III Assessment involves further sampling and establishing limits of the contamination and developing a plan for remedial action and clean up.

The horror stories involving environmental clean air pollution are legion. The liability is unlimited, while many of the concerns are real. Some areas of environmental legislation involve enormous expense with very little result. One can be assured this will remain a hot area of litigation, controversy, and federal legislation for the coming years.

REVIEW QUESTIONS

Answers to these questions are found in the Answer Key section at the back of the book.

1. Through zoning, a community can protect existing land users from all of the following, EXCEPT:
   A. encroachment by undesirable uses.
   B. uncontrolled development.
   C. incompatible uses of land.
   D. competitive business establishments.

2. Through an enabling act passed by the Texas legislature, authority to control land use is given to
   A. counties.
   B. towns and cities.
   C. local governments.
   D. all of the above.

3. Land-use controls may be imposed by
   A. state governments.
   B. local governments.
   C. subdivision developers.
   D. all of the above.

4. Zoning laws may NOT be used to regulate which of the following?
   A. The purpose for which a building may be constructed.
   B. The number of persons a building may accommodate.
   C. The placement of interior partitions.
   D. The height and bulk of a building.

5. The basic authority for zoning laws is derived from a state's
   A. powers of eminent domain.
   B. right of taxation.
   C. both A and B.
   D. neither A nor B.

6. Zoning laws
   A. tell a landowner the use to which she may put her land.
   B. compensate an owner for loss of property value due to zoning.
   C. both A and B.
   D. neither A nor B.

7. Applied to land use, zoning laws may do all of the following EXCEPT:
   A. encourage uniformity in land usage.
   B. set minimum square footage requirements for buildings.
   C. determine the location of a building on a lot.
   D. dictate construction standards for buildings.

8. A use of property that is not in agreement with present zoning laws
   A. is called a nonconforming use.
   B. may be permitted under a so-called "grandfather clause."
   C. both A and B.
   D. neither A nor B.

9. Permission to use a building for a nonconforming use may be accomplished by
   A. amendment of the zoning ordinance.
   B. obtaining a zoning variance.
   C. both A and B.
   D. neither A nor B.

10. A zoning variance
    A. allows an owner to deviate from existing zoning law.
    B. involves a change in the zoning law.
    C. both A and B.
    D. neither A nor B.

11. When a small area of land in an existing neighborhood is rezoned, this is known as
    A. downzoning.
    B. spot zoning.
    C. conditional zoning.
    D. a zoning variance.

12. A garden apartment development is situated between an office park and a subdivision of single-family residences. These apartments are in a
    A. buffer zone.
    B. down zone.
    C. spot zone.
    D. commercial zone.

13. Minimum standards for materials and construction of buildings are set by
    A. zoning laws.
    B. building codes.
    C. deed restrictions.
    D. subdivision regulations.

14. Before a newly constructed building can be used by tenants, the owner must secure a certificate of
    A. inspection.
    B. utilization.
    C. approval.
    D. occupancy.

15. Building codes may be enacted
    A. by local governments.
    B. at the state level of government.
    C. both A and B.
    D. neither A nor B.

16. A subdivider wants to limit the height to which trees can grow so as to preserve views. He would most likely do this with a
    A. zoning amendment.
    B. conditional use permit.
    C. buffer zone.
    D. deed restriction.

17. The effect of a proposed development on a community is determined by the preparation of
    - A. a property disclosure report.
    - B. an environmental impact statement.
    - C. a prospectus.
    - D. the community's master plan.

18. An environmental impact statement will NOT reveal the effect of a planned development on
    - A. air quality.
    - B. automobile traffic.
    - C. property values.
    - D. school enrollments.

Chapter 25

KEY TERMS

Cash flow: the number of dollars remaining each year after collecting rents and paying operating expenses and mortgage payments

Cash-on-cash: the cash flow produced by a property divided by the amount of cash necessary to purchase it

Downside risk: the possibility that an investor will lose money in an investment

Equity build-up: the increase of one's equity in a property due to mortgage balance reduction and price appreciation

Investment strategy: a plan that balances returns available with risks that must be taken in order to enhance the investor's overall welfare

Leverage: the impact that borrowed funds have on investment return

Negative cash flow: a condition wherein the cash paid out exceeds the cash received

Prospectus: a disclosure statement that describes an investment opportunity

Straight-line depreciation: depreciation in equal amounts each year over the life of the asset

Tax shelter: the income tax savings that an investment can produce for its owner

Investing in Real Estate

IN THIS CHAPTER

This chapter introduces you to the benefits and dangers of investing. Cash flow, tax shelters, loss limitations, capital gain, tax law changes, equity build-up, and leverage are just a few of the topics covered. The chapter also deals with property selection, investment timing, developing a personal investment strategy, valuing an investment, limited partnership, and disclosure laws. The chapter concludes with a brief discussion on the effort and courage it takes to be an investor.

The monetary returns that are possible from real estate ownership make it a very attractive investment. However, at the same time the real estate investor takes two risks: He may never obtain a return on his investment and he may never recover his investment. There are no simple answers as to what is a "sure-fire" real estate investment.

Rather, success depends on intelligently made decisions. There is an old maxim established by one of the great real estate professors: How many real estate deals does it take to lose your shirt? One. How many real estate deals does it take to make you rich? Many. Real estate is a long-term business. With that in mind, we shall consider investment benefits, tax consequences, property selection, investment timing, investment strategy, and limited partnerships.

BENEFITS OF REAL ESTATE INVESTING

The monetary benefits of investing in real estate come from cash flow, tax shelter, mortgage reduction, and appreciation.

Appreciation is the increase in property value that the owner hopes will occur while owning it. Enough appreciation can offset underestimated expenses, overestimated rents, and a rising adjustable rate loan. Without appreciation, a property should at least produce enough rental income to pay the operating expenses and loan interest, cover wear and obsolescence, and give the investor a decent return.

Mortgage reduction occurs when an investor uses a portion of a property's rental income to reduce the balance owing on the mortgage. At first, the reduction may be quite small because most of the loan payments might be applied more to payments of interest rather than the reduction of principal. But, eventually the balance owing begins to fall at a more rapid rate. Some investors invest with the idea that if they hold a rental property for the entire life of the loan, the tenants will have paid for the property. This presumes the investor is patient, and that the other elements of cash flow and income tax consequences are conducive to holding the property. Let's look at cash flow, tax shelter, depreciation, taxation of gains, and other real estate tax topics.

CASH FLOW

Cash flow refers to the number of dollars remaining each year after you collect rents and pay operating expenses and mortgage payments. For example, suppose you own a small apartment building that generates $30,500 per year in rents. The operating expenses (including reserves) are $10,000 per year and mortgage payments are $20,000 per year. Given these facts, your cash flow picture is shown in Figure 25.1.

The purpose of calculating cash flow is to show the cash-in-the-pocket effect of owning a particular property. In Figure 25.1, $500 per year is going into your pocket. When money is flowing to you it is called a **positive cash flow**. If you must dip into your pocketbook to keep the property going, you have a ***negative cash flow***. For example, if in Figure 25.1 the mortgage payments were $21,000 per year, there would be a negative cash flow. A negative cash flow does not automatically mean a property is a poor investment. There may be mortgage reduction, tax benefits, and appreciation that more than offset this.

Two terms that are related to cash flow are net spendable and cash-on-cash. **Net spendable** is the same thing as cash flow and refers to the amount of spendable income a property produces for its owner. ***Cash-on-cash*** is the cash flow (or net spendable) that a property produces in a given year divided by the amount of cash required to buy the property. For example, if a property has a cash flow of $5,000 per year and can be purchased with a $50,000 down payment (including closing costs), the cash-on-cash figure for that property is 10. For many real estate investors, this is the heart of the investment decision, namely, "How

FIGURE 25.1 Cash flow picture

Rent receipts for the year	$ 30,500
Less operating expenses	10,000
Less mortgage loan payments	20,000
Equals cash flow	$ 500

Source: © 2012 Cengage Learning

much do I have to put down and how much will I have in my pocket at the end of each year?"

TAX SHELTER

For years, Congress encouraged investment in real estate by giving special tax treatment to those who took the risk of building and developing real estate. However, the theory has changed and Congress has discontinued most tax incentives. Real estate investment is no longer the tax shelter it once was. Broadly defined, ***tax shelter*** describes any tax-deductible expense generated by an investment property. Examples most often used for real estate investment are interest, maintenance, insurance, property taxes, and depreciation. More narrowly defined, tax shelter refers only to ***depreciation*** (a noncash expense, discussed later in this chapter) that a taxpayer can report as a deduction against other income.

The U.S. Congress has a decades-long history of tinkering with depreciation rules for income tax calculation. In 1993, the depreciation period for commercial real estate was extended to 39 years for property placed in service after December 31, 1993. (Property already owned and being depreciated before that date continues to use whatever rules were in effect when its depreciation was started; that is, they were *grandfathered-in*.) Also, as of January 1, 1987, accelerated depreciation is repealed and only straight-line can be used. (Again, existing investments continue to use whatever depreciation method they started with.)

Loss Limitations

Congress has enacted much stricter limits on how much loss can be deducted from a person's other income. This is now a major consideration in whether to buy or sell or hold real estate as an investment and in choosing what types of real estate to own. Using our investment example, suppose that the $20,000 mortgage payment consists of $19,500 in interest (which is an expense for tax purposes) and $500 in loan reduction (which is not an expense for tax purposes). Suppose also that tax law allows $8,000 in depreciation on the property for the year. The result is a taxable loss as shown in Figure 25.2.

FIGURE 25.2 Example of taxable loss

Rent receipts for the year	$ 30,500
Less operating expenses	10,000
Less interest on loan	19,500
Less depreciation	8,000
Equals taxable income	$ (7,000)*

*In accounting language, parentheses indicate a negative or minus amount.
Source: © 2012 Cengage Learning

There are substantial restrictions, and a distinction is made between passive investors and active investors. If you are a *passive investor*, you can deduct your loss only against income from other passive investments. A passive investor is one who does not materially participate on a "regular, substantial, and continuous basis"; for example, a limited partner.

If you are an *active investor* (e.g., you manage the rentals you own), it is possible to use as much as $25,000 of your losses to offset your other income (such as your job income). However, only this applies to taxpayers with up to $100,000 of adjusted gross income (as defined on one's annual IRS Form 1040). For those with higher adjusted gross incomes, the loss deduction is gradually reduced, and is eliminated at $150,000 of adjusted gross income. This aspect of the tax law change has little effect on the middle-income person who owns a rental house or two, or a small apartment building, and has a hand in managing them. But, for persons with larger income who are affected by the new Internal Revenue Code, there has been a restructuring of investments and more investor participation. For example, nonactive investors with passive losses look for properties with passive income, such as parking lots. Those who do not actively manage their real estate holdings may take a more active role so as to qualify as an active investor. Loss-producing partnerships may be attractive acquisitions only for income-producing investors.

Congress created another class of taxpayers who have the ability to offset their active income with passive losses. These are referred to as *eligible taxpayers*. Eligible taxpayers are individuals in closely held C corporations who must materially participate in rental real estate activities. To satisfy the eligibility requirements, the individual must have performed: (1) more than 50% of the individual's personal services during the tax year in real property trades or businesses in which the individual materially participates, and (2) more than 750 hours of service in real property trades or businesses in which the individual materially participates.

DEPRECIATION CALCULATION

As noted several paragraphs earlier, under tax rules effective January 1, 1987, depreciation for real property must be straight-line. ***Straight-line depreciation*** is calculated by taking the total amount of anticipated depreciation and dividing by the number of years. For example, a building valued at $275,000 for depreciation purposes and depreciated over 27.5 years using straight-line will have $10,000 in depreciation each year. (Note that only improvements are depreciable, land is not. Therefore, when buying investment real estate, it is necessary to subtract the value of the land from the purchase price before calculating depreciation.) One should be cautious, however; depreciation lowers the basis of the property and the amount deducted for depreciation purposes becomes income or resale income taxable at a 25% rate. Good tax advice is always needed.

In contrast to straight-line depreciation, **accelerated depreciation** is any method of depreciation that allows depreciation at a rate faster than straight-line during the first several years of ownership. Although this is not allowed for real property placed in service starting January 1, 1987, it is retained for certain types of personal property used in business (such as a real estate agent's automobile) and for real property started under accelerated depreciation before 1987.

Passive losses (including depreciation) that are unusable in any given year can be carried forward from year-to-year and used later. Any losses carried forward into the year of sale can be deducted in full at that time.

CAPITAL GAINS

Congress reinstated capital gains as a major tax benefit in 1997. Prior to that time, the maximum capital gains tax rate was 28%. The new maximum tax rates were cut to 20% for sales made after May 6, 1997. For individuals in the 15% tax bracket, the capital gains rate has been lowered to 10%. The asset must be held more than 12 months. Another rate for property held longer than five years became effective on December 31, 2000. Tax on an asset that qualifies for the five-year period was lowered to 18% and 8% for individuals in the 15% tax bracket.

There was no rate reduction for corporations with capital gains. A corporation's top rate stays at 35% and their holding period remains 12 months.

For whatever reasons, every time Congress cuts the capital gains rates, total revenue from income taxes increases. It encourages the sale of capital assets, which in turn encourages income-producing business for all those who deal with the sale, a good thing for the economy.

AT-RISK RULES

Over the past several years, Congress has enacted **at-risk rules** for investors. The issue was that an investor could invest $1, borrow $4 that did not require personal repayment, and take tax write-offs on the full $5. Congress passed rules that limited write-offs to the amount actually invested plus *recourse financing*, that is, the investor is personally obligated to repay. Under the old rules, this applied to nearly every investment, except real estate. Under the current rules, it applies to real estate. But real estate sales nearly always require financing, and it is often *nonrecourse financing*, that is, there is no personal obligation, only the value of the property secures the debt. Therefore, Congress considers the amount at risk in real estate to be the sum of third-party financing (note that this does not include seller financing), recourse indebtedness, and cash.

INSTALLMENT SALES

In the past, a seller of real estate who had a substantial gain might choose to sell on the *installment method* to spread out receipt of the gain and therefore the taxes on it. The new rules limit the benefits of using installment sales. The wise seller will seek competent tax advice before agreeing to carry back a mortgage. **Dealers** in real property may not use the installment sales benefit.

CONSTRUCTION-PERIOD EXPENSES

In past years, Congress has set various policies as to whether or not interest paid during construction could be taken as an immediate expense or had to be added to the cost of the building and amortized. Currently, the interest must be amortized over the depreciable life of the asset, even though the interest is an actual, paid expense during the construction period.

REHABILITATION TAX CREDITS

In an effort to encourage individuals to rebuild older structures rather than tear them down or let them decay, Congress has had a policy of giving rehabilitation tax credits. Historic structures are allowed a credit of 20%. (This effectively means the federal government will pick up 20% of the cost of rehabilitating an historic structure.) Nonhistoric structures constructed prior to 1935 receive a 10% tax credit. (The investor needs to have other income against which to claim the credit, and the passive loss rules apply.)

LOW-INCOME HOUSING CREDIT

One area of tax law has loosened: low-income housing. A number of inducements such as tax-exempt bond financing, accelerated depreciation, and five-year amortization have been used in the past. The rules now allow a tax credit to owners of buildings that provide low income rental housing. On new and newly rehabilitated housing the credit is a maximum of 9% per year for 10 years. (Effectively, the government pays for most of the building.) On existing housing the credit is a maximum of 4% for 10 years.

WATCH LIST

Tax law changes have been made in the past decades with increasing frequency and impact. In fact, one of the biggest risks in real estate has been, and continues to be, tax law changes. The values of land and buildings can, and do, go up and down with changes in tax rules. (This is in addition to the marketplace risks that an investor must take.) Therefore, it is of great importance that you stay abreast of tax law changes, impending tax law changes, and even swings in the mood of Congress toward real estate. Keep this in mind as you continue to read this chapter. Also keep in mind that because approximately two out of three households in the United States own their homes, home ownership is likely to continue its favored tax status.

EQUITY BUILD-UP

An owner's **equity** in a property is defined as the market value of the property less all liens or other charges against the property. Thus, if you own a property worth \$125,000 and owe \$75,000, your equity is \$50,000. If you own that property

FIGURE 25.3 Calculating equity build-up

Equity at Time of Purchase		Equity 5 Years Later		Equity Build-up	
Purchase price	$200,000	Market value	$220,000	Current equity	$100,000
Mortgage loan	−140,000	Less loan balance	−120,000	Less beginning equity	−60,000
Down payment equity	$ 60,000	Equals current equity	$100,000	Equals equity equity	$ 40,000

Source: © 2012 Cengage Learning

with your brother or sister, each with a one-half interest, your equity is $25,000 and his/her equity is $25,000.

Equity build-up is the change in your equity over a period of time. Suppose you purchase a small apartment building for $200,000, placing $60,000 down and borrowing the balance. Your beginning equity is your down payment of $60,000. If after five years you have paid the loan down to $120,000 and you can sell the property for $220,000, your equity is now $100,000. Because you started with $60,000, your equity build-up is $40,000. Figure 25.3 recaps this calculation.

LEVERAGE

Leverage is the impact that borrowed funds have on investment return. The purpose of borrowing is to earn more on the borrowed funds than the funds cost. For example, suppose you are an investor and you have $250,000 to invest in an apartment building. If you use all your money to buy a $250,000 building there is zero leverage. If you use your $250,000 to buy a $500,000 building, there is 50% leverage. If you use your $250,000 to buy a $2,500,000 building, there is 90% leverage.

Whether or not to try leverage depends on whether the property can reasonably be expected to produce cash flow, tax benefits, mortgage reduction, and appreciation in excess of the cost of the borrowed funds. The decision also depends on your willingness to take risk. For example, the $250,000 building would have to fall to zero value before you lost all your money. Moreover, the building could experience a vacancy rate on the order of 60% and there would still be enough cash to meet out-of-pocket operating expenses. In other words, with zero leverage there is very little likelihood of a total financial wipe-out.

In contrast, if you buy the $2,500,000 building, a 10% drop in the property's value to $2,250,000 wipes out your entire equity. Moreover, even the slightest drop-off in occupancy from 95% down to 85% will cause great strain on your ability to meet mortgage loan payments and out-of-pocket operating expenses.

But, suppose apartment building values increase by 10%. If you had bought the $250,000 building with borrowed funds, it will now be worth $275,000, an increase of $25,000 on your investment of $250,000. Similarly, if you had bought the $2,500,000 building it will now be worth $2,750,000, an increase of $250,000 on your investment of $250,000. As you can see, leverage can work both against you and for you. If the benefits from borrowing exceed the costs of borrowing, it is called **positive leverage**. If the borrowed funds cost more than they are producing, it is called **negative leverage**.

PROPERTY SELECTION

The real estate market offers a wide selection of properties for investments, including vacant land; houses; condominiums; small, medium, and large apartment buildings; office buildings; stores; industrial property; and so forth. Selecting a suitable type of property is a matter of matching an investor's capital with her attitudes toward risk taking and the amount of time she is willing to spend on management. Let's begin by looking at the ownership of vacant land.

Vacant Land

The major risk of owning vacant land as an investment is that one will have to wait too long for an increase in value. Vacant land produces no income, yet it consumes the investor's dollars in the form of interest, property taxes, insurance, and eventually selling costs. The rule of thumb is that the market value of vacant land must double every five years for the investor to break even. If this increase does not occur, the owner will have spent more on interest, insurance, property taxes, brokerage fees, and closing costs than is made on the price increase.

The key to successful land speculating is in outguessing the general public. If the public feels that development of a vacant parcel to a higher use is 10 years in the future, the market price will reflect the discounted cost at current interest rates and property taxes for that waiting period. If the land speculator buys at these prices, and the higher use occurs in five years, there is a good chance the purchase will be profitable. However, the speculator will lose money if the public expects the higher use to occur in five years and it actually takes ten years.

Finally, land speculators expose themselves to an extra risk that owners of improved property can usually avoid. When it comes time to sell, unless buildings will immediately be placed upon the land by the purchaser, very few lenders will loan the purchaser money to buy the land. This may force the seller to accept the purchase price in the form of a down payment plus periodic payments for the balance. If the interest rate on the balance is below prevailing mortgage rates, as often happens in land sales, the seller is effectively subsidizing the buyer. Furthermore, if the payments are made over several years, the seller takes the risk that the money he receives will buy less because of inflation.

Houses and Condominiums

Both single-family residences and condominiums can offer advantageous locations plus amenities, ensuring a good long-term investment. Condominium owners, however, may have more restrictions because of their obligation to abide by homeowners' associations' covenants (including highly restrictive rental policies). But there are usually fewer management headaches because the homeowners' association takes care of the exterior maintenance.

Houses and condominiums are the smallest properties available in income-producing real estate and as such are within the financial reach of more prospective investors than apartment buildings, stores, or offices. Moreover, they can usually be purchased with lower down payments and interest rates because lenders feel that loans on houses and condominiums are less prone to default than those on larger buildings. With a small property, the investor can fall back upon salary and other income to meet loan payments in the event rents fall short. With larger buildings, the lender knows he must rely more on the rental success of the property and less on the owner's other sources of income.

Houses and condominiums are usually overpriced in relation to the monthly rent they can generate. This is because their prices are influenced both by the value of the shelter they provide and the amenity value of home ownership. Thus, an investor must pay what prospective owner-occupants are willing to pay, yet when the property is rented, a tenant will pay only for the shelter value. However, when the investor sells, the sale price will be higher than would be justified by rents alone. What this means is that the investor can usually expect a negative cash flow during ownership. Consequently, there must be a substantial increase in property value to offset the monthly negative cash flow and give the investor a good return on investment.

Small Apartment Buildings

Because considerable appreciation must occur to make house and condominium investments profitable, many investors who start with these move to more income-oriented properties as their capital grows. Particularly popular with investors who have modest amounts of investment capital are duplexes (two unit), triplexes (three units), and fourplexes (four units).

If it were necessary to hire professional management, such small buildings would be uneconomical to own. However, for most owners of two to four-unit apartment buildings, management is on a do-it-yourself basis. Moreover, it is possible for the owner to live on the premises. This eliminates a cash outlay for management and allows the owner to reduce repair and maintenance expenses by handling them himself. Also, with the owner living on the property, tenants are encouraged to take better care of the premises and discouraged from moving out without paying their rent. Finally, the ownership of a residential rental property provides the owner with a wealth of experience and education in property management.

Medium-Size Buildings

Apartment buildings containing 5 to 24 units also present good investment opportunities for those with sufficient down payment. However, in addition to analyzing the building, rents, and neighborhood, thought must be given to the matter of property management before a purchase is made. An apartment building of this size is not large enough for a full-time manager; therefore, the owner must either do the job or hire a part-time manager to live on the property. An owner who does the job should be willing to live on the property and devote a substantial amount of time to management, maintenance, and upkeep activities. If a part-time manager is hired, the task is to find one who is knowledgeable and capable of maintaining property, showing vacant units, interviewing tenants, collecting rents on time, and handling landlord-tenant relations in accordance with local landlord-tenant laws. As the size of an apartment building increases, so does its efficiency. As a rule of thumb, when a building reaches 25 units, it will generate enough rent so that a full-time professional manager can be hired to live on the premises. With a live-in manager, the property owner need not reside on the property nor be involved in day-to-day management chores. This is very advantageous if the owner has another occupation where time is better spent.

Larger Apartment Buildings

As the number of apartment units increases, the cost of management per unit drops. Beyond 60 units, assistant managers can be hired. This makes it possible to have a representative of the owner on the premises more hours of the day to look after the investment and keep the tenants happy. Size also means it is possible to add recreational facilities and other amenities that are not possible on a small scale. The cost of having a swimming pool in a 10-unit building might add so much to apartment rents that they would be priced out of the market. The same pool in a 50- or 100-unit building would make relatively little difference in rent. As buildings reach 200 or more units in size, it becomes economical to add such things as a children's pool, gymnasium, game room, lounge, and a social director.

Because larger apartment buildings cost less to manage per unit and compete very effectively in the market for tenants, they tend to produce larger cash flows per invested dollar. However, errors in location selection, building design, and management policy are magnified as the building grows in size. Also, many lenders, particularly small- and medium-size banks and savings associations, are simply not large enough to lend on big projects. Finally, the number of investors who can single-handedly invest a down payment of $500,000 or more is limited. This has caused the widespread growth of the limited partnership as a means of making the economies of large-scale ownership available to investors with as little as $2,000 to invest.

Office Buildings

Office buildings offer the prospective investor not only a higher rent per square foot of floor space than any of the investments discussed thus far, but also larger cash flows per dollar of property worth. This is because office buildings are costlier to build and operate than residential structures, and because they expose the owner to more risk.

The higher construction and operating costs of an office building reflect the amenities and services office users demand. To be competitive today, an office building must offer high grade finishes and services to all tenants, thus adding to construction and operating costs. Office users also expect and pay for daily cleaning services, such as emptying wastebaskets, dusting, and vacuuming. Apartment dwellers neither expect these services nor pay for them.

The need for office space has increased in the United States over the last several years because the U.S. economic base has shifted to a high percentage of service providers (lawyers, accountants, psychologists, etc.). Planned office developments often attract the service-related businesses because their client or customer base is interrelated. In addition, office building tenants are reluctant to leave their locations because of costs of relocating and moving, and they don't want to change their business address.

You should note, however, that "return" has many different measurements and many different definitions. A "7% return" can be calculated as a return on cash invested, a return on a down payment (including closing costs), and to more sophisticated investors, a before-tax or after-tax return on their investment. An investor needs to know how to ask the right questions and how to evaluate the response to those questions.

Tenant turnover is more expensive in an office building than an apartment building because a change in office tenants usually requires more extensive remodeling. To offset this, building owners include the cost of remodeling in the tenant's rent. Another consideration is that it is not unusual for office space to remain vacant for long periods of time. Also, if a building is rented to a single tenant, a single vacancy means there is no income at all. To reduce tenant turnover, incentives such as lower rent may be offered if a tenant agrees to sign a longer lease, such as five years instead of one or two years. Care must be taken on longer leases however, so that the owner does not become locked into a fixed monthly rent while operating costs escalate.

The risk in properly locating an office building is greater than with a residential property because office users are very particular about where they locate. If a residential building is not well located, the owner can usually drop rents a little and still fill the building. To do the same with an office building may require a much larger drop; then, even with the building full, it may not generate enough rent to pay the operating expenses and mortgage payments. Finally, the tax shelter benefits available from offices may not be as attractive as comparably priced apartments. This is because compared to office buildings, residential properties tend to have a higher percentage of their value in depreciable improvements and less in nondepreciable land.

INVESTMENT TIMING

The potential risks and rewards available from owning improved real estate depend to a great extent on the point in the life of a property at which an investment is made. Should one invest while a project is still an idea? Or is it better to wait until it is finished and fully rented? That depends on the risks one can afford and the potential rewards.

Land Purchase

The riskiest point at which to invest in a project is when it is still an idea in someone's head. At this point, money is needed to purchase land. But beyond the cost of the land, there are many unknowns, including the geological suitability of the land to support buildings, the ability to obtain the needed zoning, the cost of construction, the availability of a loan, the rents the market will pay, how quickly the property will find tenants, the expenses of operating the property, and finally, the return the investor will obtain. Even though the investor may have a feasibility study that predicts success for the project, such a report is still only an educated guess. Therefore, the anticipated returns to an investor entering a project at this point must be high to offset the risks he takes. As the project clears such hurdles as zoning approval, obtaining construction cost bids, and finding a lender, it becomes less risky. Therefore, a person who invests after these hurdles are cleared would expect somewhat less potential reward. Nonetheless, the investor is buying into the project at a relatively low price; if it is successful, he will enjoy a developer's profit upon which no income tax must be paid until the property is finally sold. Against this, he takes the risk that the project may stall along the way or that, once completed, it will lose money.

Project Completion

Another major milestone is reached when the project is completed and opens its doors for business. At this point, the finished cost of the building is known, and during the first 12 months of operations the property owners learn what rents the market will pay, what level of occupancy will be achieved, and what actual operating expenses will be. As estimates are replaced with actual operating experience, the risk to the investor decreases. As a result, the investor entering at this stage receives a smaller dollar return on her investment, but is more certain of her return than if she had invested earlier.

First Decade

A building is new only once, and after its first year it begins to face competition from newer buildings. However, if an inflationary economy forces up the construction cost of newer buildings, existing buildings will be able to charge less rent. Furthermore, newer buildings may be forced to use less desirable sites. During the first 10 years, occupancy rates are stable, operating expenses are well established, tax benefits are good, and the building is relatively free of major repairs or replacements.

Second Decade

As a building passes its tenth birthday, the costs and risks it presents to a prospective investor change. Before buying, he must ask whether or not the neighborhood is expected to remain desirable to tenants and whether or not the building's location will increase enough in value to offset wear and tear and obsolescence. A careful inspection must be made of the structure to determine whether poor construction quality will soon result in costly repairs. Also, the investor must be prepared for normal replacements and expenses such as new appliances, water heaters, and a fresh coat of paint. As a result, an investor buying a 10-year-old building will seek a larger return than the buyer of a younger building.

Third and Fourth Decades

Larger returns are particularly important as a building reaches its twentieth year and major expense items such as a new roof, replacement of plumbing fixtures, repair of parking areas, and remodeling become necessary. As a building approaches and passes its thirtieth year, investors must consider carefully the remaining economic life of the property and whether rents permit a return on investment as well as a return of investment. Also, maintenance costs climb as a building becomes older, and decisions will be necessary regarding whether or not major restoration and remodeling should be undertaken. If it is, the cost must be recovered during the balance of the building's life. The alternative is to add little or no money to the building, a decision the surrounding neighborhood may already be forcing upon the property owner. Older properties may offer attractive tax benefits and have been a strong magnet to real estate investors who hope to find properties that can be fixed up for a profit. However, care must be taken not to overpay for this privilege.

Building Recycling

More buildings are torn down than fall down, and this phase in a building's life also represents an investment opportunity. However, as with the first stage in the development cycle, raw land, the risks are high. In effect, when the decision is made to purchase a structure with the intention of demolishing it, the investor is counting on the value of the land being worth more in another use. That use may be a government-sponsored renewal program, or the investor may be accumulating adjoining properties with the ultimate intention of creating plottage value by demolishing the structures and joining the lots. Because the risks of capital loss in this phase are high, the potential returns should be too.

DEVELOPING A PERSONAL INVESTMENT STRATEGY

The objective in developing a personal ***investment strategy*** is to balance the returns available with the risks that must be taken so that the overall welfare of the investor is enhanced. To accomplish this, it is very helpful to look at lifetime income and consumption patterns.

FIGURE 25.4 Lifetime income and consumption patterns

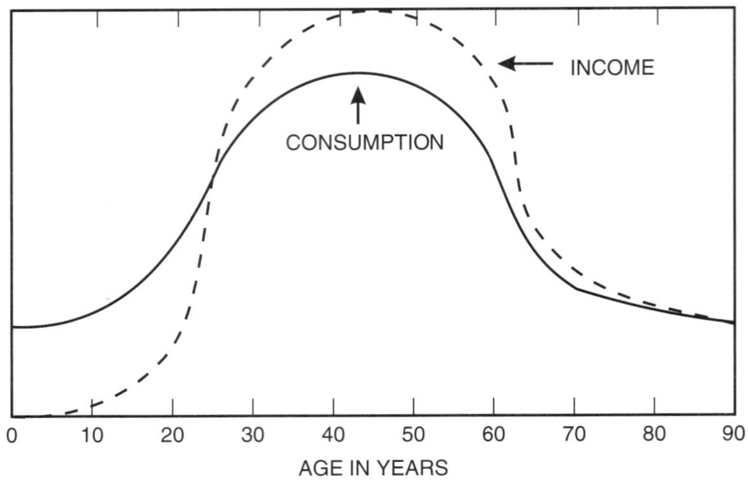

Source: © 2012 Cengage Learning

In Figure 25.4 the broken line represents the income that a person can typically expect to receive at various ages during his or her life. It includes income from wages, pensions, and investments. The solid line represents a person's lifetime consumption pattern. Taken together, the two lines show that during the first 20 to 25 years, consumption exceeds income. Then the situation reverses itself and income outpaces consumption. If one is planning an investment program, these are the years to carry it out.

Risk Taking

Figure 25.4 shows that an investment opportunity offering a high risk of loss is better suited for a person under the age of 45. Then, even if the investment does turn sour, the investor still has a substantial amount of working life remaining to recover financially. An investor between 45 and 55 years of age should be somewhat more cautious in terms of risk taking because there is less time to make a financial recovery if the need arises. Above the age of 55, high-risk investments are even less appropriate for the same reason. Therefore, as a person reaches 55, 60, and 65, there should be a program of moving toward relatively risk-free investments, even though the returns will be smaller. Upon retirement, the investor can live off the investments he or she made when younger.

Debt Repayment

Mortgage debt commitments that require a portion of the investor's personal income should also be considered in light of one's position on the lifetime income and consumption curves. This is done to ascertain whether or not there will be sufficient income in the future to meet the loan payments. Not to consider the future may force a premature sale, perhaps in the midst of a very sluggish market at a distressed price. For the investor who has passed his income peak, financing with less debt and more equity means a higher probability that the properties will generate enough income to meet monthly loan payments. Also, with fewer dollars going to debt repayment, more can be kept by the investor for living expenses. By comparison, a relatively young investor may be handicapped by the lack of starting capital; however, she has the advantages of time and increasing income on her side.

The same points made here in connection with investments can also be applied to one's home. If a homeowner can purchase a home with a mortgage and then pay down the mortgage during those years in life when income substantially exceeds consumption, the home can be carried debt free into retirement to provide a place to live without mortgage payments. The home then becomes an investment in every sense of the word.

VALUING AN INVESTMENT

Chapter 19, "Real Estate Appraisal," discussed value from the standpoint of an appraiser or listing agent who uses current marketplace facts to estimate the value of a property. An investor's valuation problem is somewhat different. An investor knows the seller's asking price, can find information relating to the current income and expenses of a property, and can project future income based on these. Additionally, an investor will have information on how the property can be financed and will have some figure in mind as to how much appreciation to expect. From these, the investor calculates the anticipated return on investment. If this return is more appealing than alternative investments, the property is purchased. If not, no sale results. Figure 25.5 illustrates the different viewpoints of the appraiser and the investor.

LIMITED PARTNERSHIPS

As discussed earlier in this chapter, large investment properties have a number of economic advantages over small ones. Yet the vast majority of investors in the United States do not have the capital to buy a large project single-handedly. Moreover, many persons who would like to own real estate do not do so because they wish to avoid the work and responsibilities of property management. As a result, the United States has witnessed the widespread use of limited partnerships for real estate investment. This popular form of investment offers investors the following advantages:

1. Management of the property and financial affairs of the partnership by the general partner.

FIGURE 25.5 Contrasting an appraiser's vs. an Investor's viewpoint

Appraiser's viewpoint	Investor's viewpoint
$\text{Value} = \dfrac{\text{Net Income}}{\text{Return}}$	$\text{Return} = \dfrac{\text{Net Income}}{\text{Price}}$
The appraiser solves for value.	The investor solves for return.

Source: © 2012 Cengage Learning

2. Financial liability limited to the amount invested.
3. The opportunity for a small investor to own a part of large projects and to diversify.

The organizers of a limited partnership are responsible for selecting properties, putting them into a financial package, and making it available to investors. As a rule, the organizers are the general partners and the investors are the limited partners. For their efforts in organizing the partnership, the general partners receive a cash fee from the limited partners and/or a promotional interest in the partnership.

Property Purchase Methods

Property is purchased by one of two methods. The organizers can either buy properties first and then seek limited partners, or they can find limited partners first and then buy properties. The first approach is a **specific property offering**. The second is a **blind pool**. The advantage of the specific property offering is that the prospective limited partner knows in advance precisely what properties will be owned. However, this approach requires the organizers either to find a seller who is willing to wait for a partnership to be formed or to buy the property in their own names using their own capital. If they use their own capital, the organizers risk the chance of financial loss if limited partners cannot be found.

The advantage of the blind pool is that the organizers do not buy until money has been raised from the limited partners. This requires less capital from the organizers and avoids the problem of holding property but not being able to find sufficient investors. Also, the organizers can negotiate better prices from sellers when they have cash in hand. However, if the organizers are poor judges of property, the investors may wind up owning property that they would not have otherwise purchased.

Property Management

Once property is purchased, the general partners are responsible for managing the property themselves or selecting a management firm to do the job. In addition, the general partners must maintain the accounting books and at least once a year remit to each investor his portion of the cash flow, an accounting of the partnership's performance for the year, and profit or loss data for income tax purposes. With regard to selling partnership property, the partnership agreement usually gives the limited partners the right to vote on when to sell, to whom to sell, and for how much. In practice, the general partners decide when to put the matter up to a vote, and the limited partners usually follow their advice.

Financial Liability

The word *limited* in limited partnership refers to the limited financial liability of the limited partner. In a properly drawn agreement, limited partners cannot lose more than they have invested. By comparison, the general partners are legally liable for all the debts of the partnership, up to the full extent of their entire personal worth. Being a limited partner does not eliminate the possibility of being asked at a later date for more investment money if the properties in the partnership are not financially successful. When this happens, each limited partner must decide between adding more money in hopes the partnership will soon make a financial turnaround, or refusing to do so and being eliminated from the partnership. By way of comparison, an individual investor who buys real estate in his own name takes the risks of both the limited and general partner.

Investment Diversification

Investing with others can provide diversification. For example, a limited partnership of 200 members each contributing $5,000 would raise $1,000,000. This could be used as a down payment on one property worth $4,000,000 or on four different properties priced at $1,000,000 each. If the $4,000,000 property is purchased, the entire success or failure of the partnership rides on that one property. With four $1,000,000 properties, the failure of one can be balanced by the success of the others. Even greater diversification can be achieved by purchasing properties in different rental price ranges, in different parts of the same city, and in different cities in the country. Regarding income tax benefits, a very important advantage of the limited partnership is that it allows the investor to be taxed as though she is the sole owner of the property, because the partnership itself is not subject to taxation. All income and loss items, including any tax shelter generated by the property, are proportioned to each investor directly.

Service Fees

The prospective investor should carefully look at the price the organizers are charging for their services. Is it adequate, but not excessive? To expect good performance from capable people, they must be compensated adequately, but to overpay reduces the returns from the investment that properly belong to those who provide the capital. When is the compensation to be paid? If management fees are paid in advance, there is less incentive for the organizers to provide quality management for the limited partners after the partnership is formed. The preferred arrangement is to pay for management services as they are received, and for the limited partners to reserve the right to vote for new management. Similarly, it is preferable to base a substantial portion of the fee for organizing the partnership on the success of the investment. By giving the organizers a percentage of the partnership's profits instead of a fixed fee, the organizers have a direct stake in the success of the partnership.

Pitfalls

Although the limited partnership form of real estate ownership offers investors many advantages, experience has shown that there are numerous pitfalls that can separate investors from their money. Most importantly, a limited partner should recognize that the success or failure of a limited partnership is dependent on the organizers. Do they have a good record in selecting, organizing, and managing real estate investments in the past? Are they respected in the community for prompt and honest dealings? Will local banks and building suppliers offer them credit? What is their rating with credit bureaus? Are they permanent residents of the community in which they operate? Do the county court records show pending lawsuits or other legal complaints against them?

With reference to the properties in the partnership, are the income projections reasonable, and have adequate allowances been made for vacancies, maintenance, and management? Overoptimism, sloppy income and expense projections, and outright shading of the truth will ultimately be costly to the investor. Unless there is absolute confidence in the promoters, one should personally visit the properties in the partnership and verify the rent schedules, vacancy levels, operating expenses, and physical condition of the improvements. Consideration should also be given to the partnership's ***downside risk*** (i.e., the risk of losing one's money).

The careful investor will consult with a lawyer to make certain that the partnership agreement does limit liability to the amount invested and that the tax benefits will be as advertised. He will also want to know what to expect if the partnership suffers financial setbacks. Are the partnership's properties to be sold at a loss or at a foreclosure sale, or do the general partners stand ready to provide the needed money? Will the limited partners be asked to contribute? The prospective investor should also investigate to see if the properties are overpriced. Far too many partnerships organized to date have placed so much emphasis on tax shelter benefits that the entire matter of whether the investment was economically feasible has been overlooked. Even to a 28% bracket taxpayer, a dollar wasted before taxes is still 72¢ wasted after taxes.

Finally, to receive maximum benefits from his investment, the investor must be prepared to stay with the partnership until the properties are refinanced or sold. The resale market for limited partnership interests is almost nonexistent, and when a buyer is found, the price is usually below the proportional worth of the investor's interest in the partnership. Moreover, the partnership agreement may place restrictions on limited partners who want to sell their interests.

Master Limited Partnerships

One major problem with limited partnerships has been that they are illiquid. Once an investor invests, the commitment is to stay in until the partnership dissolves, and this can be 5, 10, or even 15+ years later. Until then, the limited partner can convert to cash only by selling to someone else or sometimes back to the partnership. This is usually done at a substantial discount to the value of the property in the partnership, assuming a sale can even be arranged. Into this need has come the **master limited partnership (MLP)**. MLPs are limited partnerships that can be traded on a stock exchange nearly as easily as corporate stock. Thus, an investor can buy into a partnership after it has been formed and sell out of it before it is dissolved. Meanwhile, the investor receives the available tax advantages of a limited partnership. However, if the underlying partnership is not well run, has poorly operating properties, or is uneconomic, simply making the partnership easily traded is no magic. MLPs do offer liquidity, but you must still carefully analyze the partnership's ability to perform before investing in it.

DISCLOSURE LAWS

Because investors are vulnerable to unsound investments and exploitation at the hands of limited partnership organizers, state and federal disclosure laws have been passed to protect them if the investment qualifies as a "security." Administered by the Securities & Exchange Commission at the federal level and by the Texas Securities Board at the state level, these laws require organizers and sales staff to disclose all pertinent facts surrounding the partnership offering. Prospective investors must be told how much money the organizers wish to raise, what portion will go for promotional expenses and organizers' fees, what properties have been (or will be) purchased, from whom they were bought, and for how much. Also, prospective investors must be provided with a copy of the partnership agreement and given property income and expense records for past years. They must be told how long the partnership expects to hold its properties until selling, the partnership's policy on cash flow distribution, the right of limited partners to a voice in management, the names of those responsible for managing the partnership properties, and how profits (or losses) will be split when the properties are sold.

The Prospectus

The amount of disclosure detail required by state and federal laws varies with the number of properties and the partners' relationship. For a handful of friends forming a partnership among themselves, there would be little in the way of formal disclosure requirements. However, as the number of investors increases and the partnership is offered to investors across state lines, disclosure requirements increase dramatically. It is not unusual for a disclosure statement, called a ***prospectus***, to be 50 to 100 pages long.

Blue-Sky Laws

The philosophy of disclosure laws is to make information available to prospective investors and let them make their own decisions. Thus, an investor is free to invest in an unsound investment so long as the facts are explained to him in advance. An alternative point of view is that many investors do not read nor understand disclosure statements; therefore, it is the duty of government to determine the economic soundness of an investment before it can be offered to the public. The result has been the passage of **blue-sky laws** in several states. The first of these was passed by the Kansas legislature in 1911 to protect purchasers from buying into dubious investment schemes that sold them nothing more than a piece of the blue sky. Texas has retained these laws and applies them to limited partnerships and other securities offered within its borders.

EFFORT AND COURAGE

As the opening paragraph of this chapter suggested, you can become rich by investing in real estate. It should be pointed out, however, that success won't drop in your lap; it takes effort and courage. Good properties and good opportunities are always available, but you will look at many opportunities to find one good investment. You will also need to know which ones you don't want, and why. That is the part that takes effort. All investors need to know what a good opportunity looks like, and this book is a step in that direction. After you finish this text, start reading articles and books on real estate investing, and take courses on the subject as well. But most importantly, get out and start looking at properties right away if you have not already done so. Begin to get a sense in the field for what you are learning from your books and classes. Always ask questions as you go along, and demand straight, reasonable answers. After you've viewed several dozen properties and talked to appraisers, lenders, brokers, property managers, etc., you will begin to get a feel for the market—what's for sale, what a property can earn, how much mortgage money costs, etc. As you do this, you will see everything you've learned in this book come to life.

As you continue, you will recognize what a good investment property looks like. At this point your next big step is to muster the courage to acquire it. All the real estate investment education you've received will not translate into money in your pocket until you make an offer—until you put your money, reputation, and good judgment on the line. There is no "get rich quick" formula, so don't expect one. If you have a good, informed investment strategy and the courage to take the risks, the rewards are certainly attainable.

REVIEW QUESTIONS

Answers to these questions are found in the Answer Key section at the back of the book.

1. ABZ Realty offers you a four-unit residential building in which each unit rents for $500 per month. Given a 5% vacancy rate, operating expenses of $700 per month, and mortgage payments of $1,500 per month, you can anticipate a monthly
   A. net spendable of $200.
   B. net spendable of $300.
   C. negative cash flow of $200.
   D. negative cash flow of $300.

2. Monetary benefits of investing in real estate come from
   A. cash flow.
   B. tax shelter.
   C. mortgage reduction.
   D. all of the above.

3. A negative cash flow may be offset by
   A. tax shelter.
   B. appreciation.
   C. both A and B.
   D. neither A nor B.

4. Mortgage balance reduction
   A. is an out-of-pocket expense.
   B. is a deduction for tax purposes.
   C. is tax exempted.
   D. is quite large at the beginning of the loan period.

5. The value of depreciation on an investment property is
   A. inversely proportional to the investor's tax bracket.
   B. the same to all investors, regardless of their tax bracket.
   C. directly proportional to the investor's tax bracket.
   D. not a factor in the investment decision.

6. Tax laws allow depreciation on a building to be
   A. started over each time the property is sold.
   B. more than its value.
   C. both A and B.
   D. neither A nor B.

7. Equity build-up in a property can be the result of
   A. mortgage reduction.
   B. appreciation.
   C. both A and B.
   D. neither A nor B.

8. Negative leverage occurs when
   A. borrowed funds cost more than they produce in benefits.
   B. an investment property depreciates in value.
   C. both A and B.
   D. neither A nor B.

9. What is the cash-on-cash ratio for a property that has a cash flow of $16,900 and could be purchased with a down payment of $130,000?
   A. 7.69%
   B. 0.219
   C. 0.12
   D. 0.13

10. To be considered a good investment, when a property that generates a negative cash flow is sold,
    A. there must be a substantial increase in property value.
    B. there need be a little increase in property value.
    C. the investor is best off if the property has decreased in value.
    D. none of the above.

11. Tax shelter in real estate
    A. refers to the income tax savings that an investor can realize.
    B. is possible because depreciation is deductible as a cost of doing business.
    C. both A and B.
    D. neither A nor B.

12. For most people, when is the best time in life to undertake high-risk investments?
    A. Under age 25
    B. Age 25 to 45
    C. Age 55 to 65
    D. Over age 65

13. In a typical limited partnership, the
    A. organizers are the limited partners.
    B. investors are the general partners.
    C. both A and B.
    D. neither A nor B.

14. In a limited partnership, which cannot lose more than the amount they have invested?
    A. General partners
    B. Limited partners
    C. Organizers
    D. Managers

15. A disclosure statement given to prospective investors in a limited partnership, outlining the plans and prospects for the partnership, is called a
    A. prospectus.
    B. forecast statement.
    C. cash flow.
    D. binder.

Appendix A

Rules of the Texas Real Estate Commission

CHAPTER 531 CANONS OF PROFESSIONAL ETHICS AND CONDUCT FOR REAL ESTATE LICENSEES

§531.1 Fidelity

A real estate broker or salesperson, while acting as an agent for another, is a fiduciary. Special obligations are imposed when such fiduciary relationships are created. They demand:

(1) that the primary duty of the real estate agent is to represent the interests of the agent's client, and the agent's position, in this respect, should be clear to all parties concerned in a real estate transaction; that, however, the agent, in performing his duties to the client, shall treat other parties to a transaction fairly;

(2) that the real estate agent be faithful and observant to trust placed in the agent, and be scrupulous and meticulous in performing the agent's functions; and

(3) that the real estate agent place no personal interest above that of the agent's client.

§531.2 Integrity

A real estate broker or salesperson has a special obligation to exercise integrity in the discharge of the licensee's responsibilities, including employment of prudence and caution so as to avoid misrepresentation, in any wise, by acts of commission or omission.

§531.3 Competency

It is the obligation of a real estate agent to be knowledgeable as a real estate brokerage practitioner. The agent should:

(1) be informed on market conditions affecting the real estate business and pledged to continuing education in the intricacies involved in marketing real estate for others;

(2) be informed on national, state and local issues and developments in the real estate industry;

(3) exercise judgment and skill in the performance of the work.

§§531.10-531.17. Minimum Appraisal Standards.

§531.18. Consumer Information Form 1-1.

(a) The Texas Real Estate Commission adopts by reference Consumer Information Form 1-1 approved by the Texas Real Estate Commission in 1991. This document is published by and available from the Texas Real Estate Commission, P.O. Box 12188, Austin, Texas 78711-2188.

(b) Each real estate inspector or active real estate broker licensed by the Texas Real Estate Commission shall display Consumer Information Form 1-1 in a prominent location in each place of business the broker or inspector maintains.

§531.19. Discriminatory Practices

No real estate licensee shall inquire about, respond to or facilitate inquiries about, or make a disclosure which indicates or is intended to indicate any preference, limitation or discrimination based on the following: race, color, religion, sex, national origin, ancestry, familial status, or handicap of an owner, previous or current occupant, potential purchaser, lessor, or potential lessee of real property. For the purpose of this section, handicap includes a person who had, may have had, has, or may have AIDS, HIV-related illnesses, or HIV infection as defined by the Centers for Disease Control of the United States Public Health Service.

Appendix B
Practice Exam I

1. The requirement that real estate contracts be in writing is called:
   A. Statute of Frauds
   B. Law of agency
   C. Regulation Z
   D. Specific performance

2. The use of land that produces the greatest current value is called:
   A. market value
   B. highest and best use
   C. income approach
   D. projected gross income

3. If a salesperson lists and sells a property for $90,000 and receives 60% of the 7% commission paid to her employing broker, how much does the salesperson receive?
   A. $2,520
   B. $3,780
   C. $5,400
   D. $6,300

4. Sara Seller is satisfied with all of the terms of an offer to purchase her property from Bill Buyer except the date of possession, which she changes from April 9 to April 10. Which of the following is correct?
   A. Sara's acceptance creates a valid contract
   B. Sara cannot make a counteroffer
   C. Sara can always accept Bill Buyer's original offer if the April 10th date is not accepted
   D. Sara has rejected Bill Buyer's offer

5. The best method to appraise a residential property is the:
   A. cost approach
   B. income approach
   C. market approach
   D. highest and best use

6. At the time of listing a property, the owner specifies that he wishes to net $65,000 after satisfying a mortgage of $25,000 and paying a 7% brokerage fee. For what price should the property be listed?
   A. $90,000
   B. $94,550
   C. $96,300
   D. $96,774

7. When an option is exercised, it becomes which of the following?
   A. lease
   B. offer
   C. multiple listing
   D. contract of sale

8. The person borrowing money to purchase real estate is the:
   A. mortgage
   B. mortgagor
   C. mortgagee
   D. grantor

9. A real estate broker sells a tract of land (described in the figure below) for $1,600 per acre and earns a 9% commission. How much does the broker receive? (answers rounded)

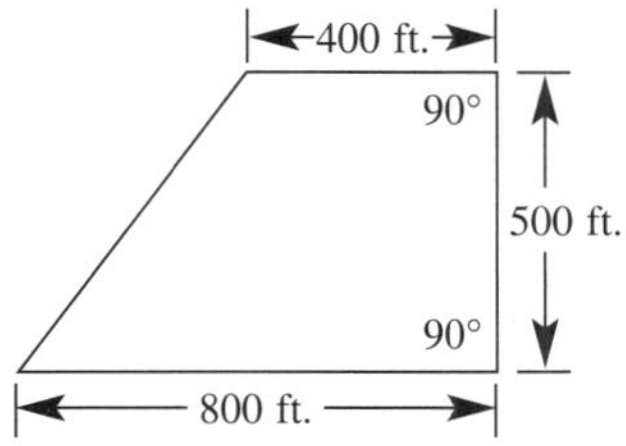

A. $661
B. $952
C. $992
D. $1,983

10. Charging a rate of interest higher than permitted by law is called:
A. usury
B. Fannie Mae
C. alienation
D. adjustable rate

11. The real estate secondary market for mortgages includes all of the following EXCEPT:
A. FNMA
B. GNMA
C. FHLMC
D. mortgage brokers

12. Texas Home Equity mortgages are limited to of market value.
A. 70%
B. 50%
C. 80%
D. 125%

13. The practice of not lending money in a specific area is called:
A. disintermediation
B. redlining
C. intermediation
D. channeling

14. The party who assigns a contract interest to another is the:
A. grantor
B. assignee
C. assignor
D. grantee

15. From the standpoint of both the agent and the seller, the best type of listing contract is:
A. open
B. exclusive agency
C. net
D. exclusive right to sell

16. The Texas Real Estate Commission members are appointed by the:
A. Texas legislature
B. Texas Association of REALTORS®
C. Governor of Texas
D. Texas attorney general

17. If the monthly payment on a $60,000 fully amortizing mortgage loan at 12% APR for a 20-year term is $660.65, how much is the principal reduced by the first monthly payment?
A. $60.65
B. $72.00
C. $600.00
D. $612.20

18. Hypothecate most nearly means:
A. selling real estate
B. pledging real estate as collateral for a loan
C. leasing real estate
D. giving an easement

19. Texas real estate brokers must notify consumers and service recipients of the procedures for directing complaints to the commission:
A. with a TRELA posting
B. on a sign prominently displayed in place of business
C. no notice is required
D. on a salesperson's business card

20. Which of the following most accurately describes the major purpose of a mortgage or a deed of trust?
    A. to secure the payment of a note
    B. to convey a title to the trustee
    C. to provide for equity of redemption
    D. to prevent assumption

21. The acceleration clause provides for which of the following?
    A. equity of redemption
    B. prepayment penalty
    C. right of lender to require immediate payment of principal balance when borrower is in default
    D. alienation by borrower

22. Which of the following liens takes priority over mortgage foreclosure sale proceeds?
    A. mortgage lien
    B. second lien
    C. property tax lien
    D. mechanic's lien

23. The TREC may assess an administrative penalty against a licensee for each violation of the TRELA for an amount not to exceed:
    A. $100
    B. $500
    C. $1,000
    D. $5,000

24. A lending institution's sharing in the appreciation in value of property and sharing in the equity of property is called:
    A. shared appreciation mortgage
    B. amortization
    C. liquidation
    D. hypothecation

25. All of the following may be required prepaid items by the mortgagee EXCEPT:
    A. real property taxes
    B. hazard insurance
    C. property owner's assessment
    D. broker's commission

26. FHA requires which of the following documents to be signed by borrowers purchasing a home built before 1978?
    A. commission disclosure form
    B. lead-based paint test results disclosure
    C. lead-based paint information disclosure
    D. Fair Housing Disclosure form

27. Within what period from notice must an applicant request an appeal if the commission declines to license an applicant?
    A. 30 days
    B. 60 days
    C. 90 days
    D. 10 days

28. The financing arrangement in which the borrower and lender hold equitable title to the real estate and a disinterested third party holds legal title is:
    A. deed of trust
    B. note
    C. junior mortgage
    D. contract for deed

29. To be eligible for a license under the TRELA an individual must be:
    A. a resident for 60 days
    B. a resident for 6 months
    C. 21 years of age
    D. a legal resident at time of filing application

30. Minor changes to a signed accepted offer to purchase require each amendment or change to be initialed by:
   A. all parties
   B. buyer only
   C. broker and seller
   D. seller only

31. A blanket mortgage usually contains which of the following?
   A. closed-end clause
   B. release clauses
   C. good faith estimate
   D. due-on-sale clause

32. A listing broker is permitted by law to do which of the following?
   A. make a secret profit in addition to the commission
   B. agree to reduce the asking price without the seller's approval
   C. present an offer from the broker's sister with full disclosure of the relationship
   D. accept a bonus from the buyer without the seller's approval

33. Which of the following regulates the advertisement of credit terms available for a house offered for sale?
   A. RESPA
   B. Fannie Mae
   C. Equal Credit Opportunity Act
   D. Regulation Z

34. The TREC may NOT suspend or revoke a license when it has been determined that:
   A. licensee has entered a plea of guilty of a felony
   B. licensee has engaged in misrepresentation
   C. licensee failed to make clear to all parties which party licensee is acting for
   D. licensee states the owner will accept the list price

35. If a lease specifies the rent to be 2% of the gross sales per annum, with a minimum annual rent of $8,000, what is the annual rent if gross sales are $1,200,000?
   A. $8,000
   B. $12,000
   C. $24,000
   D. $28,000

36. Which of the following provides the grantee with the greatest assurance of title?
   A. special warranty deed
   B. deed of gift
   C. general warranty deed
   D. grant deed

37. Which of the following is a benefit of recording a deed?
   A. it prevents any liens from being filed against the property
   B. it protects the grantee against the grantee's creditors
   C. it protects the grantee against future conveyances by the grantor
   D. it makes a mortgage lien subordinate

38. Under TRELA a party is not liable for a misrepresentation or a concealment of a material fact by a licensee in a real estate transaction unless:
   A. party is a subagent
   B. party knew of the falsity
   C. no exception
   D. party chooses to be liable

39. An action between two brokers may not be brought in a court in this state for recovery of a commission for the sale or purchase of real estate unless the promise or agreement is:
   A. written
   B. oral
   C. either written or oral
   D. part of purchase agreement

40. All of the following are rights of a life tenant EXCEPT:
    A. encumber
    B. use
    C. alienate
    D. waste

41. Which of the following statements is correct?
    A. an easement provides right of possession
    B. an easement in gross has no servient tenement
    C. an easement is a fixture to real estate
    D. an appurtenant easement can be obtained by necessity

42. The requirement to disclose representation at the time of the licensee's first contact with another party can be:
    A. oral
    B. written
    C. either oral or written
    D. no disclosure required

43. A meeting at which a substantive discussion occurs with respect to specific real property is called by the TRELA a(n):
    A. intermediary meeting
    B. face to face meeting
    C. settlement party
    D. subagency

44. A claim, lien, charge, or liability attached to and binding upon real property is a(n):
    A. encumbrance
    B. community property
    C. license
    D. syndication

45. An owner of a condominium office:
    A. has a proprietary lease
    B. is assessed by the property owners association for maintenance to his office unit
    C. may pledge his property as security for a mortgage loan
    D. owns a share of stock in the corporation that owns the real estate

46. Timesharing is commonly associated with which of the following?
    A. cooperatives
    B. profits
    C. joint ventures
    D. condominiums

47. Which of the following clauses in an accepted offer to purchase protects the buyer from losing her earnest money in the event financing is not obtained?
    A. habendum
    B. contingency
    C. defeasance
    D. subordination

48. The Fair Housing Act of 1968 prohibits discrimination in the rental of all of the following EXCEPT:
    A. offices
    B. apartments
    C. houses
    D. residential lots

49. The Fair Housing Act of 1968 prohibits all of the following EXCEPT:
    A. discriminatory advertising
    B. use of brokerage services
    C. steering
    D. redlining

50. Inducing an owner to list property by telling the owner that people of a certain national origin are moving into the neighborhood is called:
   A. steering
   B. redlining
   C. blockbusting
   D. profiteering

51. Representing that goods are new if they are reconditioned is a violation of the:
   A. Agency law
   B. Deceptive Trade Practices Act
   C. Statute of Frauds
   D. Parole evidence rule

52. A property manager's fee usually consists of a base fee plus:
   A. a percentage of the rental income received
   B. a percentage of the gross potential income
   C. a percentage of the net income
   D. a percentage of the stabilized budget

53. When a lessee installs trade fixtures, these are:
   A. a permanent part of the real estate
   B. owned by the lessor
   C. the personal property of the lessee
   D. real property

54. A person living on the managed premises as a salaried employee engaged to manage and lease apartments is called a(n):
   A. property manager
   B. rental agent
   C. employee manager
   D. resident manager

55. An alienation clause makes a mortgage:
   A. defeasible
   B. unassumable
   C. incontestable
   D. adjustable

56. A real estate salesperson, while acting as an agent for another, is a(n):
   A. intermediary
   B. broker
   C. facilitator
   D. fiduciary

57. A buyer assumes a seller's existing 11%, $80,000 first deed of trust on the settlement date of June 12. The seller makes the monthly payment on June 1 with interest in advance. Which of the following is a correct settlement statement entry for the interest?
   A. $293.28 buyer's credit
   B. $439.92 seller's credit
   C. $293.28 seller's debit
   D. $439.92 seller's debit

58. Which of the following types of listing contracts gives the broker commission entitlement if anyone sells the listed property during the listing term?
   A. net
   B. open
   C. exclusive agency
   D. exclusive right to sell

59. A real estate salesperson advises a prospective buyer that the property the buyer is considering is scheduled for annexation into the city limits. This disclosure constitutes which of the following?
   A. disloyalty to principal
   B. misrepresentation
   C. required disclosure to buyer
   D. violation of disclosure of information by salesperson

60. A real estate agent owes what level of obligation to his principal?
   A. no obligation
   B. very lowest obligation
   C. very highest fiduciary obligation
   D. no fiduciary obligation

61. A salesperson receives two offers for a listed property within a 10-minute period. One offer is 2% less than the listed price, and the other is 6% less than the listed price. The salesperson should present to the seller:
   A. neither offer
   B. both offers
   C. the highest offer
   D. the first offer

62. Closing on a commercial property is April 18. The property taxes for the previous year were $5,760. Which of the following is the correct closing statement entry for taxes?
   A. $1,728 buyer's credit
   B. $4,032 buyer's credit
   C. $1,728 seller's credit
   D. $4,032 seller's credit

63. The amount of a purchase money mortgage appears in the closing statement as:
   A. seller's credit only
   B. buyer's debit only
   C. seller's debit; buyer's credit
   D. seller's credit; buyer's debit

64. A seller paid an annual hazard insurance premium of $540 for a policy effective February 12. At settlement on April 16 of the same year, the buyer purchased the policy from the seller. This transaction is correctly entered on the settlement statements as:
   A. $96 buyer's credit
   B. $444 buyer's credit
   C. $96 seller's credit
   D. $444 seller's credit

65. The amount of earnest money appears on closing statements as a:
   A. credit to buyer
   B. debit to seller
   C. credit to seller
   D. debit to buyer

66. When listing real property for sale, a real estate broker:
   A. does a competitive market analysis
   B. makes an appraisal to estimate market value
   C. estimates residual income
   D. correlates reproduction cost

67. An apartment building produces an annual net income of $10,800 after deducting $72 per month for expenses. What price for the property would provide a buyer with a net return of 12%?
   A. $90,000
   B. $97,200
   C. $116,641
   D. $129,600

68. An apartment building contains 30 units. Each unit rents for $200 per month. The vacancy rate is 4%. Annual expenses are $3,000 for maintenance, $1,100 insurance, $1,600 taxes, $1,200 utilities, and 15% of the gross effective income for management fee. What is the investor's net rate of return for the first year if he paid $260,000 for the property?
   A. 6.69%
   B. 11.64%
   C. 14.94%
   D. 19.94%

69. A subagent would have to disclose to the listing broker all of the following facts about the buyer except that the buyer:
   A. has a daughter who is a real estate attorney
   B. has an option on two adjoining parcels
   C. has a known poor credit rating
   D. has defaulted on three previous transactions through the subagent

70. Which of the following methods is used to estimate the value of the land only, on which an apartment building is to be located the next year?
A. cost approach
B. income approach
C. market data approach
D. replacement cost

71. Gross rent multipliers are used in connection with which of the following?
A. condominiums
B. schools
C. vacant land
D. income property

72. Adherence to which of the following has the effect of maximizing land value?
A. principle of contribution
B. principle of change
C. principle of anticipation
D. principle of highest and best use

73. Texas law presumes that all property acquired after marriage is:
A. separate
B. community
C. unity of person
D. right of survivorship

74. An urban homestead can consist of a lot or lots amounting to no more than:
A. ten acres of land
B. 100 acres of land
C. 200 acres of land
D. one section of land

75. When land is torn away by the violent action of a river it is called:
A. erosion
B. avulsion
C. reliction
D. alluvion

76. The characteristic of land that has the greatest effect on land value is:
A. nonhomogeneity
B. location
C. indestructibility
D. immobility

77. All of the following are examples of public land use controls EXCEPT:
A. deed restrictions
B. building codes
C. zoning
D. environmental control laws

78. An estate created for the life of a person other than the life tenant is called a life estate:
A. in remainder
B. pur autre vie
C. by dower
D. in reversion

79. The person making the will is known as the:
A. devisee
B. bequestor
C. legatee
D. testator

80. A formal declaration by a person signing a deed that he or she, in fact, did sign the document is called:
A. a commissioning
B. a conveyance
C. a recorded plat
D. an acknowledgment

81. A trespass on the land of another as a result of an intrusion by some structure or other object is an:
A. encroachment
B. easement
C. estate
D. emblement

82. As a result of a salesperson's negligence in filling in the provisions in a contract of sale, the seller incurs a financial loss. Liability for this loss may be imposed on:
   A. both the salesperson and the employing broker
   B. the salesperson's employing broker only
   C. the salesperson only
   D. neither party

83. A gift of real property at death is a(n):
   A. devise
   B. bequest
   C. escheat
   D. demise

84. Of the following types of deeds, which provides the grantee with the LEAST assurance of title?
   A. bargain and sale
   B. quitclaim
   C. grant
   D. special warranty

85. Recording protects which of the following parties?
   A. grantor
   B. seller
   C. vendor
   D. grantee

86. All of the following are rights of a mortgagor EXCEPT:
   A. defeasance
   B. foreclosure
   C. equity of redemption
   D. possession

87. Which of the following gives the mortgagee the right to declare the entire principal balance immediately due and payable if the mortgagor is in default?
   A. acceleration clause
   B. alienation clause
   C. statutory foreclosure clause
   D. assignment clause

88. On June 16, a seller closes on the sale of her home. Annual taxes of $861 for the current year were paid in full by the seller prior to the sale. If these payments are prorated, which amount will be returned to the seller (calculate using the month/day proration)?
   A. $357
   B. $397
   C. $430
   D. $464

89. If the GIM is 7.5 and the annual gross income is $250,000, what is the estimated property value?
   A. $1,875,000
   B. $2,500,000
   C. $3,000,000
   D. $3,333,000

90. A salesperson licensee may receive commissions from which of the following?
   A. cooperating broker
   B. buyer
   C. seller
   D. sponsoring broker

Appendix C

Practice Exam 2

1. To foreclose on a home equity loan in Texas requires:
   A. judicial foreclosure
   B. nonjudicial foreclosure
   C. subordination
   D. fiat money

2. While a broker was inspecting a property for listing, the property owner told the broker that the house contains 2,400 square feet of heated living area. Without verifying this information, the broker listed the property and represented it to prospective buyers as containing 2,400 square feet. After purchasing the property, the buyer accurately determined that the house has only 1,850 square feet and sued for damages for the difference in value between 2,400 square feet and 1,850 square feet. Which of the following is correct?
   A. the broker is not liable because he relied on the seller's positive statement as to the square footage
   B. the seller is not liable because the broker, not the seller, represented the property to the buyer as containing 2,400 square feet
   C. the theory of caveat emptor applies; thus, neither the seller nor the broker is liable to the buyer
   D. both the broker and the seller are liable to the buyer

3. The sales associates of Executive Realty, Ltd., obtained several excellent listings in Exclusive Estates by advising homeowners that a number of Chinese families were moving into Exclusive Estates and therefore their property values would be substantially depressed. This activity is most accurately described as:
   A. steering
   B. blockbusting
   C. soliciting
   D. redlining

4. A real estate salesperson earned $48,000 in commissions in one year. If she received 60% of the 6% her broker received, what was her average monthly sales volume?
   A. $66,666
   B. $80,000
   C. $111,111
   D. $133,333

5. The type of listing contract that is most beneficial to the broker and the seller is:
   A. exclusive right to sell
   B. net
   C. open
   D. exclusive agency

6. A real estate broker is responsible for all of the following EXCEPT:
   A. acts of sales associates while engaged in brokerage activities
   B. appropriate handling of funds in trust, or escrow, accounts
   C. adhering to commission schedule recommended by the local real estate organization
   D. representing property honestly, fairly, and accurately to prospective buyers

7. A triangular tract of land is 8,000 feet long and has highway frontage of 4,000 yards. If Ajax Realty Company lists this property at 9% commission and sells it for $1,600 per acre, what amount of commission does Ajax receive?
   A. $105,785
   B. $158,678
   C. $218,160
   D. $317,355

8. When listing a home for sale, the broker advises the seller that because he owns only one house, the listing is exempt from prohibitions of the Fair Housing Act of 1968. Which of the following statements about the broker's advice is true?
   A. the broker is acting correctly in advising the seller about the exemption
   B. the broker always should give good legal advice to sellers and buyers
   C. the broker is in error because the exemption is from the Civil Rights Act of 1866
   D. the broker is acting incorrectly in that the property is not exempt because the seller is using a broker

9. A construction loan can also be called a(n):
   A. reverse mortgage
   B. blended-rate loan
   C. blanket mortgage
   D. interim loan

10. A salesperson associated with Metro Realty, Inc., obtained an offer for a property listed by Preferred Real Estate Company, which she gave to Sam Slicker, the listing agent with Preferred, for presentation to the property owner. Realizing that the amount of the offer was such that it probably would not be accepted, Sam increased the amount by $3,000 prior to presentation. Which of the following statements correctly characterizes Sam's action?
    A. to make the change a proper and appropriate act, Sam should have obtained the approval of Metro Realty before changing the offer
    B. Sam's action was in violation of his fiduciary obligations and was completely improper
    C. Sam's action would have been appropriate with the seller's consent
    D. Metro Realty, Inc. will be entitled to the entire commission because of Sam's actions

11. In the process of preparing an offer for commercial property, a broker was asked by two potential purchasers to recommend the most beneficial way for them to take title to the property. Which of the following should the broker recommend?
    A. tenants in common
    B. in severalty
    C. ask an attorney
    D. ask the listing broker

12. Upon the broker's recommendation, a seller accepted an offer that was 8% below the listed price. The broker did not disclose to the seller that the buyer was the broker's brother-in-law. Which of the following is correct?
    A. the broker violated his obligations as agent of the seller
    B. the fact that the buyer is related to the broker is not required to be divulged to the seller
    C. the broker has done nothing wrong as long as he doesn't take any commission
    D. the broker has done nothing wrong if the appraised value of the home matches the offered price

13. A VHAP loan is available to:
    A. all Texans
    B. women only
    C. men only
    D. Texas veterans

14. Combining the interest rate with other costs of a loan is known as the:
    A. trigger rate
    B. annual percentage rate
    C. finance charge
    D. amount financed

15. If the closing date is November 10 and the seller had paid the real property taxes of $2,880 for the current tax year of January 1 through December 31, which of the following is the correct closing statement entry for taxes?
    A. seller's credit of $400
    B. seller's debit of $2,480
    C. buyer's credit of $400
    D. buyer's debit of $2,480

16. RESPA requires lending institutions to provide borrowers with which of the following at the time of or within three days after application for a mortgage loan for housing?
    A. good faith estimate
    B. HUD Form No. 1
    C. disclosure statement
    D. nonrecourse note

17. The buyer assumes a 9% loan with a balance of $74,000 mortgage at closing on July 12. The seller has already made the July 1 payment; the next payment of $ 638.69, including principal and interest for July, will be due on August 1. Which of the following is the correct closing statement entry for interest?
    A. buyer's debit of $222.00
    B. buyer's credit of $638.69
    C. seller's debit of $222.00
    D. seller's credit of $638.69

18. No covenants or warranties are found in a:
    A. General Warranty deed
    B. Special Warranty deed
    C. Quitclaim deed
    D. Sheriff's deed

19. Under the right of eminent domain the government can take ownership of privately held land for all of the following EXCEPT:
    A. streets
    B. an elementary school
    C. a single family residence
    D. public housing

20. A single taxpayer sells her residence for $122,000. The original cost was $86,000. The taxpayer has lived in the home for 3 1/2 years and is in the 28% tax bracket. What is the amount of income tax due?
   A. $36,000
   B. $10,080
   C. $7,200
   D. $0

21. A property manager's responsibilities include all of the following EXCEPT:
   A. maintenance
   B. collecting rents
   C. commingling
   D. negotiating leases

22. Which of the following is one of the basic responsibilities of a property manager?
   A. appraising the property annually
   B. evicting all minority tenants to provide for a more stable complex
   C. producing the best possible net operating income for the owner
   D. preparing the annual tax returns and attending audits with the IRS

23. What net annual operating income must a property manager produce from a property to provide an 8% return to the owner, who paid $763,000 for the property?
   A. $9,538
   B. $61,040
   C. $95,375
   D. $104,849

24. Which of the following most accurately describes a property manager?
   A. fiduciary
   B. trustee
   C. escrow agent
   D. resident manager

25. When all parties agree to the terms and conditions of a real estate contract, there is said to be:
   A. mutual satisfaction
   B. sui juris
   C. meeting of the minds
   D. equitable consent

26. A roofline extending without permission onto an adjoining property is an example of:
   A. easement appurtenant
   B. encroachment
   C. license
   D. easement in gross

27. John owns an apartment building in a large city. After discussing the matter with his legal advisers, he decides to alter the type of occupancy in the building from rental to condominium status. This procedure is known as:
   A. conversion
   B. partition
   C. deportment
   D. amendment

28. The members of the Texas Real Estate Commission serve for a term of:
   A. 6 months
   B. 18 months
   C. 3 years
   D. 6 years

29. An owner's office building is producing a net annual operating income of $140,000. If the owner paid $1,166,666 for the property, what rate of return is she receiving on her investment?
   A. 8.3%
   B. 12%
   C. 14%
   D. 16.3%

30. All of the following statements about options are correct EXCEPT:
    A. they must be in writing to be enforceable
    B. they are binding upon optionor and optionee
    C. when exercised, they become contracts of sale
    D. optionor and optionee must be competent

31. Which of the following is both a contract of sale and a financing instrument?
    A. installment land contract
    B. sale and leaseback
    C. lease with option to purchase
    D. executed contract

32. A lease providing for rental changes based on changes in the Consumer Price Index is which of the following?
    A. escalated
    B. graduated
    C. percentage
    D. index

33. If the Commission proposes to suspend or revoke a person's license, the person is entitled to a hearing before the Commission:
    A. at a place the Commission selects
    B. within the county of licensee's business
    C. both A and B
    D. in Austin only

34. Public land use controls in the form of zoning ordinances are an exercise of:
    A. power of eminent domain
    B. general plan for development
    C. police power of the government
    D. Interstate Land Sales Full Disclosure Act

35. A property owner in a recently zoned area is permitted to continue to use his property in a manner that does not comply with the zoning requirements. This use is described as:
    A. exclusive-use zoning
    B. deviation
    C. nonconforming use
    D. private control of land use

36. A real estate broker, acting as an agent for another in a transaction, has a primary duty to:
    A. get the transaction closed successfully
    B. help the parties reach a mutually beneficial agreement
    C. treat all parties impartially
    D. represent the interests of his client

37. Which of the following actions of the broker is most likely to result in the creation of an agency with the buyer?
    A. show buyer an available property
    B. transmit buyer's offer to seller
    C. discuss the financing alternatives
    D. negotiate on buyer's behalf

38. A deed is made eligible for recording on the public record by which of the following?
    A. abstract
    B. avoidance
    C. alienation
    D. acknowledgment

39. The listing broker should follow all of the seller's instructions EXCEPT:
    A. show the property on Fridays
    B. extend the closing if necessary
    C. conceal the cracked foundation
    D. lease the property prior to closing

40. Which of the following provides the exclusive right of possession and control of real property?
    A. easement
    B. leasehold
    C. license
    D. encumbrance

41. A co-owner of real property automatically received a deceased co-owner's share of ownership. This is called:
    A. intestate succession
    B. inheritance by devise
    C. right of survivorship
    D. inheritance by descent

42. Four brothers received title to a large tract of land from their grandfather, who gave each brother a one-fourth undivided interest with equal rights to possession of the land. All four received their title on their grandfather's seventieth birthday. The brothers most likely hold title in which of the following ways?
    A. in severalty
    B. as tenants in common
    C. as tenants by the entirety
    D. as remaindermen

43. John and his wife, Mary, live in a community property state. Mary inherits a large shopping mall in the city where they live. Which of the following statements about Mary's ownership of the mall is correct?
    A. Mary and John hold the property as tenants by the entirety
    B. Mary may encumber or convey the title only with John's participation in a mortgage or deed
    C. Mary holds title as separate property
    D. the property is considered community property because of the marriage status at the time of inheritance

44. Which of the following statements about the creation of a condominium is FALSE?
    A. a Declaration, Articles of Association, and Association Bylaws must be recorded in the public record in the county where the property is located
    B. a parking garage with rental spaces can be converted to condominium ownership
    C. an apartment complex can be converted to condominiums only with a majority vote of the tenants
    D. a shopping center can be converted to condominium ownership

45. A real estate agent can do which of the following?
    A. complete TREC-approved forms
    B. prepare a deed
    C. draw a real estate note
    D. prepare a deed of trust

46. The state took a part of an owner's property for construction of a building. Which of the following statements about this event is correct?
    A. the property owner must be compensated for the difference in market value of the property before and after the partial condemnation
    B. the building to be constructed may be used for the sole use and benefit of a private corporation
    C. the property owner has no recourse to challenge taking his property
    D. the value established is the average of the owner's desired value, the state's desired purchase price, and an independent appraisal

47. It is unlawful for a licensed broker to compensate which of the following for a real estate sale?
   A. another broker
   B. a friend who made referral
   C. a broker licensed in another state
   D. the broker's salesperson

48. A property with a market value of $80,000 is entitled to a homestead exemption of $20,000. What is the tax rate per $100 if the tax bill is $900?
   A. $1.125
   B. $1.50
   C. $11.25
   D. $15.00

49. An encroachment is which of the following?
   A. lien
   B. party wall
   C. trespass
   D. fixture

50. In estimating the value of an office building containing 22,400 square feet, an appraiser established the annual rental income to be $400,000. The appraiser also learned that monthly expenses averaged $16,700. If the average investor in this type of property was realizing a net return of 13.5%, what would be the appraiser's estimate of the value of the property?
   A. $1,478,518
   B. $1,484,444
   C. $2,962,962
   D. $2,964,600

51. A competitive market analysis is performed when:
   A. assessing property
   B. pricing property
   C. appraising property
   D. condemning property

52. For which of the following types of property would the market data approach be the most relevant appraisal method?
   A. vacant industrial land
   B. library
   C. condominium office
   D. farm land with a large hog operation

53. The principle providing that the highest value of a property has a tendency to be established by the cost of purchasing or constructing a building of equal utility and desirability is the principle of:
   A. highest and best use
   B. competition
   C. supply and demand
   D. substitution

54. When an offer to purchase real estate is signed, the real estate broker or salesperson must give written notice that title insurance or an abstract should be obtained by the:
   A. seller
   B. title company
   C. buyer
   D. seller and buyer

55. The broker, when acting as an intermediary, must obtain written consent from:
   A. seller
   B. buyer
   C. TREC
   D. all parties to transaction

56. A real estate broker who is acting as an intermediary must:
   A. disclose to buyer that seller will accept less
   B. disclose to seller that buyer will pay more
   C. disclose confidential information
   D. treat all parties honestly

57. A building now 21 years old has a total economic life of 40 years. If the replacement cost of the building is $1,200,000, what is the value?
   A. $228,571
   B. $252,631
   C. $570,000
   D. $630,000

58. Which of the following is the most likely result of the homogeneous development of a residential subdivision?
   A. overinflated values
   B. maximized values
   C. stabilized values
   D. depressed values

59. Which of the following approaches to value is the most appropriate for estimating the value of a condominium apartment?
   A. cost approach
   B. income approach
   C. comparable approach
   D. gross rent multiplier

60. Which of the following statements by the listing broker to the buyer might lead a court to infer an agency relationship with the buyer?
   A. "This is a good buy."
   B. "Let's test the seller with a low offer and then go up if we have to."
   C. "Now is the time to submit an offer."
   D. "Let me tell you about the type of loans available at the bank today."

61. A rural homestead for a single person can consist of not more than:
   A. 200 acres
   B. 640 acres
   C. 120 acres
   D. 100 acres

62. The monthly payment necessary to fully amortize a 15-year mortgage loan of $100,000 at 8.5% APR is $984.74. How much interest will the mortgagor pay over the 15-year term?
   A. $77,253.20
   B. $127,500.00
   C. $176,892.41
   D. $276,892.41

63. A person who dies leaving a valid will is said to have died:
   A. intestate
   B. testate
   C. in succession
   D. in descent

64. A lender charges a 2% loan origination fee and three discount points to make a 95% conventional insured mortgage loan in the amount of $47,500. What is the cost of these charges to the borrower?
   A. $922
   B. $1,188
   C. $1,425
   D. $2,375

65. Which of the following could be considered separate property?
   A. dividends from husband's inherited stocks
   B. one spouse's salary
   C. rents from real estate inherited by the wife
   D. real estate inherited by the husband

66. A security device on a home rental must be rekeyed by the landlord within what time period after tenant turnover?
   A. 3 days
   B. 7 days
   C. 10 days
   D. 30 days

67. All of the following are ways in which a seller may finance the sale of her property for a buyer EXCEPT:
   A. wraparound purchase money mortgage
   B. contract for deed
   C. FHA-insured mortgage
   D. purchase money first mortgage

68. Bill and Betty Brown execute and deliver a $50,000 mortgage to Ajax Financial Associates at 10:30 a.m. on April 1. At 11:30 a.m. on the same day, they give a $10,000 mortgage pledging the same property to Fidelity Finance, Inc. Fidelity's mortgage is recorded at 1:10 p.m. that day, and the mortgage to Ajax is recorded at 1:42 p.m. on April 1. Which of the following statements about these mortgages is correct?
   A. because the mortgage to Ajax was executed and delivered first, Ajax holds the first mortgage
   B. Fidelity has the second mortgage because it was executed and delivered after the mortgage given to Ajax
   C. Ajax and Fidelity will be co-first mortgage holders because both mortgages were signed on the same day
   D. because the mortgage to Fidelity was recorded first, Fidelity holds the first mortgage

69. When a buyer signs a purchase contract and the seller accepts, the buyer acquires an immediate interest in the property known as:
   A. legal title
   B. statutory title
   C. equitable title
   D. defeasible title

70. Regulation Z specifies that the only specific credit term that may appear in an advertisement of a house for sale without the requirement of a full disclosure is which of the following?
   A. SAM
   B. APR
   C. ECOA
   D. RESPA

71. In the sale of their home, Van and Vera Vendor were required to satisfy their existing first mortgage of $40,000 so the buyers could obtain a first mortgage to finance their purchase. The Vendors' closing statement contained a debit in the amount of $800 because the Vendors paid off their loan prior to the full term. From this information, it can be determined that the Vendors' mortgage contained a(n):
   A. acceleration clause
   B. alienation clause
   C. prepayment clause
   D. defeasance clause

72. A developer gave the seller a $385,000 purchase money first mortgage to secure payment of part of the purchase price for a tract of land. The developer was able to convey unencumbered titles to the first six lot purchasers by paying only $8,000 on the purchase money mortgage because the mortgage contained:
   A. release clauses
   B. due-on-sale clauses
   C. prepayment clauses
   D. mortgaging clauses

73. In the purchase of an office building, the buyer gave the seller a mortgage for $200,000 more than the seller's first mortgage and took title to the property subject to the first mortgage. The purchase money mortgage required payments of interest only for the first five years, at which time the principal has to be paid and a new purchase money mortgage created. All of the following statements about these financial arrangements are correct EXCEPT:
   A. the purchase money mortgage is a wrap-around term mortgage
   B. for this arrangement to work satisfactorily, the seller's first mortgage must not contain an alienation clause
   C. this arrangement must be approved by Fannie Mae
   D. the purchase money mortgage has a balloon payment

74. The Texas provision that provides for the transfer of real estate belonging to any person who dies without a will and has no heirs is:
   A. eminent domain
   B. escheat
   C. right of redemption
   D. ad valorem

75. Which of the following actions of the broker is most likely to result in the creation of an agency with the buyer?
   A. show buyer an available property
   B. transmit buyer's offer to seller
   C. discuss the financing alternatives available
   D. negotiate on buyer's behalf

76. A property description reading "1/4 of the north-east 1/4 of section 22" describes how many acres?
   A. 20
   B. 40
   C. 160
   D. 240

77. The private ownership of land is known as:
   A. feudal ownership
   B. government ownership
   C. allodial ownership
   D. eminent domain

78. All of the following are powers of government EXCEPT:
   A. police power
   B. escheat
   C. taxation
   D. deed restrictions

79. An owner whose property is condemned is entitled to be compensated for:
   A. book value
   B. assessed value
   C. market value
   D. mortgage value

80. A listing contract creates an agency relationship in which:
   A. the broker is a general agent
   B. the seller is the principal
   C. the seller is a general agent
   D. the broker is the principal

81. When a real estate broker or seller conceals a known defect, this is an example of:
   A. mutual mistake
   B. unintentional misrepresentation
   C. fraud
   D. mistake of law

82. Upon application for an original license, pursuant to TRELA, the applicant shall pay a fee to the real estate recovery fund of:
   A. $10
   B. $100
   C. $500
   D. $1,000

83. A lease is all of the following EXCEPT:
   A. contract
   B. nonfreehold estate
   C. freehold estate
   D. binding obligation on the parties

84. During a licensee's period of inactive status the person may:
   A. practice real estate
   B. refer buyers for a fee
   C. list homes for sale
   D. pay annual license renewal fees

85. A licensed real estate practitioner may not:
   A. sell or exchange real estate
   B. negotiate listings
   C. advise sellers on legal matters
   D. aid in locating rental real estate

86. Which of the following enables the mortgagee to sell the mortgage in the secondary mortgage market?
   A. assignment clause
   B. due-on-sale clause
   C. mortgaging clause
   D. power-of-sale clause

87. When a buyer purchases a home using a VA-guaranteed loan, he is allowed to:
   A. pay a loan origination fee
   B. pay discount points
   C. purchase the property to be used as a rental
   D. both A and B

88. Redlining applies to which of the following?
   A. brokers
   B. developers
   C. lenders
   D. landlords

89. A lease is a contract that is:
   A. bilateral
   B. unilateral
   C. collateral
   D. trilateral

90. Which of the following is a deductible expense for homeowners?
   A. real property taxes
   B. maintenance
   C. mortgage principal payments
   D. energy usage

Appendix D

Answer Key

Chapter 2

1. C	6. B	11. D	16. C
2. D	7. C	12. B	17. C
3. D	8. A	13. D	18. B
4. C	9. B	14. B	19. B
5. E	10. C	15. D	20. D

Chapter 3

1. B	6. B	11. C	16. B
2. E	7. A	12. D	17. D
3. E	8. D	13. E	
4. A	9. B	14. A	
5. B	10. C	15. A	

Chapter 4

1. B	6. D	11. B	16. D
2. E	7. C	12. D	17. C
3. B	8. A	13. C	18. E
4. D	9. C	14. E	19. A
5. C	10. C	15. D	20. A

Chapter 5

1. C	5. A	9. B	13. A
2. A	6. D	10. C	14. B
3. B	7. A	11. A	15. C
4. C	8. A	12. D	

Chapter 6

1. B
2. C
3. A
4. B
5. D
6. C
7. B
8. A
9. C
10. D
11. E
12. A
13. D
14. C
15. A

Chapter 7

1. D
2. C
3. D
4. C
5. B
6. C
7. C
8. B
9. A
10. C
11. A
12. C
13. C
14. D
15. A
16. D
17. B
18. C
19. C
20. C

Chapter 8

1. D
2. C
3. A
4. D
5. D
6. C
7. C
8. A
9. B
10. B
11. C
12. B
13. D
14. B
15. D
16. B
17. D
18. B
19. C

Chapter 9

1. E
2. D
3. D
4. B
5. C
6. C
7. D
8. B
9. C
10. D
11. D
12. D
13. D
14. C
15. B
16. A
17. D
18. B
19. B
20. B

Chapter 10

1. D
2. E
3. A
4. C
5. C
6. C
7. D
8. B
9. B
10. D
11. C
12. C
13. E
14. D
15. B
16. C
17. A
18. A
19. A

Chapter 11

1. C	6. C	11. D	16. C
2. D	7. A	12. C	17. A
3. B	8. D	13. A	18. C
4. B	9. B	14. B	19. C
5. B	10. C	15. C	20. C

Chapter 12

1. A	4. E	7. D
2. B	5. C	8. C
3. A	6. B	9. C

Chapter 13

1. D	4. C	7. D	10. B
2. D	5. C	8. B	
3. D	6. D	9. D	

Chapter 14

1. A	4. D	7. C	10. C
2. D	5. C	8. B	
3. B	6. C	9. C	

Chapter 15

1. A	4. B	7. C	10. B
2. D	5. D	8. D	
3. C	6. C	9. B	

Chapter 16

1. A	6. D	11. C	16. D
2. C	7. A	12. B	17. A
3. A	8. C	13. C	18. D
4. A	9. D	14. C	19. A
5. D	10. A	15. B	

Chapter 17

1. E
2. D
3. B
4. E
5. C
6. C
7. B
8. D
9. D
10. C
11. A
12. D
13. A
14. D
15. C
16. B
17. D
18. B
19. A
20. A

Chapter 18

1. A
2. B
3. C
4. B
5. B
6. D
7. C
8. D
9. C
10. A
11. C
12. B
13. A
14. D
15. E
16. B
17. B
18. A
19. B
20. C

Chapter 19

1. C
2. B
3. A
4. A
5. D
6. C
7. D
8. D
9. A
10. C
11. A
12. C
13. C
14. C
15. C
16. C
17. D
18. A
19. A
20. C

Chapter 20

1. C
2. B
3. D
4. A
5. B
6. B
7. D
8. A
9. C
10. D
11. D
12. B
13. A
14. B

Chapter 21

1. A
2. A
3. C
4. C
5. D
6. E
7. B
8. A
9. C
10. B
11. C
12. B
13. D
14. D
15. C
16. C
17. B
18. E
19. D
20. C
21. A

Chapter 22

1. A
2. C
3. B
4. D
5. C
6. C
7. A
8. C
9. B
10. A
11. D
12. B
13. C
14. B
15. B
16. C
17. C
18. C
19. D
20. B
21. A
22. C
23. D
24. A

Chapter 23

1. D
2. C
3. A
4. B
5. C
6. C
7. A
8. D
9. A
10. B
11. C
12. A
13. A
14. D
15. C
16. D
17. D
18. C

Chapter 24

1. D
2. D
3. D
4. C
5. D
6. A
7. D
8. C
9. B
10. A
11. B
12. A
13. B
14. D
15. C
16. D
17. B
18. C

Chapter 25

1. D
2. D
3. C
4. A
5. C
6. A
7. C
8. A
9. D
10. A
11. C
12. A
13. D
14. B
15. A

Answer Key to Practice Exam 1 (Appendix B)

1. A
2. B
3. B
4. D
5. C
6. D
7. D
8. B
9. C
10. A
11. D
12. C
13. B
14. C
15. D
16. C

17. A
18. B
19. B
20. A
21. C
22. C
23. C
24. A
25. D
26. C
27. D
28. A
29. D
30. A
31. B
32. C
33. D
34. D
35. C
36. C
37. C
38. B
39. C
40. D
41. D
42. C
43. B
44. A
45. C
46. D
47. B
48. A
49. B
50. C
51. B
52. A
53. C
54. D
55. B
56. D
57. B
58. D
59. C
60. C
61. B
62. A
63. C
64. D
65. A
66. A
67. A
68. D
69. A
70. C
71. D
72. D
73. B
74. A
75. B
76. B
77. A
78. B
79. D
80. D
81. A
82. A
83. A
84. B
85. D
86. B
87. A
88. B
89. A
90. D

Answer Key to Practice Exam 2 (Appendix C)

1. A
2. D
3. B
4. C
5. A
6. C
7. B
8. D
9. D
10. B
11. C
12. A
13. D
14. B
15. A
16. A
17. C
18. C
19. C
20. D
21. C
22. C
23. B
24. A
25. C
26. B
27. A
28. D
29. B
30. B
31. A
32. D
33. C
34. C
35. C
36. D
37. D
38. D
39. C
40. B
41. C
42. B
43. C
44. C
45. A
46. A
47. B
48. B
49. C
50. A
51. B
52. A
53. D
54. C
55. D
56. D
57. C
58. B
59. C
60. B

61. D
62. A
63. B
64. D
65. D
66. B
67. C
68. D
69. C
70. B
71. C
72. A
73. C
74. B
75. D
76. B
77. C
78. D
79. C
80. B
81. C
82. A
83. C
84. D
85. C
86. A
87. D
88. C
89. A
90. A

Glossary

Abstract: a summary of all recorded documents affecting title to a given parcel of land

Abstract of title: a complete historical summary of all recorded documents affecting the title of a property

Abstractor (abstracter): an expert in title search and abstract preparation

Accelerated depreciation: any method of depreciation that achieves a faster rate of depreciation than straight-line

Acceleration clause: allows the lender to demand immediate payment of the balance owed

Accession: the addition to land by man or nature

Accretion: the process of land build-up by waterborne rock, sand, and soil

Acknowledgment: a formal declaration by a person signing a document that he or she, in fact, did sign that document

Acre: a unit of land measurement

Actual notice: knowledge gained from what one has seen, heard, read, or observed

Adjustable rate mortgage: a mortgage on which the interest rate rises and falls with changes in prevailing interest rates

Adjusted market price: the value of a comparable property after adjustments have been made for differences between it and the subject property

Adjusted sales price: the sales price of a property less commissions, fix-up, and closing costs

Administrator (administratrix): a person appointed by a court to carry out the instructions found in a will

Ad valorem taxes: taxes charged according to the value of a property

Adverse possession: acquisition of real property through prolonged and unauthorized occupation of another's land

Agency: a relationship created when one person (the principal) delegates to another person (the agent) the right to act on his behalf

Agency by estoppel: relationship that results when a principal fails to maintain due diligence over his agent and the agent exercises powers not granted to him

Agency by ratification: one that is established after the fact

Agency coupled with an interest: one that results when the agent holds an interest in the property he is representing

Agent: the person empowered to act by and on behalf of the principal; see also Agency; Broker

Agreement of sale. See Installment contract

Air lot: a designated airspace over a parcel of land

Air right: the right to occupy and use the airspace above the surface of a parcel of land

Alienation clause: requires immediate repayment of the loan if ownership transfers; also called a due-on-sale clause

Alienation of title: a change in ownership of any kind

Allodial system: one in which individuals are given the right to own land

Alluvion: the increase of land when waterborne soil is gradually deposited

Amendatory language: government-required clauses in FHA and VA contracts

American Recovery and Reinvestment Act of 2009: a broad package of federal provisions intended to provide economic stimulus during the recession, including tax incentives, unemployment benefits, and domestic spending worth an estimated $787 billion.

Americans with Disabilities Act (ADA): a federal law giving disabled individuals the right to access to commercial facilities open to the public

Amortized loan: a loan requiring periodic payments that include both interest and partial repayment of principal

Amount financed: amount of credit provided to the borrower

Amount realized: selling price less selling expenses

Annual percentage rate (APR): a uniform measure of the cost of credit that includes interest, discount points, and loan fees

Anticipation, principle of: what a person will pay for a property depends on the expected benefits from the property in the future

Apartment locators: firms that specialize in finding rental units for tenants

Appraisal: an estimate of value

Appraisal letter: a valuation report in the form of a business letter

Appraisal Review Board: local governmental body that hears and rules on property owner complaints of overassessment

Appraise: to generate an estimate of value

Appreciation: an increase in property value

Appropriation process: the enactment of a taxing body's budget and sources of money into law

Appurtenance: right or privilege or improvement that belongs to and passes with land but is not necessarily a part of the land

"As is": said of property offered for sale in its present condition with no guaranty or warranty of quality provided by the seller

Assemblage: the process of combining two or more parcels into one

Assessed value: a value placed on a property for the purpose of taxation

Assessment district. See Improvement district

Assessment roll: a list or book, open for public inspection, that shows assessed values for all lands and buildings in a taxing district

Assign: to transfer to another one's rights under a contract

Assignee: one to whom a right or property is transferred (also called an assign)

Assignment: the transfer of one's rights under a contract to another

Association: a not-for-profit organization that can own property and transact business in its own name

Association dues: fees paid by a condominium or PUD unit owner to the owner's association for upkeep of the common elements

Assume the loan: the buyer obligates himself to repay an existing loan as a condition of the sale

At-risk: the amount of money an investor stands to lose

Attorney-in-fact: one who is authorized by another to act in his (her) place

Automated underwriting systems: computerized systems for loan approval communication between a loan originator and the investor

Avulsion: the removal of land by the action of water

Balloon loan: a loan in which the final payment is larger than the preceding payments

Balloon payment: the name given to the final payment of a balloon loan

Banks: as mortgage lenders

Bargain and sale deed: a deed that contains no covenants, but does imply that the grantor owns the property being conveyed by the deed

Base line: an east-west or geographer's line selected as a basic reference in the rectangular survey system

Basis: the price paid for property; used in calculating income taxes

Bench mark: a reference point of known location and elevation

Beneficial interest: a unit of ownership in a real estate investment trust

Beneficiary: one for whose benefit a trust is created; the lender in a deed of trust arrangement

Bequest: personal property received under a will

Bilateral contract: results when a promise is exchanged for a promise

Bill of sale: a written agreement by which one person transfers his personal property to another

Blanket mortgage: a mortgage that is secured by more than one real property

Blended-rate loan: a refinancing plan that combines the interest rate on an existing mortgage with current rates

Blind pool: an investment pool wherein properties are purchased after investors have already invested their money

Block busting: the illegal practice of inducing panic selling in a neighborhood for financial gain

Blue-sky laws: state laws designed to protect persons from buying into dubious investment schemes

Borrower's points: charges in one-percent units of a loan, paid by a borrower to obtain a loan

Boycotting: two or more people conspiring to restrain competition

Breach of contract: failure without legal excuse to perform as required by a contract

Broad market: one wherein many buyers and many sellers are in the market at the same time

Broker: a person or legal entity licensed to act independently in conducting a real estate brokerage business

Budget mortgage: features loan payments that include principal, interest, taxes, and insurance (often called PITI)

Buffer zone: a strip of land that separates one land use from another

Building codes: local and state laws that set minimum construction standards

Buyer's broker: a broker employed by, and therefore loyal to, the buyer

Buyer's market: one with few buyers and many sellers

Buyer's walk-through: a final inspection just prior to settlement

Bylaws: rules that govern how an owners' property association will be run

Call clause (due-on-sale clause): a clause in a note or mortgage that gives the lender the right to call the entire loan balance due if the property is sold or otherwise conveyed

Canons: standards of conduct

Capital gain: the gain (profit) on the sale of an appreciated asset

Capitalize: to convert future income to current value

Cash flow: the number of dollars remaining each year after an investor collects rents and pays operating expenses and mortgage payments

Cash value: the amount of money a policyholder would receive if the policy were surrendered

Cash-on-cash: the cash flow produced by a property divided by the amount of cash necessary to purchase it

Caveat emptor: let the buyer beware

CC&Rs: convenants, conditions, and restrictions by which a property owner agrees to abide

Certificate of deposit: a saver's commitment to leave funds on deposit for a specific period of time

Certificate of occupancy: a government-issued document that states a structure meets local zoning and building code requirements and is ready for use

Chain of title: the linkage of property ownership that connects the present owner to the original source of title

Characteristics of land: fixity, immobility, indestructibility, modification, nonhomogeneity, scarcity, and situs

Characteristics of value: demand, scarcity, transferability, and utility

Chattel: an article of personal property

Chattel mortgage: a pledge of personal property to secure a note

Check: a 24-by-24-mile area created by guide meridians and correction lines in the rectangular survey system

Client: principal

Closing: the act of finalizing a transaction

Closing date: the day on which title is conveyed

Closing into escrow: a closing where all parties sign their documents and entrust them to the escrow agent

Closing meeting (settlement meeting): a meeting at which the buyer pays for the property, receives a deed to it, and all other matters pertaining to the sale are concluded

Cloud on the title: any claim, lien or encumbrance that impairs title to property

Codicil: a written supplement or amendment to an existing will

Color of title: some plausible, but not completely clear-cut indication of ownership rights

Commingling: the mixing of clients' or customers' funds with an agent's personal funds

Common elements: those parts of a condominium in which each unit owner holds an undivided interest

Community property: property co-ownership wherein husband and wife are treated as equal partners with each owning a one-half interest

Community Reinvestment Act: federal statute encouraging federally regulated lenders to encourage their participation in low-income areas

Comparables: properties similar to the subject property that have sold recently

Compensation: for brokers and salespersons

Competent parties: persons considered legally capable of entering into a binding contract

Competitive market analysis: a method of valuing homes that looks not only at recent home sales but also at homes presently on the market plus homes that were listed but did not sell

Computerized loan origination: originating loans through the use of a networked computer system

Condemnation proceeding: the legal action of eminent domain

Conditional sales contract. See Installment contract

Conditional use permit: allows a land use that does not conform with existing zoning

Condominium: individual ownership of separate portions of a building plus joint ownership of the common elements

Condominium declaration: a document that converts a given parcel of land into a condominium subdivision

Conformity, principle of: maximum value is realized when there is a reasonable degree of homogeneity in a neighborhood

Connection line: a survey line that connects a surveyor's monument with a permanent reference mark

Consequential damages: an award to a property owner whose land is not taken but which suffers because of a nearby condemnation

Consideration: anything of value given to induce another to enter into a contract

Construction loan (an interim loan): a loan wherein money is advanced as construction takes place

Constructive eviction: tenant breaks the lease because the landlord does not keep the premises habitable

Constructive notice: notice given by the public records and by visible possession, and the legal presumption that all persons are thereby notified

Contour lines: lines on a topographic map that connect points having the same elevation

Contour map (topographic map): a map that shows land elevations

Contract: a legally enforceable agreement to do (or not to do) a particular thing

Contract for deed: a method of selling and financing property whereby the buyer obtains possession but the seller retains the title

Contract rent: the amount of rent specified in the lease contract

Contractual intent: precludes jokes or jests from becoming valid contracts

Contribution, principle of: we should invest dollars whenever they will return to us more than $1 of value and should stop when each dollar invested returns less then $1 in value

Conventional loans: real estate loans that are not insured by the FHA or guaranteed by the VA

Cooperating broker: a broker who, acting as an agent of the listing broker, procures a buyer

Cooperative: land and building owned or leased by a corporation which in turn leases space to its shareholders

Corporation: a business owned by stockholders

Correction deed: a document used to correct an error in a previously recorded deed

Correction lines: survey lines used to correct for the earth's curvature

Correlation process: a step in an appraisal whereby the appraiser weights the comparables he is using

Cost approach: land value plus current construction costs minus depreciation

Counteroffer: an offer made in response to an offer

Covenant: a written agreement or promise

Credit report: a report reflecting the creditworthiness of a borrower by showing past credit history

Credit scoring: method of evaluating credit risk

Curable depreciation: depreciation that can be fixed at reasonable cost

Curtesy: the legal right of a widower to a portion of his deceased wife's real property

Customers: third parties

Datum: any point, line, or surface from which a distance, vertical height or depth is measured

Dedication: the voluntary conveyance of private land to the public

Deed: a written document that when properly executed and delivered conveys title to land

Deed as security: a deed given to secure a loan and treated as a mortgage

Deed of trust: a document that conveys title to a neutral third party trustee as security for a debt

Deed restrictions (deed covenants): provisions placed in deeds to control how future landowners may or may not use the property

Default: failure to perform a legal duty, such as failure to carry out the terms of a contract

Defeasance clause: a mortgage clause that states the mortgage is defeated if the accompanying note is repaid on time

Deficiency judgment: a judgment against a borrower if the sale of pledged property at foreclosure does not bring in enough to pay the balance owed

Delayed exchange: a nonsimultaneous tax-deferred trade

Delinquent loan: a loan wherein the borrower is behind in his payments

Demand: a need or desire coupled with the purchasing power to fill it

Depreciation: loss in value due to deterioration and obsolescence

Dereliction: the process whereby dry land is permanently exposed by a gradually receding waterline

Devise: a transfer of real property by means of a will

Devisee: one who receives real property under a will

Diminishing marginal returns, principle of: we should invest dollars whenever they will return to us more than $1 of value and should stop when each dollar invested returns less than $1 in value

Discount broker: a full-service broker who charges less than the prevailing commission rates in his community

Discount points: charges made by lenders to adjust the effective rate of interest on a loan

Discrimination. See Fair housing laws

Disintermediation: the movement of money out of savings accounts into corporate and government debt instruments

Documentary tax: a fee or tax on deeds and other documents payable at the time of recordation

Dominant estate: the parcel of land which benefits from an easement

Dower: the legal right of a widow to a portion of her deceased husband's real property

Downside risk: the possibility that an investor will lose his money in an investment

Downzoning: rezoning of land from a higher-density use to a lower-density use

Dual agency (divided agency): representation of two or more principals in a transaction by the same agent

Due-on-sale: a clause in a note or mortgage that gives the lender the right to call the entire loan balance due if the property is sold or otherwise conveyed

Durable power of attorney: power of attorney that does not lapse because of the passage of time unless a time limitation is specifically stated in the instrument creating it

Duress: the application of force to obtain an agreement

Earnest money deposit: money that accompanies an offer to purchase as evidence of good faith

Easement: the right or privilege one party has to use land belonging to another for a special purpose not inconsistent with the owner's use of the land

Easement appurtenant: an easement that runs with the land

Easement by prescription: acquisition of an easement by prolonged use

Easement in gross: an easement given to a person or business

Economic obsolescence: loss of value due to external forces or events

Economic rent: the amount of rent a property could command in the open market

Effective yield: a return on investment calculation that considers the price paid, the time held, and the interest rate

Emblements: annual plantings that require cultivation

Eminent domain: the right of government to take privately held land for public use, provided fair compensation is paid

Encroachment: the unauthorized intrusion of a building or other improvement onto another person's land

Encumbrance: any impediment to a clear title, such as a lien, lease, or easement

Environmental impact statement: a report that contains information regarding the effect of a proposed project on the environment of an area

Equitable mortgage: a written agreement that is considered to be a mortgage in its intent even though it may not follow the usual mortgage wording

Equitable title: the right to demand that title be conveyed upon payment of the purchase price

Equity: the market value of a property less the debt against it

Equity build-up: the increase of one's equity in a property due to mortgage balance reduction and price appreciation

Equity mortgage: a loan made against the appreciated value of the borrower's property

Equity of redemption: the borrower's right prior to foreclosure to repay the balance due on a delinquent mortgage loan

Equity sharing: an arrangement whereby a party providing financing gets a portion of the ownership

Escalation clause: provision in a lease for upward and downward rent adjustments

Escheat: the reversion of a person's property to the state when he/she dies and leaves no will or heirs

Escrow account: a separate account for holding clients' and customers' money

Escrow agent: the person placed in charge of an escrow

Escrow closing: the deposit of documents and funds with a neutral third party along with instructions as to how to conduct the closing

Estate: the extent of one's rights in land

Estate at will: a leasehold estate that can be terminated by the lessor or lessee at any time

Estate for years: any lease with a specific starting time and a specific ending time

Estate in severalty: owned by one person, sole ownership

Estoppel certificate: a document in which a borrower verifies the amount he still owes and the interest rate

Exclusive agency listing: a listing wherein the owner reserves the right to sell his property himself, but agrees to list with no other broker during the listing period

Exclusive authority to purchase: listing utilized by buyer's brokers

Exclusive right to sell: a listing that gives the broker the right to collect a commission no matter who sells the property during the listing period

Executor (executrix): a person named in a will to carry out its instructions

Executor's deed: a deed used to convey the real property of a deceased person

Express contract: a contract made orally or in writing

Face amount: the dollar amount of insurance coverage

Fair Credit Reporting Act: federal law giving an individual the right to inspect his or her file with the credit bureau and correct any errors

Faithful performance: a requirement that an agent obey all legal instructions given to him by his principal

Familial status: one or more individuals (who have not obtained the age of 18 years) being domiciled with a parent or another person having legal custody of such individual or individuals or the designee of such parent or other person having such custody, with the written permission of such parent or other person

Fannie Mae: a real estate industry nicknamed for the Federal National Mortgage Association

Federal Home Loan Mortgage Corporation ("Freddie Mac"): agency providing a secondary mortgage market facility for savings and loan associations

Federal Housing Administration (FHA): government agency that insures lenders against losses due to nonrepayment

Federal Housing Finance Agency (FHFA): an independent federal agency that acts as the regulator and conservator of Fannie Mae and Freddie Mac. It also acts as the regulator of the 12 Federal Home Loan Banks which were created by the Federal Housing Finance Regulatory Reform Act of 2008.

Federal National Mortgage Association ("Fannie Mae"): agency providing a secondary mortgage market for real estate loans

Federal Secure and Fair Enforcement of Mortgage Licensing Act of 2008 (SAFE Act): a federal law enacted to enhance consumer protection and to reduce fraud in home mortgage lending that requires states to educate, test, license, and register mortgage loan originators according to national standards.

Fee simple: most extensive interest (ownership) one can hold in land; often called the complete bundle of rights; an absolute estate

Fee simple determinable estate (fee on conditional limitation): a fee estate limited by the happening of a certain event

Fee simple subject to condition subsequent: the grantor has the right to terminate the fee estate

Fee simple upon condition precedent: title does not take effect until a condition is performed

Feudal system: all land ownership rests in the name of the king

Fiat money: money created by the government, printing press money

Fictional depreciation: depreciation deductions as allowed by tax law

Fiduciary: a person in a position of trust, responsibility, and confidence for another, such as a broker for his client

Finance charge: the total dollar amount the credit will cost the borrower over the life of the loan

Financial liability: the amount of money one can lose; one's risk exposure

Financing statement: a recorded document designed to protect the rights of a chattel lienholder

FIRREA: the Financial Institution's Reform, Recovery, and Enforcement Act of 1989

First lien mortgage: the mortgage on a property holding senior priority and the first to be paid in event of foreclosure

Fixity: refers to the fact that land and buildings require long periods of time to pay for themselves

Fixture: an object that has been attached to land so as to become real estate

Flat-fee broker: a broker who for a fixed price will list a property and help the owner sell it

Forbear: not to act

Foreclosure: the procedure for taking over a pledged property and selling it to satisfy an unpaid debt

Formal will: a will that is properly witnessed

Four unities of a joint tenancy: time, title, interest, and possession

Franchiser: the party giving the franchise

Fraud: an act intended to deceive for the purpose of inducing another to give up something of value

Freddie Mac: a real estate industry nickname for the Federal Home Loan Mortgage Corporation

Freehold estate: an estate in land that is held in fee or for life

Front foot: one linear foot along the street side of a lot; lot appraisal

Fructus industriales: annual plantings that require cultivation

Fructus naturales: trees, perennial plants, and uncultivated vegetation

Functional obsolescence: depreciation that results from improvement that are inadequate, overly adequate, or improperly designed for today's needs

Funding fee: a charge by the VA to guarantee a loan

Fungible: freely substitutable

Gain: the profit on the sale of an appreciated asset

General agency: an agency wherein the agent has the power to transact the principal's affairs in a particular business or at a certain location

General lien: a lien on all of a person's property

General partnership: a form of co-ownership for business purposes wherein all partners have a voice in its management and unlimited liability for its debts

Gift deed: a deed that states "love and affection" as the consideration

Ginnie Mae: a real estate nickname for the Government National Mortgage Association

Good consideration: consideration without monetary value, such as love and affection

Government National Mortgage Association ("Ginnie Mae"): a government agency that sponsors a mortgage-backed securities program and provides subsidies for residential loans

Government survey: a system for surveying land that uses latitude and longitude lines as references

Graduated payment mortgage: a fixed interest rate loan wherein the monthly payment starts low and then increases

Graduated rental: a lease that provides for agreed-upon rent increases

Grant: the act of conveying ownership

Grantee: the person named in a deed who acquires ownership

Grantor: the person named in a deed who conveys ownership

Grantor-Grantee indexes: alphabetical lists used to locate documents in the public records

GRM (Gross rent multiplier): a number that is multiplied by a property's gross rents to produce an estimate of the property's worth; an economic factor used to estimate a property's market value

Gross lease: the tenant pays a fixed rent and the landlord pays all property expenses

Ground lease: the lease of land alone

Ground rent: rent paid to occupy a plot of land

Groundwater level: the upper limit of percolating water below the earth's surface

Guardian's deed: used to convey property of a minor or legally incompetent person

Guide meridians: survey lines running north and south that correct for the earth's curvature

Handicapped: having a physical or mental impairment which substantially limits one or more major life activities; or having a record of having such an impairment; or being regarded as having such an impairment

Heirs: those designated by law to receive the property of the deceased if he leaves no will

Highest and best use: that use of a parcel of land which will produce the greatest current value

Holdover tenant: a tenant who stays beyond his lease period and who can be evicted or given a new lease

Holographic will: one that is entirely handwritten and signed by the testator but not witnessed

Home-seller program: a plan whereby FNMA will buy purchase money mortgages from home sellers

Homestead protection: state laws that protect against the forced sale of a person's home

Hypothecate: to pledge property to secure a debt but without giving up possession of it

Illiquid asset: an asset that may be difficult to sell on short notice

Illiquidity: the possibility that an asset may be very difficult to sell on short notice

Implied authority: agency authority that arises from custom rather than expressed agreement

Implied contract: a contract created by the actions of the parties involved

Impound or reserve account: an account into which the lender places monthly tax and insurance payments; also called an escrow account

Improvements: any form of land development, such as building, roads, fences, pipelines, etc.

Income approach: a method of valuing a property based on the monetary returns it can be expected to produce

Incurable depreciation: depreciation that cannot be fixed and simply must be lived with

Independent contractor: one who contracts to do work according to his own methods and is responsible to his employer only as to the results of that work

Index rate: the interest rate to which an adjustable mortgage is tied

Indicated value: the worth of the subject property as shown by recent sales of comparable properties

Informal reference: to identify a parcel of land by its street address or common name

Innocent misrepresentation: wrong information but without the intent to deceive

Installment contract: a method of selling and financing property whereby the seller retains title but the buyer takes possession while he makes his payments

Installment sale: the selling of an appreciated property on terms rather than for cash so as to spread out the payment of income taxes on the gain

Interest: compensation allowed by law for the use or forbearance or detention of money; deduction

Interest rate cap: the maximum interest rate charge allowed on an adjustable loan

Interim loan: a loan that is to be replaced by a permanent loan, a construction loan

Intermediary: a broker employed to negotiate a transaction between the parties

Intermediate theory: the legal position that a mortgage is a lien until default, at which time title passes to the lender

Inter vivos trust: a trust that takes effect during the life of its creator

Intestate: without a last will and testament

Intestate succession: laws that direct how a deceased's assets shall be divided if he leaves no will

Inverse condemnation: a legal action in which an owner demands that a public agency buy his land

Investment strategy: a plan that balances returns available with risks that must be taken in order to enhance the investor's overall welfare

Joint tenancy: a form of property co-ownership that features the right of survivorship

Joint venture: an association of two or more persons or firms in order to carry out a single business project

Judgment roll: a publicly available list of court-ordered judgments

Judicial foreclosure: foreclosure by lawsuit

Junior mortgage: any mortgage on a property that is subordinate in priority to the first mortgage

Jurat: a sworn statement by the person who signed the document that the information contained in the document is true

Land patent: a government document used for conveying public lands in fee to miners and settlers

Land trust: a real estate trust wherein the person who creates the trust (the trustor) is also its beneficiary

Land-use control: any legal restriction that controls how a parcel of land may be used

Latitude lines: imaginary east-west reference lines that circle the earth

Lawful objective: to be enforceable, a contract cannot call for the breaking of laws

Lease: an agreement that conveys the right to use property for a period of time

Leasehold estate: an estate in land wherein there is possession but not ownership

Lease option: allows the tenant to buy the property at present price and terms for a given period of time

Legacy: personal property received under a will

Legal consideration: the requirement that consideration be present in a contract

Legatee: a person who receives personal property under a will

Lessee: the tenant

Lessor: the landlord

Leverage: the impact that borrowed funds have on an investment return

License: a personal privilege to use land on a nonexclusive basis

License revocation: to recall and make void a license

License suspension: to temporarily make a license ineffective

Licensee: one who holds a license from a government or other agency which permits a person to pursue some occupation according to certain standards, such as real estate sales

Lien: a hold or claim which one person has on the property of another to secure payment of a debt or other obligation

Lien theory: the legal position that a mortgage creates a charge against property rather than conveying it to the lender

Life estate: the conveyance of fee title for the duration of someone's life

Life tenant: one who possesses a life estate

Limited common elements: common elements, the use of which is limited to certain owners; for example, walls and ceilings between individual units

Limited liability company: a company consisting of members or managers that is governed by its bylaws

Limited partner: a partner who provides capital but does not take personal financial liability nor participate in management

Limited partnership: a combination of general partners who operate the partnership and take personal financial liability and limited partners who provide the bulk of the capital

Liquid asset: an asset that can be converted to cash on short notice

Liquidated damages: an amount of money specified in a contract as compensation to be paid if the contract is not satisfactorily completed

Lis pendens: litigation is pending

Listing: a contract wherein a broker is employed to perform real estate brokerage services

Littoral right: the lawful claim of a landowner to use and enjoy the water of a lake or sea bordering his land

Loan balance table: shows balance remaining to be paid on an amortized loan

Loan escrow: an escrow account opened for the purpose of repaying a loan

Loan origination fee: the expenses a lender incurs in processing a mortgage loan

Loan points: a charge, expressed in percentage points, to obtain a loan

Loan policy: a title insurance policy designed to protect a lender

Loan servicing: the task of collecting monthly payments and handling insurance and tax impounds, delinquencies, early payoffs, and mortgage releases

Loan value: value set on a property for the purpose of making a loan

Loan-to-value ratio: a percentage reflecting what a lender will lend divided by the market value of the property

Longitude lines: imaginary north-south reference lines that circle the earth

Loose money: means that lenders have adequate funds to loan and are actively seeking borrowers

Loyalty to principal: a requirement that an agent place his principal's interest above his own

Maggie Mae: a real estate industry nickname for the MGIC Investment Corporation

Maintenance fees: fees paid by a condominium or PUD unit owner to the owners' association for upkeep of the common elements

Majority: the minimum age required for legal competency (in most states 18 years)

Maker: the person who signs a promissory note

Margin: the amount added to the index rate that reflects the lender's cost of doing business

Market approach: a method of valuing property based on recent sales of similar properties

Market value: the cash price that a willing buyer and a willing seller would freely agree upon, given reasonable exposure of the property to the marketplace, full information as to the potential uses of the property, and no undue compulsion to act

Marketable title: title that is free from reasonable doubt as to who is the owner

Marketable title acts: state laws aimed at cutting off rights and interests in land that have been inactive for long periods; not used in Texas

Master deed: a document that converts a parcel of land into a condominium subdivision

Master limited partnership: limited partnership that can be traded on a stock exchange

Maturity: the end of the life of a loan

Mechanic's lien: a lien placed against real property by any unpaid workman or supplier who has done work or furnished building materials

Meeting of the minds. See Mutual agreement

Menace: threat of violence to obtain a contract

Meridian: a north-south line running from the starting point as the correlated base line used as references in mapping land

Metes and bounds: a detailed method of land description that identifies a parcel by specifying its shape and boundaries

MGIC: Mortgage Guarantee Insurance Corporation

Middleman: a person who brings two or more parties together but does not represent either party

Mill rate: property tax rate that is expressed in tenths of a cent per dollar of assessed valuation

Minor, Infant: a person under the age of legal competence; in most states, under 18 years

Misrepresentation. See Innocent misrepresentation.

Mistake: refers to ambiguity in contract negotiations and mistake of material fact

Modification: the influence on land use and value resulting from improvements made by man to surrounding parcels

Money damages: compensation paid in lieu of contract performance

Monument: an iron pipe, stone, tree, or other fixed point used in making a survey

Mortgage: a pledge of property to secure the repayment of a debt

Mortgage banker: a person or firm that makes mortgage loans and then sells them to investors

Mortgage broker: a person who brings borrowers and lenders together, a loan broker

Mortgage company: a firm that makes mortgage loans and then sells them to investors

Mortgage Debt Relief Act of 2007: a federal tax relief provision allowing a taxpayer to exclude a discharge of debt from income when it is realized as a result of modifying a mortgage or foreclosure on ones principal residence (effectve through 2012).

Mortgage insurance: insures lenders against nonrepayment of loans

Mortgage lien: a pledge of property by its owner to secure the repayment of a debt

Mortgage pool: a common fund of mortgage loans in which one can invest

Mortgage-backed security: certificate that passes-through principal and interest payments to investors

Mortgagee: the party receiving the mortgage; the lender

Mortgagee's information letter: a document prepared by a lender that shows the balance due on an existing loan

Mortgagor: the person who gives a mortgage pledging his property; the borrower

Mortgagor-Mortgagee indexes: alphabetical lists used to locate mortgages in the public records

Multiple listing service: an organization that enables brokers to exchange information on listings

Municipal bond programs: a source of home loans that in turn is financed by the sale of municipal bonds

Mutual agreement: means there must be agreement to the provisions of the contract by all parties involved

Mutual rescission: voluntary cancellation of a contract by all parties involved

National Association of REALTORS® (NAR): the dominant real estate industry trade association in the United States

Nationwide Mortgage Licensing System: a national registry that provides a tracking system of licensed home mortgage originators who are employed by banks, savings associations, credit unions or Farm Credit System institutions, as mandated under the SAFE Act of 2008.

Negative amortization: a situation wherein a loan payment is insufficient to pay the interest due and the excess is added to the balance owed

Negative cash flow: a condition wherein the cash paid out exceeds the cash received

Negative leverage: occurs when borrowed funds cost more than they produce

Net lease: tenant pays a base rent plus maintenance, property taxes, and insurance

Net listing: a listing wherein the commission is the difference between the selling price and a minimum price set by the seller

Net operating income (NOI): gross income less operating expenses, vacancies, and collection losses

Net spendable: the number of dollars remaining each year after collecting rents and paying operating expenses and mortgage payments

Non-assumption clause: a clause in a note or mortgage that gives the lender the right to call the entire loan balance due if the property is sold or otherwise conveyed (also called an alienation clause or a due on-sale clause)

Nonconforming use: an improvement that is inconsistent with current land use zoning regulations

Nonhomogeneity: no two parcels of land are alike; also referred to as heterogeneity

Nonjudicial foreclosure: foreclosure is conducted by the lender

Nonperforming loan: a loan wherein the borrower is behind in his payments

Notary public: a person authorized by the state to administer oaths, attest and certify documents, and take acknowledgments

Note: a written promise to repay a debt

Notice of consent: allows the secretary of state to receive legal summonses for nonresidents

Notice of revocation: allows the revocation of a notice of consent

Novation: the substitution of a new contract or new party for an old one

Obedience (faithful performance): a requirement that an agent obey all legal instructions given to him by his principal

Offeree: the party who receives an offer

Offeror: the party who makes an offer

Office of Federal Housing Enterprise Oversight (OFHEO): a former agency (2002–2008) in the Department of Housing and Urban Development, charged with ensuring the financial stability of the two government sponsored home mortgage enterprises, Fannie Mae and Freddie Mac.

100% commission: an arrangement whereby the salesperson pays for office overhead directly rather than splitting commission income with his broker

Open listing: a listing that gives a broker a nonexclusive right to find a buyer

Operating expense ratio: total operating expenses divided by effective gross income

Operating expenses: expenditures necessary to operate a property and maintain the production of income

Opinion of title: an attorney's opinion as to the status of title

Option: a right, for a given period of time, to buy, sell or lease property at specified price and terms

Optionee: the party receiving the option

Optioner: the party giving the option

Origination fee: a charge for making a loan

Ostensible authority: results when a principal gives a third party reason to believe that another person is his agent even though that person is unaware of the appointment

Overall rate: a mortgage-equity factor used to appraise income-producing property

Overencumbered property: a property where market value of that property is exceeded by the loans against it

Owner's policy: a title insurance policy designed to protect the fee owner

Package mortgage: a mortgage secured by a combination of real and personal property

Parol evidence rule: permits oral evidence to augment a written contract in certain cases

Partial release: a release of a portion of a property from a mortgage

Partially amortized loan: a loan that begins with amortized payments but ends with a balloon payment

Participation certificate: a secondary mortgage market instrument whereby an investor can purchase an undivided interest in a pool of mortgages

Participation loan: one that requires interest plus a percentage of the profits

Partition: to divide jointly held property into distinct portions so that each co-owner may hold his or her proportionate share in severalty

Partnership: a form of co-ownership for business purposes

Party (parties): a legal term that refers to a person or a group involved in a legal proceeding

Party wall easement: a fence or wall erected along a property line for the mutual benefit of both owners

Payment cap: a limit on how much a borrower's payments can increase

Percentage basis: rent is based on the tenant's sales

Percolating water: underground water not confined to a defined underground waterway

Performance: principal is expected to do whatever he reasonably can to accomplish the purpose of the agency, such as referring inquiries by prospective buyers to the broker

Periodic estate: a tenancy that provides for continuing automatic renewal until canceled, such as a month-to-month rental

Personal property: a right or interest in things of a temporary or movable nature; anything not classed as real property

Personalty: things of a temporary or movable nature as distinguished from realty

Physical deterioration: deterioration from wear and tear and the action of nature

PITI payment: a loan that combines principal, interest, taxes, and insurance

Planned unit development (PUD): individually owned houses with community ownership of common areas

Plat: a map that shows the location and boundaries of individual properties

Plottage value: the result of combining two or more parcels of land so that one large parcel has more value than the sum of the individual parcels

Point: one percent of the loan amount

Point of beginning or point of commencement: the standing place at one corner of a parcel of land in a metes and bounds survey

Police power: the right of government to enact laws and enforce them for the order, safety, health, morals, and general welfare of the public

Positive cash flow: a condition wherein cash received exceeds cash paid out

Positive leverage: occurs when the benefits of borrowing exceed the costs of borrowing

Power of attorney: a written authorization to another to act on one's behalf

Power of sale: allows a mortgagee to conduct a foreclosure sale without first going to court

Prepayment penalty: a fee charged by a lender for permitting a borrower to repay his loan early

Prepayment privilege: allows the borrower to repay early without penalty

Prescriptive easement: an easement acquired by prolonged use

Price fixing: two or more people conspiring to charge a fixed fee, having an anti-competitive effect

Primary market: where lenders originate loans

Principal: a person who authorizes another to act for him; also refers to a property owner

Principal: the balance owing on a loan

Principal meridian: a longitude line selected as a reference in the rectangular survey system

Principles of value: anticipation, change, competition, conformity, diminishing marginal returns, highest and best use, substitution, supply and demand

Private mortgage insurance (PMI): a private mortgage insurance source to insure lenders against foreclosure loss

Pro forma statement: a projected annual operating statement that shows expected income, operating expenses, and net operating income

Probate court: a court of law with the authority to verify the legality of a will and carry out its instructions

Procuring cause: the agent whose efforts bring about the desired results

Projected gross: the estimated rent a fully occupied property can be expected to produce on an annual basis

Promissory note: a written promise to repay a debt

Proprietary lease: a lease issued by a cooperative corporation to its shareholders

Prorating: the division of ongoing expenses and income items between the buyer and the seller

Prospectus: a disclosure statement that describes an investment opportunity

Public grant: a transfer of land by a government body to a private individual

Public improvement: one that benefits the public at large and is financed through general property taxes

Puffing: nonfactual or extravagant statements a reasonable person would recognize as such

Pur autre vie: for the life of another

Purchase money mortgage: a loan used to purchase the real property that serves as its collateral

Qualified fee estate: a fee simple estate subject to certain limitations imposed by its owner

Quarter-section: 160 acres

Quiet enjoyment: the right of possession and use of property without undue disturbance by others

Quiet title suit: court-ordered hearings held to determine land ownership

Quitclaim deed: a legal instrument used to convey whatever title the grantor has; it contains no covenants, warranties, nor implication of the grantor's ownership

Range: a six-mile-wide column of land running north-south in the rectangular survey system

Ready, willing, and able buyer: a buyer who is ready to buy now without further coaxing, and who has the financial capability to do so

Real chattel: an interest in real estate that is personal property, such as leasehold estate

Real estate: any land and its improvements in a physical sense, as well as the rights to own or use both

Real estate commission: a board appointed by the governor to advise and set policies regarding real estate licenses and transaction procedures

Real estate commissioner: a person appointed by the governor to implement and carry out laws enacted by the legislature that pertain to real estate

Real estate investment trust (REIT): a method of pooling investor money by using the trust form of ownership and featuring single taxation of profits

Real estate lien note. See Promissory note

Real estate listing. See Listing

Real Estate Settlement Procedure Act (RESPA): a federal law that deals with procedures to be followed in certain types of real estate closings

Real property: ownership rights in land and its improvements

Real savings: savings by persons and businesses that result from spending less than is earned

Realtist: a member of the National Association of Real Estate Brokers, Inc.

REALTOR®: a registered trademark owned by the National Association of REALTOR® for use by its members

REALTOR-Associate®: a membership designation for salespersons working for REALTOR®

Realty: land and buildings and other improvements to land

Reasonable care: a requirement that an agent exhibit competence and expertise, keep his client informed, and take proper care of property entrusted to him

Reciprocity: an arrangement whereby one state honors licenses issued by another state and vice versa

Recorded map. See Recorded plat

Recorded plat: a subdivision map filed in the county recorder's office that shows the location and boundaries of individual parcels of land

Recorded survey. See Recorded plat

Recording acts: laws that provide for the placing of documents in the public records

Recovery fund: a state-operated fund that can be tapped to pay for uncollectible judgments against real estate licenses

Rectangular survey system: a government system for surveying land that uses latitude and longitude lines as references

Redlining: the practice of refusing to make loans in certain neighborhoods

Regular mortgage: a pledge of property to secure the repayment of a debt

Regulation Z: a federal law requiring lenders to show borrowers how much they are paying for credit

Release of lien: a certificate from the lender stating that the loan has been repaid

Reliction (dereliction): the process whereby dry land is permanently exposed by a gradually receding waterline

Remainder interest: a future interest in real estate held by a remainderman

Remainderman: one who is entitled to take an estate in remainder

Rental value: value of property expressed in terms of the right to its use for a specific period of time

Replacement cost: the cost, at today's prices and using today's construction methods, of building an improvement having the same usefulness as the one being appraised

Replacement value: value as measured by the current cost of building a structure of equivalent utility

Reproduction cost: the cost, at today's prices and using today's construction methods, of building an improvement having the same usefulness as the one being appraised

Reserve account (impound account): an amount of money collected by a lender each month so as to have enough to pay for property taxes and property insurance when they become due

Reserves for replacement: money set aside each year for the replacement of items that have a useful life greater than one year

Resort timesharing: exclusive use of a property for a specified number of days each year

RESPA (Real Estate Settlement Procedure Act): a federal law that deals with procedures to be followed in certain types of real estate closings

Restrictive covenants: clauses placed in deeds to control how future landowners may or may not use the property; also used in leases

Reverse annuity mortgage. See Reverse mortgage

Reverse mortgage: the lender makes monthly payments to a homeowner who later repays in a lump sum

Reversionary interest: the right to retake possession of a leased property at some future time

Right of first refusal: the right to match or better an offer before the property is sold to someone else

Right of survivorship: a feature of joint tenancy whereby the surviving joint tenants automatically acquire all the right, title, and interest of the deceased joint tenant

Riparian right: the right of a landowner whose land borders a river or stream to use and enjoy that water

S Corporation: allows limited liability with profit-and-loss pass-through

Sale and leaseback: owner-occupant sells his property and then remains as a tenant

Sale by advertisement: allows a mortgagee to conduct a foreclosure sale without first going to court

Sales associate: a salesman or broker employed by a broker

Salesperson: a person associated with a real estate broker for the purposes of performing acts or transactions comprehended by the term of Real Estate Broker as defined in the Texas Real Estate Licensing Act

Salvage value: the price that can be expected for an improvement that is to be removed and used elsewhere

Scheduled gross (projected gross): the estimated rent a fully occupied property can be expected to produce on an annual basis

Second lien mortgage: one which ranks immediately behind the first mortgage in priority

Secondary mortgage market: a market where mortgage loans can be sold to investors

Section: a unit of land in the rectangular survey system that is one mile long on each of its four sides and contains 640 acres

Seller financing: a note accepted by a seller instead of cash

Seller's affidavit of title: a document provided by the seller at the settlement meeting stating that he has done nothing to encumber title since the title search was made

Seller's market: one with few sellers and many buyers

Senior mortgage: the mortgage against a property that holds first priority in the event of foreclosure

Separate property: spouse-owned property that is exempt from community property status

Servient estate: the land on which an easement exists in favor of a dominant estate

Settlement: the process of consummating a real estate transaction

Settlement statement: an accounting of funds to the buyer and the seller at the completion of a real estate transaction

Severalty ownership: owned by one person, sole ownership

Severance damages: compensation paid for the loss in market value that results from splitting up a property in a condemnation proceeding

Sheriff's deed: a deed issued as a result of a court-ordered foreclosure sale

Situs: refers to the preference by people for a given location

Sole ownership: owned by one person

Special agency: an agency relationship created for the performance of specific acts only

Special assessments: charges levied to provide publicly built improvements that will benefit a limited geographical area

Special warranty deed: contains only one covenant—the covenant against encumbrances

Specific lien: a lien on a specific property

Specific performance: contract performance according to the precise terms agreed upon

Specific property offering: property purchase method whereby the organizers buy properties first and then seek partners

Spot zoning: the rezoning of a small area of land in an existing neighborhood

Square-foot method: an appraisal technique that uses square-foot construction costs of similar structures as an estimating basis

Standard mortgage: a pledge of property to secure the repayment of a debt

Standard parallel: a survey line used to correct for the earth's curvature

Statute of frauds: a law requiring that certain types of contracts be written in order to be enforceable in a court of law

Statute of limitations: a legal limit on the amount of time one has to seek the aid of a court in obtaining justice

Statutory estates: estates created by law and including dower, curtesy, community property, and homestead rights

Steering: the practice of directing home seekers to particular neighborhoods based on race, color, religion, sex, national origin, nonhandicapped, or adult only housing

Step-up rental: a lease that provides for agreed-upon rent increases

Straight-line depreciation: depreciation in equal amounts each year over the life of the asset

Subject property: the property that is being appraised

Subject to the existing loan: the buyer of an already mortgaged property makes the payments but does not take personal responsibility for the loan

Sublease: a lease that is given by a lessee

Sublessee: a lessee who rents from another lessee

Sublessor: a lessee who rents to another lessee

Subordination: voluntary acceptance of a lower property priority than one would otherwise be entitled to

Substitution, principle of: maximum value of a property in the marketplace tends to be set by the cost of purchasing an equally desirable substitute property provided no costly delay is encountered making the substitution

Subsurface right: the right to use land below the earth's surface

Sunk cost: a cost already incurred that is not subject to revision

Surface rights: the right to use the surface of a parcel of land

Survey books: map books

Survivorship, right of: a feature of joint tenancy whereby the surviving joint tenants automatically acquire all the rights, title, and interest of the deceased joint tenant

Syndication (syndicate): a group of persons or businesses that combine to undertake an investment

Tack on: adding successive periods of continuous occupation to qualify for title by adverse possession

Take-out loan: a permanent loan arranged to replace a construction loan

"Taking back paper": said of a seller who allows a purchaser to substitute a promissory note for cash

Tax basis: the price paid for a property plus certain costs and expenses

Tax-deferred exchange: a sale of real property in exchange for another parcel of real estate to affect a nontaxable gain

Tax lien: a charge or hold by the government against property to insure the payment of taxes

Tax shelter: the income tax savings that an investment can produce for its owner

Teaser rate: an adjustable loan with an initial rate below the market

Tenancy at sufferance: the result of a tenant who stays beyond his legal tenancy without the consent of the landlord

Tenancy by the entirety: a form of joint ownership reserved for married persons; right of survivorship exists and neither spouse has a disposable interest during the lifetime of the other

Tenant: one who holds or possesses property, the lessee

Tenants in common: shared ownership of a single property among two or more persons; interests need not be equal and no right of survivorship exists

Term loan: a loan requiring interest-on-payments until the maturity date (due date), at which time the entire principal is due

Testamentary trust: a trust that takes effect after death

Testate: to die with a last will and testament

Testator (testatrix): a person who makes a will

Tester: an individual or organization that responds to or tests for compliance with fair housing laws

Texas Fair Housing Act: Texas statute enforcing federal and state guidelines against discrimination

Texas Real Estate Commission: the state board that advises and sets policies regarding real estate licensees and transaction procedures

Thin market: a market with fewer buyers and few sellers

Third parties: persons who are not parties to a contract but who may be affected by it

Tight money: means that loan money is in short supply and loans are hard to get

"Time is of the essence": a phrase that means that the time limits of a contract must be faithfully observed or the contract is voidable

Timesharing: part ownership of a property coupled with a right to exclusive use of it for a specified number of days per year

Title: the right to or ownership of something; also the evidence of ownership such as a deed or bill of sale

Title by descent: laws that direct how a deceased's assets shall be divided if he leaves no will

Title by prescription. See Adverse possession

Title closing: the process of consummating a real estate transaction

Title cloud: a title defect

Title commitment: obligates the title insurance company to issue a policy of title when curative requirements have been satisfied

Title insurance: an insurance policy against defects in title not listed in the title report or abstract

Title plant: a duplicate set of public records maintained by a title company

Title search: an inspection of publicly available records and documents to determine the current ownership and title condition for a property

Title theory: the legal position that a mortgage conveys title to the lender

Total payments: the amount in dollars the borrower will have paid after making all the payments scheduled

Townships: a six-by-six-mile square of land designated by the intersection of range lines and township lines in the rectangular survey system

Tract index: a system for listing recorded documents affecting a particular tract of land

Trade fixture: a business or trade-related article attached to a rental building by a business tenant

Treasury Constant Maturities: an index published by the Federal Reserve, of average yield rates on various U.S. Treasury securities, which are adjusted to constant maturities for a period of time.

Trigger terms: credit advertising that requires compliance with Truth in Lending rules

Trust: ownership by a trustee for the benefit of another

Trust account: a separate account for holding clients' and customers' money

Trust deed. See Deed of trust

Trustee: one who holds property in trust for another

Trustee's deed. See Sheriff's deed

Trustor: one who creates a trust; the borrower in a deed of trusts arrangement

Truth in Lending Act: a federal law that requires certain disclosures when extending or advertising credit

UCC lien: lien which attaches pursuant to the provisions of the Uniform Commercial Code

U.S. Public Lands Survey: a system for surveying land that uses latitude and longitude lines as references

Undivided interest: ownership by two or more persons that gives each the right to use the entire property

Undue influence: unfair advantage to obtain a contract

Unenforceable contract: a contract barred by the statue of limitations or the doctrine of laches

Unilateral contract: results when a promise is exchanged for performance

Unilateral rescission: innocent party refuses to perform his contractual duties because the other party has not performed his

Unit deed: a deed to a condominium unit

Unity of interest: all joint tenants own one interest together

Unity of person: the legal premise that husband and wife are an indivisible legal unit and a requirement of tenancy by the entirety

Unity of possession: all co-tenants must enjoy the same undivided possession of the whole property

Unity of time: each joint tenant must acquire his or her ownership interest at the same moment

Unity of title: all joint tenants must acquire their interests from the same deed or will

Universal agency: an agency wherein the agent empowered to transact matters of all types for the principal

Up-front mortgage insurance premium (UFMIP): a one-time charge by the FHA for insuring a loan

Urban homestead: a homestead in a town, city, or village

Usury: charging a rate of interest higher than that permitted by law

Utility: the ability of a good or service to fill demand

VA: Department of Veterans Affairs

Valid contract: one that meets all requirements of law, is binding upon its parties, and is enforceable in a court of law

Valuable consideration: money, property, services, promises not to act, or anything worth money

Valuation of real property. See Appraisal

Variable rate mortgage: a mortgage on which the interest rate rises and falls with changes in prevailing interest rates

Variance: a permit granted to an individual property owner to vary slightly from strict compliance with zoning requirements

Vassals: tenants of the lord and subtenants of the kind

Vendee: the buyer

Vendor: the seller

Vested: owned by

Void contract: a contract that has no binding effect on the parties who made it

Voidable contract: a contract that binds one party but gives the other the right to withdraw

Voluntary lien: a lien created by the property owner

Walk-through: a final inspection of the property just prior to settlement

Warranty: an assurance or guarantee that something is true as stated

Warranty deed: a deed that usually contains the covenants of seizin, the covenant against encumbrances, and sample document

Waste: abuse or destructive use of property

Water right: the right to use water on or below or bordering a parcel of land level

Water table: the upper limit of percolating water below the earth's surface

Words of conveyance: the grantor's statement that he is making a grant to the grantee

Worst-case scenario: shows what can happen to the borrower's payments if the index rises to its maximum in an adjustable loan

Wraparound mortgage: a mortgage that encompasses any existing mortgages and is subordinate to them

Writ of execution: a court document directing the county sheriff to seize and sell a debtor's property

Zoning: public regulations that control the specific use of land in a given district

Index